THE FIFTH GLOSTER GAZETTE

A Chronicle, Serious and Humorous, of the Battalion while serving with the British Expeditionary Force

With an Introduction by
CHRISTINE BERESFORD

and
CHRISTOPHER NEWBOULD

ALAN SUTTON

poke equal fun at themselves, their seniors and their enemies and made light of intolerable conditions, of fear, dirt, hunger and disease.

Some time after the war a complete collection of *The Fifth Gloster Gazette* was published privately, but without photographs, as the plates had been lost in France. The current book is a slightly reduced facsimile of the first bound edition, with the addition of the missing photographs, which modern printing technology has enabled us to reproduce from original copies of the *Gazette* held in the museum. It serves as a poignant memorial to the indomitable spirit of the young men who gave their best years, if not their lives, for their country.

Christine Beresford
Curator
Regiments of Gloucestershire Museum

A SHORT HISTORY OF THE 5TH BATTALION, THE GLOUCESTERSHIRE REGIMENT

Britain has never been comfortable with a large standing army, preferring to base its defences on the Royal Navy backed up by a small force of regular soldiers which was expanded during times of crisis by a call for volunteers. Even during the First World War, which made extraordinary demands on the country's manpower, Britain survived from 1914 to 1916 with a wholly volunteer Army.

The unbroken line of the part-time Volunteers in Gloucestershire began in 1859. By 1908 the country's various Volunteer bodies, some of whom served in the Boer War, had been incorporated into a new Territorial Force as the 5th Battalion The Gloucestershire Regiment. Raised for home defence, the new force's administration, training and equipment were much improved on earlier arrangements which had depended largely upon the generosity of the public or money from the Volunteers' own pockets.

The highlight of the year's training was a two week camp. For many men it was the only holiday they knew. Understandably, the 5th Glosters preferred the camps by the sea, such as at Lulworth Cove in 1911 and Shorncliffe in 1913, to places like Salisbury Plain where they manoeuvred in 1910 and 1912. On 2 August 1914 the Battalion set off for their annual camp at Marlow-on-Thames. The next day war was declared and they were sent home, only to be mobilized twenty-four hours later. By the evening of 6 August the weary Territorials were at their war station on the Isle of Wight. A few days later they were mustered at Swindon, where a call for volunteers for active service was made. Every officer and 90 per cent of the men responded. They then marched to Essex, where they were later joined by a newly raised battalion of the 5th Glosters, named the 2nd/5th. Here they guarded the east coast and trained the new recruits who had answered the call to the Colours. Almost the whole of the Gloucester rugby team enlisted, and for the duration of the war, the Battalion team was unbeaten!

In March 1915 the 1st/5th Glosters sailed to France to take their place at the Front which stretched from the Swiss Alps to the Channel. Their first year abroad was spent alternating between the trenches in Belgium and northern France and the rest billets behind the line. Untested in any major operation, they nevertheless made life difficult for the enemy. Regular patrols were carried out, usually at night into No Man's Land between opposing trenches.

Although the Battalion was spared the terrors of the opening stages of the Battle of the Somme, by late July 1916 it had fought several fierce actions. In August it suffered over five hundred killed, wounded and missing out of a total strength of one thousand. In November it began its second winter in the trenches, with all its attendant horrors. Constant sniper and artillery fire restricted movement to the hours of darkness. Although no major attack took place, in one month the Battalion's casualties were 22 killed, 64 wounded and 3 missing. Mud was everywhere and sickness was rife.

The German retreat from the Somme in March 1917 brought welcome relief. The *Gazette* observed laconically that 'the change to open warfare was much appreciated'. By August static warfare had resumed and the 5th Glosters suffered terrible casualties during the 3rd Battle of Ypres. The ground was so sodden and churned up by artillery fire that they fought in a sea of mud.

In November 1917, after a period of rest, the Battalion moved to Italy and fought on the Austrian Front until September 1918. Much of their time was spent in ordinary trench routine and patrol activity. In June 1918 the 5th Glosters were prominent in stubborn fighting to defeat an Austrian attack in thickly wooded and hilly country. Eventually, in September 1918, the long years of trench warfare in France and Flanders were rewarded with a German collapse and the Battalion returned to the Western Front to take part in the great Allied advance. In the final month of the war, a series of hard fought but successful actions took place. In one of them, the diminutive Private F.G. Miles from the Forest of Dean destroyed several German machine-guns, single handed and under heavy enemy fire. For this he was awarded the Victoria Cross, one of five to be awarded to members of The Gloucestershire Regiment during the First World War.

After the Armistice the Battalion was demobilized and returned to Gloucestershire. In the war cemeteries of Flanders, France and Italy they left behind 587 of their number. That the survivors endured the appalling conditions and fought with stoic good humour is a tribute to the comradeship developed within this typical county Territorial battalion. Loyalty is a strong impulse among Volunteers, particularly to comrades in the same company. The fear of letting them down was often greater than that of becoming a casualty. These bonds of friendship were developed in peace on the rifle range or in the local drill halls and forged in the fire of battle. Contrary to the views of many of the professional soldiers, who often regarded the Territorials as 'Saturday afternoon soldiers', and even 'those b—— Amateurs', they joined because they thought there was a job worth doing, and they 'laid down their lives with the same readiness as they abandoned their businesses at the beginning of the war'. The spirit of Territorials such as the 5th Glosters had a special quality, an enthusiasm and zest for life undaunted by the horrors of the trenches. Their indomitable character and sense of humour is reflected in the pages of their gazette.

Their spirit endures to this day. Men of the 5th Glosters answered the call again in 1939 and fought throughout the Second World War. Although their title disappeared in the Territorial Army reorganization of 1967, their successors soldier on today in the ranks of the Wessex Volunteers.

Colonel Christopher Newbould CBE
Chairman, Board of Management
Regiments of Gloucestershire Museum

5th GLOUCESTER GAZETTE

A Chronicle, serious and humorous, of the Battalion while serving with the
BRITISH EXPEDITIONARY FORCE

" Happy is he who dies for his earthly city, for it is the body of the city of God ".
Charles Pegou, *killed in action 1915.*

" All honour give
To those who, nobly striving, nobly fell,
That we might live ".

1. 3411 L/Cpl. R. E. BARTLETT, Killed, 14/9/16.	7. Lieut. W. FREAM, Killed, 21/7/16.
2. 8623 Pte W. JARVIS, Missing, bel. Killed, 23/7/16.	8. 2563 Pte. A. E. ROBERTS, Killed, 6/7/16.
3. 2nd Lt. R. MADDER, Killed; 20/7/16.	9. 2nd Lt. C. V. N. PUCKRIDGE, Miss., bel. Kill., 21/7/16.
4. 2nd Lt. D. G. DURRANT, Killed, 16/8/16.	10. 2174 Pte. A. E. JELFS, Missing, 23/7/16.
5. 1998 Pte. G. F. FEAR, Killed, 21/7/16.	11. 421 Sgt. P. T. COOKLEY, Killed, 21/7/16.
6. 463 Sgt. H. YOUNG, Killed, 23/7/16.	12. 2nd Lt. J. FARRIMOND, Miss. bel. Killed, 21/7/16.

[This number was originally issued in typewritten form and has been printed in response to a general desire.]

No. 1.

APRIL 12, 1915.

5th Gloucester Gazette.

A Chronicle, serious and humorous, of the Battalion while serving with the
BRITISH EXPEDITIONARY FORCE.

IT is with a light heart that we launch out a new periodical into the vast whirl of competing journalism, confident as we are that the " Fifth Gloucester Gazette " will serve to maintain a highly useful purpose.

But at the same time we say at once that such success as it will win must inevitably depend on the efficiency with which our band of numerous correspondents perform their various duties. To them we look for a steady stream of articles on such subjects as " Prattlings from the Potsdam Purlieus," " Heard at Headquarters," " Les bons mots du Colonel," " Les jeux d'esprit de l'Adjutant," " La causerie de la maison Cavendish " and other engrossing topics.

It may be of great interest to many to learn that, although the editorial packing case unhesitatingly reserves to itself full powers, comfortable seats on the Board of Management may nevertheless be obtained if applications be accompanied by the presentation of a pair of gum boots (size 11) or a young horse (under 18), gifts indeed so modest that they would at first sight seem but to tarnish the escutcheon of the Editor's armorial bearings.

We would counsel our readers to offer their services on the above terms at once, seeing that with a wise prudence it has seemed good to withhold final allotment of shares in the Gazette until—we quote the prospectus—such time or times as the combustion of the Printing Press through the agency of Mr. Jack Johnson or Miss Busy Bertha shall ensue.

Meanwhile contributions are earnestly invited. We are quite sure when we issue this invitation that the supply will more than equal the demand. For instance, we can with but slight imagination picture the readiness of the Q-rt-rm-st-r's horse to discuss through the medium of our columns certain weighty matters of no negligible girth which concern his creature comforts very closely.

Let the company wags get busy ! ! Many men will be anxious to contribute to a Gazette which will record the sayings and doings, the tears and the smiles of Gloucestershire men. We have, in the words of as the Elizabethan, " hearts of high emprise." Get a move on then, boys, and earn the title of " The Fighting Fifth," and our Gazette shall at once be great and glorious. That the regiment will win that title we are confident. And even though we may not appear by our own individual efforts to be gaining any ground for the Allied cause, yet

" . . . while the tired waves, vainly breaking,
    Seem here no painful inch to gain,
Far back, through creeks and inlets making,
    Comes, silent, flooding in, the main."

We have no cause for anxiety. The national character has re-asserted itself, in spite of false prophets. We never stood better in the eyes of the world than we stand to-day, and with that spirit our Regiment is instinct.

THE BATTALION A. B. C.

A. is the Adjutant's horse, who foretells
    Our real destination to be Dardanelles.

B. is the beer over which 'twas discussed
    To edify Germany's agents we trust.

C. stands for Chelmsford, the town of our training,
    And where it is almost continually raining.

D. is the word which all of us said
    When the billets were changed and we hadn't a bed.

E. is for England, now distant and dear,
    When we see her white cliffs again, how we will cheer.

F. is the Frenchman who answered " quite so "
    To our "S'il vous plaît Monsieur, donnez-moi l'eau"

G. is the Glo'sters—those grim gory fighters
    Who've cleared all the trenches from Bailleul to Ypres.

H. is for Hell, the place where the Hun
    Sings " Wacht am der Styx " when his fighting is done.

I. is the Indian who cries " Souvenir "
    With a Teutonic head on the end of his spear.

J. is for Joffre—we haven't yet met him
    But thousands of Germans will never forget him.

K. is for Kitchener—humorous bloke
    Who conceals all his flippancy under a cloak.

L. is the letter he wrote to the trenches—
    Beware of the wine, and keep clear of the wenches.

M. is our money—exactly eight bob—
    Paid us on Fridays to finish this " job."

N. is the nominal labouring man
    Who strikes for more wages whenever he can.

A

O.   is the output on which we depend
      To bring this detestable war to an end.

P.   is the pack and the pick that we carry
      With hurdle and sandbag the foeman to harry.

Q.   is the query " What will he do,
      Should he also pick up a comrade or two ? "

R.   is the French road well studded with cobbles
      O'er which the perspiring warrior hobbles.

S.   is the Sergeant, familiarly " Serg,"
      Whose temper is short, his vocabulary large.

T.   is the trench where they safely abide,
      Glad that it's deep, and sufficiently wide.

U.   is for Uhlan who's scarcer by far
      To-day than he was at the start of the war.

V.   is Vin Rouge which 'tis foolish to buy
      On a route march in front of the Officer's eye.

W.   is the water which no one should drink
      In spite of what rabid teetotalers think.

X.   is last Xmas.

Y.   is next year.

Z.   is the end of this alphabet 'ere.

                                    F. W. H.

CHIT-CHAT.

The Commanding Officer is very anxious to order paper covers in which the succeeding issues of this Gazette may be inserted. It would be very suitable to have a design engraved on these covers. Will men please send in specimens of such designs as soon as possible that the covers may be ordered from Gloucester. The successful Competitor who gains the honour of adorning the cover with his handiwork is much to be envied.

The number of aeroplanes which flew over Meteren one day when we were in that neighbourhood was noticeable. As a matter of fact our airmen was engaged in pursuing a Taube which came very near to playing havoc with members of the Divisional Staff. Congratulations to Captains Crawshay and Girdwood, D.S.O., on their narrow escape from the bomb which dropped close to them.

Our persistent sense of humour must be a source of severe trial to the German nation. On April 1st one of our Aeroplanes appeared over the aerodrome at Lille and dropped a football. At the sight of the dark thing dropping thro' the skies the good Germans hurried and took what cover they could find. Even after the bomb bounced they were still suspicious. But how angry when then they read at last on it—"April 1st, Gott strafe England."

All Troops are warned to let sleeping dogs in the shape of unexploded shells severely alone. The members of a certain Battery in our vicinity went through Mons, Le Cateau, etc., without even the proverbial scratch. But one member picked up one of the sleeping shells, placed it between his knees and proceeded to unscrew the cap, with disastrous results to some of his mates.

The course of instruction in the trenches was admirably conducted for us by the officers and men of the two Regiments whose trenches we visited. We were very sorry for Private Lea having the misfortune to be wounded in his eye through no fault of his own. Before Sergt. Lloyd was able to focus his glasses he had received a rap on his knuckles. Congratulations to the Commanding Officer and to Sergt. Young on their immunity from the glass of broken periscopes.

Those days and nights occupied in Trench instruction were interesting if only for the homely nature of Trench occupation. Even the animal world in the shape of a cat which preserved a strict neutrality by spending the day in the English Trenches and the night in the German Trenches illustrates the " Home from Home " atmosphere of some Trenches.

" IN THE PINK "—A LETTER.

Dearest Florrie. Came to anchor after 10 miles on a road
Which for stones would beat a quarry and for mud a
         bloomin' sink,
I am lying in a farmyard,where we're making our abode,
And I hope you're doing nicely, as this leaves me in
         the pink.

Well, we've marched for miles on cobbles, which is
         dreadful for the feet
Past the fertile fields of France, which have a most
         peculiar stink ;
And we've smoked that French tobacco, and it much
         resembles peat,
And we've tried a few French liquors which they leaves
         me in the pink.

We haven't seen a German, but we're getting pretty
    near :
And we haven't been in Trenches, but we're just upon
    the brink,
And when I write again, you need not be surprised to
    hear
We've been at 'em with the bayonet, and been dabbling
    in the pink.

Well, whatever comes, keep smiling, for, whatever
    comes, I'm true,
And so are all the Glo'sters and they're not the boys to
    shrink,
And when the Kaiser's busted, I'll be racing back to
    you,
And trust as shall find you as this leaves me in the
    pink.

THE CHAPLAIN'S COLUMN.

The Bishop of Gloucester writes as follows :—
" Please give the 5th a message of God speed from me,
and tell them that we have been thinking much of
them, and remember them constantly in our prayers."

Some Platoons inaugurated Prayers at night in
their respective barns. It is hoped that five minutes'
silence will be the rule in all barns or billets throughout
the Regiment.

Members of " C " Company must have noticed the
grave of Captain Ainsworth, of the Eleventh Hussars,
which lay close to one of their barns at Meteren. A
Trooper in that Regiment told me that the Captain
met his death after killing a German Officer in a scrap
between patrols at night. A bullet passed through the
flap of his saddle and entered his lung. It was nice to
see that some of our men laid some primroses on his
grave, a touching witness to the reality of the Communion of Saints, the Brotherhood of the Baptised. We
can shew our belief in it by sharing a hymn book or
laying a wreath on a grave. Meanwhile the little
graveyards we pass are beautifully kept, as they should
be, for they are part of God's Acre.

THE BABE B. A.

(Oxford and Cambridge have led the way in coming
    forward to do their duty to their Country.)

Daily Press.

There's a Babe B. A. whom you met one day,
You christened him thus of old,

He was full of fun—was he twenty-one,
    Or twenty two all told ?

Would you know him now with his puckered brow,
His putties all muddy and torn ?
You've seen him grapple with dim Whitechapel
And eke with the hunter's horn.

For a sportsman true was the man we knew
You should see him pot the red !
As deft with the cue as with driver true
He would lay them all stone dead.

Did a rabbit race at lightning pace ?
Did a pigeon steal swiftly by ?
Did a snipe zig-zag—They would join the bag
Where pheasant and partridge lie.

But his back's to the wall at his country's call
He's ready to do his job,
He has learnt to fight in the cause of right,
To scupper the Kaiser's mob.

So here's to the fame of the noble game
Of life as is lived by you,
For nine out of ten of your fellowmen
Would swear you are good and true.

As three-quarter back, he carries his pack
And forty odd things in tow,
And though he wobbles on stony cobbles
He's ready to meet his foe.

And so in the day when we're far away
From the boys of the Old Brigade,
We'll think of this rhyme and the good old time,
In the days when we are old and staid.

CASUALTIES.

No. 1619 Pte. R. Lee, C. Company. Wounded 9. 4. 15.

No. 381. L.-Sergt. R. E. Lloyd. C Company. Slightly
    wounded. 9. 4. 15.

THINGS WE WANT TO KNOW.

Who wrote to two ladies the same love letter by
carbon ?

Who described the Scottish Regiment as " The Sea force " ?

———

Which Platoon seized their rifles hurriedly in dead of night to answer back the fierce German rifle fire, when it was only the mules indulging in kicking practice to keep their hoofs in ?

———

SPORT.

RUGBY FOOTBALL.

On Wednesday, the 14th April, the South Midland Division played the Fourth Division. The Battalion was well represented :—

Pte. C Cook	Pte. Harris
Pte. Washbourne	L-Cpl. Millard
Pte. S. Hamblin	Lt. Sumner
Pte. F. Webb	Pte. A. Cook
Pte. S. Sysum	Pte. S. Smart
L-Cpl. A. Lewis	

—no less than 11 of its players appearing. The team was captained by Lt. Poulton Palmer and the Fourth Division also included several Internationals.

The Fourth kicked off with the wind and immediately began to press, their forwards doing splendid work. Then Sysum broke away and scored after a bout of passing. The goal kick failed.

The Fourth returned to the attack and almost scored, but after some loose play our forwards broke away and " got over." Hamblin converted. Soon after Washbourne intercepted and a combined movement with Hamblin resulted in the ball being taken over the line by J. Harris. The score at half time was 11 points to nil.

The South Midlands continued to keep the upper hand and Harris again scored. Five minutes before time Washbourne scored a brilliant try leaving us victors by 17 points.

Despite the difference in the scoring the game was most interesting and thoroughly enjoyed by all the spectators, especially by the Welshmen who had turned out to see a football match after many months in the trenches.

———

CRICKET.

The inauguration of the cricket season was attended with great success. A bevy of company cooks at once chic and bizarre in their zephyrous and coloured costumes occupied one corner of the yard and some young officers looking more than usually smart in their well fitting gum boots and well groomed Burberries did the honours most gracefully and assiduously. The opposing elevens—the Privates and the Police—contained some interesting names. A great deal had been expected from young Ike White and much discussion had taken place as to how he would shape against the cunning wiles of the famous lobster—Sergt. Huggins.

A corduroy wicket beautifully laid on cobbles rolled out so well that practically no " gardening " was required—in not a single case did the batsman have to pat the ground—and as far as could be seen from the Press Parlour the wicket was in capital order thanks to superhuman exertions of the sapper section.

It was indeed a happy inspiration which led Pte. White, on winning the toss from Sergt. Huggins, to take first knock, as the wicket was bound to wear a bit, and indeed the Captain of the Privates XI. set his side an excellent example, gracefully deflecting the left hand trundler to the leg terminus—in this case the main cess pool—three times in the first over.

At the time of going to Press he was still undefeated with 101 to his credit—so far a most excellent display, despite a marked tendency to be " c and b," but a trifling fault in a free display of late back chat and open defiance of the eleven Police.

Stop Press.—June 30th.—White not out 251.

G. F. H.

———

ADVERTISEMENT COLUMN.

BOOTS.—Messrs. Truefit and Co. Limited.
Messrs. Blister and Co. Un Limited.

The above may be seen without appointment at the Quartermaster's Stores any morning between 2 and 4.

———

MISSING ARTICLES.—Messrs. Grabbital, Snatchem and Keepit beg to state that they have active agencies in each platoon. Officers' kit inspections successfully negotiated.

———

Several advertisement spaces open.
For Terms, etc., apply to the Office Boy.

———

BATTALION RIDDLE.

Of what battle in English history do two officers of the Regiment remind you ?

A prize of 5/- will be awarded for the first correct answer that reaches the Editor, C/O Orderly Room.

———

All communications and illustrations to be sent to the Editor, C/O The Orderly Room. Please make the Gazette " go " by sending in your contributions.

Another issue of the Gazette will be published as soon as sufficient matter is sent in.

[This number was originally issued in typewritten form and has been printed in response to a general desire.]

No. 2.   MAY 5, 1915.

5th Gloucester Gazette.

A Chronicle, serious and humorous, of the Battalion while serving with the BRITISH EXPEDITIONARY FORCE.

ONCE again the unexpected has obviously happened. The "Fifth Gloucester Gazette," in spite of obstacles which at one time threatened to be overwhelming, has at length seen the light of day.

There were many difficulties in the way. In the first place, Pte. Pyne had to be lured and enticed—and it was no easy task—from one of his favourite forms of recreation—the pastime of route-marching—at the point of the Editorial Pencil (uncut). And then only thanks to the kind offices of Quarter-Master-Sergeant Mayne was a strange typewriter at his disposal. It is true that patient readers found themselves the innocent victims of a combined Missing Letter and Mangled Word competition—but that was the fault of the office-boy's handwriting. Anyhow, in the case of the present issue, we hope that persevering readers will be suitably rewarded, if not agreeably surprised.

Over the actual conflict of printing, we will draw a decent veil. Suffice it to say that only a Keats, in the act of describing the emotions of Cortez, as a new planet swam into the latter's ken, could have described the feelings of the Printer and Editor as they gazed on their handiwork. But it was only the midnight mouse and the peeping stars who marvelled, as hour after hour the staff covered themselves with imperishable glory, and their hands—and most of the Gazette—with smudges of indelible ink.

Meanwhile, as we thank our readers for the kind reception they have accorded to the Gazette, we plead for ever-increasing interest in it throughout the Battalion.

TRIOLET

(With apologies to Austin Dobson)— The French Roadmenders.

They intended a road,
But lumps grew upon it :
The map plainly showed
They intended a road :
But marching be blowed
For the surface is chronic.
They intended a road,
But lumps grew upon it.

                                        F. W. H.

CHIT-CHAT.

The "Morning Post" published a review the other day of Dr. Shipley's book on "The Minor Horrors of War," these horrors being the flea, the louse, the bug, and other undesirable insects. And the article appeared under the headline, "Little Brothers of the Prussian."

A wounded soldier was asked recently if he had been treated well in the Hospital. "Oh ! yes," he said, "Rather ! Why, they bathed my head with vinegar, put a bag of salt on my little Mary and my feet in hot mustard and water. I only wanted a bit of pepper in both my ears, then I should have been a blasted cruet."

We much regret that our Armourer-Sergt.-Major has left us to take over, we believe, a post at the Ordnance Headquarters.

All Platoon Sergeants are personally responsible to the Commanding Officer for seeing that all N. C. O.'s and men of their Platoon have the opportunity of reading the Gazette. In several cases, men had not seen the First Number a week after publication. Don't be selfish ; the other man wants to see the Gazette as much as you do.

The following sent in some excellent specimens of designs for the cover :—Lieut. King, L-Cpl. Biddle, Pte. W. J. Wood, Pte. Robertson, and some member of the Machine Gun Section. The design chosen was that of Pte. Robertson. Lieut. King's will, we hope, be printed as a separate cartoon.

The "Gloucestershire Echo," the "Gloucester Journal," and the London "Evening News" (some of our many esteemed contemporaries), gave us good "notices." We certainly did need some encouragement, and we are indeed grateful. But we can only hope to maintain the standard of the first issue if every member of the Battalion will do his best to send in contributions. Our esteemed contemporary—"The Cheltenham Chronicle "—is a little disappointed with the title of our paper, and suggests a more "frightful" title—*e.g.*, "The Asphyxiator," Surely the "Fifth Gloucester GAZ-ette " is practically the same.

SCISSORS AND PASTE.

In connection with the recent operations in British and German East Africa, the following extract from the "East African Standard" is interesting :—

"A man in the K. A. Rifles attached to a machine gun—he was a Christian and called himself Charles Matthews—was engaged in the attempted relief of the post. When the attack failed, he succeeded in bringing the gun away with him. Arrived at the main camp he reported himself, stated that he had brought away the gun, but apologised profusely for having left the tripod behind."

That's the right spirit, chaps.

————

The following verses recently gained a prize in a " Westminster Gazette " competition.

THE LAY OF THE LONELY SOLDIER.

I am wearin' Mary's gloves upon me 'ands,
Round me Tummy is Eliza's woolly bands,
    Isabella sends me shag,
    An' any time I wants a fag
There is diff'rent gals as sends me diff'rent brands.
       (Gimme a Woodbine !).
Yes, there's 'eaps o' gals as sends me diff'rent brands.

With Eva's pen to all the gals I write,
I puts on Gertie's 'elmet every night.
    An' each time I wash me ears
    It's with Clara's scented Pears',
And there ain't no blooming bit o' fluff in sight.
      ('Ow is your fawther ?).
Gawd ! I wish there was a bit o' fluff in sight !

It is quite true about the Claras and the Gerties, etc. " The people at home have been very good to us. They kept us going through the winter "—a seasoned Tommy remarked the other day.

————

In " The War Men-Agerie," Mr. St. John Hamund sings prettily of " The Censaur " :

    " The Censaur is half beast, half man :
    Which seems a reasonable plan ;
    Since if there's blame for what is done,
    Each puts it on the other one.
    The man gets news and passes it,
    The beast suppresses very bit.
    (Or if you are in any doubt,
    Put it the other way about)."

————

CHAPLAIN'S COLUMN.

" Keep on looking for the bright, bright skies ;
Keep on hoping that the sun will rise :
Keep on smiling when the whole world sighs :
    And you'll get there in the morning.

Keep on sowing when you've missed the crops :
Keep on dancing when the fiddle stops ;
Keep on faithful till the curtain drops :
    And you'll get there in the morning."

To the Bishop of Pretoria we owe probably more than we can tell. No one who heard him could fail to realise the important part that religion is destined to play in this war. The man who is not going to crack in a tight corner, the man who is going to do his job best, is the man with the right spirit. It is the man that matters—that was the burden of his message, and one which will help us all to do our own particular work, when we grasp the close personal relationship which can exist between God and man.

————

THE ROUTE MARCH.

(With apologies to Dr. Browne.)

This route march is a blighted thing—God wot.
    The sun—
    How hot !
    No breeze !
    No pewter pot !
He is a blooming pool
    Of grease—
    " The Sarge,"
And yet the fool
    (He's large)
Pretends that he is not.
    Not wet !
Foot-slogging over Belgian ways—
    In summer blaze !
Ah ! but I have a sign ;
    The sweat
Keeps dripping off this blessed nose of mine.

                F. W. H.

————

NATURE NOTES.

Birds somtimes select queer nesting places. A lark built a nest and laid three eggs therein at the top of a trench parapet. One day our sapper section indulged in a little trench mortar practice over the nest, and, immediately after a bomb had been fired, it was found that one of the eggs had hatched out. Evidently the young bird was anxious to know what was the matter.

It seemed strange, while heavy shell fire was in progress recently, to hear the bursts of shell fire punctuated by the homely call of the cuckoo.

We hear that one of our Company Commanders dislikes the rats which have quartered themselves in his dug-out, but it affords a fine opportunity for the acquisition of a Company Mascot. They are rumoured to be as large as rabbits.

Did a certain officer enjoy the boiled blackbird's egg with which he regaled himself at breakfast ?

Quite a feast of song is afforded by the nightingales in the vicinity of our trenches.

————

CORRESPONDENCE.

To the Editor of the 5th Gloucester Gazette.

Sir,
    I beg to enclose (with Alice's permission) the following letter received by her from the front, and I venture to believe that you and your readers will be astonished at the dangers our brave boys face—and survive.

        Faithfully yours,

           F. W. H.

        Somewhere in France.
        (Date censored].

Dearest Alice,
    Well, we are here at last—less than a dozen yards from the Germans—shells bursting all round. Bang ! Bang ! —there go two more. (Oh, Alice, where art thou ?). It is night, dark and stormy. Standing at

my post I can hear the Huns gnashing their teeth and turning over the leaves of their books prior to singing the " Hymn of Hate." How terrible for our listening patrols who are now standing with their ears resting on the enemy's parapet. I've " 'ad some."

Besides that, these devils have taken to exuding blue gases—directly against the advice of the Bishop of Zanzibar.

I must now chuck it.

Upon my vigilance depends the lives of my comrades, and the enemy is advancing by short rushes.

PERCY.

P.S. I forgot to say how proud we are of our officers.

P.P.S. Am expecting a stripe.

THINGS WE WANT TO KNOW.

The Transport Section would like to know who was responsible for the following :—

How to become a Transport man :

1. Put your puttees on upside down, so as to be different from anyone else.

2. Beg, borrow or pinch 2 or 3 chin-straps, wear them on top of your cap, at the back, or any way except the right one.

3. Get your clothes so dirty that it is difficult to recognise you, and you are complete.

Was the following letter (extracted from a daily paper) written by a 5th Gloucester ?

" My Darling Wife,

I sends in this letter half-a-crown.

P. S. There's a censor bloke wot opens our letters, so I sends no half-a-crown.

(a) Who ties a piece of string round his forehead to shave in the morning ?

(b) Is he in C. Company ?

Does the line—

" the sods with our bayonets turning "

occur in a recent poem on the war written by Mr. John Masefield ?

THE BAILLEUL CUP.

The course presented a very gay appearance on the great day of the Bailleul Cup. Considerable interest had been aroused among racing men owing to the fact that the form of many of the starters was merely conjectural. During the preliminary parade on the Pavé, an unusually large crowd had assembled in the Barbed Wire Enclosure, among whom we noticed Auntie Typhoid clinging tightly to the gallant Major's arm. The keen eyes of racing enthusiasts speedily marked down Quartermaster as an ugly customer where the favourite's chances were concerned. That fine three-year old, Adjutant by Blas Tit out of Da Mnem was noticeable for length of stride, and his excellent condition aroused much sympathetic comment, while the Quartermaster showed undoubted signs of great staying powers, his neck and quarters being significant of just that strength required for five miles races. The Doctor, too, was in fine fettle, having grown an excellent mane since mobilization.

Quite a fashionably dressed set of people arrived by the early ration carts, in time for bully beef and beer in gaily decorated billets, and several farm yards were quite en fête. An adjournment having been made, the chief item of the programme took place. Owing to superior initial velocity in starting, Dacre by Jam Pot out of Trench Mortar at once assumed the lead, hotly followed by Adjutant and Quartermaster, a large field tailing off with Doctor and Relief in rear. But ere Hyde Park Corner was reached it was evident that Dacre had shot his bolt, the punishing nature of a long course being too much for him. Colic, too, was soon in difficulties and had to loose his girth, thereby losing several lengths. The race had now resolved itself into a contest between Quartermaster, Adjutant, and Home Sweet Home, the first-named winning by a short ration from Adjutant, who was in hot pursuit. Quartermaster, with In Dent up, then received a great ovation as he was led back to store by his owner, J. Tickler, Esq. Adjutant, the favourite, came in for a good bit of cheering, his colours of Red and White being very popular. The crowd took his defeat very well, in spite of the fact that a lot of money changed hands.

G. F. H.

RESULT,

Quartermaster	by Prophet out of Rations	1
Adjutant	by Blas Tit out of Da Mnem	2
Hit	by Walking out of Trenches	0
Blown	by Shell out of Existence	0
C. B. the IV.	by Tardy out of Billets	0
Safety	by Clearing out of Wood	0
Relief	by Number Nine out of Action	0
Colic	by Fruit out of Season	0
Show a Leg	by Sergeant out of Revielle	0
Regent Street	by Path out of Wood	0
Padre	by Gum Boots out of Wagon	0
Gripes	by German Band out of Tune	0
Home Sweet Home	by Germ. Hun out of Belgium	0
Empty Jar	by Stand Down out of Rum	0
Doctor	by Shelled out of Chateau	0
Iron Ration	by Tin opener out of Armour	0
Kaiser Bill	by Slashers out of Berlin	0
Dacre	by Jam Pot out of Trench Mortar	0
Shrapnel Nigger	by Jack Johnson out of Black Maria	0

FROM THE EDITOR.

" True Tilda " and " Bee." Were the contributions intended for the Gazette, or for my personal use ?

R.I.P.

" And every mound of Flemish earth
Shall witness bear, as men pass by,
That greater things than life and death,
Are Truth and Right, which never die."

To some men, perhaps, even more than to others, this war has entailed great sacrifices. Charles Barnett, the very day war was declared, was one of those who offered themselves willingly. To him, situated as he was, the sacrifice was indeed a great one. A painstaking and efficient officer, we all knew him to be a very gallant gentleman, and we had all learnt to like him for his sterling qualities. And as his own platoon and all available officers stood round his grave on that starry night, amid the little clearing in the wood, we knew that the sacrifice in his case, as in that of others who lay down their lives for King and Country, could never be in vain.

Those beautiful lines by Canon F. G. Scott, one of the Canadian Chaplains, are true :

" At last, O Christ, in this strange, darkened land,
Where ruined homes lie round on every hand,
Life's deeper Truths men understand.
For lonely graves along the country side,
Where sleep those brave hearts who for others died,
Tell of Life's union with the Crucified."

CASUALTIES.

KILLED IN ACTION.

2nd Lieut. Barnett, C. F. R.   A. Company   19/4/15

DIED OF WOUNDS.

| No. 2647 | Pte. | Cummings, E. G. D. | ,, | 26/4/15 |
| 2229 | Dmr. | Mobley, A. | C. ,, | 5/5/15 |

WOUNDED.

2345	Pte.	Giddings, C. W.	D. ,,	17/4/15
790	,,	Howell, H. G.	A. ,,	18/4/15
2578	,,	Johnson, J. G.	D. ,,	19/4/15
1673	Dmr.	Goddard, L. E.	D. ,,	19/4/15
3338	Pte.	Phillips, C.	D. ,,	24/4/15
1932	,,	Timms, H.	D. ,,	24/4/15
2446	,,	Kingscote, A. W.	A. ,,	25/4/15
1789	,,	Phillips, J.	A. ,,	26/4/15
2098	L.Cpl.	Seabright, A.	B. ,,	26/4/15
2471	Pte.	Doyle, F. L.	A. ,,	27/4/15
2514	,,	Branford, H.	A. ,,	3/5/15

Lt.-Colonel A. P. Birchall, of Saintsbridge House, Gloucester, was well known to many of our readers, and will be affectionately remembered by all who knew him. In their great battle we read the " 4th Canadian Battalion at one moment came under a particularly withering fire. For a moment—no more—it wavered. Its most gallant commanding officer, Lieut.-Colonel Birchall, carrying, after an old fashion, a light cane, coolly and cheerfully rallied his men, and at the very moment when his example had infected them, fell dead at the head of his battalion. With a hoarse cry of anger, they sprang forward (for, indeed, they loved him) as if to avenge his death. The astonishing attack which followed, pushed home in the face of direct frontal fire made in broad daylight, by battalions whose names should live for ever in the memories of soldiers, was carried to the first line of German trenches. After a hand-to-hand struggle, the last German who resisted was bayoneted, and the trench won !

No officer could have been more deeply and probably none more widely beloved and admired."

—*Times.*

To RUPERT BROOKE

Dead in the Defence of Beauty.

(Sub-Lieutenant in the Hood Battalion of the Royal Naval Division, died of disease in the Dardanelles.)

Sweet singer of this latter day
Whom Death unkindly takes away,
Yet in the Spring-time of thy power,
Take thou in this mournful hour
The thanks of one whom often thou
Hast helped to rapture. Take the praise
Of all who in these sordid days
Have needed loveliness. Though now
Thy songs are ceased, and though their wine
Of Beauty that is all divine
No more brings holy drunkenness
Into the Soul ; yet ne'er the less
Thy end's sheer glory. Evermore
Joy diadems thy death to all
Who loving thee—love beauty more,
Since in thy death thou showest plain
Though Songs must cease and Life must fall
The things that made the songs remain.

F. W. H.   30/4/15.

ADVERTISEMENTS—RECEIVED TOO LATE FOR CLASSIFICATION.

HOUSE PROPERTY.

5th Gloucester Gazette.

A Chronicle, serious and humorous, of the Battalion while serving with the
BRITISH EXPEDITIONARY FORCE.

THE Bishop of Pretoria's visit to this land where History is being made afresh, has not been in vain. His letter to the *Times* has become a classic. It is a clear call to our country to do what our enemies, the Germans, and our friends the French, have long since carried out, namely, to mobilise herself, her workers and her shirkers, that she may fight with all the available material that is at her command. For the industrial army has yet to be organised and mobilised. And, indeed, by a strange and almost paradoxical turn of events, the eyes of all the world have of late been focussed on that island home of ours, " crowned with the sunlight, cradled in the seas," rather than on the Flats of Flanders. There, the advent of a Business or National Government, " for the saving of the Nation," has come as a relief to ourselves, and is a shock to the Germans. They never bargained for a united and a determined England. We hope and trust that by this time such flagrantly wicked cries as " Business as usual," will be no more heard in the land. The time calls for " collective action," which may yet heal " our unhappy divisions."

"The war may teach us how, in the past, we have wasted our energies upon a wrong ideal, or rather upon no ideal at all. It may make us substitute an ideal of harmony for one of conflict ; and if it does that, we shall get more from it than any victory can give us."

—Times.

CHIT-CHAT.

The Germans reckoned on a disruption of the British Empire. But the slender threads have now become chains of steel.

AUSTRALIA TO CANADA.

Round battered Ypres your men lie thick—
 Mine lie at Sari Bair.
Snow sister, we have followed quick
 Your pride of death to share.

Much grain our hands have harvested
 For Britain : the ripe math
Of continents shall all be shed
 For her while each one hath.

And this our woe shall be a spur
 While needs our Mother ; then
Must we ope wider yet to her
 Our granaries of men.

—Thorold Waters.—*Daily Chronicle.*

For never have Australia, New Zealand, Canada, India, seemed quite so near to us as they are to-day, when they fight side by side in Flanders and the Dardanelles.

The Italian Military Authorities have many thousands of savage buffaloes at their disposal. Hundreds of Italian lives have already been saved by buffalo charges in the narrow mined passes which bar the entrance to the Austrian Trentino. To start the stampede of buffaloes, bombs are only occasionally used, since an injection of serum rouses the animals sufficiently. Having achieved their purpose, they are then eaten by the Italian soldiers. Truly a buffalo in its time plays many parts !

A Captain and a Subaltern, after getting back safely with their wounded, decided to go forward to rescue their guns. " It's certain death," said the subaltern. " Yes, it's certain death," said the captain, " but it doesn't matter." " No," replied the subaltern, " it doesn't matter."

Towards the end of January, a German Pole, Kiskouski, of 56th Regiment of Infantry, was taken prisoner near La Bassé. While in the Canadian Hospital at Le Touquet, he gave the chaplain his " Tornister Worterbuch "—a Knapsack Dictionary and Phrase Book of English, destined to render valuable service when " The Day " came for the great invasion of England. The British uniforms described are the patterns in use in the summer of ·1912 ? Yet the members of the happy, happy Fatherland deny any premeditation.

It is instructive to note that this Pole was stationed at Kiel. Was he aboard one of those transports which did make a short dash for our coasts, and as quickly returned to their own ?

This Book is published as " The Huns' Handbook," and amusingly illustrated by Chas. Graves.

" One breakfast time, while Sir Henry Irving was on an American tour, he was feeling rather cheap as the result of a late supper party, when a rat ran across the room and, in consequence, he started. " You needn't mind him, Mis' Irving," said the negro waiter, " he's a real one."

The above story, culled from the pages of a lately published book, might be of consolation to an honoured member of A. Company. Did he not, with his quick intelligence, designate a certain object as a species of snake, belonging to the silver genus ? And it was only a piece of candle, after all, elongated by a practical joker.

It is proverbial that the bystander sees more of the game than either or any of the combatants. In eloquent proof of this, we quote a tit-bit from Dr. Dernberg's newspaper " The Fatherland, "published in Germany :

" As a matter of fact, the Belgians are happier under German government than they have ever been before. Belgium was a nation of industrial slaves before the entrance of the Germans. Germany brought with her not only her 42-centimetre guns, but also her social welfare legislation." ! !

By an appropriate coincidence, it was the same day that brought us the news both of the stoppage of racing and of the deficiency in the supply of Epsom Salts. In the double predicament we may yet see Epsom reviving its old industry of evaporating the waters to obtain the salts to which it gave its name.   *The Observer.*

We presume, to start racing again.

———

" Boys in Khaki " (Supply Column). All we know about Tickler, M.P., is that his politics belong to Grimsby, and his jam goes to the front. May you also be preserved.   " John Bull."

———

Though the trenches are no longer wet (owing partly to the cutting off of rum rations), we print the following song which has appeared in a daily paper.

I've a little wet home in the trench.
Where the rainstorms continually drench.
There's a dead cow close by
With her hoofs toward the sky
And she gives off a beautiful stench.
Underneath in the place of a floor
There's a mass of wet mud and some straw,
And the Jack Johnsons tear
Through the rain-sodden air
O'er my little wet home in the trench.
There are snipers who keep on the go,
So you must keep your napper down low.
And the star shells at night
Make a deuce of a light
Which causes the language to flow.
Then the bully and biscuits we chew,
For it's weeks since we tasted a stew.
But with shells bursting there
There's no place can compare
With my little wet home in the trench.

———

THINGS WE WANT TO KNOW.

1. Who asked for a kilometer of tobacco ?

2. The name of the polite private who, on being served with a stale egg, handed it back with the words : " Madame, c'est magnifique mais ce n'est pas un œuf."

3. (a) Name of the soldier who inquired at a shop for a Lee Martin.

    (b) Name of the shop girl who supplied him with " Le Matin."

    (c) If that was what he really wanted ?

4. How many perambulators are there in Rotten Row?

5. Which Corporal reported that the German sandbags had been whitewashed ?

6. What section was advised to dig itself in, owing to excessive caution displayed when the enemy opened fire with a machine gun ?

7. And who killed the Blackbird ?

8. Do the Germans call our Maxim (Wood pecker) the Night Jar ?

BY THE WAY.

" It is stated by a refugee recently escaped from Lille, that, as a result of a fancy dress ball given there by the Germans on Christmas Eve, one of the Local Ladies who had participated in the festivities, found the next morning that the words " Gott Strafe England " had been tattoed on her person."

—*Official Summary.*

A young lady from Lille, so they say,
Went out to a Ball, and next day
      " Gott strafe England " was found
      Tattooed plainly all round
Her person, in quite the Huns' way.

Meanwhile, a Tommy sympathises with the girl as follows :—

Look 'ere, Sir, dear Cap. Uzielli,
It's a terrible thing, I do tell 'ee.
      This poor girl's taboo
      Cause of that there tattoo
That the Huns painted all round her— —

(You must call it " person," Thomas : the word that rhymes is too Byronic for polite literature.—Editor).

———

THE PRIVATE'S LITANY.

From 3 days of fatigue under the name of rest ; from parcels on the last day ; from fog till 8 a.m. (or after) ; and from all things that prolong stand-to ; from flies ; from sentimental songs and from " Tipperary " ; from trench-inspection by staff-officers and the Colonel ; from French beer ; from people that refuse to lend, and from people that borrow ; from Sergeant Peter Huggins ; from listening patrols and from dead Germans ; from the lady who takes your money and says " no compris," Deliver me !

———

RUTHLESS RHYMES FROM ROTTEN ROW.

(May 14-15).

Here's to you—" Phiz ! Bang ! "
   Light as a feather, heavy as lead,
Wherever you go, don't light on my head,
      " Phiz ! Bang "

Here's to you, " Pip ! Squeak ! "
Where are you going ? Whom do you seek ?
You're travelling some, you're off lik a streak
      Of Lightning, " Pip ! Squeak ! "

Here's to you "Phiz! Bang !" and "Pip! Squeak"! all !
Tales are told of you, far too tall
To be entered here, but it's certainly clear
We don't care a hang for either or both—
      " Pip ! Squeak ! " " Phiz ! Bang ! "

———

BALLADE OF BEELZEBUB—GOD OF FLIES.

Some men there are will not abide a rat
  Within their bivvy. If one chance to peep
At them through little beady eyes, then pat
  They throw a boot, and rouse a mate from sleep
To hunt the thing, and on its head they heap
  Curses quite inappropriate to its size.
I care for none of these, but broad and deep
  I curse Beelzebub—the God of Flies.

Others may hunt the mouse with bayonet bright,
  And beard the glittering beetle in his lair,
And fill the arches of the ancient night
  With clamour if a stolid toad should stare
Sleepily forth from the snug corner where
  They fain would rest. But I will sympathise
With beetle, rat and toad. I have no care.
  I curse Beelzebub—the God of Flies.

The ting gnats they swarm in many a cloud
  To tangle their small limbs within my hair
And sting. The blood-flies dart ; and buzzing loud
  Blue bottles draw mad patterns on the air.
The house flies creep, and what is hard to bear,
  Feed on the poison papers advertised,
And rub their hands with relish of such fare !
  I curse Beelzebub—the God of Flies.

ENVOI.

Prince—Clown of Europe—other shall make haste
  To call damnation on your limbs and eyes.
Spending good oaths upon you were a waste,
  I curse Beelzebub—the God of Flies.
                                    F. W. H.

TO THE PATRIOTS OF POPLAR

and other places where England's honour was upheld by mob law.

The 'uns is usin' pison—the Loositania's sunk.
We reads the dily pipers, so we knows
                          (All abaht it).
Come show yer patriotic spirit, let's get drunk.
'Eave 'alf a blooming brick at someone's shop—then do
It may be kept by one of England's foes.   [a bunk.
It's easier nor route marchin' and shootin' in a dry
Dusty land where we doesn't know the lingo.
                          (Rool Britannia !)
This is the kind o' warfare for the likes o' you and I :
We doesn't want to fight (as the dear old verses sy)
But if we do we've got the bricks—by jingo !
                                    F. W. H.

OUR PORTRAIT GALLERY.

1. To P.H.

(With apologies to George Macdonald.)

Where do you come from, Peter, dear ?
Out o' the reg'lars into 'ere ;
Whence take your eyes such depth of blue ?
Defaulters feelins is of that hue.
Lose they ever that innocent stare ?
When I walks with the girls in Barton Fair.
How come you so rotund and fine ?
I perseveres when I starts to dine.
Why do you wear that scarlet band ?
Only because it looks so grand.
Bogey are you, or fairy feat,
Or a plain M. P. upon his beat ?
No fairy I aint, nor plain d'ye see,
But a pleasant, popular, plump M. P.
                                    F. W. H.

THE PLUG STREET EMPIRE.

6-50   TWICE NIGHTLY   9

SPLENDID PROGRAMME
Fresh Bill each Week.

1. Overture—" A." Company Orchestra.
    Conductor—Drummer LAPPINTON.
    Instruments :
    First Mouth Organ ... Pte. WALKER.
    Second ,, ,, ... Pte. BUNDY.
    First Biscuit Tin ... C. S. M. WAGSTAFF.
    Mandoline ... ... Pte. SPIERS.
    *Massed Triangles and
    Concertinas under the
    direction of ...* ... Drm. CARPENTER

2. Screaming Farce—" *Brigade Time* "
            Watches by Ingersoll.

3. The Three Alkalis in their Smoke Swallowing Act
    Thyo, Hypo, and By Carb.

4. Great Wire Walking Act
    *by Slip Over, Trip Up, and Dammit,
    who will put their foot in it twice nightly.*

5. Little Willie in his Lightning Act, entitled
    " *Pop off*," or " *Phiz Bang.*"

6. Cresol and Chloride will appear in their realistic
    Fly-catching Act.

7. Great Fight for the Championship of the World
    *Special engagement of Jack Johnson and White
    Hope. 15-inch gloves, 17 yards ring.*
    Referee—President WILSON—if not too proud.
    Time-keeper—A. FUSE.

8. Great Looping the Loop-hole Scene
    by Telly, Scopic and Snipem.

9. Song—Frosti's Good-bye
    " *When Little Willie comes.*"

10. Thrilling Yarn, entitled : " *The Ship that
    foundered*," or " *The Smack that reached the
    Bottom*," by U. 19.

11. The famous Cross-talk Comedians in their patter
    Song—
            " *Kay & Kayenne.*"

Wigs and Beards by N. O. CLIPPER.

NEXT WEEK ; Special arrangements have been
made by our patrols for a visit from the Famous
Saxon Troupe of Wire Walkers.

POPULAR PRICES ; Sandbags . . . frs. 1.50
                    Dug-outs 50
                    Parapets . . . Free.
    Admission by identity disc only.

Respirators are damped each evening instead of
fire-proof curtain being lowered—by arrangement with
the Lord Chamberlain.

ODE TO THE RUM RATION.

Wine ! 'Tis but a comprehensive term
For nectar of whatever form or fashion,
Beer, Whisky (" Johnnie Walker," " Black & White,")
   Or Rum, good honest Rum, my favourite Ration.

Oh Rum ! Thou com'st from isles amidst whose groves
   Each dusky Strephon woos his dusky Phyllis,
Heedless alike of war and war's alarms,
   All heedless, too, of " Big and Little Willies ! "

I love me not the wine of our Allies,
   Ni blanc ni rouge—(I'm very hot on French,
Although my comrades, jealous of my gifts,
   Threaten to inter me in some distant trench.

That's by the way. My ode is now to Rum
   On which I could discourse with much sagacity.
And Rum, I find, when liberally supplied,
   Tends to increase my usual loquacity.

Heed, not then, any Temperance crank,
   Who fears thy influence upon the weak.
We are no babes who " face the music " here,
   But men who fight as e'er fought ancient Greek.

So let us pour thy generous spirit forth,
   And let each Strephon lift his glass to Phyllis.
And while we dream of those fair eyes we love,
   We'll quite forget to curse both German Willies.

NOTICE.

" NO ISSUES."

Lectures on the above subject will be given next Tuesday by Dr. Skinner, the famous rationer, appointed by the Board of Higher Technical Education.

That section which was recently left short of bread, owing to double rations having been served out to a sister section, is required to attend the first lecture :

" HOW TO LIVE WITHOUT GRUB."
                  (Biscuit Collection).

The second

" HOW TO CLEAN BUTTONS WITHOUT
   POLISH "
                  (Pinka Collection).
is optional, but it is hoped that many of the troops will attend, as the subject is of exceptional interest.

With the possible exception of Professor Haybread —who is a German—Dr. Skinner is the greatest living authority on the subject.

On Wednesday, Professor B. Lister—the famous evolutionist—will lecture to the Battalion on

" MAN'S DESCENT FROM MULES."
                  (Zam—buk Collection).

Pte. Hayward in charge of the lantern.

GIFTS.

The Battalion's most grateful thanks are due to :—
   Lieut.-Colonel S. S. Marling, for 4 telescopic rifle
      sights.
   Colonel J. C. Griffith, for many things, including
      periscopes, sun curtains and tobacco.
   Colonel E. B. Jeune (Commanding 3/5th) for
      periscopes.
   All those ladies who so kindly made sun curtains,
      particularly those of the Cheltenham Ladies'
      College.
   All who have sent tobacco and cigarettes.
   Canon Brewster—for hymn books & mouth organs

LITERARY COLUMN.

We have received the following books for review. With great reluctance we have refrained from quoting from their contents, as the mere mention of the names of their distinguished authors is more than sufficient to guarantee a ready sale and a wide circulation.

HOW TO SELL THE "CITIZEN."
   By one who knew . . . Pte. KNOCKER.

HOW TO B-B-BAYONET THE B-B-B-B-BOSCH.
   By one who hopes . . . A. SERGT.

HOW TO PRESERVE THE FIGURE.
   By one who doesn't. . . " D " Company Cook.

HOW TO KEEP THE UNIFORM CLEAN.
   By one who might   .. . Pte. F. W. H., Editor
      of the Battalion " Tailor & Creaser."

HOW TO MANAGE MULES.
   By one who does   . . .Pte. Darkie HAYWARD.

EDITOR'S HAVERSACK.

J. R. Your poem on " Trenchitis "—you did well to apologise to " Excelsior "—does not scan. At the same time it is a most interesting pamphlet, dealing as it does with a new disease which you have unearthed with most praiseworthy persistency. Meanwhile, we are in consultation with the Medical authorities who hope in the course of a few days to bring out a new serum—prophylactic in character,—which will effectually choke off your own and similar outbursts I hope these remarks are sufficiently trenchant.

Thank you, No. 13 Platoon, for reminding us of those splendid lines you quote :

  " If the day looks dark and dreary,
    And your prospects sort o' slim ;
  If you're getting kind o' weary,
    And the future's awful grim ;
  And you feel inclined to chuck it,
    When all hope is nearly gone.
  Just bristle up and grit your teeth,
    And keep on keepin' on."

Platoons 1, 2, 3, 4, 5, 6, 7, 8, 9, 10, 11, 12, 14, 15, 16
Please send in contributions.

CASUALTIES.

" No easy hopes or lies
Shall bring us to our goal,
But iron sacrifice
  Of Body, Will and Soul.
There is but one rank for all,
  For each one life to give.
Who stands if Freedom fall ?
  Who dies if England live ? "

KILLED IN ACTION.

2229	Dmr. Mobley, A.	A Company	5/5/15
378	Sgt. Morgan, H. H.	C ,,	13/5/15
664	Pte. Franklin, T.	D ,,	13/5/15
1819	Pte. Aston, J.	D ,,	13/5/15
2650	Pte. Romans, C. H.	D ,,	13/5/15
2554	Pte. Middleditch, H.	D ,,	13/5/15
169	Sgt. Hearl, W.	A ,.	21/5/15
2306	Pte. Sleeman, J.	A ,,	21/5/15
3243	Pte. Hawkins, A.	B ,,	6/6/15
2179	Pte. Thompson, I. H.	D ,,	7/6/15
2350	Pte. Smith, A. S.	D ,,	15/6/15

ACCIDENTALLY KILLED.

| | 2nd Lieut. Guise, H. G. C. | C Company | 6/5/15 |
| 3335 | Pte. Bates, J. E. | C ,, | 6/5/15 |

DIED OF WOUNDS.

1844	Pte. Cole, R. W.	C Company	12/5/15
1906	Pte. Silvester, L. J.	C ,,	20/5/15
2256	Pte. Coulthard, E.	D ,,	28/5/15
2664	Pte. Clarke, W. B.	C ,,	15/6/15
2426	Pte. Angell, H. V.	B ,,	13/6/15

WOUNDED.

1543	Pte. Peacey, F.	C Company	6/5/15
459	Sgt. Portlock H.	C ,,	6/5/15
2666	Pte. Cromwell, W.	C ,,	6/5/15
2873	Pte. Robertson, G. S.	C ,,	6/5/15
1998	Pte. Fear, G. F.	C ,,	6/5/15
	Lieut. Sprague, F.H. (R.A.M.C. attached)		11/5/15
2536	Pte. Hobbs, F.	C Company	12/5/15
365	Cpl. West, G.	C ,,	19/5/15
2529	Pte. Faulkner, J.	C ,,	19/5/15
2517	Pte. Hodgson, A.	A ,,	19/5/15
2751	Pte. Curtis, T. B.	B ,,	26/5/15
3298	Pte. Greenwood, C. H.	C ,,	27/5/15
1266	Pte. Yates, H. J.	C ,,	27/5/15
2509	Pte. Vickery, T.	A ,,	28/5/15
1679	Pte. Mace, W.	C ,,	29/5/15
1897	Pte. Black, A.	C ,,	4/6/15
2334	Pte. Turner, L.	B ,,	4/6/15
2518	Pte. Ingles, W. H. S.	A ,,	5/6/15
3250	Pte. Reay, L.	B ,,	5/6/15
2763	Pte. Lewis, E.	B ,,	6/6/15
2467	Pte. Simmons, P.	A ,,	7/6/15
1481	Pte. Organ, L. W.	A ,,	12/6/15
1647	Pte. Wyatt, F. J.	D ,,	13/6/15
2589	Pte. Lane, G.	D ,,	15/6/15

R.I.P.

2nd Lieut. H. G. C. GUISE.

Together Christopher Guise and Charles Barnett came to us in those early days of August. Not many days separated their deaths, and but few inches their graves. For they lie side by side in the Battalion Cemetery, so that even " in death they were not divided." A born soldier, a natural leader of men, " he leaves behind him." in the words of the Elmore Parish Magazine, " an unsullied reputation, and sustained the best traditions of an honoured family." His great popularity, with officers and men alike, was genuine, and fully deserved, and it is not too much to say that we can never forget him.

———

A SECOND LIEUTENANT.

Somewhere in Flanders he lies,
The lad with the laughing eyes,
    And I bade him goodbye but yesterday !
He clasped my hand in a manly grip ;
I can see him now with a smiling lip,
    And his chin held high in the old proud way.

Salt of our English earth,
A lad of promise and worth.
    Straight and true as the blade at his side,
Instant to answer his country's call,
He leapt to the fray to fight and fall,
    And there, in his youth's full blood, he died.

Victor yet in his grave,
All that he had he gave ;
    Nor may we weep for the might have been,
For the quenchless flame of a heart aglow
Burns clear that the soul yet blind may know
    The vision splendid his eyes have seen !

Weep but the wasted life
Of him who shrinks from the strife.
    Shunning the path that the brave have trod ;
Not for the friend whose task is done,
Who strove, with his face to the morning sun,
    Up and up to his God !

           Touchstone—*Daily Mail.*

———

5th Gloucester Gazette.

A Chronicle, serious and humorous, of the Battalion while serving with the
BRITISH EXPEDITIONARY FORCE.

SINCE those hot days when patient compositors at Bailleul wrestled with English obscurities and finally achieved the impossible and printed the Gazette, the Allies have been joined by another Friend in their great campaign of anti-barbarism. No one who read the Italian Prime Minister's speech could but feel that here was a nation which has not merely " run to the succour of the victor." She has counted the cost, and the whole nation has gone into the war. " It is a moral revolution—the soul of Italy has awakened from a long trance of materialism and indifference." She has realised, like Belgium, that there are some things worth fighting for. Emile Verhaeren in his book, " Belgium's Agony," describes a similar crisis in his country. " I saw the King go into the parliament House and I saw him coming out. He had taken counsel with the representatives of his people on the eve of his and their blood-stained Easter Day. And, indeed, it was for us Belgians nothing short of an Easter morning. It was our Resurrection. We did our duty, and in the doing of it we were born again." It is to be hoped that Shelley's great prophecy from the last chorus in " Hellas " may yet be literally fulfilled—" Another Athens shall arise and—to remoter ages—bequeath the glory of her skies;" and that Greece, before it is too late, may join the Allies, and once more be in the vanguard of Liberty Triumphant.

KEEP SMILING ! The Germans, who hoped to spend a pleasant holiday in Switzerland, have had to get home " quick " because the Swiss Hotel keepers would not take their Paper Money ! ! !

THE PRIVATE'S STORY.

The night was dark and dreary, and the moon shone through the sky ;
I was sitting on Plug-Street Station when I heard a startling cry ;
My mate stood there before me, and through many a tear did say ;
The rustic bridge a mile off, sir, has just been blown away.
The midnight mail is due sir, and even as we spoke
She thundered through Plug Street Station, a'belching sparks and smoke.
Something had to be done, sir, to save a fearful smash.
From a thousand yards in the air, sir, that train would soon fall crash.
Then I pulled out my last " Woodbine " sir, and I sat me down to smoke,
When I thought of the lives at stake sir, that fag half made me choke.
But I sat and pondered and pondered, till my brain was scorched with the sun,
Then I came to the sudden conclusion that something would have to be done.
So to study the situation I brought forth my Bradshaw guide
With the waves rising higher and higher, it was washed away by the tide.
The express was dashing along, sir, at a mile and a half an hour,
When I jumped on a transport mule, sir, and prayed for more strength and power.
Then I galloped away in the darkness, till I reached the brakes with my hands :
Then, tugging away at the buffers, I brought the train to a stand.
And that's how I was promoted from obscurity, so to speak,
To a full-blown railway porter at the rate of a franc a week.
Well, that's the end of my story, the telling'll never tire,
Though everyone that hears it seems to think I'm a bit of a...

" Private" No. 1 PLATOON.

EXTRACTS FROM THE DIARY OF O. C., RECONNOITRING PATROL.

Sunday,.... ..day of......

6.0 p.m.	Waked from sound sleep. Feeling very fit. Don't believe any Germans in trench opposite at all.
6.15 p.m.	Met Company Commander. Told him I didn't believe any Germans opposite. C.C. said in that case I was just the man he wanted, and would I go across at 9.30 p.m. and find out ?
6.25 p.m.	Said I would ; but how? C. C. suggested patrol, as I might feel lonely in German trenches by myself.
6.30 p.m.	Said I would think about it.
6.32 p.m.	Went to think about it in secluded spot.
6.50 p.m.	Still thinking in s.s.
6.55 p.m.	Thought I might have left unsaid remark to C. C. about no Germans.
7.0. p.m.	Went to tell off patrol.
7.15 p.m.	Patrol went to think it over in secluded spot (same one).
7.20 p.m.	Observed with telescope four Germans in trenches opposite. Seemed to be large, cheerful men.
7.30 p.m.	Went to think it over in secluded spot.
7.35-8 p.m.	Pretended to eat hearty dinner. Discovered C.C. had finished whisky. Most annoying. C.C. promised rum " if " we came back all right. Thought C.C. might have said " when " instead of " if." Asked C.C. whether patrol was necessary, in view of four Germans seen by me. C. C. not having any. Said four Germans probably caretaker, wife, and two children locking up for the night. Dislike C.C.
8-8.30 p.m.	Found my Platoon Sergeant and arranged work for night. P. Sgt. said he didn't believe any Germans in trench opposite us. Dislike P. Sgt. A tactless N. C. O.
8.40 p.m.	Noticed one of patrol writing on black edged note paper. Said it was his last will and testament, and would I censor it as he wished to send it off to-night. Dislike O. of P. A pessimist. Refuse to censor last will and testament.
8.45-9 p.m.	Discussed weapons with Patrol. Company bomber insisted bombs-lemon, two in number. Gave way reluctantly. N. B. To patrol as far as possible from Company bomber. C.C. lent me his Colt automatic pistol and explained mechanism.
9.5 p.m.	Let off Colt accidentally. Severely frightened C.C. Felt happier.
9.15 p.m.	Met Machine-gun Officer who said " the hate was just beginning." Explained he meant Machine-gun hate at 9.15. to night. Expostulated with M. G. O. M. G. O. said bullets would probably go high if patrol lay down. Dislike M. G. O. A reckless young officer.
9.15 9.25 p.m.	Listened to Machine gun firing. Unpleasant weapon.
9.25-9.30 p.m.	Still listening to Machine-gun, plus three German machine-guns.
9.30 p.m	M. G. O. told me " hate " was over, and I could start. M.G.O. seemed amused at something.
9.30 p.m.	Counted two more German Machine-guns firing.
9.35 p.m.	Rifle grenades—German—six in number.
9.40 p.m.	Went to look for patrol.
9.45 p.m.	Found Patrol whistling " Dead March " in unison Tell Patrol we will wait a bit.
9.50 p.m.	Less wind up now. Tell Patrol I thought we would start.
9.55 p.m.	Tell Patrol we ought to start.
10.0 p.m.	Tell Patrol we must start.
10.5 p.m.	C. C. came and asked why we hadn't started. Produced Colt as if to load.
10.6 p.m.	C. C. noticed Colt and pretended Adjutant wanted him on telephone.

10.10 p.m.—Patrol started. Night very dark. Fell into
11.30 p.m. large shell hole getting over parapet. Lost C. C's Colt, probably at bottom of shell hole. Felt happier. Company Bomber suggests I should carry the bombs as am now unarmed. Reprove Company Bomber for talking. Tread on our listening patrol (all five of us). Listening patrol annoyed. Reprove listening patrol for swearing. Their duty to be seen and not heard. Remember have not warned our sentries, so shall probably be shot by them on returning. Discover one of patrol punctured in leg by bayonet of listening patrol. Happy thought ! Send him back with message to senteries and take his rifle. Discover rifle unloaded. Reach our wire front line. Curious smell. Crawl under wire into decaying cow. Believe patrol pulled me through dead cow. Remove portions of dead cow from my face. Patrol complains of smell of dead cow. Corporal suggests more open formation. Flare from our line just misses my head, and burns furiously on the ground. Suspect C. C. of having fired it. Very dark beyond wire. Patrol crawls. Very wet and muddy. Find rifle barrel choked with cow. Hope for the best. Patrol reports four Germans (one each advancing from front, flank and rear. Fail to see Germans myself. Reprove patrol for getting the wind up.

Distinctly see two Germans myself. Patrol fail to see any Germans. Reprove patrol for being unobservant. Flare shows my Germans to be trees. Suspect patrol of grinning.

Patrol, in succession from the right, fall into disused trench full of water. Fell in myself. My orderly reports his rifle lost. Reprove him for carlessness. Find I have lost my own rifle. Prolonged search for rifles. Patrol find orderly's rifle but fail to find mine. Believe orderly has my rifle. Say so. Patrol light matches to verify number of rifle. Rapid fire on us from English and German trenches. Find disused trench handy, but still full of water.

Interval.

Ask Corporal whether he knows way back. Answer in the negative. Collect opinions of patrol as to direction of our lines. Patrol quite positive on four points of the compass (one each). Take my own line. Crawl. Fall over trip-wire into several tin cans. Suspect Corporal of using bad language about me. Order Corporal to lead the way. Corporal falls over another wire into golconda of tin cans. Swear at Corporal. Feel happier. Crawl through more wire. Lose seat of breeches in wire. Orderly suggests we are going towards German lines and are in German wire. Halt patrol hurriedly. Debate on subject with patrol. Orderly gloomy but firm. Decide to lie low and listen. Do so. Distinctly hear Pte. Jones imploring to be allowed to shoot. Also hear my Platoon Sergeant demanding flare pistol. Also hear sound of men standing to, and loading. Crawl nearer in despair. Shout to Platoon Sergeant by name. Hear Pte. Jones still reasoning with P. Sgt. P. Sgt. inclined to think it safer to shoot first and enquire afterwards. Recollect telling P. Sgt. that was the thing to do. Wish I hadn't told P. Sgt. that. Shout again P. Sgt. answers. Saved. Rally patrol and fall over parapet on to fixed bayonet.

11.35 p.m. Demand rum from C.C. C.C. promises anything if I will take the smell of dead cow away with me.

11.45 p.m. My servant brings me rum in my dug-out. Notice he is wearing respirator. Overhear sentries complaining that someone "don't half stink". Notice strong smell of dead cow myself. Discover a good deal of dead cow still adhering.

11.55. p.m. to 12.30. a.m. Remove chunks of dead cow from clothes, boots, etc.

12.30. Write report for Headquarters. Report very well drawn up.

2.15. a.m. "Distance covered by patrol estimated at five hundred yards. German trenches overcrowded. Object of patrol attained, etc."

2.15. a.m. Went to observe path of patrol by daylight.

2.30. a.m. Observe seat of trousers fluttering on wire.

2.45. a.m. Observe furthest point—the disused trench. Distance appears less than it seemed at night.

3.0. a.m. Fetch C. C. and ask him how far it is. C. C. says about 50 yards. Dislike C.C. C.C. asks for his Colt. Feel happier. Tell C.C. of its loss. C.C. bad tempered about it. Fed up with C.C.

3.30. a.m. Retire to sleep.

4.0. a.m. Waked by C.C. who asks me if I realise that I am on duty till eight a.m.

The C. C. be—"Strafered."

IN FLANDERS.

I'm homesick for my hills again
—My hills again !
To see above the Severn plain
Unscabbarded against the sky
The blue high blade of Cotswold lie ;
The giant clouds go royally
By jagged Malvern with a train
Of shadows. Where the land is low
Like a huge imprisoning O
I hear a heart that's sound and high,
I hear the heart within me cry :—
" I'm homesick for my hills again
—My hills again !
Cotswold, or Malvern, sun or rain !
—My hills again ! "

F. W. H.

SCISSORS AND PASTE.

The Only Way.

An officer, seeking places to billet his men, called at a wealthy lady's house, and inquired if she could take in two recruits.

" Certainly not ! " replied the lady. Then, after a moment's thought, she added, " But there's a nice dry shed at the end of the garden."

The officer, accustomed to this kind of reply, asked to be allowed to look over the house. Seeing the dining room, he remarked, " Nice room this."

The lady agreed it was a nice room.

" Well." said the officer calmly," have it ready for two of my men on Monday "

" But it's impossible " shrieked the lady. " The room's full of costly furniture. Where shall I put it ? "

After gazing out of the window, the officer replied :
" Well, you know, there's a nice shed at the end of the garden."

Sunday Telegraph.

Pears are in—that is, they are in France, the nice sweet little pears with a ruddy glow on them. A Territorial, knowing this, decided on dessert, and being off trench duty for a day or two ordered some pears in his best public school French, which had up till then served him well enough. It was true that he was doubtful about the gender of " poire " but made it masculine, and explained that he wanted the " petit " sort. Then after the bully beef course he invited his messmates to share his contribution to the feast, opened his bag and displayed—peas in the pod ! It was another case of the " beggars not understanding their own language."

Daily Chronicle.

This actually did happen in the Battalion, and in C Company.

German attempts at humour being usually very feeble indeed, we rejoice to see what they call " The Amusement Calendar ". Included in their " Latest Programme " are the following items :—

"Hansel and Gretel " — The Grand Duke Nicholas and General French.
"The Dollar Princess"— Strict American Neutrality.
"The Seer of Visions "— The English . Eye-Witness.
"How to win a war " — Please send receipe by return-Kitchener.

From *Daily Express*.

Yet another parody of our " Little Grey Home in the West," this time secured personally by the Editor from " La Plus Douce Ferme," the scene of modern frescoes. All rights reserved.

" There's a little wet trench near Messines,
It's the wettest that ever was seen.
There are bullets that fly,
There are shells in the sky,
And smells, like a German has been !
My dug-out's a haven of rest,
Tho' 'tis only a tumbled-down nest.
But with Johnson's around
I must keep underground,
Till the golden sun sinks in the West."

He (Smart young subaltern), pointing to an imposing looking tent : " That is the Officers' Mess."
She (Smart French girl) : " Ma foi, why have they not cleared it up ? "

THINGS WE MUST KNOW.

1. Ginger, dear, how DID you kill that pig ?
2. (a) What sergeant told the girl to call him papa ?
   (b) Why ?.
3. (a) Who bought the chair for " Peter " to sit down on while he was putting a defaulter through his drill ?
   (b) And why ?
4. Who was the " grand " cricketer. who nevertheless put his pad on the wrong leg.
   (Was he in the Transport ?—Their drivers always ride with right leg well padded ; or was it because he thought he was going to bat the other end ?)
5. Which sergeant rouses his Platoon with " Come on, lads, the sun is well in the Heavens, and the day is far spent " ?
6. Who is the cook who asks, when you go to him for rations, "if you want j-j-jam on it" ?
7. Who was it who ordered a Stretcher-bearer to go down a 60-feet well on a chain ⅝ in. in diameter and 30-ft. in length, to rescue an old riddle of a bucket ?
8. (a) The number of runs by which the men won in the cricket match between the officers and men, AND,
   (b) The exact number of men on pack drill next day, and how many were members of the victorious team.
9. (a) Who brought rations up to the Trenches in a coke bag ?
   (b) What was the colour of the bacon in the morning ?
10. (a) Why, oh why, did you tell your Platoons to extend inwards ?
    (b) Will you give detail for same ?
11. (a) Why did the Doctor condemn the meat ?
    (b) Was it in revenge for the previous evening ?

Meanwhile, in view of the keen desire for knowledge as evinced by the above questions, it is proposed to open an Information Bureau, under the heading of "They say that."

EXAMINATION PAPER.

1. "The old soldier has a card-board box to bulge his Pack on route-marches." Has he ? Have you ? If not, why not ? State reasons and draw map.
2. Who is the officer whose name most easily answers to the saying " Multum in Parvo ? "
3. To what base uses can the semaphore be put in D. Company ?
4. Trace the growth and girth of Company Quartermaster Sergeants, giving dates and measurements in all cases.
5. A groom at G. H. Q., many miles behind the firing line, writes home as follows :—" and now, Mother dear, I must close. The bugle note rings clear and true, calling me back to the trenches. So I must lay down my pen and take up the rifle. Whether I shall return or not, who can tell ? " What treatment do you advise for those who write home this and similar tosh ?
6. The distance from Cranham to Gloucester is 10 miles. A starts walking to Gloucester at 2.30 p.m. on a very hot afternoon, at the rate of 4 miles an hour. His bosom pal leaves the Cross at 2.29 p.m., walking 3¾ miles an hour. Where and why will they meet ?
   (To save pencil, paper, loss of temper, brainfever, etc., the answer is, we regret to state— " The King's Head," Upton St. Leonards).

THE SONG OF THE RECONNOITRING PATROL.

Oh ! its roaming in the gloaming
When the birds have gone to roost ;
When the evening hate's beginning,
And machine guns do a boost ;
When you're crawling on the ground,
While the bullets flick around,
Oh ! it's very jolly roaming in the gloaming.

Just roaming in the gloaming
When the flares drop on your head.
And you wonder if your friends at home
Will know that you are dead ;
When before your straining eyes
Countless Huns appear to rise,
It's a merry business roaming in the gloaming.

Oh ! it's roaming in the gloaming
On an old decaying cow,
When your head gets in it's stomach
And you're mixed up anyhow ;
When enveloped by the smell,
You can only whisper " H."
It's a weary business roaming in the gloaming.

Just roaming in the gloaming
When the rain begins to fall ;
When you feel convinced you've lost your way
And won't get home at all ;
When you shiver and perspire,
And trip over German wire.
Oh ! it's then you're fond of roaming in the gloaming

Oh ! it's roaming in the gloaming
When you're safely back at last ;
When your sentries haven't shot you,
And the rum is flowing fast ;
When you write a grand report
Saying more than all you ought,
That's quite the best of roaming in the gloaming.

OUR LIST OF BENEFACTORS.

On Wednesday, June 23rd, " Les Ouvriers ' Concert Party, from the 48th Division A.S.C. M.T., provided an entertainment for the Battalion. This took place in the open-air, and was much enjoyed.

The Vicar of Tewkesbury.—Sundry comforts.
Cirencester, per *Wilts and Gloucester Standard*— Pipe, ¼ lb. tobacco, 100 cigarettes, chocolate and cake to each Ciceter man : also shirts and socks.

OUR BENEFACTORS—*continued.*

The Ladies' College, Cheltenham.—Periscopes and concertinas.

Various Gloucester Friends (per Mrs. Collett).— 150 pairs canvas shoes.

The Gloucester Women's Suffrage Society.—5 baths and heater.

Mr. Harley Butt (Gloucester).—Tobacco and Cigarettes.

From the Powers that Be. A much enjoyed REST—
" When the squat and sullen howitzer is quiet,
    And his diet
Of cordite and of lyddite is at rest
      In the nest,
While the gunners at the limber come and go
      To and fro."

2nd Lieut. J. P. Winterbotham for preparing an excellent wicket with an entrenching tool.

Unknown Genius.—Designs of air pillow to puff packs.

OUR PORTRAIT GALLERY.

II.—THE Q.M.

(After an old Nursery Rhyme).

1. I love little Quartie
His coats are so warm
And though he will curse me
He'll do me no harm.

2. He changes my bags
With a patriot zeal
When they're wearing away
To the land o' the leal.

3. When out of the trenches
Upon the green sward
He stands up to bat—
And the fielders are awed.

4. And chasing the leather
He murmurs " O blast ! "
" It's very hot weather
To double so fast ! "

5. More often we notice
He chooses to stand
As umpire—the fate
Of the match in his hand.

6. So I'll not pull his leg,
Nor hint he is stout,
And in the next game
He'll give me " not out ! "   F.W.H.

BRICKS FROM THE EDITOR'S PACK.

The Editor does not think that his readers are quite alive to the seriousness of the situation. Were it not for the untiring and delightful efforts of " F. W. H." this paper would have had to discontinue publication.—If England requires more munitions, we need more contributions. All the same we are glad to welcome some fresh contributors this month.

There appears to be a wish in certain influential circles, notably that in which the Transport lives and moves, that Nos. 1 and 2 of this Gazette should be reprinted. The Board of Directors, after receiving reports from their auditors, are of unanimous opinion that such publication is desirable, provided that Platoon Commanders—that already overworked body—could furnish lengthy lists of intending purchasers.

Meanwhile it is satisfactory to be able to state that No. 3, adorned with Lance-Corporal Robertson's splendid cover, as executed by Mr. John Jennings, has sold like hot cakes. In the event of any difficulty in obtaining your copy, please forward your complaint to O. C., Publishing Dept., Headquarters Mess.

The Directors feel that interest in the columns of the Gazette would be doubly increased by the insertion of more " personal pars," " Company doings," "Platoon patter," etc. A well-known Barrister will revise the Personal Column every month, so that there will be no chance of shareholders being mulcted in heavy damages. So please send in some of those horrid truths hitherto concealed in those green envelopes, which enclose nasty bits about your sergeant, and nice bits about your packs.

Next Month.—Fumes from the Editor's Water Bottle ! !

Nos. 1 and 4 Platoons.—Compositions received with many thanks. Regret that lack of space compels us to hold over same.

A PIRATICAL DITTY.

(With apologies to Gilbert and Sullivan.)

1. When the enterprising sniper's not a-sniping (not a-sniping)
    And Billy's final fury has begun (à la Hun)
He loves to see the little Taube a-flying (Taube a-flying)
    And to listen to the rattle of the gun (Maxim-gun).
Chorus : When youv'e military duties to be done
      (to be done)
    Our life in France is such a happy one (happy one).

2. When in our cosy bivvys we are lying (sometimes lying)
    And we whistle comic songs when day is done
      (day is done) ;
And with periscopic glances we see if the foe advances
    And so on till this bally war is done (war is done).
Chorus : When you've many irksome duties to be done
      (to be done)
    Our Terrier's life is such a varied one (varied one).

3. When down to bathe through dusty lanes we're marching
    (we are marching)
    With our packs upon our backs we curse the Hun
      (in the sun).
Over cobble-stones galore, with limbs jarred stiff and sore
    And the rifle's almost like a blooming ton
      (like a ton).
Chorus : When all fatigues and duties soon are done
      (quickly done)
The Private's life is quite a happy one (now duty's done).

                O. L. W.

ANSWERS TO CORRESPONDENTS.

" Worried " writes us in melancholy vein. He appears to have fallen foul of his C.S.M. for keeping the maul in his dug-out to kill flies with. Personally, we have found the old method of two ladders, one with a rung missing ; and a block of granite, as efficacious as any for dealing with these pests.

" Tiz " asks us whether it is usual for Officers to wear respirators on foot inspections. No, not usual, but often.—Well, the roads are trying for the feet, aren't they ?

ROUND ABOUT THE HALLS.

Having a few hours to spare one evening recently. I strolled down to the Empire well-known to the inhabitants of Plug Street.

This magnificent building has been considerably improved in the matter of ventilation since my last visit. Large portions of the roof having been removed.

The extraordinary rapidity with which such alterations have been carried out was remarked upon by all.

As might be expected, an excellent variety entertainment was provided, and an expectant house awaited the raising of the waterproof sheet.

Only in the parapet seats was there any thinning out noticeable, and here not more than one in every three seats were occupied.

The performers in " Brigade Time," not having recovered from the shock of appearing on the stage

C

within 7 minutes of their scheduled time at the previous house, their place was taken by " The Three Alkalis," in a really clever turn. Unfortunately, there appeared to have been some disagreement as to their " get up," which resulted in three distinct patterns of respirator being represented. However, apart from this slight contretemps, their performance was admirable, and imbued everybody with a sense of safety.

Item 9 " When Little Willie comes " was tastefully rendered, and the inimitable Kay and Keyenne kept the whole house rocking with laughter. Their performance went off without a jamb, and many of the audience were seen to wipe the tears from their eyes with 4 by 2.

The boxing match for the championship of the World, which was postponed until the following evening, is dealt with in our sports column.

CRICKET BEHIND TRENCHES.

The very best thanks of the whole Battalion are due to a large number of " Gloucester Sports," who very thoughtfully clubbed together and sent out a complete set of Cricket gear for the use of the Battalion.

In order to commemorate the receipt of such a splendid gift, a match was arranged between " Gloucester men " and the rest of the Battalion, which, after a very pleasant game, ended in favour of the Gloucestrians. The match, which was opened with the " Alex. Matthews " ball, was played on D. Company's field in which a very carefully selected pitch was preserved with matting, which somewhat unsettled some of the " cracks." Lieut.-Colonel J. H. Collett, and several other officers, together with a good sprinkling of N.C.O.'s and men, were present to watch the doings of some of their old favourites.

Needless to say, the kit, which is available for any enthusiasts of the Battalion, has been in great demand since, as the record of matches shows.

Gloucester XI. v. the Rest of the Battalion.

Rest.

Sergt. Gardner, b. Smith	10
Cpl. Field, b. Lt. Sumner	6
Lt. Snowden, c. Harvey, b. Lt. Sumner	0
Lt. King, b. Smith	18
I.-Cpl. Millard, b. Cpl. Knight	1
Lt. Durrant, c. and b. Smith	6
Pte. Timms, b. Smith	0
Pte. Tilley, b. Smith	0
Pte. Sindrey, b. Smith	9
Pte. Stinchcombe, c. Lt. Sumner, b. Smith	0
Lt. J. P. Winterbotham, not out	0
Extras	6
	56

Gloucester XI.

Pte. Hamblin, b. Lt. Snowden	19
Pte. Harvey, c. Lt. Snowden, b. Lt. King	6
Pte. Pollard, l. b. w., b. Sindrey	6
Pte. Sysum, b. Sindrey	7
Pte. Egerton, c. Gardner, b. Lt. Snowden	0
Pte. Mansell, b. Lt. Snowden	3
Capt. Sessions, b. Sindrey	4
Lt. Sumner, b. Miliard	11
Cpl. Knight, c. Gardner, b. Sindrey	0
Pte. Webb, not out	8
Pte. Smith, stumped Lt. Durrant, b. Millard	4
Extras	10
	78

Bowling.

Bowlers	Total overs	Total maiden overs	Total runs	Total wickets
Pte. Smith	8	2	21	7
Lt. Sumner	4	0	21	2
Cpl. Knight	3	0	8	1
Lt. King	3	0	17	1
Lt. Snowden	4	0	17	3
Pte. Sindrey	5	0	12	4
L.-Cpl. Millard	2	0	6	2

Umpires :—Lieuts. C. F. Foote and C. W. Winterbotham.

CRICKET MATCH—OFFICERS V. MEN.

Officers :		Score.
Capt. V. N. Johnson	b. Egerton	13
Lieut. H. P. Snowden	b. Smith	1
Capt. R. J. C. Little	c. Gardiner, b. Egerton	0
2nd Lt. J. P. Winterbotham	c. and b. Smith	9
2nd Lt. C. W. Winterbotham	b. Egerton	2
2nd Lieut. H. S. King	c. Smith b., Egerton	0
Capt. H. C. B. Sessions	b. Egerton	0
Capt. G. F. Collett	c. Sysum, b. Egerton	15
Lieut. L. R. C. Sumner	b. Smith	9
Capt. Visct. Campden	b. Smith	0
2nd Lieut. K. G. Durrant	not out	0
Capt. R. M. F. Cooke	b. Smith	0
Extras		15
		64

BOWLING.

Pte. G. Smith, 5 wickets for 30.
Pte. W. Egerton, 6 wickets for 19.

Men :		
Pte. L. Hamblin	b. 2nd Lt. J. P. Winterbotham	14
Pte. F. Mansell	c. Capt. Little, b. Capt. Collett	16
Sgt. A. Gardiner	run out	27
L-Cpl. S. Millard	b. Lieut. Sumner	18
Pte. W. Egerton	c. and b. Lieut. Sumner	1
L-Cpl. F. W. Harvey	c. Capt. Johnson, b. Lt. Sumner	1
Pte. H. Pollard	b. Capt. Collett	4
Corpl. A. J. Field	b. Capt. Collett	1
Pte. S. Sysum	b. Lieut. Sumner	4
Pte. R. Sindrey	not out	19
Pte. G. Smith	b. 2nd Lt. J. P. Winterbotham	1
Extras		44
		150

BOWLING.

2nd Lieut. J. P. Winterbotham, 2 wickets for 49.
Lieut. L. R. C. Sumner, 4 wickets for 19.
Capt. G. F. Collett, 3 wickets for 24.

Other Matches played during the Month.

No. 12 Platoon	75	No. 11 Platoon	53
1/5th Glo'ster Transport	28	1/4th Ox & Bucks Transp.	72
"C" Co.	111	'B' Co.	66
No. 9 Platoon.	50	Rest of "C" Co.	54
1/5th Glos. Machine Gun	93	1. Bucks. Machine Gun.	39
No. 14 Platoon	57	No. 13 Platoon.	57
No. 9 Platoon.	135	No. 4 Platoon	88

BOXING.

On Wednesday last at the Plug Street Empire, the fight for the Championship of the World was held.

Before a crowded house the two greatest terrors of modern times stood face to face.

Jack Johnson, trained to a hair, without a superflous grain of cordite in his composition, and The White Hope.

From the start it was seen that The White Hope was working for a smack at the Black's time fuse.

After gentle sparring the Black landed a glancing blow on the i of White Hope, but with a smart right parry the W. H. delivered the point and sent J. J. tottering back to his *basket*.

The Black's seconds were seen to scratch the Black's head during the interval, and in the second round the W. H. going all out for a knock out blow, landed a heavy blow on the Black's fuse cap.

From pieces picked up at C 6 d 4-9 it is thought that the Landsturm " seconds " must have set J. J. for percussion.

Our reporter is getting on as well as can be expected, and is lucky to have escaped.

TO MY LITTLE MARY.

We Tommies get some decent grub
  And are not hard to please,
With assorted Army biscuits
  And varieties of cheese.

Jams of different coloured hues,
  (A tin goes round to four).
Oh for the courage of Oliver Twist
  To go and ask for more !

Some days a little butter, too,
  But it goes on very thin,
With a dozen fellows waiting round,
  The last one gets the tin.

Of bread we have 'bout half a loaf
  Near a month old, they say.
So in the shop we get " le pain "
  When we've been and drawn the pay.

Then scores of tins of bully beef
  Are dished up as a stew.
Boiled " piéce de resistance " steak,
  And the spuds are very few.

The funny thing about this diet,
  It does not make us thinner,
Yet back to England once again,
  Heaven help that good square dinner !

OUR MONTHLY FRENCH LESSON FOR BEGINNERS.

A Prize is offered for the best translation of the following :

LEUR NOUVEAU PAS !

...Les Boches voudraient à tout prix Calais...

Fatigué du pas de parade,
Qui fait sourire le Français,
Le bon Germain, dans sa bravade,
Voudrait notre Pas-de-Calais.
Pour l'apprendre, à Kalais, qu'il vienne,
On lui montrera la méthode,
Et bientôt, de Berlin à Vienne,
Il pourra en lancer la mode.
C'est un pas coquet, difficile,
Un " pas sage," mais dangereux ;
A marcher, il n'est pas facile,
Et le Germain est trop gâteux !
Aussi : S'il ose s'en saisir,
Ce grand pas sera son trépas :
Et pour contenter son désir,
Nous lui ferons sauter le pas.

        ALBERT SAUTTEAU.

1/5th Bn. Gloucestershire Regiment.

Roll of Officers, N.C.O.'s and Men employed with the Brigade Grenadier Coy.

Lieut. W. Fream.

A. Company.		C. Company.	
1183	L.-C. Nash, E. F.	1999	Cpl. Lippett, G
2453	Pte. Thomas, A. C.	2768	L.-Corpl. Ross, G. E.
2486	Pte. Pepperel, W. F.	2742	Pte. Wintle, A. H.
1366	Pte. Marshall, H. R.	2602	Pte. Webb, C. F.
2480	Pte. Smart, S.	3014	Pte. Crosby, C. F.
2315	Pte. Jackson, L. E.	3571	Pte. Ireland, A. D.
2444	Pte. Ellson, D. M.	1434	Pte. Pyke, A. C.
2489	Pte. Doogood, H. A. C.		

B. Company.		D. Company.	
405	Sergt. Bishop, P. C.	2177	L.-Cporl. Hensley, G.
2091	L.-C. Coton, J.	1413	Pte. Dyer, H.
2341	Pte. Barnett, E.	1417	Pte. White, I.
1987	Pte. Blandford, C. E.	1372	Pte. Smith, F. W.
2182	Pte. Hemmings, C.	2614	Pte. Clift, G. A.
2544	Pte. Jeenes, H. P.	2594	Pte. Russell, G.
1474	Pte. Sully, G. E.	1961	Pte. Elliott, H.
1474	Pte. Jeynes, H. C.		

A. Company.
59 L.-Corpl. Cresswell, C. Cook to Company.

1/5th Bn. Gloucestershire Regiment

Warrant Officers and Sergeants.

1st Class, Warrant Officer.
Bn. Sergt.-Major :
    4656 Dennis, T.
    2nd Class, Warrant Officers.
Bn. Qr.-Master-Sergt. :
    86 Webb, W.
Coy. Sergt.-Majors :
    456 Tibbles, W. G.
    602 Horne, L. H.
    204 Wagstaff, G.
    325 Attwood, C.

Coy. Qr.-Master-Sergts. :
    497 Lance, T. P.
  1857 Locke, W. N.
  2539 Humphris, H.
    466 Wilce, F.

Sergeants :

30	Brown, D.	1643	Chandler, H. J. R
2005	Huggins, A.	599	Webb, C. H.
410	Armstrong, R.	892	Ayres, A.
238	Huxford, J.	405	Bishop, P. C.
154	Jennings, J. C. W.	242	Hill, F.
539	Preater, W. H.	988	Jefford, F.
66	Durrett, T.	904	Hinch, G.
661	Chapman, H.	1129	Pyment, H. G.
352	Jordan, A.	413	Wonson, R. C.
463	Young, H.	2340	Cook, H.
133	Faville, A.	1068	Stevens, S.
200	Hill, W.	2412	Cook, G. E.
770	Jones, H. V.	1531	Gardiner, A.
23	Taylor, E.	433	Patrick, S. G.
203	Heaven, J.	492	Cook, E. W.
379	Morris, A.	506	Owen, J. G.
2420	Richards, R. E.	1465	Knight. E.
242	Liddiatt, L.	1654	Conduit, D.
75	Proctor, F.	381	Lloyd, R.
392	Finch, F.	2218	Maisey, F.
2416	Bailey, W. W.	1524	New, D.
58	Meadows, J.	1300	Groves W.

PROMOTIONS.

Lieut. R. M. F. Cooke	To be Captain (Tempy)	dated	10/5/15
2nd Lt. T. H. Moore	To be Lieut.	,,	dated 29/3/15
2nd Lt. Brenan	To be Lieut.	,,	dated 29/3/15
2nd Lt. F. Conder	To be Lieut.	,,	dated 29/3/15
2nd Lt. Nason	To be Lieut.	,,	dated 29/3/15

PROMOTIONS AND APPOINTMENTS.

The following promotions and appointments take effect from the dates stated :—

To be Company Quartermaster Sergeant :
466   Sergt. F. Wilce   dated 20/6/15

To be Sergeants :
2218	L.-Sergt. F. Maisey	,,	20/6/15
1524	Corpl D. New	,,	20/6/15
1300	L.-Sergt. W. Groves	,,	14/7/15

To be Lance-Sergeants :
1999	Corpl. G. Lippett,	,,	20/6/15
111	Corpl. P. Speck	,,	14/7/15

To be Corporals :
2114	L.-Corpl. F. Kibby	,,	27/5/15
1724	L.-Corpl. F. Coole	,,	20/6/15
1156	L.-Corpl. J. Apperley	,,	20/6/15
1628	L.-Corpl. R. C. Jackson	,,	14/7/15
2331	L.-Corpl. G. W. Chandler	,,	14/7/15
1183	L.-Corpl. E. F. Nash	,,	14/7/15
2487	L.-Corpl. W. J. Abbott	,,	14/7/15

To be Lance-Corporals :
2693	Pte. A. H. T. Lewis	,,	27/5/15
1521	Pte. J. Hayward	,,	20/6/15
2272	Pte. F. W. Reeves	,,	20/6/15
2428	Pte. F. H. Butcher	,,	14/7/15
2746	Pte. H. Buckle	,,	14/7/15
2787	Pte. F. Davis	,,	14/7/15
1557	Pte. A. C. Rice	,,	14/7/15
1142	Pte. S. M. Santer	,,	14/7/15
2684	Pte. A. Holloway	,,	14/7/15
2678	Pte. J. W. Gray	,,	14/7/15
1813	Pte. D. A. Watts	,,	14/7/15
1427	Pte. B. W. Fisher	,,	14/7/15
2609	Pte. A. Rigby	,,	14/7/15

CASUALTIES.

Wounded Accidentally.

2717	L.-Corpl. Hensley, G.	12/7/15	Coy. D.
2652	Pte. Webb, C. F.	12/7/15	Coy. C.
1417	Pte. White, I.	12/7/15	Coy. D.

Wounded.

2542	L.-Corpl. Holland, J.	16/7/15	Coy. B. (Slight)

5th Gloucester Gazette.

A Chronicle, serious and humorous, of the Battalion while serving with the BRITISH EXPEDITIONARY FORCE.

"The Bloater in the Adriatic
Idly pursues his course erratic,
Nor dreams that fate will lead him to
The hungry poet in his attic.

The same, of course, may be said of the sardine and the hungry soldier. Little does the peach, nursed by summer suns, think of her future in the shape of a tin gleely opened in an English trench. The polo pony never bargained for a corpulent Company Commander, and I do not suppose the German Emperor a year ago had any conception of what his future is going to be before long !! Such is the inability of the mind to project itself into the future.

No. 1 of this "Gazette"—how it gasped for breath ! What a fight for life !—never imagined that "Gazette No. 3" would be bedecked in so handsome a cover, still less that it could attain to the dignity of print and enjoy in this area a circulation greater than any other Threepenny Paper !!

Born 'neath a lucky star, blessed by many less fortunate contemporaries on the other side of the silver streak, once again it makes its bow, and wishes its readers "bonne chance."

ANNIVERSARY.

1. BELGIUM.

An outcast in grey worlds had Freedom grown,
(You gave your soul to right,
Your blood to the beast called Might),
You sheltered him in the night
And made a throne.

Who doth not see it now,
    Belgium ?
And the light on your brow,
    Belgium ?

The large fat lands that blinked with lazy eyes
Look upward at the glory, and arise :
Burnish their rusty arms and ride away.
The state aloof
Feels now the cloven hoof
Of Prudence, driven back into its face ;
And—ease grown terrible—leaves the market place,
To clank, high-hearted, and singing in the fray.

This have you done,
    Belgium,
And tho' the Hun
Makes palaces mere smoke,
And burns the shrines
Through all your lands : there shines
And stands unbroke,
More high and brighter than that height of flame,
Your everlasting name.

2. FRANCE.

The spirit wise and witty
Of France in the golden morning,
Arose at the glimpse of a city
And the sun-bright towers adorning—
Frozen music and history
Mingled together in mystery.

The fair young face of France
Kissed by the glowing sunlight,
Forth (by some happy chance)
Peered from the mirror of one bright
Pool that the trees were arching—
Water we passed in our marching.

Lo, we have seen you France ;
We have seen the soul that made you !
Above all evil chance
And the guile of those who betrayed you
You still shall sit secure
As long as the worlds endure.

3. GERMANY.

Foul shame be on you who did violate
Flanders, the obese old woman...God
Avenge the treacherous deed and with a nod
Dismiss your plea, "Necessity." The hate
Of all men is upon you, and disgust
Sickens us as we think upon the deed.
France—the fair woman who escaped your will,
And we, her friend to whom she called in need,
And Russia, firm of spirit whom we trust
To add the chastisement which is your due,
Strong Italy, and Serbia suffering still
But still defiant—We together swear
By all that still is undefiled and fair,
To hunt you and to beat you down until
Your swinish body turn to finer dust,
Your tall pride bend
To break, and all your lust
Come to a bloody end.

F. W. H.

FOREWORD.

To The Editor,
    5th Glo'ster Gazette.

Dear Sir,
    I feel that the 5th Glo'ster Gazette is incomplete without a short story. My little effort has been rejected by numerous Editors who seemed to doubt its probability. This, Sir, only shows their ignorance. I feel that you, with a knowledge of Trench warfare gained at the Front, will have better taste.

Yours faithfully, and truthfully, B. F.

THE GIRL AT THE GUN,
or
PENELOPE AND THE PRUSSIANS.

A short story of the Great War, not hitherto published. All rights of translation and reproduction strictly reserved throughout the World, including the Cannibal Islands and St. Helena.

THE grey light of dawn broke wanly over the Trenches at Washoutegen. The carrion crow from his perch upon a ruined periscope croaked a hoarse greeting to the day. "Curse that bird; how I hate him !" exclaimed sentry Alf. Cockles (formerly well-known in London Society as Sir Bramble Blackbrush, Bart.) "Curse him !" he repeated, "he shall croak no more." He hastended to a machine gun, and with trembling fingers inserted a clip of K. and KN.S.A.A.

His keen eye glinted along the sights. "Three thousand, five hundred, and forty three yards" he murmered, quickly estimating the range. "A long shot, but I will have him yet." He glanced down the bore of the gun. "Bother !" he exclaimed harshly, grinding his teeth. The barrel was choked by a blue-bottle. The weapon was useless ! He began searching his pockets for a pin. The blue-bottle must be removed immediately. He found his iron ration, three different patterns of respirator, his identity disc, a box of matches (empty), a pipe, a candle, a tin of tobacco, two packets of Woodbines, three shell heads, a German helmet, four photographs signed "Mimi," "Mabel," "Suzanne" and "Mary" respectively, a large yellow slug, a mouse, a piece of cheese, and two holes.

"A pin," he cried, raving with the blood-lust, "A pin !" "Can I lend you one ?" said a pleasant voice from the other side of the parapet. Instantly his soldierly instincts were on the alert. He cleared his throat, and called in a manly ringing voice, "Halt-who-are-you-advance-one-and-be recognised pass-friend-alls-well." He paused breathless, and waited for the applause. He was now glad to think of the midnight oil he had burnt learning the correct way to challenge. There was no reply. Keeping one finger on the trigger, he peered over the parapet, regardless of the bullets which all this time were streaming over him.

There, crouching beneath the sandbags, he saw a slight girlish figure clad simply in......(deleted by the Censor.)

"Won't you come in ?" he said gently. "I will," she replied, doubtfully, "if you will stop swearing at me." He helped her over the parapet, and his heart beat too fast to notice......(deleted by the Censor.) She smiled prettily, showing a pearly set of teeth, probably her very own. "Here is a pin," she said, pulling out her hair pin, and releasing masses of golden red hair.

He longed to kiss her, but remembered that during six months' continuous trench warfare he had grown a bristly beard, and other things such as (refer to advertisements of Keating's—Editor.) "Thank you," he said, simply, quickly removing the blue-bottle with a few quick, skilful movements.

"But what are you doing here ?" he continued. Her childish face dimpled. "I'm a spy," she said, laughing. Cockles scratched his head. The situation puzzled him "A spy ?" he gasped "Oh ! a spy for England," she answered, merrily waving a a small Union Jack. "That's right," said Cockles. in a relieved tone of voice. Her face clouded, "But oh !" she cried, "I came here to warn you, The Germans are attacking you at 9-30 a.m., and it is now 9-25."

"Gracious goodness !" exclaimed Cockles, losing all control of his language, "why did you not tell me this before. Now it may be too late."

Madly he beat his brow. The minutes passed 9.26.—9.27.—His brain reeled. He remembered that he must wake the General at all costs, He remembered too, his last attempt on a previous occasion. He remembered how he had burst into that veteran's bedroom, and shouted "To arms, to arms, the Germans are upon you !." He remembered how the General had said to him (deleted by the Censor) ......, and had hurled him through a second storey window with the aid of the Divisional Cyclists. 9.28.—9.29.—9.30.—A long drawn yell burst from the enemy's lines. Volumes of gas a hundred feet high rolled from their trenches. Over that green-grey wall flew clouds of Jack Johnsons, White Hopes, Black Marias, Portmanteaux, Little Willies, Very Lights, Whizzing Jennies, Crumps, Coal boxes, Whiz-Bangs, Pip-Squeaks, pink rockets, jam-pots, and several patterns of bombs and aerial torpedoes. Through it all a strong smell of sauer-kraut, and lager beer ever increasing in volume, told that behind the gas the German hordes were advancing on the English line.

Cockles glanced at the girl besides him. She was white as a sandbag. Her mouth was firm, and tightly compressed as she hastily adjusted her respirator and goggles. How should he gain time to wake the General and his own comrades still peacefully asleep, and at the same time hold the Huns at Bay ? That was the momentous question for Cockles !

An idea struck him. There was the girl, there was the gun (now free from the blue-bottle), and there were the enemy. He grasped her arm roughly. "Can you use a machine-gun ?" "You mean a Maxim" she replied calmly. Oh ! yes, I've often used one on the moors for fun."

"Quick !" he said, "Fire this gun till I return. Keep the enemy at bay for an hour and a half till I wake the General, and the day is ours !"

He dashed wildly off, only stopping to catch a glimpse of the girlish figure, her hair streaming in the draught of the shells bending over the deadly quick-firer.

Penelope (for that was her name) opened fire. She shot away the emplacement ; she shot away the parapet and wire ; she riddled the carrion crow (at 3543 yards) ; she shot away a Taube in mid air ; she shot away the gas ; she shot away the Germans behind it ; she shot away the smell of sauer-kraut and lager beer ; she shot away the German trenches. Her "tir de barrage" stopped the shells (all sorts), bombs, Very lights, and rockets.

By the time that Cockles returned with the General, and all his comrades, followed by the officers of his regiment, the attack was ended. The line was saved !

Over the smoking gun, surrounded by a huge pile of empty cases, and broken firing pins, round which the Salvage Corps was already hovering, bent a pale, slight, girlish figure. She had taken off her respirator and goggles, but a Union Jack still fluttered bravely from the crank handle of the gun.

A dreadful fear clutched the heart of Cockles. He sprang forward, handing off the General, who showed signs of doing the same thing.

Was she dead ?

He clasped her in his arms. No ! Her heart beat still. Her eye-lids fluttered and raised. He looked into her deep brown orbs.

Was it love ? It was !

"Dearest," she whispered.

"My own," he murmured.

* * * *

Cockles was promoted on the spot to the rank of unpaid Lance-Corporal, and attached to the staff of the Nth Brigade (for Home Service only) as N. B. G.

He was also awarded the P. T. O. (for valour in waking the General.)

And Penelope ? Ah ! she has—Cockles.

BALLADE OF THE RICH HEART.

What thief is he can rob this treasury
  Which hath not gold but dreams within its gates ?
What power can enter in to take from me
  My treasure ? While upon the threshold waits
"Courage " my watch-dog, keeping back the Fates
  Which follow close until I do depart
With safety from their little loves and hates,
  Singing of all I carry in my heart.

Guarded of dreams against all evil chance
  With young Adventure arm in arm I go,
Laughing at Luck and silly Circumstance,
  And counting naught that comes to me, my foe.—
I change, if 'tis my whim, the winter snow
  To blowing blossom ; and with that same art
I fashion, as I will, life's weal and woe,
  Singing of all I carry in my heart.

Let me go lame and lousy like a tramp
  But feel the wind, and know the moon-lit sky.
What matter if the falling dew be damp ?
  Still it is dew. And well content am I,
Among my dreams in seeming poverty,
  Far from the cities, and the noisy mart,
With Life and Death—my dearest friends—I lie,
  Singing of all I carry in my heart.

Envoi.
Prince of this world, high monarch of all those
  Who deem reality life's better part,
Careless I tweak thy crooked royal nose,
  Singing of all I carry in my Heart.   F. W. H.

THINGS WE WANT TO KNOW.

Who boiled a tin of jam in mistake for a Maconachie ? And was he a Sergeant ?

Did a well-known Lance-Corporal improve his French at Allouagne ?

What Regiment gets Abdulla cigarettes sent out to it ? (The advertisement in Abdulla's boxes is as follows :—
    " There is a mistaken idea that " Tommy " doesn't know a good thing in cigarettes when he sees it, but I can assure you that every-one was simply bubbling over with excitement when the Quarter Master Sergeant shouted as he drove in with the ration cart, 'Good news, boys, a case of Abdulla cigarettes for you' ".)

Is it true that there is an old lady in D Company ?

Who made the OXO with lemonade ?

Was there a report current in the German lines that one of their patrol had been chased by a Ghurka ?

Is it true that the author of that rumour is suffering from a swelled head ?

Who bayoneted the mouse ?

Who brought back the rumour that the streets of A. remind one of the Burlington Arcade.

Who had a bath in a sump hole ?

A sentry, on seeing a dog on the other side of the parapet, said " Halt ! Hands up ! " who was he ? To what Company did he belong ? And was he surprised when the dog didn't paws ?

Who tried to roof the dug-out before it was dug-out ?

Who blew the candle out and then pinched the onions and the kitty ?

Who said he had haricot veins ?

What Company Cook refuses to peel the spuds ?

To what Company did the three men belong who were seated outside the baths, clothed with one identity disc, searching for " small deer ? "

And is it true that French fleas have the annoying habit of jumping backwards, to evade capture ?

Is it true that the one-man-band is to be fed on " oatmeal porridge " as it is so fond of Scotch music ?

Is it really true that D Co's Sergeants had to stop up the key hole and cracks when the " nuts " were " cracking " their after-supper jokes ? And why ?

Who asked for " a kilometre of Glen Rush with a grenadier in it " when all he wanted was a " Litre of Vin Rouge with a dash of grenadine ? "

How long it took to get to the First Division, and was the route selected a choice one ?

Is it true that a rifle with telescopic sights is being procured for the fat L. Corporal.

Who complained that we had " none of them rikoshay bullets wot was served out to the Allymands ? "

When will the War be over ?

Who ordered the section to fire at an angle of 45 degrees, so that the Germans might not know the direction from which the bullets came ?

Which N. C. O. says " Hurry up, chaps, for dinner ; it's all gone ?

OUR PORTRAIT GALLERY.

No. 3—THE M.O.

Who says " Ye've got a nasssty cough
A number nine will take that off " ?—
    The Doctor.

Who mixes Epsom with my tea
Because he thinks it's good for me ?
    The Doctor.

Who cures the pain in Little Mary,
And pulls out teeth when necessary ?
    The Doctor.

Who, when his favourite forceps fell,
Cried " —and—the thing to—" ?
    The Doctor.

Of cold, the flea, and other horror
Who rids my body vile ? Begorra,
    The Doctor.

                  F. W. H

HIAWATHA ON PATROL.

Through the fresh and chilly evening,
Through the damp and sloppy clover,
Ere the sun had scarcely sunken
In his rose and golden splendour,
Outward crept the quaking trackers,
Pockets full of Mills' lemons
(Cunning Messrs. Mills, of London).
Detonators neatly fitted,
Each one steering clear of other
Lest by any sad misfortune
He should bump his neighbour's pocket,
(Dangerous things those bombs like lemons).
Through the wire of barbed description,
Ripping many pants and tunics,
Stole the doughty German snatchers,
Silently as prowling pussies,
Straight towards the German trenches.

On through wire and past chevaux-de-
Frise and still more clinging tendrils,
Slipping into murky shell holes,
Roundly cursing German gunners,
Onward crept the would-be baggers,
Urging on each other bravely,
With the vision of a tot of
Rum to warm their chilly innards
When the dirty work was over.
Only now a bit more labour,
Passing wire of barbed description.

See ! The wire is now behind them,
They are now in fields untrammelled,
By this wire of clinging nature,
Thick with points that scratch all over.
Cunningly bestrewn by Frenchmen.
Down they drop as through the darkness
Streaks a rocket, tail all fiery,
Launched from out their trench back yonder.
Soaring up and up and onwards,
Bursting out in light so brilliant,
Neatly hung beneath a para-
Chute which floats with graceful leisure,
Out across the dark and dreary
Space between the lines of trenches.

Cautiously they raise their heads and
Gazing hard across the clover
Seek the telltale " pickel-haube,"
Which denotes the noxious presence
Of a prowling Bosch or even
Two or three intent of mischief,
Such as cutting, for amusement,
Lengths of wire of barbed description,
Cunningly bestrewn by Frenchmen.

Unbeknown to Hiawatha
(Who, of course, is now a Corp'ral)
Number one of our patrollers,
Feels a nasty sense of sickness
Creeping through his sopping person,
Can it be that when the rocket,
Artfully despatched by Someone,
Waved its dazzling light above them,
He had seen a pickle-haube
Sticking up amongst the clover ?
When at length the deadly nausea,
Which assails our quaking snatcher,
Overrides control of muscles,
And his teeth began to chatter,
He approached Hiawatha,
(Corp'rals have no fear, of course not),

Whis'pring loudly in the organ
Specially designed for hearing,
And with shaking and he forthwith
Gave the " just about " direction.

Suddenly across the heavens,
Brilliantly with stars bespangled,
Streaks a coruscating Something
From a kicking Very pistol,
Safe behind protecting sandbags.
Sure enough our Hiawatha,
Gently raising head and shoulders,
Gazes hard with eyes outstanding
At the spot (as near as nothing)
Pointed out by the patroller
With the chattering teeth (by Boodles).
Sure enough the dazzling star shell,
Artfully despatched by Someone,
Parabola-wise above them,
Shows the hawk-like eye of Hia-
Watha something gently moving
To and fro amongst the clover,
Scarcely more than thirty yards or
Thirty-five from where they cower.

Surreptitiously they extract
From their pockets, fingers trembling,
Lemon bombs by Mills of London,
(Crafty Messrs. Mills of London),
And with safety pin they fumble,
So that on the slightest provo
Cation they can hurl their weapon
At the creeping cursed Germans.
Murmuring " Gott strafe Deutschland,"
Grasping hard their lemon missiles,
They proceed to crawl and creep a
Little closer to the pickle—
Haube that the soaring star-shell
Had disclosed amongst the clover.
Shall we praise or blame the Sergt.
Or the members of his party,
(Likewise grasping jam tins, lemons,
Frictions Heavy, Automatics),
Who upon another errand,
Of the same nerve racking nature,
Wandered from his right direction.

No ! My brothers, let a water-
Proof sheet hide this wretched picture,
Of our worthy Hiawatha
Creeping back with all his party,
Muttering in vitriolic
Language, awful maledictions,
Cursing hard at his misfortune,
And the stupid lack of reason,
Shown by Sergeants who, patrolling,
Wear in place of Service caps a
Woolly helmet with a button.

Let us then, O worthy brothers,
Ere we curse our luck unduly,
Stipulate with our Commanders,
That some sort of understanding
Should be made in hours of daylight,
So that those of us who offer
(Secretly 'gainst hope still hoping
For a month of furlough, medals),
Outwardly to go and capture,
Lurking huns and other vermin,
May not waste our latent powers
Stalking after one another.   H. S. K.

FUMES FROM THE EDITOR'S WATER BOTTLE

It has for some time been customary to predict that " everything will be different " après la guerre." Ideas are in the melting pot. Party cries are being tested, and from out the crucible of conflict will emerge all that is noble, good and true. It is quite possible, for instance, that some members of this Battalion will process, demanding " Votes for Women " as a slight return for the Baths presented by the Gloucester Women's Suffrage Society. A hot bath is a sure way to the heart of a Trench-worn Territorial.

The experiment of printing 1,000 copies of the Gazette has proved an admirable one, and the sale has been quick and ready. The desire that the first two numbers should be reprinted is so widespread that steps will be taken to that effect.

Meanwhile it is a matter for much congratulation that our most industrious contributor, " F. W. H.," distinguished himself in a conflict, as David did, against a Philistine. The pen MAY be mightier than the sword ; it cannot be said to excel the " little man's " Kosh.

How the Piano came to S.

Who thought of it ? Captain Scott Williamson.
Who financed it ?
    Brigadier-General McClintock and the Brigade Staff.
    Colonel Serocold and officers of the 1/4th Bn. Royal Berks Regt.
    Lt.-Colonel Collett and officers of 1/5th Bn. Gloucestershire Regt.
    Lt.-Colonel Doig and officers of 1st. Bucks. Bn. Oxford and Bucks L.I.
    Lt.-Colonel Dugmore, D. S. O., and officers of 1/4th Bn. Oxford and Bucks. L. I.
Who brought it ?
    Major Baron and his merry men.

One night an officer and his orderly, while going his rounds, came on a sentry at a Barricade. The sentry challenged as follows—
    " Alt ! 'oo are you ? "
    To which the officer replied—
    ' Friends."
    " Pass on, hall's well ! " from the sentry.
    However, the officer was not at all satisfied, and told the sentry that he was to recognise everyone before allowing them to pass and after challenging them, say—" Advance one, and be recognised."
    About an hour later the officer returned, and the following dialogue took place—
    " 'Alt ! 'oo are you ? "
    " Friend."
    Pause.
    " 'Alt ! 'oo are you ? "
    " Friend."
    Pause (longer).
    " 'Alt ! 'oo are you ? "
    " Friend."
    Pause (longer still.)
    ' Danged if I aint gone and forgotten the rest ! "

Overheard at the Bomb School :
(a)   Bang ! ! !
(b)   The man who throws the lemon is the man who gets the pip.

(a)   " A little goes a long way," said the gunner as he despatched a pip squeak.
(b)   " Not so far as you think," said the infantryman as it burst in his own trench.

Copy of Message received by Gunner Officer from O. C. Infantry in trenches—
    " Your shell W.A.1.5. just received. Shall we return same, or hand it to Salvage ?

Overheard in a dug-out :
    " Blimy, Bill these 'ere trenches must be safe ; 'ere's our Quarter Bloke, coming along."
    " Strike me pink ! So 'tis. Tell yer what, Tubby, bet yer boots (and, blimy, if they'd be much loss to yer) we've got a full ration issue, else, safe or no safe, 'e 'ouldn't show 'is " goggles " up 'ere."

    " Any rags ? Any old iron ? " Cried the dealer in these commodities, as he knocked at the suburban villa. " No, go away " snapped the householder irritably, " There's nothing for you. My wife's away." " Any old bottles, then ? " enquired the dealer blandly.

IN FRANCE.

1. NŒUX-LES-MINES.

There stands a town named Nœux-les-Mines,
Raised by no mortal hand I ween.

There did we stay a live-long night ;
And sad and ev l was our plight.

Like water from a water butt
The rain poured down.   And doors were shut.

Therefore we built us bivvies in
A bank––but Ah ! the roofs were thin.

And soon the rain through all the cracks
Dripped in and trickled down our backs.

Each weary soldier robbed of sleep,
Frighted the night with curses deep.

Or strove with loud and hideous song
To make the darkness seem less long.

One, like unto Diogenes,
Betook him to a tub—and fleas.

His name I cannot quite recall,
But what *he* said was best of all.

With Satan and his powers in league,
A sergeant then did cry " Fatigue,'

And out into the lashing rain,
We all must tumble once again.

To dig in trenches and to wish
We were not human men, but fish.

When we returned outworn––chill,
No rum was there our cares to kill.

And so until this very day,
Talking of town, our soldiers say :—

" Of all the towns that we have seen,
Vilest by far is Nœux-les-Mines."

2. GONNEHEM.

Of Gonnehem, it will be said,
That we arrived there late and worn
With marching, and were given a bed
Of lovely straw.   And then at morn
On rising from deep sleep saw dangle––
Shining in the sun to spangle
The all-blue heaven––branch loads of red
Bright cherries which we bought to eat,
Dew-wet, dawn-cool, and sunny-sweet.
There was a tiny court-yard, too,
Wherein one shady walnut grew.
Unruffled peace the farm encloses
I wonder if beneath that tree
The meditating hens still be.
Are the white walls now gay with roses ?
Does the small fountain yet run free ?
I wonder if that dog still dozes....
Some day we must go back to see.   F. W. H.

AFFAIRE DE LODGEMENT.

SCENE.—Estaminet dans lequel un officier, faute
de mieux, a d'occuper le lit du cabaretier qui se
trouve être parti en voyage.

OFFICIER (dans son lit rèpondant à quelqu'un
cognant à sa porte).—" Qui est là ? "

VOIX (provenant d'une charmante servante à
l'extérieur).—" Avez-vous de la place pour deux
dans votre lit ? "

O.—" Plutôt ! ! "

V.—" Parce que le cabaretier est revenu "

O.— ! ! !

WHIST DRIVE.

On Monday, July 26th, No. 12 Platoon held
a Whist Drive. Entrance fee 2d.

Thirty-two players, including distinguished
visitors in Sergt. Finch and Corpl. Watkins, sat
down to the tables, or rather the waterproof sheets,
the ladies being members without hats.

As usual at whist drives there was quite a merry
buzz of conversation, but as soon as Lance-Corporal
Robertson arrived with a continuous string of prizes
and it began to be whispered round that the booby

prizes were eminently desirable and numbered three,
the play became very tense and keen.

Lance-Corpl. Harvey was ever casting a wistful
eye on the bottle of champagne, while Pte. Draper
was not unobservant of the pot of jam.

The programme was varied with " Klondyke,"
" Misere " and " Kimberley."

As the lights failed Lance-Corpl. Robertson
supplied each set with candles, an action which
pleased all until they found at bedtime that it
was their own candles which had been burnt.

The prize winners were as follows.

First prize for top score

(Ladies or Gentlemen(L-Corpl. Harvey.		Champagne.
1st Lady	Corpl. Watkins.	Tin of Apricots.
2nd Lady	Pte. Parr.	Tin of téte de porc.
1st Gentleman	Sergt. Young.	Tin of peaches
2nd Gentleman	Pte. A. G. Davis.	2 tins of sardines.
1st Booby	Pte. Draper.	Pot of Stephens' jam.
2nd Booby	Pte. Elliott.	1 biscuit.
3rd Booby	L-Corpl. Brien.	1 Rough Rider cigarette.

Sergt. Finch was graciously asked by Sergt.
Young to present the prizes, and proceeded to do
so with all his well-known esprit and bonhomie.
He so praised up the skilful play of Corpls. Harvey
and Watkins, expatiated on their generous natures
and fondled their prizes so lovingly, that these two
winners felt very relieved when at length they did
hold the prizes in their own hands.

Other prizes were likewise handed over with small
sermons on the evil of greed, and each winner was
called upon for a speech.

One joke of Corpl. Harvey's kept the room
rocking for five minutes. But the sardine winner
was somewhat stage struck, for he thrice could get no
further than the middle of his opening sentence—
and then Sergt. Finch struck in " The gentleman
wishes to say how pleased he is to be the fortunate
recipient of this beautiful prize, whose magnificence
has overcome his utterance." etc., etc., etc.

" Those were the sentiments you wished to
express my lad, weren't they ? Very good, to your
seat. ' Quick March ' ! "

Sergt. Finch ended by congratulating all and
sundry upon the most enjoyable evening they had
spent, and hoped another drive would take place
shortly.   R. E. K.

TRENCH NURSERY RHYMES.

(For a wet day.)

Slip about ! Slip about !
        Sanitary man.
Clean up the trench as quick as you can.
Sump it and pump it and sprinkle with " C."
And then get it d- - -d by the A. D. J. T.

The Poilus had a little trench,
        Also a Trench Store cow.
The Gloucesters tried to milk the brute,
        And look at the d- - - -d thing now.

Lieutenant Snugowt sat by his dug-out
        Censoring letters galore.
There came a Hun bullet and stuck in his gullet,
        And censored the censor still more.

Stand to !
German Shell ! !
Didn't burst ! ! !
All's well ?

Hello ! Lloyd George !
Have you any shells ?
Yes, lads ! Yes, Lads !
Guns as well.
Some with high explosive
And lots more with shrapnel,
And some to drop from aeroplanes
And blow the Huns to — bits.

———

Old Kaiser Will'um
Went out to kill 'em.
 To place the Crown Prince in the sun.
Arriving at Ypres
He found British snipers,
 And so the young pip squeak was done !

———

Phizzle ! whizzle ! little flare !
Who the devil sent you there ?
While we stumble through the grass,
How we " strafe " you as you pass.

———

Boschety Hunty had a desire,
For Boschety Hunty to cut up our wire.
But Kaiser Bill's horses and Kaiser Bill's men,
Can't render effective his breeches again.

G. F. C.
H. S. K.

———

WAR NOTES.

1. OUR EMPIRE.

India wished to help us in the African trouble.
Debarred from fighting, Indians of high caste
formed a Bearer Corps and did the work of coolies.

———

German South West Africa, which General Botha
won for the Empire, is six times the size of England,
and it was conquered by brilliant tactics on the part
of gallant men.

———

Who says the Empire is rotten ?

2. OUR ALLIES.

It is a three-day match, and it is the afternoon
of the second day. Russia has a large number of
runs to make, and she has lost three wickets. But
every moment sees an improvement of the wicket, and
if she can play out time, she will have a plumb
wicket and tired bowlers to face on the Great Third
Day. And both her present batsmen are well set,
though they are content to pick the ball to hit.

3. OUR NAVY.

" If their duty to the Allies was to free the
waters, they have done their duty brilliantly......
the waters represent nine-tenths of the best strategic
positions, which, thanks to these Britons, are now
in our possession, but which, without these Britons
had certainly been in German hands.

The Samonprava (Serbian Newspaper.)

JARGES POEM.

The young gent who edits this blighting Gazette
 Said to I just a day back, or two
" Jarge, I take it as lucky as you and I met,
 For I'd like to have something from you."

" Right you are, Sir," says I, " wot be yours, beer or stout
 I don't mind for myself which you name.
In this 'ere blighting country to which we've come out
 I can ne'er get enough of that same."

But the young gent, says he, with a very broad grin,
 " Jarge, my meaning I fear you've mistook.
I said 'from ' you, not ' with ', and I want you to spin
 Me a poem or yarn for my book."

Then I laughed till the tears washed my beautiful face
 As it ain't 'a bin washed for a week.
An' my ribs ached as if they'd gone out of their place
 An' 'ad slipped back again with a creak.

Says I " Sir, you ain't asking much, I don't think,
 From a bloke which 'is real job is fightin',
I don't say as 'ow I aint good at a drink,
 But I aint any good, Sir, at writin'.

" And yet, Sir," says I, " I often do feel
 That if only I COULD write a story,
I'd tell 'em such tales of these chaps true as steel
 Who are out here a fightin' for glory.

As would make the folks 'ome 'ardly know which to do,
 'Eave their chests out with pride, Sir, or cry.
For I know what 'eroes my pals are, and you
 Know that too, Sir, the same just as I.

You know as it aint any picnic we're at.
 You've been in the trenches like me,
An' you've seen my pals bleeding and dying ; and that
 Aint the pleasantest sight you can see.

You've seen 'ow we stands facin' death night an' day,
 An' these slackers at 'ome, I could show 'em,
If only I COULD say all I could say
 In the style of a yarn or a poem.

But you, why don't YOU, Sir, write home and just say
 'Ow we need every man who is fit.
An' the chaps must come out an' take part in the play
 An' not watch other chaps do their bit.

If they're too old to fight, Sir, or can't pass the Doc.
 Let them stay an' make shells, Sir, or guns.
Then we'll give Kaiser Bill such a 'ell of a shock.
 — 'Ow I 'ates Kaiser Bill an' 'is 'Uns !

If I had a few of 'em 'ere by the neck
 In that dirty old 'orse-pond I'd throw 'em.
But lor, Sir, it's time as I passed in my check.
 An' I'm blowed if I aint writ a poem ! "

" Y."

———

CHAPLAIN'S COLUMN.

There is now a piano in the village where the
Battalion rests and another is expected shortly.
Brigadier-General McClintock and the staff of the
145th Brigade have promised to support the above
scheme, as have the Officers commanding the four
Battalions. To them we are most grateful for their
moral support and financial assistance.

———

Canon and Mrs. Brewster have sent a Brass
Altar Cross, to take the place of the wooden one
which was unfortunately broken during one of the
moves. They have also given 50 yards of Butter
muslin for the 3rd Field Ambulance Hospital.

———

The Countess Bathurst and Mrs. Berkley Powell
have kindly sent supplies of Illustrated Papers.

———

The appointment of the Bishop of Khartoum
as Bishop in charge of the Forces is a welcome one.
There are still some men who have not been confirmed
who may yet like to avail themselves of the Bishop's
forthcoming visit to our area.

D

NONSENSE RHYMES.

A fellow who lived at Bailleul
Was so deeply in love with his geul
That the military post-
Man gave up the ghost,
And now she has married an Eul.

A subaltern known as Colquhoun,
Was considered, at home, a buffoquhoun,
He would not have been
If his parents had seen
Him drilling his Scottish Platolquhoun.

H. S. K.

BATTALION LIMERICK.

There was a C. Company swel
Who said " What a h— of a smell.
But whether from drains
Or human remains
I am really unable to tell."

C COMPANY DEBATING SOCIETY.

This society originated in No. 12 Platoon, but so many came from other platoons in the company that it was decided to christen it as above.

The first meeting was held on Monday, August 9th.

During private business, Lance-Corpl. Harvey read two excellent poems, and Pte. Lee-Williams told some waggish stories.

The subject for debate was " that in the opinion of this Society, Trades Unions, are a menace to the country, and should be abolished.

Corpl. Harvey in moving the motion briefly sketched the history of Trades Unions, and argued that whereas once so useful they had now fallen into a decline.

Pte. Sheppard in opposing, congratulated himself on the fact that Trades Unions had given him shorter hours.

Pte. Lee Williams desired co-operation as a substitute, while against him Pte. Martin urged that Trades Unions made for efficiency.

Sergt Proctor then gave the House an intellectual treat. He spoke at great length on how he had suffered after 16 years as a member of a Trade Union, and every word of his was listened to with intense interest.

Corpl. Knight gave a history of Trades Unions, and regretted they had now lost their old uses. He envied the lot of the country-man, and dilated upon the evils of strikes.

Sergt. Cook submitted Trades Unions achieved their purpose in aiding their fellow-men, while Corpl. South spoke of the Post Office and Trades Unions. Pte. Pyne desired the good of the people, and Sergt. Lippett co-operation.

Corpl. Furley endorsed this sentiment, and Pte. Roddis also spoke. In summing up, Pte. Sheppard reiterated his former arguments, while Corpl. Harvey, in an eloquent speech denounced Trade Unionists as traitors to their country in a time of crisis and peril. The motion was lost by 19 votes to 31.

Subject for next debate—" That bachelors should be taxed."

WITH APOLOGIES TO TENNYSON.

Blow, blow, cuss and blow
'Skeeter, and fly, and flea.
Go, go, down below.
Insects that pester me.
Souvenir bites you give as you go.
Lumps on the head, spots on the toe—
Never a limb goes free.—
While the creepy man, while the sleepy man, sleeps.
Pants and vests, legs and chest,
(Keating's would come as a boon).
Many a pest these infest
Banishing slumber soon.
Madly we slaughter the louse in his nest,
Bayonet bugs, and hope for the best,
Under the silver moon—
Ere the creepy man, ere the sleepy man, sleeps.

ADVERTISEMENTS.

OUT OF THE TRENCHES.

THE REST FARM.

Into this quiet place
Of peace we come.
The War God hides his face,
His mouth is dumb.

All reckless wild decrees
His lips repeat,
Are hushed by a little breeze
In waving wheat.

And like the penance-peace
In a heart forlorn,
Trills the word of the trees—
The sigh of the corn.

CRICKET (The Catch.)

Whizzing, fierce, it came
Down the summer air,
Burning like a flame
On my fingers bare,
And it brought to me,
As swift, a memory.

Happy days long dead
Saw I then once more.
Childhood that is fled :
Rossall on the shore ;
Where the sea sobs wild
Like a homesick child.

O the blue bird's fled,
Never man can follow.
Yet at times instead
Flies this scarlet swallow :
And upon its wings
Sweet time-strangled things.

BACK TO THE TRENCHES.

Unrest is in the trees
And billowy clouds drive by :
The curved moon rides high
Like a ship midst stormy seas.

Beneath her fitful light,
To the trench's treachery.
And all Fate may decree,
Fearless we march to-night.

The reflected life of man
'Neath the moon's reflected light,
Riding its stormy night
To an end no eye may scan.

F. W. H.

PROMOTIONS.

Lt. L. R. C. Sumner to be Captain (Temporary) dated 10/6/15

Lt. F. E. Francillon to be Captain (Temporary) dated 10/6/15

2nd Lt. H. S. King to be Lieut. (Temporary) dated 10/6/15

2nd Lt. C. W. Winterbotham to be Lieutenant (Temporary) dated 10/6/15.

To be Acting Company Qr-Mr.-Sergt.

30	Segt..	Brown, D.	Dated 1/8/15

To be Acting Sergt. :

2717	L-Sergt.	Thomson, R. O.	,, 1/8/15

To be L-Sergt. :

908	Corpl.	Wyatt, J.	,, 18/7/15

To be Acting L-Sergt. :

2355	Corpl.	Harvey, M. J.	,, 1/8/15

To be Corporal :

717	L-Corpl.	Eden, J.	Dated 18/7/15

To be Acting Corporal :

2339	L-Corpl.	Green, W. A.	,,	1/8/15
1767	,,	Parrott, E.	,,	1/8/15
1739	,,	Slatter, F.	,,	1/8/15

To be Acting L-Corporals :

2760	Private	Hill, R.	,,	1/8/15
2575	,,	Thomas, H. G.	,,	1/8/15
2569	,,	Sullivan, D. W.	,,	1/8/15
1901	,,	Furley, C.	,,	1/8/15
2755	,,	Goatman, E.	,,	1/8/15
2348	,,	Phillpots, F.	,,	1/8/15

To be Unpaid L-Corporals :

2467	Private	Simmons, P.	,,	24/5/15
2315	,,	Jackson, L. E.	,,	26/7/15
1366	,,	Marshall, H. R.	,,	26/7/15
2535	,,	Garner, E.	,,	1/8/15
2275	,,	Burkenshaw, V. J.	,,	1/8/15
2681	,,	Harris, J.	,,	1/8/15
2729	,,	Wise, R.	,,	1/8/15
1052	,,	Philips, C. H.	,,	1/8/15
2550	,,	Moxon, J. E.	,,	1/8/15
2776	,,	Wilkes, W. G.	,,	1/8/15
2558	,,	Paynter, W. F. L.	,,	1/8/15
2621	,,	Bromage, W.	,,	1/8/15
2368	,,	Robertson, K. A.	,,	1/8/15
2371	,,	Harvey, F. W.	,,	1/8/15
2365	,,	Morgan, W. W.	,,	1/8/15
1585	,,	Nicholls, W. A.	,,	1/8/15
2726	,,	Washbourne, W. P.	,,	1/8/15
2697	,,	Middlecote, H.	,,	1/8/15

A CASUALTY.

" Come for the cause is good. Stout heart, strong hand."
" England needs now. Death—for your native land ? "
" The cause is good."

Poor hackneyed words. But yet his manhood woke,
And held it true—it matters not who spoke.
The cause was good.

Poor hackneyed words. We heard them once again
From dying lips, teeth clenched against the pain.
For thus he spoke, and so his loss was gain,
" The cause is good."

CASUALTIES.

Officers—Wounded—

2nd Lieut. G. Hawkins	17/8/15	D Coy.

Other Ranks—Wounded—

3287 Private C. A. Teale	1/8/15	C Coy.

All contributions, which should be written on one side of the sheet only, should be sent to the Editor, c/o the Orderly Room, Battalion Headquarters. The Editor cannot be responsible for the return of rejected M.S.S.

5th Gloucester Gazette.

A Chronicle, serious and humorous, of the Battalion while serving with the
BRITISH EXPEDITIONARY FORCE.

THE C. O.

(With apologies to Herrick)

A sweet disorder in the dress
Kindles in him small kindliness.
My slack puttees him oft have thrown
Into a fine distraction.
An erring lace he cannot bear,
Nor the neglected flowing hair.
Did he command that splendid force
The W. V. T. C. - of course
He'd see they dressed with careful art,
Very precise in every part.
And would, I'm certain, never dote
On the tempestuous petticoat.

F. W. H.

LEAVE.

I.—The Soldier Speaks.

Within my heart I safely keep,
   England, what things are yours :
Your clouds, and cloud-like flocks of sheep
   That drift o'er windy moors.
Possessing nought, I proudly hold
   Great hills and little gay
Hill-towns set black on sunrise-gold
   At breaking of the day.

Though unto me you be austere
   And loveless, darling land :
Though you be cold and hard, my dear,
   And will not understand.
Yet have I fought and bled for you,
   And by that, self-same sign,
Still must I love you, yearn to you,
   England—how truly mine !

II.—The Awakening.

At night, in dream,
I saw those fields round home
     Agleam.
Drenched all with dew
Beneath day's newest dome
     Of gold and blue.

All night—
All night they shone for me, and then
     Came light.
And suddenly I woke, and lovely joy !
I was at home, with the fields gold as when
     I was a boy.

. . . .

Thus shall all men rise up at last to see
Their dearest dreams golden reality.

III.—Land of Heart's Delight.

Glory's a temple open wide.
   Content, a little shrine.
But Heart's Delight is a land so bright
   We reckon it half divine.
It lies wherever man has lived,
   But wheresoe'er you find it,
Its skies are blue with dreams come true,
   And Heaven is just behind it.

Glory's the universal gleam
   Of all God gives to men.
Content, the little silver dream
He sends to one in ten.
But Heart's Delight, all golden bright,
   Is given to those alone
Who have hidden their hearts in the deepest parts
   Of a place called—Home.
               F. W. H.

FUMES FROM THE EDITOR'S WATER BOTTLE.

We know that he who tries to please all pleases no one. The 48th Division has always endeavoured " to give satisfaction." It is a little hard, therefore, that people complain at home because there are not enough casualties !

Some people ARE hard to please.

We are always grateful for information ; it need not even be second-hand. Thank you, No. 15 Platoon, for letting the world know that the following Battalions are being raised :—

The Pawnbrokers' Battalion—they know how to advance.

The Shop-Assistants' Battalion — They can counter-attack, can't they ? And, lastly, most formidable of all—

The Boarding-House-Keepers' Battalion—they have learnt to charge ! ! !

A story comes from the Dardanelles anent a Captain in the gallant Australian Contingent.

" Now boys," he said, prior to an inspection, " these English Staff Officers are coming to size us up to-day, so look-smart......And look here, for the love of Heaven, don't call me Alf."

It is said that the Turkish Sniper is rewarded with money according to a fixed tariff. Whether the same tariff holds good on the Western Front, we do not know, but it is said that the Terrible Turk is recompensed as follows from the German Treasury :

For every English 2nd Lieutenant ...   5 marks
              Lieutenant 10   ,,
              Captain   15   ,,
              Major   20   ,,
              Colonel   25   ,,
              General   30   ,,
              Staff Officers ...   20 days
                       Field Punishment.

With the praiseworthy exception of Pte. S. E. Barton, No. 15 Platoon, no one attempted to translate the French poetry. A prize of 10 francs has been awarded to the above.

During the last two months there has come to light the existence of weird ideas concerning the doings of the Fifth Gloucesters. Officers on leave in Gloucestershire have been encouraged with some such leave-takings as this from friends : " Well, good-bye, old chap. Hope you will get on all right, Of course, if you are lucky you may get on to the Line of Communication. But we know you can never get to the Front ! ! ! !" Is this the result of ignorance pure and simple, or comes it from over-burdened loyalty to the Second Line ?

Arnold Bennett tells us of a French soldier who, in an engagement, was left between the opposing lines. When hit he cried " Vive la France !" When he was missed he kept silent. He was hit again and again, and at each wound he cried " Vive la France !" He could not be killed. At last they turned a machine gun on him, and raked him from head to foot. " Vive la   !"

Most of our readers are by this time aware that " F. W. H.," who has contributed so much to this Gazette, is none other than Lce-Corpl. F. W. Harvey, D.C.M. We are very glad to think that although he will shortly be in " another place "—i.e., forsaking the Lower for the Upper House—he will still help to make this Gazette just what it has always claimed to be : " A record, serious and humorous, of the Fifth Gloucestershire Regiment." While we congratulate him and Lce.-Sergt. Knight on being awarded the medals they have so thoroughly deserved we wish them, and Lce.-Corpl. Robertson, every success in their new rôle.

Overheard in France.
        " Butter ? "
        " No compree ! "
        " Burrrrrr ? "
        " Na poo ! ! "
        " No blooming bon ! ! ! "
        " Goood—byeee."

Overheard in England. Scene : Oxford Circus.
   Old Lady : " A ticket to take me to the Bank, if you please, young man."
   Booking-clerk : " Tuppence."
   Old Lady : " Is this escalator safe."
   Attendant at top : " Yes, if you don't step off 'ead first."
   Old Lady to Attendant at bottom : " Is this the Bank ? "

Major General A. I. Samashko, member of the Russian Special Committee appointed to enquire into cruelties perpetrated by the Germans, publishes in the *Novoe Vremya* of August 11 (24) the following story, told under oath, by Prokop Koldobenko, private in a Russian infantry regiment, who succeeded in escaping from a German internment camp :

In the middle of October a party of 200 British soldiers was brought into the camp. On the very first day one of them refused to eat the unsavoury mixture called soup, and poured it on the ground. The German guards became enraged, and one of them attempted to bayonet the Englishman. He, however, succeeded in evading the blow. Then the chief of the Guards of the camp, a German officer, ordered a big barrel to be brought. Then he assembled all the prisoners of war, British as well as Russians, and ordered the British soldier to be put on the barrel, and struck him three times with his sword, ordering his soldiers afterwards to strike him with their batons. Neither cries nor prayers for mercy stopped this act. Only when the soldier fell down from the barrel, being unconscious, the punishment stopped. He was then lifted up and bound to a lamp-post, so that his feet could not reach the ground. In such position he was left for more than an hour, so that his arms became quite twisted. On the next day the poor soldier died."

MORNING POST.

These are the people you are up against, Boys.

It is high time that attention be drawn to the childish belief in "mascots." It is nothing less than rank paganism and silly superstition to believe that the "lucky charm" is going to protect one from danger. "We laugh at the Southern races for dreading the evil eye...but our own reliance upon a bone, a metal animal, or a wooden doll, is every whit as pagan."

All the copies—and there were 1000—of No.5 are "off the strength." This is very gratifying. Thank you all, and C. Company especially, for the way you have supported the Gazette. It is something to be able to spot a good thing, isn't it ?

Once again we thank our contemporaries on the other side of the silver streak for their very kind notices of issue No. 5 of this Gazette.

From PUNCH :—
Balm for Lord Kitchener.
Extract from 2/1 S. Midland Brigade Orders :—
"The Brigadier congratulates all ranks in the Brigade on the smart appearance presented at the Inspection to-day by the Secretary of State for War."

THE D.C.M.

From THE LONDON GAZETTE.

The Distinguished Conduct Medal has been awarded to.

2382 **Corpl. R. E. KNIGHT,** 1/5th Gloucestershire R. (T.F.)

For conspicuous gallantry on the night of Aug. 3-4, 1915, near Hebuterne, when, in command of a patrol, he went out to reconnoitre in the direction of a suspected listening post In advancing he encountered the hostile post evidently covering a working party in the rear. Corpl. Knight at once shot one of the enemy, and with Lance-Corpl. Harvey, rushed the post shooting two others, and, assistance arriving, the enemy fled. Three Germans were killed and their rifles and a Mauser pistol were brought in. The patrol had no loss.

2371 **Lance.-Corpl. F. W. HARVEY,** 1/5th Gloucestershire R. (T.F.)

For conspicuous gallantry on the night of Aug. 3-4, 1915, near Hebuterne, when, with a patrol, he and another non-commissioned officer went out to reconnoitre in the direction of a suspected listening post. In advancing they encountered the hostile post, evidently covering a working party in the rear. Corporal Knight at once shot one of the enemy, and, with Lance-Corporal Harvey, rushed the post, shooting two others, and, assistance arriving. the enemy fled. Lance-Corporal Harvey pursued, felling one of the retreating Germans with a bludgeon. He seized him, but, finding his revolver empty and the enemy having opened fire, he was called back by Corporal Knight, and the prisoner escaped. Three Germans were killed, and their rifles and a Mauser pistol were brought in. The patrol had no loss.

We publish a more detailed account as follows :

The Patrol was commanded by No. 2382, Corporal R. E. KNIGHT, assisted by No. 2371, Lance Corporal F. W. HARVEY, and 6 other men.

Corporal KNIGHT and 4 men were armed with Rifles and Bayonets. Lance-Corporal HARVEY carried a revolver and bludgeon. The remaining two men carried revolvers and bombs.

The Patrol went out from a trench to reconnoitre some bushes suspected of being a listening post.

On the way out, about 350 yards from our trenches the patrol heard coughing on their right.

They moved towards it and came on a hostile listening post apparently put out to cover a working party which was at work about 400 yards away. One of the hostile post having heard our patrol came towards it and Corporal KNIGHT shot him.

Corpls. KNIGHT and HARVEY then rushed the post, shooting two others.

The rest of our party then came up.

Meanwhile Lance-Corporal HARVEY had followed a German who was running away and coming up with him felled him with his bludgeon, The man then made signs of surrendering, but as Lance-Corporal HARVEY seized him by the collar and pointed a revolver at him, the prisoner became frightened and struggled for the revolver. When Lance-Corporal HARVEY pulled the trigger he found he had used all his rounds.

The enemy from behind opening fire, Corporal KNIGHT shouted to Lance-Corporal HARVEY to return. The prisoner wrenching himself free and bolting. Lance-Corporal HARVEY decided not to follow him, and the patrol withdrew, reaching our lines at 11.15 p.m.

Three Germans were undoubtedly killed ; our casualties were nil.

THE SOLDIER'S DOG.

A little vagrant cur,
　He had a noble heart ;
He met us on the road,
　And chose the better part.

It may be Belgium's wrongs
　Beneath his weskit burned ;
Or visions of a home
　The Huns had overturned.

And so he sought our camp,
　And followed to the trench.
For Englishmen to him
　Were much the same as French.

The soldier's dog, he shared
　The soldier's daily bread,
And howsoever short
　The rations, he was fed.

And in return he warred
　Against the soldier's pest,
The vermin great and small
　Which rob them of their rest.

Sometimes he would patrol
  Along the parapet,
To scent the creeping guile
  Of Huns on mischief set.

And had Hunny snake
  Through barbed fences crawled,
He would have had his bags,
  And bit him till he bawled.

They why, oh why, when you
  Had made your footing sure
Did you mistake the road,
  Or fall to alien lure ?

I cannot think that you
  Did willingly desert,
Still less that to Kultur
  You were a base pervert.

I fancy when the fight
  Is raging on the plain,
Beside the old platoon
  You will be found again.

THE WORKING PARTY.

It was a perfect day. So much was quite obvious. But why our Company was called upon to " supply 1 Officer, 10 N.C.O's, and X men to parade at the cross-roads, 1500 yards S.W. of the second L. in (censored) at 11 ack emma AAA " was not quite so apparent. However, in due course, and punctually at 11 a.m. (Brigade time) we reached the cross-roads 1500 yards, etc., etc., etc., having observed the first sine qua non of invisibility, " single file at 200 yards distance."

At 12 noon the R. E. officer pedalled briskly up and explained how sorry he was, but breakfast being rather late had upset things slightly.

Assuring him of our absolute indifference to such minor contretemps, he proceeded to detail his working parties. This finished, he rode vigorously on to find out what work was to be done. 30 men under Sapper A., with 20 shovels and 10 picks, were led away duly whistling strongly. Another 20 men armed with " Hooks, bill," under Sapper B., headed NNE. and the remainder, under yet a third sapper, with entrenching tools and clasp knives only, proceeded under his able guidance to a distant clump of trees.

Now it is manifestly impossible for one officer to be in 3 places at once, so the only alternative was to detail myself to a suitable position where it would be possible to enjoy the weather with as little discomfort as possible, and yet remain central.

The cunning way in which the parties had been detailed by the master hand filled me with admiration, and after a short rumination in my selected position, I proceeded to perambulate with a view to observing how things were proceeding.

Following a trail of Woodbine packets and trampled grass, No. 1 working party was soon run to earth erecting a magnificent field of barbed wire. Several of the party were securely pinned by the over-growing maze. Ripped tunics, pants, and puttees were everywhere, and here and there shirt-coloured pennants floated lazily in the sluggish air.

Apart from a slight argument between one of the N. C. O's., and Sapper A. as to which were most useful on this kind of work, wire cutters or picks and shovels, things seemed to be working pretty smoothly, so I headed for No. 2 working party, who were found busily cleaning bricks with their bill-hooks, to the accompaniment of a torrent of vitriolic language and irrelevant repartee.

The third party, under cover of the clump of trees, was resting when I approached. The reason was obvious. The N. C. O. in charge explained that to them had fallen the lot of cutting down trees and undergrowth prior to building a model redoubt. The sunlight glittered here and there on the broken blades of knives which had proved unequal to their task.

A mild suggestion that it might prove advantageous to change the tools round so that parties should have what was wanted was answered by— " Oh, well, they will be relieved in an hour's time." But as long as Messrs. Cook and Son get their 1 franc per head after the war, what DOES it matter."

A COMMON PETITION.

I crave not of the wonder
Of thy full plan to see :
No secret would I plunder
Of guarded destiny :
This only grant to me :

To hear the rolling thunder
Of Life—be man alive :
Yet through no body's blunder
To drag the bright soul under
—Drowned where it needs must dive.

Keeping against all Fate
What Thou hast given me—
The dual mystery
Of man—inviolate.   F.W.H.

THINGS WE WANT TO KNOW.

Who ate the dubbin which had been put into a disused butter tin ?

And did it account for his boots being dirty on inspection ?

Who mixed the tooth powder with water and swallowed it, for a dose of salts ? Was it effective ?

Is it true that the recipe for " shakkles " is as follows :—Put some fat on a piece of 4×2 and draw it through water ?

What Sergeant, in his endeavour to prove that France was fighting Italy, said Napoleon's army crossed the Alps on Nestle's Milk ?

Will our esteemed contemporary, "The Gloucester Journal," publish the version of the Battle of St. Julien, as related by a sergeant who, whilst on leave from this Battalion, stated he was " there."

Who asked the mule for a light ?

Why did the butchers annoint their rifle bolts with cresol instead of rifle-oil for their rapid firing ?

Are the impromptu debates held in the A Company's Sergeants' Mess occasionally of a rowdy order ?

Does a certain Sergeant " let himself go," and use words which remind one of Disraeli ?

Did a certain Private in A. Company, in the course of an argument on the war, state that Germany had called up all her " unmedically fit " ?

Is a certain Sergeant the subject of a great deal of admiration because of his intimacy with a General ?

Does the friendship exist simply in his own mind ?

Does he wear crossed-rifles ?

Is he a Maltese potato expert ?

How many G.S. wagons were required to take home the Doctor's bag when he went out shooting, and how many limbers brought up the cartridges ?

Who told them to put the lid on the dixie to keep the tea dry, when it began to rain ?

Who stopped the cricket match because of the cow ?

Why two of the senior officers had stiff necks the same morning, and if the mantlepiece in C. Company's Officers' Mess had anything to do with it ?

What the Quartermaster said when he made a misdeal the other evening ?

Is it true that there is an air raid every Sunday in Chelmsford ?

And how do the brave 2/5th like it ?

How does the M. G. Section like the new order re shorts ?

Which Private in No. 6 Platoon dreamed dreams ?

And if they came true ?

Who wrote home—" We have left the place I mentioned to you in my last lettter in the green envelope ? "

And who wrote—" God bless and keep you from your loving husband........." ?

And who signed the letter to his old schoolmaster, " Your old scohlar " ?

What Corporal was jubilant at receiving his first love-letter ?

Who was the senior N. C. O. who woke at 7 a.m. and asked what time breakfast was ?

OUR BENEFACTORS.

The Committee of " Soldiers' Day," Cheltenham, who sent each Cheltenham man a parcel, and who have also sent a large number of canvas shoes.

Barnwood House, Gloucester (per Dr. Townsend), Mr. Harley Butt, and Mr. and Mrs. A. Slater Gloucester, cigarettes.

Soldiers' and Sailors' Association Clothing Depot, Gloucester, shirts.

Mr. Jack Margetson (Stroud), " Times " Broadsheets. Also Woodbines.

Mr. Harley Butt yet more tobacco.

Owing to the difficulty of obtaining arm title badges to replace those worn out, Mrs. J. H. Collett has organised working parties in Gloucestershire to make these.

A TRUE TALE OF THE LISTENING POST.

(Dedicated to R.E.K.)

Men are queer things right through—whatever make—
But Tommy Atkins really takes the cake.

Which said, see in your mind (my point to prove)
Two soldiers, frozen and afraid to move,
On listening patrol. For four dead hours
Afraid to move or whisper, cough or sneeze.
Waiting in wonder whether 'twas the breeze
Moved in the grass, shaking the frozen flowers
Waiting in wonder whether 'twas the breeze
Just then. Germans were out that night, we knew,
With bombs to throw, and so we lay, we two,
With rifle ready at shoulder, and... What's that
Twanging the wire (both heard the sound)—a rat ?
Or the Bosch bomber creeping, creeping nigher
To hurl death into the trench behind us ? Both
Turned barrels 'gainst the unknown, ready to fire,
Waiting to fire should ever it take form
Of human body.—Waiting, being loath
To shoot at nothing, making so alarm
And laughter in the trench we guarded. Here
Sounds a hoarse whisper against my ear :
Something it utters—" What is it ? " I hiss,
Soft as a serpent ; and upon my oath
My comrade covering still the sound, said—this
This, while the unknown stalked, and fear was chilly
Like ice around our hearts—" I say old chap "
(My laughter followed like a thunder-clap)
" Couldn't I do some beef and piccalilli.

Men are quaint things world over, willy nilly.
But R. E. K.—you take the—piccalilli.

F. W. H.

VIR TENAX PROPOSITI.

There was a time when the Broomfield Road at Chelmsford and a motor bicycle knew him. Sometimes, when the road was greasy, the connection was intimate. But that time is now long past, and a horse has supplanted the motor. He is ubiquitous : there is no place which may serve as a refuge. He searches carefully, and those gold-rimmed glasses make his vision keen. Once we welcomed him as he came along with that bulky haversack, but now many of us wish that we might hide behind a blade of grass and chirp like a grass-hopper. And why ? He is a man with a purpose,

stern, unwavering. It has become an obsession, yet he is a kind man, with a word of cheer for all. Is it a feeling of work undone that makes us quake ? Often it is. " Have you anything for me for the Gazette ? " Ah ! The Secret is out. This is the reason of our trepidation. We know our guilt, and so does he, and he ruthlessly hunts us down, making life a burden, till we have seen the error of our ways. Allowances must be made for him. The Israelites of old complained that bricks could not be made without straw. No more can the Gazette be published without contributions. The editorial scissors are rusty ; we need not fear them. Far more terrible is the look of reproach when we confess our article is still a thing of the future. The Gazette is the only paper of its kind produced at the Front, and the fact that most of the Daily Papers have thought it worthy of notice ought to make us do our utmost to make " Him happy by making the Editorial task an easier one.

" A Convert."

FROM AN OUTPOST.

I've tramped West England up and down,
    Down Severn way, Down Wye way,
Through every little country town
    Down every lane and bye-way.
I mind the old stone churches there,
    The taverns 'round the market square,
The cobbled streets, the garden flowers,
    The sundials, telling peaceful hours.
Down Severn way, Down Wye way.

The meadow lands are green and fair,
    Down Severn way, down Wye way.
The clover scent is in the air,
    Down Severn way, Down Wye way.
I mind the gabled homesteads there,
    The noble uplands clean and bare.
The chatter of the building rook,
    The soft low babble of the brook.
Down Severn way, Down Wye way.

Mayhap I shall not walk again
    Down Severn way, Down Wye way.
Nor pick a primrose in the lane,
    Down Severn way, Down Wye way.
But though my bones, unshriven rot
    In some far distant alien spot,
What soul I have shall rest from care,
    To know that meadows still are fair
Down Severn way, Down Wye way.

(Adapted from a contemporary).

AT A HOSPITAL IN ENGLAND.

" Ah, my poor man, and how did you come to get wounded ? I suppose in one of those bloody battles we read of, which cannot help but make us feel so proud of our dear brave men."

" Lor' bless yer, no mum. I wasn't wounded at hall, Lidy. Dontcher fretcher' self abaht me, mine is only one o' them there o' dahn-roight bad luck.

" But why are you bound down in bed like this if you haven't been wounded ?."

" Well, yer see, Lidy, it was like this 'ere. I got rarver run dahn, so I goes to our doctor, I does, and I ses to him, I don't feel me blooming self I ses. Well, ses he, stick this under yer tongue, and he puts a thermometer in me marf, caught 'old o' me wrist, ses 'cough' say 'ninety-nine' and do it agen all at once loike, and I was so took aback oi was, that I sneezed, sed " swazzon-kanze " and bit the end off ther thermometer, and swallered so much mercury that they can't keep me from slipping off the bed wivaht binding me dahn."

H.S.K.

No. Q/C/R/2233.

"HINTS ON COOKING IN THE FIELD."

(How it was written.)

I.

The greatest of the audience heard somebody complain
The food we get is good, but yet it's very very plain.
We get the same stuff every day again and yet again.

II.

The greatest of the audience declared " If this be true,
" Come here the junior Brigadier, I've got a job for you.
" Compose a little treatise just to tell 'em what to do."

III.

The Junior Brigadier felt ill. " A job of work for me ?
" Well, 'pon my Sam, Oh, blast and d......, why this can
      never be."
I'll get old Colonel What's-his-name to do it after tea.

IV.

The Colonel called a Major, and they puzzled all they knew
To find a cook who'd write a book worthy of G. H. Q.
But all the cooks they came across made nothing else but
      stew.

V.

" Well, d...... it," said the Major, " Sir, it's time we got a
      dash on,
Or, else I fear the Brigadier and we shan't be the fashion.
But first of all we ought to know what is and is not ration."

VI.

" I quite agree," the Colonel said, " but don't be in a hurry,
Three weeks or more should pass before there's any need to
      worry.
But if you really want to start, why not begin with curry ? "

VII.

" By Gad, of course," the Major cried, " that's quite a happy
      thought.
Let's say " This dish is good with fish—when any can be
      caught,
If curry isn't issued—well, no doubt it can be bought."

VIII.

" And what about the biscuits, Sir ? I hear they're using
      them
For paving floors and dug-out doors, so let's put down a mem.
' Eat biscuits next, as issued.' That's good enough, pro.
      tem.

I.X

" There's one more thing we ought to say, and that's the use
      of jam.
I've heard it said it's good with bread—or was it with roast
      lamb ?
Or make a jam-roll if you like ; the Staff don't care a d......

X.

" A top-hole book," the Colonel said, and slapped his thigh
      with glee.
"Ten thousand prints of Cooking Hints, to please the C.-in-C.
And d...... the lazy beggars of the Printing Co. R.E. ! "

B. H. Q.

29th August, 1915.

1st Printing Co. R.E. ? Army 53.

MONKEY LORE.

" There's something in that," said the A.D.J.T.
as he fell in the sump-hole.

" Enough is as good as a feast," chortled the Q.M.
as he sent up three blankets amongst five.

" All's fair in love and war," said the N.C.O. as he
addressed the two envelopes containing carbon copies
of a letter to his wife.

"Now they're off " said the M.O., as he handed the
man back his fumigated shirt.

" Things are not always what they seem," said the
two Platoons who consumed their dubbin ration in
mistake for butter.

H. S. K.

E

THE GREEN ENVELOPE.

The colour's poor, the paper rough,
The yarns it holds are very tough.
They come from Gunner, Private, and Sapper,
And all are dumped in the poor green wrapper.

The tales they write to Maude and May
Will raise their hair, and turn it grey.
They weep and cry and cannot think
How their soldier-boy can keep in the pink.

Tales of derring do and woe,
Thrilling adventures wherever they go ;
Tales of joy and tales of hope,
All refugees in the green envelope.

But sad to say, I'm much afraid,
Far from the Trenches they're mostly made.
Experiences do not get their due
In the modest wrapper of pale green hue.

The Editor says he would like to get
Some of the contents for his Gazette.
Those tales of things that have never been,
And horrible sights that nobody's seen.

C. G. K.

THINGS WE WANT TO SEE.

The teeth of a biting wind.

Jockeys for the chevaux-de-frises.

The signaller who can send a barbed wire.

The " madame " who can darn a sump-hole.
      (We know many men who can d...n them when
      the lid doesn't fit).

A French girl who is not " mobilisee."

One of Sammy's angels.

Leave continuous and extended.

Peace with honour and a piece in Gloucester.

NEW WORLDS FOR OLD.

I.—The Olden Peace.

(In England, 1913).

What is it says the breeze
In London streets to-day
Unto the troubled trees
Whose shadows strew the way—
Whose leaves are all a-flutter ?

" You are wild," the rascal cries.
The green tree beats its wings
And fills the air with sighs.
" Wild ! Wild ! " the rascal sings,
" But your feet are in the gutter."

Men pass beneath the trees,
Walking the pavements grey.
They hear the whispering tease
And at the word he utters
Their hearts are green and gay.

Then like those gay green trees
They beat proud wings to fly.
But like the fluttering trees
Their footprints mark the gutters
Until the beggars die.

II.—The Newer Peace.

(In Flanders, 1915).

For that this thing hath purged the ancient sunlight
Of guile. And trees sing with primœval voices ;
And that there hath came back to us through danger
(As lovely stars laughing up out of one bright
Lone lake) the fires of Faith, and that fair ranger
Romance—dear child of Beauty and Terror—; rejoices
Once more man's soul e'en from beneath the sod,
Finding, in wildest war, peace and its God.

III.—A People Renewed.

Now these like men shall live,
   And like to princes fall.
They take what Fate will give
   At this great festival.

And since at length they find
   That Life is sweet indeed,
They cast it on the wind
   To serve their country's need.

See young " Adventure " there
   (" Make-money-quick " that was)
Hurls down his gods that were
   For Honour and the Cross !

Old " Grab-at-Gold " lies low
   In Flanders. And again
(Because men will it so)
   England is ruled by—Men !

F. W. H.

CORRESPONDANCE.

Reedbank,
Lough na brack derragh.

Sir,

On the 14th of this month, while I was quietly swimming in my ancestral lake, I foolishly swallowed what appeared to be a fly. Immediately I felt a sharp pain in my jaw, and I was violently jerked into a boat, when a man dressed in a yellow overcoat, and wearing a yellow cap, wrenched open my mouth and extricated a hook. He then threw me back into the lake, saying " You dirty little devil, where the blazes do you think you are going to ?" I felt, and still feel, very much insulted, as although not fully grown, my figure and red spotted scales are much admired by my relations. Also such language was quite unfit to be addressed to a lady.

Another man in the boat, also armed with a fishing rod, but who was quite inoffensive, said " Do they swear like that in the Gloucesters ?"

I noticed that my assailant's cap was decorated with a badge shewing an eel or a serpent crawling up a stick. I trust that from this clue you may be able to identify the man who insulted me so grossly, and I beg you will inform him that all my family, and my cousins the Fry's, the Smelt's, the Parr's, the Sprat's and the Minnow's, are firmly resolved to have no further dealings with so rude an angler.

Your sincere well-wisher,
TINY TROUT.

(The M. O. was on leave from the 11th to the 19th and it is believed to have proceeded to Ireland. But no, it cannot be !—Ed.)

To the Editor.

Sir or Madam,

Would you be so good as to bring to the notice of the authorities the pressing need for a revised field post-card on the following lines, as I feel sure that, by its adoption, platoon commanders and other minor censors would be saved much labour and weariness of the flesh.

I am, etc.,

H.S.K.

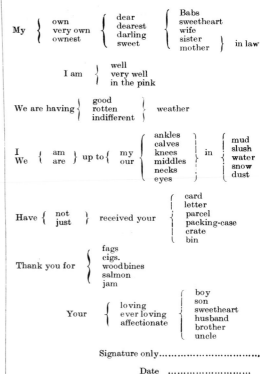

Signature only..................................

Date ....

(We will forward your suggestion to the proper quarter. Ed).

CRICKET.

Played on 19th September, 1915, within 900 yards of the German Trenches.

No. 14 Platoon v. No. 13.

No. 14.

Dunce, C.	c. Hardiman	b. Hill	2
Turner, W.	c. Smith	b. Tilley	21
James, J.		b. Millard	7
Hill, E.	Run out		6
Watts, D. A.	c. Cross	b. Dovey	11
Clift, G.		b. Millard	6
Russell, G.	c.	and	b Dovey	2
Bennett, H.		b. Dovey	5
Rabenhill, H.		b. Smith	3
Popjoy, G.	c. Millard	b. Dovey	2
Jordan, M.	Not out.		2
	Extras		14
		Total	82

No. 13

	1st Innings.		2nd Innings.	
Smith, H.	Run out	3	b. James	0
Hardiman	b. James	1	b. Popjoy	2
Millard, S.	b. James	0	Not out	9
Cross, A.	b. Popjoy	6	b. James	6
Tilley	b. James	0	b. James	7
Wyatt, A.	b. Popjoy	3	b. James	2
Philpott, J.	b. James	1	b. James	0
Hill, C. R.	b. James	1	b. James	2
Bransdon	b. James	0	b. James	0
Verget	b. James	0	b. James	0
Dovey	Not out	1	b. James	0
	Extras	2	Extras	8
	Total	18	Total	36

No. 14 won by an innings and 28 runs.

FROM THE EDITOR'S POST BAG.

G. E. C.

Very many thanks for letting me know that Cascara has been taken by the enemy. I fear it is an ancient wheeze.

Intending Subscribers in England.

The Gazette will be forwarded to any address in England on the receipt of the minimum subscription of 10s., paid in advance. Cheques, etc. are payable to the Mess President of the Battalion.

1/5th GLO'STER REGIMENT.

PROMOTIONS.

To be Sergeants :—

No. 2717 Act./Sergt. Thompson, R. O. Dated 15/8/15.
No. 1999 L./Sergt. Lippett, G. J. Dated 16/8/15.

To be L/Sergeants :—

No. 2355 A/L/Sergt. Harvey, M. J. Dated 15/8/15.
No. 2382 Corpl. Knight, R. E. Dated 16/8/15.

To be Corporals :—

No. 2339 A/Corpl. Green, W. A. Dated 15/8/15.
No. 1777 A/Corpl. Parrott, E. Dated 16/8/15.

To be Acting Corporals :—

No. 2308 L/Corpl. Fudge, A. A. Dated 15/8/15.
No. 1511 L/Corpl. Perry, G. Dated 16/8/15.

Appointed Acting L/Corporals :—

No. 2654 Pte. Ayliffe, F. W. Dated 7/9/15.
No. 2714 Pte. Stinchcombe, H. T. Dated 7/9/15.

Commissions from the Ranks :—

No. 2370 L/Corpl. Nixon, P. Promoted 2nd Lieut. into 2nd. Glos. Regt. Dated 15/8/15.
No. 2699 L/Corpl. Oxley, G. M. To be 2nd Lieut. in the 2nd Glos. Regt. Dated 15/8/15.
No. 1473 Corpl. Twine, W. H. To be 2nd Lieut. in York and Lancaster Regt. Dated 15/8/15.
No. 1643 Sergt. Chandler, H. J. To be 2nd Lieut. in York and Lancaster Regt. Dated 15/8/15.

BATTALION GRENADIERS.

Roll of Qualified Grenadiers who have passed Tests at Brigade Grenadier School.

Lieut. W. Fream. 2nd Lieut. J. P. Winterbotham.
Lieut. H. S. King. 2nd Lieut. C. V. N. Puckridge.

A. Company :—

58	Sergt.	Meadows, J.
111	L/Sergt.	Speck, P.
1345	Corpl.	Partridge, A. E.
1183	,,	Nash, E. F.
1366	L/Corpl.	Marshall, H. R.
2787	,,	Davis, P.
1557	,,	Rice, A.
2444	Pte.	Ellison, D. M.
2453	,,	Thomas, A. C.
2489	,,	Doogood, H. A. C.
2486	,,	Pepperell, W. F.
2506	,,	McKee, H. J.
1346	,,	Aldridge, F. G.
2495	,,	Bircher, W. G.
1347	,,	Davis, W. C. F.
2515	,,	Blackwell, H.
2499	,,	Barnes, R. C.
1858	,,	Brisland, R.
1940	,,	Ireland, C. H.
3343	,,	O'Neil, C.
2503	,,	Done, A.
49	,,	Kemp, R.
2463	,,	Jones, L.
1831	,,	Miller, W. F.

B. Company :—

203	Sergt.	Heaven, J.
242	,,	Hill, F.
864	Corpl.	Turner, E. W.
2091	L/Corpl.	Coton, J.
2558	,,	Paynter, W. F. L.
1987	Pte.	Blandford, C. E.
3310	,,	Sully, G. E.
2341	,,	Barnett, E.
2182	,,	Hemmings, C.
3139	,,	Butt, R.
1753	,,	Bassett, A. E.
2752	,,	Cook, C.
2626	,,	Cocks, J. A.
2572	,,	Taylor, G. F.
1667	,,	Yelverton, H. R.
2767	,,	Parham, W. G.
2322	,,	Harding, W.
2619	,,	Ayris, W. L.
2766	,,	Milne, W. J.
2433	,,	White, J. H. C.

C. Company :—

438	Sergt.	Patrick, S. G.
2693	L/Corpl.	Lewis, A. H. T.
3031	Pte.	Medlicott, W.
3571	,,	Ireland, A. D.
2555	,,	Mullis, E. J.
2708	,,	Sampson, A. E.
3127	,,	Timms, W. J.
3014	,,	Crosby, C. T.
2623	,,	Bridgman, F. F.
2642	,,	Young, H.
3216	,,	Price, J. W.
3752	,,	Wiltshire, F.
2963	,,	Sindrey, R.
1723	,,	Turner, G. E.
1434	,,	Pyke, A. C.
2628	,,	Cooke, D. E.
3299	,,	Lewis, R. W.

D Company :—

1129	Sergt.	Pyment, H.
1608	Corpl.	Bignell, G. R.
2348	L/Corpl.	Philpotts, F.
2729	,,	Wise, R.
2735	,,	Millard, S.
1813	,,	Watts, D. A.
1427	,,	Fisher, B. W.
2697	Pte.	Middlecote, H.
2726	,,	Washbourne, W. P.
2614	,,	Clift, G. A.
1961	,,	Elliott, H.
1413	,,	Dyer, H.
1966	,,	Lockier, E. S.
1589	,,	Lewis, L. W.
2656	,,	Baylis, J. W.
2607	,,	Organ, S. T.
1609	,,	Bennett, H.
1597	,,	Grimes, P. J.
2088	,,	Hardiman, G.
2612	,,	Smith, W. J.
2613	,,	Tanner, J.
2649	,,	Rea, W.

CASUALTIES.

Officers :—

Wounded Accidentally :—

Lieut. W. Fream 21/9/15

Other Ranks :—

Wounded :—

3299	Private Lewis, R. W.	31/8/15	C. Co.
1810	,, Preston, W. H.	17/9/15	A. ,,
30	Coy. Q.M.S. Brown, A. F.	22/9/15	A. ,,
2665	Private Collorick, H.	28/9/15	D. ,,

Wounded Accidentally :—

| 1375 | Private Harris, A. T. | 7/9/15 | D. ,, |

No. 7.   OCTOBER, 1915.

5th Gloucester Gazette.

A Chronicle, serious and humorous, of the Battalion while serving with the BRITISH EXPEDITIONARY FORCE.

OF CENSORING LETTERS.

(An unpublished Essay of Francis Bacon.)

YOU maye read in an ancyent historyan howe in the Gallick Warres a certayne Roman Soldyer wrote to hys wyfe at Brundusium, tellyng her of many and wonderfull deedes of prowesse, the whych dyd not in all thyngs corresponde to the truth of whatte hadde verilie befallen. You shalle reade also howe the generall who in those dayes was the sole **censor epistolarum** in a hygh wrathe tooke an axe and destroyed the letter (whych accordynge to the custom of that tyme was inscrybed on a greate stone of granyte) and summonyng the author to hys presence said weightylie and wyth some showe of displeasure—" Miles vera et magna fecisti ; scriptor necnon falsa dixisti : versus ante in sanguine, mendax erumpis sanguinarius," the whych was ryghte well said. Many men do greate thynges, but wryte them falselie, makyng theyre myndes a magnyfying glass and theyre imaginacioun an artyste's brushe, so that the thynge tolde is in muche respecte differente from the thynge done. And thys is as true of letters of the presente warre as in all paste warres : human nature changeth not in this inclinacioun. The censor of letters at ye presente tyme not only vetoeth dangerous informacioun : he studieth also the nature of the human soule, whych in despyte of ye devyce of fielde poste cardes and ye covering of one's honoure in an enveloppe of greene, ever seeketh prayse and flatterie at ye expense of truthe and would fayn appear heroick in the eyes of others.

It is no lesse worthie to observe that greate myndes eschewe thys sillie means of promocioun of selfe : it is always little mynds that would appeare greate : " parvi magna fingunt," as Tully hath it, " magni videri volunt." A greate mynde standeth secure on its owne foundacioun and needeth not the aide of paynted proppes.

Exaggeracioun in a soldyer's letter may be very paynfull to hym that readeth it, and thys is so when the character and worke of the wryter belieth the thynges he wryteth. You would well thynke that some had come nigh to utter extinctyon by the havock of shelles, who had only seene theyre explosion from a safe distaunce ; and others caught vilely at the throate by ye furies of gass, who forsooth had never experienced any worse smelle than that of an ancyent dung-heape.

In defense of thys lying it myght well be sayd that the soldyer only provydes for the sublyme expectation of those who receive hys letters ; they are proude that he is fyghting, and looke for letters from hym and newe whych they can telle to the mattronnes of theyre acquayntance. It myght also be argued that the soldyer desyres sympathy from his friends, to the quickenyng whereof he must perforce give coloure to actual dangers and conjure up dangers whych do not exyst, and make playnts

whych have no bases in fact. But thys defense is hollow, for weakness in one doth not excuse weakness in another, and, as Scripture saith—Truth is prime, " Magna est Veritas et praevalebit."

Howbeit the censor of letters who is also the reader of heartes hath often much joye in hys worke, for he cometh upon letters from a devoute lover to hys ladye, from a fayther to his lyttle chylde, or from sonne to his mother : and these are documents worthe many chronicles of fyttes and valoure. They are fulle of resignacioun to an enforced partynge, fulle of hope for a speedie returne, written with affection and tendernesse. These are whyte lyghtes of faith in the darke horrors of warre.

TRIOLET.

(The Crossing.)

I'm not feeling well,
And the waves wont be quiet.
My companions can tell
I'm not feeling well.

And I'm going to — Oh hell !
Supply fishes their diet.
I'm not feeling well,
And the waves won't be quiet.

F. W. H.

VVth CORPS SUMMARY

31-9-19.

OUR OWN FRONT.

Right Division.—Enemy found to be holding their trenches running N and E of 6k7125.

Parties of enemy working on Right, Leftand Back sides.

Enemy prisoner told our patrol that lighting up time was 7.3 p.m. and that the moon refused to show owing to clouds.

Centre Division.—Aerial reconnaissance reported enormous edifice behind SAHIOBWA. From enquiries it was found to be merely the dug-out for a Field Ambulance. Being home-made, this great work will be allowed to stand, subject to some interference by gravity or weather.

The same aircraft report lighting-up time in BOLIVAR as 8.19 p.m. and that the sun does not rise in HONG KONG till 7.22 a.m.

Left Division.—Enormous activity. Our men fired 6 shots, and the enemy retaliated by playing a band.

Later Germans took our trench away, but we caught hold of it in time and hung on. Unhappily, in the struggle our trench was torn in two, and the enemy hold one half at present. It is expected that they will retreat, as the half they hold is mined with old Winning Post Annuals. At any rate, we do beat them by knowing that the lights should be lit at 6.23 p.m. in the event of there being no moon ; and this superiority will in time prove invaluable.

Corps South of Somewhere.

It is found that steel loop-hole plates are useless as trouser buttons.

An order has been issued forbidding the habit of hanging pictures on wire entanglements.

In this Corps a regrettable incident occurred. Two men refused to accept the time for lighting up, as putting the moon out.   Both were shot at sunrise.

Still Further South.

The A. S. C. hotly attacked the enemy's position with sparking plugs, bacon and flaming Machonochies. Enemy faltered and fell back. The Corps of R. T. O's. pressed on, and by a wonderful distribution of Movement Orders completely routed 8-feet of German trench. Meanwhile, the Mobile Veterinary Corps on the left inflicted severe loss on enemy, who had never seen such troops in the fighting line, and their appearance awed the Huns completely.

At this stage several Staff Officers of various armies, corps, divisions and brigades, appeared, and one A.P.M. This dash of colour on the sombre fields pleased the enemy immensely, who cheered heartily, and amidst cries of " What pieces of grandeur ! " laid down their arms and surrendered. It is both awkward and unfortunate that the real victors, i.e., the assorted staff, did not realise that it was they and they only who achieved the victory But in point of fact, a German prisoner was heard to exclaim as he looked at the brassards " There's not an umpire among them. It's not fair, we aren't playing any more." And so the coloured bands really did the trick. The enemy were further discomfited on learning that the sun did not set before 5.19 p.m. and that there were no orders issued on this point before the battle began.

In Russia the sun and moon continue to rise and fall at various times on different days.

Correspondence.

Letter found on a German prisoner—
......we have had no food for 3 weeks. Again I say that we have had no food for 3 weeks. I ought not to tell you, but I must say that for 3 weeks we have had no food. It is nearly a month, 3 weeks to be exact, since we had any food. It is no good sending me food as there are men who would eat it before it reached me, they having had no food for 3 weeks.........

Other fronts.

If BULGARIA declares war on anyone, it will most certainly have a tremendous effect on BULGARIA.

On the other hand, it may not. However, it will be interesting to see if BULGARIA does declare war or does not. What will happen ? Can we say ? I don't know. Let us wait.

SARK maintains a strict neutrality, in spite of pressure from the owner of ST. MICHAELS MOUNT.

Sun rises 8.3 a.m. and sets 7.5. p.m.
Moon ,, 6.40 p.m. ,,   ,, 12 noon.

OUR PORTRAIT GALLERY.

THE S.M.

His mien is fierce and Kaiser-like,
He does not walk, but rides a bike,
Up to the trench and back.
And all the boys from Coombe to Bristol
Envy him 'cos he has a pistol,
But does not wear a pack.

He chronicles your every error.
Even the sergeants go in terror
To catch his evil eye.
So labours he with great reward :
The pen is mightier than the sword
Unless the poets lie.

And when the guards come on parade,
He sees their trousers are not frayed,
And notes the lengthy sleeve.
I wish him luck, and (when I'm dressed
For duty in my shabby best)
A sudden eight days' leave.

Then with renewed and quiet mind
May he return to us, and find
Naught to excite his rage or
Cause that bristling lip to pout.
For what is life in France without
The gallant sergeant major ?

F. W. H.

THE MYSTERY OF 2643, PTE. CHUGWATER.

CHAPTER I.

" A most interesting case, my dear Potson," said Chublock Bones as he returned noisily to our dug-out one wet September afternoon. " Most interesting, and at present I can see no light on the matter." At once I was keenly awake, every nerve strained to breaking point, the excitement of another case presenting unexpected relief from the tedium of our sedentary life.

Great as was my excitement, I refrained from interrupting my friend Bones' meditation. He was seated, as was his custom, on a pile of sand-bags, with his gum boots on my pack, carefully filling his aged briar from my tin of ration tobacco. Meanwhile I nervously chewed my " Rough-rider " and watched my companion closely.

" Most interesting " he again remarked in an abstracting-semi-detached-don't-care-if-it-snows kind of mood.

At last I could stand the strain no longer, and broke the silence. " Of course, I do not presume to be able to throw any light on the case as yet," I remarked, " but the saying that two heads are better than one might prove true for once."

Bones pulled hard at his briar, filling the dug-out with an acrid blue smoke which set me fumbling nervously for a few of my respirators.

" Well," said he, ' it appears that, briefly, No. 2643, Pte. Chugwater has disappeared. His company commander can find no clue of him, and up to the time of appearance of the last Summary nothing has been heard. He was last heard swearing in the kitchen adjoining the officers' mess at about 10.15 on the morning of the 28th."

" Let me see," I said, " that would be just about high water at Southend, wouldn't it."

" Exactly, and that is what makes the case more remarkable," observed Bones. " As far as can be ascertained he was in good health and had drawn 5 francs the day previous. There is no doubt that it is his own signature on the acquittance roll, so that disposes of any suspicion of foul play which might attach to his company commander.

" Most extraordinary and most interesting," he soliloquised, and sank into a brown study, from which I had learned it was useless to try and rouse him.

CHAPTER II.

When I came back to the dug-out once more after an intimate inspection of sumps in the fire trench, I found Bones eagerly scanning the pages of the field service pocket book.

"What is the height of a fire platform, Potson? he queried, as I stumbled over his foot and cannoned heavily against an upright.

"Oh! about 6 to 10 days" I replied, looking through my letters just received.

"Ah: I thought so," he ejaculated crisply, and darted from the dug-out.

Next morning at stand-down he re-entered the dug-out and smiled knowingly.

"It is most gratifying to be thought so much of by one's grandmother, isn't it?," he queried.

"Most," I answered, and then it dawned on me that by some abstruse working of his power of deduction he had divined a very pungent truth.

"Marvellous," I added, "how do you manage it, my dear Bones?"

"It's quite simple. You know my methods, Potson," he replied. "I observed you rubbing yourself against the support as I entered, and a glance at your pained expression decided me that you were wearing a red wool cholera belt, knitted by your grandmother."

"Superb," I ejaculated, "but you will pardon me if I don't quite follow your deduction. How could you tell it was red, and from my grandmother.

"Well, my dear Potson, by careful observation, and by guarded questions, I elicited that you had received in the course of the week cholera belts from all your relations with the exception of your grand-mother, so when I saw you showing the usual symptoms, I diagnosed at once."

"Incredible," I replied, "but how on earth did you find out it was red?"

"My dear Potson, that I admit was a bow at a venture, but by watching you give an angry start when I purposely switched on the red light in my pocket torch, I was satisfied."

"Stupendous," I murmured weakly.

CHAPTER III.

A tot of rum put new life into me, and I soon had strength to ask, "What news of the missing Private?" "Ah! yes, that reminds me" he answered, "great events may happen shortly, so carry your revolver handy always. In the course of the last few hours I have discovered some interesting facts which shed a ray of light on the proceedings. There is a strong suspicion of foul play. Briefly, the facts are these. It appears that some days ago, 2nd Lieutenant Bryman had occasion to be severely spoken to by a Brigadier for carrying too much in his pack, and at the end of the route march roundly abused Pte. Chugwater for not filling his pack with an air cushion. That night all the officers in the mess were seriously indisposed, and it is thought that the missing man must have poisoned the food. At any rate, next day No. 2643 Pt. Chugwater disappeared and has not been seen since. He is known to have been a keen purchaser of silk-woven cards, which he despatched to one, Emilina Brown, at Gloucester. Careful enquiries at Gloucester bring to light the fact that at Barton Fair a man answering to the description of the missing man was seen firing "rapid" at bottles in plain clothes.

"What an extraordinary side-show," I cried.

"Of course, you understand the man was in plain clothes. Nothing else occurred, and no further facts have come to light yet, but any minute I am expecting to be called away or upon."

As he spoke a tap was heard on the waterproof sheet, and a messenger, all steaming with the exertion of keeping up with ration parties in the communication trenches, entered and handed Bones a note. Like a flash he pulled on his gum boots and darted up the steps, brushing aside the gasping orderly.

CHAPTER IV.

When I awoke next afternoon the air was heavy with tobacco smoke, and I became aware of a peculiarly contented look on Bones' face.

"What news?" I asked.

Without answering he handed me a pink form, on which I read the mystic sentence "Our guns will open fire at 11-30 a.m. AAA."

"But I don't follow the connection in the least," I replied. "What time did this come?"

"Just now 3.30 p.m." he answered, "the mystery is solved, and we are relieved to-morrow."

Pinching myself to dispel any doubts, I motioned to him to continue.

"In a few words it amounts to this. Private Chugwater is a cook at Brigade Headquarters."

The dug-out formed fours, and I swooned silently away. Recovering slowly I repeated the continue motion, and lay back on my waterproof sheet.

"By careful reconnaissance," continued Bones, "I entered the orderly room, first raising the alarm outside by saying that the Sergeant Major was WALKING down the road."

"In the general stampede which followed I went through all the pink forms I could find, and at length get on the trail!"

"On the afternoon of the 28th all Company Officers and M.C.O. were circularised for the name of a potential cook for Brigade Headquarters. It appears that this form was taken to the H.Q. of Pte. Chugwater's company commander, who was out, Lieutenant Bryman, however, was in, and, doubtless still sore from the cutting remarks about his equipment he convinced the brilliant plan of sending in the name required. To submit Pte. Chugwaters' name was the work of a moment, and there remains little more to relate. In due course the movement order came, and by an oversight, Lieut Bryman omitted to tell his company commander."

"But," I queried, "what was the cause of the officers' indisposition?"

"Oh," replied Bones, that was a mistake on the part of one of the Mess servants, who put the butter supplied by Battalion H.Q. Mess on the table, instead of that bought locally."

"But who was the man who was seen at Barton Fair firing rapid at bottles?" I persisted.

"Ah! that was a man named Smith, from London."

———

THINGS WE WANT TO KNOW.

Which is the fastest horse in the Battalion?

Who was the Private who said "Here's old Mother again in full marching order," when an old lady, with a basket on her back, came begging for bread in A Company Mess?

Who was the jocky in D Company who was overcome by Black Bess?

Which N.C.O. in D Company mistook a bay number board in the trench for a periscope?

Did the Ghurka weep in the mail bag?

Who is the individual in B. Company known as the human gramophone?

Who was the sentry who fired at the moon?

Who said that if he intended to be a regular soldier he should join the Navy?

Which Company Officer asked his servant if he had mixed dubbin with the mashed potatoes? Is he in A Company.

Who was the officer who forgot the rule of the road when he brought a fatigue party back?

Now that the Q. M. Stores are at No. 9, will there be any diminution in his figure?

Which A Company N.C.O. declared vociferously in his sleep thet he was "Mahomet," and seemed more than half inclined to believe his statement when awake?

Did a certain well-known member of A Company attempt to appease the wrath of the Mayor of the village by presenting him with a tin of mustard?

Was the attempt successful?

Does the Mayor anticipate a cheap cruet supply for the future?

Was the football match between the Sergeants and Corporals of A Company a screamingly funny farce, and did the antics of a rotund and popular Non. Com. add to the piquancy of the affair?

Which of our Warrant Officers is madly in love with a young French Madame, and does he find a slight difficulty in pouring forth into her ears the story of his devotion, owing to the smallness of his French vocabulary?

Does the said vocabulary consist solely of the words " Oui " " Bon " and " Compris "?

What did the M.G.O. do to the rat?

Who wrote to ask if his brother was coming out in the next drought?

Did a certain popular Officer appear on parade with his ribbed stockings inside out, to the great amusement of his platoon?

Would it not be as well if A Co. Cooks were informed that paraffin oil is not by any means a necessary or palatable addition to shackles.

What did the officer get for losing his respirator?

What did the Doctor say when he found his pyjamas sewn up?

How did some Platoon Sergeants come off against their Platoon Commanders in the Football Match? And how did some Platoon Commanders come off against their Platoon Sergeants?

Who was the N.C.O. who went to find the Policeman to get " Brigade Time "?

What time was it when he found it?

Who is the Corporal who waxes his moustache with bacon fat?

How does he manage when the bacon is short?

What drummer would like to have his blanket and novel!

Is he a Lance-Corporal?

Who was the Corporal who sang in his sleep that nice song, " Eileen, Eileena, etc."?

Who tries to catch rats with fly papers?

Who is the N.C.O. in A Company whose double is Charlie Chaplain?

Is he in No. 2 Platoon?

Which section was it that made a pudding with bread and a tin of condensed milk?

And is it right that they caught flies and put in for currants?

Was this section in No. 16 Platoon?

How did the Sergeants enjoy their rocket display in the trenches?

Were they in "A" Company?

Who was the officer who told his men to make a noise like a piece of cheese if they wanted to catch rats?

Is it true that you can find in the Navvies Battalion a father and son who are both in receipt of the Old Age Pension?

Is it a mark of intelligence to suppose Boadicea to be another name for Joan of Arc?

Is it a fact that a certain popular N. C. O. is anxious to know why a brace of L. were taken into the Ark?

IN MEMORIAM.

Why should we mourn the dead (since death
Will come to everyone)
Who go in valiant youth, and yet
Unspoiled with life and living's fret,
While still the seasons run
Ever more wearily and weak for him who tarrieth?

They never crept into the night
That lurks for all mankind.
Joyous they lived, and joyous leapt
Into the gaping dark where slept
Their fathers all : to find
Honour, the jest of fools, yet still the soul of all delight.

SONNET.

(To H.M.)

Him, the gods, loving, took while life was young.
Say rather (clinging to a wiser creed)
God takes and suddenly on wings of speed
Bears to the utter quietness far flung
Of fields Elysian where the horrid tongue
Of battle is not. For He knew his need
Better than those who knew him well indeed,
Loving him best. Above his grave is rung
The death bell of all things which hurt the sense
And vex the mind and plague the soul of man,
Tinging the rainbow colours of his best
Dreams drably : and hath cried a voice, " Go hence !
Old Angel Time, to weary whom you can,
The while my well beloved child hath rest."

RONDEAU.

If we return, will England be
Just England still to you and me—
The place where we must earn our bread ?
We, who have walked among the dead,
And watched the smile of agony.

And seen the price of Liberty
Which we have taken carelessly
From other hands. Nay, we shall dread ;
If we return.

Dread lest we hold blood guiltily
The things that men have died to free.
O, English fields shall blossom red
For all the blood that has been shed
By men whose guardians are we,
If we return.

F. W. H.

FUMES FROM THE EDITOR'S WATER BOTTLE.

It has often been alleged that the pen is mightier than the sword ; it would seem to be true that the boot is greater than the bark. One who is a familiar figure in the Regiment was accustomed, in the old Chelmsford days, to greet in dulcet tones applicants for clothing, etc., in the following encouraging terms :

" Young man, d'you know my name ? "

" Yes, Sir, " came from the blanched lips of the frightened youth.

" Well then, get out or you'll get it," was the energetic reponse.

So far the Boot had to acknowledge—through lack of opportunity, solely—the supremacy of the Bark.

However, our hero's recent display between the posts has reversed the old order of things, and the Boot has pride of place, easily.

" Halt ! Who goes there !"

" Merry Party."

" Pass, Merry Padre."

But was the Padre really merry ? Ed.

" The enemy then fired several explosive shells into our trenches."

Weekly Times.

We presume that this was to distinguish them from the variety filled with porridge and sawdust, sometimes known as " duds."

In the reign of Charles II. it was laid down that a Candidate for the office of Quartermaster " Should be a man of metal who has learned some arithmetic, he should be an understanding man."

The Quartermaster's arithmetic is " some arithmetic," as he alone knows how to divide two shirts among three men.

Major Baron was most kindly about to give us another of his excellent concerts. But unfortunately the " Alarm " came just as the entertainment was beginning.

Overheard at the Canteen—

" Corporal give me a three-penny loaf, please "
" Sorry, but we haven't any."
" Well then, give us 3 candles instead."

" Any Tooth paste ? "
" Don't stock any."
" Give us a Tin of Brasso, then."

How stew is served to the companies of a certain regiment " somewhere in England "—

The stew is delivered to the platoons via tubes, a tap being placed in each hut. In the event of a portion of meat entering the tube, it rings a bell, returns to the butcher, and reports. So far there has been no report ! !

We shall soon have to start an " Old Boys' Column " in our Gazette. Many members of the Battalion move off from this humble planet to more exalted spheres. Perhaps they will oblige us from time to time with side-lights on their doings.

A former Adjutant of the Battalion has had a fortunate escape—

" Lieut.-Colonel R. V. G. Brentell, of the Suffolk Regiment, who has arrived at Brighton suffering from six wounds, lay helpless and alone for three days and nights between the British and German lines in France, during which time he was robbed by the Germans.

Some years ago he had the distinction of being the tallest man in the Indian Army."
Daily Paper.

" And after the Germans had been through his pockets he was one of the shortest."
Punch.

As an old school-fellow of three brothers not unknown to fame—Captain M. T. Johnson, killed, alas, on the banks of the Aisne, Captain D. Johnson, D.S.O., wounded seriously at the Dardanelles, Captain V. N. Johnson, once Adjutant of this Battalion and now Brigade Major of the 12th Brigade—the Editor from his easy chair would like, on behalf of his readers, to wish the last-named every success in his new rôle. The Battalion knows what it owes to his hard work.

An old friend of the Battalion in Sergt.-Major G. N. Chapman has been given a commission in the 2nd Bn. Gloucestershire Regiment. As a former Colour-Sergeant Instructor attached to this Battalion, he did a great deal for the efficiency of the Battalion.

Of No. 6 of this Gazette, 1,250 copies were printed, and we hope that our circulation will increase month by month.

" To a German the course adopted by the London County Council a few years ago of refusing to allow Empire Day to be celebrated, and forbidding the use of the Union Jack in the schools under their control, would be inconceivable."
Lord Cromer, *Spectator*, Oct. 2nd, 1915.

Germany's debt to that Love of the Fatherland, so carefully instilled into her sons and daughters from their earliest years, is a great one.

It is tragic to think that we have so neglected our opportunities that even at this time there are Englishmen who openly profess their willingness to acquiesce in a German domination. But it is refreshing to know that two such enlightened gentlemen, the employes of a Corporation in England, have been dismissed as being unworthy of receiving Ratepayers' money.

A correspondent, who notes that contributions are demanded by the Editor, writes to know what sort of " copy " is required. Articles " serious or humorous "—we quote from the title page—verse, light or heavy, would be acceptable. But may I remind my readers that we cannot accept Prose cut into lengths as Poetry.

THE DILEMMA.

VERSES ON THE DIVERS CHARMS OF TWO YOUNG WENCHES.

Erstwhile, in pedagogic garb,
I felt the urgings of the Muse.
But now I feel Love's stinging barb,
And, loving, know not where to choose.

For Julia's charms my heart entwine,
Alas ! I owe her kisses sweet—
Yet while I strive to make her mine,
Long for the arms of Marguerite.

Her unforgetable embrace
Makes throb my heart, my pulses beat,
Yet while I gaze on her fair face
I fly, in winged fancy fleet,

To where my Julia stands aglow
For me, her amorous dolt, to fly
From fettering wires and indents slow,
To lay me fettered to her eye.

Humble their birth, yet great their grace,
What though they thump the yeasty flour
When Julia lifts to me her face,
What man but envies me my hour ?

And when, a strolling at my ease,
I look to pass the time away,
At Marguerite a shelling peas,
What dog but envies me my day ?

Ah ! pity me, poor luckless wight,
Thus envious envied, much bemused,
Yet, should I strive to set wrong right,
Who knows I were by one refused ?

So deeply pledged to Marguerite,
So basely bound to Julia's nod,
My only hope's a shell to meet,
And hide my shame beneath the sod.

CHAPLAIN'S COLUMN.

On October 3rd, the Senior Chaplain to the Division dedicated our new Field Altar. It is the gift of Lieut-Colonel Collett, Lieut-Colonel Marling, and Major Tarrant, to whom we would express our grateful thanks. It makes our services more home-like, and the Divine Presence more real.

We expect the Right Reverend Bishop Gwynne shortly. He has promised to hold a Confirmation Service. If there are men who would like to have a talk to the Chaplain about the matter, will they please let him know. While he is "in residence" his dug-out adjoins the Square.

In "Love and War" the following verses, which have the merit of being both simple and appropriate, occur—

A Soldier's Prayer.

"God give me but the grace to stand
Patient and strong, with sword in hand,
To do my share for this dear land—
Perchance to die.

No earthly gifts I crave, dear Lord,
But that I may still bear this sword
Until the day when, Peace restored,
I lay it by.

"STAND TO."

(With apologies to F.W.H.)

At dawn, half dream,
I see those fields in front,
Like steam,
Drenched all with fog,
And start my daily hunt
For louse and bug.
All day—
All day it hangs about, and then
Comes night.
And, in my soaking togs, I dreams enjoy.
But not at home by the fire's glow as when
I was a boy.
. . . .
Thus shall all Tommies, rise next morn to see
Their Dearest Friend, pitted and all rusty.

K. A. R.

WAR.

Dawn was just breaking on the fair land of France. The long rows of trees stood out gaunt and grey against a threatening sky and the mist lay heavy on roadside and hedge.

Away in the distance the guns still boomed and crashed, and the flicker of the star shells showed pale against the sullen sky. An old woman knelt before a wayside altar, her hands clasped and her eyes turned heavenwards in prayer.

Little heeded she the damp grass that had soaked through her worn and patched dress, or the crashing of the guns. Far behind her lay what remained of her little home and her only property reposed by her, wrapped in a cloth.

God and the poor old creature alone could tell how hard it was after 80 years of hard and underpaid toil to be turned from the little house where she had hoped to end her days in peace. It was very hard after all the little economies and schemings to buy the new stove and the picture of the Madonna, to say farewell to it all and go out into a cold world to seek new friends. And as she prayed—prayed to her God who understood it all, and as she murmured her supplications her face was once again

that of a young woman, and her rheumy eyes shone with the light of youth once more.

It was broad daylight now, and over the hill a cock crowed stridently. A despatch rider hummed past and a motor lorry came lumbering up the road. The poor dejected figure moved not. A dog nosed among the bundle and howled, but he was not driven away. Old Germaine still gazed at the plaster saints and the wax flowers, but her face had the repose of death and the happiness of life ever-lasting.

A woman came along the road leading a cow by a halter, and high up in the sky a lark burst into its throbbing song of happiness, and old Germaine was with her God.

J.S.P.

OUR BENEFACTORS.

The following have sent Newspapers :—
The Countess Bathurst.
Miss Parr.
Canadian Field Comforts Commission—per Lieut. Plummer.
Mrs. Temple Cook.
Mr. W. R. Voller.
N.B.—Picture Papers, Magazines, are most welcome.

Mr. and Mrs. Tubbs, Wotton under Edge	- Woodbines.
Mr. Jack Margetson, Stroud.	- Woodbines (every week.)
	- "Times" Broadsheets.
	- Books for Recreation Room.
	- Library.
Miss Pagan, Penzance	- Parcel of comforts.
Colonel Griffith.	- Hand-bayonets.
Gloucester Women's Suffrage Society.	- Steriliser.
Mr. Hawkins ("Uncle Jack") Bristol Times and Mirror	- Cigarettes.
Messrs. Moreland and Sons, Ltd., Gloucester.	- "John Bull" Matches.
Canon Brewster	- Hymn sheets.

THE HUN.

How strange are the ways of the Hun !
He lived upon sausage and beer.
Now that "harmless" old son
Bad and mad all in one
Makes hell of this agonised sphere.

How strange are the thoughts of the Hun !
"Ja, ja," he is "god-like and grand."
Though that we see no fun
In the murders he has done
Is a thing that he can't understand.

How strange is the swank of the Hun.
Is there room on this planet for him ?
With his latest big gun
He will capture the Sun
And use the old star as a "glim."

And what is the end of the Hun ?
And will it be torrid, or chill ?
There's a furnace begun
Which is second to none
They've marked it "Reserved for our Bill."

AFTER THE WAR.

A Few Rules of Golf.

(With apologies to the Royal and Ancient, St. Andrews.)

1. The players will parade at 10.30 a.m. and carry haversack rations. Clubs will be slung on the right shoulder.

2. Parties will move off at the "slope" at 150 yards interval.

3. Caddies will "present" at all times, except when giving advice.

F

4. Caddies will see that all balls are clean, so as to prevent a jamb (Ticklers').

5. Parties should make use of all possible cover when approaching the " green."

6. A single player has no standing through the green. He must " halt," stand to attention and " present " arms to all armed parties. Any offenders will be compelled to replace all divots on the links after "stand to " at night.

7. Every foursome must be accompanied by a range-finder and the class of shot given, either a (Mashie) Howitzer or a brassie (Soixante-quinze) to be used.

8. A ball which has fallen into a " sump-hole " may be lifted out without penalty, but the water must be sterilised by the R.A.M.C. and the ball sent to Sappers for fumigation.

9. When approaching a green it is most necessary that players should avoid enfilade fire, especially near the 4th and 6th greens. Any players suffering from enfilade fire should report at once to Headquarters, when the Chaplain to the Society will take notice of exact language used for future reference.

10. Any balls found lying about to be returned to the B. S. M. the professional at the club-house, those marked K.14 especially valuable.

11. Any player noticing mist or fog coming from any part of the surrounding country must sound alarm (Fore), when all players will put on Smoke Helmets and " stand to."

12. The exact position of the barbed wire and other defences guarding the green must be carefully noted, as these defences are likely to be altered owing to the state of the course and the discretion of Colonel Bogey.

13. The Club-House is open from 8 a.m. to 9.30 p.m. summer and winter. Refreshments provided Luncheons by Machonochie Ltd. Teas by the Management Coy. Cooks.

SMOKING CONCERT.

No 4 Platoon held a smoking concert in their own Barn in celebration of their victory over No. 3 at football by 19 points to 3.

Lance. Corpl. Hopson took the chair, and discharged his onerous duties to the satisfaction of all.

After the toast of the King, Sergt. Stevens took the Barn by storm by singing several good songs.

After " order " had been obtained, Sergt. Durrett, of the victorious team, in a few well-chosen words, expressed his pleasure at being present at such a gathering, commented upon the sporting way in which " No. 3 " had taken their defeat, and promised to turn out for the next match and " work the scrum."

Songs were sung by

L/Corpl. Hopson   ... "My Little Grey Home in the Trench."
L/Corpl. Davis   ... " The Rosary."
L/Corpl. Jackson   ... " If I were a Blackbird."
Pte. W. Bundy   ... " My Heart is with you to-night."
Pte. Doyle   ... " Thora."
Pte. R. Barnes   ... " Tipperary."
Pte. P. R. Davis   ... " It was Night on the Bloodstained Battlefield."

and others.

On the proposition of Pte. A. Cook, the Captain of the winning team, a hearty vote of thanks to the chairman, and to all who helped to make the evening so enjoyable, including Pte. Stock, who " totted."

PROMOTIONS.

Promotions and Appointments. Officers:—

2nd Lt. L. W. Moore to be Lieut, dated 28/9/15.
2nd Lieut. J. P. Winterbotham to be Acting Adjutant, dated 6/10/15.

Commissions from the Ranks.

To be 2nd Lieut. 5th Glos. Regiment :—

L/Sergt. R. E. Knight, C. Coy.
Dated 16/9/15.
L/Corpl. K. A. Robertson, C. Coy. Dated 16/9/15.
L/Corpl. F. W. Harvey, C. Coy. Dated 16/9/15.

Promotions N.C.O'S.

No. 2741 Corpl. J. W. Watkins, C. Coy., to be Sergeant, dated 2/10/15.
No. 1739 A/Corpl. F. Slatter, D. Coy., to be Corpl., dated 2/10/15.
No. 2760 A/L/Cpl. R. Hill, B. Coy., to be L/Corpl., dated 16/8/15.
No. 2569 A/L/Cpl. D. Sullivan, B. Coy., to be L/Corpl., dated 8/9/15.
No. 1901 A/L/Cpl. C. Furley, C. Coy., to be L/Corpl., dated 20/9/15.
No. 2755 A/L/Cpl. E. Goatman, C. Coy., to be L/Corpl., ʻ ed 27/9/15.
No. 2348 A/L/Cpl. F. Philpotts, D. Coy., to be L/Corpl., dated 2/10/15.
No. 2535 A/L/Cpl. E. Garner, C. Coy., to be L/Corpl., dated 2/10/15.
No. 2528 A/L/Cpl. A. W. G. Enoch, B. Coy., to be L/Cpl., dated 10/10/15.

Promotions and Appointments:—

To be Sergeants :—
No. 908 L/Sergt. J. Wyatt, D. Coy., 12/10/15.
No. 1506 Corpl. A. E. Richardson, A. Coy., 17/10/15.
No. 427 Corpl. M. Bailey, C. Coy in B. Coy, 29/10/15.
To be Corporals :—
No. 2308 A/Corpl. A. A. Fudge, A. Coy., 15/10/15.
No. 1511 A/Corpl. G. Perry, A. Coy., 12/10/15.
No. 2557 L/Corpl. C. W. Norris, C. Coy., 17/10/15.
No. 1627 L/Corpl. J. Boughton, A. Coy., 29/10/15.

Appointments:—

To be L/Sergts. with pay :—
No. 2414 Corpl. F. Kibby, C. Coy., 12/10/15.
No. 1628 Corpl. R. C. Jackson, B. Coy., 15/10/15.

To be L/Corpls. with pay :—
No. 2404 Pte. (L/C) R. Fowler, C. Coy., 17/10/15.
No. 1978 Pte. (L/C) H. C. Price, C. Coy., 29/10/15.

GRENADIERS.

The undermentioned Officers, N.C.O.'s and men qualified as Grenadiers at the recent examination.

Lieut. H. P. Snowden.
No. 2712 L/Corpl. Minett, A. Coy.
No. 1381 Pte. Bateman, F., B. Coy.
No. 1892 Pte. Sterry, J., A Coy.
No. 2156 Pte. Stephens, A. R., A. Coy.
No. 1772 Pte. Aston, C., D. Coy.
No. 2447 Pte. Michael, E. A., A Coy.
No. 2791 Pte. Bartlett, H., A. Coy.

CASUALTIES.

Lieut. T. H. Moore killed in action, 27/9/15.
L/Corpl. W. G. Rodway killed in action, 27/9/15.
Pte. C. W. Smith died of wounds, 19/10/15.

Lieut. C. W. Winterbotham   Wounded slight   18/10/15
Corpl. H. Page   ,,   ,,   17/10/15
Pte. B. S. Sansom   ,,   ,,   17/10/15
Pte. G. Walker   ,,   ,,   17/10/15
Pte. B. W. Fisher   ,,   ,,   17/10/15
Pte. W. C. Bingham   Missing   27/9/15

R.I.P.

LIEUT. T. H. MOORE.

"Somewhere in France"—we know not where—he lies,
'Mid shuddering earth and under anguished skies !
We may not visit him, but this we say :
Though our steps err, his shall not miss their way.

. . . .
To him has come, if not the crown and palm,
The kiss of Peace—a vast sufficing calm.

. . . .
From our small limits, and withholdings free,
Somewhere he dwells, and keeps high company :
Yet tainted not with so supreme a bliss
As to forget he knew a world like this."

Lines from " Somewhere in France "—
John Hogben—*Spectator.*

War has its victories no less than Peace. The Battalion has to mourn the loss of one whose qualities were signally developed by the work he carried out amidst the difficulties and dangers of "No Man's Land." His daring reconnaissances had earned the commendation of the Divisional General.

He gave up his life in endeavouring to rescue Lance-Corporal Rodway, and thus made the supreme sacrifice. His men loved him, and his tradition will not die.

"He went," as the Vicar of Tewkesbury said at the Memorial Service," straight from communion with his Lord at the Altar of the Abbey back to the trenches, and on the third Sunday came his last and highest call. Not one of the illustrious dead who lie round the Altar of this Abbey is worthier of honour and of imperishable remembrance : not one lived a more honourable life, or died a more glorious death...Not even the bestowal of the Victoria Cross could add honour to his name or the manner of his passing, for it was the King of Kings Himself who welcomed him on the other side with the accolade of valour and the words of supreme commendation—"Greater love hath no man than this, that he lay down his life for his friend."

One who knew him well writes : He was of the type which is England's peculiar glory. To say that is to say all—good friend, good leader, good man. To praise what we have lost is stoic comfort, but no comfort is so true as the memory of a stainless life and a noble death, and the sure hope that death is not the end of all. This we offer with our sincere sympathy to those who mourn him at home.

It is pleasant to report a kindness from an enemy. We hear that the wife of one of the German officers in the trenches opposite wrote to Tewkesbury to say that Lieut. Moore had been given an officers' funeral.

LCE-CORPL. W. G. RODWAY.

Lance-Corporal W. G. Rodway joined the Stroud Company in 1910. He made his name in the Battalion in the Regular Soldiers' Musketry Course fired at Chelmsford in November last. He shot splendidly under difficult conditions, and earned the distinction of being "best shot in the Battalion." His score of 155 under the conditions prevailing was a very fine one, and it is very doubtful if there was a better in the Brigade. During the last few months he had done some excellent patrolling with Lieut. T. H. Moore, who always took him with him.

Quiet and retiring, he was popular with all who knew him, and especially in his company.

Good soldier, true friend, devoted son, good Christian, he "loved not his life to the death," and the promised reward we know is his.

R. I. P.

2nd Lieut C. F. R. BARNETT
Killed 19 April 1915

Lieut T. H. MOORE
Killed 26 September 1915

2nd Lieut H. G. C. GUISE
Killed 6 May 1915

" Qui ante diem periit,

Sed miles, sed pro patria. "

" They are commemorated not only by columns and inscriptions in their own country, but in foreign lands also, and by memorials graven not on stone but on the hearts of men."

5th Gloucester Gazette.

A Chronicle, serious and humorous, of the Battalion while serving with the
BRITISH EXPEDITIONARY FORCE.

A CHRISTMAS PRAYER FROM THE TRENCHES.

Not yet for us my Christmas bring
 Good-will to men, and peace ;
In our dark sky no angels sing,
 Not yet the great release
For men, when war shall cease.

So must the guns our carols make,
 Our gifts must bullets be,
For us no Christmas bells shall wake ;
 These ruined homes shall see
 No Christmas revelry.

In hardened hearts we fain would greet
 The Babe at Christmas born,
But Lo, He comes with pierced feet,
 Wearing a crown of thorn.
 —His side a spear has torn.

For tired eyes are all too dim,
 Our hearts too full of pain,
Our ears too deaf to hear the hymn
 Which angels sing in vain
 " The Christ is born again."

Oh Jesus, pitiful, draw near.
 That even we may see
The Little Child who knew not fear.
 Thus would we picture Thee
 Unmarred by agony.

O'er death, and pain triumphant yet
 Bid Thou thy harpers play ;
That we may hear them, and forget
 Sorrow, and all dismay
 And welcome Thee to stay
 With us on Christmas day.

Nth CORPS SUMMARY.

Right Division.—A noise resembling a trench pump or a German consuming soup was heard at 9.30 p.m.

Our Artillery opened fire on the GORGE in X, and about half an hour later the noise ceased.

Rainfall for last 24 hours—4.3836 metres.

High tide.—6.40 p.m.

Centre Division.—A prearranged provocative scheme was successfully carried out by our Artillery in conjunction with our Infantry.

A German opposite the STUNTED OAK fired a shot at 10.23 p.m. This breach of promise was preceded by a salvo of variegated lights from the enemy's third line.

An excellent system of shower baths has installed itself in all dugouts.

Weather—Showery.

Rainfall.—(We regret that the graduated mess tin was inadvertently buried in one of innumerable land slides.)

Left Division.—An Officer's patrol **Again** penetrated the enemy's system of artificial lakes. Whilst the enemy's attention was distracted by an (Unpaid)

Lance-Corpl. imitating a flight of wild geese rejoicing over an unopened egg, the officer rammed and sank four ration punts lying alongside the Company (?) headquarters.

The stewards were drowned in their sleep, so know nothing about the matter at present. The Officer reports the punts to have been in a bad state of repair. In addition two Unteroffiziers were snared with caviare sandwiches and brought into our lines.

All remaining trenches in this sector are supported by telephone wire revetment only.

Russian Front.—Although news from this front is scarce we hear that PONSK has fallen (this is not to be wondered at considering our own trenches).

The German casualities are said to be as many as, if not more than, per day.

Several cases of madness are reported from this theatre, where the conditions are terrible. Men have been observed to fling themselves flat in front of section leaders, imagining themselves sump covers. Two men were seen standing close together. One, who claimed to be a revetment hurdle, was removed when his companion sank to the ground with a graceful motion, being convinced he was a trench falling in. In one case ten men were found bound together under the impression they were sandbags.

Other cases too numerous to mention could be cited.

Balkans.—Each State is still pushing ahead, and all the friends have not lost half as many as all the enemies, and vice versa.

Italian Front.—Count ITCHI has assumed complete control of the forces in the mountains. Boulder rollers are urgently required.

From correspondence found on a captured prisoner:

S......t., 6. 12. 15.

...... it is awful. Every day another one goes. Where will it stop ? Why will it stop ? They say that..., but who knows ? Can he ?

(Unposted)   7. 12. 15.

Many thanks for the parcel. The Leberwurst would have been fine, but the skin was only tied at one end. Please send another pair of waterwings. Mine was hit by a much-to-be-cursed-and-despised-pig-dog of an ...ish sniper.

X......t 4. 9. 15.

... Only men with a very well developed and powerful side stroke can get along our communication trenches. Others have to walk outside and risk being hit by the (?) maxim which fires at 5 minutes past and 25 minutes to every hour.

SUN RISE } Suspended until further notice, or
MOON RISE }   for duration of war.

A GLOUCESTERSHIRE WISH.

Here's luck my lads, while Birdlip Hill is steep :
As long as Cotteswold's high, or Severn's deep
Our thoughts of you shall blossom and abide
While blow the orchards about Severn side.

While a round bubble like the children blow
May Hill floats purple in the sunset glow.
Our prayers go up to bless you where you lie
While Gloucester town stands up against the sky.

To write old thoughts of loveliness and trace
Dead men's long living will to give God praise
Who of His mercy doth His own son give
This blessed morn that you and all may live.

Christmas, 1915. F.W.H.

SUITABLE CHRISTMAS PRESENTS.

For RUSSIA.—Frozen German, complete with chilblains.

For FRANCE.—Her own back and a bit more.

For BELGIUM.—Belgium.

For ITALY.—Some old port (in the Trentino).

For SERVIA.—A silver lining.

For TURKEY and AUSTRIA.—A strong emetic suitable for dealing with a surfeit of Hohenzollern sauce.

For BULGARIA.—A Russian bear, complete with bite.

For GREECE.—A strong comfortable fence with collapsible seat firmly attached.

For the Navy.—A German Fleet at sea with Davy Jones' locker to receive the same.

For the Army Staff.—The head of Lord St. Davids, with or without charger.

For the Artillery.—More iron rations, English made —not to be used on relief days.

For the Cavalry.—A gap in the German line—large size—unwired.

For the R.E.—A convertable dugout and sump hole—Suitable for any weather wet or fine.

For the Infantry.—(1) An outfit comprising webbed feet, wings, and waterproof plumage, or (2) Trenches complete with waterproof dug-outs, pipe drainage, sufficient revetting material and pumps.
(We must warn our readers, however, that No. 1 is probably the more easily obtainable present of the two. Ed.)

For Lord Derby.—The last eligible slacker properly enlisted, equipped, and trained.

For the 1/5th Gloucesters.—A new Cow.

For the Intelligence Officer.—A picture of Joan of Arc and her two daughters leading the ancient Britons to victory against the Romans.

For the M. O.—A dressing station where German shells don't attend sick parade.

For the Padre.—Another anti-aircraft cigarette holder.

For the Quartermaster.—A Company Quarter-master Sergeant without " deficiencies."

For the Germans.—We have no gifts suitable for Christmas.

For the M. G. O.—A comic carrying party (German pattern) fitted with dixies and shell hole.

For the Transport Officer.—Hard lines.

For the A. D. J. T.—Bottle of Patcho.

For G. F. C.—Another 18 years service.

For C. S. N.—A spare platoon.

For the Cow.—An express Delivery.

For the Sanitary Corporal.—A Consultant's salary.

For Lieut. W. Fream.—A lemon.

For Lieut. H. S. King.—A Queen.

For Drummer Jackson.—Five seconds with Jack Johnson.

For Lieut. C. W. Winterbotham.—£400 per annum.

TO MARGUERITE.

Oh beautiful, I found thee once
When summer winds blew warm, and sweet.
I said " The fellow is a dunce
Who does not love my Marguerite."

Thy form symmetrical, and clean,
Made my poor heart with rapture beat ;
Birds, mice, and insects—N'ere so mean
A thing but loved by Marguerite.

" And here," I said " The winter blast
I shall not fear. The snow and sleet
Shall harm me not while I hold fast
Unto my love—My Marguerite."

I guarded thee with tender pride
By day and night, and all too fleet
The summer and the autumn died,
And left me still with Marguerite.

Then came the equinoctial gale,
The rain descended like a sheet,
Followed by frost, and snow, and hail,
And Oh, the change in Marguerite !

Her symmetry went with the wind,
Her beauty was a wreck complete,
Befouled, disordered, who could find
Ought but disgust in Marguerite ?

Thy ruin is beyond repair.
Deep in the mud, a good five feet,
Object of horror, and despair,
I leave thee now, My Marguerite.

Oh, blame me not that rain should quench
The love that throve in summer heat,
You're known as " That d...d awful trench,"
—Na poo ! Na poo ! My Marguerite !

A CHRISTMAS CAROL.

" Good morning, Sarj., is the old man in ?

" Yes, round in 'is orfice. That's the door, jest walk in."

" Well my good man, what do you want me to do for you this morning ?

Anything you take a fancy to you can have."

" Well sir, ccc-can I..."

" Come don't be afraid to ask, I can give you as much of my time as you like. I've only got to make out the ration indents and check three or four other similar jobs, but I'm in no hurry. I can easily go without my lunch to-day."

" Well Sir, could I have a noo toonic ?"

" Of course you may. Here, Holbein, give this fellow the best tunic you can find. Measure him carefully first and get one that really fits."

" Oh, thank you Sir, I didn't."

" Don't mention it, quite a small matter, and while you're down here how are you off for trousers and puttees ? "

" Well Sir, I could do......"

" Of course, of course, and those boots don't look as good as they might be, and why surely you don't like to be seen in a dilapidated hat like that."

" Here, Holbein, give this man a new set of every-thing, and a couple of tins of strawberry jam and a bag of coke."

" Oh, thank you Sir, may your shadow never..."

" Tut, tut, that's all right, always pleased to do anything I can for you or any of your pals."

. . . .

Then I awoke.

POETRY.

The poems of Earth are lived,
  Not scratched with the dirty pen,
They are writ in the sense of things,
  And sung in the hearts of men.

Sensuous strains of Spring,
  Flowing in silver flood,
Summer's golden delight
  Warming the waiting blood.

Colour and scent and sound,
  Of all the changing year,
These are the poems of Earth
  Which every man must hear.

Sorrow, and pain, and love,
  Joy, and fear, and regret,
These are the burning poems
  That all our hearts beget :

These are the poems of Earth
  Which every man must pen,
That you and I make up
  And straight forget again.

                                    F. W. H.

From the "Division on our Left."

HENRY AND THE HELMET.

Henry was patrolling. He had been patrolling for some time. He was alone,—alone beneath the enemy's parapet. Reader, have you ever been in that position ? You haven't ? Well don't then.

There had been quite a lot of men on the patrol, for Henry belonged to that famous regiment the Southend Scatterers, whose promiscuous daring is a bye-word throughout the British Army.

The difficulty was to keep them off the enemy's parapet. In fact, it had been found necessary to post Military Police there to do this, and give the English Artillery a chance.

On this particular night, in spite of the strict secrecy observed, the news had leaked out that a patrol was going out disguised as knife-rests, and several sentries joined the patrol as they crept into the dark. The start, however, had been unfortunate. The bombers had been blown up just over their parapet, and were not expected to come down for some time. The Company Commander was still at the telephone waiting to report to Head Quarters that they were all present.

Then, the night being dark, some of the patrollers had mistaken the parados for the parapet, and climbing over the former were instantly lost.

They were found to have reconnoitred strongly towards an estaminet in rear of the second line trenches, capturing en route (with the best intentions) the C. O. and the Adjutant, and bombing the Brigadier. For this,—so strict is the discipline of the British Army—they were put under arrest. The remainder of the patrol, after fighting a white cat, a black dog, a covey of partridges, some rats and a patch of thistles that had run out of ammunition, and had returned to report the utter rout with great loss of five German patrols.

They were, at the moment our story opens, imbibing rum in the Company Head Quarters, and describing how the white cat in its death agonies sang the Hymn of Hate.

Only Henry remained. He was very calm, and chuckled at the bombs which the Germans flung at him from time to time. For he was a seasoned veteran. Do you think, my readers, that our gallant lads care for little things like bombs ?

(Not if they use Sullivan's Soothing Syrup, and Anti-Swear Word Spray for Shaken Systems.—Advt.)

From time to time Henry shot a German, but his real task was listening. Like many English soldiers

he was an accomplished linguist. German was to him as familiar as his native tongue.

(And this after only four days study of Lee-Williams' Lightning Lore for Little Linguists. Advt.)

As he pressed his megaphone to the German parapet he could hear all that passed in their trench. He heard the Quartermaster refusing to issue any more hats or hold-alls that night. He heard the Doctor realising that a Sanitary Policeman had been put on fatigue ; he heard what the C. O. said when he fell into a sump ; he heard what the Subaltern said when he tripped over a pair of legs belonging to a private who was sleeping on the fire platform, and what the Private said as he rubbed his shin after the Subaltern had passed ; he heard what the Sergeant thought of the friendly natives in his shirt who woke him up ; he heard what the Adjutant thought of men with long hair, and what the men with long hair thought of the adjutant ; he heard the Company Commander shooting at rats in his dug-out, and he heard the rats giggling and dropping chunks of earth on the Company Commander's head ; he heard a Listening Post getting the wind up ; he heard the Sentry going to tell the Corporal ; he even heard a Fatigue Party discussing ration-carrying at night. He heard all this—

(He would not have heard it had he not been using a Mackintoshs' Mammoth Megaphone—Makes Mice Move like Mountains. Advt.)—he made careful note of it, but yet he was not satisfied. To-night he determined he would not return without information of real value. So he waited while the bullets ricochetted off him in all directions.

(Henry would doubtless have been severely wounded had he not been wearing Poots' Patent Projectile Proof Pants for Potted Patrols. Advt.)

So still he lay that a yellow slug built its nest behind his ear, and a hungry German louse stalked him cunningly through the grass.

At last, as the first faint lines of dawn streaked the Eastern sky—

(" At-Sky " inclusive, extracted from the "Daily Mail's " Handbook of Phatuous Phrases for the Phatigued—No young Author should be without it. Advt.)—Henry's chance came.

A hush fell upon the German lines. A ponderous step approached, and halted opposite Henry. A deep German voice sounded in the stillness :— "Germans ! Before we sing the Morning Hymn of Hate (omitting verses 25 and 26), I will read you a very private-from-our-Greatly-Beloved-in-his-Potsdam-now-residing-All-Highest-Message."

This was Henry's opportunity. He realised that he must obtain that message. How to do it ? A thought, nay a brain-wave, struck him. He had on him his gas helmet. (Pattern 156087 912) the latest, and most deadly instrument of torture that the brains of the English Army had yet devised.

Readers, have you ever mixed up together an Acetylene lamp, one hundred-weight of rotten eggs (smashed), a decaying cabbage, some dead worms and a bucket of cresol ? You havn't ? Well you don't know what the helmet smells like.

Holding his nose with one hand, Henry drew the dreadful thing from its case (first being careful to mark the date on it with indelible pencil). Instantly a deeper silence fell upon the German trench,—a silence only broken by the laboured breathing of strong men in agony.

(See Phatuous Phrases for the Phatigued. Advt.)

Henry stood up. Before him leant a German General struggling for breath, but still clutching the document containing the precious message in his hand.

It was the work of a moment to seize the paper, place the deadly helmet over the General's head and face, secure him with a halter rope, and pull him through the German wire.

Commander-in-Chief von Koffemup—for it was he, no less—was incapable of resistance, and was hauled to the English line by the triumphant Henry. Never a shot was fired ; the deadly helmet had done its work.

There was joy among the Scatterers.

The document proved to be of immense value.

(Buy the 5th Gloucester Gazette—Every story has a happy ending. Advt.) It showed conclusively what is the correct way to pronounce DVINSK, and even PREMYSL.

Von Koffemup, during the strong delirium in which he lingered for some days, disclosed many valuable secrets.

And Henry. Ah ! The discipline of the British Army is strict. Henry was given one year's F.P. No. 1 for taking his helmet out of the trench.

GLOUCESTERSHIRE.

(Tune—" The Slashers.")

I. "The Slashers."

(Dedicated to the Gloucestershire Regiment.)

O hark to " The Slashers," O hark to the drum !
'Tis the Gloucesters a-marching, and marching they come.
From cities and fields whence their fathers went out
To meet the King's foes and to put 'em to rout.
Africa, Flanders, and Egypt, and Spain,
Giving them glory to keep without stain ;
Giving them honours to bear to old England
When victory-crowned they sail homeward again.

From land of the elver, and land of the pear,
They go never grieving war's hardships to wear.
Be't vin rouge or perry they always are merry
They fight and they die, but they never despair.
Ever the vision of homeland they keep,
Vivid in thought, but more vivid in sleep,—
Valleys of corn where the reaper is singing,
Blue coloured Cotteswold made white with it's sheep.

These be the things that they fought for in Spain,
These be the things that we fight for again.
Two gallant thousand they mustered of yore,
We count our comrades ten thousands and more.
Onward, then onward till victory's won !
England shall never bow down to the Hun.
Gloucestershire, guarded of Gloucestershire's lovers,
Stands, and shall stand, while the centuries run.

II. Song of Gloucestershire.

(Dedicated to the Gloucestershire Society.)

North, South, East and West,
Think of whichever you love the best,
Forest and vale and high blue hill
You may have whichever you will,
And drink one cup to the love o' your soul
Before you drink to the lovely whole.

Here are high hills and towns of stone
(Did you come from the Cotswolds then ?)
With an architecture all their own
And a breed of sturdy men.

But here's a forest old and stern
(Say do ye know the Wye ?)
Where sunlight dapples green miles of fern
A river wandering by.

Here's peaceful meadowland and kine
(D'ye see an old grey tower ?)
Where all together close entwine
Grass, clover and daisy-flower.

Here stretches the land towards the sea
(Behold the castle bold !)
Where men live out life merrily
And die merry and old.

North, South, East and West,
Think of whichever you love the best
Forest and vale and high blue hill
You may have whichever you will,
And drink one cup to the love o' your soul
Before you drink to the lovely whole.

III. Song of Minsterworth.

(Tune—" The Vicar of Bray.")

(Dedicated to my home.)

In olden, olden centuries
On Gloucester's holy ground, sir,
The monks did pray and chant all day
And grow exceeding round, sir ;
And here's the reason that they throve
To praise their plesant fortune,
" We keep our beasts "—thus quoth the priests—
" In Minsterworth—that's Mortune ! " *

CHORUS :

So this is the chorus we will sing
And this is the spot we'll drink to
While blossom blows and Severn flows
And Earth has mugs to clink to.

O there in sleepy Summer sounds,
The drowsy drone of bees, sir,
And there in Winter paints the sun
His patterns neath the trees, sir ;
And there with merry song doth run,
A river full of fish, sir,
That Thursday sees upon the flood
And Friday on the dish, sir.

CHORUS.

The jovial priests to dust are gone,
We cannot hear their singing ;
But still their merry chorus-song
From newer lips runs ringing.
And we who drink the azure air
And see the blossom drifting,
May sit and sing the self-same thing,
Until the roof we're lifting.

CHORUS.

* The ancient name of the parish was Mortune—that is, the village in the mere, and the name was changed to Minsterworth early in the 14th century because it belonged to the Minster or Abbey of Gloucester and was the Minster's " Worth " or farm where the cattle were kept.

F. W. H.

DIARY OF OFFICER ON DUTY.

9 p.m.   Thawing hard and raining slightly.   Come off duty. Wonder how trenches will stand it.

9.45 p.m.   Jones comes into Mess dug-out for dinner.   Says trenches look more like taking it lying down. Reprove Jones for pessimism.

10 p.m.   Turn in.   Jones reminds me am on duty again, 3 a.m. till " Stand to."   Night very dark, raining very hard.

12 midnight.   Rats seem to be very noisy in dug-out roof.

12.30 a.m.   Awakened by heavy thud.   Reprove servant for calling me too early.   Find it isn't servant but dug-out falling in.

12.30   Try to get out of valise and bed, but find it difficult. to

12.45 a.m.   as plank-revetting has collapsed on a slant over bed.

12.45 a.m.   Give up trying to get up.   Decide to sleep till called by servant.

1 a.m.   Small cascade on face.

1.15 a.m.   Pool of water under head.

1.30 a.m.   Two small cascades on face.

2 a.m.   Valise getting full of water.

2.30 a.m.   Begin to feel very moist underneath.   Find about a foot of water on dug-out floor.   Notice sky through hole in roof, but can't see door in usual place.

2.45 a.m.   Sounds of digging outside.

3 a.m.   See hole appearing near doorway.

3.10 a.m.   Begin to think I shall be drowned in bed.   Call out.   Am answered by Pte. Arthurs, my servant. Says he is digging his way in. Reprove Pte. A. for not coming in by door. Pte. A. says he is, but the door is buried.

3.15 a.m.   Loud crash and rush of water. Enter Pte. Arthurs through hole in wall.   Explain situation to him.   Pte. Arthurs inclined to be downhearted.

3.30 a.m.   Extricated from ruins of bed by Pte. Arthurs. Reprove him for pulling me out head-first into two foot of water.   Pte. A. explains that he didn't know which end of me he had hold of.

3.30-3.45 a.m.   Light candle produced by Pte. A.   Use three boxes of matches.   Find wading boots hanging up above flood.   Try to put them on.   Fail.

3.45 a.m.   Discover reason of failure. Wading boots full of (1) Loose earth from side of dug-out. (2) Three refugee kittens. Empty out earth and kittens, and put on waders.

4 a.m.   Crawl out of dugout after unearthing stick, hat, coat and respirator. Tell Pte. A. to "tidy up a bit." Wonder how he'll do it. Leave Pte. A. very down-hearted.

4.5 a.m.   Night very dark. Decide to go round trenches. Proceed along trench "Rosalie." "Rosalie" seems altered somewhat. Find myself falling over buckets, must have taken the wrong turning. Turn back and fall into sump-hole (?) Find it isn't a sump-hole but "Rosalie." No use for "Rosalie" as a name. Think of several others more appropriate. Fall over prostrate revetting hurdle into large mound of earth. Think of more names for "Rosalie" and say them. Climb up large mound of earth and fall down other side. Really a sump-hole this time. Swim strongly with the tide towards floating object. Find it a sump cover.

4.20 a.m.   Reach "Rosalie" again. Find myself entangled in six different telephone wires.

4.20-4.30 a.m.   Remove telephone wires. Wonder how Pip-Emma and rest of the family will carry on.

4.30 a.m.   Fed up with "Rosalie." Make for fire trench.

4.45 a.m.   Hear sounds as of someone in pain. Make towards them, via several sump-holes. Find Pte. Binks criticising (1) the trench, (2) the weather, (3) the men who made the trench, (4) their ancestors, (5) himself, for ever leaving happy home.

        Ask Pte. Binks what the trouble is. Pte. Binks says he's stuck, has been stuck for an hour ; and expects to be stuck for ever. Go to assistance of Pte. Binks.

5.5-5.15 a.m.   Dig out Pte. Binks.

5.15 a.m.   Pte. Binks emerges less one boot. Find I am stuck myself.

5.15-5.30 a.m.   Am dug out by Pte. Binks and others.

5.30 a.m.   Determine to proceed. Rescue party tell me this part of trench is best. Proceed along fire platform and parapet.

6 a.m.   Reach end of line. Start back Trench "Mimi" to give "Stand to" and issue rum from Mess dugout. Try to remember how many sump-holes in "Mimi."

6.20 a.m.   Find all the sump-holes in Trench "Mimi" didn't know there were so many.

6.30 a.m.   Find more sump-holes but no Mess Dugout. Decide to wait till daylight.

6.35 a.m.   Found by Pte. Arthurs. Pte. A tells me he has just dug himself out of my dugout. Says my dugout is "Na-poo." Hopes to recover some of my kit when the weather clears up. Pte. A. says he knows where Mess dugout was earlier in night.

6.45 a.m.   With aid of Pte. A. find a large hole like a badger earth. Crawl through hole into large sump-hole. Turns out to be Mess dug-out.

7 a.m.   Growing light but still raining. Issue rum through "badger earth" after digging out jars. Notice that prevailing current in Mess dug-out is N.N. by E. to S.S. by W.

7.10 a.m.   Pte. A. and other Officers' servants try to light fire to cook breakfast. Appear to find mud very incombustible. Leave them digging out bacon for breakfast.

7.20 a.m.   Issue large ration of rum to Officer on duty.

7.30 a.m.   Meet Company Commander. C. C. asks why I forgot the "Situation Report." I wonder.

7.35-7.40 a.m.   Rally fatigue to dig out breakfast carrying party.

7.50-8 a.m.   Listen to carrying party. Feelings much relieved by their remarks.

8.15 a.m.   Breakfast. Enter Jones. J. says his dugout is all right, and "thinks it might be worse." Hate such idiotic...optimism, and say so. J. amused. Think J. a d......d fool and say so.

8.20 a.m.   Message from H. Qrs. to O. C., Company to say that two Companies of 59th Royal Bally MacCrunch Fusiliers will be attached to us for instruction arriving at 12 noon and that accommodation must be found for them in our trench.

8.25 a.m.   Discover even suicide impossible, as revolver and Verey pistol both buried.

9 a.m.   Go to sleep on table of Mess Dugout.

I/5th BATTALION GLOUCESTERSHIRE REGIMENT.

The undermentioned N. C. O's and Men have been granted Commissions since Mobilization.

Sergt	Gorton, P.	Divisional Cyclists Company.
Pte	Moore, L. W.	1/5th Gloucester Regiment
Sergt	Priestly, S.	10th Gloucester Regiment.
L/Cpl	Jones, S. T. H.	
Pte	Rouse, F.	

L/Cpl	Thomas, H. G.	8th Gloucester Regiment.
Pte	Clarke, W. E.	10th Gloucester Regiment
Pte	Clarke, F.	10th Gloucester Regiment.
Pte	Tubbs, S. B.	2/5th Gloucester Regiment.
L/Cpl	Morgan, D. P.	3rd Gloucester Battery, R. F. A.
L/Cpl	Paulson, J. J. R.	1st Hereford Regiment.
L/Cpl	Coulson, D. J.	R. G. A.
Pte	Thomas, H. V.	South Midland R.E.
L/Cpl	Ridler, W. F.	1st Gloucester Battery, R. F. A.
Pte	Barling, C.	Worcester Regiment (since killed in action).
L/Cpl	Hawkins, G.	1/5th Gloucester Regiment.
L/Cpl	Hone, J.	9th Gloucester Regiment.
L/Cpl	Oxley, G. H.	2nd Gloucester Regiment.
L/Cpl	Nixon, P.	2nd Gloucester Regiment.
L/Sgt	Knight, R. E.	3/5th Gloucester Regiment.
L/Cpl	Harvey, F. W.	3/5th Gloucester Regiment.
Pte	Kingscott, H. G.	Royal Navy
L/Cpl	Robertson, K. A.	3/5th Gloucester Regiment.
Pte	Fielding, J.	Gloucester R. F. A.
L/Cpl	Morgan, W. W.	1st Gloucester Regiment.
L/Cpl	Ross, G. E. H.	8th Gloucester Regiment.
Sergt	Chandler, H. J.	York and Lancaster Regiment.
Corpl	Twine, W. H.	York and Lancaster Regiment.
Coy S. M.	Chapman, G. N.	2nd Gloucester Regiment.
Pte	Harvey, E. H.	3/5th Gloucester Regiment.
Pte	Clarke, B. C.	A. S. C.
Pte	Berry, W.	
L/Cpl	Davis, F. C.	10th Gloucester Regiment

OUR PORTRAIT GALLERY.
No. 6. "TIM."

He's a popular sergeant you bet,
For he'll rough it along with his men,
And start up a song in the wet
To set 'em all smiling again.

His stories are naughty I'm told.
His voice has a sonorous sound.
But the envy of all who behold
Is the way that his puttees are wound.

Blue-eyed, debonaire, with a hat
Cocked sideways the eight of an inch,
He's sparrow-like ; but for all that
The name in his pay book is Finch.

                                    F. W. H.

[At great personal inconvenience and enormous expense we have been able to procure the following lucid explanation of the present military situation on the Eastern front. Every eye is (or should be) turned on this front, and we feel that it needs the profound military knowledge, literary capability, and inherent perspicacity of our premier fiction writer adequately to cope with the complex intricacies of the kaleidescopic metamorphoses undergone by the German forces in course of the pursuit of their tactical manipulatory stunts. Ed. 5th Gloucester Gazette.]

THE WAR IN THE EAST
by
Hollow Billhook.

(*Copyright in Channel Islands, Scilly ditto and Asia Minor.*)

This article has been submitted to the Press Bureau, which, although not objecting strongly to its publication, cannot vouch for the accuracy of the statements, nor will it associate itself with the views expressed by the contributor.

It is with a certain feeling of trepidation that I write upon the latest phase of the operations on the Eastern front. This feeling is engendered not so much by the uncertainty as to the numbers engaged on either side, but by the muddy state of the wicket, which appears from all the summaries (received up to the time of going to press) to be worse than I had been led to believe when writing for the Summer Number of " Home Notes," or " Deeds of Daring for the Young."

Everybody, without exception, will remember that in this article I expressed a doubt as to the ability of the Germans to bring to a successful conclusion their meteoric descent on PLOVSK, which, on reference to Sketch I. will be found situated amongst grassy knolls 387° (magnetic) East of OPOPOV. From personal knowledge of this town, and here I may say that some of the happiest days of my youth were spent amongst its grey lichened walls and moss—(Thank you, that will do. Ed.)—which, as every schoolboy knows is called, and I may say justly so, the key to the Adriatic, it seems incredible to think that the Russian hordes should have experienced a difficulty in dislodging the enemy.

SKETCH I.

(censored)

And before pursuing this necessarily brief survey of operations in this theatre, it will be as well if we turn aside for a moment to discuss and consider the numbers actually engaged on both sides.

The Numbers.

A. **Russians.**—From official reports via Flushing and the West End, General VLITOF'S forces appear to be considerably over strength, and we may safely say without fear of contradiction that his numbers must closely approximate, if not surpass, even more than that. From these figures we must deduct those without respirators and 2d. Tube Helmets, which in itself reduces our numbers to about 40,000,000. See Sketch II.

SKETCH II.

(censored)

Of these, probably not more than ONE TENTH have a really serviceable pair of webbed feet, which my knowledge of the district enables me to pronounce as indispensable. So we see, on referring to Sketch III. that our forces actually available, excluding ration-parties and men not yet inoculated a second time, scarcely total 3,000,000.

SKETCH III.

(censored)

What this number represents can best be grasped by imagining 3 million pennies, piled on top of one another. This would form a tower, at least, and I think we shall not be overstating the fact if we say probably more than, 16 times the height of the season and of which the pieces, if laid end to end, would pave a path 3 feet broad on BOTH sides of the road from Selfridges to the Field Service Canteen. See Sketch IV.

SKETCH IV.

(censored)

B. **German.** (ugh !).—Here we are up against a greater difficulty still, for with their now well-known deceitful tactics, false lists of casualties are published, but from private sources of information, I am assured that Field Marshall von PUFFENSCHLAGER and Field Marshal Graf von BLUTWURST are bewailing the ever-increasing numbers of men withdrawn for (a) Divisional duties, (b) Brigade duties and (c) H.Q. details. Excluding (I.) (a) the 40,000 killed in action at the crossroads last May (Sketch V.)

SKETCH V

(censored)

(b) tne 30,007 killed in the counter-attack, July 10th, (Sketch VI.)

SKETCH VI.

(censored)

and (II.) 2,800 odd details (see Sub-Section B. paras. (a), (b), (c), we arrive at the astonishingly small number of 268,064,001 active bearers of arms.

In addition to this must be borne in mind the fact that the German soldier no longer has rations, but when dinner-time arrives (every third day), he is handed a leaflet on which is printed a revised version of the Hymn of Hate (Mark VIII.)

SKETCH VII.

(censored)

So much for the question of numbers, which having settled, we can dismiss (at the slope, that man).

Other factors have to be considered in so gigantic an undertaking as this, and favourable weather in ONE portion of the frontage might easily impede the progress in ANOTHER portion, and vice versa.

SKETCH VIII.

(censored)

Consequently, a suitable day must be chosen, and owing to their failure to take advantage of the 4 hours continuous sunshine of June 15th they are still standing to.

In the interim, we learn from our old friend WIRELESS that the 80 inhabitants of PERLOFSK (English PLOVSK) have fled to the neighbouring grassy knolls (see Sketch I.)

Organisation.

Before closing such a brief summary of momentous events, it may be advisable, and, at the same time simplify matters, if we compare the two belligerent armies in minor details.

A. (I.) **Arms.** (a) The Russians are now armed almost entirely with captured German MAUSERS taking real ball ammunition, whereas. (b) The Germans are armed almost entirely with captured Russian rifles. So great is the German's love of his rifle that millions of Huns have been captured simply through loitering in the purlieus of battle sights searching for their own rifles.

(N.B. The nose-caps of German bullets are greatly prized by the Slavs.)

(II.) **Equipment.** Whereas (a) The Russians carry *only* the unexpended portion of their day's ration (b) the Germans have, in addition, spare boots (3 different sizes), mess tin, drinking cup, wire cutters, prismatic compass, corkscrew and hammer, roll of wire netting, and in some cases ready-made sumpholes with lids which actually fit. Cases have been known where machine gunners had, in addition to a pair of shorts, a complete machine gun padlocked to their leg.

From these particulars, then, it is quite clear that owing to the extreme difficulty of any definite decision being arrived at before the spring, we see NO reason why leave should be stopped, and in view of the fact that BULGARIA has declared her intention of siding with the CUBISTS in the event of a reply to their ultimatum to the Poles being unsatisfactory, I see no objection to stating as my own personal and private opinion that should PLOVSK fall within the next few days, all hope of our victory in the OLYMPIC Games must go.

And now let us turn—

[No, not in this number. Ed.]

H. S. K.

CHRISTMAS, 1915.

Babe of the stable cold and bare,
Babe of the winter night,
Babe of the snow and freezing air—
(And Joseph had no brazier there,
And only a candle light)—
Poor wee little mite.

Out o' the East a star aflare,
Clomb up in the silent sky,
And wonderingly it tarried where,
In tumbled straw the baby fair,
Mary put to lie,
With the oxen nigh.

Lo, on the hills a flash of wings,
And the sudden stir of a song—
" To men of good-will this Infant brings
Store of peace and good tidings."
(And what if the war be long ?
Were the Angels wrong ?)

Kings from afar with gifts of gold,
Of myrrh, and of incense sweet,
Came with the star to the stable cold
And save the child by writ foretold,
And with honour meet,
Knelt down at His feet.

— — —

O Little Jesus, look on me
Observing Thy Nativity !
See, on this Christmas eve I lie
On straw in a broken barn ; on high
Star-shells bright
With a trail alight,
Gleam in the Eastern sky.
And when I shepherd my thoughts at night,
Angels come to my darkened sight,
And sing when the noises of war are still—
" Peace on earth to men of good-will,
Peace to the hearts from evil free,
That love both friend and enemy."
You know I cherish no lust to kill,
But only my life to give
That others may live.
Alas, the Kings of the earth proffer
To Thee and Thy people only myrrh,
But look, dear Child, I give to you,
The gold of a heart untarnished and true,
And the fragrant spice
Of my sacrifice.

P.

THINGS WE WANT TO KNOW.

Who was the Co. Q. M. S. who, while eating a pork chop for dinner asked the cocks whether it was beef or mutton ?

Which Cook lit a fire in a wooden box ?

And did he think it would burn up quicker ?

Was it hard lines on C. Co. having to close their concert so abruptly ?

And is it true that the language of some of the performers in the sketch was not exactly episcopal ?

Is the best recipe for obtaining a new shirt—Play in a Rugby Match ?

Who was the N. C. O. who tried to explain to the young lady in the Cafe Parisien how the Provost-Sergeant carried his baton ?

Was the N. C. O. in D. Co. ?

Who carried his valise upside down ? Does he want his ticket ?

Which N. C. O. is known as " Pudding," and does his real name render the nickname singularly appropriate ?

Is it a fact that the N.C.O. referred to as "Charlie Chaplain " possesses a considerable power for sarcasm, and was the nickname simply given him by his victims as a weak means of " getting their own back ? "

Did the Officer of No. 3 Platoon find the boxing of his men delightfully funny to watch ?

Who first boiled a couple of eggs, and afterwards used the water to make tea ?

Which member of No. 3 Platoon is known as " The Budget ? "

Who put two nose-bags on one horse ?

Who was the N. C. O. who put a bran poultice on the wrong leg ? and what did the horse think of him ?

Who hog-maned the Battalion postman ? and what did they say when he dropped the rat ?

Who was the groom who put Salts in the Cocoa in mistake for sugar ?

Was an extra man required for Sanitary duty ?

Who is it in B Coy. who can ride a bike with the handle-bars locked ?

Who was the shoemaker who swallowed rivets while drinking tea ? Did he fancy it was his iron rations ?

Who was the N. C. O who could not go on leave without a short rifle ?

Who told the K. E. H. we were off to Siberia ?

Who is the Major in the Artillery whose telegraphic address is " Girders Steel ? "

Who thought he was taking two " dialogues " down to the Sappers when all the time they were only " Diagonals " ?

Will the author of the Command " Two paces right turn " give detail for same ?

What did Ginger say when he fell in the sump hole ?

Was it " Don't mench " ?

Who was the cook who made a pudding and put it in the coal box ?

Was he a Company Cook ?

Who was the Sergeant who said he could see to do his hair and shave without looking in the glass ?

Is he in C. Company ?

Who asked if he had to take his boots off to rub in anti-frostbite grease ?

Was he in No. 13 platoon ?

Who rubbed the water cart with anti-frostbite grease to prevent the water freezing ?

O.C. PLATOON ENQUIRES.

I once had a lovely platoon, Sir,
The finest platoon ever seen,
They could drill 'neath the sun, or the moon, Sir,
They were fit, and their rifles were clean.

They could march, and they knew how to shoot, Sir,
And to bayonet sacks upon sticks,
Equipped from the cap to the boot, Sir,
—Their number was fifty and six.

They were infantry right to the core, Sir,
They trusted in bullets and steel
To finish the terrible war, Sir,
—It bucked them all up a good deal.

But as soon as we landed in France, Sir,
Such terrible changes began
That hardly a man had a chance, Sir,
Of being an Infantry man.

For some for the transport have left, Sir,
And one cuts up beef for the Staff,
And others, of whom I'm bereft, Sir,
Mend trousers that suffer from " STRAFE."

There are some who are Sanit'ry men, Sir,
—(We tread upon dubious paths)—
And some became sappers, and then, Sir,
They lived among boilers and baths.

The M. G. O. pinched a few more, Sir,
—And blood-thirsty beggars they be—
They're especially out for the gore, Sir,
Of Huns that are carrying Tea.

One's running a photograph show, Sir,
Another is making a map,
There are servants and grooms, one or two, Sir,
They all leave a bit of a gap.

There are some who are Officers now, Sir,
While others wield clippers and shave,
There are bandsmen all under a vow, Sir,
To hearten the steps of the brave.

The few that remain use the bomb, Sir,
Proficient in anarchist lore
They handle H. E. with aplomb, Sir,
I look on with obvious awe.

If my men are all details am I, Sir,
A detail myself ? and if so,
Am I O. C. Platoon still, and why, Sir,
Is what I should just like to know.

C. W.

IT IS SAID THAT

The Quartermaster is too old a bird to dish out new shirts in exchange for Football flags.

Skylights belonging to inhabitants are best left alone.

(No. 3 Platoon ! Please note.)

Although " B " Company may enjoy it, yet " Lead Kindly Light " and " Landlord fill the flowing bowl " do not blend at all well.

Honest Labour is not always useful, as Lance-Corporal...... thought when he discovered that he was carrying three bricks in his valise.

It is never too late to mend, as the Q. M. said of the tattered overcoats handed in by " A " Company.

No one has ever seen an R. E. sump with water in it.

One of the numerous Battalions of the Gloucestershire Regiment desires to be addressed as " The Gloucestershire Regiment," and that this Battalion resides at Chelmsford.

CHAPLAIN'S COLUMN.

There are a good many familiar sights and sounds which we shall miss this Christmas—the Church decorations, the Christmas peal. We would give the world to hear the Painswick Bells again.

But we have the Angel's Hymn " Peace on earth and goodwill amongst men," and it is because we are determined to translate these words into deeds that we are away from our own firesides at the Festival of the Home. For this, the graves at Gallipoli—for this, the little Cross in the Belgian Chateau, or the French orchard—for this, our own little cemetery at " Plugstreet "—that the Kingdoms of this world may become one day the Kingdoms of Christ and His God.

We shall make our Communions then on Christmas Day and bring the Little Child, the Hope of All the World, the greatest present a man can give, our lives, ourselves, that we may be given the strength to do His work, to fight His battles and so help to achieve " peace on earth and Good Will amongst men."

There has just been formed in England " The League of the Spiritual War." It aims at " collecting the names of men in the King's Forces whose heart God has touched, and who, in the words of the membership card, " mean, if God spares them, to fight on His side in that second campaign, and would like to help and be helped by one another."

The Spirit of the League is expressed in William Blake's lines,

I will not cease from mental fight,
　Nor shall my sword sleep in my hand
Till we have built Jerusalem
　In England's green and pleasant land.

This League would seem to be the outcome of a real determination to build up a more genuinely Christian civilisation. For those who will one day return to England will have it in their hands to make or to mar the England they love, and they are going to make it ; and this League, which anyone may join, is going to help things on.

EDITOR'S POST BAG.

We have received the following poem, written to his home by an Indian soldier of the Indian Expeditionary Force. It gives his impressions of Armageddon.

The cruel German tyrant on Belgium laid his hand.
Patiala, Nahba, Russia, France and England bade him stand.
Came India to the rescue and Canada as well,
Teli and Turkey lent their men the German host to swell :
And so the war is waging by sky, and land, and sea,
And underneath the Water. Five kinds are fighting three.
Praise to the men of Europe, the Masters of Machines,
With flying craft and twelve mile guns, their mines and their
　　　　　　　　　　　　　　　　　submarines.
And praise to the beasts of Europe who share the people's art,
To the cat that churns the butter and the dog that draws the
　　　　　　　　　　　　　　　　　cart.
And horses speed the ploughshare and shops are faced with
　　　　　　　　　　　　　　　　　glass,
And the rain it never ceases and the fields are green with grass.
The cannon roar like thunder, the bullets fall like rain,
And only the halt, the maimed, the blind, will ever see home
　　　　　　　　　　　　　　　　　again.

For we are all as kittens in the kiln of destiny.
Perchance the Guru may save us, but what will be, will be.
We have eaten the salt of the Sirkar before when times were
　　　　　　　　　　　　　　　　　good,
Let us fight like valiant soldiers and pay the debt with our
　　　　　　　　　　　　　　　　　blood.
The Germans deal in numbers, the Frenchman has a trench,
And bodies are heaped upon bodies till all the air is a stench,
Bodies are heaped upon bodies like stones in a river bed,
The trench is seven hundred miles long, and who can count
　　　　　　　　　　　　　　　　　the dead ?
Only potatoes and cabbage are grown upon English ground,
Some things you can do for a penny, but butter's a shilling a
　　　　　　　　　　　　　　　　　pound.

Patiala and Nahba —Sikh States in the Punjab.
Teli—Austria.　　　　Guru—Founder of Sikh religion.

A LETTER.

(The following letter which has just been received in England will, we hope, give no clue as to the nationality of the Battalion which has recently been in the trenches with us. Ed.)

Dear M—

Shure, I'm in the thrinches, an' its meself thats not so shur that its the shant I'd be afther wantin' to be spindin' me honeymoon in. Phwat wid the spalpeens ov all kinds at all, and the devil knows phwat they wor sint for, and its meself thats meanin thim creepy crawly varmints, wid whiskers on, phwats foriver ticklin the hide ov a man an makin him look loike a tirrible dhose ov maisles. An, be jabers, phwen a bhoy gits a chance ov dacent slape, be me powers, out come the rats an mice, to have a look roun an see phwat kind ov tormint they cud put thro a dacint man—lavin out the spiders an slugs an worms that'd glad the heart ov ony fisherman an thim there devils on t'other side ov the fince, won't let a chap av a promenade without thrying to blow off the top of his cranium wid thim beastly little spit-fire masheen ghuns, an its the same thats no bigger than me auld shillalagh as can rip away so fast that me poor head gits dizzy countin the first two.

Be me ould hat, an faith 'tis the only one I've got, its not in the thrinches I'd come for me week-end holiday. But I'm afeared I'm not telling yez phwat I intinted to phwen I shtarted this letther, that I'll be afther telling yez phwen I've had a scratch at me back—the creepy itchin cant catch thim aslape darlints.

We've just come in the thrinches with the Glo'ster's for insthruction and nice bhoys they are, tho there ain a dacent dhudee amongst them—shure iviry mither's son iv thim got a fag shtuck in his face inshtid av a swate little black cuddy. Howiver we come in wid thim and ov course expected to av our heads blown to smithereens at once, but be jabers it woz alright, sartinly we woz worried at night by ivry son of a ghun, first twas " Go there and cum here, crawl out to some unourthly place phwats called a " listenin post "— I sthrained me eyes in th' dark an looked an listened but divil ov a post cud I see at all, at all.

Phwen I wint and thold the sargint, dear,—he called me all the blanked cuss words he cud lay his hans on, an by me ould bhoots, he can cuss.

That there was no woodin post there at all, at all, barrin me own woodin skull—but that listnin post was to go out in the front an listhin, to see phwat I cud hear ; and thin he thritined to run me in for lavin me phost, just as if I cud av brought it in wid me ; so back I wint agin to see phwat I cud listhin—phwen—smack comes a bullet an whizzed past me ear 'ole into a lump av airth aninst me. Faith an I'd heard enough ! so I laid down wid me ear on the groun for a few hours. Shure ! I'd foun out phwat listhinin phost woz. Anyhow—the first night passed off widout me head bein blown off tho no thanks to thim across that field av praties. I racaved th parcel you sint me, an its contints, or some ov it, av gone where it'll take sum findin agin. And may the saints reward yez for yer kind thought in sinding it on. An wid luck—I'll be afther seein yez in a wake or so—as the praste—I'm meanin the captin, av told me that me name's down in the list to go, as soon as I git a chance, so hopin yez are all kap'n up your spirits—and its meself that wishes I was puttin ov some ov it down me throat. Top o th marnin to yez me darlint.

　　　　　　　　　From ye're livin,
　　　　　　　　　　　　Pat.

THE TWA TOMMIES.

(Being an old Ballad without a moral)

As I went walking all alane
I heard twa tommies making a mane
The ane unto the ither did say :
" How shall we get a drink to-day ? "

" In my pocket burns my pay
" But every estaminet
" Is closed—alas—to you and me
" And guarded by a fierce M. P."

" In the Quartermaster's store
" Lieth a keg of rum and more
" And naebody kens 'tis there to-day
" For the Quartermaster's gone away.

" I there will softly pull
" The cork and fill our bottles full.
" And one gulp of that good rum
" Shall light a fire in your tum.

" We'll find some quiet place and drink,
" And maybe we will sleep in clink
" To-night—Who knows ? But anyhow
" We'll have a blooming good time now."

F. W. H.

FUMES FROM THE EDITOR'S WATER-BOTTLE.

That some confusion of ideas should exist in connection with the rights and wrongs of this war is inevitable. But at the same time it should be impossible for a man to say that " I feel sorry for the Germans, because I look at them from a Christian standpoint." It is just because we look at Germany and the war from a Christian point of view that we are out here to kill as many Germans as possible in the shortest possible time. Such a menace to Christianity cannot for one moment be tolerated by a Christian country. And men " who profess and call themselves Christians " are determined to see that in Galilee, not in Berlin, lies the hope of the world, and the salvation of Mankind.

" There can be no hope for Europe except in grinding Germany to powder, even though the task take ten years." (Professor J. H. Morgan.)

It is the first nine years of the war that will be the worst ! !

But seriously, diaries of German soldiers almost uniformly betray a common sentiment of lust, rapine and ferocious credulity. One says, " It is the Infantry who are to blame ; " another says " The Pioneers are the worst, and those brigands of Artillerymen ;" a third writes : " It's all the fault of the Transport." The cumulative effect of these several recriminations is to inculpate the whole.

So it is no good saying or believing that the " good " Germans were only obeying their cruel leaders.

Professor Morgan's article—" The Brutality of the Bosche," in the Graphic of October 30th, should be read by everyone who has a sneaking sympathy for our friends opposite. As a man in A Company expressed himself during the rains of last month " I'd like to see the blinking trenches fall in on top of the blighters."

Personally, one has always kept a blank space on the page of one's diary reserved for July, to note down the appearances of " Christmas Numbers." We feel, therefore, that the publishing of a Christmas Number in December is indeed a strange and unheard of chimera. It should have been a matter of history by this time. All the same, it gives us an excellent opportunity of wishing our readers the old, old wish, A Happy Christmas and a Bright New Year.

At a Convent in Flanders, it was announced that the Germans were approaching. Thereupon the Abbess sent all the nuns to the British trenches for protection, during the passage of the Germans through the town. On some one remonstrating with her for sending a number of defenceless women into the trenches, the Abbess retorted, " The soldiers there are British."

A good many of our readers seem to have a complete set of the Gazette with the exception of No. 3, which is very scarce. It is proposed, therefore, to reprint " No. 3," if Company Quartermaster-Sergeants will inform the O. C. Publication Dept., Headquarter Mess, how many they require, so that an estimate may be formed of the number to be printed.

Among a number of German prisoners reaching Southampton recently was an officer, and the observation was made to him by a gentleman watching the procession : " You want the world, don't you ?" " Yes, and Kitchener wants you," came the reply in broken English ; but even the sharpness of this retort was a little dulled by the wit of a boy standing on the pavement, who, with a chuckle, smartly said to the officer : " But he's got you, ain't he, guv'nor ?"

The following are extracts from the diary of a German soldier captured by the French ; they refer to an officer of his company :—
" Lieutenant REINACKER is drunk...'
" Lieutenant REINACKER is again drunk."
" This evening our Lieutenant REINACKER went sick..."
" To-day we made an attack......Lieutenant REINACKER could be heard ceaselessly shouting " Vorwearts " (Forward) from the second line dug-outs."

A final entry briefly mentions the fact that :—
" Our Lieutenant REINACKER has been awarded the Iron Cross."

Perhaps he had pinched his Platoon's Pill-ration.

The Phraseology of the British Tommy has ever been a favourite theme of Novelists and story-writers. And the words he is made to use are generally a medley of half-clipped slang interspersed with a string of oaths. Literary purists, therefore, and stylish generally, who have ventured to credit him with more orthodox vocabulary, will rejoice to hear that a Platoon Sergeant was heard to tell his men to fall in " on the site selected for the absolution benches."

It is good to hear the new Divisoinal Band practising. Our troops did not leave Southampton "with bands playing and colours flying," and hitherto there has been practically no opportunity of hearing music of any kind.

" After months of warfare, when we have grown accustomed to the idea that thousands of our men are dying that England may be free, bands for recruiting purposes were thought of, because it was found that the appeal of music was wanted to stir the consciousness of the people. And in France the inspiration of noble sounds and memories has been needed. They have been asking for music, to march the men off to battle. The bands are being sent at last, though thousands have marched off in silence."

MISS LENA ASHWELL,
" Nineteenth Century," August, 1915.

Recent Order from the Q. P. I. D. Department.
" A Junior Subaltern has written to the Minister of Agriculture complaining that there is an absence

of LOVE (Calf). You will therefore render a nominal roll of Officers and Other Ranks in the Unit under your Command, in need of same."

Staff Officer. " What's the name of this trench ?"
Sentry. " Oi dunno sir what its *real* name is but we calls it 'Land and Water.' "

From a Contemporary—
" God made the Bees,
The Bees made the honey.
The Gloucesters do the work
And the R. E.'s get the money."

This Number of the Gazette is printed, as its predecessors have been, in France.
It is on sale at the Battalion Canteen."

Conversation between Sergeant returned from leave, and a comrade. Time 4.15 a.m.
Comrade : " Well, Bob, how did you get on, old fellow, at home ?"
Sergt. : " Oh, alright !
C. " How's yer mother ?"
S. " Bin dead some years."
C. " Well, how's yer old man, then ?"
S. " Oh, olright !" (sulkily).
C. (in undertone) " Did yer bring a bottle back wi' yer ?"
S. " Yes, I had a decent time at home."
C. " Glad to hear it. What colour's the label ?"
S. " Went over to Gloucester twice."
C. " Did'st see anyone as knew I ? Is it Black and White ?"
S. " No, I was with the girl."
C. " Isn't it time to get up, Bob ? We could have some in our tea."
S. " Damn ! it's snowing."
C. " I allus did say as how a nip in yer tea puts yer right on a mornin' like this."
S. (in despair) produces bottle, both drink.
Comrade : " Ah.........Bon ....."

To Lieut. King's clever pencil we owe the cover which encloses, while it adorns, our Christmas Number. We are fortunate in being able also to publish an excellent illustration by Sec. Lieut. Robertson. The Editor is always ready to consider any drawings which may be sent in. He would like to be able to publish a sketch every month. Artists please note !—and the only reason why he has not done so is that no sketches have been sent in.

We have been the recipients of two very handsome presents. The Ladies of Cirencester, through The Countess Bathurst, sent us 81 articles of clothing of various descriptions and beautifully and strongly made. Mr. Voller has also sent a fine consignment of football shirts and shorts which he has procured for us with the help of friends in Gloucester. Our best thanks are due to those who have thus done so much to increase the comfort and enhance the pleasure of many in the Battalion.

A Battalion Christmas card has been ordered, and we hope that by the time these lines are in print it will be on sale in the Canteen.

Overheard in the Trenches—
" Heard the news, Bill ? "
" No."
" Well, the Navy is coming up here next week."

There was a time, not so very long ago, when the Territorials were regarded as " Saturday afternoon soldiers." And those who should have known better spoke of this particular branch of His Majesty's Force as " Those b...... Amateurs." Now that our old neighbours of the Ploegsteert area—the North Midland Division—have justified their existence, according to all accounts, in their great attack on the Hohenzollern redoubt, the opinions of those openly hostile to the Territorial Force may possibly undergo some modification. They have laid down their lives with the same readiness as they abandoned their businesses at the beginning of the war.

We trust that the appearance of Trench Mc-Clintock, Trench Nicholson, Fort Clissold, etc.. will not be followed by " Trench Foot (*e*)."

OUR BENEFACTORS.

Ladies of Cirencester, per The Countess Bathurst.	81 articles of Clothing.
The Countess Bathurst.	Papers and Books.
Miss Parr.	Papers and Magazines.
Mr. E. D. Compton	,, ,,
Mr. W. R. Voller	,, ,,
Miss Grace Armstrong	Books and Magazines.
Friends in Gloucester per Mr. W. R. Voller.	Football Shirts and Shorts.
Canadian Field Comforts Commission.	Papers.
Mrs. Kerr.	Papers.
" Daily Express "	Footballs.
Camps Library	Books and Magazines.
Ladies of Gloucester	200 arm-badges a month.
Miss Gobey's Pupils (Tuffley)	Comforts.
Canon P. L. Park, per the Mayoress of Gloucester	Furber wheeled stretcher.
Mr. Harley Butt	More Tobacco.
Mr. Jack Margetson	More " Woodbines."
Miss Pagan	Comforts
Rev. H. M. Roxby	Gymnasium.

4th DIVISION FOLLIES.

We fell in, under Lieut. Durrant, punctually at 4-45 p.m. and set out for A....... The party was not so large as we expected it to be, nor had the idea caught on so well as we might have wished. The M. G. section, however, was well represented and altogether we formed a very merry party. The march was accomplished in record time, the march music (?) being supplied on a mouth organ by a member of No. 4 Platoon. Upon arrival at A...... we found the Music Hall to be a splendidly set out room with seating accommodation for about 1,500. The programme was an excellent one, and the two lady performers received quite an ovation. The pianist was very good, and his comic song entitled " That's All " brought forth roars of laughter and applause. Altogether the songs and patter were excellent, being really funny and not too vulgar. A corporal of the " Royal Dubs." gave a very clever club and knife swinging display, and when closing time arrived and we wended our way back to B..., we were all agreed that the evening had been a most enjoyable one. Certainly our comrades of the 4th Division have done splendidly to organise so efficient a place of amusement. On the way home many of us, in talking over the matter, came to the conclusion that what the 4th Division have accomplished we of the 48th Division could surely emulate. Now then boys, as the cockneys say, " What abaht it ? "

E. K.

ALL FRIENDS SHALL TASTE THE WAGES OF THEIR VIRTUE,

AND ALL FOES THE CUP OF THEIR DESERVINGS.

—SHAKESPEARE.

1915 CHRISTMAS 1916

(Supplement to the Xmas No. 5th Gloucester Gazette.)

FROM MY DUG-OUT.

When the weather is bad, and we're soaking wet
When the farther we go the deeper we get
In mud and in water ; what comforts us yet ?
    " A pipe."

When watches are long and the night is dark,
And life seems to hold of hope not a spark,
What keeps our spirits just up to the mark ?
    " A pipe."

When peace comes again and the war's at an end
And we recall the past as o'er fireside we bend,
Who shall we say was our very best friend ?
    " Our pipe."

———

C COMPANY WHIST DRIVE.

On Saturday, Nov. 6th, "C" Company held
their third Whist Drive, fortunately securing the
loan of "Marie" which, by the way, is a room used
for ablutionary purposes. The room was brilliantly
lit by candles judiciously placed on the window sills
and tables, the latter consisting of "waterproof
sheets" placed on the floor. The brick floor
provided admirable seats which were softened by the
use of blankets. The latter were scrupulously
carried round from "table" to "table." The
majority of players, not being tailors, found the
cramped position not quite as comfortable as they
would wish. As usual the noise was not suggestive
of the name "Whist."

To distinguish the Ladies from the Gentlemen
the former removed their headgear. Many beautiful
creations were crushed or spoilt owing to the lack
of suitable receptacles for the same.

Sergt. Finch in his own inimitable manner
distributed the prizes, passing various jocund
remarks to the happy recipients. At the conclusion
of a very successful and pleasant evening thanks
were rendered to the organisers Sergts. Finch and
Watkins, and the donors of prizes for hidden numbers.

List of prizes and winners.

1st Prize (for best score) Bot. Champagne.
Pte. Palk. score 177.

LADIES.

1st	Pte	Roddis.	159	Tin of Salmon.
2nd	,,	Attwood.	157	Tin of Herrings.
3rd	,,	Price, A. E.	156	Bottle of Sauce.

GENTS.

1st	Pte	Whitworth.	162	Tin of Three Castle Cigarettes.
2nd	,,	Merrell.	159	Tin of Tomatoes.
3rd {	,,	Harding.*	157 }	Two packets of Gold Flake
	L/pl.	Lewis, T. H.	157 }	

HIDDEN NUMBERS.

These prizes were given by members of the Company
who wished to remain anonymous.

1st	Pte	Martin, E. F.	145	Tin of Abdulla Cigs.
2nd	,,	Rudman. *	142 }	Tin of Sausages.
3rd {	,,	Evans.	142 }	
	,,	Teale.	139	Tin of Apricots.

BOOBY PRIZES.

1st	L/Cpl. Lewis, M.E.*	129	Tin of Sardines
2nd	Pte. Lane.	129	Small Bottle of Sauce.
3rd	L/Cpl. Gray.*	132 }	Caramels.
	Pte. Davis, S. T.	132 }	

Won after cutting *

                                    T. H. R L

WHIST DRIVE.

**A Company 1/4th R. Berks and A Company 1/5th
Gloucesters.**

Very few preliminary arrangements were
necessary for the carrying out of a most successful
and enjoyable whist match and social evening,
between the Sergeants of A Company, 1/4th Royal
Berkshire Regiment and the Sergeants of A Company,
1/5th Gloucester Regiment.

Four tables were conveniently arranged in the
Gloucester Sergeants' Mess, and punctually at 6.30

p.m. the Royal Visitors put in an appearance. Without further ado, it was decided to play until 11 p.m., with an interval for refreshments (the extension of time being due to the kindness of Captain Collett). Sixteen games were completed by 8.30 p.m. when one of the visitors (much to the surprise of the Gloucester Sergeants, who had prepared a dixie of stewed fruit) suggested an adjournment to the Royal Berks' Mess for refreshments. Arrived there, we were so amazed at the extent of the preparations which had been made in our honour that we scarcely knew whether we were awake or dreaming. Sergt. Wonson specially was observed to give a skip, in a manner quite out of keeping with his dignity. After a neat little speech of welcome by Sergt.-Major Hogarth, we commenced to do justice to the really excellent spread provided. One well-known speaker has sighed for a business Government, but as we sat down to that feast our sigh was for cooks equal to those who had prepared the meal before us. There was something quite unique about the liquid portion of the refreshments. Suffice it to say that it in no way resembled Vin Blanc or Vin Rouge.

The meal being at length at an end the Berks Sergeants rendered some really excellent choruses, and then Sergt.-Major Wagstaff, on behalf of the Gloucester Sergeants, made a fitting speech of thanks in which he remarked that " he trusted that this would not be the last occasion of the kind."

The whist match was then continued, cigarettes and other luxuries kindly provided by Captain Collett being handed round meanwhile. Everyone seemed in the best of spirits, and Sergt. Meadows' deep voice could be heard reverberating round the Keep almost without cessation. Some very keen play was in evidence, and the evening resulted in a win for the Berks by eight tricks.

Before dispersing the whole company joined in singing " Auld lang Syne," and the National Anthem brought to close a most enjoyable evening.

I may say that as we curled up in our blankets our thoughts were far from the war, and all connected therewith. This was due in no small measure to the fact that both A Company of the Royal Berks and ourselves were very much " off duty," and it is a surprising fact that not even one attended sick parade next morning.

G. H. W.

TO THE BATTALION GRENADIERS.

The rifle is by all agreed
To be the soldier's friend in need.
For bullets fly without a tack,
And never think of coming back ;
And so a man without alarm
May use his trusty old firearm.
But when you come to hand grenades,
You're playing with such fickle jades
That men may be, as saith the bard,
Oft hoisted with their own petard.
A careless swing with number one
Is certainly a thing to shun,
For should you hit a wondering friend
'Tis like of both to be the end.
Again the lively fulminate
With which your bombs you detonate
Is most susceptible to blows,
And spiteful : you may lose your toes
By treading on it in a trench,
Or if you give the thing a wrench
Inside the bomb, it may reply
By sending bits of you on high.
So pray be careful when you use
The harmless looking inch of fuse,
The silly jam tin full of nails,
Those neat contrivances of Hale's,
The lemon made by Messrs. Mills,
The friction bomb that always kills
Within six yards, and most of all
That fulminate mercurial.
For these beneath a fair outside
A very deadly devil hide,

Which fears no foes, but knows no friend,
Resolved of all to make an end
Who meet him in his angry mood
With something fiery in his blood :
But by himself he's like a lamb
Who'd think it wicked to say d...,
Until the wicked fulminate
Wires into him and starts a hate.
If then you hurl it at the Hun
Both hard and high, you'll see some fun.
But don't forget that he will bite,
The hand that fed him, and sit tight,
With which precautions bombs will be
A friend in need to you and me.

GRENADIERS.

The undermentioned Officer, N. C. O's. and men qualified as Grenadiers at recent examinations—

	Lieut	Nason, C. S.	
413	Sergt	Wonson, R. C.	A Company
2480	Pte	Smart, S.	do
159	L/Sgt	Jones, G.	do
1400	Pte	Cousins, F. G.	do
1917	Pte	Trigg, L.	do
2478	Pte	Hayward, W.	do
2487	Corpl	Abbott, W. J.	do
1810	Pte	Preston, W. H.	do
1628	L/Sgt	Jackson, R. C.	B Company
2528	L/Cpl	Enoch, A. W. G.	do
2297	Pte	Stephens, J.	do
506	Sergt	Owen, J. G.	do
3167	Pte	Smith, T.	do
1842	Pte	Nash, E. M.	C Company
1486	Pte	Heath, H. S. J.	do
2374	Pte	Barnes, H. C.	do
1875	Pte	Davis, S. J.	do
2549	Pte	Matthews, H.	do
3281	Pte	Brint, A.	do
2355	L/Sgt	Harvey, M. J.	D Company
646	Corpl	Keeley, T.	do
3304	Pte	Fisher, W.	do
2680	Pte	Hamblin, L.	do
1576	Pte	Reynolds, C.	do
2702	Pte	Pollard, H.	do
2637	Pte	Woolley, M. J.	do
2180	Pte	Wyatt, F. G.	do
2223	L/Cpl	Bolter, H.	do
546	L/Cpl	Allen, F. S.	do

1/5th GLOUCESTER REGIMENT.
Promotions and Appointments.

		13-11-15	
1724	Cpl	Coole, F. A.	To be L/Sg with pay 3/11/15
2735	L/Cpl	Millard, S.	To be Cpl dated 1/11/15
1108	L/Cpl	Cuzner, J.	To be Cpl dated 3/11/15
2593	Pte (L/C)	Over, J.	To be paid L/Cpl 1/11/15
2467	,,	Simmons, P.	To be paid L/Cpl 3/12/15
		20/11/15	
1813	L/Cpl	Watts, D. A.	To be Cpl dated 9/11/15
2223	Pte (L/C)	Bolter, H.	To be paid L/Cpl 9/11/15
1585	,,	Nicholls, W. A.	To be paid L/Cpl 9/11/15
1366	,,	Marshall, H. R.	To be paid L/Cpl 19/11/15
2480	Pte	Smart, S.	To be L/Cpl without pay 9/11/15
2632	Pte	Turner, E. M.	do
2322	Pte	Harding, W. M.	do
1441	Pte	Steel, W. G.	do
2533	Pte	Fry, H. H.	do
2667	Pte	Cullis, R. H.	do
2366	Pte	Maddock, W. H.	do
2591	Pte	Miles, A. E.	do
2707	Pte	Saunders, E. C. S.	do
2673	Pte	Gardner, H.	do

CASUALTIES.

Pte	A. E. Sampson Killed	1/11/15
Sergt.	J. Heaven Wounded Accidentally	30/10/15
Pte	E. M. Nash Wounded	5/12/15
Pte	B. Cumming Wounded Accidentally	7/12/15

R.I.P.

Pte. A. E. Sampson enlisted in the 2/5th at the outbreak of the war and was among the first draft of recruits sent to us, being posted to F. Company.

He was one of the Battalion Grenadiers and was always ready to do his best in whatever part he was required to play.

Immensely popular he will be greatly missed by all who knew him.

He was one of the Patrol under Corpl.—now 2nd Lt. Knight, which did such good work on the night of August 3rd.

H

5th Gloucester Gazette.

A Chronicle, serious and humorous, of the Battalion while serving with the BRITISH EXPEDITIONARY FORCE.

THE NEW YEAR, 1916.

Oh ! Thou, who bringest after rain
A sky of perfect blue again,
And from the earth so seeming dead
Raiseth the snowdrop's drooping head,
First of that host of simple flowers
That far outmatch all human powers
      For Beauty.

Thou, who from village and from shrine
Dost somehow make Crusaders come,
Dost break the chains of wealth and ease,
And from base fears the heart release,
Dost in the hour of peril cry
On sleeping souls to live and die
      For duty.

Thou, too, these wrecked and wretched homes,
These churches, with their shattered domes,
Shalt raise again in the new age
When evil powers have spent their rage.
And war no longer can erase
Families with their dwelling-place.
      Peace giver !

And thou the bodies of those slain
Self-sacrificed shalt bring again
Fairer than all, when as the rose,
Again the shell-swept desert blows,
As souls are quickened by thy breath,
And Spring succeeds to Winter's death,
      Life giver !

TO 1916.

Oh, little babe that now adventureth forth
On thy brief sojourn in the lap of time,
What have the fates in store for thy career ?
What will they write throughout the coming year ?

Thy baby innocence is cast adrift
Upon a sea of mortal woe and strife.
Passion, let loose, and hatred, foul and grim,
Fill up our cup of sorrow to the brim.

But as thy days increase we pray that thou
Wilt, with thy warmth and sunshine, drive away
The Cloud of Horror which obscure our sight,
And give us back once more the blessed light.

For that glad time in all humility we pray,
And ask for Victory in the sacred cause of Right,
That "Peace on Earth" may once again be found,
And hymns of Praise throughout the world resound.

1st January, 1916   T. A. G.

AFTER THE LETTERS OF BLANCHE.

(A day report we may expect if the contributor to one of our well-known illustrated papers were given the job of Intelligence officer)

Dearest old Brigade Majorkins.

It was such a hateful day yesterday, and I was so frightened of the horrid dark last night that I have been in bed most of to-day, but in spite of it all I owe you a letter, and so, in a perfect dream of a dressing-gown, I have made up my mind to write.

Just about 10 p.m. last night the enemy put up the dinkiest duck of a red light. This was followed by some divine green and blue ones, and I loved it so. I suppose some old German lady must have sent a box to her son or something, because there were only five altogether. It was a pity they sent them up so quickly, as the true beauty of the colours was not apparent to its full effect. I rushed in to tell Uncle Charles, but he was clearly not interested.

Of course, dear old thing, I forgot all about looking to see if anything happened, but that doesn't matter a bit, does it ?

Did you ever stroll along between the lines, I wonder ? I did last night, and ran right into five great big men. I don't know who they were, of course, but they looked nice, kind sort of men, and were dressed very quietly in sort of grey lounge suits and bowler hats. Two of them had caps on, just like our chef used to wear, only smaller.

Meeting five strange men in the dark rather embarassed me, and so I at first pretended I hadn't seen them, and then I glanced shyly round and saw they had stopped. I noticed the three men in bowlers had a funny sort of spike in their hats, and thinking they had perhaps been drinking, or at a carnival or something, I thought it would be better if I went straight on back to the old trench. Funny meeting them out there, wasn't it ? I told Uncle Charles, and the dear silly old man growled, "Probably a Bosche patrol." Of course, it wasn't ; we know better than that, don't we, old B. M. ?

About 3 a.m. a lot of old carts rumbled along the road from one of those villages in their lines. I can't think what they were doing out so late, and the poor dear horses must have hated it so. I am sure they weren't those delicious carts like we have ; "good-sized" isn't it, or "G.S." or something ? Nor were they those darling little limbers our khaki boys adore so.

When this is all over I shall hope always to drive about in one with Uncle Charles in the little truck thing behind. Wouldn't people stare? But I forgot, I must not wander away from my work.

Anyhow, we'll forget all about the rotten old German carts, and talk about something else.

The enemy dug a jolly little place and put a lot of such ripping timbers on it, but would you believe it, our silly old left division scored 15 direct hits on it almost at once, and before it was light !

Have you heard the rumour that there's nothing remaining in front of the left division to get a direct hit on and that they are going to see what they can do with poor little B-s and A-e and C-s. Oh ! you poor old thing, I DO hope they won't bang away at C-n too.

Well, ta-ta, best wishes and all that sort of thing. There's heaps more to tell you, but I'm TOO tired.

Ever your loving
EVELYN.

What lovely souvenirs the new gas-gongs make !

" MINNIE."

For a gunner to write in an Infantry "mag"
Is serious, but please regard this as a "rag,"
And as you all know—
It's so often been said—
Fools will rush in, where wise men fear to tread.

For several months, when observing, I'd seen
A look of displeasure—you'll know what I mean—
Come over the faces
Of all of the "feet,"
And the words that were muttered I dare not repeat.

This worried me greatly, so one sunny day
I plucked up my courage, and spoke in this way
To an Officer, who
I thought looked very kind,
"Why do you hate me ? Oh, please ease my mind."

He glanced down, and shuffled—he really was kind—
Then coughed, and said gently " I think you will find
"It's only your firing
"Displeases my men,
"As for each round you fire, the Bosches fire ten."

"And also you choose such peculiar times
"For registering targets—the chief of your crimes—
"With all the day open,
"You shoot just when we
"Are changing, or dining, or having our tea."

I sympathised greatly with all that he said,
But answered him bravely with uplifted head,
"Our job is to shoot,
"And the shortage of shell
"Is no fault of ours, as you must know well."

As time rolled on, and we got shells in plenty,
If the Bosches fired ten we handed them twenty ;
And friendship made strides
Between gunner and "feet,"
Just one thing was needed to make it complete.

Suddenly, one day from out of a wood
Was heard a short "cough," and the Infantry stood
And gazed with amaze
As, from out of the spinney
There issued a shell from a "Werfer" called "Minnie."

There was a merchant, named Beecham, whose pills
"Worth a guinea a box" are a cure for all ills,
But a gross of such boxes
Although worth a guinea
Wouldn't give the result obtained by one "Minnie."

The first shell went off with a terrible "crump."
Just when stagnation had given the hump
To the Officers who,
In the wet trenches,
Were cursing their luck, and thinking of wenches.

The windows of dugouts were smashed, and a man
Who hails from a city :—last syllable " ham "—
Who was dreaming of home
And a well-known distillery,
Woke up shouting " Hell " and " Where's the artillery ? "

The first shell was followed by several others,
So they called for the help of the gunners—their brothers !—
Who stood to their guns
(As true gunners should)
And "strafed" the "Minnie" which fired from the wood.

For many long weeks the Bosches kept firing
With " Minnie " on trenches and roads—never tiring—
And the Infantry shouted,
Both early and late,
" Ring up the gunners to retaliate."

And now, when I go observing, a smile
Of welcome and friendship, greets me all the while,
And gunners by Infantry
Now understood,
All through the " Minnie " which fired from a wood.

During peace, of all quarrels that do us men vex,
The greatest is caused by the opposite sex,
But here it has taken
A woman we hate,
To bring us together, and put matters straight.

FORWARD OBSERVING OFFICER.

A CHRISTMAS TRUCE.

It was Christmas Eve, wet and windy. Thoughts of other Christmas Eves as I left my dugout after a hasty supper, to patrol the trench.

So busy was I with my thoughts that I forgot the trench was not floored with polished oak, till I found myself up to my knees in mud and water. Dug out of this I dreaded to continue my tour along the parapet, where it might be easier to combine my duties with dreams that would not be denied.

Up and down, up and down, all seemed quiet on the Western front. What should I have been doing then, if the Huns had refused to become the Devil's dupe ? By jove, this was a rotten sort of Christmas ; even worse than last year, when exhausted human nature welcomed an unofficial truce for a few days. This year the guns were going to strafe any attempt at that sort of foolery.

Ha, what was that ? A sentry says he has just heard a noise like the snapping of wire. Mere wind, I suppose, but we must listen. Certainly there's a rustling sound. Wind in grass no doubt, but Hark ! That's an unmistakable whistle. I was just going to put up a flare, when I got the shock of my life. A full Military Band started a German carol which we all knew, just in front of our wire. All the garrison of the trench were up on the fire platform in a second, but not a shot was fired. However, I sent for the searchlight and set it up on the parapet, and by its light saw more Huns than I have seen before ranged in a cirlce about 50 yards away, with every kind of musical instrument, playing the carol quite regardless of their audience. At the appearance of the light an Officer seemingly left the party and asked in guttural English if he might come through our wire. I stepped out to meet him, with a hand on my revolver, only to be greeted as Kamerad with wishes for a Happy Christmas. What could I do ? The men had already generously applauded the music. So I thanked him for his kindness and offered his party a spare jar of rum, saying at the same time there must be no more of it— War was war, and we could only accept peace on our own terms. After much clinking of mess tins, accompanied by " Hoch's" and " Cheer Oh's," the visitors withdrew. I reported the incident to my Company Commander, who still slept the sleep of the weary in his dugout. My story amazed him somewhat, and roused suspicion in his anxious breast. " I think you had better take out a patrol later on and see if there's anything behind this show of heartiness," he said. " Very good, Sir," I replied, resolving inwardly to let sleeping dogs lie in future.

I set about choosing the party. It occurred to me that we also had been practising some carols, and some of the choristers were in the trench at the time, including our musical director, who I knew, could do two or three parts himself if necessary.

I did not definitely intend to serenade the Huns, but still we were sent out for information, and could get it in more ways than one. We crashed and stumbled through our wires in the usual light-hearted way, and began with stealth to approach the solitary tree, in front of our trench, long known as the Christmas Tree. While still some distance from it, we became aware of sounds, plainly indicating the presence there of an enemy party. We decided to push on, trusting to the chance of approaching unheard which the noisiness of the enemy offered. With infinite caution we got near enough to see—a strange sight. The enemy party was busy dressing the Christmas Tree. They were hanging bags, suspiciously like the containers of tube helmets upon the stouter branches (stray sausages trailing from some of these revealed their secret), bombs (doubt-less on the same analogy filled with chocolates), illuminated wurzels, and festoons of coloured paper from top to bottom. Seeing the enemy so pleasantly occupied, I rose and went towards them. They were not a bit dismayed "You come too early, Kamerad," said one of them turning to me, "We meant to invite you all when we had finished the decorating." "Never mind" said I, "Let me and my few men help." So we set to work and further embellished the tree with a few Very light cartridges, which should serve as sconces for candles, souvenir postcards, and other small treasures, which we happened to have. I had to inform them that there was little chance of our getting leave to join them next day, also that our guns would probably be active. They deplored our stern intention. Their own gunners, they said, had entered into the spirit of the thing, and made dummy shells for the occasion, which we need not be afraid of, since the cases were only cardboard and the contents ration jam and sauerkraut. They were having a dance at P.........the night after Christmas, and most of them had their girls up. The palatial set of dugouts in the second line had been set apart for them, a fact which they trusted us not to reveal to the bloodthirsty gunners. We were welcome to the dance if we cared to come. I made the excuse that we were plastered with mud from head to foot and not in a fit state to meet their ladies. If there was really nothing doing we might arrange football matches with the company on our left on some suitable bit of ground between the lines, at which we hoped to see them and their young ladies.

The decorating was finished and we strolled on with them just as far as their wire, which looked very nice in ivy and berried holly. However, the barbs remained, as I discovered on carelessly cocking my leg over the first strand. Well, it seemed that I had got the information I had been sent for, so I withdrew with my party after an excellent glass of lager and went back to our trench.

Splosh ! ! I am back in the trench again lying on my back in the mud and water. Where's the rest of the patrol? They seem to have vanished entirely. Did I go out at all, or did I fall asleep on the parapet and dream it all?

THE FIRST SPRING DAY.

(To A.E.S.)

We laid you fast in frozen clay
When Winter had enchained the land.
(Lad, was it but three weeks to-day ?)
And now comes Springtime's messenger
    With golden tidings in his hand.

A mist blows off the thawing earth,
And drips from every budding tree,
The springs are loosed, and mad with mirth
Run lisping in the fallen leaves,
    Or laughing in the sunlight free.

Oh you who loved the song so well
Do you not hear the throstle's note ?
Nor heed the lovesome light that fell
As warm five thousand years ago when
    Solomon, the wise king, wrote ?

" Sweet "—wrote he—Yes, the light is sweet !
And maddening sweet to walk in Spring :
Yet is the pleasure incomplete—
How should the living understand the melodies
    That dead throats sing ?

Thinker and poet clutch in vain
The secret of a laughing rill,
And Shakespeare's self could never again
The message blow so mockingly by trumpet
    Of a daffodil.

Dear lad, for you I will not call,
Nor let a foolish dread be born.
A thousand years is still too small
To learn the secrets you must learn ere
    You arise on Doomsday morn.

For you have set your ear to earth
To list the growing of the flowers :
And catch the strains of Death and Birth :
And take the honey that is stored by all
    The flitting bee-like hours.

And you must put to memory
The silver music of the stars
That raineth down so silently,
And all the mighty harmony scrolled on
    The sky in glittering bars.

The music that no man can make,
The colours that he cannot see,
These out of darkness you shall take
And nourish up your growing soul with
    Manna of their mystery.

And then when you awake again
(And I have slept a little too)
How we shall rise to peace anew
An earth—Where every dream is true
    And nothing is unknown but pain.

                    F. W. H.

CHRISTMAS.

Christmas was spent out of the trenches at the rest village, and our celebration of the festival began on Christmas Eve when a party from the Bucks Battalion gave a capital concert, which was much enjoyed by a large audience. The Bucks are to be congratulated on possessing so good a party of entertainers.

On Christmas day, the powers that be cancelled all working parties, and consequently the day was a real holiday. Several Church services were held and at the parade service at 10 o'clock, the new Divisional Band distinguished itself by its accompaniment of the musical portions of the service and its playing of the opening and closing voluntaries. In the evening, our own carol party, under Captain Mitcheson, gave an excellent rendering of carols. During the day two football matches were played.

Christmas fare was provided for the Companies, though a roast dinner was postponed until the new year. Altogether the day was spent in as joyous and festive a manner as was possible under the circumstances, though many thoughts naturally turned towards home.

No. 2 Platoon.

A rollicking and merry Christmas was spent especially by Nos. 7 and 8 Sections of No. 2 Platoon.

In the evening they arranged a dinner and a Concert which was most ably presided over by Corporal Harries. The menu consisted of Chicken, Rabbit and Fish, etc. Nobody enquired as to how the rabbits were obtained. This was followed by

Sweets, which included Pears, Pineapple, Mince Pies, Xmas Pudding, etc. (Bravo! Transport.) At the finish of dinner the men in their most comfortable positions started the Concert. Cigarettes and suitable drinks were supplied at intervals and songs were sung by prolific artists, among whom are included Corpl. Nash, who rendered "Take me back to dear old Portland," Corpl. Harries, "My Silver Bell," and Pte. Smith, "Little Grey Home in the West" etc.

The artists among the guests included Sergt. Speck, whose song "Take me back to your garden of love" was vigorously applauded. Lce. Corpl. Sysum gave "Hey Ho! Can't you hear the Steamer Blowing" and was so loudly encored that he bashfully gave "Don't cry, Mammy" (Good old Sysum!)

But the memory of Pte. Pittaway's sleight of hand tricks will live for ever in the minds of his comrades. He mystified them, he astounded them and left them wondering. When he had finished all they could feebly murmur was "Good old Pitty" and later deafened him with rounds of cheering.

Coy. Qr. Master Sergt. Brown caused shrieks of laughter with his "I am L......y" and order was only restored by Corpl. Partridge (a guest) giving a pathetic rendering of "Asleep on the Deep." Others gave invaluable aid to the merriment of the party but their names are too numerous to report.

Sergt. Thompson spoke to the gathering very ably on their valuable work in the trenches, etc.. and stated he was proud to belong to the platoon.

Colonel Collett and Captain Collett paid the sections visits during the progress of the Concert and both wished the platoon a Merry Xmas and a Happy New Year.

The toasts were "The King," "Our Officers," "Our N.C.O's" and "The Men."

Merriment reigned supreme until "Lights Out," when the gathering dispersed after singing "Should Auld Acquaintance be Forgot" and concluded with "God Save the King"—which seemed to carry an undercurrent of threat to the Kaiser.

S. M. S.

No. 3 Platoon.

The N. C. O's and men of No. 3 Platoon had decided some time before Christmas to have a Royal spread and a real good time when that important day arrived. The arrangements (which were largely due to Ptes. Gough and Blackwell) were very complete and excellent. Lieut. Durrant, who gave the affair his very hearty support, took his seat at the head of the table. The cooking of the joint, chickens, etc., had been splendidly performed, and the meal very much appreciated and was voted excellent. At the end of the meal Lieut. Durrant, who was unfortunately obliged to leave early, said that he wished to take this opportunity of thanking the N. C. O's and men of the Platoon for the loyal manner in which they had helped him ever since he had known them. He wished them all to know that he appreciated what they had done, and thanked them from the bottom of his heart.

Sergt. Knight called upon all present to drink to the health of Lieut. Durrant, and as the officer left everyone rose and sang lustily, "For he's a jolly good fellow."

The table was then cleared, and liquid refreshments and smokes having been produced, Sergt. Meadows rose to propose the first toast, "The King." Then Pte. Gough rose and called upon all to drink to "Our fallen comrades." He referred to those comrades who had made the supreme sacrifice, whom those of us who knew and loved them can never forget. This toast was drunk in silence. Pte.

Blackwell then proposed "The friends at home" and the toast having been drunk, the real fun commenced!

Our old friend and late Platoon Sergeant, Provost-Sergeant Stevens, rendered several comic songs in his inimitable style, and L–Corpl. Jackson obliged with the old favourite "If I were a blackbird." Songs were also rendered by Sergt. Meadows and Pte. Griffiths, and the redoubtable "Emma" also assisted in the fun of the evening. The Commanding Officer looked in during the evening and expressed himself as being delighted to see the men having such a good time. We had received a visit from Captain Collett earlier in the evening and he also seemed astonished at the manner in which the barn had been decorated, and at the excellence of the catering. Altogether the evening was a most enjoyable one, and although this has of necessity been very different from previous Christmastides, I think we can say that No. 3 Platoon at any rate spent "A Happy Christmas."

[The Editor is always ready and anxious to publish accounts of company doings and matters connected with the Battalion in general. He can only do so if readers will kindly send in contributions without waiting to be asked.]

CHRISTMAS.

SPECIAL ORDER OF THE DAY.

By Lt.-Col........., R. F. A.

Commanding.........Brigade.

1. The C.O. wishes all Officers, N.C.O's, and Men of the Brigade a Happy Christmas and a Happy New Year. This order is to be read out on three successive parades, and certificates to this effect will be rendered in duplicate.

2. The C.O. considers that one Officer in each unit should be sober on Christmas Day. Names of Officers selected for this duty will be submitted to this Office to-night.

3. The C.O. reiterates his conviction that successive Christmasses will find the Brigade which he has the honour to command still adding to its laurels on the historic fields of France.

.................Captain R. F. A.

Adjt..........Brigade R. F. A.

December 24th.

Appendix to Special Order of the Day.

By Lt.-Col.......... R. F. A.

Commanding .... Brigade R. F. A.

Erratum. In para. 1, line 2, the words

"A happy Christmas . ."

should read

"A Merry Christmas . ."

Captain, R. F. A.

Adjt..........Brigade, R. F. A.

Dec. 24th, 1915.

Reference special order para No. 2 AAA Nil return order received too late for compliance AAA.

(signed) O. C. Amm. Col.

OUR PORTRAIT GALLERY.

No. 7. THE THREE PADRES.

(An Acrostic.)

R. C. Chaplain.

Pale faced, brown eyed, slight,
Upon a lanky bay
Rides this modern knight
Down rain-beat road to-day ;
In a little broken shrine
Emptying out the blessed wine.

Wesleyan Chaplain.

Much loved by all who know you,
Especially you seem
Envied for smiles that show you
Kindness in a gleam.

C of E. Chaplain.

Helm of our literary ship,
Editor of this Gazette,
Luck be yours, although you whip
My muse into an awful sweat.

TRIOLET ON ACROSTIC.

Acrostics are the devil to compose,
Let no one contradict and say they ain't.
Sonnets are rather difficult, but those
Acrostics are the devil to compose,
Take it from me, for I'm a man who knows,
They'd stain the shining soul of any saint.
Acrostics are the devil to compose,
Let no one contradict and say they ain't.

F. W. H.

BUCOLICS.

There was a time when we were accustomed to see cows standing about listlessly in green English meadows, staring aimlessly, cropping grass, and ruminating moodily. So common was the sight that it became part of the daily round and was noticed and forgotten in the same moment.

Then for a period we endured well-nigh intolerable odours handed over as part and parcel of the trenches. Everywhere there appeared to be decomposed cows. Some buried anything down to six inches beneath the soil, others overtaken by a more sudden fate, lying out in the open, but always the odour. Occasionally it became so insufferable that a party with " cow-respirators " stole out over the parapet under cover of darkness, armed with tins of chloride of lime, in a vain endeavour to mitigate the obnoxious effluvia.

Time passed, during which we once again lived within sight of live, browsing, staring, ruminating cows.

Then joy of all joys, we became possessed of one, Rival battalions claimed ownership, " cow-guards " were paraded, but despite all endeavours the cow remained with us.

Milk was obtained. Fine, fresh milk. No tinned glutinous, sugary, semi-solid diluted to look like the real article. Real milk flowed.

In course of still more time, noticeable structural alterations became apparent. Internal accommodation appeared to be inadequate. Graceful contours gave place to ominous bulges. The bulges became bulgier. Excitement and expectation ran riot amongst those intimately associated with it.

Once again M.M. Nestle profited.

Then, early on the morning of the memorable 5th of January, excitement and expectation were satisfied.

The Bull Calf had arrived.

HONORIS CAUSA.

Mentioned in Despatches.

The following Officers and Non-Commissioned Officers were mentioned in Despatches dated January 1st, 1916.

Lt. Colonel J. H. Collett.
Captain V. N. Johnson.
Captain (Temp. Major) N. H. Waller.
2nd Lieut. (Temp. Lt.) E. Conder.
No. 392 Sergt. F. Finch.
,, 2741 Sergt. J. N. Watkins.

We also note with pleasure the name of Captain F. A. Bruel, a former Adjutant of the Battalion.

The following awards for service in the Field have been conferred :—

Military Cross.

Captain (Temp. Major) N. H. Waller.

Distinguished Conduct Medal.

No. 133 Sergt. A. Faville.
,, 154 Sergt. J. C. W. Jennings.

THE DEPUTY CHAPLAIN GENERAL.

The Deputy Chaplain General, the right Reverend Bishop Gwynne, of Khartum, will hold a Confirmation Service at 3 p.m. on the afternoon of Saturday, February 26th. He hopes to be able to remain in the Divisional area over the following Sunday.

PASSION.

All life from passion springs.
In holy escstacy
Midst whirr of angel wings,
Did God decree
The golden stars that shine :
The flaming morn :
And that this flesh of mine
Should once be born.

And all the works of men
That live indeed :
Joyance of sword or pen,
High thought or deed,
Are in such primal fashion
Contrived and wrought,
God grant me fire of thought
To work Thy will—With Passion !

F. W. H.

BRICKS FROM THE EDITOR'S PACK.

From the Artillery :—

" The O. C. Brigade hopes that more attention will be paid to the condition of ammunition wagons than has been done in the future.

Verbal reply from Battery Commander.

" I will see this is done yesterday."

Ignorance among people at home on some points is amazing. Thus we read in a London Contemporary that " Bread is the Staff of Life, but the life of the Staff is one long loaf."

" The French fire opened large breeches in the German trenches."

Corps Summary 11–1–16.

In other words, it caused a rapid movement to the rear.

———

Newly joined Subaltern reporting to C. O.

" I have come to report myself to you Sir, Lt.... Rugby and Balliol."

C. O. (drily) :—

" Oh yes ! Allow me to introduce you to my interpreter, M. Blank of F.........and Amiens, chiefly Amiens."

———

The Navvies Christmas.—The navvies had dined well and drunk deep of the cups of Lethe. The C. O. comes to wish them good cheer and a Happy New Year. " The G. O. C. says he is very pleased with your work." To which from the corner of a billet " Yes and he......well ought to be."

———

We hear on good authority that the Driver of the Leave Train is shortly coming up to H............ for a week's instruction on our Light Railway.

———

It is a commonplace that Trade follows the Flag. It is equally true that Cricket and Football follow hard on the tracks of England and her Empire. But football received a very great filip throughout the Division when it was announced that General Fanshawe had offered a cup for competition.

It has excited a great deal of interest and some very keen football. The Final will be " some " Final.

———

We are most grateful to Colonel Smyth-Osbourne, A.A. and Q.M.G., for bringing over the 4th Division Follies. All ranks enjoyed the performance hugely.

———

The Soldiers and Sailors Families Association during the month of December sent

" to the Gloucester Battery
06 pair socks."
" Gloucester Journal."

No wonder the Germans state that we are getting short of wool.

———

A story reaches us anent a certain service which was being held in a barn. At the back were two men who found the time hanging heavy on their hands, albeit the sermon was a short one. " And now," said the Padre, " we will sing God save the King." " It cannot be done Guv'nor, nohow, as I've got the ace."

———

We hear on good authority that a rat is at the present moment having a very happy life at B. He has been carefully fed on the ration rat poison. He has now grown fat and sleek in consequence, and his coat is particularly fine.

———

The goose dinner, provided regimentally, proved a great success and was enjoyed by all ranks, with the exception of the Headquarter Mess, which drew THE gander of the flock, and consequently retired from the fray.

We understand that a large requisition for dentures has since been submitted by that mess.

———

We should indeed be ungrateful if we did not acknowledge the very kind notices of our Christmas Number which appeared in many of our contemporaries. One day, perhaps, it may be our pleasant privilege to conduct representatives of the Press over our large and spacious offices that they may obtain a glimpse of·the romantic life as led

by each piece of copy till it arrives at the mouth of the Editorial separator, finally to achieve a " Place in the Sun."

———

It was very nice, and reminiscent of other days, to hear Carols at Christmas. Under the leadership of Captain Mitcheson the singing was excellent. Carols were sung at the Divisional and Brigade Headquarters and the Bucks Battalion. Visits to the Berks and Oxfords had to be cancelled owing to a change in the relief day.

———

SAPPER TO TRANSPORT DRIVER Hello ! got a job for you to-night. Got any empty limbers up here ?

DRIVER. Ah, two, what do you want 'em for ?

SAPPER. Well, we got half a dozen post holes to go down, think you could get 'em on somehow ?

DRIVER. Oh, Ah, how long be 'em Sapper ?

SAPPER. About six feet.

DRIVER. I can put 'em on easy, let 'em go down on the coal limber.

SAPPER. Right oh, that's another job done.

———

From the Transport. A DIALOGUE. 1.30 a.m.

NIGHT PICKET (hurriedly) " Corporal, Corporal, Corporal ! ! ! "

CORPORAL (sleepily) " Hullo."

NIGHT PICKET. " Come at once, there's a horse down. We don't know whether he is tired or has got the colic."

———

PUZZLES.

My first is :—
What you feel at dinner.
My second is :—
What you feel after dinner.
My whole is :—
What you feel before dinner.
ANSWER.
APPE–TITE.

———

Q. What is the difference between a 5th Gloster and the Kaiser ?

A. One makes Will ill, the other ill will.

———

What the Kaiser sent to Kitchener :—

Stand take to taking
I you throw my.

———

There was an atmosphere of suppressed excitement on the opening night of the 48th Division " Curios." The stalls were crowded, and there was a very fair sprinkling of well known " first nighters." The whole entertainment went with a " go " from start to finish, and as one discussed the various turns in the foyer while smoking a cigarette in the interval, nothing but praise was accorded to the performers as a whole. When all the players tried so hard to amuse us, it would be invidious to single out any for special praise.

Our gratitude to those who organised such an admirable troupe is great and we feel sure that all ranks who have the opportunity of seeing " THE CURIOS " will fully appreciate their efforts.

To the Deputy Lord Mayor of Birmingham and to Sir John Holder we are especially grateful for the way in which they have financed this scheme, and to Colonel Smyth-Osbourne, who has been the moving spirit, and to Captain Hawkins, who has supervised the training. Major Danielson has been indefatigable.

A PRESENT FROM FLANDERS.

Where dewfall and the moon
Make precious things
On every small festoon
A spider slings :

Treading—like dead leaves, under
All drifted days
Happy the lovers wander
In Winter ways.

No thought of pain perplexes
The peace they hold.
No wordly sorrow vexes
The lovers. Gold—

All golden gleams the way,
How strange such riches
Drawn from rough men should be,
Seven or eight worlds away
Fighting, and carelessly
Dying in ditches !

F. W. H.

OUR BENEFACTORS.

Children of North Nibley Schools (per Mrs. Mostyn
Pritchard) :—Socks and mittens.
The D. M. Department, Lenton's Ltd. Gloucester :—
Cigarettes.
Master Reggie Chappell, Dursley :—A mouth organ.
Mr. J. Margetson, Stroud :—" Times " Broadsheets
and Woodbines.
Hempstead Working Party (per Rev. the Hon.
C. A. Sinclair) :—Mufflers and mittens.
Miss Gobey's pupils, Tuffley :—Christmas presents.
Mrs. Gosse, London :—Palliasses.
Mr. E. L. Seward: —Tobacco and cigarettes.
Mr. J. F. Thorpe (formerly Captain of A Company) :—
Tobacco and cigarettes.
Mr. R. Beckingsale, Gloucester :—Nestle's milk.
Mr. C. Lee-Williams :—Part song music.
Queen Alexandra's Field Force Fund :—300 parcels
of comforts and 300 cakes.
" Daily News " :—Plum puddings.
Patrons of the " Palladium " Gloucester :—
Christmas parcels.
Canadian Field Comforts Commission :—Papers.
Mrs. Temple Cooke :—Papers.
Miss Grace Armstrong :—Magazines.
Mr. E. D. Compton :—Papers.
Miss Parr :—Papers.

A REMEMBRANCE.

O'er Dorset's vale and Thorncombe hill
The wintry sun gilds seascape still,
From Lulworth Cove to Lyme's steep vales
Her shores still face the western gales.

Her sons have gone across to France,
That land oft named for sword and lance,
Our Northern seas on silent watches shield ;
Their country's homes to none they yield.

In winter time their thoughts oft roam
O'er sea to dear ones left at home,
Old farmstead nestling, silent, still,
Mid Dorset's vale and Thorncombe Hill.

And when at last this war is done,
Old England rests—'neath summer sun,
Her ships steam home, with favouring gale,
Joy comes again in Dorset's Vale.

THINGS WE WANT TO KNOW.

Who was the N. C. O. who, when directed to enquire
for " pommes-de-terre frites," asked for " Armen-
tiere chips " ?
Who is the Sergeant who is firmly of the opinion that
" you can't get drunk on nuts " ?
Who is the Coy. Q. M. S. who got under the bakehouse oven when the Germans were strafeing ? Is
he an old soldier ?   Was the Coy. S. M. with him ?
Who was it who remarked that " T-t-t-the b-b-
bottom o-of the w-w-well w-was o-o-o-out " ?
Who is the Private of No. 12 Platoon who tried to
cut a sandbag with a meat saw ?
Who had black on his forehead on Dec. 26th, and
why ?
Who is the Sergeant who tried to number his Platoon
when they had drill tube-helmets on ?
What was it the first man said ?
Who is the officer who said that the Lewis gun was
a cross between a Colt revolver, a Barr and Stroud,
and a gramaphone ?
Which N. C. O. reported to his Sergeant that the
Commanding Officer had instruced him to erect a
sheet of " congregated iron " over the dug-out
entrance, and to dig a " thump hole ? "
How did the Company S. M. enjoy the gorgonzola ?
Did a certain Company Officer find his men's views
on the War of an instructive nature ?
Who is the " A " Company sergeant who suffers
from rheumatism, and has he received an offer
from a young lady in England, of a quantity of
" Thermogene " wool ?
Is the seat of pain unusual ?
Which " A " Company sergeant has been very much
in the limelight this Christmas ?
Which " A " Company Sergeant used the " Rum
sauce " with his meat ?
When the baricade guard shot a mongrel, did the
self appointed executioner choose an unusual
portion of the dog's anatomy at which to direct
his bullet ?
Which Sergeant upon being presented with a " Peps "
tablet, attempted to consume it plus the lead
paper covering ?
Who is the Adjutant (Infantry) who mistook a five
inch Howitzer shell for a Chinese cracker ?
Did the subaltern (Artillery) kiss the sentry as well
as shake hands with him ?
Who was on duty at the incinerator and tried to dig
out a " dud " shell.
Why have the " Hows " got to support the
Gloucesters with rifle fire ? Is an aspersion being
cast on the Gloucester's snipers ?
And when are the Gloucesters going to fire the
" Hows."
Has the leave train been found to exceed the speed
limit of five miles per hour ?
Who spoke of efficiency as being the Kerb stone of the
new National Policy ?
Who is the gunner who talks about casement ?
Who said he was as happy as a sandbag ?
Now that men have been ordered to play football in
their spare time, will the Quartermaster supply
the candles ?
Or must we wait for a full moon ?
Is there a very talkative parrot in No. 11 Platoon ?
Who kissed the A. P. M. ?
Who woke up to find that he was hugging a pig ?
Who was the N. C. O. in " A " Company who tried to
borrow a fur coat before going home on leave ?
Who is the officer who considers port to be a teetotal
drink ?
Who is the Officer who had to take off his spurs when
riding ?
Who is the drummer in " C " Company who put a
sack in the skylight to stop the shells ?

Who boiled a tin of Cafe au lait and one of jam in mistake for water ?
Who said " Let's give one good three cheers " ? Was he in No. 10 ?
Who was the sanitary man who put a bugle on the incinerator ?
Who was the Officer who tried to milk the cow and was cleared out of the shed by her ?
Which Platoon is so very fond of Berming ?
Who was the N. C. O. who said " We have been on three days night sentry ? "
Which N. C. O. in singing the " Bandoliero " rendered the word " dislocate " as " discolate " ?
During the festive season did a certain old lady sell a member of A Company 3 rabbits minus their skins, although she was only known to possess two ?
Has the said old lady's cat (a remarkably fine one) since vanished ?
Who is the N. C. O. in D. Company who forgot to post the first page of his letter ?
Who tried to dry himself under the shower bath ?
Who asked if it was true that the big drummer is a little man ?
Which stretcher bearer slept for 70 hours out of 72 and then got up for a rest ? Is he in No. 16 ?
Who was the D Company cook who put bacon fat on the tea to keep the flavour in ?
Did a Corporal in B Company ever receive that parcel he talked so much about ?
Who got a rise out of a Company Commander by saying that his Company had " got the wind up " ?
Who spoke of a " plume de nom " ? Did he say it was a " lipsus languae " ?
Who tried to stack the water round the pump ? Is he in No. 13 Platoon ?
Who put on his full pack to be inoculated ? Is he in D Company ?
Who stripped to wash in a tea cup ?
Who is the N. C. O. in B Company who is not forced to use anti-frostbite on account of his nationality ?
How many so-called German " Minnies " arrived near certain Artillery dugouts, and how much did it cost the Major of the battery to repair his temper and windows ?
How was it that the virgin shot of a certain Battery with new equipment could hit a tree at 25 yards, when they could not hit one at 3,300 yards in 40 rounds with their old equipment.
Who is the Officer who lost his Trousers in the train while coming back off leave ? Where did he want to go to recover them ?
Who is the Officer who objects to criticism on his clothing by a " very Junior Officer " ?
Who put the toasted cheese on the end of his bayonet and kept the safety catch up ? Did he catch anything ?
Who said that he could not clean his candle by rifle light ?
Which are the badges usually worn by " British Officers " in A—S. ?

APRES LA GUERRE.

(Tune, " Home, sweet Home.")

I dream of a time of gladness,
  When toil and strife is o'er,
And hearts now filled with sadness
  Will throb with joy once more.

I dream of faces beaming,
  Of eyes, long moist with tears,
Now bright and clear and gleaming
  With love light—Gone are fears.

Home, dearest place on earth :
  Now, far we have wandered
We've learned your true worth !

I dream of arms extended,
  To welcome him so dear,
Love, joy and pride, all blended,
  From those sweet lips, so near.

I dream, but no, I'm waking ;
  The past is gone ; I'm here,
With loved ones—past all quaking,
  I'm home. Apres la guerre.

Home, dearest place on earth :
  Now, far we have wandered,
We've learned your true worth.

G. E. K.

CORRESPONDENCE.

To the Editor,
  " Fifth Gloucester Gazette "
  Dear Sir,
We think you deserve every congratulation for having brought out in the Christmas Number of your Gazette the timely suggestion that the 48th Division should form Follies of their own. It shews the power of the Press as exemplified by the " Fifth Gloucester Gazette " (3d) and its less valuable, though equally powerful contemporary, the D...M...
As a notice in your valuable paper will surely have the desired effect, we beg to offer our services at a salary not exceeding £25 per week.

Your sincerely.

Lanoline and Vaseline, Serio Comics.
Somewhere outside the 4th Divisional Area.

TRIOLET.

Winter has hardened all the ground
But flowers are on the window-pane ;
  No other are there to be found
Winter has hardened all the ground
  But here while Earth is bare and bound
Bloom ghosts of those his frost has slain.
  Winter has hardened all the ground
But flowers are on the window-pane.
F. W. H.

" THE CURIOS."

The 48th Division " CURIOS " gave their first performance on Wednesday, January 19th. There was a full house and an excellent entertainment followed. The whole Division has been looking forward for a long time to the appearance of a Variety Entertainment of its own, on the understanding of course, that it must be as good as, or better than, any other in the neighbourhood. In consequence the audience was not by any means uncritical. It is therefore a high tribute to " THE CURIOS " and their Manager to be able to say without any flattery that everyone present went away highly delighted with the entertainment. Naturally, there were a few signs of nervousness in the early part of the evening, but these disappeared very quickly and the programme went with a remarkably good swing.
" THE CURIOS " have all the makings of a very good Concert Party. The Comic Songs of Gunner Thompson were an instantaneous success, and he will be better still after a few more performances. He was well backed by Pte. Cruikshank and the two together were very amusing indeed in their joint

I

turn which included " Out in the open " as a duet. The comic side was very well balanced by the songs of Pte. Rayner and Pte. Cooter. Pte. Rayner's solos were particularly good. He has a very pleasant voice, and sings with expression and spontaneity. His rendering of " So fair a flower " was delightful, so also was " Good-bye, Virginia," which he and Sapper Palmer sang as a duet. Pte. Cooter has a good voice and will improve with more experience. " The Roll on the Open Sea" was a difficult song for his first item, but he did much better with " The Yeoman's Wedding." Gunner Sander's dancing was very popular and is a valuable asset to " The Curios " programme.

The concerted items of the programme were also well performed by all the Party. " The Wedding in the Moon " was a rather ambitious piece, but it was perhaps the best of all. The " Tin Can King " quite brought down the House. Gunner Thompson's costume and dancing were amazing. He has obviously studied Maud Allan.

The part of the Pianist is such Concert Parties is generally as difficult as it is important. Pte Brooks has a good deal to learn yet, but he showed promise and will find more experience invaluable.

The Opening Chorus and Finale gave the whole performance a good start and finish. It is impossible to mention every item of the 24, but we most heartily congratulate " THE CURIOS " jointly and individually on their debut. The greatest credit is due to them for giving such a good first performance after so short a period of training.

Finally, the thanks of the whole Division are due to their Manager, Captain Hawkins, for his successful production of such a promising Concert Party.

The " 5th Gloucester Gazette " would also like to convey to him best wishes and congratulations on his recent wedding.

Programme.

1.	Opening Chorus	
2.	" Oh to-morrow night " . . .	Sapper Palmer.
3.	" Until "	Pte. S. Rayner.
4.	" No more stopping out late " .	Pte. Cruikshank.
5.	" Pride of the Pier "	Corpl. Herbert.
6.	" Roll of the Open Sea " . . .	Pte. E. Cooter.
7.	" Blue Hungarians Band ". . .	Gr. G. Thompson.
8.	" Mr. Bottomley "	Concerted.
9.	" Double Dancing Act " . . .	Corpl. Herbert and Gr. Sanders.
10.	" So fair a flower "	Pte. S. Rayner.
11.	" I followed her "	Sapper F. Palmer.
12.	" The 5.15 "	Corpl. Herbert and Pte. Cruikshank.
13.	" The Ragtime Curate " . . .	Gr. Thompson.
14.	" Wedding to the moon " . . .	Concerted.
15.	" Out in the Open "	Gr. Thompson and Pte. Cruikshank.
16.	" Yeoman's wedding song " . .	Pte. E. Cooter.
17.	" Good-bye, Virginia " . . .	Pte. S. Rayner and Sapper F. Palmer.
18.	" Shipwrecked "	Gr. Thompson.
19.	" Peru "	Corpl. Herbert.
20.	" Song at Piano "	Pte. Cruikshank.
21.	" Sunshine of your smile " . .	Pte. S. Rayner.
22.	" Banjo solo "	Gr. Thompson.
23.	" Dance "	Gr. Sanders.
24.	" Tin Can King "	Concerted.
Pianist.	. . . .	Pte. W. C. Brooks.

FIRST MILITARY EXPERIENCES.

I have a wife. I mention it because it might help to explain what follows. As a relief from my wife I have a garden, and one day not long ago I sallied forth into my garden, partly because I was sick of reading all about " what Sir John French ought to do " by a local editor, partly because I wished to feel I was doing something useful, and last, but not least, because my wife had ordered me out of doors.

While I stumped about, in and out and roundabout, in my clogs, up and down steps, doing everything hind before, and incidentally listening to caustic and unmannerly remarks from sundry windows of the house, the thought suddenly struck me that I might just as well do my bit for King and Country. I made my way to the wash house (where the beer is kept) in order to think the matter over, and finally decided to join at once. I also thought that I should thereby get out of the gardening, which does not agree with my back. I talked the matter over with my wife, who, not seeing through it, fell upon my neck with pride at my determination in such a way as to make me remark (sotto voce) " this is a bit of alright." But now the question was " What was I to join " ? At last I decided to try the Red Cross, but here I was told that inasmuch as I knew nothing about the job I should be no good. At last in desperation I joined the rival show, the V. T. C., and Oh………So I enrolled in their ranks and became one of them, even as they themselves, and began to do my bit. I was told where to stand and how to stand, and when to stand, and what to do with my eyes, hands, feet, and middle. I formed fours, reformed two deep, marched slow, and " as you were'd " times without number, and I became a very blank file more than once, to the intense delight of my fellows. My spirit sank within me and I sighed often for the awkwardness of my feet, and my right hand never knowing what my left was doing. Nevertheless I buoyed myself up with the thought that someone else was doing for my garden, and someone else listening to my wife. So with fresh heart I learnt to " slope pip " and " order ip " and trail the ......thing, and present it to someone (how willingly would I have presented it to anyone, free, gratis, and for all time) and " Fix......bayonets " by numbers, and every other old thing, times innumerable. And I went for route marches and doubled, and got out of step, and put every one else out, and drew words of import from the Platoon Sergeant, who was the very man for the job, and uncouth withal, and who played Rugby, which covered a multitude of sins.

Then came a night when we assembled to have gorgeous green uniforms served out to us, and to get into them, which was another matter and was done as best might. But the colour suited us right well. Nevertheless the puttees were a fearsome sight, and no two legs were alike ; but the populace was well pleased.

Now the order went forth that there should be shooting at the butts, which caused much searching of hearts, and when the time came for me to lie prone upon my...I had no breath left in me, but to the wonder and amazement of all I scored a " What ho " bull. Then gathered the elders together (before each of whom in turn the red flag had waved) and questioned me with unbated breath. " How did you do it " ? But I answered them never a word, being bereft of speech, for I had pulled off with both eyes shut. My score was 22 all told in five rounds, being half the years of my age. They were all amazed that I, being in private life a brewer of beer, should possess such a straight eye and steady hand. But I, slipping softly away, stepped out smartly along the road picking my feet up six inches at each step, and yet for some time afterwards I could not purchase a cap to fit, they all being three sizes too small. The remainder of my doings in training, and how we had skeleton company drill with skipping ropes, and tried to learn " changing guards " and relieving sentries, two by day and three by night, as if it were Beecham's Pills, and how the portly members found the place too hot and their faces wept, and sundry other mischances, with the arguments when wrong orders were given and right ones obeyed wrongly, and the revilings and admonitions, and every man doing that which was wrong in every-one else's sight, are they not burnt in to the memories of us till our dying day ?

GRENADIERS.

The undermentioned Officer, N.C.O's. and men have passed the test laid down for Grenadiers—

2nd Lieut. L. J. Clayton.

183	Pte.	White, H. G.	159	Pte.	Apperley, J.
2483	Pte.	Richardson, H.	352	Sergt	Jordan, A. C.
1978	L/Cpl.	Rice, A. C.	669	Corpl	Godson, R.
1860	Pte.	Walker, J.	1527	Pte.	Sproat, A. L.
2742	Pte.	Wintle, A.H.	2675	Pte.	Gardiner, W.
1864	Pte.	Davis, A. E.	1649	Pte.	Walters, V. N.
2781	Pte.	Haydon, G.	1465	Sergt.	Knight, E.
3441	Pte.	Bartlett, R. C.	2223	Pte.	Holbrook, J.
1627	Corpl.	Boughton, J.	2347	Pte.	Lockier, M. C.
2593	L/Cpl.	Over, J.	1656	Pte.	Ryder, E. J.
1726	Pte.	Weaver, F. H.	2465	Pte.	Martin, W. B.
2467	L/Cpl.	Simmons, P.	1820	Pte.	Roche, W.
2490	Pte.	Spiers, J.	1732	Pte.	Wager, H. W.
2639	Pte.	Wright, A. E.	1992	Pte.	Creed, E. D.
2951	Pte.	Merrell, E. W.	2714	L/Cpl.	Stinchcombe, H. T.
2339	Cpl.	Green, W. A.			

PROMOTIONS AND APPOINTMENTS.

2nd Lieut. J. P. Winterbotham. Appointed adjutant, dated 7/10/15.—Promoted Lieutenant 18/11/15.

965	L-Sgt.	Hill, E.	To be Sergt. dated		24/11/15
2293	Cpl.	Field, A. J.	,,	,,	22/12/15
111	L-Sgt.	Speck, P. L.	,,	,,	5/1/16
2557	Cpl.	Norris, C. W.	To be L-Sgt. with pay		5/1/16
1920	,,	Jackson, A.	,,	,,	24/11/15
2272	L-Cpl.	Reeves, F. W.	To be Corpl., dated		24/11/15
2404	,,	Fowler, R.	,,	,,	22/12/15
2562	,,	Ricketts, G. H.	,,	,,	27/12/15
2075	,,	Wheeler, G. H.	,,	,,	29/12/15
1557	,,	Rice, A.	,,	,,	5/1/16
1980	Pte. (L-C.)	Stone, A.	To be L-C with pay		10/11/15
1386	,,	Davis, F.	,,	,,	16/11/15
2726	,,	Washbourne, W. P.	,,	,,	24/11/15
2697	,,	Middlecote, H.	,,	,,	4/12/15
2512	,,	Minnett, H.	,,	,,	22/12/15
2709	,,	Saunders, E. C. S.	,,	,,	27/12/15
2715	,,	Sysum, S.	,,	,,	8/1/15
2621	,,	Bromage, W.	,,	,,	29/12/16
2322	,,	Harding, W. M.	,,	,,	3/1/16
2315	,,	Jackson, L. E.	,,	,,	5/1/16
2493	Pte.	Blackwell, E. S.	To be L-Cpl. without pay dated		11/1/15
2516	,,	Gough, T. W.	,,	,,	11/1/16
3343	,,	O'Neil, C.	,,	,,	11/1/16
1363	,,	Hopkins, W. C.	,,	,,	9/12/15
1200	,,	Bennett, A. C.	,,	,,	9/12/15
2754	,,	Etherton, G. H.	,,	,,	16/12/15
2067	,,	Mitford, H. J.	,,	,,	9/12/15
2629	,,	Challenger, A. E.	,,	,,	8/1/16
1976	,,	Wilcox, S. J.	,,	,,	8/1/16
2635	,,	Wood, S. C.	,,	,,	8/1/16
2579	,,	Dennis, A.	,,	,,	16/12/15
2670	,,	Egerton, W.	,,	,,	8/1/16
2705	,,	Rea, W.	,,	,,	11/1/16

CASUALTIES.

405 Sergt. Bishop, P. C. Wounded Accidentally 19/12/15
3051 Pte. Wasley, A. Wounded (Slight, at duty) 30/12/15

No. 10.   MARCH 12, 1916.

5th Gloucester Gazette.

A Chronicle. serious and humorous, of the Battalion while serving with the
BRITISH EXPEDITIONARY FORCE.

TO THE KAISER—Confidentially.

I met a man—a refugee
    And he was blind in both his eyes, Sir,
And in his pate
    A silver plate
(' Twas rather comical to see !)
    Shone where the bone skull used to be
Before your shrapnel struck him, Kaiser,
    Shattering in the self same blast
(Blind as a tyrant in his dotage)
    The foolish wife
Who risked her life,
    As peasants will do till the last,
Clinging to one small Belgian cottage.

That was their home.   The whining child
    Beside him in the railway carriage
Was born there, and
    The little land
Around it (now untilled and wild)
    Was brought him by his wife on marriage.
The child was whining for its mother,
    And interrupting half he said, Sir,
I'll never see the pair again
    Nor they the mother that lies dead, Sir.

That's all—a foolish tale, not worth
    The ear of noble lord or Kaiser,
A man un-named
    By shrapnel maimed,
Wife slain, home levelled to the earth
    That's all.   You see no point ? nor I, Sir,
Yet on the day you come to die, Sir,
    When all your war dreams cease to be
Perchance will rise
    Before your eyes
(Piercing your hollow heart, Sir Kaiser !)
    The Picture that I chanced to see
Riding (we'll say) from A to B.
                   F. W. H.

ON LEAVE.

IT was delightful to be home, of course. First time too. So I sallied forth at 11.30 a.m. on the first morning to spread myself a bit—after all we had been in front line trenches for seven long months. I had a few good original jokes too.

The morning was fine, and everything surprisingly as I had left it. The same ancient dog was parading in the sun at the house at the corner. The same ancient man, who always came on Thursdays, was making the day hideous with " Tom Bowling " on the same impossible cornet. The same ancient road man was performing mystic rites with a juicy-looking pat of mud.   I remembered in my childhood wondering why it wasn't good to eat.   I couldn't see any sign of the dashing damsel (the owner, I believe, of the ancient dog) but an earnest young woman in nurse's kit on a bicycle who nearly knocked me down at the crossing may have been she.   It was just as I was wondering about this and looking back that I collided with Mrs. Vic. Mrs. V. is a remarkably good talker. She got off the mark at once.   " So glad to see you, Arthur. How well you look ! What, on leave ? How nice ! And when do you expect to go abroad ?   Soon,

I suppose. I'm afraid you won't look so well after you have been in those dreadful trenches.   Really, I can't think how those poor dears stand it.   Fancy shells bursting all round them day and night, and no pyjamas to sleep in !   Well, good bye, I hope you'll get out soon.   I expect you're looking forward to it " —and off she went.   I took a deep breath, and went on somewhat stunted, but then, I reflected, Mrs. Vic. was not a genius anyhow.

Eventually I laughed and was hailed at the same time by the Vicar.   " Hullo, Brown," quoth he, " What are you doing here ? " I replied that I was " back on leave."   He paused and I could see that he was wondering how to conceal the fact that he hadn't the foggiest notion whether I had been out of England, or not.   " Oh ! " he began, " Let me see. What Regiment are you in ? Oh, yes, the Gloucesters, of course " (making a plunge) " they're abroad aren't they ? "   I told him they were, and had been for seven months.   He looked doubtful.   " I suppose you haven't been in the-er'-firing line yet ? " he queried.   " You have ? really !   O had no idea.   I suppose the trenches are very warm spots. Continual fighting, eh ? Well, well, and when is the war going to end ?   You fellows out there must know much more about it than we do."   I told him I didn't know, and he seemed disappointed.   " One of our wounded tells me the Germans can't last another month.   Such an interesting man with wonderful experiences—an Irishman.   He tells me the stories of German atrocities are perfectly true.   He says himself that he found in a village captured from the Germans during the retreat from Mons, a large case addressed to the Crown Prince and marked immediate and perishable.   When they opened it it was full of children's hands."   He looked at me obviously expecting me to play up, but I felt that Pte. O'Callaghan (that was the wounded man's name) was probably uncappable, and the Vicar hastened on, obviously suspecting me of prevarication.   I felt puzzled, and several sizes smaller.

Still pondering, I spied James. James is a bachelor, and unfit for service, but leads an active life during the war doing a variety of amazing jobs.   He was in a hurry, but crossed the road, and shook me warmly by the hand.   " Heard you'd gone out, old man. How are you ?   I suppose you haven't been in the front line yet ? " I explained, somewhat hopelessly.   " Well, well.   When's the war going to end ?   You ought to know.   Heard the story of that trench at Wipers ? They were so close to the Boches,—so the chap who told me said—that they had one parapet, and took turns at the loop holes.   So long, I must hurry on now."

And so on.   Things went from bad to worse.   I talked to 18 people, of whom 3 asked me when I was going to the front, 9 asked me when we were going into the firing line, and all asked me when the war was going to end.   Finally I met Smith.   " Tell me," he said, " all about the trenches."   " Well, of course," I replied, " We haven't really been in the firing line yet. There is such a demand to be sent into the front line, that there is a long waiting list at G.H.Q. of Battalions waiting their turn. Every month there is a ballot for the privilege, though no Regiment who has not been out at least twelve months can enter. It is wonderful to see the joy when the news comes that a regiment has succeeded. They march up with bands playing, and colours flying— you must have seen the pictures. Bayonets are fixed, and all the fuses of the bombs lighted. Often the bombers, out of sheer light-heartedness throw bombs at each other, and other less fortunate regiments on the road. Soon they pass through the 10th, 9th, 8th, 7th, 6th, 5th, 4th, 3rd, and 2nd lines and reach the goal of their march—the firing line. They are of course shelled all the way. If they are not shelled it is pathetic to see their disappointment. Often they refuse to proceed until a proper baptism of fire is theirs. (Oh, yes, I like shelling. It is a glorious and exhilarating sensation. Any of the London Daily Papers will tell you so). Finally they reach the front line. Often there is a struggle with the Regiment already there, who are of course reluctant to move out. However, fighting begins at once. Every rifle bursts into rapid fire, every bomb is hurled at the hated enemy. The roar of rifles, bombs, shells and minenwerfers is continuous by day and night. Hardly can the men be persuaded to eat, or take a sip of rum. From time to time an attack is made on the German trenches, when the uproar is double. By night the sky is lit up from sea to sea with star-shells. Any of the papers will tell you what a star shell is. So the war goes on day and night. That is what the Official Communiqués mean when they say " On the Western Front all is quiet." Then you should see the dug-outs. Wonderful places they are. The walls are hung with pictures by the most famous artists, and carefully papered. The ceilings are in many cases beautifully frescoed. Baths with hot and cold water are provided. The floor of the trenches themselves are always covered with oil-cloth—provided by the R.E."

Smith was openly interested, but puzzled about something. " I thought the Gloucesters had had some casualties," he remarked. " One lad I heard of, was, I know, shot through the head. I don't understand —— "

" Oh, yes," I replied, " we have had casualties. Not from German bullets, of course—mostly from falling down stairs—terribly dangerous these continental stairs. The man you heard of may have been one of those who committed suicide because he couldn't live always in the firing line."

Smith pondered. I could see his last doubt was removed. " Most interesting," he murmured ; " what you tell me all agrees with those splendid accounts in the Daily Hum. And when will the war end ? " " February 29th, 1917," I answered, and left him pondering.

It was not kind to Smith but I felt better as I walked back home to enjoy a civilised meal and people who did understand.

OUR PORTRAIT GALLERY.

No. 8. Major Waller.

Nonchalantly he stands
   On every step of life
Tapping his legging.

It is just the same
   Whether we're expecting
A Boche attack
   Or Church Parade.

Nothing flusters him. Men
   Confidently go
To do his bidding :
   While he stands there

Revolving stunts ;
   And nonchalantly
Tapping his legging.

F. W. H.

NTH CORPS SUMMARY.

OUR OWN FRONT.

Right Platoon : On the evening of the –th our right group repulsed an attack, estimated at from 10 to 97 strong, by the Germans opposite. A barrage of light frictions and bully beef tins was kept up by the men composing this group, and it is believed that the results exceeded all expectations. Several of the enemy were heard to complain bitterly of the strength of the English line.

Our snipers claim etc., etc.......

Centre Platoon.—At 10.20 a.m. 15th instant, a solitary partridge was observed inside our wire. Two platoons were " stood to " and a heavy tir-de-barrage was put down whilst selected shots with telescopic sights turned their attention to the bird itself. After 400 rounds, signs of fatigue and fright became apparent, and a patrol which issued from Sap X was enabled to bring the partridge in unhurt. Nothing of an incriminating nature was found.

Most of the enemy's fire trench in front of GOO GOO farm appears to have been thrown over the parapet. Baling still continues.

Our machine guns made good practice with a ration party S. S.E. of HITCHY KOO Farm.

Five rockets rapid were fired from the second line trenches opposite the BOATHOUSE at 1.36 a.m. yesterday morning. Nothing untoward happened.

Our snipers claim etc., etc.......

Left Platoon.—Officer's patrols (which leave our trenches thrice nightly regularly) have had some exciting encounters.

A sentry who challenged one of our patrols was handcuffed whilst offering cigars to a sergeant who answered " Freund."

Twenty-three loop-hole plates have been located in the hedge running from the WINDMILL to the Bois de TIZ.

Our snipers claim to have hit three sappers who were wiring the 3rd line.

Loud cheers were heard opposite our left sector on the afternoon of the 18th and shortly after, an officer wearing a green cap with silver-plated peak and bright yellow collar bands looked over.

A deserter was found sleeping on a disused fire platform during the night of the 12th. On being cross-examined he stated that, although he promenaded our wire for two hours the previous night with hands up, no notice was taken of him. Cramp in the arms forced him to return to his own trenches.

POLDHU WIRELESS.

Messrs. Poldhu announce that peace overtures have again been made by Appendrodts' and Schnitzlers' who complained that a continuance of hostilities will seriously jeopardise their ability to show a profit for the past year.

RUSSIAN FRONT.

The great Russian offensive still makes slow progress, despite the mud which, in places, attains a depth of 8 feet. The Germans have evacuated

MUHDSKI, captured by them in January, 1915, April, 1915, and November, 1915, and re-taken by the Russians in March, July and December.

The Germans claim great victories all along their front.

The morale of our troops has never been better. In a recent night raid we captured 87 guns, 4 machine guns, 30,000 prisoners and a member of the Russian ballet taken prisoner last June. This latter was employed by the enemy as physical drill instructor.

ITALIAN FRONT.

An Alpini skirmishing party who removed their boots and socks and scaled a precipitous slope spiked an Austrian Howitzer without casualties. They have since been sent down to the Base with frostbite.

Otherwise no alterations.

PERSIAN FRONT.

A strong patrol of Medes and Persians, whose system of patrolling altereth not, was ambushed by our forces near Ali Baba. Their equipment included cats, for night work presumably.

Serbian Front.
Egyptian Front.
Bulgarian Front. } Bad weather has prevented any further movements.
Montenegrin Front.
Greek Front.

CAPTURED CORRESPONDENCE:

Bonn, Jan. 4, 19——.

Beloved Gottfried. How glad you must be to have met Karl Schnitzel-Wurzel. Everyone is delighted at the good news, but when will it to an end come? The price of food is colossal. Sugar is 20 M. a pound, and bread is issued only on presentation of season tickets. Thank heavens the accursed Russians are at last crushed......

How happy we shall be to welcome you all home as victors.

———— 4. 2.15.
(delayed in post).

......This is too awful to last. We cannot go on and on for longer as we have gone on and on up till now. Little Heinrich was 8 the other day and has been warned that he may be called up any day for service. We have no bread, and in fact everything is short beyond belief.

Information obtained from Hans Lochputz, of the 666th Regt. of Prussian 121st Corps, captured opposite......

Prisoner is a Swede by extraction aged 18. Chest 28 (expanded 29), educated at Wapping and Zurich, employed as a waiter at the Walditz Hotel, London. Size in hats 5 5/8, collar 17, has a slight cast in his port eye, also a port nose. Speaks with a pronounced English accent and was found in possession of several unexpended portions of the day's rations. Says their food is bad by the time they get it up in the trenches. He has had no leave yet and sees no chance of getting it. Has been awarded the Iron Cross 3 times and states that they have no straw in their billets. He considers it is improbable that the war will last for ever. He appeared much impressed by the state of the roads on this side of the line and admits they have nothing like it on their side.

————

High Water, Southampton, 1.1 p.m.
Moon First Quarter, 2nd inst., 10.43 a.m. invisible at Greenwich.
Snow-drops, -drifts, -flakes and -storms in season.

A GLOUCESTERSHIRE LAD.

The Day.

In thunder and thick hail
 Of Death's on-driving storm
The day of battle breaks.

Now earth beneath us shakes
 Threshed with a hellish flail
For granary of the worm.

Lo, here at last the hour
 Wherefore our prayers were said
Whereto my fate has moved.........

God of the living and dead
 O gird us now with power
For all that we have loved!

To his Maid.

Since above Time, upon Eternity
 The lovely essence of true loving's set,
Time shall not triumph over you and me,
 Nor—though we pay his debt—
 Shall Death hold mastery.
Your eyes are bright for ever, Your dark hair
 Hold an eternal shade. Like a bright sword
Shall flame the vision of your strange sweet ways,
 Cleaving the years ; and even your smallest word
Lying, forgotten with the things that were,
 Shall glow and kindle, burning up the days.

The Return.

The unimaginable hour
 That folds away our joys and pain,
Holds not the spirit in its power.
 Therefore I shall come home again—
 (Where ever my poor body lies)—
 And whisper in the Summer trees
Upon a lazy fall and rise
 Of wind : and in day's red decline
Walk with the sun those roads of mine
 Then rosy with my memories.
Though you may see me not, yet hear
 My laughter in the laughing streams—
My footsteps in the running rain...
 For sake of all I counted dear
And visit still within my dreams
 I shall at last come home again.

F. W. H.

————

LT.-COLONEL TARRANT.

We congratulate Lt.-Col. Tarrant on being given the command of the 3/5th and we congratulate the 3/5th on having him for a commander.

Lt.-Col. Tarrant joined the ranks of the old 2nd V. B. G. R. 26 years ago, rose to the rank of Sergeant and was granted a commission in 1898 in the old E. (Cheltenham) Company. He raised and commanded the Cyclist (L) Company, and eventually commanded the Cheltenham detachment of two Companies. He was promoted to Major in 1913. We are happy to know that one whose whole heart and soul has been in the Regiment has been appointed to command the Reserve Battalion, as it will lead to that very close entente between the Service and Reserve Battalions which is so essential.

We wish Col. Tarrant every success in his new appointment.

OUR FIGHTING MEN.

R.E.

We all admire the sapper,
  He is so full of brains ;
He makes the most tremendous sumps
  That keep out all the rain ;
And happy should I be if I
  Could find a dug-out half as dry.

He works both day and night
  With fierce and furrowed brow—
Or, rather watches others work
  And tells them why and how ;
And, with a muffled kind of sob,
  Gives someone else the hardest job.

R.F.A.

The Gunner's on a higher plane—
  His hours are 10 to 3,
He takes a day off when there's rain,
  Because he cannot see.

You find him seated on a knoll,
  Dreaming of range and fuze,
And wishing that the Div. Amm. Col.,
  Were like the widow's cruse.

He loves his little weekly hate,
  And once he's fairly set,
He rarely puts much more than eight
  Rounds through the parapet.

SIGNALS.

The Signal man wears blue and white
  Most gorgeous on his arm,
And causes heaps of fun at night
  By spreading Gas Alarm.

He bangs your wire—a thing I'd hate
  To do behind your back,
And when you gently remonstrate
  He murmurs "A(c) A(c) A(c)."

A.S.C.

Some men I know have billets fine
And motor cars galore,
They live—oh, miles behind the line...
The Army Service Corps.
They often go to A......s
To pass the time away ;
Their life must be one constant grind
To earn their extra pay.

THINGS WE WANT TO KNOW.

Who were the two gallant Captains who took shelter in a 6 ft. deep sump-hole from a flight of " Little Willies " ?

Is there a L/Cpl. in No. 7 Platoon who is responsible for the Orders " By the right, quick forward," and " Pick up arms " ?

Will some chef kindly give the B. Company Cooks (?) a few lessons in Tea-making, or failing this, the recipe ?

What do the Stroud lads think of the letter recently published in their local paper by members of another Battalion ?

Which Sergeant has a unique way of pronouncing the name of Dumas' heroes and was his Company Officer vastly amused when he heard it ?

Who is the Officer who dismounts on the right side of his horse ?

Who is the Officer who wants to take home an exploded bomb ?

If standing to at H. is not better than standing half a dozen at the Café Parisien ?

Who said buildings at H. were being demobilised ?

Who thought of curing a Ham from the Battalion Calf ?

Which Sergeant stated that artillery observers watched a recent bombardment through a pair of strong BICOLOURS ?

Which N.C.O. on a working partly recently asked the way to the " ravenous " and did he mean " rendezvous " ?

What Officer can give us information about a permanent shovel ? Is he in " A " Company ?

Why does the R.E. get (1) Ordinary pay, (2) pay for being Corps Troops, (3) Pay for work done ?

Who put on his sheep-skin as an undershirt ? Is he in No. 2 Platoon ?

Who is the " A " Company Private who asked the way to spell " promenade " in French ?

Is it true the 2/5th are relieving us and going nearer the Fighting Line ?

What did the Duc de G——t say to the M.O. at 2 a.m. ? And what does he think of the M.O.'s H. E. ?

Whether " R. O. Y." was pleased or otherwise when certain members of the Artillery mistook him for an Officer ? Was his acknowledgment of their salute carried out correctly ?

Have the Signal Company really decided to make experiments in crossing parrots with carrier pigeons for the purpose of carrying verbal messages ?

How did the Russian General show his coolness ?

What did " Ginger " say when he found the parcel of eggs were hardboiled when he was trying to break them for an omelette ?

Which N.C.O. of " A " Company sat on a chair in a dug-out for 11½ hours without moving ?

Which Stretcher Bearer said " Here's a dug-out, and there's room for six more ? " Was it a dug-out or a latrine ?

Where the *Daily Mirror* artist saw the Officer " set the fuze " of a rifle grenade ?

Where the *Daily Mirror* artist obtained the photo of " Tommy and his cat in the trenches " seeing that the aforesaid " Tommy " is obviously a member of the A.S.C. ?

Where are the trenches in which the photos were taken ?

If French windows are not very expensive, and whether a certain N.C.O. found that snowballing, although exciting, has its detractions ?

Re Natural History Notes in News Sheet. What's the elephantine accoucheur's fee per month ?

Who's the Derby Recruit who had an appointment and was passed first ? What else did he get through besides the Medical examination ?

Who is the wrecker of " gigs " ? Had he too got his spurs on upside down ?

What " lonely " subaltern forgot to send both wires for his luncheon party when on leave ? Did he get the goods ? Was the bulk up to sample ?

Who was the Officer who asked if it was a " Whizz pink " ?

Who asked for " weak nerves " when all he wanted was " huit œufs " ?

Who was the Officer who dug out the M.O. and his boots ? Is it true that when the boots came out there was a gas alarm ? Or was it the socks ? "

Who was it who sent home an edition of this Gazette, praising it up to the skies, and got the following reply from his wife, " It is very good and nearly vulgar enough to have been edited by you " ?

Who is the Company Commander who, on opening a parcel from home and expecting to find a bottle of Créme de cacao, unearthed a bottle of Eno's wrapped up in a roll of Broncho ? And by the bye, isn't chlorodyne at a premium in the village where this parcel was received ?

If won by the same team three seasons in succession, will the Fanshawe Cup become their property ?

Who is the Arch Wangler ?

Why do " No. 2 Mess " wear smoke helmets at Mess ?

Who is the officer who warmed the whiskey ?

Does every officer dining at " No. 2 Mess " receive a stuffed bird as a souvenir ?

Is it true that the D. A. C. are now adopting tri-hyphenated names ?   Is it a result of their figuring in the Tatler as a " Fine unit in the New Army " ?

Did the warm baths of St. L— revive the tired Major ? Why does he so strongly recommend someone else to take the cure too ?

What happened to the " 4th How. Fish " ? And how much sand was put into the carburettor by the scheming prelate ?

Will the M. G. Company's Lenten penance consist in letting off 1000 less rounds per diem ?

Which Trout in the Brigade rises quickest ?

Who was the subaltern, whose hair would have done credit to a poet, who, when in charge of a Company, reminded them that there was a Battalion Hair-cutting Shop ?

Who was the Officer who took cover in the Corps Line ?

What was the cool thing the Sergeant in A Company did during the recent cold weather ? Would it have been possible in summer ?

Why has so much anti-have bite grease been required at Hdqrs. Mess ? Is it for the feet ?

Why talk about " stunts " when you are on leave, as there are at least 12,000 uninterned aliens ?

How are the " empties " getting on without their faithful friend ?

What does the Padre think of the Russian General ?

Who is the Trench Mortar Battery Officer known as the " Dud King " ? Is it true that when his battery fired 16 rounds, of which 15 were duds, the Germans shouted out, " If you send us over the gun we'll send 'em back to you " ?

Who was the Senior Officer, very irate at being an hour late for dinner and completely lost, who asked a working party in a trench " Pimlico " ? and was answered, " No ! Next bus." What was his answer, if any ?

Who is the Officer who broke a mirror while at the Army School ?

Who is our " Sexton Blake " ? Will he shortly have to report to Scotland Yard for Duty ?

Who cooked two eggs in a frying pan which he had previously greased inside with anti-frost bite grease ?

Which " A " Company Officer found the aim of one of his bombers very effective during a recent snow-ball fight ?

Has his nasal organ resumed work yet ?

Who asked for " six sous de bon-jour," and was that what he really required ?

Did his request bring forth a torrent of " Bon-jour, monsieur's " ?

Whether our editorial staff havr not redoubled their efforts since the 2/5th have issued their mag " The Ghurka " ?

Which Sgt. is now known as the " Fighting Parson " ?

If the experience related to a local newspaper man by a certain Non Com. home on leave, were not a trifle lurid ?

What is the Romance of H— ? Why were the Junior Officers of the Battery ordered to take charge of the suspected Officer ? And WHERE was the Major ? Is the mud guard a comfortable seat ?

What is a Pracon ? Which National History Book was consulted ?

Who is Blanche's Correspondent ?

THE CANTEEN AND KRUPPS.

A soldier does not grow fat, on Army Rations alone :
If he searches the dixies of shackles, he may find a hefty bone.
And when parcels are not regular, and bread a loaf for three,
He tries to fit his uniform with bully-beef and tea.

With prospects like those for a month, they hailed with great delight,
The rumour passed round the trenches, " The canteen opens to-night.
The much splashed troops poured in, to spend their five franc notes,
And peaches and fags were stowed away in pockets of overcoats.

The men bought all the stuff, in unmolested peace.
The profits went up with a rush, and showed a large increase,
But within range of the German gunners, it will be clear to you
That this delightful state of things would shortly be na poo.

One day a German gunner, an evil minded Hun,—
Sighted with great accuracy, and fired his — gun ;
An eight point two came over, and hit the canteen fair,
Spreading it over the landscape, with chocolate everywhere.

Oh, mourn for the pears and peaches, the Woodbines scattered about,
The cake and biscuits vanished, a fearful bloodless rout !
Amidst the awful ruin, satisfaction was derived
And we laughed aloud at the Boche, the BEER had not arrived !

The enterprising steward was not dismayed a bit,
He sold bent tins of sausages, and things not badly hit,
And now down in the cellar, the Huns may strafe away.
He rooks each muddy soldier of all their hard-earned pay.

D. B.

———

BRICKS FROM THE EDITOR'S PACK.

A Field Officer notices that a sentry does not present arms to him as he should, but merely salutes in the ordinary way. The F. O. therefore returns to see what the sentry will do the second time. The sentry still salutes as if he were saluting a junior officer.

F. O. " Is that the order ? "
Sentry : " No sir, it's the slope."
F. O. " Well, how long have you been out ? "
Sentry : " Since Reveille, Sir."

Overheard in the Barn :
" We are going into Reserve, chaps."
" Well, that's one consolidation, then."

Overheard at the Bomb School :
Instructor : " What is in this bomb ? "
Instructed : " Animal and blaspheme."

From an Orderly Room :
" Please impress on all ranks the importance of never being unharmed."

" To C. O.'s. SOLICITOR, Public School, attested, group 19, posted Home Service only ; Colonel R.A.M.C. advises seek POSITION as Hon. Lieut. and Quartermaster Staff Sergeant. Capable : excellent references : motor : motor cycle.
                              Box E. 415."
                              The Times.

" Lady offers ASSISTANCE for few hours daily, to read and write for blinded or incapacitated OFFICER.
                              Box F. 154."
                              The Times.
The above, coming as they do next each other in the Agony Column of *The Times,* January 20th, 1916, might help each other.

Others have been before hand in telling this story. However it is worth repeating.

A senior officer, about to go out and about, discovered that he had no tube helmet. Forthwith he commandeered his servant's. In the course of the morning he came across a man without his tube helmet. Not being satisfied with the replies of the delinquent, he said to the latter: "Take mine, and let me see if you know how to use it correctly." The delinquent took the helmet, undid it, and out came a pair of socks! Tableau!!

It is not a new story, but it is a good instance of quick repartee. At Sandhurst it occurred to some of the cadets to endeavour to pull the Sergeant's leg.

"Number."

"One, Two, Three, Four, Five, Six, Seven, Eight, Nine, Ten, Knave, Queen, King."

Quick as lightning came the order,

"All Court Cards report to the Major at once."

In another Brigade.

"Which way is the wind?"

"From the Brigade, of course."

We are sorry to see that some discharged soldiers have already been compelled to go to the workhouse. The " Daily Mail " instanced three cases a short time ago. We look to the people at home who are to " keep the home fires burning " to see that such things are not allowed to occur. There were quite enough scandals after the South African war.

"Me that have been where I've been,"
"Me that have seen what I've seen."

Men who have stuck it out, have who risked their lives, wrecked their constitutions, and lost their limbs because

"The Hun is at the gate,"

scarcely deserve to be treated in this fashion.

"In time of danger and in time of war
God and the soldier we alike adore.
The danger o'er, the grievance righted,
God is forgotten and the soldier slighted."

It is up to the people of England to create a firm public opinion on this matter. It is after all only fair. We are not asking you at home to send additional parcels, much as we appreciate them, but we do ask you to undertake that the maimed, the halt, the blind, the broken men, men who are perforce the flotsam and jetsam from the cruel waves of war, men who have toiled and moiled in danger that you might live in safety, and in some cases amass some nice war profits, that these men should be cared for now that their usefulness is over and their capacity for wage-earning at a low ebb. Do not let it be said of you that you were ungrateful or that you let slip the opportunity of doing what you could for those who had done so much for you.

Many congratulations to the "Curios," who are "going very strong." They have fully justified our expectation and have not flattered only to deceive. With the experience they have gathered they have ceased to be an experiment. They charm away Trenchitis and rejuvenate the weary. That's the style.

Stories reach us anon of the tales spun in the Bar parlours of heroic deeds that never were done. We did not think that you, of all people, Sergt. H—., would have averred that you tore your Little Mary in the barbed wire, during the first charge. And what's this, we hear, Cressy, about that piece of shrapnel in your eye? You know very well you were out cutting up wood behind the Quartermaster's Stores, and a piece chipped up into your eye. Those

K

sort of yarns may go off like hot cakes in the " Rose and Crown," but we shall not forget you aprés la guerre, when next we meet.

We much regret that the Arch Wangler has received a month.

" I don't think much of this 'ere country, Bill. One 'arf of it be in sand-bags, and t'other 'arf be under water."

FROM ANOTHER BRIGADE.—In the trenches.

Brigadier (Infantry).—" You are very young to be a Colonel."

Colonel (Artillery).—" Oh, I don't know about that, Sir."

Brigadier (Infantry).—" If you were in my Brigade you would be merely a Platoon Commander."

Colonel (Artillery).—" That might be so, Sir, but in the Artillery it is brains that count."

FROM ANOTHER DIVISION.

Bty. Commdr. to Infantry.—" Are they firing on your trenches?"

Infantry.—" Have you no Forward Observing Officers there?"

Battery.—" Yes, but they are sitting on a Board."

Infantry.—" That's all very well, but there'll be a Board sitting on them jolly soon."

We have to lament the departure of one who has carried out the important and onerous duties of Office Boy ever since we acquired our spacious premises in Fleet Street. Sgt. B. Conduit has left us for G. H. Q. He has typed our tortuous handwriting, and what he did not know about the many journalistic coups achieved by this Gazette is scarcely worth recording. Sgt. Turner reigns in his stead.

Now that Newspaper rations are at such a low ebb, will our friends at home please forward as many papers as they conveniently can? We have not really enough to go round, and all ranks are very glad to get hold of something to read.

It is not at all a bad scheme to put an occasional " fat " order with your newsagent. Mrs. Kerr, of the Manor, Dursley, has done that more than once, with the result that a nice bundle of picture and other papers came along. While others—those whom we mention in our list of benefactors—never fail to send a weekly contribution.

We were very glad to receive a copy of " The Ghurka," the Gazette which " A " Company of the 2/5th Battalion have just brought out. It is very well got up and nicely printed. We hope that it will meet with the success that it deserves, and will enjoy an ever increasing circulation. But we fear that " Battalion Orders " if they are to appear each issue, will have to submit to censorship; or the " Battalion Orderly Room " will indeed be " The Lion's Den."

The last few months have witnessed a marked rapproachment between the gunners and the " feet." If the accurate shooting of the guns has won respect, the jolly fellows behind the guns have promoted the camaraderie and mutual understanding that should exist between two branches of the Service which are so inter-dependent upon each other " Right into the cup each time," G. P. Huntley used to say in " The Three Little Maids." Bang, bump, into the trench go the sprightly field guns and the stately Hows. Go on bumping them, boys.

Not a little excitement and considerable amusement was caused by the antics of the Leave-train

Driver as he endeavoured to negotiate the right-angled turn opposite the pond on our Light Railway. However he soon got into the way of things and, for one who obviously had had but slight experience in driving, he showed not a little skill. We hope to see a vast improvement in the pace of the Leave Train. No more nosing about at junctions please, but get along a bit faster. You've spent so much time on the road, that you ought to know the way by this time, Mr. Engine Driver.

Overheard in H............
I do not mind " Right Turn," nor " Left Turn ": I can stick " About Turn " but I can't stand H........

Overheard after 9.15 p.m.
M.P. " What's that light doing there " ?
Voice from Barn : " Burning you......, of course "

Good luck ! Welsb old boy We hadn't known you a long time but we were all very fond of you and shall follow your career with interest. Cheer Oh !

" The old order breaketh up." As O. C. Publication Department, Major Tarrant rendered invaluable assistance, not the least being that of protecting the Editor from being lynched by the maligned, the libelled, the rejected (and therefore infuriated) poets, as well as that of spotting " printer's errors." He was about to take over the command of the 3/6th Battalion, when he was posted to the 3/5th, and therefore is really still very much in touch with " The Fifth." While all ranks congratulate him on obtaining a promotion to a command as responsible as it is coveted, it is not too much to say that they will miss him very much. They know, however, that he has only gone to inspire " The Third " with the traditions of " The First " line, so that the former may the more easily take their place besides their more experienced comrades, not untutored in the arts of war, and permeated with the same dogged determination to " stick it."

THE SOLILOQUY OF AN OLD SOLDIER

You need not watch for silver in your hair,
  Or try to smooth the wrinkles from your eyes,
Or wonder if you're getting quite too spare,
  Or if your mount can bear a man your size.

You'll never come to shirk the fastest flight,
  To query if she really cares to dance,
To find your eye less keen upon the sight,
  Or lose your tennis wrist or golfing stance.

For you the music ceased on highest note,
  Your charge has won, you'd scattered them like sand,
And then a little whisper in your throat
  And you asleep, your cheek upon your hand.

Thrice happy fate, you met it in full cry,
  Young, eager, loved, your glitt'ring world all joy—
You ebbed not out, you died when tide was high.
  An old campaigner envies you, my boy.

O. C. A. CHUD.

CHAPLAIN'S COLUMN.

The Deputy Chaplain General, The Right Reverend Bishop Gwynne, of Khartoum, paid a very welcome visit to the Division on Sunday, Feb. 27th. He held Confirmation Services, at one of which some members of this Battalion were con-firmed. He has promised to come again, when we hope that he will be able to spend more time with us.

Endeavours have been made of late to put into some sort of repair the French graves which lie scattered about in our Brigade area. In not a few cases the crosses have disappeared, and often there is nothing to read or decipher on those that remain.

A good bit of work has been done in the cemetery. Graves have been returfed, paths made and the whole railed off.

A suggestion has been made that members of this Battalion might like to follow the example of other units and contribute a regular sum—however trifling—towards the maintenance of our unfortunate fellow soldiers who are prisoners in the miserable German prison camps, and are living on very scanty and bad food. The Chaplain will be only too glad to forward any sums that may be sent him for this purpose.

LINES TO A DUG-OUT.

With sunset's ray again day's task is done,
The trenches clean, the night's work not begun.
An hour's sleep. Perchance it may be nice
To cook a frugal supper, mid mud and rats and mice.

The Sergeant's voice is heard. What ! No fatigue to-night ?
(Ten hours of rest and sleep. A real delight.)
Yet, may be, carrying planks, revetting down Trench Revel,
A boring job if fine ; if wet, the very devil.

Our dug-out's warm, yet oft times full of smoke.
Is't French Briquettes, or even English coke ?
And so we pass the live long days, until reliefs arrive.
The —th Battalion, last time up, a rest from long trench life.

ADVERTISEMENT.

SOUVENIRS FOR ALL

Read these testimonials :

" Company Cook " writes : I used to be unable to stoop ; in your circus I can bend and duck readily.'

" Indigestion " : ' I can always get wind up in your performance.'

" A. S. C. " : ' I always write my letters by the light of your shells bursting round me.'

———

Front Seats . . . **Free**
Back Seats . . . **One franc**
Cellars (reserved) . **3 guineas**

(furnished with every convenience.)

———

TO SLACKERS.

I hope I'll ne'er get leave again
To see the English flapper swain,
With trousers creased and swishy cane,
    In mufti.

When England's empire is at stake,
When brave men die for England's sake
Why should these " Pip-squeaks " poodlefake
    In mufti ?

Lord Derby's scheme is loopholed wide
For cowards with conscience, or with pride
Of Wilson's tap, to 'scape and hide
    In mufti.

When this war's o'er, and peace has come
For future wars let's swear it " some "
That all shall share the " tot of rum "
    In khaki !

No use to hang on apron strings
Or say their job's munitioning
They'll take their part in the real thing
    In khaki.

                                G. F. C.

———

THE " CONSCIENTIOUS " SHIRKER.

The Conscientious Shirker
Slanders fighting as a sin ;
His duty to his King implies,
His duty to his skin

He need not be a combatant
If conscience bars the way ;
And the conscience of the shirker
Is the voice of self to-day.

True patriots for principles
Their lives would gladly give ;
The false for quibbles, creeds and qualms
Would much prefer to live.

And since the verb " to kill " should not
Be " actively " fulfilled,
What better could the slacker do
Than " passively " be killed.

Some parents give their sons without
A murmur to the war ;
And others give their influence
To keep them where they are.

To such it seemeth good and well
That fairest flowers should die
While worthless weeds and noxious seeds,
Should grow and fructify.

From outpost of the Empire
Troops the Anzac to the flag.
And scornful wave their emu plumes.
At laggards where they lag.

They know no country here below,
The Army Corps of cranks,
And reap the fruits of liberty
Without returning thanks.

For men will prate and men will preach
And prophesy and dream,
But aye there comes the vital day,
When fighting is supreme.

And save for those who kept the gate,
When warring heathen rage.
How few the sweets for freeman left
In Freedom's heritage.

Britannia rules the guardian waves,
And trusts her sailor sons
If Jack could have his way he'd ship
The shirkers to the Hun.

———

OUR BENEFACTORS.

Miss Parr.	Papers.
Miss Backhouse.	,,
Mrs. Kerr.	,,
Mr. W. R. Voller.	,,
Canadian Field Comfort Commission.	,,
Lieut. Col. Marling.	,,
Lieut. Col. L. Winterbotham.	,,
Mrs. Temple Cooke.	,,
Dickens Fellowship, Gloucester Branch.	Books.
Mr. Jack Margetson.	Woodbines.
Mr. T. R. Pritchard.	Cigarettes.
Camps Library.	Books, Magazines, Papers.
Bishop Frodsham.	Papers.
Colonel Griffith.	Mouth Organs, Books.

———

GRENADIERS.

The undermentioned N. C. O's. and men have passed the test laid down for Grenadiers.

2717	Sgt.	Thompson, R. O.	1748	Pte.	Iles, J. C.
2893	Pte.	Brooks, E. O.	1663	L/Cpl.	Abel, J.
1859	Pte.	Baker, J.	2584	Pte.	Hopkins, P. J.
2716	Pte.	Tandy, F.	2636	Pte.	Wilson, A. G.
2520	Pte.	Merchant, A. H.	1395	Pte.	Workman, H.
2701	Pte.	Phelps, F.	1928	Pte.	Pugh, F. E.
499	Sgt.	Webb, C. H.	2955	Pte.	Parker, H.
2542	L/Cpl.	Holland, J.	2784	Pte.	Powell, W. H.
2871	Pte.	Reed, S. F.	238	Sgt.	Huxford,
2833	Pte.	Harris, E. J.	2155	Pte.	Smith, J. E.
392	Sgt.	Finch, F.	2665	Pte.	Collerick, H.
3312	Pte.	Holtham, A. E.	1192	Pte.	Newman, G. E.
2663	Pte.	Burlton, W.	2518	Pte.	Ingles, W.
2115	Pte.	Doyle, B.	2603	Pte.	Hopkins, H.

———

PROMOTIONS AND APPOINTMENTS.

EXTRACT from LONDON GAZETTE dated 23/2/16. 3/5th Battalion Gloucestershire Regiment.

Major John Frederick Tarrant, from 1/5th Battalion Gloucester Regiment, to be Temporary Lieutenant-Colonel, dated 7-3-16.

Extract from supplement to the LONDON GAZETTE of 25th February dated 26th February, 1916.

The South Wales Borderers.

Lieutenant Arthur Conrad Robert Welsh from the Gloucestershire Regiment, T. F., to be Second Lieutenant.

Second Lieutenant A. C. R. Welsh, to be Lieutenant (temporary) dated January 11th, 1916.

From Battalion Orders Part II.

1139	L/Sgt. Harris, F., to be Sergt.	dated	14/1/16
1628	L/Sgt. Jackson, R. C.,	,,	8/2/16
2557	L/Sgt. Norris, C. W., to be A/Sergt.	,,	11/1/16
1629	Corpl. King, A. D., ,,	,,	11/1/16
2331	Corpl. Chandler, G. W., to be L/Sgt. with pay	dated	31/1/16
2487	Corpl. Abbott, W. J.,	,,	14/1/16
1550	L/Cpl. Welch, H., to be Corpl.	,,	14/1/16
2467	L/Cpl. Simmons, P.,	,,	31/1/16
1069	L/Cpl. Spencer, E. J., to be A/Cpl.	,,	11/1/16
2348	L/Cpl. Philpotts, F.	,,	11/1/16
2091	L/Cpl. Coton, J., ,,	,,	11/1/16
2714	Pte. (L/C.) Stinchcombe, H. T., to be L/Cpl. with pay	dated	14/1/16
2579	,, Dennis, A. ,, ,,	,,	16/1/16
2516	,, Gough, T. W. ,, ,,	,,	31/1/16
1441	,, Steel, W. G. ,, ,,	,,	12/1/16
2729	,, Wise, R. ,, ,,	,,	13/1/16
2486	,, Pepperell, W. F., to be Actg. L/Cpl. with pay	dated	11/1/16
2480	,, Smart, S. ,, ,,	,,	11/1/16
2558	,, Paynter, W. F. L. ,, ,,	,,	11/1/16
2748	,, Brien, C. ,, ,,	,,	11/1/16
2366	,, Maddock, W. H. ,, ,,	,,	11/1/16
2376	Pte. Horlick, R. A., to be L/Cpl. without pay	dated	20/1/16
2386	,, Payne, H. A. ,, ,,	,,	20/1/16
2892	,, Voller, H. W. ,, ,,	,,	20/1/16
1556	,, Bundy, W. ,, ,,	,,	31/1/16
1527	,, Sproat, A. L. ,, ,,	,,	31/1/16
2767	,, Parham, W. G. ,, ,,	,,	31/1/16
2711	,, Smith, F. C. ,, ,,	,,	31/1/16
2364	,, Lee-Williams, O. ,, ,,	,,	31/1/16
2669	,, Dovey, W. ,, ,,	,,	31/1/16

CASUALTIES.

KILLED.

| 2481 | Pte. Adams, E. A. | | 25/1/16 |

WOUNDED.

1027	Pte.	Midwinter, J. P.		9/2/16
1527	Pte. (L/Cpl.)	Sproat, A. L. (Slight)		10/2/16
1976	Pte. (L/Cpl.)	Wilcox, S. J.		12/2/16
2728	Pte.	White, A. J. (Slight)		13/2/16
2114	Pte.	Clarke, C. J. (Shell Shock)		8/2/16
3161	Pte.	Pike, A. R.	..	10/2/16
2766	Pte.	Milne, W. J.	..	10/2/16
2542	Pte. (L/Cpl)	Holland, J.	..	10/2/16
661	Sgt.	Chapman, H.	..	11/2/16
1791	Pte.	Price, E. D.	..	14/2/16

Previously officially reported missing, now unofficially reported Prisoner :—

| 1989 | Bingham. W. C. | Official List | February 26, 1916 |

R.I.P.

2481   Pte. Adams, E. A.

There was a widespread feeling of regret among his old comrades in " A " Company and in the hearts of those who were Lewis Gunners with him, when it was known that Pte. E. A. Adams had been killed instantly beside his gun just before his relief was due. Unselfish—he always thought of others before he considered himself—invariably cheery, he has left behind him happy memories which will be cherished by a multitude of friends.

One who knew him well writes. " Always willing to do all or more than his share, and ever ready with words of sound advice, he was loved and is now sadly mourned by those who were honoured with his friendship. We realise now his true worth and how great is the gap caused by his death.''

5th Gloucester Gazette.

A Chronicle, serious and humorous, of the Battalion while serving with the
BRITISH EXPEDITIONARY FORCE.

APRIL, 1915—APRIL, 1916.

There is always something memorable in connection with an anniversary. Another year in the life of somebody, or another page of history written. It forms, as it were, a landmark.

"———," our starting point, the milestones tells us is " X kilomètres." But how many kilomètres is it to Berlin ? That " ridiculous " March to Berlin is coming off some day, Mr. Press-Croaker, though it may not take place till peace is declared. How many kilomètres to Berlin ? That's what we want to know.

It is now 12 months since the GAZETTE was launched on its adventurous career. How many more years of glorious life will add fresh lustre to its escutcheon ? Subscribers of Five Francs " for the Duration " may well turn over in their minds the question as to whether they will be " up " or " down " on their bargain. It may be even now rather a near thing, seeing that all such subscribers get their money's worth if they secure 17 copies—we only wish we had more back numbers to supply them with —and this Number is No. 11 ! Or, on the other hand, it may not. Quien sabe ? In any case, it is perhaps a matter for congratulation that the circulation has risen from the paltry, but now priceless, 50 copies of April, 1915, to the creditable 1550 of April, 1916, so that we can still, with truth, repeat our boast that our circulation is greater than that of any other threepenny paper in our area.

Seeing that gratitude, like the milestone, both looks back on the past with satisfaction, and looks forward towards the future with anticipation, we will take this opportunity of thanking all those contributors who have helped in the task—and the Quartermaster will tell you it was no small one—of hauling the Editorial valise along summer's dusty roads, and winter's slippery trenches, especially Lieutenants Harvey, King and C. W. Winterbotham —for they, indeed, have made the bricks while providing their own straw—in the hope that they will, with many others, " carry on," and that, while they wear the laurels of Literature, they may win further distinction on the Field of Fame.

F. T. BLANK BLANK.

A whisper wandered around
    Of a plan of the G. O. C.'s,
And figures surveyed the ground
    In stealthy groups of threes ;
But the whole Brigade was there
    Or pretty well all the lot,
When we dug a trench at Never-mind-where
    On April the Never-mind-what.

The What's-a-names dug the trench,
    The Who-is-its found the screen,
And we mustn't forget to mench
    The Thingumies in between ;
The Tothermies built the fence
    And the R. E.'s " also ran,"
For we didn't spare any expense
    With labour a shilling a man.

There isn't much else to tell,
    Though the enemy made a song
And tried to blow it to Hell,
    But got the address all wrong,
For you'll find it is still out there
    In the bally old self-same spot !
That trench which we dug at Never-mind-where
    On April the Never-mind-what.

W. O. D.

APRIL—FRANCE AND ENGLAND.

It was a real Spring morning—at last. Not merely a matter of sunshine and blue sky, but a day with hope astir, and a smell of life in the air itself. But being in the trenches, and having been up a large part of the night, I had only thought that it looked as if the snow had gone for good, and that later in the day the Artillery, German and English, would probably enjoy themselves. I could picture the Bosch Gunner Officers finishing a hearty breakfast, and rubbing their hands together cheerfully—just as ours were doing at the prospect of abundant targets. However, I stumbled towards my dug-out, feeling quite content that another night was over and my ration of sleep at hand.

Then I stopped to notice a wren singing with amazing shrillness in a bush covered with golden catkins. That set me thinking how green the grass was in the little orchard through which the trench ran, and I noticed that the ruined hedge was quite covered with fragile little leaves. So I began to think of England, and realise that it was April, and then overhead I saw an aeroplane. It was that which made me think of trout-fishing, for the bi-plane against the blue of the sky had just the transparent appearance that a trout in good condition has when you see him from above in a clear stream with sun shining through on to the gravel bed. So my thoughts turned to a split cane rod which it is a joy to handle ; to the music of the reel ; to the grace of the tapered line gliding out, and to the flicker of a well-thrown fly before it drops lightly on the stream. As I pulled empty sandbags over my feet, and laboriously screwed myself between the blankets, I sighed remembering April mornings like this when I and Nat had foregathered on a Cotswold trout stream. It seemed distant as a dream of heaven, and much too good ever to have happened. For Nat, best of fishermen and good friends, has gone where those who love peace (as he did) will assuredly find it, and there also we are told there is a very lovely river, " clear as crystal," though trout are not specifically mentioned. So I went to sleep amidst the endless scrambling and squeaking of the rats and mice. But now I seemed to be awake and full of an amazing cheerfulness—the joyful anticipation of sure happiness. Then I realised that I was in a Cotswold village on a perfect April morning of warm wind and sun, and high white clouds against a blue sky. Also I knew that the whole peaceful day lay before me, that a stream I knew and loved was mine to fish, and that Nat was with me again. It was early yet, and there would be no rise for another hour and a half at least, but all things were ready. I had had the best of breakfasts, my tackle was all in order, and my rod glinted in the sunlight where it stood spiked into the green lawn in front of the Inn. So now I could lean over the grey stone bridge and thank God who made me with eyes, ears and nose, and let me live on such a day.

For the village lies along a little valley which wanders with the stream through a bold, open, upland country. The stream runs beside the village street until they part company, and orchards take the place of the road where the waters make a wide bend under a copse of beech and ash growing up a steep slope. So all the valley and grey stone village is full of the music of running water, and this morning there is little sound else.

The children are in school, and the men out on the hills at work. An occasional voice, the clink of a bucket, or the clucking of a hen, are all that is audible of the life of the village. But from the fields above there comes the distant bleating of sheep and lambs ; in the beech copse a rookery is enjoying some crowded life, and occasionally the cry of a nesting plover carried to the bridge. Through all runs the music of the stream, and of the clear lime-stone springs that feed it.

At present its waters slip along with no rings to break its swirls and glides, and proclaim the rising trout only a water vole swims across just below me, and plops nervously under, on seeing the figure on the bridge. Underneath the right-hand arch lives an aged ruffian of a trout, black and scarred, uncatchable, and darkly suspected of cannibalism, though fond of bread crumbs. I amuse myself looking for signs of his nose, which can sometimes be seen poking cannily out of cover. But he is not showing up, so·my eyes watch instead the wonderful dance of the water weeds. It goes on for ever. Hard not to believe that these swaying rippling streamers of green are not alive. There is an influence almost hypnotic in their everlasting movement in water so clear that you cannot see it. Then Nat joins me on the bridge with his morning lecture on the advantage of trying one's own flies—at which he has been busy most of last night, and ever since breakfast. I tell him that life isn't long enough and point out what he has been missing. He accuses me of being frivolous and launches out on the inevitable discussion of " What will they take to-day." The hot debate rages over Tups Indispensables, and the whole family of Duns—olive, grey, and blue, and ends as usual in strong disagreement. And so we wish each other " Tight Lines," and off to our respective beats. Mine is in the orchards along the bend under the beeches on the horse-shoe slope, where the clamour of the rookery rages merrily. So I stroll leisurely down the sunny street, stopping now and then to look into the clear water over the low stone parapet that buttresses the footpath. It is good, too, just to breathe the air which is full of faint sweet scents. There is nothing doing yet ; only a moorhen picks her way along the bank with comic jerks of her head and neck. But I know where my fish will be— by Mayfly time he would be 1¼lbs. or more—but I want him to-day, and guess that he will clear the pound. So I look for him on his feeding ground, and as I look, a grey shadow appears in the right place just below the little thorn bush over the gravel that shows between the weed bed and the far bank. He is not feeding yet, for he is not on the surface, but he is only waiting for the fly to come down. So I sit under an apple tree and listen to the Hallelujah Chorus of the rooks, and watch some placid rabbits skipping about among the Marsh Marigolds on the opposite bank of the stream, and a still more placid water vole grooming his face with his fore-paws. There are some wood pigeons too, who leave the high beech tops with a sudden clatter of wings flying upwards, and then, breast out and wings steady, plane

across to the high trees of the old Manor House beyond the church tower. At last there is a splash, a little trout's undignified rise. But he has risen at a fly, and some more follow—fine olive duns— gliding and circling in the maze of water eddies. I look for my fish (called by me " Charles ") and he has risen to the surface ready for business I can see him now—every fin and almost every spot. Presently a fly comes circling over him. He tilts up and flashes forward, taking it indeed with a greediness that warms my heart. Two more he has in peace, and then I creep up well behind him feeling not a little tense. The reel screeches merrily as I get the line out, and then too hurriedly I make the cast. The fly falls two feet out, and the only question is whether Charles will be badly scared, for the fly will certainly be dragging before it reaches him. And so it is. Just as he had tilted up his head for a rise, Charles saw the first telltale ripple round the fly as the catgut-cast and line were caught by the faster current of the nearer waters. Even so, he followed it down longingly, and snapped at it from a safe distance in disgust. He then slinks perceptibly lower and takes no notice of three healthy Olive Duns that pass over him one after the other. Plainly he wants a rest, so I light a pipe and wait.

Charles is busy again, so now for a second attempt. The rise is at its height, the flies are coming down in flotillas at a time, and all the reach is broken by the rings and ripples of rising fish. A ridiculous sparrow is inspired to masquerade as a swallow, makes a complete fool of itself, and chirps proudly about it. Less hastily this time, I get my line out, and when I let the fly go for it, behold it is that rare thing (for me), a perfect cast. The fly floats to an inch, and I know in that glorious moment that my olive dun will pass over Charles perfectly, and that Charles must surely be mine if he rises. The fly falls down, surely Charles must see it now. There is nothing in the world for me but that little speck of grey flotsam and the long trout by the weeds. Then just as I am thinking that Charles is going to fail me, with a drive of his tail up he goes surely and confidently. I can see the white of his open mouth and a flash of bronze and silver in the sun, and then my line and rod make one quivering curve and the smooth waters are broken into foam by Charles' thwarted rush for his stronghold in the bank under the thorn bush. For me it is a moment of victory— an ecstasy to remember even in dark hours. Now he is in the net, and in another moment—the sunny land and flashing water slide from me ; the music of the water is jangled and confused, and out of chaos emerges a human voice, " Nearly 1.30, Sir " " Time to get up."

The glory is departed.—How could my rat-ridden dug-out be glorious, anyhow ? The day has clouded, and as I crawl out feeling liverish and peevish, a light drizzle begins to fall.

And so to lunch, and—sight to shudder at—dear heap of tinned salmon. Was it ever part of a fish, a mighty vivid creature, master of the frozen Northern rivers ?

<hr />

WHAT GOD SAID.

" This be a lesson " said life with a frown
As it knocked me down.
And " Serve him right," cried the goodly men.
While I—I picked myself up and then
    With all my prospects looking blue
Went on just as I used to do.
But the good God smiled as he shook His head
" It's a troublesome child " said He " But yet
Not quite so altogether dead
As those solemn old fools that laughed. Don't fret."
(At least , I think that's what He said).

TRIOLET.

The snaring of dreams
Is a delicate sport.
How simple it seems—
  The snaring of dreams :
Till you find all the gleams
On the wonder you've caught
Dead. Snaring of dreams
Is a delicate sport.

A PHILOSOPHY.

Only in pages of men's books I find
Swart villain and fair knight
Closing in fight.
Not piebald is mankind
The soul is hued to such swift varying
As flying hornet's sunshine-smitten wing.

Therefore, dear brother men (where'er ye be)
Who strive for right
With such short sight
'Tis wise for little folk like you and me
Neither too much to praise nor yet to blame
Since in our different ways we're all the same.

OUR PORTRAIT GALLERY.

No. 9. F.W.H.

A thick-set dark haired dreamy little man
  Uncouth to see
Revolving ever this preposterous plan—
  Within a web of words spread cunningly
To tangle life—no less.
(Could he expect success ?)

Of life he craves not much, except to watch.
  Being forced to act,
He walks behind himself, as if to catch
The motive :—An accessory to the fact
Faintly amused, it seems,
Behind his dreams.

Yet hath he loved the vision of this world
  And found it good.
—The faith, the fight 'neath Freedom'd Flag unfurled,
  The friends, the fun, the army brotherhood.
But, being crazed or worse
He turns it all to verse.

                                   F. W. H.

AN ODE TO THE " CHARGE " OF THE TRENCH MORTAR.

Half a Gun ! Half a Gun ! Just a
    Trench Mortar
All down our beastly trench,
    Grimly they loiter,
Stormed at with shot and shell
Minnies, Six-inch as well ;
" Isn't this b———— hell ? "
    Say the Trench Mortar.

When the emplacement's made
With pick and shovel, spade
Many a man's dismayed
    In the In*fantry*.
For when they've laid their gun
And fired their only " one "
WE get back ten to one
    Into our " pantry ! "

Each time they try to fire
We say " Not here, good Sire,"
And raise their ruddy ire,
    For we are averse ;
But with persistence rare
They seek another lair
Pooping their shell in air,
    From the next traverse.

At last with heaving sigh
They shoot their shell on high,
For the Hun trench they try,
    To spill the Boche blood !
Was there a Hun abashed ?
Was there a German smashed ?
Short of their wire it crashed
    Na pooh ! It's a dud !

Observing with faces set,
Saying, " We'll strafe 'em yet
If only more shells we get,
    Than one " diurnum,"
There comes a German yell
From the spot where it fell,
" Send us the gun as well
    And we'll return 'em."

Now their day's work is done,
Seizing their strafing gun
Back from their post they run
    Out of the trenches,
Out of the range of shell
Out of the mouth of hell
Into their billets,—well
    Back to their wenches !

                                   G. F. C.

WAR, MODERN WAR.

'Ave yer ever carried rations to the trench at dead of night,
When yer curses and yer grumbles,
Yer trips, and then yer stumbles,
And falls down in a 'eap, when a star shell shines out bright ?
    That's war, modern war.

'Ave yer ever been on sentry, when the 'ours they seem like
    weeks,
When yer curses and yer swears,
Yer grip yer gun and stares
Out in the thick black darkness, when its only rats that
    squeak ?
    That's war, modern war.

'Ave yer ever been for water, when it's mor'n a mile to go,
And yer cusses and yer fumbles,
With the pump, which loudly grumbles,
And seems to tell the 'Uns yer there, and the bullets whistle
    low ?
    That's war, modern war.

'Ave yer ever been out listening, when the night's as black
    as 'ell,
And yer cusses at a tree trunk,
And yer feels, well, in a blue funk,
Fer a minute, then yer laughs, and yer mates yer never tell ?
    That's war, modern war.

'Ave yer ever 'eard the screaming of a shell up in the air,
And yer cusses, when it's nearer,
And nothing else seems dearer
Than yer life ! She butts ahead ! The devil did y'care !
    That's war, modern war.

'Ave yer been out with a party, in the dark and in the rain,
And yer cuss when with a thud,
Yer slips 'eadlong in the mud
And yer've got another 'our to go on digging just the same ?
    That's war, modern war.

Yes ! its war, just modern war,
When the rations yer are lugging,
And yer breaks the water jar,
When the rats squeak in the bushes,
And the fireworks sky 'igh rushes,
When yer smothered up from head to toe,
With thick, grey, slimy mud,
When yer mate gets 'it beside yer,
And yer splashed up with his blood.
That's when yer 'now yer in it,
And yer out to reach the limit,
And ye'll " carry on " and win it,
Well ! that's war, just modern war.

OUR BENEFACTORS.

Citizens of Gloucester, per The Mayor
800 Tommies Cookers.
Mr. Berkeley Powell   Papers.
Mrs. Russell Kerr   ,,
Mrs. Temple Cooke   ,,
Mr. W. R. Voller   ,,
Miss Parr   ,,
Miss Backhouse   ,,
Miss Grace Armstrong   Magazines.
Canon Brewster   Hymn Sheets.
Camps Library   Magazines and Papers.
Lt. Col. Winterbotham   Papers.
Bishop Frodsham   ,,
Lt. Col. Marling   ,,
Canadian Field Comforts Commission   ,,
South Zeal Working Party—per Mrs. Cann
and Miss Tucker   Comforts.
" Daily Express Cheery Fund "
Cards, Mouth Organs and Boxing Gloves.
Mr. Harley Butt   Tobacco.

" CHAOS."

'Tis evening o'er the trenches.
  The silent sentinels stand
Thinking of home and loved ones
  As they gaze o'er No-man's land.

The night is still and eerie
  And the moon from behind the clouds
Makes the lank and ghostly pollard trees
  Look like dead men in their shrouds.

Of a sudden the silence is shattered
  By a deafening crash of sound !
Liquid fires courses through the trenches,
  Bursting metal hurtles around ;

The trenches are full of panting
  Multitudes trying to pass,
Whilst from the void behind them
  Comes the hiss of escaping gas.

Be not alarmed, O reader mild,
  'Tis caused by no Hunnish lust
But rather one of the Gloucesters
  Whose Primus Stove has " Bust."

J. S. P.

TO A CHILD.

All that God wills for you I pray you know,
Love and delight of this green joyous earth,
Innocent thoughts as white as winter snow,
Content of heart and the red wine of mirth.
'Ere they depart as last year's swallows flew,
Wild song of gladness let the days sing you.
I pray sweet things upon you, yet I'd have
No stagnant pool of pleasure mar your life.
Troubled and dancing in diviner strife.
Each day shall be to you a tribute wave
Royally set towards a farther shore.

F. W. H.

YE MERRIE GLEVUM YEOMEN.

We have been fortunate enough to acquire from a well known historian details of an inspection, held just before the battle of Agincourt, of " A " Muster of the 1/5th Glevum Archers, its chief muster(d) Commander being present.

" Ho, ye varlets, odd's bodikins. What is this I see ? Bowyer Watt with his jerkin undone ! Thou art half naked, Sirrah.

String me him, Sergeaunt, to yon sapling oak, then strike him on the withers thrice, with thy pikestaff.

By my halidom, how now ? Archer Dicken, thy clothyard shaft is but two feet length. In truth a sorry sight, by my fay. An he mend it not, within the coming hour, mark you, Sergeaunt, he will e'en clean the muck from yon stables for the space of two long and weary hours, in the company of Bowyer Llewellyn. A Menial job, in sooth, fit alone for those cravens who would secure for themselves the safety of old England's shores, rather than face such dangers as appertains to this grand emprise and high adventure.

'Sdeath, Sergeaunt. Are my men to port themselves, like women-folk, with unshorn locks lying greasily on their sleek necks, harbouring the very pests we would heartilie avoid ! Out upon them for lousy lechers. See to it that the swift shears of one Mytteforde are busy anon.

Byr Lakin ! Pikeman Perkin, thy jerkin is lurking behind thy baggage. Place me him in the stocks and shower upon him eggs of scant value, first stripping him of his habiliments, which our noble King hath right royally equipped him withal. A murrain on him and ekeall such !

THE SENTRY —

AS THEY PICTURE HIM AT HOME

AND

AS HE IS

And thou, Pikeman Rogers, seemingly hast lost thy stoup of mead, thy venison pastie and thy bag of oats which are given thee against the time of grievous necessity. Hast thou indeed bartered them upon thy housing dame in mart for such consolaciouns as she hath no right to proffer ? "

" O gracious Master Commander, these were but stolen from me with subtletie by the goodman of the house of my sojourn, what time I did busy myself with burnishing of my arrow heads."

" Sergeaunt, look to it that his monies be lessened by one groat, wherewithal to replace the losses.

" Now, my merrie men, our great leader hath this day bidden me go forward stoutly in small parties by which the easier to cozen the enemy of our approach, and to minish our losses from arrows of our adversaries. Verilie these our strategems afford certaine promise of bringing to our armies great prowess and glorious victory, whereby our enemies will be mightilie discomfited and sore smitten. Have a care ye wander not in your journeyings, for many and divers footfalls ye will perforce encounter. Take ye the occasiouns of covert such as the verdure of the land may provide, but pass ye speedilie by such places where virtue tarryeth not. Flee, as it were the very pestilence, the wine they offer, the high wassail they bid you keep, the gladsome eyen that would fain entice you. Strain ye upon the start, follow thy spirit (not rum) and cry—

" God for merrie England and St. George."

Muster ! Bows to the left hand ! To your duties, oh my merrie yeomen."

THE ORCHARDS, THE SEA AND THE GUNS.

Of sounds which haunt me, these
Until I die
Shall live O, first the trees
Swaying and singing in the moonless night .
The wind being wild
And I
A wakeful child
That lay and shivered with a strange delight.

Second—less sweet, but thrilling as the first
The midnight roar
Of waves upon the shore
Of Rossall dear.
The rhythmic surge and burst :—
The gusty rain
I loved to hear
Flung on the pane,

And now another sound
Wilder than wind or sea
When on the silent night
I hear resound
In mad delight
The guns......
They bark the whole night through
And though I fear,
Knowing what work they do,
I somehow thrill to hear.

F. W. H.

THINGS WE WANT TO KNOW.

Did a certain member of No. 5 platoon enjoy his parcel ? Did it contain what he expected ?
Which member of No. 5 platoon had two flares put up because he had seen two rats on the parapet ?
How about les boutons noirs ? Yes, but what about le deuxième étage ? Eh !

L

What stopped " That reminds me " from telling his story ?
Who is known as the walking Q.M. ?
Are the trenches a TRANSPORT of delight ?
Which recruit said '" That's more than one man firing " when the Hun M. G. commenced its evening hate ?
Which member of A. Company in order to learn the French language has commenced with a history of the 1870 affair ?
Which recruit in No. 1 Platoon challenged thus— " Halt ! Who bist " ?
Which Sgt. gave out in orders, that there would be a box of platoo-uns for them as do roll up their " Woodbines " in bundles of ten, the best ?
Who was the reinforcement who thought the Regulars were in the German Trenches, and that being merely a Territorial he was therefore in the second line trenches ?
How many Officers discovered traces of Irish blood in their veins on St. Patrick's Day and whether the A. D. S. did not make a very passable imitation of a camouflage ?
What member of a Coy. Mess while proceeding up " Pas de Tir " remarked " The Silly Blighters have built the fire platform on the wrong side " ?
Is it correct he was trained at a well-known seaside resort ?
Is it true it cannot rain at W. S. M. on Sundays ?
Did they always put a bucket of washing water under cover when it rained at Cranham ?
Why is there a shortage of jam at Headquarters ?
Who is known as the " Dud King " ? When and how did he acquire the title ?
How many months have the D. A. C. been " in action " ?
How many officers have tried to ride the Major's horse and failed ?
Did they keep a pack of spaniels ?
Did the name " Sally " on Easter Monday remind any men in " A " Company of Hempstead Lane ?
Did they not wish they were at Highnam-au-bois ?
What did the Hen say when the Ford Ambulance ran over her ?
Was it " Ghee Whizz ".........?
Is it true that the Kaiser has a partiality for " Woodbines " ?
Is it due to the fact that he does not like his Navy Cut
How many barns has the T.O's horse pulled down ? And is it safer to tie his horse to a clothes line ?
Did the Padre get the right address ?
Was the visit of the Parisian Dancing Girl and her husband a complete success ?

PIPER'S WOOD.

In Minsterworth when March is in
And spring begins to gild the days,
O, then starts up a joyous din
For Piper's Wood is full of praise
Because the birds deem winter done
And welcome the returning sun.

Blackbird and thrush and robin dear
Within this wood try over all
The songs they mean to shout so clear
Before green leaves go red and fall :
And, hearkening in its shadows, you
Must needs sing loud of Summer too.

F. W. H.

THE FLAG.

" About three years ago I had an argument with a notable man who preached to me the then by no means uncommon rubbish about the flag being mere school boy jingoism, the country merely a vulgarity, and Patriotism merely a conceit of Feudalism—to-day, to-day his son has died for these things and my friend is an internationalist no longer."

AUSTIN HARRISON,—*Sunday Pictorial.*

The power of the human mind to project itself into the future is notoriously weak. We can never again then, allow ourselves to be content with a narrow range of outlook. Granted for the time being the Huns actually in front of us naturally form the chief object of our study yet there must ever be before our mind's eye vistas of countries which we may never see, the whole pulsing Empire whose life has at certain periods in their momentous months been in most grave and serious danger. Henceforward it can never be a crime to fly England's Flag on those occassions when circumstances demand it ; never the thing to do to throw cold water on things imperial. Too long have superior people sniffed at any outward observance of Empire Day. The Colonies have given us lavishly of the very best. Anzac, Canadian and South African alike are for all time associated heroically with Gallipoli, Ypres and the German Colonies ; and many a man has travelled more miles than we can estimate, from southern palm, or northern pine, leaving his estate in hireling hands that he may give himself, body and soul, to the great cause for which the flag stands, and over which it shall ever fly.

Mr. Hughes, with the farseeing eye of an Imperial Statesman, understands the situation and says " All the Dominions are looking to Great Britain, for we expect a plain statement of what the policy of Britain is. Every Britain should understand therefore " the absolute importance of so uniting and welding together in common interests as well as in common British sentiment, the whole mighty framework of the Empire, or so solidifying and consolidating it by some common bond of mutual interest and sentiment, as to render it along with all its component, scattered and diverse parts, INVINCIBLE and immeasureably prosperous throughout."

So precious then is the Empire of ours, too sacred to be played with, too great to be ridiculed. The blood of our colonies will surely be the seed of our Empire.

NEVER AGAIN.

It is Peace, say five years ago. The Blue Lagoons are still. It is the Peace too of the Southern Cross, and the magic spell of a summer's evening holds us content with the glories of Nature and the wonders of the Island Kingdoms which dot the Archipelago. One thing alone jars upon us. For some hours two steamers—liners both—have been waiting outside the bar which runs all round the harbour of a British Colony. One has the yellow funnels of the North German Lloyd—S.S. Zieten—accounted for by the Navy many months ago now—and the other of a more slender build shows the black funnel of the P. and O. line. Side by side, almost, they lie, representatives of two great commercial nations. But a steamer is leaving harbour, having discharged her cargo of beads, bully beef tins and beer, and has loaded herself with palm oil and bananas. So a string of flags is run up the flag staff on the quay by the Harbour master—signifying that the wharf is now empty and that the "dampfer Zieten" is to occupy the vacant space. And this, mark you, at a British Port ! Never again, please, Mr. Hughes.

MINNIE.

I'll sing you a song of a lady,
  A song about Minnie the maid—
Though Maid in Germany's all she is
  For here we call her a jade ;
And her pedigree runs :—" By Johnson
  Out of a hand Grenade."
        Oh, it's " Look out !
        Minnie's about,"
            CRUMP !!
        My ! What a lump
        Of poor old France
        Is obliged to dance !

She's a jolly fine game to play at,
  A sort of Diabolo ;
But the fellow who tries to catch her
  Is after a D. S. O.
And I reckon he'd spend the rest of the war
  Making the daisies grow.
        Run for your lives
        Minnie arrives
            CRUMP !!
        She's dug us a sump
        But don't you forget
        There'll be yards to revet.

To be chivalrous minded to women
  Is a Britisher's natural code
But you can't feel kind towards Minnie
  When once you've heard her explode.
For she'll do more harm to your morals
  Than the whole of the Charing Cross Road.
        Here she comes,
        Hooray ! Thumbs
            UP !!
        Fraulein B. Krupp
        Hasn't shed blood—
        Minnie's a dud.

O. D.

BRICKS FROM THE EDITOR'S PACK.

If you do not get your copy of the Gazette, please inform the Editor, c/o. The Orderly Room, 5th Gloucestershire Regiment, B.E.F.

There comes a story about the attempt made by young Von Tirpitz to escape. Discovered and kept under guard he spat in the face of a sentry, a Scotchman of some strength. Laying his rifle down by his side, and slipping off his equipment, he too spat, but on his hands, and administered a sound thrashing to young Von Tirpitz, who demanded reprisals. The sentry was Court-martialled, and the demands of Justice met by a sentence of 24 hours' imprisonment for laying aside his arms while on sentry-go.

We want the Old Boys Club of ours to wake up a bit. Will those ex-members of the Battalion write occasionally to the Editor ? We have heard from 2/Lieut. J. W. Watkins, 2nd Battalion Lancashire Fusiliers and 2/Lieut. Harvey sends us of his best each month. Now then, next please.

" Of course all the talk about German atrocities has been very much overdone. It is ridiculous to suppose that there is much truth in these allegations, and directly the war is over they will all be forgotten." One is sorry to find any ideas such as these current in the minds of educated persons. We have had occasion to refer before now to the " fable of German atrocities " and we shall continue to do so until the end of the chapter. We are not, be it said, encouraging a spirit of revenge. We want to ensure that never in the history of the world should anything occur again to rival the deeds of the Hun, as they came through Belgium and France, on the tide of their great advance, when they thought they could do what they liked with impunity, and considered that frightfulness would pay. " German Atrocoties " are official. Professor Morgan, the Home Office expert, has published a book containing actual extracts from the Diaries of German soldiers. What do you make of this ? Extracts from a Diary of a German soldier of the 13th Regt., 13th Division, VIIth Corps.

December 19th, 1914. " the sight of the trenches and the fury, not to say brutality of our men in beating to death the wounded English affected me so much that, for the rest of the day, I was fit for nothing." And so on. We are not going to reprint what the women went through. But O! superior person, is it worth while winning a reputation for wisdom etc., at the expense of truth, at the expense of your own country? Don't dare to say that the German Atrocities are untrue till you have read the book above referred to written by Professor J. H. Morgan, who gives DOCUMENTARY evidence of " a leisurely barbarity which proves great deliberation, cases such as the discovery of bodies of despatch riders burnt with petrol or " pegged out " with lances." There are still people who have not yet realised that we are at war with the HUN, and that the issues are tremendous.

We are winning the war, boys. Don't forget that the failure of the Huns at VERDUN, in the greatest, largest, most terrific battle the world has ever heard of, has had a tremendous effect, morally and strategically. The Huns had circularised Switzerland, giving time table for arrival at Verdun and Paris. " The Germans have suffered the greatest reverse they have experienced in the war."

A spy story during the German advance, from " Back of the Front " by Phyllis Campbell. We walked to the station for a paper and stood waiting there till the boy would arrive on his bicycle. While we waited we saw a very familiar figure standing by the pavement—a man with a tray of nuts suspended round his neck. He was a tall, soldierly figure of a man—distinguished in appearance but shabby and soiled to a degree. Gossip said he was an English Officer who had been ruined by a famous Paris actress.

For seven years he had stood between the Chateau and the Church selling nuts—never looking one in the face, never speaking. As we watched him, suddenly from among the soldiers came a typical Paris gamin—ragged, hatless, impudent and bare-footed—evidently drunk. He reeled on the edge of the pavement and cannoned against the seller of nuts, whose wares were flung broadcast by the contact. Instead of apologising he thrust a hand through his hair and said something in Argot—and there was a roar from the soldiers. The seller of nuts looked wizened with rage—and his retort, when it came, was bitingly satirical. The gamin wheeled round and spat in his face—like a flash, the seller of nuts became a soldier, an officer—a gentleman—a spy! The soldiers closed round him—that volley of horrible cursings was in pure, high German. The gamin was a famous French detective, and the seller of nuts a Prussian nobleman, an officer of high rank.

Une jeune demoiselle dans une papeterie demande des nouvelles de la santé de l'Editeur de la Gazette. Le Major répond " Il a mal à la gorge." " Comment a-t-il eu ce mal à la gorge ? " " Trop de serments probablement," dit le Major, ceci a la grande hilarité de la demoiselle.
For the benefit of those who are not French scholars, " serments " means " an oath."

He was a Senior Officer. He had been attending a course of map reading and had learned how to find the true north from his watch. Unfortunately a good dinner and a night's sleep drove this recondite method from his mind. Meeting the instructor the next morning he asked him if he would mind giving the details once more.

" Not at all Sir, not at all. A gold watch is necessary and eke a gold chain ; swing the watch round the head till the chain breaks. The watch then goes west. If you then set off at an angle of ninety degrees this will give you the true north."
Exit the instructor at the double.

A good many of us laughed loudly at the pictures in Punch entitled " Mule Humours." A certain Senior Officer not altogether unconnected with the Artillery quite thought the picture the funniest he had ever seen. On second thoughts, however, he decided that the last one in which the Mules celebrate the kicking of the Colonel was in doubtful taste. It therefore hangs in his office, minus the funniest picture of the lot and shorn of more than half its glory.

There can be no two opinions about the Competition for the Fanshaw Cup being an unqualified success, and the Final, which long ago we foretold as certain to be " Some " Final, and played as it was by teams representing the 144th and 145th Infantry Brigades, was a fitting climax to a long and well fought struggle for the cup. It was indeed unfortunate for the Bucks that a goal, which was to many of us quite obvious, should have been disallowed, as the score have been one all at half time. However the Bucks would be the very first to admit that the better side won in virtue of the pronounced superiority of the Worcester forward line.

The game was admirably refereed by Corpl. (" Why not give him another stripe ? ") Deakin—such a change from the constant and unnecessary whistling which marred our match with the Bucks when every charge entailed a free kick for somebody.

General Fanshawe, who had followed with the keenest interest the course of this and other games in the competition, before presenting the cup and distributing the medals, complimented both teams on their football as being of a very high order.

Cheers and counter cheers and the curtain fell on Football, as far as this season was concerned. Who will win it next year ? ! ! ! ! !

The Navy have always had a soft spot for Football. Was not G. D. O'Lyon sent back especially on a destroyer, so that he might be able to take part in an International? (Vide question in House of Commons by Non-Sportsman.)

It was no surprise therefore to find the Press box well nigh full with representatives from the London Dailies, as the Army too, like the senior service, has a distinct penchant for sport. Unfortunately, owing to lack of space, we are only able to print the account of our own reporter. But we would merely say that the M......Pst had its usual article on " Real Rugger " in commenting on the " carrying off " of the Cup. The D......M...... described the admirable service of trains, etc. The D......M-r-r reproduced photographs of the house where the scorers of the goals lived, their ancestors, their Sunday Schools, and the Boot Shop where they bought the boots they used to wear in peace time! And all hoped that the same venue would witness similar titanic struggles for many years to come !

There are some happenings since August, 1914, that we can never forget ; they are indelibly fixed on our memories. The gallant Captain rushing down the Swindon streets loading his revolver as he ran, to round up an alleged spy—a poor Italian organ grinder. The evacuation of the Padre's gum boots—they tell us he has not yet realised the humour of that situation. Washbourne's try at Nieppe—a dazzling effort. The M.O's luck at Allouagne—golden days, those, for him. The Staff Officer of Loos. And now there is something else we do not seem able to forget, and that is ......H......

Those keen partisans—and they were many—who braved the snowstorms to watch "A" and "D" Companies settle (temporarily) their Rugby differences, were rewarded with a hard fought game. "A's" pack at once asserted itself so that the loss of the redoubtable Sergeant Thompson, after the first five minutes, may well have had an almost decisive effect on the ultimate result of the struggle, in spite of "D's" pronounced superiority "outside." Anyhow, the embraces of the Brothers Hamblin were both picturesque and proper.

Now that the cricket season is rapidly approaching, we hope that some good wickets may be obtainable. The last match recorded in the columns of the GAZETTE was played 900 yards from the German lines on September 19th, when play suffered from the roughness of the pitch. Efforts are being made therefore to acquire on a 99 years' lease a permanent pitch. We are quite sure that all sportsmen in the Battalion will do their very best to get the wicket into good order, if only that their son's sons may in their turn become adepts at England's summer game.

The following application for special leave was made !—" To O.C. —— I beg to apply for special leave, as I am being married on the 23rd inst., and should like to be present at the ceremony.

(sd.)————

Overheard on the road.
An A.P.M. to Captain H. driving at his usual pace, "Who are you?"
Capt. H.—"I am Captain H."
A.P.M.—"If you were a general, you have no right to go that pace, I don't care who you are."
Capt. H.—"I know you don't care who I am, now you know I am only a Captain."

We offer a prize of 20 francs for the best short story up to 1700 words, and a prize of 10 francs to the sender of the best yarn published in "Bricks from the Editor's Pack."

The "Daily Express" have recently sent us a set of Boxing gloves. Can they have heard of the ferocious arguments which are carried on between the two H.Q. Sergeants as to the length of the war?

His old comrades in the "Fifth" will be pleased to see the following award of the Military Cross.
Temp. Sec. Lieut. WILFRED WYNTER-MORGAN, 1st Gloucester R.
"For conspicuous gallantry when rescuing four men who had become imprisoned in an old mine under very heavy shell fire.
His name has previously been noted for gallant conduct."

From Lady Poore's Reminiscences.
An Australian soldier at Gallipoli who was on sentry duty took off his helmet and hung it with his rifle on a tree.
A passing Officer asked, not unnaturally :—
"And what may you be?"
"Oh, I'm a bit of a picket," drawled the sentry, unabashed. "And what may you be?" "Oh, I'm a bit of a Major," was the answer. "Well," rejoined the sentry genially, "If you'll wait a jiff I'll get my rifle and give you a bit of a salute."

Many congratulations to Temp. Major F. M. Hext, who was for 21 years in the Royal Irish Fusiliers and subsequently was Adjutant and then 2nd in Command of the 1/5th Gloucesters, on being promoted Temp. Lieut.-Colonel to command a service unit of the Devonshire Regiment. He saw field service in the Egyptian Expedition of 1884.

———

———

There was a young Captain named Blair
Who demanded a cab "A la gare" (guerre)
Said the Cabby "O lor,
I'm not for the war,
Why not try the Café Gobert?"

!

There is a young Padre who lives in a trench,
Who's uncommonly fond of a beautiful wench.
He frequently visits a city near by
Whose initial is " A " and whose girls are not shy.

He usually goes in an A.S.C. car,
As the distance to footslog is rather too far.
In future the latter will be his sad lot,
As the last monthly " Mag " was a trifle too hot.

He has slandered his friends, and he plainly will see
Why, when asked for a lift, they say " Napoo ! Compree ? "
No more are free " pads " now given away,
But were they all free, or had he to pay ?

A word of advice to this Padre we offer,
If again to the printer his proofs he would proffer,
He'd better endeavour to make some amends
To those " lucky young devils " he used to call friends.

A. S. C.

(We welcome help from our friends in the other
branches of the Service, but the Editor would point out that
ordinary, as well as **All Silly Contributions** should come
DIRECT to him, who can take a knock as well as give one.)

PROMOTIONS AND APPOINTMENTS.

Extracts from LIST No. 72 of appointments, commissions, etc., approved by the General Officer Commanding in
Chief, dated 4/3/16.

Appointments, Commissions, etc.

2nd Battalion Lancashire Fusiliers.

No. 2741 Sergeant J. W. Watkins, from 1/5th Battalion
Gloucestershire Regiment. To be Temporary 2nd Lieutenant
dated 5/3/16.

8th Battalion Gloucestershire Regiment.

No. 2667 Lance Corporal R. H. Cullis, from 1/5th
Battalion Gloucestershire Regiment. To be Temporary 2nd
Lieutenant dated 5/3/16.

No. 2654 Lance Corporal F. W. Ayliffe, from 1/5th
Battalion Gloucestershire Regiment. To be Temporary 2nd
Lieutenant dated 5/3/16.

10th Battalion Gloucestershire Regiment.

No. 2591 Lance Corporal A. E. Miles, from 1/5th Battalion Gloucestershire Regiment. To be Temporary 2nd
Lieutenant dated 5/3/16.

Extracts from Supplement to London Gazette, dated
18/3/16. Captain G. F. Collett to be Temporary Major
26/1/16.

Extracts from Supplement to London Gazette, dated
30/3/16. 2nd Lieutenant G. Hawkins to be Temporary
Lieutenant 25/2/16.

Extracts from Supplement to London Gazette, dated
1/4/16. 2nd Lieutenant (Temporary Lieutenant) E. F.
Brenan to be Lieutenant 28/8/15.

To be Coy. Q. M. S. :—

410	Sgt.	Armstrong, R.	29/3/16

To be Sergts :—

2557	A/Sgt.	Norris, C. W.	22/1/16
1629	,,	King, A. D.	5/3/16
1536	L/Sgt.	Coward, W. J.	17/2/16
1920	,,	Jackson, A.	2/3/16
2331	,,	Chandler, G. W.	29/3/16
2487	,,	Abbott, W. J.	29/3/16
1348	Corpl.	White, W. H.	14/3/16

To be L/Sgts. with pay :—

1921	Corpl.	Brick, J.	17/2/16
864	,,	Turner, E. W.	2/3/16
717	,,	Eden, J.	29/3/16
1159	,,	Apperley, J.	29/3/16
1627	,,	Boughton, J.	8/3/16

To be Corpls :—

1069	A/Cpl.	Spencer, E. J.	16/2/16
2348	,,	Phillpotts, F.	22/1/16
2091	,,	Coton, J.	5/3/16
2568	L/Cpl.	Salter, E. G.	17/2/16
2787	,,	Davis, P.	17/2/16
2760	,,	Hill, R.	17/2/16
2535	,,	Garner, E.	2/3/16
2223	,,	Boulter, H.	8/3/16
1386	,,	Davis, F.	8/3/16
2697	,,	Middlecote, A.	14/3/16
2315	,,	Jackson, L. E.	17/3/16
2748	,,	Brien, C.	29/3/16
1441	,,	Steel, W. G.	29/3/16
2516	,,	Gough, T. W.	29/3/16
2711	,,	Stinchcombe, H. T.	29/3/16

To be L/Cpls. with pay :—

2486	A/L/Cpl.	Pepperell, W. F.	5/3/16
2366	,,	Maddock, W. H.	22/1/16
2480	,,	Smart, S.	16/2/16
2558	,,	Paynter, W. F. L.	17/2/16
2635	Pte (L/c)	Wood, S. C.	17/2/16
3343	,,	O'Neil, C.	17/2/17
1527	,,	Sproat, A. L.	2/3/16
1556	,,	Bundy, W.	8/3/16
2776	,,	Wilkes, W. G.	8/3/16
2550	,,	Moxon, J. E.	21/3/16
1363	,,	Hopkins, W. C.	13/3/16
2632	,,	Turner, E. M.	29/3/16
2067	,,	Mitford, H. J.	29/3/16
2533	,,	Fry, H. H.	29/3/16
2386	,,	Payne, H. A.	29/3/16
2705	,,	Rea, W.	29/3/16
2669	,,	Dovey, W.	29/3/16
471	,,	Tovey, J.	29/3/16

To be L/Cpls. without pay :—

2997	Pte.	Warwick, F.	19/3/16
2453	,,	Thomas, A. C.	,,
3557	,,	Butler, A. C.	,,
2277	,,	Higgs, A.	,,
1476	,,	Coopey, A.	,,
1189	,,	Gibbons, C.	,,
2742	,,	Wintle, A. H.	,,
3014	,,	Crosby, C. T.	,,
2695	,,	Lewis, T. H. R.	,,
2680	,,	Hamblin, L.	,,
2663	,,	Burlton, W. G.	,,
2653	,,	Watts, E.	,,
3999	,,	Niblett, W. E.	21/3/16
4008	,,	Hook, W. H.	,,
2972	,,	Turner, C. J.	,,
4196	,,	Kiddle, A.	,,

GRENADIERS.

The under-mentioned Officer, N.C.O's and men have
passed the test laid down for Grenadiers :—

2nd Lieutenant Cruickshank, H. W.
908 Sgt. Wyatt, J.
2705 Pte. Hopkins, W. T
2340 Sgt. Cook, H.
1935 Pte. Tilley, W.
1750 ,, Chandler.
1563 ,, Oldland, E.
2682 ,, Hiam, E. J.

CASUALTIES.

Killed in Action
66 Sergt. Durrett, T. 13/3/16.

Wounded

4369	Pte.	G. Edwards (Slight at Duty)	18/3/16
2614	,,	G. A. Clift (Slight)	20/3/16
1681	,,	A. Godwin	23/3/16
1787	,,	W. F. Jennings (Slight)	23/3/16
2317	,,	E. J. Carter	24/3/16
4346	,,	E. A. Eaketts (Slight)	9/4/16
1527	L/Cpl.	A. L. Sproat do.	9/4/16
4	Dmr.	R. Gurney (Shell-shock)	10/4/16
1550	Cpl.	H. G. Welch	12/4/16
2578	Pte.	L. Davis (Slight)	12/4/16

CASUALTIES.—continued.

2318	Pte.	A. Gainer (Slight)	13/4/16
2334	,,	L. Turner	,,
1707	,,	V. Haug	,,
4486	,,	A. J. Warren	,,
2944	,,	J. A. Kitching	,,
2864	,,	R. F. Phillips	,,
506	Sgt.	J. G. Owen (Shell-shock)	,,
1935	Pte.	E. Tilley ,,	,,
4247	,,	A. Kemmett ,,	,,
8821	,,	R. W. Evans ,,	,,
4143	,,	C. W. Hook ,,	,,
1936	,,	A. E. Browning ,,	,,
1794	Dmr.	A. W. Brick ,,	,,
3250	Pte.	L. Reay (Slight)	,,
4426	,,	A. E. Cole ,,	,,
2480	L/Cpl.	S. Smart	15/4/16
2527	Pte.	E. Eden	,,
2551	,,	G. L. Martin	,,
4141	,,	P. Stevens	,,
1538	,,	C. Apperley (Shell-shock)	,,
3792	,,	P. J. Jackson (Slight)	,,
154	Sgt.	J. C. W. Jennings ,,	16/4/16
2594	Pte.	G. Russell ,,	,,
4393	,,	C. Hewlett	,,
2693	L/Cpl.	A. H. T. Lewis	,,

R.I.P.

No. 66 Sgt. T. Durrett. Killed in action 13/3/16.

Sergt. Durrett will always be remembered by " A " Coy. and his numerous friends in the remainder of the Battalion for his optimism and cheerfulness even under the most trying circumstances. He was one of those men who possessed the gift of dispelling gloomy feelings in others, and even the worst grouser after a few minutes in his society could see the brighter side of things. He was quite an "old soldier," having served nearly 20 years ; he held the Territorial Efficiency Medal and was one of the oldest men serving in the Battalion. Before the war he was well known as a rifle shot, and captained the team that won Colonel Bathurst's Cup at the Battalion Rifle meeting for two successive years. He had held the rank of Sergeant since 1910 and for two months just before his death he was acting as C.Q.M.S., which duties he carried out very efficiently. His death is a great loss to his company, every one of whom will deeply sympathise with Mrs. Durrett in her bereavement.

EPITAPH.

(T.D.)

A shallow trench for one so tall.
" Heads down ! "—no need for that old call
Under the up turned sod.
Safe is his body, never fret,
Behind this foreign parapet ;
And over all the wind and wet
His soul sits safe with God.

F. W. H.

R.I.P.

No. 277 Pte. A. R. Cook.

March 21st, at Suffolk Hall, Cheltenham, Pte. Albert Reginald Cook (Reg.) 1/5th Gloucester Regt., only and dearly loved son of Mr. and Mrs. Cook, The Rowans, St. Mark's, aged 21.

No. 12.

MAY, 1916.

5th Gloucester Gazette.

A Chronicle, serious and humorous, of the Battalion while serving with the
BRITISH EXPEDITIONARY FORCE.

VICTORY.

Whether you shall see it, or I,
We cannot tell
Now. And it doesn't matter.

For 'twill come when Hell
Is covered, and the batter
Of guns fades :—Victory !

Remember then, you who have followed the dead
Through the worst, loudest, last
Thunder before the sun—

Remember—Though the Hun
And his brute power has passed—
There are more wars to be won !

O, while Life's Life to all eternity :—
Brothers press on, GO ON TO VICTORY !

F. W. H.

FOR A WORD AND A SCRAP OF PAPER.

Not for defence, and not for fame,
Neither in fear nor pride
The men who boast a British name
Are marshalled side by side ;
For outraged homes, for nameless wrongs,
For violated laws,
God shall repay ; to us belongs
A more resistless cause.

To keep " a scrap of paper " white.
To make the " word " we penned
A thing closed eyes may read aright,
Stopped ears may comprehend.
Our dearest blood shall write it plain
On many an outland grave,
While England's cannon roar again
The word that England gave.

Thus, e'en though 'whelmed by land and deep,
Though death and ruin come,
And murder—sullied myriads sweep
Over our island home,
Firm in our cause—though fate be cross,
We'll stand with hearts unstirred,
Enhancing still with every loss
The worth of England's word.

G. G. H., AUGUST, 1914.

HONORIS CAUSA.

Appointment to the Most Distinguished Order of Saint Michael and Saint George, for services rendered in connection with military operations in the field :—

Lieut.-Colonel J. H. Collett.

The Military Cross :
Captain H. C. B. Sessions.
London Gazette, June 2nd, 1916.

The following were " mentioned " in the despatch from General Sir Douglas Haig, G.C.B., dated April 30th, 1916 :—

Lieut.-Colonel J. H. Collett, C.M.G.

No. 1139, Sergt. C. F. Harris.

No. 2717, Sergt. R. O. Thompson.

WAR PRAYER.

Lord God of Hosts, Thou see'st that our cause,
Despite the meaner claims of self's dread lure,
Is just, and seeking thine eternal laws,
Through all our earthly frailty, is pure.

Thou knowest, Lord, our enemy's desire,
His lust of power, his pride's insanity,
And rising to Thy Throne in anguish dire,
O Lord ! the groaning of humanity.

Our nation, and the nations by our side
Who with us stand for freedom's sacred right,
Their rulers, and our own, in mercy guide,
And lift our spirit upward to the height

Where dwells the vision of a future blest,
Where wrong shall cease, and where the tortured heart
Of untold multitudes shall be at rest.
Help with Thy strength those who are torn apart.

From loved ones fighting upon land and sea,
Who having heard and answered duty's call
Are ready, leaning humbly upon Thee,
To make the greatest sacrifice of all.

Look down in pity, Lord, on all who bear
A load of grief, whom cruel death has crushed
'Neath burning misery, or cold despair,
And let the anguish of their soul be hushed.

Let this thought hold us, that all those who fight,
And all the people of the conquered lands,
And they who wait and watch—by day or night,
Through life and death are ever in Thy hands.

Hear Thou the voice of agony that cries
From widespread battlefields, in noontide heat,
Or 'neath the solitude of moonlit skies
Where o'er the sinking ship the closing sea-waves beat.

O let Thy Holy Presence be beside
All those who help with heart or hand or brain
The suffering and oppressed ;—of those who died
Make us more worthy, Lord, we who remain.

Until with solemn sound shall strike the hour
We too shall have to face the last dread fight.
O grant we may be, by Thy saving power
For ever with them, Lord, in Thine eternal light.

20th April, 1916.

M. L. G.

The undermentioned N.C.O's and men, having become time expired whilst on Active Service with the Battalion, have voluntarily re-engaged for four years or the period of the War.

713	Pte.	Langley, R.	23/9/15
717	L/Sgt.	Eden, J.	23/9/15
1108	,,	Cuzner, J.	1/9/15
1189	Pte.	Gibbons C.	20/12/15
1192	,,	Newman, G. E. A	20/12/15
1441	,	Steel, W. G	9/11/15
1465	Sgt.	Knight, E.	19/9/15
154	,,	Jennings, J. C. W	1/4/16
602	C. S. M.	Horne, L. H.	,,
456	,,	Tibbles, W. G.	,,
410	Sgt.	Armstrong, R.	,,
392	,,	Finch, F.	,,
379	,,	Morris, A. L.	,,
1171	Pte.	Gould, C. A.	3/1/16
1468	,,	Mason, W.	24/1/16
1386	L/C.	Davis, F.	9/2/16
1401	Pte.	Halliday, H. A.	31/3/16
1378	,,	Brown, C. E.	6/3/16
864	Sgt.	Turner, E. W.	5/3/16
325	C.S.M.	Attwood, C. H.	1/4/16
238	,,	Huxford, J. H.	,,
904	,,	Hinch, G.	26/2/16
617	Pte.	Powell, E.	1/4/16
1273	L/Sgt.	Wiggall, P.	8/2/16
1363	Pte.	Hopkins, W. C.	27/3/16
1348	Cpl.	White, W. H.	3/12/15
1027	Pte.	Midwinter, J.	4/12/15
1358	,,	Brindley, A. E.	7/12/15
530	,,	Wintle, C. H.	,,
1412	,,	Marsh, A.	,,
133	Sgt.	Faville, A.	8/12/15
1369	Pte.	Green, A. H.	,,
1372	,,	Smith, F. W.	,,
1349	Cpl.	Ashbee, J. A.	,,
1356	,,	Gardner, R. H.	,,
1069	L/C.	Spencer, E. J.	9/12/15
1436	,,	Jones, F.	8/12/15
75	Sgt. Dmr.	Proctor, F. W.	10/12/15
1354	Dmr.	Jordan, M. G.	12/12/15
466	C.Q.M.S.	Wilce F.	9/12/15
965	Sgt.	Hill, E.	22/12/15
2297	Pte.	Stephens, J.	26/12/15
1344	,,	Brookes, E. G.	21/12/15
413	Sgt.	Wonson, R. C.	10/1/16
908	,,	Wyatt, J.	10/1/16
2134	Pte.	Hopkins, C. H.	31/1/16
30	Sgt.	Brown, A. F. D.	14/2/16
471	L/C.	Tovey, J.	27/2/16
1361	Pte.	Brown, K. D.	1/3/16
499	Sgt.	Webb, C. H.	19/3/16
86	Q.M.Sgt.	Webb, W.	22/3/16
1317	Pte.	Sansom, B. S.	20/4/16
1430	,,	Harris, C. M.	24/4/16
1486	,,	Heath, H. S. J.	28/4/16
1274	,,	Davis, P. R.	2/5/16
1288	,,	Smith, G.	6/5/16
1454	Cpl.	Whyham, A. R.	27/4/16
1280	Pte.	Trenfield, W. E.	25/4/16
1298	,,	Speke, J. C.	24/4/16
1300	Sgt.	Groves, W.	24/4/16
2293	,,	Field, A. J.	28/4/16
1475	Pte.	Peacey, W.	3/4/16
1476	,,	Coopey, A.	1/4/16

SICKNESS AND HEALTH.

(I) Foreboding.

The year grows lean :
The dwindling days
Come wrapt in haze.

And I have seen
Crouched by the fire
Of old Desire

A figure lean
Who layeth brands
With shaking hands

Upon it. (Keen
In very truth
The wind !) Ah stay !
What doth he say ?—
" My-name-was-Youth."

(II) An Adventure with God.

Far worse than pain
Unutterable weariness
Of blood and brain—
Intolerable dreariness
Of days, God gave me.
And I bethought
The first fresh blood of youth that rose to leave me,
And how in those brave days—
Virgin of lust and sport—
I had forgot
To render any praise
Then as I thus looked upwards through the net
Wherein both soul and flesh lay cunningly caught,
God ('twas like Springtime calling from the earth
The flowers to birth !)
Smiled down and did restore
All that I had before.

(III) Song of Health.

For friends to stand beside, for foes to fight,
For devils' work to break, for wrong and right
And will to choose (however hard) between them :
For merry tales, no matter where you glean them :
Songs, stars, delight of birds, and Summer roses,
Sunshine, wherein my friend the dog now dozes :
Danger—the zest of Life—and Love, the lord
Of Life and Death : for every open word
Spoken in blame or praise by friend o' mine
To spur me on : For old good memories
Keeping in my soul's cellar like good wine :
For Truth so strong, and Beauty so divine :
For animals and children, and for trees
Both wintry black and blossoming in white :
For homely gardens, and for humming bees :
For drink, and dreams, and daisies on the sod,
Plain food, and fire (when it will light),
                              Thank God.

(IV) The Ballade of Damnable Things.

I do not like a horse to throw me off,
I do not like the motor bike to skid,
I do not like a nasty hacking cough,
Nor influenza. And I never did
Enjoy the thought of frizzling on a grid
The while wee flaming devils dance and sing.
But, short of simple Hell without the lid,
I think that jaundice is the damndest thing.

Fleas, faintness, famine, stomach-ache, the feel
Of flies upon your face, rats in your bed,
Lice, dusty roads, a blister on your heel,
The taste of salts, the scent of things long dead.
Home-sickness, chilblains, grief uncomforted,
A hollow tooth with cold, a hornet sting :
These are unpleasant, yet when all is said,
I think that jaundice is the damndest thing.

See you the whole bright world before your eye
Dwindle as ugly as a wrinkled pea.
See Beauty, a pricked bubble : Truth, a lie :
Achievement, foam on muddy water. See
Yourself a yellow devil suddenly,
And all the zest of youth gone journeying :
See you all this !—and then you will agree
(I think) that jaundice is the damndest thing.

ENVOI.

Prince of the damned, I ransacked my supplies
To find a fitting wish at you to fling.
Now may you look on Hell through yellow eyes !
I think that jaundice is the damndest thing.
                              F. W. H.

A MINOR AFFRAY.

This is the story of a minor war which took place in my dug-out between myself and Fritz. Fritz was not a Hun, but a rat—not the common grey beast of the English barn or sewer, but a real black specimen. At first I did not regard him as an enemy. He seemed mild, and inclined to mind his own business—like the German before the war. I liked his sleek appearance and apparent trustfulness. He was a bit of a gymnast too, his best performance being to crawl along between two beams in the dug-out roof which were a few inches apart. This meant that he had to do a " split " all the way, right legs along one beam, left legs along the other. Viewed from below it was a very remarkable effort, and the first time I saw it I applauded so vigorously that Fritz nearly fell on to my face, over which he happened to be at the moment. Also, he had a very odd habit of sneezing. I never discovered whether it really was cold in the head—it may have been indigestion—anyway, it was a most surprising noise which amused me at first. So in the beginning I suffered Fritz and thought no evil of him. Then he began to show signs of moral obliquity. One night—or rather early morning—I woke under the impression that something was annoying me. It was true. Fritz was annoying me by dropping large lumps of the dug-out roof on my face. Even as I turned over on my back to look up, a stream of dust and earth fell accurately into my right eye. By the time I was able to see again, Fritz had taken cover, sneezing derisively. He spent the rest of my sleep in mining a large part of the dug-out wall, and pushing it out so that it fell with a thud on top of all my washing kit, and an open tin of cigarettes. After this it was clear that Fritz was at war with me. It was obvious that he was a treacherous and very malignant rat, probably of German origin, with preposterous ideas about super-ratishness. Possibly he even imagined himself to be a super-rat, impelled by a moral duty to occupy my dug-out, and force his " Kultur " on the inferior human being he found there. I began to suspect that his whiskers were trained à la Hohenzollern, and that his sneeze was his way of shouting " Hoch." I wondered whether he could do the " goose-step." At any rate, it was plain that F. M. G. (Fritz Must Go). I considered the tactical position. I had to admit that Fritz held the offensive, and that I had been taken by surprise. On the other hand he was the sort of overbearing, self-confident rat who would underestimate the strength of his enemy. Very likely he thought I shouldn't put up a fight at all, but just evacuate the dug-out and pay an indemnity of cheese. His conduct bore this out, for as I was shaving he looked out of a hole just over my head, dropped a lump of earth into my cup, sneezed loudly twice, and winked. As I had a shaving brush in one hand and a razor in the other, there was nothing to be done at the moment, but later in the day I laid for Fritz with an automatic pistol cunningly disguised as a novel. But Fritz did not show up. During my next morning sleep he devised a new form of attack. This was in the nature of the Zeppelin raid. Doing his famous split-crawl to a point just over my face, he dropped with a loud " Hoch." I confess that he shook my morale badly the first time he fetched up all standing on my nose. The next time he tried it Fritz made a miscalculation somewhere, for he fell on my feet. I flatter myself that the counter attack was quickly and vigorously delivered. Fritz must have flown yards. The only drawback was that the mighty kick which sent him flying nearly broke all the toes of my right foot on the dug-out roof. However, the incident obviously impressed Fritz, for as I was preparing to get up, and thinking how much I hated pickled salmon for lunch on a cold day, I saw him

hop down through a hole in the door, followed by reinforcements—four of them.

Some time during the next twelve hours Fritz sank to the lowest depths of petty spite. He and his reinforcements gnawed :—

(1) my haversack, in which there was nothing but an oil-bottle.

(2) a novel I was reading. (They removed the critical chapter, and now I shall never know why the heroine, who was a really nice girl, married the hero, who was quite an impossible person, and wore white spats).

(3) a nice new map of Berlin with which we had just been issued. (So now I shall never find my way to Potsdam when the great advance gets there).

That day I waited long and patiently for Fritz, cutting short my sleep. I also put down some cheese to tempt him out. Fritz probably regarded the cheese as the first sign of surrender, but he was very cautious. He sent out his reinforcements one at a time to reconnoitre, encouraging them by sneezing " Hochs " from the background. Fritz also treated one of them, who returned at the double with a bit of cheese, with the greatest brutality. As far as I could hear he bit his reinforcement and pinched the cheese from him. At last, Fritz himself appeared when all his reinforcements had been scouting about unmolested for some time. But he was canny. He moved in short rushes, taking care never to halt where I could get a shot at him. I bided my time Then I fired. What Fritz thought of it I do not know (he was about a yard away). His reinforcements vanished. He himself seemed to bound all round the dug-out. Perhaps he suffered from shell shock, but when I looked for his mangled remains there was no sign of his corpse on the field of battle. Only a large dark pool spread from the corner where he had been. At first I thought it was his gore, until I recollected that rats' blood wouldn't smell of rum punch. Too late I remembered a parcel labelled " medical comforts " which I had put there unopened the night before. The sadness of defeat settled upon me. Fritz shaken perhaps, but alive, and a bottle—a whole bottle—of the very best gone hopelessly West.

But unknown to me the silver lining was even now through the dark cloud shining. If I had had an old kit bag I could have started packing at once, smiling incessantly (as per advice in modern ballad).

What frantic deed Fritz was contemplating I know not, but he was undoubtedly reckless, otherwise he wouldn't have sat outside the dug-out entrance with his back to me. Perhaps, too, he was slightly deafened. In any case, he never knew what hit him (it was my stick, as a matter of fact).

I buried him. His tombstone is a broken bottle of—medical comforts.

OUR BENEFACTORS.

Bishop Frodsham	Papers
Miss Backhouse	,,
Mr. W. R. Voller	,,
Heathville House, Gloucester	,,
Mr. Berkeley Powell	,,
The Hon. Mabel Gye	,,
Privates Shaw and Pine	Typing
Lt.-Colonel Marling	Papers
Lt.-Colonel Winterbotham	,,
Camps Library	,,

M

KINGS OF THE AIR.

I. Peace Song of the Aeroplanes.

Upward and upward with quiver and whirr,
Onward and upward, our pulses astir,
Higher and higher to heaven's clear blue,
Clearing the rain-cloud we swiftly skim through.
Joyous and fleet as a bird on the wing,
"Faster and faster" we hear the wheels sing;
Swift through the air as a swallow we swoop,
Turn a clear somersault, looping the loop;
Onward and upwards through limitless space,
Challenge the breezes to outstrip our pace;
Flecked with the sunbeam's bright ripple of mirth,
Up to the sphere where the snowflakes have birth.
Bathing our planes in a shimmer of light,
Gliding along in the silver of night,
Earth far below us in mystery fades,
Ghost of a dream-word enwrapped in the shades;
Clear as a songbird's most glorious note
Peals of a church bell in harmony float,
Rising like incense to regions above,
Melting away in a vision of love,
Onward and onward, a speck in the sky,
Dimmer and dimmer to man's watching eye,
Moving through sunlight of brightness untold,
Losing ourselves in a river of gold.

II. Song of the Fighting Airman.

Following fast in the wake of the Huns
    Hard on the foeman's trail,
In the threatening rattle and roar of the guns
    And the scream of the shrapnel hail;

Borne up aloft over earth's abyss,
    Burning to do and dare,
Mindless of bullet's shriek and hiss
    And the scathing searchlight's flare.

Heedless of all save the gaping gash,
    Rending the flanks of the foe
And to see him dash with headlong crash
    Three thousand feet below.

On field or wave 'tis a joy to fight
    But joyful beyond compare
Is the rapture to fight for the cause of right
    And to conquer—in the air!

III. The Lay of the Zeppelins.

    Stealthy and sinister we start
    Upon our country's mission grand,
    To aim a blow at England's heart
    In honour of the Fatherland.

    Grim and majestic, on we sail
    Till cursed England's cliffs are scanned;
    Now all her pride will not avail
    'Gainst servants of the Fatherland.

    We cross her coast line, sailing high,
    Her gunners' shell-fire to withstand;
    Her cities unsuspecting lie
    'Neath zeppelins of the Fatherland.

    'Gainst homestead, town, and Church tower old—
    Helpless or no—we raise our hand
    And hurl destruction, to uphold
    The good name of the Fatherland.

    What care we for defenceless lives,
    For fierce flames by the sea-wind fanned,
    If through our deeds of hate yet thrives
    The glory of the Fatherland?

    Yet should we, met by shell's close screech,
    In peril of reprisal stand,
    We homeward turn, full glad to reach
    The shelter of the Fatherland.

                    M. L. G.

TRIOLET.

If Beauty were a mortal thing
That died like laughter, grief and lust,
The poet would not need to sing
If beauty were a mortal thing
It would not wound us with its sting.
We should lie happy in the dust
If Beauty were a mortal thing
That died like laughter, grief and lust.

                    F. W. H.

OUR PORTRAIT GALLERY.

No. 10. THE PRUSSIAN.

(*A critical study*)

Though he can lift a manly quart,
Small gaiety is in his soul
That burrows like a garden mole
In earthly matters: and his heart
Is hard and little, like a pea,
And empty of humility.

He boasted learning—kulture—rank:
Slated the Bible most severely:
Laughed when the Lusitania sank:
Nor even guessed that he was merely
The dullest and the most unsavoury lout
That ever fared on "wurst und sauerkraut."

No. 11. "C" COMPANY COOK.

"Do you want j-jam on it?" he'll reply—
Twirling a red moustache,—
When chaffed about the rations' quality:
"Say, is this tea or hash?"
"Jim, tell us, do
Why you put sugar in the blooming stew!"
"And here's a heap of coal in mine, not half!"
    To all our chaff,
"Do you want j-jam on it?" he'll reply.

                    F. W. H.

THE REAL FEELING

WHEN ON "TOUR"?

THE BALLAD OF THE NOTARY.

A notary lived down " Funky " way
And he was sleek and he was gay ;
    The excellent feller
    Kept a good cellar
Of wine, as a prosperous notary may.

A notary fled from " Funky " way
But he was thoughtful and wily—trés.
    The provident soul
    First dug him a hole,
And buried his bottles in two feet of clay.

A shell came visiting " Funky " way,
And burst just where those bottles lay.
    We heard the thud,
    Saw pools of blood—
Red liquor that oozed from the stricken clay.

And we were happy down " Funky " way,
For most of the bottles survived the fray.
    And many a wight
    Drank deep that night
To the notary who was sleek and gay.

                A. B. P.

EDITOR'S POST BAG.

Truly the art of letter writing is with us still, if we may judge from the following priceless effort which was sent to the War Office :

" Respected Sir, Dear Sir,

Though I take this liberty as it leaves me at present I beg to ask you if you will kindly be kind enough to let me know where is my husbin through he is not my legible husbin as he a wife though he says she is ded but I do not think he knows for sure but we are not married though I am getting my allotment reglar which is no fault of Mr. Lloy george who would stop it if he could and Mr. Makena but if you know where he is belong to the Royal Nava. Fling Corps for ever since he joined in jan when he was sacked from his work for talking back to his Bos which was a woman at the laundry where he worked I have not had any money from him since he joined though he told Mrs. Harris what lives on the ground floor that he was a pretty ossifer for six shillings a week and loots of underclose in for the bad weather and I have three children what he has been the father of them though he say it was my fault. Hoping that you will write to me soon and you are quite well as it leaves me at present I must close now hoping you are well,

            MRS. JANE JENKINS."

The Editor, 5th Glo'ster Gazette.

Dear Sir,

I very much regret that the publication of my few ribald rhymes should have so gravely injured the feelings of our friends of the Commissariat.

Written in great haste to fill a vacant column, they lacked, I fear, any pretence of revision either on my part, Sir, or on yours, and it never occurred to me that my weak attempts at caricature could possibly arouse any sentiment other than that of pity for the author. Still less did I imagine that animosity would be cherished against my good friend the Editor, or that vengeance would take so terrible a form as that hinted by " A. S. C. " last month.

Mea culpa ! And upon me also be the blame which I hasten to detach from you. My excuse must be my ignorance of the fact that I was wounding the susceptibilities of some of the best of the **All Sorts and Conditions** of people that go to make our fighting men.

Trusting that you will pardon the palpable plagiarism, and that you will still be able to visit the gay city in comfort.

    I am, Sir,

        Yours to command,

            (Signed) B. F.

DEATH—THE REVEALER.

Within this dim five-windowed house of sense
I watched through coloured glass
The shapes that pass.
Soon must I journey hence
And meet the great winds of the outer world.
And see
(When God has turned the key)
The true and terrible colours of that scheme
Which now I dream.

            F. W. H.

THINGS WE WANT TO KNOW.

Who was the Brigade Ammunition Column Commander who was seen in Piccadilly at 1 a.m. the other morning, sprinting furiously in the wake of a brewer's dray and shouting—" Stop trotting those heavy draught horses, I tell you " ?

And whether anyone, to look at him now, would give him credit for being in such good training ?

Who was the M. P. who lost his hat ? And where was he ?

Who is the C. S. M. who tried to keep step with a horse ?

Who said " All horses in the new Division are mules ' Is he in No. 7 ?

Who is the reinforcement in D. Company who offered his chum 2d. to chase a ghost away ? Is he in No. 14 Platoon ?

Can anyone add another pull-through to this one ? Of all the pull-throughs I ever pulled through, I never pulled a pull-through through that pulle through like this pull-through pulls through.

Who is the mounted subaltern who thought he was commanding the Brigade while on the march ?

Who threw the M.O.'s. breeches off a Maltese cart ? Was it the T.O. or the C.O., or did the twain conspire, combine, confederate and agree together ? Had this M.O. two nose-caps which " he would not lose for anything " ? Or did they belong to his batman ?

Who is the S. O. who was reprimanded by an A.P.M. of a neighbouring Division for riding over growing crops ?

Who failed to fire at some Huns on a working party for fear of dirtying their rifles ?

What did the Padre's horse think of the march ?

What does the Mademoiselle think of the senior officer ? Did not the whole battalion envy him ?

How much did the billeting officer find " sticking out" for some of his placings ?

Did not the Padre's horse spring a surprise on the acting T. O. by chucking him off ?

Which important box was found to contain a pair of boxing gloves, a concertina, a tube helmet, and a " 75 " case ?

Why did some Company mess servants try to get their ammunition, etc., carried on the mess cart ?

How did the acting L. G. O. hope to salute the Corps Commander, and how did he actually do it ?

Who wore the red handerchief in D. Company ?

Was a neighbouring H.Q. mess jealous of 102 ?

Where does the S......usually have tea in A......?

Is it necessary to know Morse to be able to dig ?

Is the M. O. thinking of joining the Artillery ?

Did the grooms grin when our acting T. O. mounted the quondam winner of the Chester Hunt Cup ? Were they not thoroughly disappointed ?

Did the M. O. and L. G. O. compare notes on coming back from leave ?

Who is the private who cleans the sergeant's mess tin ? Is he in No. 2 platoon ? Is he working his ticket for leave ?

Who is the senior officer (lonely) who wrote to three lady-loves and " got the bird " from all three ?

If two strafes make one stunt, three stunts one boost, twenty boosts one push, five pushes one advance, how many wash-outs make one napoo ?

What was the reason for such a display of party favours on Saturday, May 6th, at H......? Are they intended to help the 8th M. to distinguish us from the Huns ?

How many fixed bayonets did the 8th M. see glistening in the western sun ?

Who was the private who, in spite of his wound, wished to go back in the trench and report sick next morning ? Had the rum issue anything to do with it ? Does he wear a green badge ?

Who was the Hun who got a rise out of the L.G.O. ?

Who spotted a fat German V.A.D. lady with telescope ? Did he say "Let me see ? " Is he at H.Q. mess ?

Who is the private who unlaced his boots to wash his neck ? Is he in No. 3 Platoon ?

Who is Mr. Boon, and what does he know about Mrs. Gray ?

What did the landlord of a well-known pub in England say to George Robey when the latter asked for the loan of a pair of pinchers ?

Who asked if they began to brick the well from the top or bottom ?

Who said he could whitewash a cellar with a scaffold-pole ?

How many Officers, on hearing the " SLASHERS " at reveille thought they had been left behind ?

Who is always being asked to make a fourth at Bridge ? And why ?

Who is the officer who has a pair of spurs for sale ?

Who is the officer who asked the groom to hold the pedals for him while he essayed to mount ? Did the bell ring ?

Did a certain Field Ambulance feel very pleased at its present of jelly ?

Who were the officers who failed to answer roll call at B...? Were they held up by the Berks ?

Who is the man in " B " Company who stirred his coffee with a candle ? Is he in " No. 7 " ?

Who is the " gunner " who tried to " fix bayonets " on the Lewis gun ? Is he, too, in " No. 7." ?

Who is the C. Company drummer who wanted to know how tall a 4-feet deep hole was ?

Who is the " C " Company drummer who used Harrison's pomade to clean his shoes with ?

Who is the newsagent in " No. 7 " ?

Did the T.O. win as many first prizes at B., as at G......?

What did the Bomb Officer think of the grenades a main ?

Who is the prominent citizen of London who returned home sober one night and was (therefore) bitten by his own dog ?

Who is the Bandsman who used bloater paste to wax his moustache ?

Who is the drummer who used brown boot polish to clean his buttons ? Did it have the desired effect ?

Who is known in No. 15 Platoon as the "Interpreter," and why ?

Who is the " A " Company man who said he heard the Germans say in plain English " Ah oui " ? Is he in No. 4 Platoon ?

Is he the same man who said one ought to have a rifle in case you get " intact " from the rear ?

Who is the sergeant, now with the 3/5th because of a sprained ankle, who has shell shock and short sight when there is a draft to come out ?

What did the Corporal Tailor say when he found they had sent him sewing needles for his gramophone ?

Who is the sergeant who declares he cleans his buttons for his own personal beauty ?

Who was found in a funk hole by R. E. ?

What Battalion took three hours to bale 15 yards of trench ?

Who cooked the cheese in a Gold Flake tin ? Was it Ellen ?

Who is the cook's mate who remarked " I had better not boil these carrots any more, or their skins will come off " ?

Who is the officer who asked if his Bready was Reakfast ? Is he an exponent of a new language ? Is he in H. Q. Mess ?

Who is the Acting S-M. who leaned against a waterproof sheet, and remarked " C...... it ! I thought it was corrugated iron " ? Is he in " A " Company ?

Is it true a well-known hunting man bought a farm to escape serving ?

What Battalion, preferring open fighting, never digs ?

Who went to the Field Cashier seven times during a nine days convalescence at ROUEN, and why ?

How long has the M.O. been telling fortunes from tea-leaves ?

Who was the officer who, on a guest-night, said good night to the C.O. at 8–30 p.m., and was found still having a French lesson at 11.30 p.m. ?

Where was a certain cook during the last Zeppelin raid in England ?

Who's the man in " B " Company who posts a sentry to watch for " German Gun Flashes " whilst on working parties ?

And was he an Ex-Guardsman and did he do the sentry's task ?

What private in " B " Company said he had lost his " Identical disc " and did he look for it in the " Sunday Portugal " ?

What Corporal was heard to say " There's five in this four already." Is he in No. 7 Platoon ?

Was it " WIT " of signalling fame that amused the R. G. A., at S... or was it the wine ? and would not the aforesaid " WIT " (with his hat off) be an asset to an overworked chaplain ?

Which " Officer's servant " told the French Lady " Boko Allemand chase me." ? And did the Allemand go to the Mess after him ?

Who was the Sergeant in " A " Company that moulded his landlady's potatoes ? And what did he get ?

Is it true that a certain Company's Sergeants are fond of watching the sights by nights ? And is the centre of attraction someone connected with the School ?

Who does the Provost Sergeant think would qualify for a Peeping Tom ? Is he an " A " Sergeant ?

Who thought he had a woman spy shadowed, but found it was an Officer ? Was it the Provost ?

Which Officer walks in his sleep ?

Who's the No. 1 L. G. who forgot to put the Gas Cylinder into the gun when putting it together ? Is he in " B " Company.

What did the first Romeo think of Juliet ? And what did the second Romeo say to her ?

Which Officer is known as a " petit cheval " ? And why ? Which Officer prefers a heavy draught ? And why ?

Do all Padres salute with left hand ?

Which Officer's Mess said that the beer is used for cooking purposes ?

Who is the Officer who gives lessons in Map-reading ?

When are Cross roads not Cross roads ?

Who, in his endeavour to show that he required a small bottle of wine, asked for " un picanin bottle vin " ?

What did the Corps Commander ask the T. O. ? Was the answer in the negative ?

What was the bet the M.O. took on, on the river bank ?

Who is the Officer who found a use for Field Glasses at 10.30 p.m. and why ?

Who is the Transport man who eats a Maconachie and then looks round for more ?

Who oiled three hooves and left the fourth ?

Who was ducked by Ginger as he stood unsuspectingly beneath the window ? Was he serenading ?

What does a Subaltern in " B " Company think of the Riding Master now ?

Why did the Company Commander drop the Jackdaw ?

Which of the " A " Company Officers' servants bought a tin of beauty-cream and used it for hair oil ? Did he also keep his pack on the mantel piece ?

Who is the private who said—It isn't so far going up Villon Lane as it is coming down ? Has he been outside Headquarters yet ?

Who is the cheerful Private in No. 1 Platoon who said he was glad he had signed on for four years, and not " for the duration " ? Does he imagine the war is going to last for years ?

HOME-THOUGHTS FROM ABROAD.

I. Song of Minsterworth Perry.

When Noe went sailing with his crew
And waters covered over the earth,
Trees that in Eden-orchard grew
Got washed away to Minsterworth.

Now every year they bloom again
(All of the trees have taken root)
And after Summer's r pening rain
We gather up the blessed fruit.

And of it brew a heavenly drink
(Two I should say) to make us merry.
Oh, cider's one, and I do think
The name o' t'other one is Perry.

II. Ballad of River Sailing.

"The Dorothy " was very small—a boat
Scarce any bigger than the sort one rows
With oars. We got her for a five pound note
At second-hand, yet when the river flows
Strong to the sea and the wind lightly blows—
Then see her dancing on the tide, and you'll
Say she's the prettiest little craft that goes
Up stream from Framilode to Bollopool.

Barefooted push her from the bank—a-float :
(The soft warm mud comes squelching through your toes)
Scramble aboard and find an antidote
For all the care a jaded spirit knows
While round the boat the broken water crows
With laughter, casting pretty ridicule
On human life and all its little woes,
Up stream from Framilode to Bollopool.

How shall I tell you what the sunset wrote
Upon the outspread waters gold and rose,
Or how the white sail of the little boat
Looked on the Summer sky the hills enclose
With blue solemnity—each white scar shows
Clear on the quarried Cotswolds high and cool,
And high and cool the fevered spirits grows
Up stream from Framilode to Bollopool.

ENVOI.

Prince, you have horses, motors, I suppose
As well. At finding pleasure you're no fool.
But have you got a little boat that blows
Up stream from Framilode to Bollopool ?

III. Defiance.

I saw the orchards whitening
To Easter in late Lent.
Now struck of hell's own lightning
With branches broken and bent
Behold the tall trees rent :—
Beaten with iron rain.
And ever in my brain—
To every shell that's sent
Sounds back this small refrain :—
" You foolish shells, come kill me,
Blacken my limbs with flame.
I saw the English orchards
(And so may die content)
All white before I came ! "

F. W. H.

ONCE BITTEN——

I guess I've learned a lot of things
I didn't know before,
And one at least is very plain
Which is, unless I'm quite insane,
I shan't be such a fool again
When next we go to war.

No longer shal I yearn to do
" The wounded hero " stunt.
To do my bit, of course, I'm keen,
But both from what I've heard and seen,
A lot of soft jobs lie between
The slacker and the Front.

I'd like to be an R. T. O.
At Havre or Leicester Square
I'd be a mass of red and blue
And look as though I'd lots to do—
And then I'd have a drink or two—
'S'n awful game, la guerre !

Or perhaps I'll join the R. F. C.
And run a Kite Balloon.
And, like a great mis-shapen star,
I'll watch the Bosches from afar
Or go to A...... in a car
To spend the afternoon.

But yet, I shouldn't like to be
Away when foes are near,
And after all, one's sure to find
It's really very dull behind,
And so I think I'll change my mind
And be a Field Cashier.

As D. A. D. A. D. M. S.
I think I ought to shine ;
Or A. P. M. or M. L. O.
Would suit me very well, you know ;
In fact, to any branch I'll go,
But not the ......Line.

EMMA KEW.

BRICKS FROM THE EDITOR'S PACK.

He who dislikes criticism is lost. For Criticism creates. We believe that the D. Company cooks make some quite nice tea nowadays, after having suffered, in company with many other cooks, a good deal of that criticism which spurs us on to renewed efforts by pointing out our weaknesses and suggesting fresh developments.

We have duly noted the criticism of the local paper which states that No. 11 of the Gazette is not up to the standard of its predecessors.

We must confess at once that it is a bit of a blow to receive a stab in that part of our anatomy which had hitherto received a pat so regularly. But is not candour a privilege of friendship ?

Bearing this in mind we too will stretch out the hand of the friend and critic. For instance, the *Echo* tells us in the summary of recent events that the Bucks defeated the Worcesters in the final for the Fanshawe Cup. We only wish they had.

We were also very surprised to read that a certain " Corporal Collett " has been promoted to " Temporary Major." Pretty quick, that, eh ? And how about the Sergeants, Sergeant-Majors, both Company and Regimental, Lieutenants, primary and secondary, Captains galore, hopped over by this agile " corporal " ! Such a case should demand the intervention of the Army Council at once.

Universal regret will be felt at the departure of our genial A.P.M., but that regret will be tempered by sincere delight at his winning a well-deserved promotion to be A.P.M. of a Corps.

A Territorial, too, and one who has soldiered for many years in the Territorial ranks ! ! ! Ye gods and little fishes ! !

He himself would like it to be a matter of common knowledge, we know, for the sake of the men who served under him in this Division, that at the Inspections which Divisional Police underwent, the highest compliments were paid to the general turn-out and efficiency of their personnel.

There is not much limelight to illuminate this kind of work. It lies chiefly behind the scenes. But the widow of T......has cause to be grateful to you, Mr. Holmes, and we shall all miss you very, very much.

Good luck to you, Major !

Cœlum non animum mutant qui trans mare currunt. In other words, Gloucester boys are Gloucester boys wherever they go. We of the " feet " have thought much about you of the Yeomanry, and have followed your gallant footsteps sympathetically, whether you were engaged in the Great Adventure at Gallipoli or occupied in chasing the wily Arab or truculent Turk in the desert. And while we ask to be allowed to congratulate you on your gallantry, we would like to say how much we sympathise with the relatives of those who have made the supreme sacrifice.

Is it true that the following is a correct list of the orders issued on the opening day of the Sergeants' Mess ?

Breakfast	7.30 a.m.
Lunch	12.30 p.m.
Tea	4.30 p.m.
Dinner...................	7 p.m.
Sick Parade	8 o'clock.

Overheard on the March :

" Blimy, Bill and there are some poor......being frozen to death in Siberia ? "

" See that there—plane ? If the Almighty had meant us to fly, He would have given us wings ! "

" Yes, and if He had meant us to carry these—packs, He would have given us four legs ! "

From an Intelligence summary—

" the attack nowhere reaching our trenches. Several dead Germans are lying in our trenches, and two wounded prisoners remain in our hands."

A little sub-editing required here, please.

The way they have in the French Army :—

" Le général Galliéni décidait, il y a quelques mois, que tous les officers d'état-major iraient prendre leur tour de tranchées et qu'ils seraient remplacés dans leurs emplois par des officeris de l'avant, blessés ou malades."

Le Cri de Paris, 7 Mai 1916.

Well done, Royals, you stuck it jolly well, and made a splendid fight of it.

We publish in this number of the Gazette a list of all those who have signed on, feeling, as we do, that they have " deserved well of the State," and that their names should be handed down to posterity.

For five francs you can have this Gazette posted to any address, as long as the War lasts.

Overheard between H...and S...

A General.—" Why are you riding on this road ? Don't you know any other road ?

T. O.—" It is usual, Sir, to ride on this road.

A General.—" What......!!!!! And how long have you been out in this line ? "

T. O.—" Only ten and a half months, Sir."

Exit General.

A little episode which happened a few days ago :

Scene : Billets near Headquarters. Provost Sergeant in doorway playing (?) a mouth organ. Enter a Private of No. 1 Platoon.

Pte.—" Can you play " Far, far away," Sergeant ? "

Sergeant.—" Oh yes ! "

Pte.—" Then make it about nine miles ! ! "

The Editor regrets the late appearance of the Gazette.

But he feels that no apology is needed. The Gazette has been the victim of circumstances. The printing and Publication, carried out as it is in France, involves many difficulties. And there are always the " exigences of the military situation " to contend with.

The List of Casualties will not be published henceforward, in obedience to a General Routine Order.

Once again he would like to take the opportunity of thanking the industrious people who continue to type the various handwritings in preparation for the Printer.

A true story reaches us from England—

An Officer was recently appointed to the Staff as Superintendent of Musketry Training. When he came to tea arrayed in his new attire, his little daughter, aged 8, greeted him with these words :— " Will they all hate you now, Daddy ? "

A Staff Officer's motor car was held up recently by a transport column. The Officer was in a hurry, and excitedly addressed himself to a company who were taking refreshment by the roadside : " Where's the delay—where's the delay ? Came the answer from a disgruntled Tommy : " Well, it ought to be in the blinking tea, but it ain't."

" Normally, if a high proportion of officers fall, the unit will go to pieces, even though its total lossses may not be extravagent. But even this rule has striking exceptions, such as the performance of the 7th Gloucesters at Gallipoli, who fought from midday till sunset on August 8th without any officer."

" Nelson's History of the War,"

Vol. XII. John Buchan.

The Deputy Chaplain General has promised to come once a month to our area to hold Confirmation Services. The Chaplain hopes that any man who has not been confirmed will let him know, and will come and have a talk about it.

A good many things go through the hands of Quartermaster Sergeant Mayne of the 145th Infantry Brigade, so that he has many acquaintances and friends throughout the Brigade. We therefore offer him our congratulations on being mentioned in the Despatch of April 30th.

We hope that Ruskin's prophecy at Sandhurst will one day be realised : " Gentlemen, I tell you solemnly that the day is coming when the soldiers of England must also be her tutors ; and the captains of her army, captains also of her mind."

It was the first autum of the War, and a Territorial Battalion—famous now for its charge—had just come out from England. It was some 20 miles behind the line. Before the night march began, the C.O. harangued his charges and ordered no smoking, no singing, no rattle of accoutrements. On reaching Poperinghe they passed a Battalion of old hands coming back from the trenches, whose passage was marked with mouth organs and song, what time that pipes and cigarettes were also busy. As a cooker passed the C. O.—referred to above—the cook lifted off the cover, and a spurt of flame shot up.

" Put that light out at once, you fool," shouted the C. O.

" And who the blinking h...... might you be, with the wind up yer," replied the Cook.

There was no one throughout the length and breadth of the Empire who heard of Lord Kitchener's death without a sharp pang of regret. London just held its breath in dumb amazement at the news.

Such success as has already attended our arms, and as will eventually crown the efforts of our armies, is due, in no small degree, as all the world knows, to the untiring efforts and organising genius of him whom every soldier in the allied ranks mourns to-day.

The Kitchener Test of India bids fair to be as famous as the Nelson Touch of Trafalgar. And no one ever preached more vigorously or more successfully the Gospel of efficiency, as not a few knew to their cost. He lived to see an army of 500,000 converted into 5,000,000, thanks to the magic of his spell and the splendour of his renown. The Allies will miss him from their Council Chamber at Berlin when terms of peace are arranged, but they will one and all admit that he helped them—as no one else could have—on that long, long road.

We gratefully acknowledge the receipt of two copies of the 5th Royal Sussex Gazette. While refraining from wishing it a long life—that would entail a long war—we wish it a prosperous one. The first issue is undoubtedly an earnest of great success in store.

The Brigade Horse Show, enlivened as it was by flashes of dazzling jumping on the part of the M. O., was a great and unqualified success. Our best thanks are due to the judges, Colonel Harris, Lt.-Colonel Cossart, and Lt.-Colonel Roberts, and to the organisers of so jolly an entertainment.

The way of the Conscientious Objector is not always smooth, *e.g.*,

X, a certain employer of labour not noted for deep piety, pleaded before the Tribunal that deep religious convictions prevented him from fighting. This plea succeded, to the great annoyance of the local recruiting authorities, who knew the man in private life.

They therefore laid their heads together and hit on a plan.

They discovered a dismissed workman who was particularly objectionable to X, and him they induced to walk up and down outside X's office. After a day or two of this, the ruse succeeded. X emerged, purple with fury, and in the presence of several handy witnesses told his persecutor that if he "...... well didn't clear off he (X) would knock his...... head off."

X is now a conscript.

We hope that we may be allowed to share with his old Battalion in expressing our deep regret at the death of our old friend Major Haddon, who died at Abbeville after an operation for appendicitis.

His vigorous cheerful personality made him a general favourite throughout the Brigade, and we all recognised in him the type of officer that every Battalion desires. His death is a great loss to the whole Brigade.

"A Corps leader, being informed that certain decorations would be allotted to his command, started his staff to compile a list of recommendations, which they despatched, says a correspondent. When the "Gazette" appeared it contained none of the names sent in, but a selection of unknown heroes. Enquiry disclosed that a roll of conscientious objectors to inoculation had got into the wrong envelope."

The Globe, June 6th.

Yes, but that's how some officers, it is alleged, were awarded a French decoration, with the difference that they formed a list of volunteers for vaccination, which was also forwarded by mistake.

I reckon that if in the future we see a soldier drunk or otherwise misbehaving, we shall do well to remember, before sitting in judgment on him, that if he doesn't hold his present appetites in order, he at any rate, held his bit of parapet with jovial grimness against what is still odds of five to one.

"Wagger," in "*Battery Flashes*."

Perhaps this war may result in some amelioration of the British Soldier's position. Before the war there were many who declared that any girl seen walking with a soldier had lost her character! It is quite true that soldiers were not treated with a proper respect. "We don't serve soldiers here: this is a respectable House." A strange contrast, this, to the German custom. Let a route march of German recruits pass through the streets, and shopkeepers would leave their customers, and run and look with pride on the raw recruits in training. With them, the army was everything; with us, nothing. We hope our countrymen will strike a happy mean between the two extremes.

It has been stated in the American Press, more or less on the authority of the American Navy, that 127 " U " boats had been accounted for by the end of April. The good work undoubtedly still goes on.

RUDAI RAT (Fragments of).

I.

Awake ! for Minnie in the Bowl of Night
Has flung the Bomb that puts the Rats to flight,
And Lo ! the Huntress of our Peace has caught
The Captain's Dug-out in a Noose of Light.

II.

Dreaming when Dawn's Left Hand was in the Sky
I heard a voice beyond the Traverse cry
" Awake, you ......fools, and get to Ground
Before the Boche bullets o'er the ground do fly."

X.

With me along yon Strip of Herbage strown
That just divides the Boche Trench from our own
Where name of Kings and Kaiser scarce is known,
And curse old Kaiser Wilhelm on his throne.

XII.

" How sweet the noise of battle is," says one,
Others—" How fine to strafe the beastly Hun ! "
Ah, keep the trench you've got and d......n the rest,
Oh, the brave music of a DISTANT gun !

XIII.

Hark to the Shell that whistles round us—" Lo,
Screaming," she says, " into the world I go :
At once the metal nose cap of my case
Burst, and its shrapnel on the Boches throw."

XXVI.

Oh, come with Emma Kew, and leave the wise
To talk ; one thing is certain, and that flies :
One thing is certain, and the rest is Lies,
That he who's wounded either lives or dies.

LXIII.

Ah Love ! could I with the R. E. conspire
To cast this sorry Hut of Logs and Mire
Would we not shatter it to bits—and then
Rebuild it stronger, larger, and much drier ?

LXIV.

Ah soon will come the night —(I know 'twill rain)—
The Moon of Heaven is rising once again :
And if she grows much brighter, she will look
Through No Men's Land for me to-night—in vain !

LXXV.

And when the Boys with joyous Foot shall pass
Across the Boche, toes upward, on the Grass,
And reach the journey's end for which we strive,
I'll join with you—but not an empty glass.

DAMAN BLUD.

EMMA KEW.

PERSONAL COLUMN.

Marriage.

May 19th, at St. George's Church, Claines, Worcester, by Special Licence, Lieut. H. P. Snowden, 1/5th Battalion Gloucestershire Regiment. son of the late Dr. Snowden and Mrs. Snowden, of Halford, Shipston-on-Stour, to Dorothy Morgan, youngest daughter of the late Joshua Crabtree, of Kidderminster, and Mrs. Crabtree, of Worcester.

As the majority of our readers are aware, Major Waller has for some weeks now been attached to Divisional Headquarters as Divisional Bombing Officer.

Captain Stuart, who left us many months ago now for the Trench Mortars, has been wounded for the second time.

Captain Mitcheson still continues to combine the duties of O. C. Salvage, and Town Major of ......

Lieutenant Symonds has left us for the Trench Mortars.

Captain Viscount Campden is on the Staff of Lord French.

Lieutenants Vaughan and Clayton have recovered from their illnesses, and the former has proceeded to the 2/5th, and the latter through the 3/5th Battalion, Gloucestershire Regiment, has rejoined his old Battalion.

Captain Francillon has been training men at the Base for some weeks. We were glad to see him back once more.

We are glad to see Captain V. N. Johnson has been given his Brevet.

All ranks throughout the Brigade were very pleased to note that Brigadier-General H. R. Done, D.S.O., had been granted the rank of Brevet Lieut. Colonel.

JEWELS.

Wondrous gleaming star.
In radiant height
Watching from afar
Jewel of the night.

Sparkling crests of foam
Joyful dance and leap
'Round our island home,
Jewels of the deep.

Flowers of every hue
Herald summer's birth,
Crowned by crystal dew,
Jewels of the earth

Acts of kindness done
Of our day a part,
Rays of Heaven won,
Jewels of the earth.

Thoughts of love that sing
High above the strife,
Peace to hearts to bring,
Jewels of our life.

Words of prayer that rise
To their heavenly goal,
Deeds of sacrifice,
Jewels of the soul.

M. L. G.

BOMBERS.

The undermentioned Officers, N. C. O's. and men have passed the test laid down for Bombers :—

2nd Lieutenant K. G. Durrant.

3741	Pte.	May, A. R.	2755	L-Cpl.	Etherton, G. H.
4277	,,	Skuse, G. H.	3324	Pte.	Smith, S.
2695	L-Cpl.	Lewis, T. H. R.	2592	,,	Neale, T. G.
2688	Pte	Johnsey, G.	2926	,,	Draper, C.
3126	,,	Swanborough, A. F.	2598	,,	Young, H. T.

PROMOTIONS AND APPOINTMENTS.

Extracts from London Gazette dated 22nd May, 1916—

Lieutenant (Temp. Capt.) Cooke, R. M. F., to Regular Forces, Gloucestershire Regiment, from Territorial Force.

Extract from London Gazette dated 2nd May, 1916.

Sergt. Major Dennis, T., to be Quartermaster with Hon. Rank of Lieutenant in Gloucestershire Regiment, dated 4/5/16.

204 Coy. Sergt-Major Wagstaff, G. H. Appointed Acting Regt. Sergt-Major with Pay and Rank of Warrant Officer, Class I, dated 4/5/16.

133 Sergt. Faville, A. Promoted Coy. Sergt-Major W. O. Class II., dated 4/5/16.

D Coy.	774	Sgt. Smith, V. G.		To be C.Q.M.S. in D Coy, dated 20/4/16
B ,,	864	L-Sgt. Turner, E. W.		To be Sgt. Orderly Room Clerk, dated 13/4/16
A ,,	1627	L-Sgt. Boughton, J.		To be Sgt. in D. Coy., dated 20/4/16
D ,,	2735	Cpl. Millard, S.		To be Sgt. in C. Coy., dated 20/4/16
B ,,	2428	L-Cpl. Butcher, P. H.		To be Cpl. dated 13/4/16
D ,,	2593	,, Over, J.	,,	,, 20/4/16
A ,,	2486	,, Peppere l, W. F.	,,	,, 20/4/16
A ,,	3999	Pte (L-Cpl) Niblett, W. E.		To be L-Cpl. with pay dated 1/4/16
B ,,	2767	,, Parham, W. G.	,,	,, 1/4/16
B ,,	2711	,, Smith, F. C.	,,	,, 13/4/16
C ,,	2742	,, Wintle, A. H.	,,	,, 15/4/16
C ,,	3014	,, Crosby, C. T.	,,	,, 16/4/16
D ,,	2663	,, Burlton, W. G.	,,	,, 20/4/16
D ,,	2653	,, Watts, E.	,,	,, 20/4/16

To be L-Corporals without pay :—

A Coy	1982	Pte. Sterry, J.		Dated	3/5/16
B ,,	2571	,, Taylor, M.		,,	3/5/16
B ,,	3241	,, Barnett, E.		,,	3/5/16
C ,,	2628	,, Cooke, D. E.		,,	3/5/16
C ,,	3299	,, Lewis, R. W.		,,	3/5/16
C ,,	1842	,, Nash, E. M.		,,	3/5/16
C ,,	2638	,, Wells, W.		,,	3/5/16
C ,,	2921	,, Cummings, P. B.		,,	3/5/'16
C ,,	1992	,, Creed, E. D.		,,	3/5/16
D ,,	2772	,, Stevens, H. C.		,,	3/5/16
D ,,	1750	,, Chandler, E.		,,	3/5/16
D ,,	1578	,, Robinson, W. G.		,,	3/5/16

2512	L-Cpl.	Minett, H.	To be Corpl.	dated	19/4/16
2322	,,	Harding, W.	,,	,,	19/4/16
2569	,,	Sullivan, D. W.	,,	,,	19/4/16
2694	,,	Lewis, M. E. L.	,,	,,	19/4/16
1978	,,	Price, H.	,,	,,	19/4/16
2177	,,	Hensley, G.	,,	,,	19/4/16
1663	,,	Abel, J. W.	,,	,,	19/4/16
3127	Pte.	Timms, H. J.	To be unpaid L-Cpl.,	,,	19/4/16
3281	,,	Brint, A.	,,	,,	19/4/16

R.I.P.

They shall not grow old as we that are left grow old :
Age shall not weary them, nor the years condemn,
At the going down of the sun and in the morning
We will remember them in Christ.

5th Gloucester Gazette.

A Chronicle, serious and humorous, of the Battalion while serving with the
BRITISH EXPEDITIONARY FORCE.

ON LEAVING ——

Tune—Regimental March of the 1/4 Bn. Royal Berkshire Regiment.

The Forty-eighth are going away
To find some Prussian Guards to slay,
And won't that be a glorious day
When the Forty-eighth get into the fray !

Here they came and here they stayed
For all but a year and ne'er dismayed.
Tho' Hun burst shrapnel, winter sent rain
The latter brought work, the former pain.
They worked all day and they worked all night
And encouraged each other as well they might,
For no word of approval e'er came through
From those behind who never knew
What days of work the trenches swallowed
When sentries all in sump-holes wallowed,
With water in places up to the waist,
And all the rations with mud to taste.
But when Spring arrived and the weather should mend
By every rule of foe and friend,
They dug a trench in " never mind where."
And the Huns they straffed them nightly there
For ever a week but they didn't mind,
And to show them so they let them find
Still farther out another line,
Dug by them to the same design.
But the offensive came and they had to go
In another region to face the foe,
And they let at last the well-known trench
Taken over at first from the gallant French.

The Forty-eighth are going away
To find some Prussian Guards to slay,
And won't that be a glorious day
When the Forty-eighth get into the fray !
                                                    C. V. N. P.

(We are very sorry indeed to say that within a very few days of writing these lines, Second Lieutenant C. V. N. Puckeridge was reported " wounded and missing.")

THE BATTLE OF THE SOMME.

It was on the Morning of Saturday, July 1st, the memorable day of the great Infantry attack, that the last number of the Gazette was placed in the hands of our readers.

It did not fall to the lot of our Brigade to take any active part in the initial stages of this colossal struggle, albeit it was on the very point of carrying out an attack to help our friends from Ulster on the night of Sunday, July 2nd.

It was not indeed until the Battle of the Somme had entered upon its third week that our Brigade was called upon to attack and consolidate some German trenches. Eventually, after many gallant attempts, the objective was gained. But many of the old hands have shed their blood, many have made the supreme sacrifice, and we mourn the loss of many good comrades.

It is then a Battalion somewhat bent and battered which publishes this Gazette. But every Officer and man is glad to know that " D " Company of the Bucks Battalion, gallantly led by Captain Birchall, followed hard upon our attacks, and crowned the operations with success.

God be with you and us who go our way
And leave you dead upon the ground you won.
For you at last the long fatigue is done,
The hard march ended.   You have rest to-day.

You were our friends.   With you we watched the dawn
Gleam through the rain of the long winter night,
With you we laboured till the morning light
Broke on the village, shell-destroyed and torn.

Not now for you the glorious return
To steep Stroud Valleys, to the Severn leas,
By Tewkesbury and Gloucester, or the trees
Of Cheltenham under high Cotswold stern.

For you no medals such as others wear
—A cross of bronze for those approved brave.
To you is given, above a shallow grave,
The wooden cross that marks you resting there.

Rest you content.   More honourable far
Than all the Orders is the Cross of wood,
The symbol of self-sacrifice that stood
Bearing the God whose brethren you are.

EXAMINATION PAPER.

(a) General Knowledge :

1. Describe briefly the increase in weight of a pack on a route march of 15 miles.

2. If one company working 25 hours per day can dig two trenches (fire), and wire them on the second night, each man removing 80 cubic feet of soil every 4 hours, calculate

    a. the number of rounds of S. A. A. fired by the Germans ;

    b. the average deposit of " 5.9 " per foot run of trench ;

    c. probable satisfaction given, and betting for and against an " encore."

3. How many times, and in how many different ways, can a party of 25 men be told off into other parties of 25, without leaving a balance of three.
    (Party of 25 to include 2 S.M's. and 1 C.Q.M.S.)

4. Discuss in as few lines as possible the rise and fall of the bread ration.

5. A munition worker works 5 hours a day, 5 days a week, and draws £5 pay per week. Compare the scale of pay of those who make shells with those who deliver them.

6. If parading at 4 a.m. with field operations ensuing until 9 p.m. comes under the heading of " rest," describe your ideas as to how *busy* day should be spent.

7. Explain the following :

D. A. M. N. Q. G. R. S. V. P. N. B. G. B. F.
D. A. S. S. C. B.

Lemon, Minnie, crump, dud, napoo, blighty, cushy.

(b) Trench Warfare :

1. Is it correct to refer to the " parrokeet " and " parachute " of a fire trench ? If not, why not ? Draw a map to illustrate your answer.

2. If an Engineer and a half dig a sump and a half, in a month and a half, how soon can you expect to get the necessary sump cover and a half, and will it fit when provided ?

3. Assuming the mean velocity of a Very Light to be x feet per second, draw a graph showing the percentage error of shrapnel bursts in terms of y (Brokerage $1/8$ %.)

(c) Rest Billets.

1. Discuss the comparative nutritive values of margarine and dubbin.

2. A barn contains 30 wire beds for 36 men and 4 N. C. O.'s. Give a rough sketch showing how

    (i) the 4 N. C. O.'s. will arrange the platoon.

    (ii) how you would do it.

3. What is the price of " oofs " per dozen if, when the price is raised 40 centimes a dozen, madame replies " napoo fineesh, compree ? "

(d) Fatigues.

1. State the probable charge asked for by Messrs. Cooks Tours Ltd. to view the Corps Lines. Do you consider it sufficient ?

2. Having dug 500 yards of cable trench, laid the cable and filled in the trench again you are given a board with the words " R. E. buried cable " painted on it. State briefly any remarks you consider suited to the occasion.

3. From your experience in such matters, how many hurdles would you be able to construct out of Cranham Woods ?

CONSOLATOR AFFLICTORUM.

" Must ever I be so
Yellow and old " you asked,
" With living overtasked,
Ugly and racked with pains ? "
I answered " Even so,
Dearest, yet love remains."

               F. W. H.

" RESTING."

(In two parts : The Beginning and—The Rest.)
(PART I. MAY)

If you're wakin' call me early
    Brigadier,
Ere the dewdrops bright and pearly
    Disappear.
We've a month away from trenches—
No more saps and sumps and stenches !—

O, a chance to air our French is
    Gettin' near.
At the Bosches we've been firin'
    For a year ;
(We have also done some wirin',
    Brigadier.)
There's been *always* something doin',
From that bullet-ridden ruin,
Dear old " HERBY," right to C. ...N,
    Pretty near.

We shall do a route-march gaily—
    We shall cheer—
If it takes us out from S......Y,
    Brigadier.
For we've tramped that blinkin' Plain a—
Long " the corduroy by JENA "
Till we're gettin' most profane (" A
    Shell-hole 'ere ")

" PASTEUR'S " fed up *and* " REVEL,"
    Very near.
We will gladly give the Devil
    " PAS DE TIR."
Other blighters can revet 'em—
For a month we'll love to let 'em,
We are going to forget 'em,
    Brigadier.

No more diggin' like a navvy—
    No damn'd fear ;
No—it's " *Compree, Mam'selle, Avez-*
    Vous de Beer ? "
While across the cafe table
We'll recall, with merry babel,
How the " R. E. buried cable "—
    (The idea !)

Yes, at " midnight-stunt " rehearsin'
    We've no peer,
And we do love keepin' " VERCIN-
    GET'RIX " clear,
But Fatigues can be heart-breakin'—
For a real good rest we're achin'.
Call me early, if you're wakin'—
    Brigadier.

      PART II. (JUNE)

" Call me early, if you're wakin' "
    Well, it's queer
But you *did* do (no mistakin')
    Brigadier ;
And between me and the mess-tin,
After thirty days of Restin'—
Well, you won't mind my suggestin' ?
          (Censored here.)

Every morning why should slumbers
    Interfere ?—
We'd proceed to Rest (by numbers)
    Brigadier.
Hours and hours we'd Rest—Salutin',
Bay'net-fightin', Marchin', Shootin'
(There is really something cute in
    The idea.)

How we *loved* that Shrapnel-helmet !
    You could hear
Muttered blessings overwhelm it
    (From the rear.)
Yes it's hot, I own ; it stifles
(And we'd picks, and spades, and rifles)
But, when Restin, who minds trifles,
    Brigadier ?

Then you took us on manœuvres,
    Cher monsieur,
Where like furniture-removers
    We'd appear.
We took food and ammunition—
We took flags to show position—
We took cover in addition
    (Am I clear ?)

Well, it's over ; Napoo ; *Fini*;
    And I fear
(Now we're back with dear old " Minnie,"
    Brigadier)
We would all declare it *bon* to
See again the towns we've gone to—
Well, I know *I* rather want to—
    Think it queer ?

But we're " in the pink "—we own it
　　　(Put it here !)—
You knew best ; our Rest has shown it
　　　(That's sincere.)
With this Big Push on we're *all* in—
Ready waiting for the " Fall in."
When you want us, do the callin',
　　　Brigadier !

　　　　　　　　　　　　F. R. B.

(We much regret that Second Lieutenant F. R. Bell has been wounded.)

THINGS WE WANT TO KNOW.

Who went to bed without even unlacing his breeches round the knee ?

And why ?

Who is the Split-King ?

How does the Mascot manage to shave with an ordinary razor without a looking-glass ?

When will the stitches be taken out of the Padre's horse by the Veterinary ?

Is it best to join the D.S.C. if you want to get an extra stripe ?

Why was a limber ordered to fetch the Q. M's valise ?

Who were the TWO who got their valises respectively down to par and 33 lbs. ?

Has a match for the Divisional Heavy Draught been discovered yet ?

Or are they still WAITING ?

Are they still using Beer for cooking purposes in C Company Mess ?

Who was so very grieved at having to give up the yellow on his shoulder strap ?

Who was the Officer's servant who, while taking up food to the Officers in the Trench, said to his mate " Where's the stump-hole mate ? " and then found himself in a sump-hole ? Is he in D Company ?

Which Officer doses his horse with " Woodward's Gripe Water " ?

Who asked the Artillery on " The Day " for the number of boots repaired during the past month ? Was the message marked Urgent or ordinary ?

Who is the Colonel of the Field Ambulance who has lace-edging to his pillow ?

Who is the Officer who while on leave, on the morning of the night after, drank his bath ?

What is the firm of Pat and Co. doing without its senior partner ?

Has the conversation anent the Russian gun been more subdued of late ?

Who is the Lance-Corporal who is in love with Emmie Gration ? Is he in No. 6 Platoon, B Company ?

Who is the Company Commander in the Royals who found himself in Command of " C " Company of the Oxfords during a practice of Night Operations ? What did he say when he discovered it ?

Are we Incomparables or merely Incompatibles ?

What did the L. G. O. say when the pole broke ?

What did " we " see ?

Who opened all the Champagne and the Perrier at 6-30 p.m. ? And why ? Has he another job now ?

When is a Souvenir-hunter not a Souvenir-hunter ? And what is the connection between Souvenir-hunting and salvage ? Has a brass valuer been appointed ?

Why did the Sergeant dislike drawing his pay from the Salvage Company ? Is he known as "Happy J........." ?

What made the M.O. think the Machine Guns were Stokes Guns ?

What Corporal in B Company was heard to ask for a mirror to see if his eyes shone ? And was it due to an extra dose of rum ?

CORPS SHIPPING INTELLIGENCE FROM LLOYDS,

JULY, 1916.

Overdue Market.

S. S. BACK BADGE—due August, 1914.

S. S. LEAVE—service practic..lly suspended.

Steamship movements :
S. S. BLIGHTY (France-England.) Special cheap fares.

S. S. CUSHY. Sailings not guaranteed.

Arrivals :
S. S. NEW ARMY (Second Line), May.

Wrecks and Casualties :
S. S. BREAD—Wrecked on Dogger Sand Bag.

S. S. REST—All hope abandoned.

KOSSOVO DAY.

From this sweet nest of peace and Summer blue—
England in June—a sea bird's nest indeed
Guarded of waves, and hid by the sea-weed
From envious hunter's eye, we send to you
Our flying thoughts and prayers, our treasure too,
Poor though it be to bandage wounds that bleed
For country dear belovéd. There the seed
Of homely loves and occupations grew
To wither in the flame of Godless might,
Kindled by hands of treachery, yet reeking
With blood of friends and neighbours. Serbia, thou
Hast thought us careless and far off ; know thou
Thy name to us is sudden drums outspeaking
And tortured trumpets crying in the night !
　　　　　　　　　　　　F. W. HARVEY.
From the Westminster Gazette—June 28, 1916.

BOXING NEWS.

T. ATKINS, the Hebuterne Hope v. FRITZ, The Bucquoy Basher

Round 1. (July, 1915).

Very little doing. Both sides appeared to be manœuvering for position. Atkins fairly confident but Fritz avoided.

Round 2. (February, 1916).

The Hope scored a few points with some light taps but was heavily countered. Entirely out-fighting. Fritz put in a tremendous lot of work and got some direct hits on the Point. Atkins felt the strain and was visibly tiring towards the end and welcomed the call of time.

Round 3. (July, 1916).

Both men very strong. Our man discarded his pipsqueak tactics and hit hard. Fritz got home with some 5.9 but Atkins countered with a straight 15" and cross hit with a 9" and cleverly dodged Fritz's well-known Minnie upper-cut. Atkins attacked furiously and broke down his main defences. Fritz got a bit dicky in the wind. The round closed with some hurricane infighting. Fritz only being saved by time.

Fourth Round,

(The Editor regrets that his contributor being suddenly put on fatigue could not finish the account.)

THE DIGGERS.

It is our fate that we must wait
    And sit in a ditch and gaze
All weary wet, o'er the parapet,
    Until we end our days
In slow decline (where neither wine
    Nor women cheer us up.)
Exchanging cards with Prussian Guards
    Via Kynochs, Paine and Krupp.

Each day we clean with ardour keen
    (Or leave may hang in doubt)
Our rifles which the watery ditch
    Could almost do without
For though the hype may serve to snipe,
    It's really rather tame
To see each day's Communiquès
    Remark " Our snipers claim—"

We get no chance when great advance
    Goes battering down the Hun ;
Though once we thought the dawn was fraught
    With trenches to be won.
They marched us out and none had doubt
    Objectives we'd attain
And do dam well ; but then—Oh hell !
    They marched us home again.

As days go by the gum boots (thigh)
    Will issue from the store,
And in the floods of Winter's mud
    We'll wallow as before,
Whilst " Unterstande " contrives to guard
    The Huns from all we do ;
Though when the war is almost o'er,
    We may have dugouts too.

Yet now and then we patient men
    Creep softly out o' nights,
A whole Brigade with pick and spade,
    Despite the Very lights ;
And never pig did ever dig
    For truffles with his snitch
With heartier glee than foolish we
    Another blasted ditch.

Where 'tis our fate that we must wait
    Knee-deep in slush and gaze
All weary wet o'er the parapet
    Until we end our days
In slow decline (where neither wine
    Nor women cheer us up.)
Exchanging cards with Prussian Guards
    Via Kynochs, Paine and Krupp.

July 11th.   W. O. D.

(We much regret that Second Lieutenant W. O. Down has been wounded.)

OUR BENEFACTORS.

Bishop Frodsham.	Papers
Lt.-Colonel Winterbotham.	,,
Lt.-Colonel Marling	,,
Mr. W. R. Voller.	,,
Mrs. Russell Kerr.	,,
Mr. and Mrs. Balfour.	1000 Canvas shoes
Miss Backhouse.	Papers
Miss Parr.	,,
Sergt. Turner.	Typing.
Pte. Shaw.	,,
Pte. Orchard.	,,
The Echo.	(Echo) daily.
The Hon. Mabel Gye.	Papers.
Miss Karn.	,,
Colonel Griffith.	,,
Mrs. Temple Cook.	,,

WONDERS.

What magic is in common grass
To bring this miracle to pass,
That within it one should find
Salves to give him peace of mind ?
—It's very queer that garden weed
Should minister to my soul s need.

What fairy in the falling rain,
Takes the robin's small refrain
And twists it to a tiny charm
To keep a tempted heart from harm ?
—It puzzles me a wild bird's song
Should save my soul from doing wrong.

     F. W. H.

BRICKS FROM THE EDITOR'S PACK.

For the edification of its readers the Continental Daily Mail stated that the Hem which the Allied forces captured was Two and a half miles W. S. W. of Doullens.

We presume that this was the objective of the Supply Column in the Push.

From......Divisional Intelligence Report, 7th-8th July,

    " Miscellaneous "

" SMOKE—Much smoke arose from dugout at ......" They must have been singing the Hymn of Hate.

" Then came a powerful officer who performed prodigies. One Bosch hesitated about following him, when beckoned to do so, and paid the penalty. He then took another prisoner, and just that moment a shell hit him in the neck and for a second he was stunned. The prisoner tried to escape only to be caught by this fearless wounded officer and brought back in triumph."

How the German Lines are Raided.

    Letter to the *Times* July 4th, 1916.

Some neck ! eh ?

We always knew that we were facing the Hun, but we little thought that the Vandal was on our Flank. Yet such indeed would appear to be the case. The French dug their trenches at some cost. They " called the lands after their own names," naturally " thinking that these dwelling places shall endure from one generation to another."

But such old and familiar names as Montvallier and Remaun. Rouget de Lisle—Trenches, we should have thought that anyone would have held sacred to the memory of our Allies—have now been replaced by a new fangled and meaningless nomenclature. Rouget de Lisle, too, so called in memory of the author of La Marseillaise, once harboured " The Vicarage " in its midst.

Captain Konig commanding the German Submarine Liner " Deutschland " on reaching Baltimore U.S.A. was interviewed by a number of Newspaper Representatives.

" Did you have any accidents coming over ? "
" None," came the reply from the Bridge.
" Did you see any British Ships ? "
" None."

With admirable tact the interviewers refrained from asking the Captain of this Submarine Liner how many German ships he had seen at the bottom of the sea.

Fas est ab hoste doceri. Some of us witnessed a most remarkable piece of organisation on the part of the Huns. One of our aeroplanes on its way back from a visit to an important French town, now well behind the German lines, swooped down to 200 feet and turned its two Lewis guns on to a Battalion of Huns marching in column of fours. The strafe was very successful, but our machine had no time to rise high over the German trenches, with the result that by the joint action of many machine guns the pilot was compelled to land with his wounded observer about half a mile behind our lines. Instantly salvoes of pip-squeaks were fired " anywhere " on the chance of hitting the wounded machine. Within three minutes no less than three sausages appeared and the 5-9's knocked the aeroplane out at once. In fact there was only just time to get the wounded observer—very faint from loss of blood—and the Lewis guns, away when the machine was " napoo." A magnificent example of organisation. We wonder how long we should have taken.

From another Battalion Orderly Room. The following order was issued : " Officers will personally see that their Kids do not weigh more than 35lbs." Do any of these Officers travel for P. Jones and Co. of Chicago ?

" With 32 prisoners they (a small detachment of the Dragoon Guards and also of the Deccan Horse) rode on slowly, still reconnoitring the open country on the skirt of Deville Wood, until they came again under machine gun fire and drew back. As they did so an Aeroplane came overhead......and in another moment stopped over the German infantry concealed in the wheat......"
Daily Telegraph, July 17th, 1916.

This evolution must synchronise, we presume, with the adoption of non-skidding tyres for aeroplanes.

Some wounded German prisoners were being conducted to an ambulance. For lack of anything particular to say, the R. A. M. C. Orderly said to one of his charges, " Well matey, what d'ye think of this war ? " His surprise may be imagined when he received the reply, " Not a b......lot, Bill."

The Company had surrendered. But it was a bitter pill for the two Prussian Guards who sulked in their dug-out. They sent a message to say that if the English wanted them they could come and fetch them. However the voice of an Officer suggesting a couple of lemons as an alternative to their surrender made them change their minds. Even then they made at first as if they would not give up their revolvers. Truly it must be a bitter pill to surrender to the Contemptibles.

It would appear that the Huns are convinced that they are " God's Own." Thus Bumptious Baron von Stengel states that " the whole present course of the war proves that we Germans have been chosen by Providence from among all the peoples to advance at the head of Kulture and to lead them to a secure peace under our protection.........we form the Crown of Kulture in all creation......there is no people richer in feeling and ideals than we Germans, and so under our protection all International Law is perfectly superfluous, because we of our own instinct give everyone his rights."

For sheer naked effrontery this boastful and impudent challenge and claim is hard to beat.

Their hideous treatment of Belgium, Serbia and Montenegro offer a splendid example of German " richness in feeling and ideals," and these ideals, as the inhabitants of those countries are fully aware, are the paving stones of Hell and not, as the Teuton proudly boasts, the coping stones of Heaven.

If it be true, as the wise tell us, that wicked things owe their existence to the prevalence of ignorance, the continued existence of the German Empire would seem to offer no exception to the rule. Germany does not know. Six months ago a party of fifty German Officers were being conducted to Havre en route for England.

They bemoaned their bad luck in being captured, but were busy consoling themselves with the inability of their captors to take them to England, as their own Navy blockaded its coasts !

Prisoners taken during the Battle of the Somme were confident (they had been officially informed) that at no time during the last six months had the Russians made any advance.

One day Germany will know, and then there will be trouble.

" LONDON and AUSTRALIA have won POZIERES with deeds of heroism that will never die."
Daily Express, July 26th.

" The British have won one of the most important successes in the new advance by the capture of POZIERES, the French village which commands the plains to the east, stretching to BAPAUME and other points of great strategic importance.

The brunt of the fighting was borne by the Australians and the London Territorials. The Australians have already been officially thanked by Sir Douglas Haig." Daily Express, 26th.

We are delighted to see that the Australians have been thanked by Sir Douglas Haig. A Territorial Division we wot of has also been thanked.

" Jack " himself would be the first to protest against the two drawings of himself which appear in this number, were he allowed to give expression to his feelings. But he has gone as far as to say that he at any rate never sat-down—as did a certain other horse—under his burden, which latter, in that case, was much over-weight. Besides, does he not carry the Split-King—far and wide across the wide Champagne of France ?

All ranks much appreciate the copies of the "Echo" which reach us so regularly from the Office of that Paper. There is a small stampede when the "Echo" boy approaches.

The liberty permitted to the cartoonist should always be generous. But we were more than surprised to see a "humorous" sketch the other day in which the fool of the family anticipates joining the Intelligence Corps, as his doctor had ordered him complete mental rest. There's no vein of humour in a cheap and wholly undeserved sneer at a body of men whose bravery has only been equalled by their intelligence.

We welcome the suggestion made in the press the other day that all those excused from Military Service on the ground of "Religious" and conscientious scruples, should be then and there disfranchised. For surely if one's country is not worth fighting for, it can hardly be worth living in. Some of the boys who come back, will have something to say about it aprés la guerre.

"Prowse Point" was once very familiar to us. Brigadier-General Prowse, of the 11th Brigade, whose gallantry at what was called the first Battle of Ypres, was thus placed on record, was killed on July 1st during the Battle of the Somme, while gallantly endeavouring to capture a machine gun.

The deeds of the Sixth and Eighth Battalions of the Royal Warwicks on the morning of Saturday, July 1st, will long be remembered. We believe that any Division will be proud to find itself shoulder to shoulder with the 48th, whose two representatives were surely "incomparable"—themselves.

On the morning of July 10th, it is stated on good authority that the Bosch Intelligence Officer, looking towards the second New Trench, was heard to exclaim, "Done again, by Jove!"

Mr. and Mrs. Balfour could have sent no more opportune present than the 1000 Canvas shoes which arrived last month. "Bon for the Troops."

OUR PORTRAIT GALLERY.

No. 12. Pte. O. Hall.

My name is Oscar Hall
—Private Hall.
I'm the darling of the girls, one and all,
And the postman staggers in
With letter, box and tin
From "Susie," "Flo," and "Min":
—Bless their eyes!

I write them all in turn,
—Each in turn.
And the phrases that I use glow and burn.
They were culled from different places
(But their origin none traces)
To brighten pretty faces;
—Bless their eyes!

When I'm Sergeant-Major Hall
—Major Hall,
And the war is finished up—good and all.
I'll put aside my gun,
And, forsaking of the Hun,
I will marry.........Everyone:
—Bless her eyes!

F. W. H.

SOCIETY NEWS.

Lady Minnie, who has been doing a lot of good work among the wounded, gave a pleasing display recently at Q. 28 d. 2. 6., where so many of our brave lads are resting.

Many spectators were so deeply moved that at the end of the performance they eagerly sought some slight token of remembrance. .

Lord and Lady Dudmore Tar are naturally proud of their gallant offsprings, Edgar, Clarence and Llewellyn. The first, who married the Lady Cassandra Headstrong, the lovely daughter of the 23rd Earl of Peckham, writes thrilling stories of his onerous duties and dangers with the 2nd line, A.S.C. His younger brother Clarence, who was a prime mover in the raising of the Home Defence Corps, has now won his spurs in the Army Pay Corps.

Little Llewellyn, who has barely finished his training with the V.A.D., and who is delicately constituted, is expected to leave for the front any day now.

Whilst chatting recently with the lovely Lady Angela Vaseline de Cinto, I was very much struck by her elegant toilette, carried out in peau de soie embroidered with diamonds, it is flung round the figure in the true oriental fashion, the flowing folds of scrumptious tulle being nattily caught up in fringe-like panels.

The skirt, delightfully fashioned in three tiers of pale flesh pink, delicately lined with rambler roses and clusters of mignonette, was as charming as it looked cool. A long black moire fob with diamond insets led the eye to a ravishing toque of bunched tulle, edged and puckered with nutty brown ninon and bands of taffeta.

The tout ensemble was wonderfully chic and tastefully a la mode.

Lady Piano Customs is probably our hardest war worker. During the last month she has taken part in two flag days, sold 33 programmes, and on the rose day sold one Gloire de Dijon and Two Allan Richardsons, thus raising for the Red Cross fund £1 12s. 7¾d. (expenses amounting to £1 12s. 1½d.)

We implore this ornament to society, not only for her own sake, but for that of the illustrated papers, not to overtire herself.

"B" COMPANY SPORTS.

Taking advantage of a slack evening (not a frequent occurrence lately), "B" Company amused themselves with some sports on Thursday, July 13th. As the running track was far from smooth and no one was feeling very strenuous, the programme contained a fair proportion of "rag" events. There were many entries, necessitating several heats in each race. The 100 yards was won by Sergt. Hill. closely followed by Pte. Iles. Ptes. Excell and Tilley stuck together like Siamese twins in the three-legged race, winning by about a yard from Ptes. Chandler and J. Taylor. The second and third pairs were separated by inches. One of the best events was the Tug-of-War, especially the second pull between 5 and 6 Platoons, won by the former, who appeared in the Final against No. 7 and soon succumbed to Sergt. Hill's vigorous stroke. The next event was described as a hobble skirt race, the make-up consisting of a pair of puttees round the knees. Competitors were divided between two styles, Kangaroo leaps and a ladylike shuffle. I forgot which style L–Corpl. Enoch and Pte. Horwood, the winners, adopted. In the All-fours race Sergt. Hill just failed to catch Pte. Tilley. Another game from the Gym.—passing the cap—was won by No. 8. As it was now getting late several events had to be left out, and a finish was made with the Obstacle race over a course laid out by Mr. King, which gave a chance to everyone, and was won by Pte. G. Harvey with Pte. Lane second. Altogether an enjoyable evening thanks to the keenness and good humour of the Company.

DYING IN SPRING.

Lo, now do I behold
Sunshine and greenery
And Death together rolled
—Yet not in mockery.

Life was a faithful friend
Shall I make other of that dark brother
Whom God doth send ?

My dear companions—you
That have been more to me
Than grief or gaiety
This sure is true—
That we shall meet once more beyond Death's door,
Again be merry friends
Where friendship never ends.

F.W.H.

(It was a saying of Pericles the Athenian that the loss of the young men in battle was like the loss of spring to the year.)

THE EDITOR.

Of course it is a great honour to be a " distinguished Contributor " to the Gazette. For one thing it leads to quite an intimate acquaintance with the editor and that is almost as good as having a friend in the War Office. One gets all the latest news. I well remember the first time I timidly approached the Editor with a little " effort." He was engaged in trying to put the Medical Officer under the table at the time, but he immediately relinquished this important work and greeted me with a jovial heartiness which is all his own. I waited anxiously while he perused the pages with contracted brows and my relief was intense when he actually smiled and called me "old man " (or was it " chap "?.) Anyway I was a proud man. Since then I have been established as a contributor and though it is a proud position, at times the life is hard. I confess with shame that I have even wished the Editor would go to .... Posieres about the period when he has ceased to be content with the promise of "something to-morrow." There is no stopping him for he is very determined. It is like this. For about a fortnight after the Gazette is out (supposing it is not more than two months late) there is peace. I meet the Editor and have friendly discussions on Welsh Disestablishment, Home Rule for Ireland and other non-contentious subjects. At the end of that time a wary look comes into his eye. " Hullo, old chap, cold better ? " or " Heard about the Russian General ? " and I know he is on my track again because I hadn't got a cold and the Russian General is just a red herring. Then out it comes " Well good-bye old chap, (pause.) Hav'nt got anything for the next Gazette, have you ?"

Later on, when I say " No " there is a pained expression of his which is hard to bear. Later still, he looks positively stern. " Must write something to morrow old chap," Later still, I cannot bear to face him. But usually there is no escape. For instance—Scene, a Trench collapsing in Sections. Time about 12-30 p.m. Dramatis persona, myself stuck up to my knees in mud endeavouring to mend a pump. Voice from the darkness. " Got that little thing for the Gazette yet old chap ? Write it out at once, can you ? " And so of course it had to be done. I have taken cover in many places during the acute period. By hiding in shell-holes and mined dug-outs I once evaded retribution for my broken promises for nearly two days, but he ran me down at last. We were digging a trench (for cables in front), and noticing a man using a pick in a way calculated to frighten if not harm his neighbour, I went up to reprove him, And lo, out of the flying sparks and bits of flint came the well-known query, " Got that thing you promised for the next Gazette, old chap ? "

OLD BOYS COLUMN.

2nd Lieut. Ayliffe has, we regret to say, been wounded in both arms.

2nd Lieut. G. H. Ross, who also gained a Commission in the 8th Battalion, fell in the same fighting. We offer our sincere sympathy to his young widow.

The engagement is announced of Captain R. S. Dacre Stuart, 5th Gloucestershire Regiment, only son of M. and Mrs. R. E. Stuart, of Dudbridge House, Stroud, to Gladys, only child of the late Rev. W. H. Gibbons, of Upton Pyne, Devon, and Mrs. Gibbons, of The Manor, Cowley, near Exeter.

Lieuts. Priestly and Cullis paid us a short visit one afternoon ; as did Lieut. Harvey of the Motor Machine Gun Corps.

Lieut. Cullis has since been wounded.

PERSONAL COLUMN.

Capt. Francillon sprained his ankle badly and has been home on sick leave.

Lieut. C. W. Winterbotham is attached to the 143rd Infantry Brigade as Assistant Staff-Captain.

Sergts. Jennings, D.C.M., Meadows, Thompson, and White, fell victims to Trench Fever. While all were shipped off to England, Sergt. Jennings was fortunate enough to land up at a Hospital at Paignton.

Capt. Sullivan, R.A.M.C., has been on the Staff of a Hospital at the Base. We wish him a speedy recovery.

Lieut. F. R. Dobson, R.A.M.C., is now attached to the Battalion.

ADVERTISEMENTS.

FOR SALE.

Lot No. 1. Fine Battalion : going for a Push.

Lot No. 2. Tired Major : going for a Whisky.

Lot No. 3. Big Push : going for ever.

Lot No. 4. Boutons noires—complete set—very rare, without reserve.

Lot No. 5. Lewis Gun—origin unknown—guaranteed to fire more than two shots in succession.

Lot No. 6. Padre's Horse—suitable for elderly Naval man.

Lot No. 7. Fine collection of Souvenir Anglais.

Lot No. 8. Complete Map of Europe $\frac{1}{10,000}$

Lot No. 9. First Edition of Sherlock Holmes, re-written, by Provost Sergeant Jack.

EXCHANGE AND MART.

Infantry Soldier about to be demobilised would part with pack cheap. No reasonable offer refused. Would accept light-weight Motor Bicycle in exchange.

Desirable Route march, complete with sweat, sun, dust, waterbottle (empty) Helmets (Hun and Shrapnel)—Pioneers perpetually pass in Lorries—What offers ?

Part share in dug-out. Would accept seat in M.T.—in exchange.

Fine opening for a young man in a German Trench. Good opportunity of a rise in the Bombing Section.

Pay (including rent Shrapnel Villa, Gas laid on) 5s. 9d. per day.

Antiques, cast off clothes of every description : apply 2-4 a.m. Dressing Station.

German Dug-outs at BAPAUME, vacant shortly. Rent free.

ON A JUNE MORNING.

In the shade of a forest giant
A wild bird sat and sang,
Swayed in the branches pliant
That downward, drooping, hang ;
The soul of a world's rejoicing
In glorious notes outpoured
Through a wonder of gladness, voicing
The freedom of heights he soared.

The leaves of the old tree quivered,
By the breath of the warm wind fanned,
And bathed in the June sun, glimmered
Like jewels of fairyland.
While clear, to the dazzling azure
Through the summer day so still,
Rose the exquisite stirring rapture
And joy of the song bird's trill.

It lifted the heart of the hearer
Narrowed by weight of care
By self-forged fetters, nearer
To the planes of gladness rare,
Where the soul of man returning
From bonds of an earth-bound shrine
Is lost in ecstasy, burning
With worship and love divine.

And ever, through depths of sorrow
Dimming the future years,
Shines forth in his sight the morrow
That shall end the day of fears ;
And 'mong the memories scorning
Sad hours that drag along
Live the vision of that June morning
And the lilt of a wild bird's song.

M. L. G.

R.I.P.

Qualis tandem Lacaena ? Quae cum filium in proelium misisset et interfectum audisset, " Idcirco," inquit, " genueram ut esset qui pro patria mortem non dubitaret occumbere."

CICERO.

How sleep the brave who sink to rest,
By all their country's wishes blest !
By fairy hands their knell is rung :
By forms unseen their dirge is sung :
There honour comes, a pilgrim gray,
To bless the turf that wraps their clay.

WILLIAM COLLINS.

They shall not grow old as we that are left grow old :
Age shall not weary them, nor the years condemn,
At the going down of the sun and in the morning
We will remember them in Christ.

O

AT THE BRIGADE HORSE SHOW.

OUR MACHINE GUN'S INACTION.

"Do you know my name?

Well, if you don't get out quick YOU'LL GET IT !"

"Where IS the O.C.R.S.P.C.A. ?"

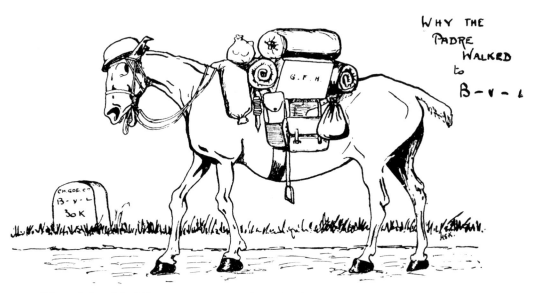

WHY THE PADRE WALKED to B – V – L

(Nevertheless "Jack" was very sorry to hear that Lieutenant King had been wounded.)

No. 14.   SEPTEMBER, 1916.

5th Gloucester Gazette.

A Chronicle, serious and humorous, of the Battalion while serving with the
BRITISH EXPEDITIONARY FORCE.

HONORIS CAUSA.

The Commander-in-Chief, under the authority of His Majesty The King, has made the following awards.

The Military Cross :

Lieutenant H. P. Snowden.
2nd Lieutenant E. H. Harvey.
456 C.S.M. Tibbles, W. G.

The Distinguished Conduct Medal :

2571   Corporal Taylor, M.
3028   Pte. Lane, J. D.

The Corps Commander has awarded the Military Medal to the following :—

2425   Pte. Trinder, A. J. (Since killed in action.)
2169   Stretcher-Bearer Merrett, F. P.
3039   Corporal Palmer, F.
2532   Pte. Fry, F. W.
1891   Pte. Millichap, P. J.
2433   Pte. White, J. H. C.
2168   Pte. Hackford, W. A.

Pte. Trinder had since been promoted to the rank of Lance Corporal.

BEYOND.

Through endless days of a weary wait,
Through age-long watching of nights,
Huns sending over their message of hate
In support of Kultur's rights ;

With choice of evils according to taste,
To each man more than his share—
Shell after shell in furious haste
Hurled through the flame-swept air ;

In the clinging mud and the drenching rain
And the cannon growling grim.
With closest friends and comrades slain,
In peril of life and limb ;

But certain, standing above it all,
The glorious goal in sight,
As one by one " the barriers fall "
O'erthrown, the fierce-fought fight.

Avenging the victims broken down
'Neath the weight of oppression's bond,
Shall lead at last to Victory's crown,
And the joy of home beyond.
                                        M. L. G.

THE BATTLE OF THE SOMME.

" No matter what test you take, the offensive on the Somme has shewn itself in every single point superior to the German effort upon the Verdun sector last February and early March. It struck against a wider front ; captured more ground more quickly, took far more prisoners and far more guns— it was at once the greater and the better of the two operations."

The part which a single Division is called upon to play in such a Battle is not great, if measured by the actual frontage upon which it operates. Nevertheless the 48th Division, our own Brigade, this Battalion, have done their bit in the Big Push. In years to come, their record, in common with that of other Divisions which operated on the La Boisselle, Orvillers and Pozieres sectors, will be famous. The men of the 48th helped to make history.

" And Gentlemen in England now abed
Shall think themselves accurst they were not here."

THE HORSES.

My Father had great horses,
Chestnut, grey and brown.
They grazed about the meadows
And trampled into town.

They left the homely meadows
And trampled far away,
The great shining horses
Chestnut and brown and grey.

Gone are the great horses
That my Father bred.
And who knows whither—
Or whether starved or fed—
Gone are the horses
And my Father's dead.
                                        F. W. H.

We are very sorry indeed to hear that 2nd Lieutenant F. W. Harvey, D.C.M., has been missing since August 19th.

RECIPE FOR ROUTE MARCH.

(With apologies to Mrs. Beeton's No. 695,
"Jugged Hare.")

Ingredients.

(a) Take 4,000 Tired Tims, well grilled in a Pozieres range.

(b) 20 miles of Route de Poussiere (Triple sec.)

(c) One jour (tres chaud), with beaucoup de soleil.

Method.

Bake the Tired Tims in Orvillers Oven, skin the feet with gratin de nutmeg. Place over all a heavy steel cover, and slowly simmer for seven hours. Sprinkle freely with bus(y) Pioneer Battalion dust. Keep the pot boiling at ebullition rate of 120 full to the minute (degrees centigrade).

Flavour with tabs cochineal en auto, at frequent intervals. Serve in billets à la maude, and describe dish as Viande du repos (Bon pour les Troupes.)

Drinks recommended (and forbidden) with this dish :

Gin and Bitters, Cocktails, Vin Blanc, Vin Rouge, Vins de toutes sortes, Biere, Portiere, Whisky et siphon, Cognac, Benedictine, Liqueurs choisies de toutes sortes.
                                        G. H.

Second Lieutenant R. E. KNIGHT, D.C.M.
Died of wounds, July 25th

IN MEMORIAM

(R. E. K.)

Dear, rash, warm-hearted friend.
So careless of the end,
So worldly-foolish so divinely-wise,
Who, caring not one jot
For place, gave all you'd got
To help your lesser fellow-men to rise.

Swift-footed, fleeter yet
Of heart. Swift to forget
The petty spite that life or men could show you ;
Your last long race is won,
But beyond the sound of gun
You laugh and help men onward—if I know you.

O still you laugh, and walk,
And sing and frankly talk
(To angels) of the matters that amused you
In this bitter-sweet of life,
And we who keep it's strife
Take comfort in the thought how God has used you.

F. W. H.

THE REGIMENTS OF THE LINE.

We hear of the Anzacs, the Highlanders, the Guards,
Their names are gilded gloriously, and sung by many bards.
But WE know—and THEY know—of other men as fine—
The good old County Regiments—the Regiments of the line.

For them no vivid writer lets loose his fluent pen ;
For them no correspondent tells where, and how and when ;
Of their glory, in story, they write the tale anew—
The old County Regiments, that fight along of you.

The Worcesters, the Gloucesters—they've done their bit.
The Warwicks and the Berkshires, as fighting men they're IT !
They show it, we know it ! they've marched and fought like Hell
Those old County Regiments and dozens more as well.

The Oxfords, the Bucks, and the Lancashires are fine,
But of their fight for days and nights we never read a line.
The Surreys, the Hampshires, the Devons, too, can fight !
And surely they might have SOME of the glory that's their
                   [right.
They've no one to boom them, they do not advertise ;
Just in Battalion Orders their hidden glory lies,
They have no Agent-General to star them in the Press,
But ask the foe ! the Germans know—and we, well, we can
                   [guess.
In lofty dim cathedrals their battle-standards blaze,
Enscrolled in gold with fights of old, and, after many days
They shall return and claim them, and newer names shall
                   shine
More proudly yet on the Colours of the Regiment of the line.

Drink to the gallant Anzacs, drink to the kilties, too !
They're bonny, bonny fighters—we know them, and its true.
Toast them, and all their valour ! and then I'll give you
                   mine—
The old County Regiments—the Regiments of the Line.

(Adapted from *The Passing Show.*)   C.M.

CHAPLAIN'S COLUMN.

Our relations at home might be spared a considerable amount of anxiety and worry if they realised two things. It is a point of honour with every officer and man, just as it is a matter of duty with the Quartermaster (a duty which is faithfully performed) to use every effort to secure and forward the personal effects of those who fall in Battle. Unfortunately it is not always possible to do so ; it would not be right to endanger men's lives in the endeavour to secure such possessions, nor would it be consonant with the wishes of the relatives so to do. But at the same time, those who mourn may rest assured that no pains are spared to forward, whenever possible, the trinkets which they naturally value so dearly.

The Regimental stretcher-bearers—and they have worked magnificently—as quickly as they can, carry or conduct, according to the seriousness or otherwise of the case, the wounded to the Advanced Dressing Station of the Field Ambulance in charge of that particular area. Then, if necessary, wounds are re-dressed, and the patients go off—the stretcher cases to a hospital, perhaps some ten miles behind the line, where they may undergo an operation, and in any case are most carefully nursed, and the "cushy" or slightly wounded, to a Casualty Clearing Station, whose business it is to forward them as soon as possible to Base Hospitals, in the neighbourhood, perhaps, of Rouen or Boulogne, whither the serious cases follow them in due course.

But the point to remember is that it is quite impossible to keep in touch with the wounded, unless one hears that they are close to the Front Line. It rests solely with the patient, who will ask the Nurse to write to his people until he can do so himself. There will still remain in many cases, we fear, cause for considerable anxiety, but we trust that relatives at home will realise the reason for our inability to satisfy their anxious enquiries.

We all deeply realise how great the strain of that anxiety must be. And we have but one wish, namely, to relieve that strain as far as possible.

A good many of the " old hands " have, for one cause or another, some because for them there can be no return, others from wounds or sickness, dropped out of the Battalion. But we hope that the same high traditions of Churchmanship will be as well maintained as in days gone by.

LET THE CENSORS SWING !

To you I write, the Guardian of the News,
A kind of uncrowned Fidei Defensor,
Secret, unknown, elusive as the muse,
                 I mean—the Censor.

Your name is Legion in each unit you
With impish conscience NOT void of offence, ill—
—natured wight, score through our billets doux
                 With large blue pencil.

A schoolboy, or " lean slippered pantaloon,"
Any old age is yours, from teens to nonage :
Some, seemingly were born this afternoon :
                 Some, in the Stone Age!

Your rank runs from Red Hat with oakleaf tip
(Swanking a bodyguard with lance and pennant)
Through crowns, down to one solitary pip—
                 2nd Lieutenant.

But star or oakleaves, all of us deplore
Your eyes profane. How can a soldier lonely
Write of his love and bare his heart before
                 His One and Only ?

How frigid must the letters be we place
Before your goggling eyes, what potent forces
Are these to aid the Breach of Promise case
                 Or cause Divorces !

How many a loving wife or maid distraught
Will each suspicious thought attempt to smother.
How many more will not, and swear in Court
             " He loves another " !

So don't you think 'twould do more good than harm
To issue once again the famous " Greenie "
And glad the heart of girl clerk and Grande Dame,
             Duchess and Tweenie ?

I write these lines now (without prejudice),
But when the war is over I'll disown 'em
For Censor, you'll be dead ! De Mortuis
             Nil Nisi Bonum !
             " WAGGER."

BILGE ABOUT BLIGHTIES.

(With apologies to the Daily Shaving Glass.)

I have just returned from the front after a short visit (with kind permission from my friends at G.H.Q.) to as forward a point as the Sickle Trench near P——S.

I saw the famous East K——S. How magnificently they all looked ! The Colonel, who told me he was not at all busy, granted me a five minute interview. He told me his splendid N.C.O.'s preferred this kind of life to rest billets and they were always itching to be at the Bosch. As he had only three attacks on that night, he took me to the army behind the army, in other words the Transport lines. Here he showed me many interesting things, and introduced me to Pte. D. F. Alter, who at that moment was engaged on the wheel of a G.S. Wagon. He was clad simply in a sporan and three strands of rope, showing how hardy are our heroes at the front.

He has been doing himself too well ; his Colonel assured me he needed a well-deserved rest and was under the watchful vigilance of Dr. Jack Richards, who, as all should know, has made a speciality of the treatment of such cases. The D.O.C. informed me that the t-t-t-t-t-t-treatment w-w-w-w-w-w-was d-d-d-d-d-d-d-doing him a b-b-b-b-b-b-bally lot of good. Pte. D. F. Alter expressed a hope to be back up among the 5.9's at the expiration of 28 days (rest).

I passed in Piccadilly the Hon. Roger Fishkin, a scion of the house Puchevillers.

This gallant Officer is now teaching bayonet fighting to the reserve depot of the Mobile Veterinary Corps. I managed to snatch a few minutes conversation with him at the Leicester Lounge and gathered that he was one of the many men who had done his bit, both in his present important position and formerly when he won his jacket as O. C. Draft Dodgers. He told me —— but that will be telling.

At this moment Miss Donkeysquith turned up flushed with her triumph at the latest reviews asking for her Elevens's.

So discreetly I left the happy couple.

I then leapt into a 60 horse-power Rolls-Royce and regardless of the price of petrol found myself at the Angel, Islington, stopping en route for lubrication (for myself and driver, not for the car) at the Café de Bon Air. Here an accident to the front door had prevented ingress, but we pushed through the back entrance. Here I met Colonel ———, of the Wangling Pals Battalion, obviously on short leave, He looked tired after much heavy work at the front, He was quite satisfied with the Progress of the Big Push and hoped to be in it again shortly (*sic.*)

Our Tommies at the Front absolutely startle one with their ingenuity. No one who has seen the way in which our soldiers carry their effects can doubt their ability as handy men. Some men even have found a novel use for superfluous jam-tins and shrapnel helmets. Inset is a typical photo of one of our troops who has been in the great advance and is longing to get at them again :—

The Pte. who is longing to get at them.

If you can place this hero a reward is offered. See our Competition Page.

Much has been written by our contemporary, the Knightly Female about the Army behind the Army, and it is interesting to hear the views of our Friend B. F. Thomas (Telegraphic Address, London, B.E.F.) who has a wide and unrivalled knowledge of this army. He informs me that there are more men of military age working strenuously for the benefit of our fighters, than have ever been seen in the Fighting line, which shows, etc. (censored) B.F. also told me (in confidence) that his job was a cushy one, he had never been allowed beyond the Corps Line, that monument of brave slogging by the R.E.'s.

THE SWALLOW'S LAMENT.

" Oh skimming swallow, swift and slight
In ecstasy of pure delight
Winging afar thy fearless flight

Athwart the scented southern air,
O'er shifting scene of beauty fair
And vision fleet of wonder rare

O'er smiling land of spreading palm
Where travellers seek shade's cooling balm
And find there noonday rest and calm

In soundless stillness reigning—save
Where gleaming foam-crests lapping, lave
The sands that sport with playing wave.

Art bringing to our sterner shore
In song of rapture to outpour
Thy golden gift of memory's store ?

The hymn of joy thy glad heart rings
To Heav'n-born realms, where freedom sings
In measure with thine outspread wings ? "

" Alas "—the swallow seemed to say,
Where'er I sped my homeward way
There raged the fury of the fray,

Of one proud land the age-long stain,
From earth and sea, from hill and plain
There rises one long moan of pain——"

—" Oh swallow, who, from out the height
Didst view death's work, answer, whose plight
Mid human woe, grieved most thy sight ? "

—" The men half clad in cold and damp,
And mourning freedom's quenched lamp,
Who languish in the prison camp ;

Who once, as swallows are, were free
And fought for death or victory,
Now held in harsh captivity ;

Away from all whom dear they hold,
Cut off from daring deeds and bold,
In grip of misery untold.

Their voiceless moaning I have heard,
And to the very depth has stirred
The spirit of a free-born bird.

Oh stranger, whosoe'er thou art,
Hear the appeal, wrung from the heart
Of one who may not bear a part

In lessening their fetters' weight !
Give thou thy help, open the gate
Of hope, that love may conquer hate."

M. L. G.

SORTES POETICAE.
SERIOUS AND HUMOROUS.

Some of our Friends :

Bully Beef.

" Chief nourisher at Life's Feast."

SHAKESPEARE.

The Padre.

" A manly man to ben an abbot able."

CHAUCER.

The Provost Sergeant.

" I've got HIM on the list,

My object all sublime,
I shall achieve in time,
To make the Punishment fit the Crime,

And (to) each Prisoner Pent,
A source of innocent merriment."

GILBERT.

Sanitary-man.

" His priestlike task of pure ablution."

KEATS.

The C. O.

" Justum ac tenacem propositi virum."

HORACE.

Lieut. E. C.

" The age is best which is the first,
When youth and blood are warmer :
But being spent, the worse, and worst,
Times still succeed the former."

HERRICK.

Brigade Route March.

" The glorious lamp of Heaven, the Sun,
The higher he is getting,
The sooner will our race be run,
The nearer he's to setting."

HERRICK.

Lieut. H. W. C.

" Get up, get up, for shame ! The blooming morn,
'Pon her wing presents the God unshorn."

HERRICK.

The Signallers.

" I babble over wiry ways,
And chatter in the dug-out."

A long way after TENNYSON.

Sergt. R. C. W.

" He is soft and tender, pray take heed,
(With bands of cowslip bind him)."

HERRICK.

To the Fluffy-Haired Lady of La Pl—y.

" Thou art my life, my love, my heart,
The very eyes of me.
And hast command of every part,
To live and die for thee."

HERRICK.

To " B and B."

Bid me to live and I will live,
Thy Protestant to be ;
Or bid me come and I will fly
By motor to La LP—Y.

A long way after H——.

Captain H. H.

" Hath no stomach to the Fight."

SHAKESPEARE.

To No. 14. B——v—l.

" She has virgins many, fresh and fair."

HERRICK.

Before a Push.

" When God knows I am tossed about
Either by (the Staff) or doubt,
Yet before the glass be out,
Sweet spirit, Comfort me."

After HERRICK.

Lieut. G. H.

" In the fell clutch of circumstance,
I have not winced or cried aloud
Under the bludgeonings of chance,
My head is Bloody, but unbowed."

HENLEY.

Base Details.

" What thou amongst the Leaves has never known,
The weariness, the fever, and the fret."

WORDSWORTH.

The Bing Boy.

" A six years' old darling of a pigmy size."

WORDSWORTH.

The Brigade Major.

" Who is the happy warrior ? Who is he ?
That every man in arms should wish to be."

WORDSWORTH

Ovillers.

" Most loathsome, filthie, fowle and ful of vile
disdaeyne."

SPENCER.

Sergeant Ed-n.

" O ruddier than the cherry."

SHAKESPEARE.

America.

" Invincible in peace, invisible in war."

A Dud.

" Full of sound and fury, signifying nothing."

SHAKESPEARE.

Q. M.

" Ethereal minister, pilgrim of the sky."

SHELLEY.

The Ovillers Hun.

" A Demned, damp, moist, most villainous body."

DICKENS.

The Regiment.

" We all their ammunition and feats of war defeat,
With plain, heroic magnitude of mind."

MILTON.

A Defaulter.

" A turn or two I'll walk
To still my beating mind."

SHAKESPEARE.

Sergeant Pr—et—r. (Band Practice).

" Heard melodies are sweet,
But those unheard are sweeter."

KEATS.

The Infantryman.

" My life's one demned, horrid grind."

The Leave Train.

" Thou still unravished bride of quietness,
Thou foster-child of silence and slow time."

KEATS.

Sergeant F—nch.

" Nature might stand up to all the World
And say, This is a man ! "

SHAKESPEARE.

The Rum Ration.

" Rarely, rarely, comest thou
Spirit of delight."

SHELLEY.

The Allies.—Certainty of Victory.

" Di patrii, quorum semper sub numine Troia est,
Non tamen omnino Teucros delere paratis,
Cum tales animos juvenum et tam certa tulistis
Pectora."

VIRGIL.

The Wolff Bureau.

" Splendide mendax."

HORACE.

To the " Derby's."

" Poor old Bill, he left this place,
With smoking gun and smiling face :
But Bill won't care, if some good chap
With FOLLOW UP and FILL the gap."

ANON.

The Conscientious Objector.

" And thou, the scorn of every patriot's name,
Thy Country's ruin and thy council's shame !
Poor servile thing ! Derision of the brave."

BRYANT

" Blighties."

" Some wandering hand in hand through arched lanes ;
Some listening to loved voices at the lattice :
Some steeped in dainty dreams of untried bliss ;
Some nestling soft and deep in well-known arms,
Whose touch makes sleep, rich Life."

CHARLES KINGSLEY.

The Anzacs.

" They tarried not to count the cost,
But came.
They came from many a clime and coast—
The slimb of limb, the dark of face,
They shouldered eager in the race
The sturdy giants of the front,
And the stalwarts of the sun.—"

JOHN OXENHAM.

Blinded-in-the-War.

" You that still have your sight,
Remember me !—
I risked my life, I lost my eyes,
That you might see."

JOHN OXENHAM.

The Wounded.

" We've paid in our toil and our woundings ;
We've paid in the blood we've shed ;
We've paid in our bitter hardships ;
We've paid with our many dead.
It's not payment in kind we ask for.
Two wrongs don't make much of a right,
All we ask is—that, what we have paid for,
You secure for us, all right and tight."

JOHN OXENHAM.

The Kaiser.

"   ...Art thou he
Who first broke peace—
For which both thou and we are here condemned
To waste eternal days in woe and pain ? "

MILTON.

" Woe ! Woe ! Woe ! —to him by whom this came.
His house shall unto him be desolate,
And, to the end of time, his name shall be
A byword and reproach in all the lands
He rapined—And his own shall curse him
For the ruin that he brought."

JOHN OXENHAM.

Prospective Peace.

" His morning hope, his evening dream.
His joy throughout the day."

OUR BENEFACTORS.

Lt.-Colonel Marling.	Papers.
Lt.-Colonel Winterbotham	—
Colonel Griffith.	Cigarettes and Papers.
Bishop Frodsham.	Papers.
Miss Backhouse.	—
Mr. Berkeley Powell.	—
Miss Parr.	—
Mr. Harley Butt.	Tobacco.
Mr. W. S. Butcher.	—
Canon Brewster	Prayer books.
Supply Column.	Strawberry Jam (ad. lib.)
Mr. Hon. Mable Gye.	Magazines.
Camps Library.	Papers.
Mr. W. R. Voller.	Prayer Books and Papers.
The Employees of F. R. Heale and Son, Whitley.	Cigarettes.
Pte. Orchard	Typing.
Pte. Shaw.	—
Pte. Wood.	—
Mr. Jack Margetson.	Cigarettes.
The Ladies of Gloucester.	Shoulder Badges.
The Echo.	" Echo."
The Archdeacon of Gloucester.	Cigarettes.
Rev. W. J. Selby.	—

SONG OF THE HUN-EAGLE.

I am the bird of birds. Of Night
The symbol and the hope.
Supreme, I bask in Kultur's light
While men in darkness grope.

My home upon Vainglory's peak
O'erlooks the lordly Rhine ;
Yet still unsatisfied I seek
The Earth—which should be mine.

Contempt I hiss at people who
Quote " Nations Law "—such stuff !
My piercing eye sees clearly through
Their sentimental bluff.

'Tis obvious that fair words conceal
Mere rank hypocrisy,
And so I answer each appeal
With just ferocity.

How righteously I strafe the foes !
— It should be told in rhyme—
And how my pent-up hate o'erflows,
Imperial, sublime !

With what a grip my claws and beak
Can fasten, clutch and tear !
Yet 'gainst the British Lion meek,
French Cock, and Russian Bear

It seems quite ineffective :
Will nothing make them cower ?
And now our Press invective
Falls flat on Neutral power.

So if I find their attitude
Towards us does not cease,
I shall take measures to conclude
An advantageous peace.

Bearing in mind this saying :
— " When luck is on the wane,
By claims of prudence weighing
You live to fight again "—

But be discreet, or else—'tis true—
My fame as sprayed sea foam
Will vanish—for it would not do
If this were known at home.

M. L. G.

THINGS WE WANT TO KNOW.

How many spare Buttons the Padre keeps ?

Who is the King of Spades ? How did he check the Knave of Hearts ?

Did the French Lesson revive the spirits and cure the headache of Le petit Duc ?

Who went beetroot hoeing with Rifles, etc. ?

What N.C.O. in B. Company was unable to distinguish between Rum and Lime Juice ?

Does he hold the rank of C.Q.M.S. ?

Who was the Sergeant in B. Company who gave the order " March at ease, on the right shoulder " ?

Which newly-made Corporal said he had put his matches in the sun and they had got wet ? Is he in No. 5 Platoon ?

Which drummer told the Frenchman that 50 was " cinq napoo " ?

How long have we been Londoners ?

If the Gazette started April, 1915, and is monthly, why is July, 1916, No. 13 ?

Who sat in the dark with the jam ? Is he in No. 8 ?

When are we going to India ?

Who said the Huns were bombarding B......with Machine guns ?

Who is the Debonair Colonel ?

Who is the great friend of the Mules ? Is he a Pioneer ?

Are the Sergeants arranging for their Mess to be Filmed, after the example of the Cabinet ?

Who is the wounded officer who was so anxious to have his kit searched by a man of understanding such as the Quartermaster ?

Who marched on a very hot march with a shirt, vest, waistcoat and woolly ?

What was No. 5's Ex-Guardsman's meaning when he said " we have got them on open-air fighting now " ?

Which private in B Company said he had to wear his kit to keep him to pieces ?

Who were the N.C.O's. in the queue ?

Why did the T.O. need a four horse waggon one morning ?

What officers missed the return Bus ?

What private at D——H.Q. had three leaves ?

Was it for gallantry in the Trenches ?

Who was the C.S.M. who did not come up for orders, because he said he might be fagged after a day at A.........?

Has anyone more than a vague idea of the doings of Le petit Duc and the Young Pretender ?

Would not an account of their Doings afford interesting Reading.

Who was the Private that tried to dry his socks by a candle ?

Who was the Private in " D " Company who was asked by an officer during bombing practice if it was a Ladies' Cricket Match ?

What was the reason for the remark ?

Who was the man who ate a tin of marmalade himself at tea-time and then asked if there was a jam issue ?

Is he in 14 Platoon ?

Who is the wittiest man in No. 14 ?

Who is the man who eats marmalade with herrings ?

Who was the man in 14 Platoon that oiled his hair with dubbin ?

Who was it said to the French Madam—" Vous coo-key Eggy " ? Is he now a Sergt ?

Who is the young officer (R.F.A.) who wanted a mutton bone ? What did he think it was ? How much did he give for it ?

What Sergt. when asked what he was before the war broke out, said he was a M.R.H.S. ?

Is he the gardener who is spoken so much of in No. 4 Platoon ?

Was it the same Sergt. who brought the Provost Sergeant to the " playing ground " of a " gambling school," but found all the gamblers asleep ?

Which drummer was it, who, at Chelmsford, could not find the " wrong " house ?

Who is the finest Map Reader of the Battalion ? Is it right he took a working party 1½ mile out of their way when sent to erect tents for the Divisional Staff ?

When does the Flower Show open ?

Who said " Rabbits " ?

Who camouflaged the white elephants ?

Is it true that the Infantry were robbed of their barbed wire to prevent the " Wind " disturbing the exhibits ?

Who was the " D-n All Consequences " officer who mistook his P.H.G. helmet for his Balaclava ? Was it comfortable to sleep in ?

Who was the officer who sang a little ballad entitled " Where's my Track " ? Were his tears due to lachrymatory shells, or merely to " Wind " ?

What did the picquet say to the Major when he found him cracking his crop in the horse lines at 2 a.m. ?

Has a certain Major discovered any fresh cases of Glanders lately ?

Why did a certain Doctor run ? Was he "ticked off " by a subaltern ?

Who is the distinguished Medical Officer who, on hearing the contact aeroplane sound its strombus horn, loudly exclaimed " Gas," donned his helmet and sought refuge in the dressing station ?

What about that Farewell Dinner Party at H. ? Wasn't S. W's. Orderly well trained in following up " doubtfuls " ?

Who is the Officer (R.F.A.) who did not know the way back through the wire ?

What did the Officer (R.F.A.) try to do with his half-crown, when he had mounted his horse ?

What is the establishment of " Fourhorsed G.S. Wagon, painted yellow " per Infantry Battalion ?

Has one unit of the Division been reconstituted as (Royal) Marine Light Infantry ?

Have you seen, while out on rest, the Beach T. Redoubt ? Is it the O.P. of the Mobile Veterinary Secton ?

Has the Provost Sergeant seen the 3,000 (Hun) prisoners he was talking about ?

Is it true three sergeants and twenty-two men stand guard over the German prisoners in Hospital at Rouen ? Is it true that most of these prisoners have lost a leg ?

Daily Report. Kite Balloon Section

What is the best way to become an Indispensable ?

Who is the D Company man who learnt to swim with a pair of rum jars ? Is he a cook ?

Who is always asking for an " economy " Ration ? Does he mean a Maconachie'? Is he in C Company ?

Who is the Lewis Gunner who asks " Do we go up this municator ?"

Who is the private who says he was not a conscript ? Did it only take two policemen and a piece of Blue Paper to fetch him ?

How much did the signallers pay for the front page the " Chronicle and Graphic " ? How many objected to sending it in ?

Who is the officer who runs his Company by Telepathy ?

What did the Sergeant say when he read that he had been to England ?

Who woke up in his bivvy and said " There's the whole Battalion in here " ? Was it nothing more than his breeches hung on the line ?

Which Divisional Mess has been turned into a Debating Society ?

What does " Garrs " have to say ?

What unit has started a racing stable ?

What N.C.O. of A Company was seen shaving in the fire trench while the Germans were shelling ? Was he trying to work his ticket ?

What Officer's servant, wearing Mademoiselle's shoes, turned his socks down over the top of his puttees ? Is it the latest military style ? Or was it swank ? Is he in A Company Mess ?

Who is the Colonel who has acquired the Bombing rights of the lake ?

Why was it that the Temporary and therefore Final destination of the Rum changed ? Why did some of you grudge the men in the Trenches, who were doing YOUR job and keeping YOU safe, their tots ?

Who is responsible for the discipline of No. 3 Mess ?

What man in B Company said that the Division had reached its objection ?

How many men in the Battalion are expecting another 6d. a day shortly ?

If the 1/5th have left the lines of communication and gone in the front line yet ?

If " Funker " was promoted at the Base, or was it a Base trick ?

Has the Tattoo of " Gott Strafe England," worn off yet ?

Has Stretcher-bearer Meyer been awarded cradle-leave yet ? Can Uzzielli tell us ?

Who dashed out after a bottle on the march from C—T to B—V—L ? What did he say when he found it empty ? Is he at H.Q. Mess ?

Who cleans out his mess-tin with permanganate of Potash ?

Who is the Blue-tabbed Officer who does not know how to salute a General ? Did the General ask him what he thought his hand had done ?

CIGARETTES.

In careless fingers loosely swung,
Up their curling smokepuffs blow,
Lightly whirling wreaths are hung,
Blue and dreaming, circling slow.

Fire-points kindle, gleaming red,
Tiny fire-sparks scatter swift,
Specks of flamelight quickly sped
E'er the lazy smoke-veils lift.

Dreams they bring of hearth and home,
Loves forgotten—all the things
Dearer now to men who roam—
Wakened by the magic rings.

Airy castles, wonder-built,
Short-lived memories that charm,
Hopes of future,'fancy-gilt,
Visioned peace and victor's palm.

Wayward, fleeting thoughts will stray,
Words, warm with the weaving spell
Wrought by winding smoke-wreaths, may
On mind's store of treasure dwell.

Spirits rising care defy,
Laughter chimes with tale or joke,
Vanish worry, woe and sigh,
In the twirling fumes of smoke,

Cigarettes ! Bear, in your wake,
Consolation, cheer and wit ;
Woodbine, Player, Golden Flake,
Truly, you have done your bit !

AN OFFICER'S WIFE HAS SUGGESTED THE FOLLOWING " RETURN POSTCARD."

I AM QUITE WELL

I AM MUCH REFRESHED AFTER

    A HOT BATH
    A COLD BATH
    A SWIM IN THE SEA

I HAVE RECEIVED YOUR $\begin{cases} \text{LETTER} \\ \text{PRESENT} \\ \text{POSTCARD} \end{cases}$

CHAMPAGNE AND WHISKEY FOLLOWS AT FIRST OPPORTUNITY

I HAVE RECEIVED NO LETTER WITH ANY NEWS AT ALL

    LATELY

    FOR A LONG TIME

(Signature only.)

BRICKS FROM THE EDITOR'S PACK.

Macaulay once wrote of Clive as being "in a painfully anxious situation." So we were. By some trick of Fortune we were presented with our dump the day before we moved. All sorts of treasures had to be parted with, including the tapestries and draperies that once adorned so tastefully "A" Company Mess at Bus. The situation was indeed desperate.

However Major Green gallantly salved our cricket stuff and the Disinfector. The Lewis Gunners took pity on 600 Hymn Books and dragged them manfully and earned the undying gratitude of a desperate Chaplain.

The situation was saved.

The news that Captain E. V. Birchall, D.S.O., had succumbed to his wounds, coming as it did after such good reports of his progress, cast a real gloom over us all. For we felt that he was associated by many ties of friendship to this Battalion.

He represented one of the very best types of the British Officer. A loyal Churchman, his marked individuality, his strength of character, his delightful freedom from the "cake of custom," were crowned with years of social service in Birmingham. He served his generation well.

England is the poorer for the death of Vivian Birchall. But the world is redeemed by the sacrifice of its best.

Of those of our Battalion who have been killed or who are missing, it is not possible now to write. For one thing our heart is heavy. For another, we are forbidden to publish that list of those who have laid down their lives, without which we should not be able to do justice to those who have fallen.

Meanwhile, we who treasure their memories very dearly, are proud that we have lived among them, known and loved them, and to their relatives at home we would say that they helped to make history, that in the hour of their trial they were not false to the Traditions of the British Army.

They went over the parapet as steadily as if on parade—to us who watched their gallantry they seemed almost to pick their way amongst the fine barrage of shells which our gunners were showering over—and they killed and captured a good many of the Kaiser's picked troops. Furthermore, while they actually were able to hand over to France some more of her rightful property, they have contributed very materially to the Final Victory which, as sure as the sun shall rise from day to day, will one day crown the joint effort of ourselves and of our Allies.

Many a time have our readers laughed heartily at the poems above the signature of "Emma Kew." The author of such jolly verses as those entitled "Our Fighting Men," "Once Bitten" and "Emma Kew" (Lieutenant Gedye, of the Gloucester R.F.A.) is dead, killed in a most gallant attempt to put out the fire which was about to ignite a "Dump" of Bombs. We should like to express our sympathy with the Brigade of Artillery of which he was Orderly Officer, on their severe loss.

The *Daily Express* of Thursday, August 3rd, spoke about the man behind the line as "straining at the leash" to go over the top.

There have been, we understand, several cases of riot and open mutiny amongst units ordered back to rest.

There is a message on the Telephone to wake up a sleeping signaller.

"The Brigade has to put up the " S. O. S."?

"Certain?"

"Yes, ain't I telling you? Did you get it?

"X2, 2A3. Repeat."

Philip Gibbs, *Daily Chronicle*, August 7th.

Some Map Reference !

" A Jolly Time at the front.

The following is an extract from the letter of an officer serving with the British Expeditionary Force :

" We are having a jolly time up here consolidating and wiring trenches recently taken from the Huns. Of course, every now and then he sends us his morning greeting in the shape of huge H.E. shells. All day long our guns are roaring.

Morning Post.

How some people take their pleasure ! !

The Corporal of a guard at a Barricade, told one of the latest additions to H-M. Forces to deliver the following message :

" Am going to advance, send Re-inforcements."
The message duly delivered was as follows :
" Going to a dance, send three and fourpence."
FACT !

We hear from letters found on German prisoners that the German cavalry are called upon from time to time to hack through hungry rioters in Munich. Our cavalry for the time being only hack down the Albert Road.

A pleasing feature of late has been the resurrection of the Band. To hear it practising makes us even look forward to the last 20 minutes of a B-V-L. CR—T. march.

The Battle of the Somme still continues. The struggle has been long and hard. But thanks to our airmen do not the prisoners speak of them coming down so low as almost to take their forage caps? and to our "heavies" (when used), good progress has been made. Prisoners have been taken in good numbers. Although we have lost more officers and men, killed wounded and missing, and the price paid has been heavy, nevertheless, there can be very few Divisions which have achieved so much in two tours under the prevailing conditions, and what the Division has taken it has kept. And it has taken a good bit.

Morning Post, August 9th :

" Will anyone kindly help me to send out (ARMY) BLANKETS to my Brother's Company of the A.S.C. which are badly needed? Grateful for any contributions, however small.

— Write Mrs. ...., Hyde Park, W."

We also hear that they are short of Shrapnel helmets, body shields and stretchers.

Before the war Soldiers in high places laid it down that Territorial Troops required six months before they could hope to compete with troops of Continental armies. Are these same soldiers responsible for sending out the present English conscript with only three months' Training? How do they reconcile the two?

THE TWO POINTS OF VIEW—overheard on the same day.

Infantryman in the Trenches (Thiepval—the foreground) "I hope and pray they'll take this Division out before Thiepval is to be attacked."

R.A.M.C.   "A real shame, I call it, taking the Division out before Thiepval is taken."

We have lost many of the "old sweats," many, Irreplaceables. We hope to publish in course of time a photograph of them all.

"If I get the D.S.O. or Military Cross, I shall be decently proud : if I get wounded I shall wear my braid with a good grace, but the distinction which I most covet does not yet exist. It is to be called 1914, to show the country that when she called for us, we did not wait."

Ex-actor now Soldier.

And so say all of us.

Many and various, if generally very unconventional, are the tributes paid by our wounded officers and men to their padres. Here are a few specimen remarks, says a correspondent, culled from those one hears every day on the lips of the wounding landing at Southampton.

"There's no mistake, one does meet some pretty sporting padres at the front. Near H.........I met one who was a sort of a Knight Templar ; he seemed to be a kind of free lance. Battalions came and went, but he stayed in his dug out in the second line as if he'd settled there for life. He knew that part of the line better than any man living ; every nook and cranny in it ; and when any party got fogged and wanted a guide, nobody could help them so well as the padre. And I'm bound to say, nobody could have been more willing to help. He labelled his dug out The Vicarage.

"One day, two men belonging to a draft fresh out from home—Cockneys they were—came along that trench. "Look here, Bill, blimy if 'ere ain't a...... Vicarage ! " said one to the other. Out pops the padre, at that, with half his face lathered, as he was having a shave at the time. "Yes," says he ; ' and here's the .... Vicar. What can I do for you ? " Imagine how the tommies looked. They say that padre applied officially to be appointed ' Chaplain of the Trenches.' Well, he belonged, all right ; he was one of us."

Daily Mail.

The Editor has been ordered by one whom he dares not disobey, no less a person than the Commanding Officer, to reprint the above extract from the columns of the " Daily Mail." Various stories anent various Padres appear to have been crystallized into a sort of mythology. But the story of the Vicarage is true if for " Cockneys " (Clever touch that : " London Territorials " again) you read." B-RKS.

PERSONAL.

MARRIAGES.

On August the 14th, at Leckhampton Church, Cheltenham, Captain H. C. Blair Sessions, 1/5th Gloucestershire Regiment, eldest son of Mr. and Mrs. Herbert Sessions, of Quedgeley Court, near Gloucester, to Olive Maud, elder daughter of Mr. and Mrs. A. H. Wyatt, of Wingrove, Cheltenham.

On August 21st, at St. George's, Hanover Square, Captain R. S. Dacre Stuart, 1/5th Gloucestershire Regiment, only son of Mr. and Mrs. R. E. Stuart, of Dudbridge House, Stroud, to Helen Gladys Dorothy, only child of the late Rev. W. H. Gibbons, rector of Upton Pyne, Devon, and of Mrs. Gibbons, of the Manor, Cowley, Exeter.

OLD BOYS' COLUMN.

2nd Lieutenant S. Priestley came over to see his old Battalion last month.

We were very sorry to see his name among the list of Missing.

We much regret to see that 2nd Lieutenant H. G. Thomas, who left us to take up his Commission, has been killed in action.

2nd Lieutenant A. E. Miles has, we regret to say, been wounded.

2nd Lieutenant A. C. R. Welsh has been awarded the Military Cross.

APPOINTMENTS AND PROMOTIONS.

To be Second Lieutenant 1/5th Battalion Gloucestershire Regiment, C. Brien, dated June 20th.

Captain (Temporary Major) G. F. Collett, to command 1/5th Battalion Gloucestershire Regiment with the Temporary rank of Lieutenant Colonel, dated September 7th.

R.I.P.

" Not theirs to triumph yet : but where they stood,
Falling to dye the earth with brave men's blood
For England's sake and duty. Be their name
Sacred among us. Would'st thou seek to frame
Their fitting epitaph ? Then let it be
Simple as that which marked Themopylae ;
"Tell it in England, thou that passest by
Here, faithful to their charge, her soldiers lie."

" PUNCH."

" They shall not grow old as we that are left grow old,
Age shall not weary them, nor the years condemn,
At the going down of the sun and in the morning
We will remember them to Christ."

" That we might live they died—
Hail !—And Farewell !
Their courage tried,
By every mean device of treacherous hate,
Like Kings they died."

JOHN OXENHAM.

5th Gloucester Gazette.

A Chronicle, serious and humorous, of the Battalion while serving with the
BRITISH EXPEDITIONARY FORCE.

ARMY

INTELLIGENCE SUMMARY.

(1) Prisoners to the number of 198 Officers and 10,633 men passed through the Corps cages up to 7-30 p.m. The Military Police have been given orders to try and induce them to come back.

(2) The following identifications were made during 24 hours ending 7-30 p.m. last night :—

(a) 4th Bn. R. W. Kents (said to be in position opposite German 1st Line).

(b) A Brigade (Probably Australian, as they are reported about POŻIERES).

Enemy Movement.

Enemy showed a disposition to push in the parapets which our working parties are said to be constructing. They were told to "go away," and finally a volley was fired (Reported by Balloon Section).

Units Fighting N. of Somme.

From prisoners' statements and aerial observation, there appears to be little doubt that the enemy forces are holding the trench system on our immediate front.

Statements of our Infantry seem to confirm this.

No actual identifications have been made during the Summer owing to unfavourable weather conditions.

Examination of a Prisoner of —— Regt.

Prisoner was very willing to give any information.

In happier times prisoner was a bricklayer and on *being closely questioned* on the "attitude of German General Staff with regard to recent developments in Trench Warfare" stated that although there could be no question of the high professional ability of Officers directing operations, yet he feared that national love for minuteness of detail might influence their decisions in Operations on a large scale.

Classes.

Prisoner stated that his half sister had an Aunt living in HAMBURG, whose younger sister has a friend engaged to an Officer in a high position in STRASSBURG.

It appears from statements of this Officer that the 1917 Class may be called up in the future.

Losses.

The Coy. lost 200 in last two days. On further examination prisoner admitted that he had been detached from his Coy. for six months, and had not seen or heard of them. He estimates the casualties from a dream which he had on the previous night. Prisoner is subject to dreams.

Trenches.

Prisoner had been told that there were many "dug-outs" on the British front.

Position.

Prisoner was able by means of an encircling movement of the forefinger to indicate his position on a map.

From position indicated it appears that his Regiment does not hold the line S of ARRAS (as at first reported), but is in Rest Billets in Russia.

Drafts.

Prisoner stated that there was a large number in the trenches.

Batteries.

States that there are a large number of Batteries on the front. He has not seen any but is confident that they are somewhere in the rear.

Officers.

Prisoner does not know his Company Commander, who never comes into the trenches except under the influence of alcohol.

General.

Prisoner was questioned closely on "Trench Mortars," Tetanus, graphy and topography, advanced thought, Advanced Theology, and Advanced Dressing Stations, Freiwilliger and Freieliebe, Made in Germany, Mormonism and Machine Guns. He seemed to have no knowledge on the last four points.

Captured Correspondence.

Extract from letter by Willi BIENZIEHER to friend at the front :—" Poor AUCHGELAUFEN was called up yesterday. He has been blind since 1870, but they fetched him in an ambulance and put him in HINDENBERG'S Group of pressed pushers.

All bricks must now be handed in to the Burgomaster at once. Yesterday they took away the last bricks from our little home and we live in tents now. Next week these will be requisitioned by the Army.

Food is very scarce—we poor ones get nothing— if you are lucky and an Officer passes in a bad temper he may throw a potato at you—otherwise there is only grass and nuts...These will now be confiscated for oil.

Here all paper must be given to the authorities to-morrow. There is great distress. What we shall do each morning I do not know...besides one must have a card...

They say here that after the Kaiser saw the Russians advancing, he returned and signed the pledge.

The barracks are quite empty now and the crops are being grown on the square...

Our poor little cat died of starvation yesterday...
I am sending you a wing...

Little Elsa WARGEWESEN was asking anxiously
for your address yesterday. I told her you were
dead.

ON RECEIVING THE GAZETTE AFTER THE
RECENT HEAVY FIGHTING.

Reared 'mid the nightingales of Plugstreet Wood,
War's rude alarms she early learned to scorn ;
And when in winter Earth was most forlorn,
In sodden trenches sang still unsubdued,
A hardy Muse ! And now, having withstood
The fiercest tempest of the strife, though worn
With mortal struggle and with feathers torn,
She cheers and comforts in her old calm mood,
Tears has she for the fall'n (herself bereft
Of some in whom she chiefly did rejoice)
Mingled with pride in their so noble death,
And mirth to cheer the heart of brothers left
Weary and sad. Hail to thee, gladdening voice,
Expressing still the soul that conquereth.

                                            C. S. N.

THINGS WE WANT TO KNOW.

Did the T. O. have to wait a long time for his French
Lessons ?

Who went twice through the window of the H. Q.
Mess ?

Who is the Padre who likes choosing Typewriters at
A—— Did he return an expert typist ? Did
he enjoy the lessons ?

Who gave an acting T. O. a map reference in No
Man's Land ?

Who is the Purple Emperor ?

Who left their Car BEHIND the Bon Air ? and why ?

Who inspects the Laundry at A—? Is it a weekly
job ?

At which Mess does the Major ask for Instructions
how to cut the tongue ?

Who tears up slips of Paper to make flags to show the
Allied advance on the map ? Do they toss up as
to who should go to A— to buy pins for the flags ?

Who is the Padre who has a pair of slacks for sale ?
And why ?

Who had his fortune told at B—V—L ?

Did not the Australians ask if the 48th was the only
Division in the British Army ?

Who fought the cook on a point of honour ? What
was at stake ?

Is it now a proverbial saying in certain circles that
" Anything is good enough for the Glo'sters ?"

Do you know the most convenient house in B—V—L
in which to wait for Lorries ?

Who is the Officer who changed his billet there ?

Who are known as the B—V—L Bombers ? And
why ?

Who is the drummer who described himself as 9 foot
6 inches ? Is he in D Company ?

Who is the drummer who woke up alive to find
himself dead ? Can he be found in D Company ?

Who is the Analyst of the Band ? Is he an expert
in eggs ?

Who is the Drummer who got lost in a mail-bag ?
Did it take two men to pull him out ?

What drummer is known as " Reveille " ? Has he
been known to get up before the G.O.C. in the
morning ? Is he in C Company ?

Which drummer is known as the Newsagent of the
Band or otherwise " John Bull's " Bully ?

Which drummer sacrificed his trousers to feed the
rats ? Is he in A Company ?

Who is " Billy " ?

Who was the Sergeant mistaken for an old Frenchman, when behind a haystack ? Is he in A Company ?

Which drummer said he would make the egg bounce ?
Is he in A Company ?

Who is the Sergeant who waited till the Q.M. had
gone on leave to get a new pair of trousers ? Is he
in the Orderly Room ?

Who is the Officer who asked, on the arrival of a
MINNIE, if it was a Rifle Grenade ? Is he in B
Company ?

Who was the man in B Company who mistook an
electric torch for a Star Shell on coming out of an
Estaminet ? Was his face very bruised and his
head very sore next morning ?

Who was heard to remark the day before we left
B—V—L that he never got a Bath ? Was he
saying the same thing 24 hours later ?

What Officer mistook his shaving water for early
morning tea ?

Who wanted to know if his letters passed the Centaur?
Was he a Corporal in B Company ?

Who is the Officer (R.F.A.) who went shopping for
the Mess and paid eight pence for Pump water ?

Who had for tea 4 pots of jam, 2 tins of butter and 1½
loaves ? Is he still an active Pioneer ?

Who was the N.O.C. in No. 7 Platoon who gave the
order " 5 rounds consecrated fire ?"

Is the fly-breeding experiment at Divisional H.Q. a
success ?

Did they realise that the Officers had Langouste in
spite of being on the horse-lines ?

Which Officer's servant carried two sets of equipment
on the march ?

Who is the Officer who inspects his platoon at the
slope ? Is he an ex-Guardee ?

Who were the heavenly twins in the horse-line
billets ? Which saw the other to bed and why ?

Was their motto " United we stand, Divided we
fall ?

Who is the Officer who left his pack behind ?

Who is the C Company Officer who changed his billet so rapidly ?   And why ?

Who is the cook who said " I have burnt the water. Where can I get some more ? "

Was it B Coy. Q.M.S. that purchased a bottle of water for Champagne ?   And did he enjoy it ?

Who was the Private in No. 5 who asked the Corporal if there was any of the piccaniny left for supper ?

Who is the Officer who left his cap behind ?

Who was the L/Corpl. in No. 5 who said he heard his Rifle fall ten minutes before he woke up ?

What Private in B Company told the Sergeant there were some men in here not come yet ?   Is he in No. 5 ?

Who is the man in the sapper section called " Gramophone " ?   Does he supply new " records " daily ?

Who is the Officer who had a compulsory hair-cut ? Is he at H.Q. Mess ?

Who are the Bridge Champions of H.Q. Division ?

Who is the popular M.O., now, alas, rather badly hurt by a fall from his horse, whom nature has so abundantly covered that no X. Ray was able to pierce the superabundant Tissues ?

Who is the prominent Pioneer, quondam King of S—y, who thinks the war was started for his benefit?

WAR CHANT OF THE HARBOUR-HUNS.

IN 1914.

Our country's pride,
  Sea-Huns we are ;
Our time we bide—
Then woe betide
  The British tar !

The foeman's fate
  And doom are sealed ;
Within our gate
We lie in wait.
  Britain shall yield !

Hail to the Day !
  Let them come forth—
Hun mines shall slay
Their hated prey
  In righteous wrath !

Then shall we sail
  To Britain's shore ;
The fist of mail
Shall make her quail
  And death outpour !

Till even she
  Proclaim our worth,
And we shall be
Lords of the sea
  And of the earth !

IN 1916.

By luck, again
  Safe back in port !
The heaving main
Strewn with our slain,
  The battle fought.

In peril's throes
  Home course we shaped
A mist arose
And from our foes
  We just escaped.

Once more we hide
  At anchor here,
While they with pride
The ocean ride
  Both far and near.

The longed for Day—
  A bubble burst !
Our land's dismay
We did allay,
  Nor told the worst.

In victory's guise
  Was failure clad ;
So through deft lies
Our nation wise
  Is falsely glad.

Once more, with hate,
  Britain to brave
We watch and wait.
By cursed fate
  She rules the wave.

M. L. G.

FRAGMENTS FROM THE CLASSICS.

(With apologies to Xenophon and his account of the March of the Ten Thousand to the Sea.)

It was now in the middle of Summer, the hot season what time the sun is very powerful indeed. By order of the Commander, the trumpet sounded early, and having had breakfast we marched.   And we marched continuously for one Twenty-fourth part of a whole day at a time, and in this way accomplished many kilometres.   Then suddenly those in the leading phalanx caught sight of the village of —— still some way off.   So that one great cry of joy went up from the parched throats of the Four thousand.   And the shout was a great one.   " The Trenches !" "The Trenches!"   And there was great joy the while, for all men knew that now at last they were in safety, and back in their old home.   For indeed they had escaped death and destruction during the great and long march, and had escaped many grievous perils.

HERODOTUS (The customs of the Onefourfivoi.)

And this to me not least, was indeed an object of wonder and surprise, to me, I say, as I came towards the peoples that dwell over against the setting sun. For the space of many moons I was living in the midst of the four tribes whose skill at tracking hateful Tribes of Prushoi—with whom they wage war—is unequalled even by any Tribe I have met.

It was about the time of the sending over of the Evening Hate, and I was wandering, as a stranger well might, down the narrow Trench, when a strange procession passed me by.   To which God or Goddess they were about to sacrifice, I was unable at first, being a stranger, to discover.   For some, that is the greater part, were bare as to their heads, upon which there was scarcely much hair growing and the others, that is by far the smaller party, had coverings for the head, both many and strange.   And now a loud cry goes up, and to me as I eagerly watch, there will come perhaps the God or Goddess, in whose honour the Festival is held.   And at the same moment as the cry goes up, behold those of the greater number bring their offerings ; sundials enclosed in priceless and yellow metal are brought forth and other things not lacking in value, such as girdles, inscribed as is the custom of that Tribe with " Gott mit UNS."   It is the Festival of the Great God Souveniros, at whose mysteries I had chanced to be present.

But very quickly is the Festival finished, for very soon a cry goes up " Nah Pu," " Nah Pu." There are no more offerings for the God, and the procession passes on its way, and the libations of Rumos are poured out forthwith.

BATTALION ORDERS.

Standing or Otherwise.
Orders by Lieutenant Colonel Grucock, C.B., D.S.M.A.C., S.F.A., Commanding 1/5 Bn. Stagshire Regiment.

Any old Night,
Any old Month,
Any old Year, Issued at 10. pip emma
(Divisional Time).

,,   ,,   10-15 pip emma
(Brigade Time).

,,   ,,   9-45 pip emma
(Battalion Time).

1   The Transport Section is detailed for Duty to-morrow.

The Sanitary Section next for Duty.

2.   Companies will parade under Sanitary men's arrangements.

3.   All men will be trained in the use of fire bombs. Certificates to this effect will be rendered to the Orderly Room within 3 days. Fire bombs should be indented for on B.F. XXX, and supplies will be issued from D.A.D.O.S. within six weeks if available.

4.   **Leave.**

All previous allotments of Leave are hereby cancelled.

The present allotment is :—

Corps Headquarters—50 to leave every Tuesday.
Division   ,,   30 to leave 1st and 15th of the month.
A.S.C.   ...   ... 15 to leave the 30th of each month.
Battalions ...   ... 5 to leave 1st April and 29th February.

5.   **Extract from G.R.O. 1.**

" It is laid down that the Liasion between the Artillery and Infantry so essential to that close co-operation between these two branches of the Service which alone can command success in major and minor operations, is not likely to be promoted by the compulsory evacuation of the latter by the former from their billets."

6.   **Extract from G.R.O. 2.**

" With a view to the encouragement of all Ranks, is has been approved, and laid down and now promulged and promulgated for the information of All Ranks that all Divisions which fail to obtain any objectives will be sent home for rest and re-equipment, and that all Divisions which may obtain, consolidate and hand over positions gained from the enemy, be called upon to carry out at least four major operations in each Battle."

7.   **Signals.**

In order that the high standard of efficiency achieved by the Signal Section may be maintained, and that it may be protected from competition, Runners will now carry Box respirators.

8.   **Comforts for the Troops.**

Blankets will be issued on 1/10/16, but owing to the inadvisability of putting a strain on Base Details, will on no account be cleaned and will be issued to the troups lousy.

9.   **Diet.**

Extract from Field General Master-Cook's Diary :

" Owing to the great popularity of the French Dish ' Pomme de Terre Fritz avec Omelettes ' among the men of the B.E.F., the Master Cooks of all Units are to make themselves acquainted with the preparation of same."

10.   **" Rest " Camps.**

While the Battalion is in rest, one Section per Company will be trained under the supervision of Company Quarter-Master Sergeants in carrying rum jars (full) along slippery corduroys.

Indents for the undermentioned should be submitted to the A.D.R.S. at once :—

Studs, rubber, special.
Jars, dummy, cast iron.
Juice, Lime, unsweetened.

11.   **Extracts from the** *London Gazette.*

Sec. Lieut. The Honble. Pip E. Squeke, 1st Fireside Borderers, to be graded for purposes of pay as a Staff Officer 1st Class and remain seconded for duty with HQrs. Home Army.

Temp. Lieut. Thomas Smith is confirmed in the rank of Temp. Sec. Lieut. while Commanding a Company in the Field.

P. CHICAGO JONES,

Lieut. and Adjt. 1/5th Bn. Stagshire Regt.

" A " COMPANY CONCERT.

On Saturday evening, September 23rd, a grand concert was held in " A " Company's Billet.

A Granary—large enough to hold 250 men—was turned into an ideal Concert Hall.   The Stage was fitted with electric light, and all the arrangements were on a most lavish scale—reflecting the highest credit on all those responsible for their organisation.

The Chairman, C. S. M. Faville, first called on Capt. Haden, O.C. " A " Company, to make a few introductory remarks.

After thanking the R.E.'s and the Band for their generous help, Capt. Haden said " In the good old West Country way—we will have more beer and music and enjoy ourselves."

The first item on the programme was a song by Pte. Shaw, followed by a recitation by 2nd Lieut. Briggs, given in the true Scotch style.   The cheering which followed showed how all ranks have taken our new Scotch Officers to their hearts.   It was a very real welcome.

The whole programme was so good that it is very difficult to single out any one performer, but special praise must be given to Ptes. Gray and Pritchard and Corpl. Thomas—whose songs quite brought down the house. As an encore Pte. Pritchard gave us the Welsh National Anthem—in Welsh.

The Commanding Officer was present, and during the interval C. S. M. Faville took the opportunity of congratulating him on his promotion and assuring him of the absolute confidence of all ranks in his leadership.

The Toast of " The C.O. and Officers " was drunk, followed by prolonged applause. The C.O. in reply said that he felt the great honour and responsibility of his high office, but that he knew he had the loyal support of every Officer, N.C.O., and man. He would do his best never to fail them, and he knew that he could always count on his old Company to do all that he asked of them.

The second part of the programme was equal to the first and the juggling of Pte. Pittaway was especially clever.

High praise is due to the Band, who added greatly to the success of the concert, and Sergt. Wonson was in his element as O.C. Smokes and Drinks.

These Concerts do much to promote that camaraderie and esprit-de-corps which has always been a feature of our best British Regiments.

E. H.

"C" COMPANY CONCERT.

On Thursday evening, September 21st, " C " Company held their first Concert of the Season, under the able Presidentship of Lieut. K. Robertson, whose efforts greatly added to the success of the Concert. The programme consisted of songs and recitations, which were both of a humourous and sentimental character.

The Star item of the programme was naturally the Battalion Band, under the able conductorship of Sergt. Proctor, which gave a much appreciated number of selections during the evening.

PROGRAMME.

Selection by Band.	
Song.—" Little Grey Home in the West "	Pte. Pearson.
Humorous Song.	Dmr. Farmer.
Song.—" Thora "	Pte. G. Barnes.
Selection by Band.	
Recitation.—" The Fireman's Wedding."	Pte. Martin.
Song.—" The Bassoon "	L-Cpl. F. Fry.
Humorous Song	Pte. E. Eden.
Selection by Band.	
Imitations of Victoria Monk	Pte. McNesby.
Song.—" Killarney "	Dmr. Farmer.
Humorous Song.—" The Ship's Captain "	Pte. Shaw.
Selection by Band.	
Recitation—" The Young British Soldier "	Lieut. Briggs.
(Rudyard Kipling)	
Song.—" When you're all Dressed up "	Pte. Rodway.
Song	Sergt. Proctor.
Selection by Band.	

We were pleased to see the Officers in the "Stalls." Their presence was very much appreciated.

Sergt. Finch, who was absent on a " Course," was greatly missed. His songs and wit have always been a feature of our past Concerts.

Votes of thanks to Lieut. Robertson, the Band and Artistes were given on the proposal of Sergt. B. Cummings.

The singing of the " King " and " Auld Lang Syne " brought a most enjoyable evening to an end.

P. B. C.

OUR BENEFACTORS.

Staff Capt., 145 Brigade.	Continental " Daily Mail."
Bishop Frodsham.	Papers.
The Vicar of Tewkesbury.	
Mr. W. R. Voller.	Cards.
Miss Karn.	Papers.
The " Echo."	" The Echo."
The Powers that Be.	Rest.
The M.O.	Inoculation.
Lieut.-Colonel Winterbotham.	Papers.
Lieut.-Colonel Marling.	,,
Mrs. Temple Cooke.	,,
Miss Backhouse.	,,
Miss Parr.	,,
Mr. Berkeley Powell.	,,
Mr. Jack Margetson.	Cigarettes.
" Daily Express " Cheery Fund.	
	Boxing Gloves and Dominoes.
The Hon. Mabel Gye.	Papers.
Pte. Orchard.	Typing.
Pte. Wood.	,,
Mrs. Russell Kerr.	Papers.

"A GLOUCESTERSHIRE LAD."

By Lieutenant F. W. Harvey, D.C.M.

With a Preface by Colonel J. H. Collett, C.M.G.

Sidgwick and Jackson. 1s. 6d. net.

Ever since the days of Tyrtaeus, the soldier-poet who fell himself amidst the men he had sung into battle " the Minstrel and the man of war, the lyre and the sword," says M. Chesterton, " are everywhere connected, and often identical."

So the world has extended a warm welcome to the Poems of Second Lieutenant Harvey, D.C.M.

The publication of his Poems in book form synchronised with the sad news that he was missing, and cast a gloom over us all. But as everyone knows, he is a prisoner in Germany, where he should be cheered by the great reception that has been accorded to his book. We reprint in this issue the review that appeared in the *Morning Post*.

" Lieutenant F. W. Harvey is " F.W.H. " of the FIFTH GLOUCESTER GAZETTE, the first journal ever published from the British trenches, and unsurpassed for literary merit by any of its younger rivals. He won the Distinguished Conduct Medal in August, 1915, for a conspicuous act of gallantry near Hebuterne, when he was a Lance-Corporal in the 5th Battalion of the Gloucestershire Regiment, and he subsequently received a commission in recognition of this and other proofs of a brilliant aptitude for the vocation of arms. He is also a poet of power and a subtle distinction, as readers of the *Morning Post* will remember, and this little collection of his poems, which has a preface by his Commanding Officer, will give him a high place in the Sidneian company of soldier-poets. " These poems," his Colonel observes, " are written by a soldier and reflect a soldier's outlook. Mud, blood, and khaki are rather conspicuously absent. They are, in fact, the last things a soldier wishes to think or talk about. What he does think about is his home." The collection is dedicated " to all comrades of mine who lie dead in foreign fields for love of England, or who live to prosecute the war for another England." The two dominant notes of the true war poetry are struck in that dedication. First, the love of country which is in the very heart's blood, a passion and a pang not to be reasoned about or defined in the cold terms of any impersonal 'ism—it is seldom, indeed, that the full-hearted patriot talks about patriotism. Secondly, the underlying thoughts that the victory which is now within our grasp, supposing we dare and endure to the end, will be no better than a defeat after all if the new sense of comradeship between all classes of the community cannot be so used as to make our country even better worth living and dying for. The least little suggestion will send the soldier-poet's winged thoughts flying back to England, his native county, his old school, the kindly life and ancient courtesies from which he is exiled for a season. The dewdrops on a spider's web, in Flanders, for example, will set the soul of "F.W.H." travelling on the road of remembrance to his West Country :—

> All golden gleams the way ;
> How strange such riches
> Drawn from rough men should be
> Seven or eight worlds away,
> Fighting, and carelessly,
> Dying in ditches !

At Eastertide he thinks of his Gloucestershire for luck, seeing its Silurian scenery as in the palm of the hand :—

> Here's luck, my lads, while Birdlip Hill is steep :—
> — As long as Cotswold's high or Severn's deep.
> Our thoughts of you shall blossom and abide
> While blow the orchards about Severn side :—
> — While a round bubble like the children blow,
> May Hill floats purple in the sunset glow.

And cricket being the most English of all English diversions (especially in the county of the Three Graces), he sees his old school again as a hot catch comes to hand :—

> Whizzing, fierce, it came
> Down the summer air
> Burning like a flame
> On my fingers bare,
> And it brought to me
> As swift—a memory.
>
> Happy days long dead
> Clear I saw once more,
> Childhood that is fled :—
> Rossall on the shore,
> Where the sea sobs wild
> Like a homesick child.

Rossall on the shore—well I know, myself an O.R., that no other school is loved better, loved longer, by its children generation after generation. But love-of-country burns brightest on its living altar, perhaps, when he sees a vision of English maidenhood, ever-young England and ever-beautiful in her keenest incarnation :—

> Your eyes are bright for ever. Your dark hair
> Holds an eternal shade. Like a bright sword
> Shall flame the vision of your strange sweet ways,
> Cleaving the years : and even your smallest word,
> Lying forgotten with the things that were,
> Shall glow and kindle, burning up the days.

Equally delightful are his impressions of comrades, both officers and men. For example, the Major who is imperturbable whatever happens, a Boche attack or a Church Parade :—

> Nothing flusters him. Men
> Confidently go
> To do his bidding :
> While he stands there
> Revolving stunts ;
> And nonchalantly
> Tapping his legging.

or C Company Cook, who also includes imperturbability among his abilities :—

> " Do you want j-jam on it ? " he'd say,
> Twirling a red moustache.
> We chaffed him over rations every day,
> " Say, is this tea or hash ? "
> " Jim, tell us, do,
> Why you put sugar in the blooming stew."
> " — And there's a heap o' coal in this—not half ! "
> To all our chaff
> " Do you want j-jam on it ? " he'd say.

In this example of several " prose poems " (let the phrase pass for once) we get a central thought of his philosophy of life :

> " Is not this the mountain of blue grass ? " asked the stranger. " Why is the grass as green as in our common-meadows ? "
> " It was never any other colour," said the native.
> " It looked blue from afar," persisted the traveller, and I have journeyed a long and difficult way to find it."
> " You had better have stayed at home," answered the native.
> " No," returned the stranger, with a sad smile, " I had better have come, but now I will go home. The grass there has become blue."

And, as for his philosophy of living, here is the gist of it all :—

> If we return, will England be
> Just England still to you and me ?
> The place where we must earn our bread ?
> We, who have walked among the dead.
> And watched the smile of agony,
> And seen the price of Liberty,
> Which we have taken carelessly
> From other hands. Nay, we shall dread,
>   If we return,
>
> Dread lest we hold blood-guiltily
> The things that men have died to free,
> Oh, English fields shall blossom red
> For all the blood that has been shed
> By men whose guardians are we,
>   If we return.

This is the underlying thought of all the true war-poetry, and it is inarticulate in millions of hearts—woe to the sleek trader and slick politicians who shall hamper the building of the better England for the sake of their pockets or to keep up Party feuds ! Woe to them, for the dust of all the valiant dead shall testify against them !

E. B. O.

Morning Post.

CORRESPONDENCE.

Dear Monsieur,

I hear that a Zeppelin has been brought down over London. Can you tell me if we have captured many Subs lately

I am, yours lovingly,

MDLLE. LE TOUQUET.

(We are inclined to think that you have captured a great number.)

Sir,

As you are out in France, can you tell me if we have got the Bosch in the soup ? Do you think it will be all over at any time now ?

I am, Sir,

Yours, etc.

A.S.C.

(Having studied our Cooks carefully we should not be surprised at what got into the soup. As regards the latter question, from a study of the mess-waiters it certainly seems likely.)

Sir,

Being something of a theorist I should esteem it a favour if you could inform me whether you could hear the guns in France the night the Zeppelin was brought down over London,

I am,

Your obedient Servant,

PROFESSOR BOOLES.

(We regret we cannot give our respected correspondent a satisfactory reply. On the night in question we were listening to the Curios.)

A DIP INTO THE FUTURE.

When the Editor of this GAZETTE assumes the Spiritual command of a Parish, we venture a forecast of his parish magazine on which his long and meritorious service in the army is bound to have an influence. Likely selections from The —————— Parish Gazette are appended.

Parish Standing Orders.

1. The Choir will parade for training every Wednesday at 7-30 under the Sergeant organist.

2. All Choir Boys will have golden curly hair and blue eyes. During the Anthem every boy will open and close his mouth together with a distinct pause between each motion, taking the time from the senior chorister present, on the right or left as the case may be.

3. It is forbidden to remove apples during the Harvest thanksgiving. These will be issued when available through the usual channels after indent on A.F. Rubric 55.

4. All sexes are warned to attend Church Parade properly dressed complete with new clothes, hymn-book and one penny (on Easter-Sunday 3d.)

5. It is forbidden to play pontoon in the aisle.

6. Article 40 is cancelled from 1.12.18.

7. G.O.C. parish views with regret the increasing habit of sucking spearmint during his sermon. This practice must cease forthwith. It is pointed out that the clearing away of the undigested residuum entails excessive labour on the sanitary sections.

8. Deficiencies in hymn-books may be made up by application to VERGER SMITH.

THINGS WE WANT TO KNOW.

Why does the Church-warden like counting the money ?

Did the Sydesman overstay his pass at the " Pig and Whistle ? "

Who put a penny in the plate and took out a half-crown ? Was he in the North Transept ?

What did the baby say when the Curate dropped it during the Christening ?

Who is the latest Member of the Mothers' Meeting ? And why ?

NOTICES.

The Senior Curate is detailed to attend a Lecture on FUND RAISING methods by the ARCHDEACON at K.17 a 9.7. (85 in the Red Book.)

Services for the Chaps on Sunday afternoon.

Collections on next Sunday for the Vicar and until further orders.

The Senior Curate is promoted acting unpaid Rural Dean.

Two Prebendaries, 4 minor canons, 16 district visitors, and 72 G.F.S. will report at the Parish Room on FRIDAY, for fatigue under O.C. working parties. The unexpended portion of the wool ration will be returned on completion to the orderly Curate.

EDITOR'S POST-BAG.

(The following letter has been received from its recipient in England.)

Oct. 1. Same.

Dear Mother and Dad and all of you,

I just got your letter I hope this will find you both quite well as it leaves me in the pink at present but for a cold. We marched about 8 miles in the pouring rain on Monday and got wet though we dont mind seeing as how its farther from the line and we may be here for some time. We're resting which means working hard all day some of them new derbyites want licking into shape. We do interesting things like Company Drill, Baynet fitering, Rifle Exercises and cetra. Dear Mother we got a lot of new Officers some of them are Scotch Officers but they seem quite decent fellows. Dear Mother and Dad so you seen the Somme film on the pictures but we whats been through it knows as it can't be like the real thing as you cant imagine what its like like we seen it. Things look bright now I think we got the bosche whacked and if this weather dont go on we'll all be back for Crismus. Dear Dad glad to hear you got the potatoes planted in the elopement alright. Theres lots of corn out in the fields mostly oats round these parts as theyve only got some old women to get it in. We'd like a turn at the job for a change and drink the cider to, what ! You ses Bill Wheelers bin called up bout time to thems the ones that ought to ave a turn some of us boys as bin out here could do munitions as well as im. I'll bet.

Dear Ma the parcel as you was going to send asnt come yet. We could do some cake to though we get good food. Dont send any more eggs though unless you can send them with the shells not broken. Well dear Ma and Dad theres no more to say as it is I'm sorry for the " censor fellow " as as got to pursue and censor this. So love to you Ma and Dad.

Your loving son,

Will————.

Also Mable and Annie.

PROFESSIONAL JEALOUSY.

Extract from " Blighty."

By a Glo'ster.

God made the bees,
   The bees make the honey ;
The Glo'sters do the work
   And the R.E.'s get the money.

The Sapper's Reply.

Who eats the honey,
   Is it Glo'sters or the bee ?
The bee gets no cash
   From the bally infantry.

Who pinches sandbags
   Required for parapet,
Drops them in the mud
   To save his feet from wet ?

When dug out, sap or bridge
  Is required by infantry,
The Glo'ster bends his knee
  To the better paid R.E.

Who taught him how to bomb,
  Revet and to demolish
To build a house or knock it down,
  The Germans for to dish ?

Why should the Glo'ster grouse
  At the R. E. and his pay ?
When the Glo'ster wants to know a thing
  The R. E. shows the way.
                " SAPPER."

We feel that the Sapper's reply requires no comment.

Poor " Twister " of the Sapper Section appears to be rather unhappy. For so would it appear from a poem by " Gramaphone "—of which we quote the first two spasms only.

" " Twister " belongs to the Sappers,
  His fighting is almost spent !
  He has pushed the Truck
  Through metres of muck
  Till now he is almost bent.

At last we're in Training and Rest-cure ;
  Some have been sent to the sea,
  And one thing is sure—
  That troubles him sore—
  It's there that he ought to be."

We trust " Twister " will either get his trip to the seaside or failing that, his old age pension, to which it would appear, he is fully entitled.

ADVERTISEMENT.

The G.O.C. presents his world-renowned troupe of variety artistes, the 48th Division.

Over 15,000 performers.

Stupendous attraction.

This Troupe has performed with success in all the principal Cities of Modern Europe, including Good Easter, Billericay, Widford, Hebuterne and Pozieres.

SPECIAL ATTRACTIONS :—

Divisional Headquateres in a Drawing Room Drama
entitled
War at the Chateau.

The R.E. in a Tight wire Act.

  Light Scenic Railway Free to All.

The 145 Bde. Glee Party :—

  That's done it

  What's the Hughes of worrying

  Battles I have known.

          By Capt. John Mountain.

A. S. C. in a recitation.

  How I won the Battle of Pozieres.

  A tale of London Gallantry.

As an encore—

  Life on 6 Bob a day.

The Infantry :—

Highly trained strong men ; great feats in walking, weight lifting, etc., etc., etc.

To conclude with a firework display by the Gunners.
    A Sure Hit.

Read these unsolicited testimonials.

  —— I was glad to have you in my Corps at Ovillers. Lieut. Rynecke. Your performance at Thiepval was very taking.

YOU MUST SEE THIS SHOW.

Everything first Class, not a wangler, not a dud.

APPLY for seats at Murky Terrace, the Cross Roads, where the Division always is.

A MAGNIFICENT SHOW.

This Troupe will perform three times every Battle.

BRICKS FROM THE EDITOR'S PACK.

" Army coats made by naturalised Germans.

Appealing to the House of Commons section of the Appeal Tribunal yesterday on behalf of an employee, a wholesale furrier made the remarkable assertion that practically all the contracts for Crimean (sheepskin) coats for the Army last year went to naturalised German firms.

Mr. Dove (a member of the Tribunal)—Did you tender against them ?—We could not compete with them ; we were turned down. The appellant added that he did not know whether it was cheapness of labour which enabled the naturalised Germans to capture the trade.

Exemption until December 1st was granted."

          Morning Post, Sept. 2nd.

They can't keep away from those Germans, can they ?

" It has been a sore grief to the relatives of the brave men who have fallen in the fight after winning the Military Cross or the Distinguished Conduct Medal that the rules of the War Office and Admiralty alike have prevented either of these decorations being handed over to the next-of-kin. To most people it would seem illogical that the greater decoration should be given to the safe keeping of relatives, and that that of secondary importance should be withheld.

Mr. Lloyd George was pressed upon the matter towards the close of the last sittings of Parliament, and he promised to give consideration to the representations made to him to permit the emblems of military honours like the Military Cross and the D.C.M. to be handed to the representatives of the brave dead. There is reason to believe that the Secretary for War has not forgotten his promise, and that in due time a favourable decision will be arrived at with regard to at least the more important of these decorations."

          Daily Telegraph.

It has always been a cause of wonder to us why the British Public has taken lying down the extraordinary ruling of the Army Authorities in this matter. Anything more illogical and absurd it is hard indeed to conceive.

Suppose for instance it should happen that an Officer and a couple of men distinguish themselves in the capture of a German trench and are wounded and succumb to their wounds in the course of a few days. They can receive the D.S.O., the Military Cross, the D.C.M., because the recommendations can be sent in at once.

But only let them fall in the Trench and then even though their work was done and the struggle finished, they are ineligible for any reward other than that of the Victoria Cross. We hope Mr. Lloyd George will carry out this much needed and crying reform and that the D.S.O. may also be included amongst the posthumous Honours. In this Department at any rate sentiment and sound sense should compel the authorities to burst the bands of red tape.

While on the subject of medals, there exists another very strange custom—that of granting no awards to Officers and men who have the misfortune to take part in operations which terminate unsuccessfully through no fault of theirs.

We have in mind the doughty deeds of a certain Battalion on the memorable First of July. They gained their objective—no mean thing that, involving as it did an advance of over 1000 yards against " original " front lines. They had to retire, owing to lack of support on the flanks. It was a most gallant affair. Officers and men were superb. But we believe that no reward of any kind was made to any of the participants in this attack owing to the fact that the scheme as a whole ended in failure.

Extraordinary, isn't it, and so very illogical.

" All classes of the people of England are unanimous in the resolve to humiliate us, from the First Sea Lord down to the most insignificant labourer at Newcastle-on-Tyne."

Kolnische Zeitung.

Wind up ! and about time, too. But there was nothing like this in the German papers six months ago. The good people of the Fatherland are being prepared for the possibility of a drawn struggle or even defeat.

G. O. 577.

The Commander-in-Chief has been informed that the practice of smoking, by the use of pipes, cigars and cheroots, has become prevalent amongst the Officers of the Army, which is not only in itself a species of intoxication occasioned by the fumes of tobacco, but undoubtedly occasions drinking and tippling by those who acquire the habit ; and he entreats the Officers commanding Regiments to prevent smoking in the Mess Rooms of their several Regiments, and in the adjoining apartments, and to discourage the practice among the Officers of Junior Rank in their Regiments.

No need to get the wind up. This is only a Routine Order issued by the Great Duke of Wellington in 1845 !

At 5-45 p.m. August 26th, an aeroplane took a photograph of our objective. By 3 p.m. next day a copy was at Battalion H.Q. in the Trench. Smart work.

At the Annual Meeting of the British Association a few weeks ago, Dr. Marett, who holds the Chair of Anthropology at Oxford, complained that the students of that science had to subsist on a " farrago of heterogeneous by-products."

Nevertheless we have written to ask him to send us a couple of tins, that we may be able to enjoy a pleasant change from the ordinary trench fare.

An Officer lately arrived from England, was walking along through the " mainstreet " of B—, after having been to the " Curios." He expressed himself pleased with the performance, but at the same time said that he was much looking forward to the " Dados," whose notice board he had passed on the way. We are looking forward to Captain Th-rnt-n's new Revue.

It takes a strong man to depart from established usage. We trust we are not guilty of revealing any secret when we remind our readers of the change of tactics in Trench warfare which marked the last few days of our stay in Flanders and the whole of that long and weary vigil in France.

The change was drastic and revolutionary, and it was neglected at one's peril. Witness the experience of a Division famous to all time for its prowess in the Great Gamble at Gallipoli ! They had a whole platoon snaffled one night. The change was none other than the holding of the Front line thinly.

The outside world has a very faint and dim idea of the tremendous advantages which accrued to the Division therefrom. Contrast, for instance, the number of casualties sustained by the Division on our left with those suffered by the skeleton Battalions which were guarding our old Home during the momentous days which preceded the memorable First of July. Our neighbours suffered more than three times as much.

For the preservation of many lives the Division has to thank the G.O.C.

From parallel columns of the *Daily Chronicle*, September 28th.

COMBLES	WITHOUT A FIGHT
Combles fell to a like tactic and like speed of action. Early in the morning the French, having carried Frégicourt by assault, so protecting their eastern flank, had got into the cemetery and the south-eastern part of Combles. At the same time British contingents broke over the last trenches in the town from the west. *Although the garrison had been reduced to about two battalions these resisted with desperate courage from cellar to cellar and from one shattered wall to another.*	For the first time in the history of this war on the western front since the Battle of the Marne and the beginning of trench warfare *the enemy has been compelled to abandon a town without a fight in it.* He has withdrawn from Combles, which is a place of some importance, and more than a mere village, and our troops have entered it from the north, while the French hold the southern half.

It is no good having an O.P. in Fleet Street, is it ?

The first Battle of Ypres.

" Many fine deeds of valour were done. In one of them Captain Rising, of the Gloucester Regiment, with ninety men, defended some point with such heroic tenacity that when, some days afterwards, the Brigadier attempted to get the names of the survivors for commendation, not one could be found."

"The British Campaign in France."

CONAN DOYLE.

Strand Magazine.—October, 1916.

Geneva, September 23rd.

It is understood that the German Government proposes to lodge a complaint with the International Red Cross Society here against the use of so-called "Tanks," as being contrary to the recognised methods of civilised warfare."

Daily Paper.

He is a poor loser, isn't he ?

"Here, as elsewhere, the Germans really ran away. 'Run,' said a famous Colonel, whom I met later in the day, 'Run'! why near Lesbœufs, you couldn't see their backs for dust.'"

Daily Mail, September 29th.

Now what were his exact words, please, Mr. Thomas ?

"—— the (the Germans) are out-gunned by hostile artillery and out-fought by enemy infantry. To both arms of the Service we owe much, but how helpless would either be if robbed of eyes and ears ! The mastership of the air has been the forerunner of victory ! "

Saturday Review, September 23rd.

We presume our airmen shut off their engines when using their ears.

Extract from XIII. Corps Intelligence Summary

" A prisoner who has been through the War almost from the commencement states that, in his opinion, one of the most effective weapons used by the British is the Mills Grenade fired as a rifle grenade. He states that apart from the casualties inflicted the moral effect is very great."

The British Army owes a not inconsiderable debt to the real author of this clever device. It is not generally known that the invention was the result of Major Waller's ingenuity.

Found, but not on a German prisoner.

Concerning Army Gymnasium Instructors

Owing to the responsibility and nature of the work and the nervous energy required to carry out the training of Instructors, it is desirable that Staff Instructors be allowed, as far as possible, to proceed on leave after every three months. Commanders and Staff should, for similar reasons, give these Instructors every assistance.

Now we are beginning to understand how the Leave Boats are filled.

The Battalion heard with great concern of the continued illness of Lieut.-Colonel J. H. Collett, C.M.G. After some few days at the Base he was given sick leave, only to have a relapse on arriving at London. It is believed that he is suffering from a mild attack of typhoid. We all wish him a speedy return to health and strength.

Lieut.-Colonel Pagan, D.S.O., commanding the 1st Battalion, whom many of us saw at Albert back in the summer, has been wounded ; and it would appear that 2nd Lieutenant Sly was also wounded and 2nd Lieutenant A. F. D. Brown reported missing the same day.

Many congratulations to our Brigadier on being awarded a Bar to his D.S.O., and to Lieut.-Colonels Harman, Clarke, Micklem and Reynolds on their D.S.O.'s.

We apologise to the many sportsmen in the Division who at very short notice were prepared to enter the Boxing Competition which we had arranged. Circumstances over which we had no control compelled a postponement. We hope to be able to entertain them at some future date.

There is a certain Colonel in the —th Division who is very keen on running anyone in for nothing. It chanced that a Canadian cantered by. As the rider paid no attention to this Colonel's calls of " Hi," " Hi there," the Colonel borrowed a horse and galloped after his would-be prisoner. Unfortunately he took a toss clean over his horse's head. The Canadian quickly turned, and, as he lopped by the Colonel, said " I canter because I can, you can't," and cantered away.

All contributions should be sent to " The Editor," c/o Orderly Room, 1/5th Bn. Gloucestershire Regiment.

If you do not get your copy, please let him know. For Five Francs you can have a copy posted as long as the War or the GAZETTE lasts.

The Gunners.

Our Artillery have covered themselves with glory and renown during the past few weeks. Some half-dozen Divisions have they shepherded across No Man's Land. Constant work like this, involving as it does observation under unhealthy conditions, has entailed the inevitable list of casualties. Among the killed are numbered Lieut.-Colonel West and Major G. D. Browne—very familiar figures through this Division. Who has not seen at one time or another Colonel West leaning against the parapet in the front line smoking that curved pipe of his, searching the while for the latest idiosyncrasies of the Boche. This intrepid gunner had the reputation among the gunners of knowing his work most thoroughly. Major Browne was one of the Majors who came out with us and will be affectionately remembered. His Battery—like many others—enjoyed a great reputation, and few O.C.'s can have taken greater care of their men.

Lieutenant W. R. F. Wyley, Adjutant of the 240th Brigade, was killed at the same time. In a letter to his father, Colonel Lord Wynford paid a warm tribute to his high qualities, both as a soldier and a man.

The same shell which proved fatal to these Officers inflicted most painful injuries to Lieutenant H. H. D'E Vallancy. It was at first feared that his injuries would prove mortal. But his many friends were delighted to hear that he was on the high road to recovery.

We should like to congratulate very heartily Lieutenant-Colonel Cossart on his D.S.O., and Lieutenant Pridmore on his Military Cross.

PERSONAL.

Many congratulations to Lieutenant-Colonel Tarrant on being selected to command Fourth Reserve Battalion, Gloucestershire Regiment.

Marriage.

On September 13th, at the Church of St. Mary the Virgin, Fretherne, Stonehouse, Gloucestershire, by the Rev. G. F. Coleridge, M.A., Vicar of Crowthorne, Captain Fritz William Cole, 5th Bn. Gloucestershire Regiment, eldest son of Mr. W. H. Cole, J.P., of Bourne House, Brimscombe, and Mrs. Cole, to Margaret Rosamund, younger daughter of the Rev. C. D. P. Davies, of Fretherne Lodge.

We were delighted to see that Captain Little and Lieutenants King and Pearce were sufficiently recovered from their wounds to be able to attend.

OLD BOYS' COLUMN.

Extract from *London Gazette.*

2nd Lieutenant A. C. Sly has been wounded and 2nd Lieutenant A. F. D. Brown, we are sorry to say, is missing. He will be remembered affectionately be members of the old " A " Company.

Sergeant H. W. Webb, a son of our Battalion Quarter-Master Sergeant, has been awarded the D.C.M. for conspicuous gallantry. He was in command of the most exposed part of the Company's line during a heavy bombardment. Later, when one hostile attack had been driven back and another was coming on, he led a bayonet charge completely routing the attackers. He is not yet eighteen years of age !

Many congratulations to Corporal Washbourne, attached to the Trench Mortars, on his Military Medal.

EXTRACTS FROM " LONDON GAZETTE."

1st Battalion Gloucestershire Regiment.

No. 30 Sergt. A. F. D. Brown, from 1/5th Bn. Gloucestershire Regiment. To be Temporary 2nd Lieutenant, dated 19/6/16.

10th Bn. Gloucestershire Regiment.

No. 2678 L-Corpl. J. W. Gray, from 1/5th Bn. Gloucestershire Regiment. To be Temporary 2nd Lieutenant, dated 19/6/16.

17th Bn. Lancashire Fusiliers.

No. 2566 Pte. J. E. Sanders, from 1/5th Bn. Gloucestershire Regiment. To be Temporary 2nd Lieutenant, dated 16/8/16.

6th Bn. Royal Berkshire Regiment.

No. 2693 L-Corpl. A. H. T. Lewis, from 1/5 Bn. Gloucestershire Regiment. To be Temporary 2nd Lieutenant dated 31/7/16.

APPOINTMENTS AND PROMOTIONS.

Lt. Tempy. (Capt.) L. R. C. Sumner, to be Captain. 22/6/16
2nd Lt. (Tempy. Lt.) C. W. Winterbotham to be
    Lieut. 22/6/16
2nd Lt. G. E. Ratcliff, to be Tempy. Lieut. dated 21/7/16
Lieut. H. P. Snowden, to be temporary Captain dated 23/8/16
1857 C.Q.M.S. Locke. To be a/R.S.M. dated 12/9/16
238 Sergt. Huxford, J. H. To be a/C.Q.M.S. of C Co. 12/9/16
774 C.Q.M.S. Smith, V. G. To be a/C.S.M. of D. Co. 16/8/16
392 Sergt. Finch, F., To be a/C.S.M. of C Co. dated 4/9/16
58 Sergt. Meadows, J. To be a/C.Q.M.S. of D. Co. 16/8/16

To be Coy. Sergt. Major :—

2416	Sergt.	Bailey, W. W.	Dated	8/6/16

To be Sergeant :—

2414	L/Sergt.	Kibby, F.	,,	21/4/16
717	,,	Eden, J.	,,	4/5/16
3010	Corpl.	Clarke, W. G.	,,	8/6/16
1777	,,	Parrott, E.	,,	19/6/16
2075	,,	Wheeler, G. H.	,,	2/7/16
2787	,,	Davis, P.	,,	3/7/16
2535	,,	Garner, E.	,,	4/7/16
2091	,,	Coton, J.	,,	10/7/16
2223	,,	Boulter, H.	,,	19/7/16

To be Sergeant :—

2697	Corpl.	Middlecote, H.	Dated	20/7/16
1663	,,	Abel, J. W.	,,	21/6/16
2177	,,	Hensley, G.	,,	23/7/16
2486	,,	Pepperell, W. F.	,,	23/7/16
2635	L/Corpl.	Wood, S. C.	,,	25/7/16
2533	,,	Fry, H. H.	,,	25/7/16
2742	,,	Wintle, A. H.	,,	25/7/16
2670	Pte. (L/C.)	Egerton, W.	,,	27/7/16

To be L/Sergt. with pay :—

2404	Corpl.	Fowler, R.	,,	13/4/16
2272	,,	Reeves, F. W.	,,	20/4/16

To be Corporal :—

2579	L/Corpl.	Dennis, A.	,,	20/4/16
2366	,,	Maddock, W. H.	,,	21/4/16
3343	,,	O'Neil, C.	,,	25/4/16
1556	,,	Bundy, W.	,,	4/5/16
2711	,,	Smith, F. C.	,,	13/5/16
1476	Pte. (L/C.)	Coopey, A.	,,	13/5/16
1525	,,	Stallard, S. G.	,,	8/6/16
2453	,,	Thomas, A. C.	,,	20/6/16
4008	,,	Hook, W. H.	,,	21/6/16
3127	,,	Timms, H. J.	,,	19/6/16
2921	,,	Cummings, P. B.	,,	2/7/16
1750	,,	Chandler, E. W.	,,	3/7/16
1842	,,	Nash, E. M.	,,	4/7/16
2571	,,	Taylor, M.	,,	3/7/16
2088	,,	Hardiman, G.	,,	4/7/16
2700	,,	Paget, T. W.	,,	10/7/16
2784	,,	Powell, W. H.	,,	20/7/16
3039	,,	Palmer, F.	,,	19/7/16
2963	,,	Sindrey, R.	,,	20/7/16
3139	,,	Butt, R.	,,	21/7/16
2558	A/Cpl.	Paynter, W. F. L.	,,	29/5/16
2726	,,	Washbourne, W. P.	,,	29/5/16

To be L/Corporal. with pay :—

2754	Pte. (L/C.)	Egerthon, G. H.	,,	21/4/16
2199	Pte.	Druce, E. C.	,,	21/4/16
2455	,,	Couldey, A. J.	,,	22/4/16
2738	,,	Jennings, A. L.	,,	25/4/16
2555	,,	Mullis, E. J.	,,	4/5/16
1772	,,	Aston, C. V.	,,	13/5/16
2425	,,	Trinder, A. J.	,,	19/6/16
1192	,,	Newman, G.	,,	27/6/16
3411	,,	Bartlett, R. E.	,,	28/6/16
1372	,,	Smith, F. W.	,,	21/7/16
5308	,,	Williams, J. (1st Glos. Attd)	,,	21/7/16
20466	,,	Terry, A. (1st Glos. Attd)	,,	21/7/16
2471	,,	Doyle. F. N.	,,	23/7/16
2677	,,	Grant, J. K.	,,	23/7/16
2679	,,	Green, F. J.	,,	25/7/16
2949	,,	Mayall, F.	,,	25/7/16
10336	,,	Oxley, A. (1st Glos. Attd)	,,	25/7/16
1879	,,	Yates, A. J.	,,	27/7/16
1982	,,	Sterry, J.	,,	4/8/16

The undermentioned are appointed unpaid L/Corporals, dated 30/7/16 :—

2465	Pte.	Martin, W. B.
2505	,,	Pike, C. R.
1856	,,	Speke, H. G.
1853	,,	White, H. G.
2374	,,	Barnes, H. C.
2630	,,	Chandler, W. J.
2951	,,	Merrell, H. W.
1696	,,	Parr, F. J.
2588	,,	Johnson, J. G.
2915	,,	Chorley, J.
2584	,,	Hopkins, P. J.
8934	,,	Hobbs, G. (1st Glo'ster, Attached)
3009	,,	Chess, E. H.
1831	,,	Miller, W. F.
3055	,,	Whitworth, A. C.
3031	,,	Medlicott, W.
3192	,,	Clemm, H. H.
3287	,,	Teale, C. H.
2816	,,	Elliott, A. W.
2798	,,	Boddington, G. H.
2944	,,	Kitching, J. A.
1596	,,	Hunt, A. W.

R.I.P.

These are the souls that chose but yesterday,
When sweet Life put her kiss into their hands,
The path of Peace along the flow'ry way,
Doing with simple grace her least commands,
Their kind hearts never passed a burden by,
That they might shoulder for a weaker one ;
Dreamers, but quick with wide humanity,
They left, for dreams, no irksome thing undone.
And they were first to heed their Country's call,
To quell their hate of strife, the stress and din,
And go, prepared to die, renouncing all,
Hiding the two-fold sacrifice within.
O sure, for these, beyond Death's Great Release
Green pastures wait, and Christ's Eternal Peace.

TANKS AGAIN!

"Why not make use of our Mobile Veterinary Section?"

5th Gloucester Gazette.

A Chronicle, serious and humorous, of the Battalion while serving with the
BRITISH EXPEDITIONARY FORCE.

THE BATTLE HONOURS OF THE GLOUCESTERSHIRE REGIMENT.

I

At the request of your Commanding Officer I am contributing a series of short articles on the County Battle Honours, and I do not think I can do better than include with the first Article the Roll which I prepared about four years ago and which hangs in most of the schools of Gloucestershire.

This Roll was prepared before the present world-wide war was upon us and without doubt, when the past two years are properly apportioned, it will be materially lengthened.

As it stands it is the second longest list in the British Army, with 34 Honours to its credit, the King's Royal Rifle Corps with 38 being at the head.

In this first article I do not propose to refer in detail to the actal Honours, but a few remarks on the origin of the various Battalions may be of interest.

The 1st Battalion was formed under Warrant date the 12th of March, 1694, and was then known as the 28th Regiment of Foot.

In the year 1782 it was officially connected with the County, being known as the 28th or North Gloucestershire Regiment.

The first Colonel was Sir John Gibson.

From 1734 to 1759 the Regiment was commanded by Colonel Philip Bragg, and for many years the 28th went by the name of the " Old Braggs."

They were also known as " The Slashers," which arose from an incident in the American War of Independence, 1775-1782.

At an engagement in 1775 at the entrances of the White plains, the Regiment were ordered to climb a cliff and being unable to carry their flint locks, threw them away. On reaching the summit they made a successful attack with their short swords, which gave rise to their nickname.

The second Battalion was raised in 1758 as the 61st Regiment of Foot and became in 1782 the South Gloucestershire Regiment.

This Regiment had two nicknames, one that of the " Silver-tailed Dandies," which arose in the Peninsular War, owing to their having retained the long-tailed coatee instead of wearing the shorter jackets used by the majority of the Regiments, the other, " Flower of Toulouse," given them for their gallant action in that Battle and the heavy losses they sustained.

The third Battalion was re-constituted in 1908 from the old 3rd and 4th Battalion of Militia into the Special Reserve.

The three Territorial Battalions were originally the 1st, 2nd and 3rd Volunteer Battalion of the Regiment and in 1908, when the Territorial Force was formed, their present nomenclature was adopted.

The 4th Battalion was formed at the beginning of the Volunteer movement in 1859, and was commanded for several years by Colonel Bush, a retired Regular Officer, it being then known as the Bristol Rifles.

The 5th Battalion was raised about the same time and was then, as now, made up from Companies spread over the County, having Headquarters at Gloucester.

The 6th Battalion was raised in 1900 at the time of the South African War, and its inception was largely due to the support of the Mardon family in Bristol, where its Headquarters are.

The new Battalions, numbered 7th to 15th, were raised during the present war.

E. S. SINNOTT,

Lt.-Colonel R.E. (T. F.)

(To be continued.)

HONORIS CAUSA.

The following have been awarded the Military Medal: —

1663	Sergt. Abel, J. W.
2331	Sergt. Chandler, G. W.
1628	Sergt. Jackson, R. C.
3127	Sergt. Thomson, R. O.
2742	Sergt. Wintle, A. H.
2528	L/Cpl. Enoch, A. W. G. (since killed in action).
2558	L/Cpl. Sproat, A. W.

THE CHRIST SPIRIT.

Gentle and strong, humble, and high, and sure,
Transcendently, thy beauty fills the soul,
As rays of glory sweep across the whole
Vast divineness of a heaven obscure
With radiance that man's gaze can scarce endure.
Joy is thy figt; and love thine aureole
Divine, and self-forgetfulness thy goal,
Of life's unrest the haven blest and sure.
Spirit of truth ! In human hearts remain
And light before them pathways still untrod ;
Restrain the thoughts that soil, the words that feign,
And break asunder self's enslaving rod,
That we may wield and hold without a stain
His temple worthy of the living God.

M. L. G.!

THE GLOUCESTERSHIRE REGIMENT.

The Sphinx superscribed " EGYPT."

1st BATTALION (28th Foot) Regulars.

2nd BATTALION (61st Foot) Regulars.

3rd BATTALION (Special Reserve).

4th BATTALION (Territorials) (First and second Lines).

5th BATTALION (Territorials) (First and second Lines).

6th BATTALION (Territorials) (First and second Lines).

7th BATTALION (Service).

8th BATTALION (Service).

9th BATTALION (Service).

10th BATTALION (Service.)

11th BATTALION (Reserve).

12th BATTALION (Service) (Bristol).

13th BATTALION (Service) (Forest of Dean Pioneers).

14th BATTALION (Service) (West of England).

15th BATTALION (Reserve).

16th BATTALION (Reserve).

BATTLE HONOURS.

Honour.	Year.	Country.	At War with	Battn. Engaged.	Commander-in-Chief.
Ramillies	1706	Flanders	France	1st	Marlborough
Louisburg	1758	N.America	France	1st	Amherst
Guadaloupe	1759	W. Indies	France	2nd	Hopson, Barrington
Quebec	1759	Canada	France	1st	Wolfe
Martinique	1762	W. Indies	France	1st	Monckton
Havannah	1762	W. Indies	Spain	1st	Albemarle
St. Lucia	1778	W. Indies	France	1st	Grant
Egypt	1801	Egypt	France	1st, 2nd	Abercromby, Hutchinson
Maida	1806	Italy	France	2nd	Stuart
Corunna	1809	Spain	France	1st	Moore
Talavera	1809	Spain	France	2nd	Wellington
Busaco	1810	Portugal	France	1st, 2nd	Wellington
Barrosa	1811	Spain	France	1st	Graham, Wellington
Albuhera	1811	Spain	France	1st	Beresford, Wellington
Salamanca	1812	Spain	France	2nd	Wellington
Vittoria	1813	Spain	France	1st	Wellington
Pyrenees	1813	Spanish Frontier	France	1st, 2nd	Wellington
Nivelle	1813	France	France	1st, 2nd	Wellington
Nive	1813	France	France	1st, 2nd	Wellington
Orthes	1814	France	France	1st, 2nd	Wellington
Toulouse	1814	France	France	1st, 2nd	Wellington
Peninsula	1808/14	Portugal Spain Frce.	France	1st, 2nd	Wellington
Waterloo	1815	Belgium	France	1st	Wellington
Punjaub	1848/49	India	Sikhs	2nd	Gough
Chillianwallah	1849	India	Sikhs	2nd	Gough
Goojerat	1849	India	Sikhs	2nd	Gough
Alma	1854	Crimea, Russia	Russia	1st	Raglan
Inkerman	1854	Crimea, Russia	Russia	1st	Raglan
Sevastopol	1855	Crimea, Russia	Russia	1st	Raglan, Simpson
Delhi	1857	India	Sepoy Mutineers	2nd	Anson, Barnard, Wilson
South Africa	1899/1902	S. Africa	S.A.Republics	1st,2nd,4th,5th	Buller, Roberts, Kitchener
Defence of Ladysmith	1899/1900	S.Africa	S.A.Republics	1st	White, Buller, Roberts
Relief of Kimberley	1900	S.Africa	S.A.Republics	2nd	French, Roberts
Paardeberg	1900	S.Africa	S.A.Republics	2nd	Roberts

OLD BORE'S ALMANACK.

Or, the Voice of the Stars for 1917.

(While not vouching for the accuracy of the following, the GAZETTE sees no objection to its publication. After all, it helps to fill up.)

JANUARY.

The opening month of a fateful year ; admission free. By arrangement with the leading planets, 1917 will simply bulge with momentous happenings, several of which will (weather permitting) quite possibly occur, and it is Old Bore's privilege to foretell them for his readers. With any luck, for instance, January will again this year have 31 days, and of these the stars (all except one little one in the corner which is so many millions of miles off that it may be ignored) indicate the 9th, as the most remarkable, though it is not clear whether this implies the suicide of the Kaiser on that date or the introduction of a new song into their programme by the "Curios." Bosches may be bombed on the 6th, 8th and 22nd of this month, but the safety-pin should first be removed from the bomb. (Safety-pins for the purpose are obtainable at twelve a dozen from any haberdasher's. ADVT.) Lighting-up time on the 17th will be one hour after sunset, but this does not apply to wiring parties. A star-shell will go up from the Hun lines on or about the night of the 28th, and London will be totally destroyed by Zeppelins on the 29th. Altogether a quiet month. The weather will be wet.

FEBRUARY.

During this month Battalion will probably on several occasions move to the right in fours. Men born on the 8th, 9th and 24th of February must beware of dark men in glasses answering to the name of Fritz, and if a visit from him is expected they should put him off by wire. The same precautions should be taken by men whose birthday is on the 2nd, or indeed any old date. London will be totally destroyed by Zeppelins on the 16th, and it is highly probable that both on that day and at least twenty-seven other days in the month several men will write home to say they are in the pink. Shells will explode on the 2nd, 9th and 22nd ; others will not. Old Bore advises any of his readers who may be entering Bosch dug-outs on the third Thursday of this month to leave cards, as this is the Bosche's "At home day." The weather will be wet, with some rain.

MARCH.

"March" is a word of ill-omen for the Battalion all this month, and several men will complain of footsoreness on or about the 5th, 31st and intervening days. Old Bore is led to think this because by means of the stars he sees the Battalion going out for a three weeks' rest early in this month. He also sees them coming back three days later. Advanced trenches will be dug on the nights of the 8th, 12th and 13th, and the Division will then attack and capture the German sixth line, their exploits being fully described in the Press by Our Special Correspondent, Mr. Fillup Fibbs, under the heading of "London Territorial's Gallantry." A serious shortage in the rum issue will occur towards the end of the month, but there will be no loss of life. London will be totally destroyed by Zeppelins on the 20th, and the weather will be wetter than usual.

APRIL.

A month full of surprises. (Try Harrison's Pomade. ADVT.) Rumours circulating on the 1st April to the effect that the Crown Prince has been captured in the English lines disguised as a film-operator should be received with caution. On or about the 14th of this month the February number of the GAZETTE may be confidently expected, and the issue will probably be found to contain one or two references to the Editor, his pack and his pick, and the horse which is his. Men falling down sump-holes on the 8th and 17th of this month should not do so, and if bringing up rations at the time they will shortly afterwards hear something to their disadvantage. A shell-hole will be discovered not far from the British front on or about the 28th ; the commands of "Fall in !" that may be given in that district about that time will not, however, have any connection with the incident. The total destruction of London by Zeppelins on the 30th will bring an eventful month to a peaceful close. Weather much about the same, thank you.

MAY.

Early this month the Battalion will receive orders to move from Q 27 d 4-5 to L 98 C 6-1 for its three weeks' rest, and will set out in Tanks. The stars are unanimous in predicting that blankets will be neatly rolled and tied in bundles of 10. On the way, news will reach the Divisional H.Q. that Mr. Truthful Thomas, Special Correspondent of the "Daily Tale," has arrived in the neighbourhood and wants to see a battle, and the Battalion will immediately return. Three advanced trenches will be dug the same evening, each one in front of the others, and Mr. Thomas will cable it all home at enormous expense under the striking title of "Anzacs' All-Night Advance !" One result of this daring effort will be that he will get the military cross (very much so). Towards the end of the month a batch of 500 plum-puddings, intended for the preceding Xmas, will arrive in a more or less weary state, having fallen by the wayside. Almost simultaneously—or perhaps a little later—the stars seem to prognosticate considerable disturbance in (and near) the Sergeants' Mess, and there seems to be some connection between these two incidents and a subsequent terrific bombardment of the German lines by 499 trench-mortar bombs, which may be expected to work enormous havoc in the enemy's trenches. The last few days of this month will see something happen to London, but old Bore is not quite certain what it will be. Weather (or not).

JUNE, JULY, AUGUST, SEPTEMBER, OCTOBER, NOVEMBER and DECEMBER.

The mixture as before. Old Bore regrets that owing to his magic crystal, Zodiac and telescopic short Lee-Enfield horoscope having been commandeered by the Ministry of Munitions he cannot foresee anything further than the first week in June, when according to the evidence of the Stars the Allied Armies will be within a mile of Berlin, but he takes this opportunity of thanking his clients for past favours and assuring them that the conclusion of Peace will find him, as before, ready to oblige with his Purple Predictions for Pallid People at Popular Prices. Address (after June) ; Old Bore, C/o GAZETTE Office, No. 1, Schlasschers-strasse, Berlin. (ADVT.)

F.R.B.

KITCHENER.

No man in England slept the night he died :
The harsh, stern spirit passed without a pang,
And freed of mortal clogs his message rang.
In every wakeful mind the challenge cried :
Think not of me : one servant less or more
Means nothing now : hold fast the greater thing—
Strike hard, love truth, serve England and the King !
Servant of England, soldier to the core,
What does it matter where his body fall ?
What does it matter where they build the tomb ?
Five million men, from Calais to Khartoum,
These are his wreath and his memorial.

CHRISTOPHER MORLEY.

Life, June 22nd.

───────

"THE GAZETTE," 5d.

At a time when it is true of almost every commodity either that the price has gone up or that its quality has decreased, it is, we think, unreasonable to expect the GAZETTE to resist the economic law indefinitely. Accordingly, the Management of the GAZETTE have been compelled to raise the price of the GAZETTE to 5d. So great a change in the history of a paper of such importance can only be justified by the pressure of urgent necessity. While our agents report an ever increasing circulation, they inform us that there is a loss on the GAZETTE of something approaching 20,000 Francs a month.

If the price were to continue to be that of the absurdly low sum of 3d., we should be compelled forthwith to discontinue the publication of Intelligence Summaries, Poems (serious and humorous), Things we want to know, Bricks from the Editor's Pack, Football, Promotions, Illustrations, Lists of Benefactors, without which the GAZETTE would no longer be what it is ; and no complete paper with the necessary official documents can be sold for 3d. without a ruinous loss. From so colossal a catastrophe, it is our earnest intention to preserve the world. Accordingly the Management, after serious consideration, have felt it incumbent on them to raise the price to 5d. The GAZETTE will therefore continue to publish full reports of everything unconnected with the war, with the publication of which it is recognised as the leading journal. Many readers have expressed their willingness to pay a higher price for the GAZETTE. It is quite likely that they will be asked to do so before the war is over. But we are not asking, and we shall not ask our friends to do more than meet the cost of the (very) raw material. Other papers, as we are credibly informed, will shortly follow suit.

Meanwhile we publish the following table as indicating the rise and fall of the price of the GAZETTE.

	PRICE.	COPIES SOLD.
April, 1915 ...	... 3d.	... 83,333
May, 1915 ...	... 3d.	... 84,444
June, 1915 ...	... 3d.	... 85,556
July, 1915 ...	... 3d.	... 86,667
August, 1915 ...	... 3d.	... 87,999
September, 1915	... 3d.	... 88,888
October, 1915 ...	... 3d.	... 89,999
December, 1915	... 5d.	... 90,001
February, 1916	... 3d.	... 91,111
March, 1916...	... 3d.	... 92,222
April, 1916 ...	... 3d.	... 93,338
May, 1916 ...	... 3d.	... 94,444
July, 1916 ...	... 3d.	... 96,999
September, 1916	... 3d.	... 99,999
October, 1916 ...	... 3d.	... 99,999
December, 1916	... 5d.	... 100,001

Already we have evidence that the readers of the GAZETTE take the same view, and welcome our decision to continue to make the journal a complete National Record.

Normally a journal which increases its price must expect a substantial reduction in circulation, but the position of the GAZETTE is, if we may say so, unique, and we do not fear any such eventuality, and look forward to the future with confidence.

" Place d'Imprimerie." E.C.

To Subscribers of Five Francs.

Dear Sir or Madam (or Other Ranks, as the case may be),

Now that the war has just started, and a long vista of GAZETTES as yet unborn looms large upon the eye of the Business Manager, it would appear that the original faith placed in the early vagaries of Hilary, Billhook, Mr. Bottomley and ground (W. Mead did not bat), as to the early cessation of hostilities, has upset the calculations of that early and enterprising group of Financiers of the FIFTH GLO'STER GAZETTE.

(Five minutes halt here. Packs off !)

The fertile minds of the present Board of Directors have given birth to the bright thought that those gallant soldiers who did or did not pay the Five Francs " for the duration," have now had their money's worth. It is hoped that they will remember the old adage " Ooops ! Let's do it again ! " Will they therefore please send p. d. q. by D.R.L.S. marked " URGENT ─── " and " confidential," another or the original Five Francs, which will last an equally long period.

Board of Directors,

Mudsome.

───────

CHORUS OF DEEP-SEA HUNS.

Our Fatherland's most trusted tool
    In all these stormy days,
We closely follow—'tis our rule—
    The underwater ways.

Our spirit daring and untired
    To hero deeds shall leap :
And fearlessly our song inspired
    Floats upwards from the deep.

Of valiant feats and bold we tell,
    Of night work fierce and black,
Of steamer's doom, and liner's knell
    And sunken fishing smack.

We cleave the water's moving wall,
    Like phantoms grim and grey ;
It closes like a mighty pall
    Upon our helpless prey.

No traveller from British port
    His quest of gold can make,
But every step with peril fraught,
    Keeps him with fear a-quake.

True, many of our Sea Huns grand—
    This has not made us wince—
Have set out from the Fatherland
    And not been heard of since ;

Numbers of these, our Supermen,
    While making history,
Seem to have vanished out of ken,
    Their fate a mystery.

Yet once again with lips set hard
    And hearts with hate aglow
We go to bring, while off his guard,
    The loathed Britain low.

Fragment of British Tar's song in the distance :—

Come on ! We're waiting the encore,
    We'll square up any debts ;
We've spoilt your little game before,
    Here's good luck to our nets !

The Hun chorus dies away.

M. L. G.

SEASIDE CAMPS OF 1917.

OPEN WARFARE.

By our Special Military Adviser—Phillip Phibbs.

(It will be noted that I have given up my position as special Correspondent of the Gaily Tonicall. I have done this at the special request of the Editor of the GAZETTE and owing to the exceptional facilities which have always been granted to me to inspect the British Army behind the lines.)

As we are now reaching a stage when open warfare may or may not be a fanciful fact of the fast approaching future, a few hints to novices on this kind of fighting will probably prove of value. The following points I have observed if put into practice should produce pleasing results.

Extending.

I have heard a whistle and seen one of our Officers wave his arms in every direction. This denotes an extension. To do this successfully you should give the man on each side of you a good hard shove—one of those shoves that made England—and you will then have extended.

Short Rushes.

Yet another use has been found for that handy weapon—the rifle. Using it as a lever raise yourself slowly, take 20 paces forward, fling your rifle down, followed by yourself and your rush is complete.

Closing.

This consist of a deluge of whistling and shouting and if these noises remind you of the famous Gloucester Hippodrome on a Saturday night, you may add your share and will then probably do right if you rejoin your platoon.

Scouting.

This is a much sought-after job owing to the amount of labour it entails—for all the lads love work. That make of man, the bug hunter, is always an ideal scouter as he is already accustomed to keep his head and eyes rigidly on the ground. A successful scout will also invariably lose himself with expedition, but he should report for duty again when cookhouse notes are heard on one of those musical instruments—the bugle.

Diamond Formation. Double.

This is adopted for scouting and has nothing to do with those 52 slips of cardboard called playing cards—at any rate until the scout has got lost. At that point however the veteran will probably see to it that packs are opened and shuffled and a nap enjoyed.

Artillery Formation.

See under Diamond formation and take away the number of Tricks you gained in the last round.

Cover.

This necessitates keeping one's head exposed to fire, thus allowing the enemy to cover you. If this is tactfully done a return to Blighty—that home of our soldiers—should ensue.

Rapid Fire.

This—(I say do shut up or you'll make the novice an old soldier at open warfare before he starts. You're absolutely corrupting his ideas on the subject, you know.—Ed.)

THINGS WE WANT TO KNOW.

Who is the gallant and dashing lieutenant (R.F.A.) who " took stables " while home on leave ? Did he have a kit inspection ?

Who was the man in the digging squad who desired to " get at 'em " ? Is he satisfied ? Is talk cheap ?

What is a pattern-maker ? Will the gentlemen who prefers allegiance to Budda please enlighten us ?

Who is the Private in No. 1 Platoon who asked what sort of an engine there was in an observation balloon ?

Who had the wind put up him while in the trenches for the first time ?

Who had a loaf of bread and a tin of bully at midnight, while on a Bombing Course ? Is he in A Company ?

How much snow was on the ground when the overloaded G.S. Wagon passed ? How was it done ?

Who has the heaviest boot-trees in the Division ? Is he at No. 1 Mess ?

Of whom did the Billet Lady say " Ah ! Mon gros " ? And why ?

Who was the Officer who paraded his Company by the advanced trench at H.E., and moved them off in fours ?

What is the difference between " remains of " and " ruins of " with reference to notes on maps ?

Who was the Deputy-acting-second-in-Command's first Victim ? And what was the T. O.'s reply ?

Who is the N.C.O. who said he would be glad when he arrived at his destitution ? Is he in the Transport ? Did he say that he was very fond of " VIN chaud hot " ?

Whose horse arrived riderless at the Stable ? Had a B. Company Officer anything to do with it ?

Who is the Officer who went into a grocer's shop in A and said " Avez-vous un bulb " ? Did he get his ears boxed ? Is he in C Company ?

A Happy Christmas to you !

Who is the Scotch Officer (teetotal) who has taken to drink, and still says he does not like it ?

Who is the new Managing Director of the Light Great Western Railway ? Is he speeding up the 4-30 express ?

Has the —— Army followed the example of the Great Eastern Railway and imported an American Railway Business Manager ?

What is the plural of *pro forma* ? Why should it be *pro formae* ?

Who is the O. C. Company who was nearly drowned in his dug-out ? Did he mistake the dug-out for a U-boat ?

Should not petrol tins have distinguishing marks ?

Who is the corporal who has developed hydrophobia ? Does he know anything about horses ?

Who is the officer who sat in his shrapnel-helmet from 2-50 p.m. till 12-30 a.m. ?

How long have the 7th R. W.'s been " a fine unit in the New Army " (Tatler) ?

Who was sitting up and taking nourishment at the American bar with his hat off ? Is that why he had his buttons polished ?

Who kept the Bus waiting 1½ hours outside a Y.M.C.A. ? Was he the Senior Officer present ? And what did the wet-through officers think about him ?

Why did the M. O. send 3 tablets with instructions to take two at a time ?

Who is the officer who was assisted by 4 Hun prisoners to regain his seat (temporarily lost) on his steed ? Where had he been ?

Who is the M.G. Officer who was found asleep by the roadside, his horse peacefully browsing the while ?

Who said he sprained his ankle by being run over by a Tank, when really it was done on the Playing Fields ?

Who was the Cook who fried the snails with the cheese ?

Who was the cook who addressed another cook as follows :—" If you had got up and helped me, I could have done it all by myself " ?

Who is the L. G. Corporal who said " Can a swim duck " ?

Who is the Officer who told the Provost-Sergeant that he had a very difficult and desperate job in getting the lights out by 10 p.m. ?

Who is the Major (O. C. Boat) who threatened to put the A.M.L.O. under arrest ?

Who is the Officer who gets Bully Beef from Fortnum and Mason ? Was he the victim of a practical joke ?

Who is the Officer who gave his batman a candle in mistake for a stick of shaving soap ?

Who was the Captain who walked 5 miles at 3 a.m. ?

Why has the T. O. acquired so delicate a French accent ?

Who is the Officer who was not allowed to pass to A unless accompanied by a C Company Officer ?

Which Company " Mess President " has instituted a Tariff of Fines for the perpetuation of innuendos ? Do the proceeds keep the Mess supplied with Drinks ?

Is it true that the German wounded get better food than our wounded at Boulogne ?

Did the Q.M. think he was going to the Front Line when he lost the Sapper Sergeant who was guiding him ?

Was the Q.M. ordered to fill up shell holes ?

Were the M. O. and the Colonel really looking for the wishbone ?

Who is the A.S.C. Officer who insists on bathing in his Sam Browne and a pair of socks ?

Who is the distinguished looking Veterinary Officer who on going to inspect Infantry Transport, loudly enquired for the " Farrier Staff Sergeant "?

Who is the Officer who is about to become Camp Commandant at the Curragh ?

Are a certain Adjutant and D. A. O. still under arrest ? Is it true that the Adjutant refused to be released ?

Who is the happy subaltern who, when last seen in D——, was surrounded by a halo of chrysanthemums ? And what did his batman think of it ?

Did Battalion H.Q. miss their rations ? Were the contents sybaritic ?

KIT AND EQUIPMENT.

Practical Hints.

From " Land and Water."

" These articles are written from practical experience of military matters with a view to keeping our readers in touch with the various requirements of active service. Changes of climate and the peculiar conditions under which the present campaign is being waged render different items of equipment advisable at different times, and we are in touch with officers at the front and others from whom the actual requirements of Officers and men can be ascertained. These articles are not intended to advertise any particular firm or firms.

STRAPS—and a Wristlet.

There are certain disadvantages attached to the use of a leather strap on the wrist watch, chief among them being the fact that one is always—and some times disagreeably—conscious of the presence of the strap. If one hole is a little too loose for a fit, and the next is a trifle too tight, the wearer almost always fastens the strap in the tight hole, with security for his watch but a certain amount of discomfort as well—and then, again, a strap takes some time to fasten and unfasten, especially if one's fingers are cold, since its position decrees that all the fastening shall be done with one hand only. All these drawbacks may be overcome ——."

Not wishing to be the least behindhand in attending to the wants and comforts of Officers and men alike, a representative of this Journal immediately called upon the Quartermaster, Transport Officer, Officers' Mess Cart, the Padre's Horse, Lewis-gun carts belonging to this Battalion, and also on the G.S. Wagons attached for rations and discipline to the Brigade and Divisional H.Q. respectively.

It is hardly necessary, nay, it is even superfluous, to say that our representative was most warmly welcomed by all the above-mentioned important personages. The Quartermaster, for instance, was wreathed in smiles, and extended a warm welcome. Later he could scarcely conceal his evident emotion when he learnt the nature of our representative's call. It is in a very large measure due to his kindly interest and consideration that we are able to publish for the benefit of " the brutal and licentious soldiery" suggestions as to kit, what should be kept, what should be thrown away, who should carry what, etc.

S

"WHEN YOU'RE ALL DRESSED UP."

PACKS, Use of.

There were, the Quarter-master admitted with engaging frankness, certain disadvantages attached to the use and carriage of packs of which he was fully cognisant. Packs could be either carried——with or without Trophies—attached to the equipment or unattached. The great advantage of carrying the Pack unattached is that it can be slipped off at a moment's notice, and placed, in the absence of the Officer's Mess Cart, or other convenient vehicle, on the Ration Cart, Blanket-Lorry or Lewis-gun cart. " I am firmly of the opinion," said the Quarter-master " that Packs will not be carried any more—(at this point our Representative was convulsed with spasms of joy—as will all our readers be. But such joy was short-lived. Let the Q.M. finish his sentence)—after this War."

FURNITURE. Porterage of.

Messrs. Daimler and Co. have just placed on the market a delightful little motor-lorry, not altogether dissimilar to those used by the R.F.C. for the special transport of Officers' surplus Furniture (Chairs, Tables, Gramophones complete with records, sofas, Boot-trees, British Warms, Gins and Bitters, Message Forms, Beds, Pianos. Whisky, cases of, Shrapnel helmets, etc.) With a pleasant-looking and affable Warrant Officer (Q.M.S. preferred) perched—cherubs always perch—alongside the driver, no Corps Commander, we are confident, would be so heartless, not even in his bitterest moments, to strafe so handy a concern, so negligible an item in a long line of Transport. Such a slight addition to the means whereby the bare comforts of our brave troops may be conveyed is as brilliant in conception as it is daring in execution, and reflects the greatest credit both on the manufacturers, Messrs. Daimler, and on their agents, Messrs. Wangle and Push.

HELMETS, Shrapnel.

Delightful as these dinky life-savers are when snugly nuzzling on one's head in the trenches, it would appear that they are somewhat cumbersome on the march. Determined to do what they could to relieve our Tired Soldiery, Messrs. Simplicity and Comfort have devised a little electrical instrument which can be coiled up inside the helmet when worn. It is a most delicate instrument and very susceptible to the influence of " Red " Rays.

Now while Tommy is marching, merely by drawing the hand across his brow, he causes the instrument to raise the helmet a couple of inches or so above his head, and by its own electrical and centrifugal force in conjunction with the Binomial Theorem, it spins the helmet round and round over his head, thus carrying the helmet and permitting the fresh air to cool his fevered locks. But—and here is the amazing cleverness of the instrument—steal there ever so quietly a Rolls Royce, or any car complete with Staff, the little instrument—so sensitive is it to " Red " Rays—immediately causes the helmet to replace itself on the head and itself neatly coils up.

No soldier's kit can be complete without the above. Meanwhile, Messrs. Simplicity and Comfort have earned the warmest thanks from the B.E.F.

SEPARATOR. Tommy's.

For some time Messrs. Ration and Blanket have been endeavouring to place upon the market some kind of machine which, while it will materially add to the Comforts of all Ranks, will effectively deal with a grave disorder. At last their continuous experiments have met with a long sought success. Not only can the sugar and the corn be speedily sifted from the Tea, but crusts of loaves are stripped of Blanket hairs immediately. All Quarter-masters will do well to furnish themselves and their Stores with one of these most useful machines, which in so far as they have been proved capable of separating " Plum " from its inveterate Tin-companion "Apple," should be hailed by all ranks with acclamation.

COMPOSITION.

As the members of the B.E.F. have experienced to their cost, ignorance of French has often proved a severe handicap. No less so is the ignorance of Military Language to Acting Adjutants, Orderly Room Clerks and others. With a view to the overcoming of this handicap, Messrs. Pidgin and English have published a little book of handy Phrases, just suited for aspirants to the seats of the mighty. A few extracts culled at random will show at once the value and the importance of their clever little Handbook.

" *Please*." Insert this useful little word as often as possible, thus :—

(1) " 1269 Pte. Orriss H., was admitted to Hospital this day, 12/12/16, please.

(2) " 23456 Pte. Whacker H. has been awarded 29 days No. 3, please, 12/12/16.

" *It would appear that*." Always begin nasty, rude, correspondence with this simple Formula, interchanging it with

" *It does not seem to be generally understood that*,"

Altogether a most useful book and an indispensable article of kit.

THE SUPER-OBSERVERSCOPE. (Known to Tommy as the " Some Scope.")

This complicated but utterly simple article, or rather combination of articles of kit, was the outcome of the clever brains of Messrs. Leiss and Goertz, two loyal Americans of U. O. (unknown origin).

It has been improved and placed upon the market by Messrs. Hedges and Butler. All Artillery Officers, G. S. O. threes, Battalion Commanders and Intelligence Officers should provide themselves with one.

The observerscope consists of :—

Prismatic glasses.
  ditto   compass.
  ditto   periscope (attachment if necessary).
Range and elevation finder.
Protractor.
Automatic ticket puncher.
  ditto   cigarette holder and magazine.

The whole so compact that it can be carried in a case slightly larger than the ordinary field glasses.

All the observer does is to look at his distant object and focus ; the " somescope " does the rest. By pressing the button on the left-hand side a small disc falls from the slot near the screw adjuster, giving full information as to ranges elevation, etc., necessary for laying the gun accurately to hit the spot looked at. No more complicated calculations ! Gunnery made easy ! !

The difficulty of smoking while observing has been completely overcome. By pressing the button on the right-hand side a magazine of 10 cigarettes comes into play and one lit by an extraordinary simple automatic petrol lighter jumps into position in the holder placed above the right eyepiece. At the same time a telescopic and flexible mouthpiece is released and faces near the observer's mouth. Refils are also supplied.

A SOLDIER-POET.

"A Gloucestershire Lad at Home and Abroad."
By F. W. Harvey.   [SIDGWICK & JACKSON.]

(Reviewed by BISHOP FRODSHAM.)

"Mud, blood, and khaki are rather conspicuously absent" from Mr. Harvey's poems. "They are, in fact, the last things a soldier wishes to think or talk about." This is the opinion of Colonel Collett, who writes the preface, and it is most true of soldiers in general. That striking person, an English Tommy, may not spend much labour upon the comfort of a dug-out, but he puts his heart into making a belated garden, where he can grow pansies and gilly-flowers, that make him sick with inarticulate longing for some little village garden in Gloucestershire or elsewhere. The secret of Mr. Harvey's power is that he says what other English lads "in Flanders" want to say and cannot.

> " I'm homesick for my hills again—
>   My hills again !
> To see above the Severn plain,
> Unscabbarded aginst the sky,
> The blue high blade of Cotswold lie ;
> The giant clouds go royally
> By jagged Malvern with a train
> Of shadows. Where the land is low,
> Like a huge imprisoning O,
> I hear a heart that's sound and high,
> I hear the heart within me cry :
> ' I'm homesick for my hills again—
>   My hills again !
> Cotswold or Malvern, sun or rain !
>   My hills again ! ' "

Similarly, Mr. Harvey voices what these same lads are thinking about the future. Men at home are busy with plans for demobilisation, for the redevelopment of trade, for all the manifold material interests of life. Those who have seen what the soldier has seen have heard a secret thing which the Lord God has whispered in their ears during the silent nights. And it is that secret thing which is to influence the future far more fatefully and beneficially than many men may guess. What must be made of the resolve, beneath this exquisite little rondeau ?

> " If we return, will England be
> Just England still to you and me ?
> The place where we must earn our bread ?
> We, who have walked among the dead,
> And watched the smile of agony,
> And seen the price of Liberty,
> Which we have taken carelessly
> From other hands. Nay, we shall dread,
>   If we return ;
>
> Dread lest we hold blood-guiltily
> The things that men have died to free.
> Oh, English fields shall blossom red
> For all the blood that has been shed
> By men whose guardians are we,
>   If we return."

The truly tragic thing for England is that so many of our best will never be able to teach what they have learnt. The wise among us, therefore, do well to listen attentively to what these " babes and sucklings " in years have to say of what God has revealed to them and hidden from us. It is only such a conviction that justifies the publication of a part of the last letter written by Lieutenant Harvey upon a matter which is now distressing many—God knows, very many—this is, the respective values of death and life in the light of love. This is his estimate : " Those who have not been in the trenches think it should create a sympathetic yearning over life and the so transitory gleam. In peace-time they could write of the " little emptiness of love," (you see, Rupert Brooke was not guiltless !) ; but that was in peace-time. Here we do not mourn the shortness of life because of love nor (more cynically) the shortness of love out-lived by living. The fellowship of death has taught us better and truer things. Yet, because death is strange, pray humanly that the cup may pass from me, dear mother. Pray that (as is permissible), but *never grieve* if it is not so, for God's ways are glorious and past finding out in His *love* for the children of men. Comment would be impertinent upon such self-revelation as this, but it is the keynote of the poems written " at home and abroad " by this one Gloucestershire lad.

The poet's portrait of himself is worth repeating in full, not only for a delicate humour of phrase :

> " A thick-set, dark-haired, dreamy little man,
>   Uncouth to see,
> Revolving ever this preposterous plan—
> Within a web of words spread cunningly
> To tangle life—no less
> (Could he expect success !)
>
> Of Life he craves not much, except to watch.
>   Being forced to act,
> He walks behind himself, as if to catch
> The motive—an accessory to the fact,
> Faintly amused, it seems,
> Behind his dreams.
>
> Yet he hath loved the vision of this world,
>   And found it good :
> The Faith, the fight 'neath Freedom's flag unfurled,
> The friends, the fun, the army-brotherhood.
> But faery-crazed, or worse.
> He twists it all to verse ! "

Sufficient has been said to show that this modest little volume has real charm, and not a little depth of thought and beauty. It contains far more real poetry than many a volume ten times its length, ushered into the world with syncophantic fanfaronade. Without doubt, Mr. Harvey himself would shrink, not without amusement, from comparison to the great ones of Olympus. He might welcome the suggestion that he resembles one of the birds in his garden at Minsterworth, who sing because they cannot help but sing. Indeed, he seems to wonder not at his own sweet voice, but at the wealth of meaning in simple things. It is no daisy, as with Alice Meynell, or " flower in the crannied wall," as with Alfred Tennyson, that speaks to him, but the tiniest, daintiest, sweetest singer in the shortening melancholy days of autumn weather.

> " What fairy in the falling rain
> Takes the robin's small refrain
> And twists it to a tiny charm ?
> To keep a tempted heart from harm ?
> It puzzles me a wild bird's song
> Should save my soul from doing wrong."

Yet does not Mr. Harvey reveal the secret of his own undoubted power in words that suggest Rabindranath Tagore at his best ? " The lean dagger had gone into the poet's heart. Shuddering, he plucked it free, lest he should die. And then—by magic—it became in his hand a shining sword fit to smite down the sorrow of the world." But the poet is "missing." This sad news was posted the very week his book was in the press.

The Saturday Review.

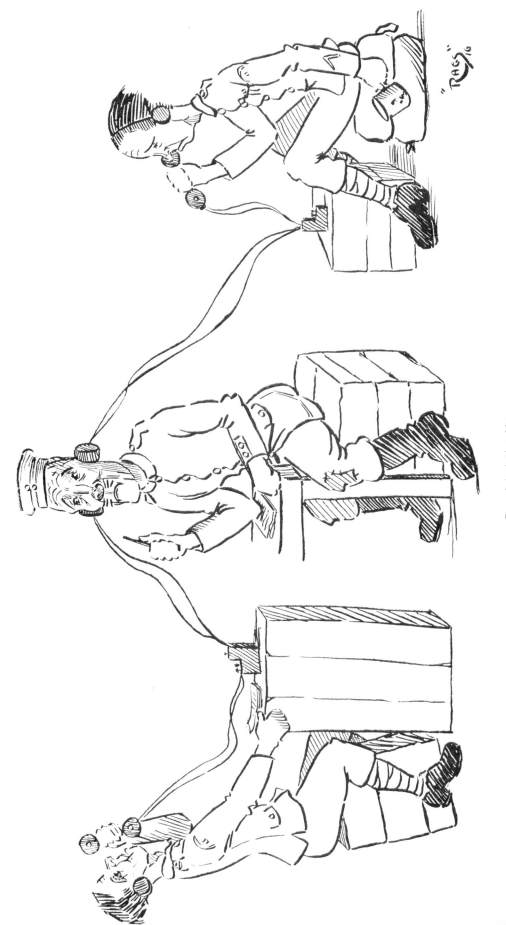

Deceiving the Hun.

' · We print the concluding portion of a long article in the Literary Supplement of the *Times* on the subject of Trench Literature :—

" It is seldom that the deeper issues of the soldier's life are touched upon. In the FIFTH GLOUCESTER GAZETTE, which is the oldest and most literary of the British trench journals, there has been much weaving of home-seeking thoughts into small, appealing lyrics. The following example by " F.W.H." whose trench poems have recently been republished in a little book, struck home to the heart of many West Country men, including an Oxford Professor of Poetry :—

> " I'm homesick for my hills again—
>   My hills again !
> To see above the Severn plain,
> Unscabbarded against the sky,
> The blue high blade of Cotswold lie :
> The giant clouds go royally
> By jagged Malvern with a train
> Of shadows. Where the land is low,
> Like a huge imprisoning O,
> I hear a heart that's sound and high,
> I hear the heart within me cry :
> ' I'm homesick for my hills again—
>   My hills again !
> Cotswold or Malvern, sun or rain !
>   My hills again ! "

There is an element of what the Russians call *prostor* (the opening of the heart to vastness) in the British soul, which cannot find full contentment in the garden labyrinths and poplar-sentinelled highways of the French countryside, but longs for the wide prospects and spacious parks and mist-veiled heights of its native islands. Yet seldom in the trench journals is there a glance at that loophole into infinity called by a name that is never printed therein. The FIFTH GLO'STER GAZETTE, however, has a proud lament over the loss of many good comrades in the Battle of the Somme :—

> For you no medals such as others wear
> — A cross of bronze for those approved brave :
> To you is given above a shallow grave
> The wooden cross that marks you resting there.
> Rest you content. More honourable far
> Than all the Orders is the Cross of Wood,
> The symbol of self-sacrifice that stood
> Bearing the God whose brethren you are.

(Extract from a poem by the late Lieutenant C. W. Winterbotham).

Nor shall you find, even if you search through all the journals treasured up at the British Museum for the future historian, any overt expression of the love that knits together all ranks in our New Army. The best beloved regimental officer gets but a scant word of regret, for it is a part of disciplined *moral* to let the dead bury their dead. The military historian has told us with what majesty the British soldier fought in the old days. These little trench papers will teach future generations how joyously a younger race of athletes, without banners or music or gay uniforms, addressed themselves to their tragic task. Time in its passing will ennoble all these ephemeral things—until they shall be seen in ages to come *sub specie æternitatis* and have for a remote posterity the beauty of memorial."

Times—Literary Supplement, October 12th, 1916.

A VISION OF PEACE.

I awoke and three times I yawned and three times I scratched my head before I bethought myself that it was Sunday—the Day of Rest. Then I turned myself and fell asleep once more and dreamed dreams. And this was one of my dreams.

It was in England—good old England—and I found myself one of a vast multitude. And there was a great waving of flags and scene of much jubilation and all the crowds were shouting for joy ! And also the business houses were closed and on every side there was evidence that some great and untoward event had taken place. And I thought to myself what is this ? Have we won some great victory ? Have our arms gained some noble decision or—and I trembled with excitement—is this PEACE ? And I sought to find the meaning of the rejoicing from someone amongst the multitude, but everywhere there was such a jostling and pushing that from no man could I obtain information. So I wandered on and beheld all around me as I have described and there was scarce a house without its decoration, scarce a building without its flags. And as I wandered I reached towards the centre of that city and ever the crowd grew thicker and the shouting louder. And then from amongst the babel one word seemed to stand out as in a louder murmur. And I strained to catch that word which for some moments defied my efforts. But at length it came out loud and clear and my heart stood still for joy at the sound of it. It was — yes it was the word " PEACE." And then I knew not what to do and I was like to have fallen into a faint had not a post supported me. And there for some minutes I remained in a state of semi-consciousness. This, then, was Peace. This was the great day for which millions—nay hundreds of millions—had waited. This was that wonderful moment. This was the end. Then I hastily began to shed my khaki. Now presently there approached a newsboy through the throng and I snatched a paper from his protesting hands and opened it. This headline caught my eye " Peace, the Independent Candidate, returned by a four figure majority." Then I sunk back into—wakefulness.

I awoke and three times I yawned and three times I scratched my head before I heard a voice calling me to arise. Then I remembered that we were moving into the Trenches for it was Sunday—the Day of Labour.

And I arose and the war continued and in England they still fought their own war—of politics.

R. F. R

CHAPLAIN'S COLUMN.

It has been the custom for some months now in obedience to an Army Order, to make no reference to our list of casualties, and to refrain from paying even a passing tribute to the memory of those who have laid down their lives in an advance which, in spite of the most stupendous difficulties, has proved victorious. But their memory will always be fresh in our hearts and minds, and alike in France and England we shall remember them—especially on Christmas Day—ever since its inception the Festival of the Family—when we " bless Thy Holy Name for all those who have departed this Life in Thy faith and fear," and receive His own power.

MILLS PILLS

WORTH
A "MINNIE"
A BOX.

GUARANTEED TO
CLEAR ANYONE OUT

Those who are left, we know, " carry on " in the same spirit as those who have gone before. Thus between those who fell and those who fight, there will be the double chain of fellowship and understanding, and " the open road of communion in a common purpose will keep us close to those whom we have lost, and whom again, because we are true to them, and because we keep alive their spirit in ourselves, we have not lost at all."

OUR BENEFACTORS.

Camps Library	Magazines
Ladies of Gloucester	Shoulder Badges
" The Echo "	The Echo
Lt.-Col. Winterbotham	Papers
Lt.-Col. Marling	,,
Miss Parr	,,
Miss Karn	,,
Bishop Frodsham	,,
The Hon. Mabel Gye	,,
Mrs. Temple Cooke	,,
Mr. Jack Margetson	Cigarettes
Miss Backhouse	Papers
Pte. Shaw	Typing
Pte. Orchard	,,
Pte. Wood	,,
Mr. W. R. Voller	Papers
Mrs. Stanley Tubb	Cigarettes

BALLADE OF MUD.

In all we see a double sway,
　In Man and Nature bad and good.
And which at last shall win the day,
　Was ever mortal understood ?
The sun may rule the Summer day,
　And Spring induce the trees to bud :
With Autumn all the leaves decay,
　And Winter owns no King but Mud.

The floor of Heaven is paved with gold,
　And even earth before the Flood
Was made of dry and decent mould.
　But with the black stains in the blood
That wretched man's happiness of old,
　The earth that was so fair and good
Knew War and Death and Dark and Cold,
　And Winter's filthy tyrant, Mud.

Darkness may bring the weary rest,
　And Death reveal beatitude ;
Cold gives to exercise a zest,
　And War with shells, both crump and dud,
Gas, minnies, bullets, billets, rest,
　By the brave soul may be withstood,
Till Hell, to work his bitterest,
　Disgorged the King of Winter, Mud.

Oh, Prince, who as the prophets tell
　Shalt harry Hell's accursed brood,
When Death and Darkness hear their knell,
　Spare not the King of Winter, Mud.

THE ETERNAL QUESTION.

The first time it happened I was quite un-prepared, but in the light of subsequent events I gained wisdom and felt prepared for it at any moment. But let me explain. After prolonged re-petition of any particular action one begins to yearn for a change, and so it happened that after many, many months of puttee winding and cartage of personal and military impediments on a species of harness, the longing for civilian clothes became so persistent that, on emerging from hospital I decided to wear civilian garments. True I also wore a pair of crutches and one foot dangled impotently some 4 or 5 inches from the ground.

In spite of this I was one day accosted at a well known railway terminus, by a doubtless very worthy old lady, and completely flabergasted by her question :—" Why aren't you in khaki, young man ? "

So taken aback was I by the suddenness of her enquiry that I scarcely know what answer I gave. All I remember is finding myself in possession of a pamphlet entitled " The shirker's duty to his King and Country," and a feeling of dizziness.

Two days later in Oxford Street I was again buttonholed and asked " Are you wounded " ?

Without a moment's hesitation I replied " Dear me no ! Oh dear no ! I was stung by my pet Pekinese whilst combing my nephew's tortoise." " Then why aren't you in khaki " ? persisted my inquisitor. " For the benefit of fatuous old busy-bodies such as yourself," I replied, " It may interest you, and at the same time save you from coming to an untimely end, if I tell you that the Guards only wear uniform when on duty."

Although quite beside the point yet none the less true, he appeared satisfied and tottered away mumbling.

The next occasion was a few days after I had taken to a couple of sticks. Suddenly I felt my arm seized and a raucous voice demanded " Where is your uniform " ? Turning round with a glint of murder in my eye I beheld a middle-aged cadaverous looking female regarding me through a pair of rimless glasses.

Heedless of all consequences I parried with " Where is your War Baby " ? I am certain she lied, but doubtless with a view to confusing me, she replied, without turning a hair, at the same time handing me a white feather :—" It's at home." " So is my uniform," I retorted, deftly cleaning my pipe with the feather and handing it back.

"PASSED TO YOU."

I sat there lonely as a cloud
That floats on high o'er hills and slopes,
And all at once there came a crowd, a host
Of yellow envelopes.
Continuous as the stars that shine,
They stretched in an unending line.

Much engaged was I but they
Demanded my attention : soon
Well I knew what all did say
Before the runner laid them down.
" Strafes " they'd be " Herewith one name."
Rolls—Reports—they're all the same.

" The G. O. C. notes with regret "
" For necessary action please "
" The General grants the leaves, submit
To this Office names of these,"
" As per minute one reply :
" With the above forthwith comply."

And oft when on my couch I lie
In vacant or in pensive mood,
There flashes on my inward eye
A thought and hope that the Staff would
Burn all their paper and begin
To think how the damn War to win.

　　　　　　　　　　　　A. A

HORTICULTURAL CANDOUR.

1st Tommy, to Ditto with Barrow :—

"Wot yer doin' to-day, Jim? Carnations?"

RATS !

The following is the translation of a document that has not yet been found on a captured German :

1. Owing to the presence of rats in the trenches, it has been found necessary to introduce cats as a protection against this pest.

2. At least 1 N.C.O. per company should be fully trained in the handling of cats and there should be 2 cat N. C. O.'s under instruction.

3. There will be an issue of cats on the first of every month from the cat-house mews, Katzenhaus, whose position will be designated later.

4. Cats should be kept in baskets when not required for use. Baskets containing Tom cats should be kept carefully apart from those containing Tabbies. It would be useful to tie up the former with jellow ribbon, the latter with green as a distinguishing mark.

5. Cats should be freed at evening stand-to and basketed again half-an-hour after sunrise. They must be kept as quiet as possible between these hours and anything in the nature of a concert must be strictly avoided.

6. At other times cat N.C.O.'s must always be prepared to release cats immediately on the rat alert sounding. The signal for rat alert will be three shots fired in rapid succession. At night it will always be rat alert.

7. Cats should be allowed to rest as much as possible during the day time owing to the keen concentration of mind which the night-work requires.

8. Cat N.C.O's. should remember that every cat has been carefully trained to its task and a judicious handling of the animal should produce excellent results, whilst a misuse of them will produce results correspondingly deplorable.

9. On moving from trenches, care must be taken to have cats well secured. On no account should they be allowed to accompany a battalion on a Route March.

10. The practice of placing cheese at the end of a bayonet and loosing a round on the approach of a rat, whilst admirable in its way, should now be discontinued, as tending to make a cat lose interest in its task.

11. Finally, every Officer, N.C.O. and man should realise that cats are provided for a military purpose and are not to be adopted as regimental pets. On one or two lamentable occasions officers have had to be severely reprimanded for issuing condensed milk in large quantities to cats during the day-time. It should be obvious that this practice will, if continued, produce inertia in the cat in a very short time, and it must cease at once.

12. Cats reported unfit for duty should be sent back to the Army Feline Training School behind the line.

BRICKS FROM THE EDITOR'S PACK.

We feel that an apology—more or less abject and couched in the most penitent language that can be devised—is due to the readers of this Gazette for our temerity in outraging the Law of the Medes and Persians in having the effrontery to publish a Christmas Number in the Month of December. From time immemorial, lovers of figures and statisticians generally, have made a practice of marking off a large space in the pages of their Diaries for July, so that they may duly observe the publication of the Christmas Number of the various Magazines and Picture papers in that Month.

Once again we can but plead the exigencies of the Military situation in extenuation for so brazenly flaunting established precedent.

This is the only Christmas Number published in December.

Good news has been received of Private Cecil H. Greenwood, of the 5th Gloucesters, who was reported killed at the commencement of the great offensive in France. On Friday last his mother received a post card from him to say that he was wounded and a prisoner of war at Munster (Westfalen) Germany. Part of his scalp was blown away, and he was unconscious for several days, but a German doctor successfully grafted part of another man's scalp on to the wounded man's head, and he is doing well.

"Wilts and Gloucester Standard."

Thank you, Doctor.

We believe that the following, in addition to the above, are wounded Prisoners of War.

3099	Pte	Dodwell, W. E.
4317	,,	Loveridge, F.
3013	,,	Cooke, V. F. W.
4775	,,	Symonds, A.
4099	,,	Curtis, A. T.
4487	,,	Drinkwater, J.
3371	,,	Davis, E. W. B.
6184	,,	Howlett, J.
2782	,,	Ing, E.
4775	,,	Symonds, A.
2926	,,	Draper, C. C.
1874	,,	Fry, V. W.

From *The Times*, Oct. 16th, 1916.

" It is important to relate that since the beginning of the Battle of the Somme there is, I was correctly informed, a marked improvement in the condition of English Prisoners all over Germany."

D. T. CURTIN.

But a German Official connected with the Military Censorship has let the cat out of the bag. " As a man of the world, you will realize that though our general public here do not know that the English have captured many Germans lately, we have had a hint from Headquarters that the English prisoners may one day balance ours and that hardship for these verfluchte Engländer may result in hardship for our men in England."

Times, Oct. 16th, 1916.

And Mr. Curtin tells us that after the War there will be terrible stories of hardships undergone by those who were taken prisoners in the earlier months of the War. " Much of it is," he says, " quite unprintable." Yet we are being encouraged in certain quarters to shake hands with the Prussian ! ! !

The goal of many—

" They have sorely wounded him,

. . . .

But no complaint has passed the barrier of his teeth,
Only he laughs and says as how he's bound for Blighty,
Instead of strafe the Allyman has given him a free
pass home,
Long leave and Duchesses to wait on him,
Pommes frites, beaucoup beer, Roll on."

Punch.

To say that we

" Opened our eyes
In mild surprise."

at reading the following WORDS—" They would do
more for their country by shaking hands. Our men at
the front gave cigarettes to German prisoners : could
they not at home be as forgiving as the men at the
Front ? "—is to put it mildly. In its Review of Trench
Journals in the *Times* Literary supplement of
October 12th, the true philosophy of the giving of
cigarettes is enunciated. " It is true that our men
took upon the German as a creature outside the pale
of humanity, but the thought that " the poor devil
knows no better " is always at work in the bottom of
the British Soldier's mind. As the toad is a toad, so
the Bosche is a Bosche, so what's the use of being
angry with him ? It is his misfortune rather than his
fault that he is a savage brute and a dirty fighter.
That is why they are so kind to the " kamerad "
with uplifted hands, give him a part of their food, or
even the last " fag," and would not mind if it could
be permitted taking them on at an improvised game
of football—a " friendly game," in fact. This
forbearance......is probably a heritage from the
" old " Army with its age long experience of little
wars with savage and half savage peoples."

Moreover it is an elementary principle of
Theology and common sense alike that forgiveness
will achieve nothing if penitence is absent.

What we dread more than anything is a general
international handshake with a Prussia of to-morrow
that bears even a faint resemblance to the Prussia
of to-day.

Why even the coddling of German prisoners is
regarded as weakness on our part ! We want this
war to be the last War. Well then what is the use
doling out forgiveness when even a *South* German
Lecturer who knows England, writes as follows :
" German culture had fully assimilated all that
deserved to live in the several civilisations of Greece
and Rome, Italy, France and England. Hence the
spreading and substitution, even by force of arms,
of this German culture, now thus become the legiti-
mate heir (because the actual quintessence) of all
these other cultures, was both no more than justice
on the part of Germany towards herself, and nothing
of loss, but rather a great gain in fruitful concentration for Europe and humanity at large."

" To preach the doctrine of forgiveness for such
people would seem to carry magnanimity beyond the
realm of sanity. The Germans themselves would be
the first to laugh at it and scornfully to abuse it to
their own advantage." American, in Daily Paper.
October 21st.

" Never has a War among civilised peoples been
waged with such entire discarding of the laws of
God and man—and never let it be forgotten that the
German Press and people have not raised a voice
against the crimes of Germany—Bethman Hollweg
said in the Reichstag that the Germans had laid aside

all sentimentality. It would be an infinite blessing
if the same could be said of certain, no doubt well
meaning, people in our midst."

A. E. Turner's Letter to *Saturday Review*,
October 14th, 1916.

Besides, listen, please listen, to the *Tagliche
Rundschau*—" The Community of Christendom
which finds its one true representative in the German
Nation, must use the sword, as the means to decimate
the ranks of the evil-minded enemy, so that the
remnant that is spared when the strife is over will
be spiritually prepared in holiness and calm to await
the coming of the rosy dawn of human fraternity."

International peace without Prussian penitence
spells International war without end.

" The German is unchanged and unchanging. He
is still, as he ever has been, the wild beast of Europe.
He embodies in his thick and portly form the very
spirit of evil. Whether he will be chastened even
by defeat is doubtful."

Blackwoods Magazine.

(Musings without Method) Nov. 1916.

Come along, boys, after that, and lets get on
towards Berlin.

On les aura !

" I saw platoons . . . . drilling in the rear
of the guns, as though they were in the Barrack yard,
" Form Fours : " " Form *Three's.*"

Saturday Review, October 14.

Special Article " With the British Army at the
Front " by G. A. B. Dewar."

What about eleven's ?

From *Punch*, October 18th.

Article " The Official Report. " Let's see ;
we'll have No. 11 Platoon on to mending the wire,
and No. 12.". . . On the *pink* slip he wrote
Situation Report. All quiet ac ac ac, O. C. D.
4 p.m."

O. C. D. Company seems to take command of the
whole Battalion. We recommend an urgent indent
for *White* Form A. F. c. 2121 Stationary Department
and not on Form Marguerite B. F. 2.

The contempt which the so-called masters of
theory have for the mere children of experience is
well illustrated by the following remark addressed
by a stay-at-home-at-all-costs officer to a wounded
Officer of 16 months' experience in and in front of the
FRONT LINE. " You fellows, of course, know all
about how to clear up a dirty trench, but technically
you know nothing at all."

We don't care a ——— about technique. We
want MEN who will fight, and who will fight OUT
HERE.

People at home who have subscribed from time
to time to the funds of the British Red Cross Society
wonder perhaps what is happening to the millions
that have been collected. They may rest happy in
the certain knowledge that they have contributed
very materially to the comfort of wounded and sick
of all ranks, and thousands have appreciated their
generosity.

Curiously enough a Motor Ambulance given by
the Gloucestershire Farmers followed the Battalion
one day last summer.

Many congratulations to our former censor—Captain Gabb, M.C.—on his appointment on the Staff of the Second Corps.

Many familiar " landmarks " in the Division have dropped out. The Doctors would be the first to acknowledge their gratitude to Major Summerhayes, R.A.M.C., for the courageous way he has fought their battles. We hope he has recovered from the serious injuries sustained from a fall from his horse. To him and to Captain Scott Williamson, who has taken up important bacteriological work at the Base, their very many friends in the Division wish " Bonne Chance." Cheer ho !

We must certainly have a Divisional Dinner once a year—say one night during the Varsity Cricket Match, the first week in July. Intending Diners please note ! No German waiters—by special arrangement—will be in attendance. In the Final Number of the GAZETTE details of the scheme will be published for information and necessary action.

That we shall also have an annual Battalion dinner in Gloucester once a year, goes without saying.

It is our pleasant task once again to wish our readers as Happy a Christmas and as Bright a New Year as circumstances—such as Huns and weather conditions—shall permit. Let's hope it is going to to be the last we shall spend away from our own firesides.

" For ourselves, if we keep the enemy slowly moving on the Somme, and maintain by means of frequent French raids our initiative over him......"

Illustrated Sunday Herald.

Nov. 12th, 1916.

The amateur strategist would appear to be playing into German hands by endeavouring to create ill-feeling between the French and ourselves.

Extract from " Blighty."

" I was talking yesterday with an Officer who was in the Jutland biz," writes my chief Naval Correspondent, " and he told me that as his vessel closed in to engage the enemy they passed through a lot of scattered debris with officers and men clinging to it. One of them shouted : " Never mind us—GET ON WITH IT ! " and then they raised a cheer. That is the way to face death, if you like. Not one of those fellows was saved. God rest their souls who died for us all and for Britain." To which we will most reverently say, Amen !

Let our last words in this present war-number be it said, seriously and emphatically :—LET THE NAVY " GET ON WITH IT " !

" The Bluejacket and Sailor."

Very hearty congratulations to Major Todd on his D.S.O., and to Captain Hayes on his Military Cross.

The sympathy of all ranks will be extended to Lieut.-Colonel G. F. Collett on his illness, coming as it did so soon after taking over the command of the Battalion. We all wish him a speedy recovery.

Several well-known people signed a round robin a short time ago—printed in the " Times "—pressing for the total abolition by Parliament of all alchohol during the war. We have also seen a letter, from one who certainly ought to know better, deprecating the sending of cigarettes to soldiers.

We presume that the abolition of alchohol applies to the men in the Trenches as well as to those who have their feet in carpet-slippers on the mantel-piece, who might well have been called upon to give it up two years ago. Well, we wonder how many lives has been saved, how many men " kept going," by the rum ration.

Some of you people at home little realise the comfort of the Woodbine.

So don't spend your time writing silly letters to the papers about things you know nothing whatsoever about, but send us plenty of cigarettes and Illustrated Papers and Magazines.

Medical Reform.

We are very glad to hear from our medical friends that that mysterious and fatal disease known as P.U.O. (Pyrexia Unknown Origin) has now been entirely exterminated. Its last organism departed this life at 2-30 p.m. on November 16th. This result was only achieved at the price of great and arduous bacteriological research. Unfortunately, at 2-31 p.m. on the same date, a new disease, strangely allied to the late lamented, made its appearance. This disease has now, we understand, been identified as that terrible scourge Pyrexia N.Y.D. (Pyrexia Not Yet Diagonised.)

Lieut.-Colonel Sinnott, C.M.G., has written a series of articles for the Gazette on the history of the Gloucestershire Regiment. We publish the first instalment.

The "Tank" driver gets 1s. 1d. a day. Bad luck old chap, but you see you are much too near the Front to get 6s. a day. Besides any old ass can drive a Tank, can't they, eh what ?

One of the discoveries of the War has been the most estimable practice of granting of leave, which has been rendered possible through the agency of the Navy. It might appear almost ungracious to criticise so beneficent a practice, were it only too true that after 20 months of service in Flanders and France, there are still men—many too, alas, had fallen after 16 months, away from home—who have had no leave, whilst sergeants at the Base who, through no fault of their own, it is true, have never seen a trench and never heard a shell, have had four leaves in 20 months ! ! ! ! No one in their senses would think of blaming these lucky men for going on leave, but we do think it hard on those who have been through so much with never a sight of home.

We know that there are many difficulties, and the situation of our island home makes it impossible for the authorities to be able to guarantee leave every four months—the practice now in vogue in the French Army—but we do plead, before it is too late, for a certain amount of fair play for the Infantry. It is their war, too, isn't it ?

The situation in the front line was causing a certain Division a considerable amount of anxiety. Great was the delight, therefore, at Divisional Head-quarters, when a pigeon flew briskly into its loft, and the Staff, eager and expectant, crowded round the pigeon-man. The message ran as follows " I'm —— well tired of holding this 'ere——bird."

One comes across strange people in strange places and not unfrequently square people in round holes. There are four M.Os.—good fellows all—in an advanced dressing station that we wot of, in constant touch with the Bosche guns. They willingly gave us the following details of their life's history. One is a decrepit family practitioner with an engaging bedside manner. A second is a consulting physician of no mean eminence. A third has hitherto made his livelihood as an operating surgeon in the North. not without success. No. 4—in command—is a struggling young dentist.

Now, by irony of fate, it fell upon a day that a tooth had to be drawn. Unfortunately there were no forceps in the kit of the advanced dressing station, so the unfortunate sufferer had to proceed many miles, and fell into the hands of a gynaecologist. Yet, in spite of this, we are winning the war.

A good many men owe their lives to the skill of Lieut.-Colonel Barling, who left us a short time ago to become a surgical specialist at the Base. We congratulate him from his own point of view, but we cannot help feeling that his departure has robbed the Division of a fine operator and a good commanding officer.

We are very sorry indeed to lose him.

So that innocent-looking place Beaumont-Hamel has at last gone the way of everything that is Bosch and is an earnest of yet further success.

This performance in the Somme Offensive must surely rank second only to the hurricane advance of our Allies from Verdun, which accomplished in hours what the Huns had achieved—at a gigantic cost—in months.

From England.—Orderly Officer on visiting rounds, to Sentry: " What are your duties ? " S. : " To march up and down in a soldierlike manner and to guard His Majesty's property in the camp."

O.O.—" Yes, anything else ? " S. : " And to prevent any improper women entering the camp except the Colonel's wife."

An Officer of the 6th Glo'sters who has been decorated for gallantry was wounded and went to the Third Line. He attended a lecture on Trench Warfare by a " homer." When the bored audience was finally released the Officer took the lecturer aside and offered to give him some hints, as his lecture was quite different to actual fact.

The lecturer said " That's like all you B. E. F. men. Just because you have been in one little bit of the line you think you know all about it. My Lecture was based on study of the whole front."

Our best thanks to " Rags " and to Second-Lieutenant Robertson for decorating this Number of the Gazette.

OLD BOYS.

Many congratulations to

Lieutenant H. W. Chandler, York and Lancaster Regiment, on his Military Cross.

Company Sergeant - Major Tibbles, M.C., on his Commission in the A.S.C.

PERSONAL.

MARRIAGE.

At Holy Trinity, Sloane St., on November 23rd, Brigadier-General Herbert R. Done, D.S.O., Norfolk Regiment, to Miss Elsie Kingham, of Glen Garragh, Co. Down.

APPOINTMENTS AND PROMOTIONS.
Part II. Orders.

To be Sergeant :—

2272	L/Sergt.	Reeves, F. W.	Dated	29/7/16
2921	Cropl.	Cummings, P. B.	,,	14/8/16
2571	,,	Taylor, M.	,,	16/8/16
2496	L/Corpl.	Hopson, F. J.	,,	19/8/16
		Appointed Sergt. Cook	,,	15/9/16
2453	Corpl.	Thomas, A. C.	,,	25/8/16
2322	,,	Harding, W.	,,	1/9/16
1752	,,	Chandler, E. W.	,,	2/9/16
1557	,,	Rice, A.	,,	6/9/16
2621	,,	Bromage, W.	,,	7/9/16
2532	,,	Fry, F. W.	,,	11/9/16

To be L/Sergeant :—

2308	,,	Fudge, A. A.	,,	21/4/16
1476	,,	Coopey, A.	,,	4/5/16
2374	,,	Barnes, H. C.	,,	13/9/16

To be Corporal :—

2621	L/Corpl.	Bromage, W.	Dated	21/7/16
2729	,,	Wise, R.	,,	21/7/16
2707	,,	Rea, W.	,,	21/7/16
3999	,,	Niblett, W. E.	,,	21/7/16
1982	,,	Sterry, A.	,,	23/7/16
2767	,,	Parham, W. G.	,,	23/7/16
1363	,,	Hopkins, W. G.	,,	23/7/16
2199	• ,,	Druce, E. C.	,,	23/7/16
2677	,,	Grant, J. K.	,,	25/7/16
2532	,,	Fry, F. W.	,,	29/7/16
2929	,,	Tolley, P. G.	,,	29/7/16
1760	,,	Caudle, H.	,,	17/8/16
1835	,,	Mustoe, M.	,,	27/8/16
20704	Pte. (L/C.)	Hobbs, G.	,,	29/7/16
2374	,,	Barnes, H. C.	,,	29/7/16
2915	,,	Chorley, J.	,,	2/8/16
2716	,,	Tandy, F.	,,	4/8/16

To be L/Corporal :—

2943	Pte.	Kitching, F. F.	,,	30/7/16
2324	,,	Harmer, H.	,,	30/7/16
20714	,,	Steeds, H.	,,	30/7/16
1722	,,	Enoch, G.	,,	30/7/16
2532	,,	Fry, F. W.	,,	30/7/16
3028	,,	Lane, J. D.	,,	1/8/16
1728	,,	Burton, R. A.	,,	19/8/16
1510	,,	Deavin, W. E.	,,	22/8/16
2680	Pte. (L/C.)	Hamblin, L.	,,	23/8/16
2997	,,	Warwick, F.	,,	23/8/16
1831	,,	Miller, W. F.	,,	23/8/16
2584	,,	Hopkins, P. J.	,,	23/8/16
2798	,,	Boddington, G. H.	,,	23/8/16
2189	,,	Doogood, H. A. C.	,,	23/8/16
2549	Pte.	Matthews, H.	,,	23/8/16
2688	,,	Johnsey, G.	,,	23/8/16
5016	,,	Prince, A. J.	,,	23/8/16

To be L/Corporal, with pay :—

2630	Pte. (L/C.)	Chandler, W.	,,	31/8/16
20250	,,	Craner, W.	,,	2/9/16
2431	,,	Lait, F. G.	,,	2/9/16
20208	,,	Fisher, W. H.	,,	2/9/16

To be L/Corporal, without pay :—

4893	Pte.	Christmas, E. G.	,,	28/11/16
20734	,,	Tonge, W. G.	,,	28/11/16
5217	,,	McNesby, E. G.	,,	28/11/16
20306	,,	Matty, A. J.	,,	28/11/16
5893	,,	Townsend, T.	,,	28/11/16
2381	,,	Stephens, W. G.	,,	28/11/16

392 A/C.S.M. Finch F. Confirmed substantive rank of C.S.M., with pay and allowances of Warrant Officer Class II., dated 4/9/16, vice 456 C.S.M. Tibbles, to England, 4/9/16.

To be L/Corporals without pay, dated 14/9/16 :—

2443	Pte	Corlett, E. J.
2307	,,	Cresswell, A.
1198	,,	Ellis, C. H.
2489	,,	Doogood, H. A. C.
2750	,,	Cambridge, B. J.
2756	,,	Webb, H.
2433	,,	White, J. H. C.
3310	.,	Sully, G. E.
5079	,,	Scott, W. J.
2745	,,	Baker, S. G.
2761	,,	Howes, A. E.
2135	,,	Roddis, F. W.
1835	,,	Mustoe, H. G.
2842	,,	Hyett, H. W.
2716	,,	Tandy, F.
2891	,,	Vergez, A.
1599	,,	Excell, W.
2728	,,	White, A. J.

To be L/Corporals without pay dated 1/10/16 :—

2955	Pte.	Parker, H.
4717	,,	Lewis, J. A.
1274	,,	Davis, P. R.
2751	,,	Curtis, T. B.
1474	,,	Jeynes, H. C.
1171	,,	Gould, C. A.
2337	,,	Hooper, H.
2431	,,	Lait, F. G.
20250	,,	Craner, W.
4887	,,	Woolger, S. T.
5274	,,	Pearson, W. J.
5056	,,	Higgins, P.
2600	,,	Davies, W. R.
4150	,,	Scutts, W. G.
713	,,	Langley, R.
1646	,,	Parker, G. G.
2583	,,	Hill, E. G.

R.I.P.

They shall not grow old as we that are left grow old :
Age shall not weary them, nor the years condemn :
At the going down of the sun and in the morning
We will remember them in Christ.

5th Gloucester Gazette.

A Chronicle, serious and humorous, of the Battalion while serving with the
BRITISH EXPEDITIONARY FORCE.

TOMMY-BY-THE-WAY.

A Sketch in miniature.

Twilight. A sunken road behind the forward trenches. Above the four foot bank may be seen the brief stems of riven trees standing gaunt against the last green daylight. They strike the note of utter desolation.

A TOMMY ENTERS in fighting kit. He is tired and has a guilty, haunted look. He sits down wearily and takes off his shrapnel helmet.

TOMMY— Oh my Gawd......Oh my......Gawd ! (*HE remains with his head in his hands in a torpor of despair. But it is not for long ; suddenly he looks up.*) Why not ?...I will...It's easy ! (*He jumps up draws his bayonet and feels the point musingly. He feels his left arm, pinching up fingers-full of muscle, looking for a fleshy part in which to make a self-inflicted wound. His hand moves up to his shoulder and it occurs to him that just under the collar bone would be a good spot. (Of course it would be a very bad spot really, but Tommy does not know that.) He puts the point of the bayonet there, but his hand refuses to give the necessary push. He hesitates, looks round, picks up his rifle and fixes the bayonet. (Then you realise that amongst the enshrouding shadows is standing a woman, for she now uncovers her face. Tall she is, mysterious you might say, for she is so garbed that her appearance suggests neither period nor age. Without further movement she stands watching the Unhappy Warrior. HE lodges the butt of his rifle against some obstacle and grasps the stock near the bayonet with both hands. With the point at his shoulder he moves to throw his weight upon it. The WOMAN takes a sudden step forward and the soldier lets fall the rifle and turns guiltily towards her. THEY stand looking at one another.*)

TOMMY.—(*Sheepishly*)   Bonjour, madame !   (*The WOMAN neither speaks nor moves*) Il fait chaud ...beaucoup, n'est-ce-pas ? Oui ? (*He tries to laugh jauntily.   Then angrily at her continued silence.*) Oh all right, if yer don't comprenny yer own blarsted lingo ! 'Op off, toute suite ! D'yer 'ear ?...'Op it !—Gor blimy, why don't you learn a decent Christian language.

WOMAN.—You poor boy !

TOMMY.—'Ow, yer can speak English can yer ! That's just like you blarsted foreigners ; learns our language and then looks down on us because we can't parlez-vous back. 'Spose yer only learnt it so's yer could spy. That's wot you are, dirty lot o' spies. But you don't come spying' on me ! I ain't nothin' ter do with you ! Oh my Gawd what the 'ell did I come to this bleedin' country for ? (*Thoroughly wrought up as he is, he breaks*

down utterly and blubbers. The Woman is beside him in a minute, supporting him, and gradually his head sinks back.)

WOMAN.—You're tired, terribly tired. A little sleep will do you good. (*She undoes the top button of his tunic. The movement rouses him.*)

TOMMY.—'Ere, what yer playing at ? Thought I was asleep, did yer ? Was goin ter see if I a'd any despatches on me, I suppose. Well I ain't, see ! But I ain't goin' to 'ave you runnin' through me pockets. I've got eight francs and you'd like 'em wouldn't yer ? I know yer ! I seen your sort at the staminets.

WOMAN.—Eight francs. They would'nt be much use to me. I possess far, far more than that.

TOMMY.—And I can well believe it ! The profits you people make out of us is somethink wicked. 'Ere give me that rifle. (*The WOMAN has been holding it*) I'm off !

WOMAN.—Have you finished cleaning it ?

TOMMY.—What !

WOMAN.—Weren't you cleaning it, just now ?

TOMMY.—Did it look as though I were cleanin' of it ?

WOMAN.—You had your back to me.

TOMMY.—J'ever see a bloke clean 'is rifle with the bayonet on ?

WOMAN.—I'm only a woman you know.

TOMMY.—What's it got ter do with you any'ow ?

WOMAN.—More than you think.

TOMMY.—Oh, 'as it, Then if it's so important for you ter know, I'll bloomin' well tell yer. I'm fed up ! I was goin' ter give meself a blighty touch.

WOMAN.—A self-inflicted wound ! Yes, I knew that.

TOMMY.—Then what yer want to ask for ?

WOMAN.—Because I wanted to hear you confess it.

TOMMY.—'Ow, did yer ! Well if yer think yer goin' to get me shot at dawn every day for a week, yer bloomin' well mistaken. Cos yer 'aven't got no witnesses, see !

WOMAN.—Why are you so fed up ?

TOMMY.—Wouldn't you be fed up if you'd gorn through what I 'ave ? Its just blinkin' 'ell for the last few weeks. Ever 'eard a shell burst ?

WOMAN.—Many thousands.

TOMMY.—Well I've 'eard millions ? Millions ! I tell yer, and that ain't no exaggeration. I've been in trenches what's been blown ter pieces all about me, and me pals all killed and wounded.

WOMAN.—Your pals all killed and wounded ! And now you're running away. A......a......

TOMMY.—Go on, say it ! A coward !

WOMAN.—Oh no ! I wasn't going to say a coward I was going to say a son of some poor mother in England who looks up to you as her hero.

TOMMY.—'Ere, 'ere, come off that ! I don't want none of your 'ero stuff thrown at me. I'm just an ordinary bloke I am. I never wanted ter be no 'ero. I was earning me 25 bob a week before this blarsted war came on. A darned good job I got in them days.

WOMAN.—And yet you gave it up.

TOMMY.—Cos why ! Cos my girl said if I didn't chuck my job and—and—

WOMAN.—And be a man ?

TOMMY.—She'd chuck me.

WOMAN.—That was the spirit of the Women of England speaking ! And so you listened to her and joined up.

TOMMY.—Well I ad to, 'adn't I ? I wasn't goin' to 'ave 'er callin'me a coward. Easy enough for 'er to jaw. She 'adn't got ter go through it. Didn't 'alf fancy 'erself walkin on me arm and lookin' at other girls whose blokes wasn't in khaki.

WOMAN.—And when you left for France were there no tears ?

TOMMY.—Well, she laughed so as I could see she was merry and bright, but I sort of noticed she kept 'er 'ead down. And when the train moved off she waved 'er 'anderchief, and I snatched it tor funlike, and... (seriously) lor' lummy, it weren't 'alf wet.

WOMAN.—And yet you say, she didn't have to go through it.

TOMMY.—Oh—well...(cheerfully) I've got 'er 'and-kerchief 'ere. (Pulls it out) It's dry now.

WOMAN.—But her eyes are not. And when you go back to her and say " I ran away " do you think she'll walk with dry eyes and a smiling face down that little street in Islington.

TOMMY.—'Ow, chuck it ! (With sudden surprise) 'Ere, Islington. I never told you she lives at Islington.

WOMAN.—But I knew it, didn't I ?

TOMMY.—You don't come from Islington ?

WOMAN.—I come from North, South, East and West.

TOMMY.—'Ere, but 'onest, do you know 'er ?

WOMAN.—I know every mother, wife, sister and sweetheart.

TOMMY.—Lor' Lummy, you are a rum' un ! Who are yer ?

WOMAN.—I've been waiting for you to ask me that, I am the Spirit of the Women of England.

TOMMY.—The Spirit......

WOMAN.—Of the Women of England ! I was when England first was. And down through all the historied years I have watched and waited whilst my men made England what she is.

TOMMY.—'Ere, but a spirit...that's what...Blimy !

WOMAN.—I know exactly. You're wondering if its shell shock. It seems so strange, doesn't it, to see me talking to you like... like your girl might. Yet I've often talked to you before.

TOMMY.—You 'ave ?

WOMAN.—There was that time when you had to join up or be chucked. Of course you didn't know it was I. Then each time letters have come from home I've been with you. And you remember that night when they were shelling the broken battered trench you had all taken so splendidly in the morning. You were sitting in a shell hole with...

TOMMY.—With ole Bill Hester. We was waiting for the counter attack. Gawd, wasn't they just crumpin' the stuff about.

WOMAN.—As you sat there, you pulled a crumpled picture out of your pocket and though you hadn't been talking about it before, you just said " that's 'er."

TOMMY.—And old Bill give a start and said 'Lummy ! I were thinkin' of my missus, too.

WOMAN.—Yes, I was with you both that night, nerving you, bidding you both be strong.

TOMMY.—Ole Bill bagged nine of 'em afore they did 'im in.

WOMAN.—You did well that night, oo.

TOMMY.—(Modestly) Oh, I—I nicked a few of 'em, (Excitedly) But we 'eld that blinkin' streak o' mud, didn't we ? They never re-took a yard of it.

WOMAN.—Yes, the Spirit of the Women of England was proud of her men that night.

TOMMY.—We was as cocky as a lot o' sparrers when we come out. (Seriously) But, by Gawd, you should have seen them as didn't come out no more.

WOMAN.—I saw them for I am with every man in his last hour of pain when he lies wounded and there be none to hear his call. And as there comes upon him the horror of a great darkness, he feels that I am at his side and Peace falls round him like a veil. And after, when the tidings come, wife, mother, sweetheart hear my voice and clutch at comfort, saying with me, " He died magnificently." Oh, if you men would only be sure of the Spirit of the Women of England there would never be sad faces when you think of home. They are so sure of you, so generous of all they hold most dear, so certain that, come what may, their men will never fail them.

TOMMY.—That's all very well, but they don't know what war is. There ain't no chance for a man at all. It's all machinery and shrapnel and high explosive. What I want to know is why the 'ell... (feeling he is talking to a lady)...s'pose I didn't oughter say that to you.

WOMAN.—Oh yes, talk to me just like you'd talk to 'er'.

TOMMY.—Well, why the 'ell should we be doin' it at all ?

WOMAN.—If a man insulted your girl, what would you do ?

TOMMY.—(Indignant)   Search me !—What d'yer think I'd do ? (Business of having a scrap) Not 'arf I wouldn't.

WOMAN.—Do you remember once when that really did happen ?

TOMMY.—(*Jauntily*) It's happened once or twice...

WOMAN.—Yes, but on this particular occasion the man hit you a bit hard and you chucked it up.

TOMMY.—It's a lie ! I've never—who told yer that ?

WOMAN.—I saw it myself.

TOMMY.—I tell yer it's a lie !

WOMAN.—Oh no, it's not. It happened just now. When...when you were cleaning your rifle.

TOMMY.—Oh come, but that...I ain't fighting for me girl.

WOMAN.—You're fighting for England. England's a woman, you know. England is just every man's girl.

TOMMY.—Oh, damn England !

WOMAN.—Certainly if you like. You've probably " damned " your girl often enough, but it doesn't make you love her any the less. That's what our enemies could never understand. They thought because we went about and " damned " our England, we wouldn't fight for her. But we did.

TOMMY.—Rather. There ain't no foreigners going to come it over us.

WOMAN.—Unless they hit a bit too hard and......

TOMMY.—(*Remembering*) Yus, you've got me all right there. (*Full of a bitter abuse of himself.*) Gawd, and you said their men never failed 'em' !

WOMAN.—Oh, you hadn't failed us then. It was your hour of agony in the garden.

TOMMY.—I was goin' to do it ! If you hadn't just... I'd 'a done it !

WOMAN.—I wonder. If you can hear my voice now, I don't think you would have failed us then.

TOMMY.—What am I to do ?

WOMAN.—Go back the way you came.

TOMMY.—But I can't. I ran away—

WOMAN.—No, you only lost direction. Anyone can lose direction in the dark, and yours was a very dark hour.

TOMMY.—I can't go back. I could never forget I've been a coward.

WOMAN.—I've known those who thought they were cowards once and have afterwards shown themselves such men that they have won the cross.

TOMMY.—Oh, I don't want none of yer V.C.'s. Any man what's been through it knows the rot of that sort o' thing.   Pictures in the papers, and girls kissin' yer !

WOMAN.—That's only one side of it. Think of all your pals who have fallen and now lie sleeping in a corner of the field they won, with forests of little wooden crosses standing sentinel above them. Wouldn't it be worth while to wear a cross in memory of the splendid dead.

TOMMY.—(*Awe-struck at the idea*) In memory...... that would be......

WOMAN.—Yes, wouldn't it.   (*SHE makes passes with her hands. Sleep begins to overcome the TOMMY.*)

TOMMY.—Phew !   I'm sleepy......In memory,...... ole Bill......lots of 'em......(*HE has settled down to sleep.*)

WOMAN.—(*Holding his rifle like a sentry*) Sleep and gather strength from me, the Spirit of the Women of England, who has kept vigil throughout all time. Never in any season has my nation's sword been drawn but I have been there too. Behind the path of the invader I have wept over desolate hearths and I have stood behind defeat to nerve the arm to victory. I have sailed in oaken ships to the outpost of the world and in ships of steel have I kept the gates of commerce clear. Little by little England has given place to Empire, and I girdle the great round world across the Seven Seas. There is no land but knows me. I have strengthened the arm of the Pioneer when he hewed his way through unadventured forests and harnessed the forces of nature to his will in each wild continent. Time was when I could be none other than a force behind my men, but in these later days I have a further part. Now it is also given to me to work with my hands in field and factory, in camp and hospital, and bear the physical burden of each day. Oh women of England and of our Empire in this your greatest hour look upon me who am but a reflection of yourselves. No little thing am I, but life and love, urging, guiding, compelling, seldom with glamour, but always in great moments of trial and sorrow and so until the world's end, a force unconquerable.

(*The TOMMY stretches himself and wakes and looks around.*)

TOMMY.—Blimey, been asleep 'ave I......'Ello, you still 'ere.

WOMAN.—Yes, I've been looking after your rifle. You were cleaning it when you fell asleep.

TOMMY.—(*Hotly*) Yes ! I was cleanin' it ! Don't you go for to say I wasn't !

WOMAN.—You still think I want to get you a Court Martial.

TOMMY.—I dunno' I s'pose not............(*laughing queerly*) I've 'ad an awful rummy dream about you. You wouldn't 'arf laugh if I told you. Strite I dreamt you was......Never mind.   But it weren't 'arf rummy. Well, I must 'op it.

WOMAN.—You don't still think I'm a spy.

TOMMY.—Oh, I was a bit narked then. 'Sides...... seems sort o' sloppy I know, but......

WOMAN.—Well ?

TOMMY.—You sort o' remind me of my girl. That's why I'm going to let you into a secret. To-night there's goin' to be the biggest scrap you ever 'eard of. Them 'Uns is just about goin' to get it in the neck, and I'm going to be one of those what gives 'em 'ell. So long.

(*HE goes off singing some popular song of the moment.   The WOMAN remains centre, her arms extended. Finally SHE sinks down as though in prayer and still you hear the song of the TOMMY going forward.*)

W. O. D.

R. I. P.

1   2   3   4

5   6   7   8

9   10   11   12

" And many of our bodies shall, no doubt,
Find native graves ; upon the which, I trust,

1.	Lieutenant C. W. Winterbotham	Killed	27/8/16.	7.	2528 L/Cpl Enoch, A. W. G.	Killed	21/7/16.
2.	Lieutenant Thomas	Killed	10/7/16.	8.	2715 L/Cpl Sysum, S.	Killed	23/7/16.
3.	1724 L/Sgt Coole, F. A.	Missing	21/7/16.	9.	3009 Pte (L/Cpl) Chess, E. H.	Missing	16/8/16.
4.	2535 Sgt Garner, E.	Killed	14/8/16.	10.	2569 Cpl Sullivan, D. W.	Killed	21/7/16.
5.	1139 Sgt Harris, C. F.	Killed	16/8/16.	11.	2562 Cpl Ricketts, G. H.	Missing	21/7/16.
6.	1485 Sgt Dunn	Killed	18/8/16.	12.	1978 Cpl Price, H. C.	Missing	21/7/16.

R. I. P.

13   14   15   16

17   18   19   20

21   22   23   24

Shall witness live in brass of this day's work :
And those that leave their valiant bones in France,
Dying like men, ...
They shall be famed. "

13. 2694 Cpl Lewis, M. E. L.	Killed 23/7/16.	19. 3084 Pte Amery, E. J.	Killed 23/7/16.
14. 2516 Cpl Gough, T W.	Missing 23/7/16.	20. 2266 Pte Palmer, S. A.,	Killed 23/7/16.
15. 3201 Pte Jenkins, E. C.	Missing 21/7/16.	21. 4018 Pte Allaway, A. E.	Killed 23/7/16.
16. 3431 Pte Carter, W. E. F.	Missing 21/7/16.	22. 3608 Pte Powis, F.	Killed 14/8/16.
17. 4020 Pte Davis, A. E.	Missing 21/7/16.	23. 2735 Sgt Millard, S.	Killed 23/7/16.
18. 2871 Pte Reed, S. F	Missing 21/7/16.	24. 4594 Pte Brazener, A. C.	Killed 3/11/16.

THE BATTLE HONOURS OF THE GLOUCESTERSHIRE REGIMENT.

II.

In the first article I gave a complete list of the Honours gained by the County Regiment.

In this and subsequent articles I purpose giving some particulars of each Honour and the circumstances under which they were gained.

The first on the list is that of RAMILLIES, 1706, which formed one of the British victories under the Duke of Marlborough in the war of the Spanish succession.

This war, which was waged over the Western half of Europe between the years 1701 and 1713, arose owing to the rival claims of Philip of France and the Archduke Charles of Austria, Great Britain fighting with Austria against France, the chief events being

BLENHEIM	1704	(Danube valley)
RAMILLIES	1706	(Flanders)
TURIN	1706	(Italy)
ALMANZA	1707	(Spain)
OUDENARDE	1706	(Flanders)
MALPLAQUET	1709	(Flanders)

followed by further fighting in Spain during 1710.

At RAMILLIES the 28th Foot, now the 1st Battalion, took part in the battle of May 23rd, 1706.

The Regiment was commanded by Lord Mordaunt and formed part of the right wing of the Allied Forces. The actual engagement lasted 3½ hours and resulted in the French, under their Commander-in-Chief Villeroi, being completely routed.

The 28th also took part in the battle of Almanza in Spain on the 25th of April, 1707, where, under the Earl of Galway, it sustained very heavy losses. No Honour was given for this engagement, which was unsuccessful.

The second Honour is that of LOUISBURG, 1758, fought on the continent of North America, the 28th under Colonel Bragg taking part in the successful siege of Louisburg under Sir Jeffries Amherst. The French garrison surrendered on the 27th of July and the island of Cape Breton was given up, together with two smaller islands in the Gulf of St. Lawrence.

It will be convenient to refer to QUEBEC, 1759, next, as the 28th Regt. sailed from Louisburg in June, 1759, with the expedition under General Wolfe.

As part of the 1st Division they took part in scaling the heights of Abraham, and in the historic engagement that followed they were on the right of the British line under Wolfe's immediate command. General Wolfe was at the head of the Regiment when the final advance was made which secured the magnificent victory for the British troops over the French and added the Dominion of Canada to the British Crown. General Wolfe was mortally wounded at the moment of victory.

The next series of Honours were gained in the West Indies during the years 1759 to 1778.

At GUADELOUPE, 1759, the 61st Foot, now the 2nd Battalion, was engaged.

The Regiment embarked for the West Indies towards the end of 1756, under Colonel Elliott, in connection with the operations against the French West India Islands under General Hopson.

The troops landed on the Island of Guadeloupe on the 24th of January, 1759, and took possession of the town of Basse-Terre.

Hostilities continued for several months, in all of which the 61st was engaged, and in the end the French were forced to surrender.

General Hopson died during the operations and he was succeeded by General Barrington.

The operations in Canada having terminated successfully, troops were despatched under General Monckton to assist in the West Indies. The 28th Regt. with other troops, arrived at St. Ann's Bay, Martinique, on the 7th of January, 1762. The operations, which resulted in the Honour of MARTINIQUE began shortly afterwards, the French Commander being forced to capitulate on February the 12th.

Operations against HAVANNAH, the capital of the Island of Cuba, a possession of Spain, were decided on in the spring of 1762, and a large force under the Earl of Albemarle was despatched from England. The 28th Foot were already in the West Indies and they joined Lord Albemarle's command.

Joint operations by the Fleet, under Admiral Pocock, and the Military Forces were at once begun, and despite of very gallant resistance by the Spaniards, the Island capitulated on August the 14th.

About 30,000 Officers and men were taken prisoners and 13 Spanish line of battleships were captured by the British Fleet.

The last of the series of Honours in the West Indies is that of ST. LUCIA, 1778, where the 28th Regt. was included in a force of 6000 men under Major-General Grant. After considerable fighting the French Commandant surrendered the Island in December.

The first entry made by the Gloucestershire Regt. into the Napoleonic wars was in Egypt in 1801, where the 28th Foot gained undying fame at battle near Alexandria.

Operations against the French were started in 1801 with a view to safeguarding our possessions in the East Indies and to restore Egypt to the Turks.

An army of 17,000 men under Sir Ralph Abercromby was despatched early in the year and the disembarkation at Aboukir Bay was effected on March 8th.

In the engagement which immediately followed this, the 28th, under Colonel Paget, took a distinguished part.

On the 13th of March the Battle of Mandora was fought, and on the 21st the French made another attack on Abercromby's army near Alexandria.

In this engagement the French attack was repulsed, but at very heavy cost.

U

The 28th fought with great determination, and at one period, being attacked both in front and rear, their Colonel ordered the rear rank to turn about, and fighting under these conditions the regiment so distinguished itself that the unique honour of wearing the badge, the Sphinx, on the back as well as on the front of the head-dress, was granted. This distinction is very rightly held in the highest estimation by the Regiment.

The 61st Foot (now the 2nd Battalion) also participated in the operations in Egypt, having been sent from India, and landed on the coast of the Red Sea. After a march of 9 days through the desert the 61st joined the British Army in time to assist in defeating the French.

During the operations the Commander-in-Chief, Sir Ralph Abercromby, was mortally wounded, and the command devolved on General Hutchinson.

General Hutchinson at once advanced on Cairo, and on June 13th the French surrendered and 13,000 troops were made prisoners.

The Battle of MAIDA, 1806, was fought in the South of Italy.

In this, the 61st Foot took part under General Stuart in defence of our ally, the King of Naples, against a superior body of French under Regnier.

The action was fought on the shores of the straits of Messina and resulted in a victory for the British.

Before proceeding to describe the long list of Honours gained by the Regiment in the Peninsular War, which was waged in Portugal, Spain and the south-west of France from August, 1808, to April, 1814, some general notes on the subject may not be out of place.

In the year 1807 Napoleon, then being at the zenith of his power, sought to impose his will upon Great Britain by closing all the continental ports against British manufactures, and in August, 1807, he called on Portugal to comply with this decree.

At the same time he persuaded the King of Spain, Charles IV., to allow a French Army to pass through Spain towards Portugal, the arrangement being that France and Spain were to divide that country between them, and that Godoy, the King of Spain's minister, was to have the Principality of the Algarve as his share in the transaction.

Portugal remonstrated, with the result that Napoleon immediately sent 30,000 troops under General Junot to Lisbon.

In the meantime the Spanish people did not fall in with the views of their King, and a rising took place which forced the King to abdicate in favour of his son Ferdinand.

Napoleon thereupon refused to recognise Ferdinand and in the end he placed his brother Joseph Bonaparte on the throne. No sooner was this done than the whole of the Spanish and Portuguese nations rose against the French and in the summer of 1808 a British force of about 24,000 men was despatched to Portugal and Spain, to assist these nations in resisting the pretentions of France.

Sir Arthur Wellesley, afterwards the Duke of Wellington, was in command. The first important battle was that of Roleia on 17th August, followed by the battle of VIMIERA, both fought in the south of Portugal, and resulting in British victories. In these battles the Gloucestershire Regt. had no part.

After these two defeats the French Commander, Junot, opened negotiations, with the result that the French agreed to withdraw from Portugal and Sir Arthur Wellesley returned to England.

This did not mean that the war was at an end, but merely that operations would be confined to Spain, and, on Sir Arthur Wellesley going home, Sir John Moore was appointed Commander-in-Chief.

On assuming command he was informed that a force of 10,000 men under Sir David Baird was being sent from England to land at Corunna in the north of Spain to co-operate with him and to act in conjunction with the Spanish Armies.

At this stage Sir John Moore was at Lisbon and he eventually decided to join Sir David Baird near Valladolid with a view to forcing the French north.

Sir John moved by two roads, part of his force marching south of the Tagus under Sir John Hope and part under himself to the north of that river.

While these plans were in progress the whole situation changed and Napoleon himself took the field at the head of 200,000 men. Sir John Moore and Sir David met at Mayorga, and feeling unable successfully to resist this large force, Moore decided to retreat to Corunna, his scheme being to embark his force there and proceed thence to the South of Spain by sea and begin hostilities afresh.

The retreat to Corunna, undertaken in the winter of 1808-1809, was accomplished under the utmost difficulties.

In the worst of weather and with an overwhelming force at its heels the British force gradually withdrew to the sea. The actual battle of CORUNNA took place on the 16th of January, 1809.

In this the 28th Foot formed part of General Paget's Division, the total Force under Sir John Moore being about 30,000 men.

Corunna can scarcely be described as a victory, but it was a great military operation which enabled the British Army to embark whilst harassed by a greatly superior force under the French Marshal Soult.

The gallant Commander-in-Chief, Sir John Moore, was killed during the battle.

The second phase of the Peninsular War began in the spring of 1809, Sir Arthur Wellesley being again in command.

After fighting at Talavera in Spain, Lord Wellington as he then became, fell back to Busaco in Portugal, and subsequently to that battle he withdrew to the south of that country and entrenched himself behind the lines of Torres Vedras. These consisted of three lines of earthworks nearly 30 miles long, from the heights of Lisbon between the Tagus and the sea.

It was here that Wellington held up the French under General Massena.

In the spring of 1811 Massena decided on a retreat. This was the beginning of the movement which led finally to the French being driven out of Spain and the War finished in 1814.

At the battle of TALAVERA fought in Spain in 1809, and referred to above, the 61st Foot under Colonel Saunders formed part of General Hill's Division.

In this engagement the British, under Lord Wellington, had about 20,000 men. The losses on both sides were heavy. The British casualties amounted to 4,000 and the French to over 7,000. Both sides claimed a victory.

Marshal Victor, the French Commander-in-Chief, was created Duke of Talavera by King Joseph, and Sir Arthur Wellesley was created Lord Wellington of Talavera.

After the battle Lord Wellington, feeling his strength was insufficient, retired to Portugal to reorganize the Portuguese and Spanish Armies.

In 1810 Napoleon had an army of 30,000 in Spain, and on the 27th of September of that year Marshal Massena attacked Lord Wellington at the ridge of BUSACO.

This engagement, in which both the 28th and 61st Foot took part, resulted in a victory for the British.

After the Battle of Busaco, Wellington despatched a Division under General Graham to support the garrison at Cadiz.

This force included the 28th Foot under Colonel Belson and on the 14th March, 1811, the Battle of BARROSA was fought. The forces in this case were unequal, the British having some 4,000 men against 8,000 French, but victory was distinctly on the British side.

As explained previously, Wellington had retired to the line of fortifications at Torres Vedras and it was not until the French withdrew in March, 1811, that active operations were resumed. As the French went north, Wellington followed up and at the Battle of ALBUHERA, under General Beresford, the 28th Foot took part. In this big engagement General Beresford had a force of 32,000 men, about three-fourths of whom were Portuguese, the remainder being British. A victory resulted, but with heavy losses on both sides.

The next Battle in which the Regiment figured was that of SALAMANCA, 1812, an engagement of first-class importance which had far reaching effects on the Campaign.

About 42,000 men were engaged on each side. In the fight for Arapiles Hill, the 61st Foot greatly distinguished itself.

Napier, in his History of the War, writes :—

" The struggle was no slight one : the men of General Hulse's Brigade, which was on the left, went down by hundreds and the 61st and the 11th Regiments won their way desperately and through such a fire as British soldiers only can sustain."

On that day no less than 6 reliefs were shot down in their defence of the Colours of the Regiment.

The winning of this Battle enabled Lord Wellington to enter Madrid, the capital of Spain, on the 12th August, 1812.

E. S. SINNOTT,
Lt.-Colonel R.E. (T.F.)

(To be continued.)

NEW YEAR, 1917.

The winter night was ghostly—quiet and strange and cold,
The trees stood sharply outlined by the moonlight hard and clear
That bathed the dreaming distance with a mist of shining gold,
Stern, in the mystic silence, thus spake the dying year :

Ye nations who have witnessed—and heard the cry go forth
Of smaller peoples helpless 'neath a savage yoke that galls,
Deliverers who have risen strong in your righteous wrath
To save the stricken countries where death's dark shadow falls ;

Ye know the desolation that with purpose fully weighed
The hands of the invader in relentless fury wreak,
Ye have heard his conquering armies, in their deadly might arrayed
Claim God Almighty's guidance—of Christ they dare not speak.

To-night my course is ended, dimly the New Year dawns
Firing to fresh endeavour, to the work that must be wrought,
Hearken and heed, O nations ! Solemn the past voice warns ;
Blest may be and fruitful the lessons the old Year taught.

Your standard hold up higher on Right and Freedom's field
Until the foe's last stronghold is levelled to earth and dust,
Till broken besid≥ their honour lies the sullied sword they wield,
Till ye have fought and conquered—and kept your sacred trust.

M. L. G.

NEW YEAR HONOURS.

The Military Cross.

Captain (Temp. Major) L. G. Parkinson.
Captain L. R. C. Sumner.

The Distinguished Conduct Medal.

238 a/C.Q.M.S. J. H. Huxford.

Mentioned in Despatches.

Major (Temp. Lieut.-Colonel) A. B. Skinner.
Captain (Temp. Lieut.-Colonel) G. F. Collett.
Captain R. J. C. Little.
Lieut. F. K. Foster.
2742 Sergeant A. H. Wintle.
3399 Private C. H. Bird (Killed in Action).

THE BATTLE OF THE SOMME.

A Cross has been placed by the side of the trench which was captured on the evening of Sunday, August 27th. It bears the following inscription :—

—IN LOVING MEMORY OF—

Lieut. C. W. Winterbotham.
Lieut L. W. Moore.
Sec. Lieut. A. L. Apperly.
3399   Pte. C. H. Bird.
3324   Pte. S. Smith.
4922   Pte. L. T. Aylesbury.
28669   Pte. D. Walters.
2781   Pte. G. Hayden.
4270   Pte. C. Stephenson.

Missing.

2nd Lieut. C. Brien.
4933   Pte. W. Pardy.
5115   Pte. J. Finch.
2131   Pte. E. L. Keen.
4105   Pte. T. Brown.
4412   Pte. E. King.

" Officers and men of the ————
Regiment who fell near this spot at the capture of this trench on August 27th, 1916."

We hope to erect similar crosses to the memory of those who fell on or about July 23rd and August 16th.

THE BUTCHER.
A MEMORY OF ENGLAND.

1.

" Any complaints ? " I asked hopefully as I entered the Billet to inspect dinners.

Apparently there was a complaint.

" One at a time ! " I shouted on my top G.

The musical intonation had the desired effect, and there was immediately a stony silence.

I pointed to one man who had a small pale growth on his upper lip and was not looking quite so ferocious as the remainder.

" Well, what's the m-matter ? " I asked—I always stutter on m's.

For reply he pushed his plate under my nose.

" That, sir ! "

I surveyed the plate for some while, trying to recall whether it was beef or mutton night. Finally I gave it up.

" It looks all right," I said.

" Ah, sir, looks ain't everything."

I could not deny this. I waited a moment.

" It's the feel, sir. It breaks one's heart. It's so tough."

I knew what I was expected to do, but instinctively I put it off.

" Ah, perhaps it's the knives," I said, still cheerful.

" Perhaps it is and perhaps it isn't. You try and bite it, sir." he said confidentially.

There was no hope of further respite, so I opened my mouth and prepared for the shock.

" It's splendid," I said a few moments later, as I vainly endeavoured to rid myself of the taste of chewed string.

Even that didn't satisfy the men.

" Oh, very well," I said, " I'll speak to the Quartermaster, but I m-must say I can't see anything wrong with it. It's as tender as a piece of sponge—something stuck to my throat—cake," I added. " I'd thoroughly enjoy it any day myself."

2.

" Really, my dear, the m-meat seems to be getting worse and worse lately," I said to my wife a few nights later, as I fiercely grappled my way with a piece of mutton.

" I can't understand that," she replied. " The butcher's wife tells me that she's always most careful to cut off meat that she knows you'll like."

" In spite of which," I said, " it's rotten ! "

Three days later the matter reached a crisis—that is to say, I lost my temper.

" Isn't there another b-bally butcher in the village ? " I asked.

" No," replied my wife, " Binx Brothers are the only ones."

" Very well," I replied firmly, " To-morrow afternoon we are off parade. I will go and see Mr. B-binx myself."

3.

I had made it up with my wife before we set out the following afternoon.

" After all, perhaps you'd better do the talking. You're best at it," I had said, and although she looked overflowing with indignation, my wife had not replied.

" Good afternoon, Mrs. Paunceston," said the butcher's wife cheerfully as we entered.

" Good afternoon, Mrs. Binx, " replied my wife. " I've called about the meat."

" I'll just ask my husband to step up," chirped in Mrs. Binx. " He's home on leave this afternoon "

Whilst he was being fetched, I suddenly had a transparent flash of memory (a bad habit engendered at the cinema).

" It doesn't m-matter," I said to Mrs. Binx. " Another time will do. Let's get on," I said, turning to my wife.

" Certainly not," she replied. " Why ? "

" Oh, you see I m-m-m--- "

My monosyllabic monologue was cut short by the entrance of Private Binx.

" Yes, sir ? " he said, saluting me smartly, and noticing that he had shaved off his pale moustache, I wondered why I ever thought Private Binx had a tame countenance.

" Oh, Mr. Binx," said my wife—the irony of that civilian title !—" My husband has been complaining about the meat lately. On one or two occasions it's been quite uneatable."

" Oh, but M'm, that's impossible ! " protested Private Binx.

" Impossible ? But why ? " asked my wife.

" Because, Madam," replied Private Binx—and here I pause to remark that Private Binx became Unpaid Lance-Corporal Binx the following day— " Because, Madam, Mr. Paunceston himself told me that that meat was as tender as sponge cake, and that he thoroughly enjoyed it every day. It was meat for the million ! "

A. A. A.

THE YULE LOG.

Captain———once looked out
In comfort at Headquarters,
Where the slush lay round about,
A waste of muddy waters.
Dully shone the moon that night
And the cold was cruel,
When a private came in sight
Gathering winter fuel.

" Hither clerk, and come to me
If thou knows't it, tell it,
Yonder Private, who is he
And where's his Regiment dwelling.'
" Sire, he lives beyond our view
Somewhere near the trenches,
A Country quite unknown to you
And full of noisesome stenches "—

" Bring my hat and bring my stick,
Bring my note book hither,
You and I will damn him quick
And we'll send him thither."
Guide and Captain forth they went,
The former roused from slumber,
The latter, stern, on vengeance bent
To take his name and number.'

" Have you chits for cutting wood ? "
" Have you my permission ? '
The private at attention stood
In soldierly position ;
" Sire, I fear I had no leave
To gather in this timber,
No supply did I receive
From my Regiment's limber."

To Headquarters back he trod
Where the fires were burning,
Heat was in the very sod
As he was returning.
Therefore, soldiers now beware,
Approaching. . . . . .
Always take the greatest care
To use red tape's precision.

G. H. P. S.

"THE GAZETTE."

The Business Manager thanks very much those readers of the GAZETTE who have been kind enough to renew their subscriptions. As something like a minimum loss of from £4 to £5 is involved in the publication of each number, these donations have been very acceptable. The GAZETTE will continue to be sold at 3d. a copy, as formerly. Both the Christmas Numbers of 1915 and 1916 were sold at 5d., in an endeavour to meet the cost of a double Number.

Contributions (cash or copy) are always welcome, cash by the Business Manager, copy by the Editor. Please send all that you have of either or both to the Business Manager or the Editor,

c/o The Orderly Room.

The accounts may be inspected at any time.

GOING HOME.

I'm goin' 'ome to Blighty—ain't I glad to 'ave the chance !
I'm loaded up wiv fightin', and I've 'ad my fill o' France ;
I'm feelin so excited-like, I want to sing and dance,
For I'm goin' 'ome to Blighty in the mawnin'.

I'm goin' 'ome to Blighty ; can you wonder as I'm gay ?
I've got a wound I wouldn't sell for 'alf a year o' pay ;
An arm that's mashed to jelly in the nicest sort o' way,
For it takes me 'ome to Blighty in the mawnin'.

'Ow everlasting keen I was on gettin' to the front !
I'd ginger for a dozen, and I 'elped to bear the brunt
But Cheese and Crust ! I'm crazy, now I've done me little stunt,
To sniff the air o' Blighty in the mawnin :

I've looked upon the wine that's white, and on the wine
        that's red ;
I've looked on cyder flowin, till it fairly turned me 'ead ;
But oh ! The finest scoff will be, when all is done and said,
A pint o' Bass in Blighty in the mawnin' !

I'm goin' back to Blighty, which I left to strafe the Un ;
I've fought in bloody battles, and I've 'ad a 'eap of fun ;
But now me flipper's busted, and I fink me dooty's done,
And I'll kiss me gel in Blighty in the mawnin.'

Oh, there be furrin lands to see, and some of 'em be fine ;
And there be furrin gels to kiss, and scented furrin' wine ;
But there's no land like England, and no other gel like mine
Thank Gawd for dear old Blighty in the mawnin' !

From *Rhymes of a Red Cross man.*

by R. W. SERVICE

FROM THE PRESS.

From *Land and Water*, Nov. 16th, 1916.

" At the moment of writing this, there is no confirmation of the holding of the ruins of Serre, the little hamlet IN THE DIP. North West of Beaumont."

Hilary Billhook, of course. For German O.P's are situated on Serre, which is a " place with wide prospect.

A recruit for the Grenadier Guards.

Mr.......of Thornbury......has joined the Army. He has been drafted into the Grenadier Guards. Possessing fine physique and a knowledge of military matters acquired in the Thornbury Platoon of the Volunteer Training Corps, he should have a successful military career."

The Dursley Gazette, Dec. 23rd, 1916.

The Guards will have to look to their laurels.

" *Nothing but the Smell.*"

The editor of the " Haller Volksblatt " has had a tragic experience in his search for a substitute for the unattainable cheese :—

" Of endless variety are the products which are being offered to the people and much belauded as satisfying food substitutes. Most of these have been discovered to be mere frauds.

One of the latest of these " substitutes " was recently purchased by us in a shop in the Brunner-strasse. It was a square-shaped packet labelled " Finest Liptauer Cheese."

On returning home and opening the packet, we found yet another cardboard receptacle, which was filled with a powdery substance that emitted a truly frightful odour. We further discovered a printed slip of paper giving directions for the preparation of the " finest Liptauer cheese." According to these from two to three boiled potatoes were to be mashed up together with the powder with the addition of six tablespoonfuls of water. A delicate flavour would then be produced, which would be further enhanced by the addition of a grated onion.

In this way then, on the payment of sixpence, we obtain the Liptauer cheese—that is to say, not the actual article but its stench at all events."

Daily Express, January 26th.

A PALINODE.

In years gone by I did not welcome Spring,
        I felt no rapture when the March winds blew
        And Daylight lengthened ; nor could even you,
Snowdrop, redeem the February's sting.
I loved the woods and hedges rioting
        With fruit and foliage of every hue
        In Autumn, and the gold sun shining through
Soft veils of mist on gorse and purple ling.
Then Hope was bold and Youth extravagant,
        Spring's promise was forgot when Autumn gave.
        But now I live from day to day, and hoard
That promise, through the long night vigilant,
        Of early dawns, warm suns, life from the grave
        To flowers and trees and beasts and men restored.

C. S. N.

THINGS WE WANT TO KNOW.

Who tried to clean his rifle with Worcestershire Sauce?

Who lost the leg of mutton, the fish and the box of tomatoes in A...? Who is really the ——est fool in the Division ?

Who lost THE Divisional fur-coat ? Why did he bring a motheaten one in the place of it ?

Who tried to remove his Stores from A——T ? And why ?

How many bottles of Brandy did the M.O. say were either destroyed by shell fire or blown up by mines ?

Which Battalion had adopted the pass word of " Chin, Chin " ? Is the usual reply " Cheer O " ?

Who is the Officer at H.Q. who booked his bed by telephone ?

Is it true that Stretcher bearer Meer has been awarded a Commission (vide Intelligence Report, December 21st) as a reward for good work done ?

How, when, why and where did a certain M. O. realise that the Emperor of Austria was dead?

Who is the wag who chalked the following famous words on a Huge Dud, "Too proud to Fight"?

Who is the sergeant who thought that Pineapples grew like Potatoes?

Did a certain C. Q. M. S. receive a Maconnachie by post from England?

How long did it take a certain M. G. Company to find out that it had an artificer in its ranks?

How many old Terrier "Gunners" have been called "Belton Parkers."

Which unit in this Division has been turned into a charitable and philanthropic institution, through which men, who cannot obtain leave in their own units, get it on attachment to the aforesaid unit?

Where did Le Petit Duc and the young Pretender go? Did they go home by any chance?

What did the Major do with his watch?

Who is the very dashing, young, and famous Lieutenant-Colonel who aspires to be "The Tank King"?

Have the efforts of a certain Battalion to turn "Scotch Redoubt" into a second Ritz, signally failed?

Who is the Distinguished Officer who is known as the "Brazier Prince."

Who had the first special train on the Light Railway? Is it true that it swept past V-LL-Station so quickly that Inspector L-g-n was unable to examine the tickets?

What was the first thing that fell out of the German Sergeant-Major's Pocket Book? And what did Lt.-Colonel D——son, D.S.O. say?

Who is the gallant R. A. M. C. Officer who salved a Bosch First Field Dressing at O......and sent it home to his wife as a souvenir? What was it really?

Who was the star turn on Christmas night?

What was the wording on the sign post confronted by an officer when emerging from a Cul-de-Sac?

Who is the Officer who scraped the mud off the Duck-pie with an entrenching tool?

Is the Padre's horse pulling a cab in A——? Does its driver wear a fur-coat?

Since when has the guard presented arms when turned out by the Orderly Officer?

Why did they hoard up all the Whisky at the Base during Christmas?

Who SEES the Bolts click when the Transport "port arms" for inspection?

Who is the Officer who does not know the difference between sherry and port? Is he Scotch? Is he at H.Q. Mess?

Who tried to throw away his cigar? Did he try to get rid of it in the fire? Is he at H.Q. Mess? Was it the Padre?

Who were the two Officers seen at A...... 3 days after their leave started?

Who is the Major who is trying to get for his Company as big a staff in his Orderly Room as is usual in a Battalion?

Who is the dashing young Company Commander who was given the "go by" at Havre?

Who is known as the Cocoa King?

Why did the Senior T. M. B. Officer spend such a long time at Havre while returning from Leave?

Who are the M. G. Officers who got shelled out of...... Camp? Is it true they did not stop till they got to Pioneer Camp?

Who is the most prominent Lance-Corporal in the Third line?

Has the order re "Wastage of Paper" reached the Third line yet?

Who is the Field Officer in the Third line who should have his crown on the top of his head?

What Church in Aberdeen uses a pitchfor-r-rk to give the note?

Who is the Staff Officer who paraded for Corps Commander's Inspection minus Sam Browne Belt, plus gum boots, thigh? Did he suck a straw?

What became of the bedroom slippers? Did they belong to an Officer in "C" Company? Did his glasses help him to find them?

Who is the distinguished Captain at Cheltenham who was ordered off Parade for wearing Field Boots?

What L/Corporal in No. 1 platoon belongs to the Ancient Order of Ye Olde Hairdressers? And who was it who said he wished to amalgamate with—in the business? Is it "Pull" or "No Pull."

Did he also undertake the agency for Raphael Tuck's silk Xmas cards for the Somme District?

Who picked out the best dug-out in B...... Wood, which collapsed a day later?

Is it anything to do with "Della"?

Which Sergeant in A Company issues out the rum in sips at intervals.?

What Private in A Company had the "Christian Herald" sent him with a "London Life" enclosed?

Which Private answers to the name of "Smoke"?

Who is the Private in the Transport who always has a tin of biscuits at his side?

Why should Blue or Red armlets be considered

Who is the Officer that was so fed up that he returned a day too soon from Leave ?

Who was the Officer in charge of a bathing party who blandly enquired of a fellow, who had just drawn a bucket of water from a well, if it was HOT ? Is he in " D " Company ?

Who is the Guide that is gloating over a few dilapidated franc notes that Madame refuses to accept ?

Who was responsible for the gassing of the Headquarter Staff one night ? Has he had previous experience at Loos ?

Which Detention Barracks in England grants weekend leave to its Conscientious Objectors ?

Who is the Leave King ?

Who is the Officer who puts salt in his Coffee ? Is he in " C " Company ? And did a " B " Company Officer follow his example ?

Who is the Battalion " Bairnsfather " ? Is he a Private in " C " Company ? When the General asked him where the Germans were, did he vouchsafe the remark " Bill, he wants to know where the Germans are " ?

Is the Sergeants Band proposing to give a series of popular Concerts ? What does O. C. Cymbals think about it ?

Who is the Company Commander who gives " Right about Turn," in spite of having been at an Army School ?

Who found a hot brick in his bed at H......l ?

Who was the Corporal who gave the order " To unfire " ? Is he in B Coy. ?

Which Battalion in the Brigade knows the way from C...Y to H......T ?

Who was the C. S. M. (single) who evinced reluctance to resume his seat in the audience during the Battalion Concert in the Palm House ? Was he afraid of his French ? Isn't it V. G. (very good) ?

Who is the Sergeant who propped and got eleven tricks Solo ?

Who is the C. Q. M. S. who said the most expensive Beer in France was Champagne ?

Was the Sergeants Mess satisfied with the Pork the C. Q. M. Ss'. (3) bought ? Could they explain why some was issued raw ?

Who thought he was skating on the pond after the Boxing ?

How many years does it take the Provost Sergeant to get through his repertoire of songs ?

Is Moreton-in-Marsh really the busiest place in Gloucestershire ? Have you perforce to follow the stream of traffic right through the village before you can turn ?

Is it true that you can turn a Warship in the Basin at Stroud ?

Who is the C. Q. M. S. who cried when they took his drum away ?

Who is the C. Q. M. S. who is jealous over the cymbals ?

Did not Mr. Rubinstein have the last and therefore the best laugh at the Battalion Concert ?

Were the Company Commanders tired after their stroll with the C. O. ?

Who is the Sergeant who is not tall enough to go bird nesting without a ladder ? Does he prefer digging worms for his Brother to go fishing ?

Is it true that a certain O. R. Sergeant has not taken advantage of the Q.M's. absence on leave ?

What size is a Lewis gun shell ?

Who said " the rifles made a funny noise this morning, because the men are shooting with their Gas helmets on ? "

Who is the Sergeant who made so many journeys to H......T to borrow music for the Concert

Who is now called PERCY ? And why ?

Who were the two Officers who marked time outside a door in the Chateau ?

What reward did they receive ?

Who were the two Officers who found it necessary to spend from 3 p.m. to 9 p.m. arranging the Concert in the Chateau ?

Who was the keen " flag-wagger " who slumbered one night in an orchard (near the training ground) in undress uniform, in order to affect a " slashing turn-out " the following morning on Field operations ? Did an inquisitive French dog wake him at 3 a.m. ?

Who is the Officer who had a small parcel of firewood sent him by post ?

Who is the man who has a " half-petrified " (hypertrophied) heart ? Does he find it cold this weather ?

Is it true that a gallant Major (R.F.A.) has the thrush?

Who were the two officers in the ———— who could not find the Fifth ? Are they in " B " Company ?

PICARDY PARODIES.

No. I.

(W. B. Y---TS.)

I will arise and go now to Picardy
 And a new trench line hold there, of clay and shell-holes made
No dug-outs shall I have there, nor a hive for the Lewis G,
 But live on top in the b. loud glade.

And I may cease to be there, for peace comes dropping slow,
 Dropping from the mouth of the Minnie to where the sentry sings,
There noon is high explosive, and night a gunfire glow,
 And evening full of torpedoes' wings.

I will arise and go now, though always night and day
 I'll feel dark waters lapping with low sounds by the store,
Where all our bombs grow rusty and countless S. A. A. ;
 I'll feel it in my trench feet sore.

No. II.

(To the tune of "They wouldn't believe me.")

Got the cutest little trench
With the acutest little stench,
Where yer've gotter stand and freeze,
Up in water to your knees,
And in there's rats beyond belief
Growing fat on bully beef,
Oh it certainly seems fine
Just to think you're in the line !

But when I tell them how sick of it I am,
    They'll never relieve me, they'll never relieve me :
My clothes, my boots, my face, my hair
    Are in a state beyond repair,
I'm the dirtiest thing that one could see,
But when I tell them, and I'm certainly going to tell them,
    That this is not what I came out to do,
They'll never relieve me, they'll never relieve me.
But leave me here until the moon turns blue.

Got the cutest little trench,
Which we undertook to wrench
From the Alleyman one day,
When the dawn was turning grey ;
And we gave those Bosches hell,
So that they turned grey as well ;
We were rather rough, I fear,
From Orvillers to Poseer.

For when they told us they wanted to give in,
    They couldn't deceive us, they couldn't deceive us,
And so with bombs and bayonits
We made an end of poor old Fritz,
    Twas the bloodiest day that one could see.
For when they told us, and they certainly tried to tell us,
    That they'd surrender if we would desist :
We wouldn't believe them, we wouldn't believe them,
But wiped them off the German Army List.
                     W. O. D.

OUR BENEFACTORS.

The Dickens Fellowship, Gloucester
                     Volumes of Dickens.
Lieut.-Colonel Winterbotham.   Papers.
Colonel Marling.   ,,
Bishop Frodsham.   ,,
The Hon. Mabel Gye.   ,,
Mr. Harley Butt.   Cigarettes.
Mr. Jack Margetson.   ,,
Mr. Nissen.   A dry Christmas.
Colonel Griffith.   Cigarettes and Papers.
Mr. W. R. Voller.   Papers.
The Powers that be.   No fatigue on Christmas Day.
Pte. Fisher.   Cocoa.
Miss Parr.   Papers.
Pte. Wood.   Typing.
Miss Karn.   Papers.
Camps Library.   Books.
Mrs. Temple Cooke.   Papers.
The Brigadier.   Brigade Library.
Mrs. Russell Kerr.   Papers.
The Countess Bathurst.   Socks.
Ladies of Gloucester, per Mrs. J. H. Collett,
        Shoulder badges and cook's suits.
" The Echo."   " Echos."
" Daily Express "   Footballs and mouth-organs.

THE LEAVE TRAIN.

In a recent issue we offered prizes for the best account of a journey in a Leave Train. We have now pleasure in announcing the results :

1st Prize (10 days leave) goes to Cpl. A. DOZER, A. S. C., Havre.

2nd Prize (1s. a day for Duration of War) is awarded to Pte .E. DUZIT, 1/5th Glo'ster, B.E.F. Handsome tins of bully-beef have been forwarded to the other competitors (full list of names to be seen at any time in the Orderly Room).

We congratulate Cpl. Dozer on his success, and trust for the sake of Pte. Duzit that the War will continue indefinitely. Below are the winning efforts.

Corpl. Dozer : " As I am at Harve, I ain't never been on no——Leave Train, thank Gawd ! "

Pte. Duzit has written his in the form of a diary, which is as follows :—

" 1st Day. Intermittent shelling in the restaurant car. Quiet along the rest of the train. Rubbed feet with whale oil.

2nd Day. Leaving restaurant car behind we moved K.P.—K.P.4, and proceeded at a steady pace for 200 yards. Am already feeling the restful effects of getting away from the line.

3rd Day. Some excitement caused by assuming with a jerk a speed of 4 m.p.h. without warning. All good effects of yesterday's rest nullified by the sudden shock. Find I am nearer the line than ever and that it is very badly laid.

4th Day. Reached a station with a glass roof.

5th Day. Towards evening time the engine driver forgot to milk the cow that clears the line in front of us. On descending there was general demoralisation on finding that the cow was out of sight ahead. Spent the night trying to find cow, but search was of no avail.

6th Day. Indented for a new cow.

7th—16th Day. Nothing doing. Rubbed feet with whale oil.

17th Day. New cow arrived. Started off again but found that the cow was a bull. A consultation followed and there was finally a decision to send out an escort of 1 N.C.O. and 10 men to clear the line in front of the engine.

18th Day. Wind up amongst some Bosch prisoners that we passed working in the line. They thought we were a tank.

19th Day. Reached a Y.M.C.A. Hut and saw the first English girl that I had set eyes on for 12 months. God bless 'er. Am beginning to weaken from strain of the last 10 days. Rubbed feet with whale oil to revive myself.

20th Day. Passed a station without stopping. Shock fearful. Rubbed feet with whale oil.

21st Day. Gramaphone in the next carriage plays " The perfect day."

22nd Day. Returned to the Station we forgot to stop at.

23rd Day. Reached Harve. Carried to Hospital with trench feet and sent to Base to await return to unit.

24th Day. Returned to unit and received 14 days F. P. for overstaying leave.

                " FIBULOUS."

WAITING.

Her part is done in the worker's day,
    She stands at the cottage door,
She watches the deepening shadows play
    And thinks of the days of yore.

She sees the face that she loves so well,
    Joyous and strong and bright :
She dreams, fast held by the woven spell,
    In the hush of the falling night.

She hears the step she has heard so oft—
    Through the fancy that longing weaves—
In the sighing kiss of the west wind soft
    And the swish of the swaying leaves.

She smiles, as the vision clear draws nigh
    Of love in the dear home nest,
The haven where peace at last may be.
    In the heart of a world at rest.

MUSIC.

A successful concert, organised very skilfully by Lieutenant Lister and C. Q. M. S. Wilce, was held in the Palm House of the Chateau at—— on January 24th.

Owing to the war, evening dress was not worn.

Whilst the vast crowds were filing into the stalls, the band under the baton of Band-Sergt. Proctor, discoursed sweet music. It was very kind indeed of Colonel Holden to come so many miles and amuse us with his Banjo.

Pte. Gray's topical song was very well received. Pte. Pittaway's conjuring skill was reminiscent of Maskelyne and Devant in their palmy days. The broad humour of the Provost-Sergeant was unmistakeable and was at once recognised by those who from time to time have had the good fortune to serve under him. Lance-Corporal Pringle told excellent tales in dialect, and the Quartette were a welcome and successful innovation. Drummer Farmer amused us with " Cheap-Deep-Sea-Trips-on-Ships." Pte. Avlemore sang that fine song " The Trumpeter " with expression and Sergt. Proctor will never cease to charm us with " The Long Trail." The stage management under Sergt. Davis was excellent.

PROGRAMME.

PART I.

Band

Pte. Rodway	...	... Song.
Pte. Gray	...	... Comic Song
L/Corpl. Warbutton	...	Recitation
Quartette ...	...	... C. S. M. Finch, Sergt Fry, Pte. Aylemore and Pte. Rodway.
Pte. Walby	...	... Song
Lieut. Cornish	...	... Comic Song
Pte. Pittaway.	...	... Conjuring
Lt.-Colonel Holden	...	Song
C. S. M. Finch	...	... Song
Sergt. Richards	...	... Comic Song

PART II.

Corpl. Pringle	...	... Song
Pte. Pritchard	...	... Comic Song
Sergt. Wyatt	...	... Song
Pte. Aylemore	...	... Comic Song
Sergt. Proctor	...	... Song
Lt.-Colonel Holden	...	Song
Sergt. Wonson	...	... Song
Quartette ...	...	... Sergt. Fry, Sergt. Wonson, Corpl. Pringle and Pte. Aylemore.
Corpl. Shellard	...	... Comic Song
Sergt. Fry	...	... Song
Drummer Farmer	...	... Comic Song

Band

GOD SAVE THE KING.

ON SENTRY.

The West has gathered day's last lingering ray,
The dreaming earth is wrapt in garment grey,
The sentinel his post of vigil keeps
While dismal through the dusk the gathering darkness creeps
With dreary sense of quiet and cold—and quaint
And shadowy—growing outlines, dim and faint.
No more the spirit, raised to utmost height,
And glad, goes forth to battle in the light,
But lonely, silent, by night's gloom oppressed,
Is called to guard o'er comrades' hard-won rest,
Each nerve, to catch the distant sound, tense-strained.
What visions on a sudden rose, then waned,
Then filled afresh the darkness with their gleam,
Elusive, real, and mocking as a dream ?
What scene of home before the watcher's eyes
Vivid as truth, one lightning moment lies,
Then changes swiftly, leaving, half confessed,
A clutching fear and longing, nameless, in his breast ?
And bracing every sense, alert and keen
For treacherous approach of foes unseen,
Stands out the path of victory through the fray
And o'er the gloom the coming glory of the day.

M. L. G.

CHRISTMAS WITH THE SIGNALS.

Christmas morning blossomed forth very promisingly, minus the snow so conspicuous on Xmas cards.

The activity commenced somewhere near dinner time when the boys—after decorating the interior of the hut with branches of fir-trees retrieved from a neighbouring wood, and fancy paper festoons from Blighty, set to and fixed up an improvised table with forms to match.

At 1-45 the gas gong sounded announcing " dinner up."

A gorgeous spread, supplemented by a ration of goose and Brussels sprouts provided by the Battalion funds, was presided over by Sergeant F. W. Reeves, who assumed the temporary rank of Chairman.

Without exception, the Signal Section " tucked in," so to speak.

The dinner was such as one conjures up in one's mind when partaking of pressed beef and " Pat-a-Cakes " in a sodden dug-out.

Pte. Whittingham was O. C. Records at the Section Gramaphone (this instrument not being a conscript by any means) which gave off the sweet music of the Bards, interspersed with dreamy waltzes.

Superior cigarettes and cigars were in abundance, thanks to the good work of the organizers, Pte. Biles and Co.

Evening came in due course. A light tea was partaken of out of consideration for the rather exceptional dinner.

The much-looked-forward-to entertainment commenced with a speech by the Chairman (Sergt. Reeves) anent the successful work of the Section during the Campaign.

Corpl. Hopkins proposed the Toast of " The King," which was reverently drunk.

The vocal efforts of the following were greatly appreciated—Pte. Wittingham (song) " The Long Trail," L/c. Burton (song), " The Mountains o' Mourne," Pte. Powell (song), " Kentucky," L/c. Shaw (comic song), " I put on my Coat and went home." At this juncture C. S. M. Finch put in an appearance and obliged with the song " When you came down the Vale."

Pte. Tuck (an ex-Member of the Section) burst forth joyously with his star song " Poppies," followed by a song by Pte. Wood, " Lighterman Tom."

At different intervals the following Toasts were drunk and responded to—" The Battalion," " Our Visitors," " Absent Friends " and " Those at Home ;" the response to the last named by Pte. Biles was very appropriate.

Pte. Saunders rose, at a given signal (not a miscellaneous one) from the Chairman and volunteered a rendering of " The Death of Caesar " from Shakespeare. The first two lines went well but then a misfire occurred through the promptings of well-meaning friends, who led him on to state that Cæsar lay dead before him in a shell-hole, this statement causing excessive laughter.

After a short absence from the festive board, L/c. T. Shaw re-appeared in a strange garb, featuring " Flora Finch " of Vitagraph Cinema fame, and amused the Company with his delightful patter appertaining to pre-war incidents, chief of them being " How the gallant crew of the good ship ' Bread Poultice ' were saved off Barking Creek.

The programme continued with a song by Pte. Clements, " Flanagan's Band "—by far the most popular song of the evening. Pte. Tonkin (song) " Sprinkle me with kisses," Pte. Rodway (song) " Until," L/c. Shaw (comic song) " A minute to Seven last Night," Cpl. Hopkins (recitation from Kipling) contributed greatly to the enjoyment of the evening.

The time came all too soon to lay the waterproof sheet down and extinguish the light that was dazzling the Provost-Sergeant,s eyes.

Taking everything into consideration, Christmas Day, 1916,will be counted amongst one of the happiest Christmasses ever spent.

W. J. W.

NURSERY RHYMES.

(A long way in front of those that have been appearing in " Punch")

1. M-RT-NP-SH.

> Martin Luther was a Hun
>   Many years ago.
> Martin was a pushful man
>   Many years ago.
>
> Martin's great great grandsons,
>   Tried to do the same,
> But the French and English,
>   Spoiled his little game.
>
> Martin pushed, Tommy pushed,
>   Poilu lent his weight—
> Martin's in another street,
>   Singing songs of hate.

2. A.........T.

> Albert was a good King,
>   Albert was a brave ;
> And his firm " No thank you "
>   Made the Bosches rave.
>
> And the town of Albert
>   Was as brave as he,
> Smashed and bashed it still
>   Repelled the enemy
>
> Albert used to suffer
>   Horrid things from Fritz,
> Till Fritz got the push, and
>   Now he seldom hits.

3. SH-LT-R W--D CAMP.

> Tommy in the trenches
>   Was rejoiced to know
> That to Sh-lt-r W—d C-mp,
>   He would shortly go.
>
> Shelter from the weather,
>   Shelter from the Bosch,
> Was a pretty prospect,
>   But it didn't wash.
>
> For the wood called Shelter,
>   Couldn't hide a wren,
> And the camp beside it
>   Was as bad for men.
>
> All the ground was shell-holes,
>   All the tents were wet,
> May the next old Taube
>   Find the place to let !

C. S. N.

WAR WORKERS.

They wear Blue. Not the light caerulean, not the deeper azure that denotes distinction at the more famous Universities, but the subfuse cyanide associated with the Police Force. But this reversion to the type of woad-wearing Briton is not their sole title to fame, for they boast an ancient lineage, being in the direct line of Spencer's hero " Who ever answereth, I do not know."

In the rush and hurry of War it is refreshing to meet such lofty indifference to the trivialities of life. So rarely does a man of thought triumph over the man of action in these modern days, that one's heart is gladdened at the spectacle of an energetic traveller full of banausic enquiries regarding trains, times of departure, hour of arrival, platform and destination, hastening to an R. T. O. who preserves an unruffled mien in face of the most stressful circumstances and who answers blandly to every question— " That I can't say."

Like all the truly great they have their detractors. There are not wanting men who describe them with an adjective which would be more applicable if they were combatant troops or wore not blue but red. Some men actually allege that the R.T.O. is to be found neither at his Office nor on the Station, and that the most highly trained Battalion scout has not a greater knack of invisibility.

Fine old world Gentlemen ! They alone have survived and derided the modern craze for specialisation. When every other Officer has had some form of training, they alone seem to be chosen for two qualifications :—Smattering of the French tongue, and a mind entirely untainted and unclouded by previous experience of Railway work.

Travelling in England will never be the same as in France. There will be no day-long waits for trains ; no hazardous leap into a truck going to an unknown destination ; no hungry application for bully beef in the Station canteen ; no adventurous uncertainty that makes a journey in France a very anabasis ; but instead, the vile sins of modernism, speed courtesy, efficiency.

G. H.

LAURELS.

> They stand for fame, for honour and renown ;
> Before prosperity and riches sought,
> By deeds of valour, skill and greatness wrought,
> Above life's changing cares and Fortune's frown.
>
> Yet not the wreathing laurels make the crown
> But the fair deed they sprang from ; nobly bought,
> They tell of sacrifice and fight well fought :
> Their soul will live through the ages down.
>
> Let them not murmer—they who heard the voice
> Of Duty, answered, firmly stood the test,
> And unrewarded know their work well done,
>
> Who scorning fear, of danger made their choice—
> Because no laurels on their brow may rest.
> What though they be not worn if they were won ?

M. L. G.

INSTRUCTIONS

for use of small box Rat-Traps and general hints as to conduct of rats in the trenches.

Issued by Subaltern Staff, December, 1916, by arrangement with the Cat N.C.O's.

PRACTICE.

Drill " by numbers " to obtain correct adjustment of the small box rat-trap.

The practice will be carried out twice nightly at 6 p.m. and 9 p.m. and daily during the rat alert period. It will also be carried out alternately with one judging the time, *i.e.*, as quick adjustment as possible. This is the most important adjustment and must be obtained by all ranks—acting or permanent—in SIX SECONDS.

D. R. O. 407. TANKS.

" Derelict Tanks in the Divisional Area are on no account to be tampered with."

I. Thumbs down between the satchel and the body and up with the satchel-flap. Immediately seize the trap with the left hand, whilst with the right hand you answer the telephone.

II. Seize the toasted cheese and thrusting the chin well forward smell it.

III. Take the cheese out of your mouth and place it on the hook then withdraw the fingers quickly.

IV. Grasp the wooden lever and adjust.

V. Place the rat trap opposite the hole as indicated by the tom cat and spring away.

VI. Carry out 2 hours leap-frog drill.

VII. Raise your rifle at full extent of arm, butt downwards, and describe a parabola with it above the head then lower into line with waist and holding it firm, point it in the direction of the rat.

VIII. Pull the trigger.

IX. Stand to again and remove dead rat. Drown it by immersing in water till it ceases to breathe.

X. Spring smartly to attention—toes inwards and legs bent, tail of the rat against the seam of the trousers.

NOTES.

I. Mice will be issued for practice purposes. As however, there is a limited number of these, they should not be removed from existing dug-outs but will be issued by the C.R.E. (Commanding Rat Emplacements.) If an officer fails to turn up within an hour of the appointed time there is a plentiful supply of mice only fit for drowning, to supply all wants if properly organised.

II. Dead rats will be dumped at the R.D. (Rat-Dump) X98.624. One extra leave will be granted for good work to each man who has seen 50 rats.

III. Rats who give themselves up should be removed forthwith under cat escort to Brigade Headquarters and should not be eaten on the way. A ration of milk, however, will be available.

PERSONAL.

The whole Division has sustained a very severe loss in the departure of Lt.-Colonel Smythe Osbourne, D.S.O., to the Headquarters of the — Army. The importance of "A and Q" in this war has again and again been clearly recognized and Colonel Smythe Osbourne did all in his power to mitigate the hardships and increase the comforts of Officers and men alike. Many will gratefully remember his many acts of kindness. There can be few members of the British Staff who have carried out more faithfully or more effectually the order of Sir Charles Munro, namely, that Staff Officers are so placed that they may do their best to help the regimental Officer.

Very many congratulations to Captain Leahy, M.C., on his appointment.

The success of the Christmas dinner was great. It was indeed a veritable triumph for the Quarter-Master; ably piloted by M. Henaud, undaunted by the alarming fact that geese were rising in price a franc a kilo every minute, he collected enough to satisfy the Battalion complete with draft, the unwelcome arrival of which had caused some feelings of dismay in the hearts and minds of the expectant soldiery. The sausages alone came in for criticism

One felt that they might contain "anything," which they probably did. Next year we shall order them direct from England ! ! !

"I see that the Military Cross has been won by Temp. Sec. Lieut. A. H. T. Lewis, Royal Berkshire Regiment. This reminds me of the fine record of the Gloucester Rugby Football Team of 1913-14, of which he was a member. Almost without exception the fifteen joined the Army on the outbreak of War and the roll of honours of this one fifteen is typical of the Rugby game the Kingdom over. Sergeants S. Millard (Forward) and A. Saunders (Forward) and L/c. S. Sysum (three-quarter) have fallen. Lieuts. F. Ayliffe and J. F. Lawson, L/c. S. Smart (England), Corpl. W. Parham, Pte. A. Cook, Pte. W. Dovev (all forwards), Pte. F. Wells (three-quarter) have all been wounded in fairly recent fighting. The Captain of the XV. G. Holford (forward) was severely wounded early in the war and has since been discharged from the Army. Pte. C. Cook (full-back) has spent months in hospital due to the exposure of campaigning. Though not actually wounded, Corporal W. Washbourne (three-quarter) has won the D.C.M. and now Lieut. A. Lewis has gained further honours for a team of which Gloucestershire may well be proud. So far L/Cpl. L. Hamblin (centre three-quarter), who has been through many months of fighting, is the only one of the fifteen to escape injury. It is a grand record on which all will congratulate one of the smartest Town Rugby Football Clubs."

Notes by "Ranger"

The Illustrated Sporting and Dramatic News.

Dec. 23rd, 1916.

(Corporal Washbourne was awarded the Military Medal.)

His many friends throughout the Division were very sorry indeed to say good-bye to the Reverend C. T. B. McNulty, one of the fast dwindling "originals"—he has held a commission since 1910. He came out as a Chaplain to his unit, the Artillery, and had been the Senior Chaplain of the Division since April last.

Major V. N. Johnson—our former Adjutant—was among those mentioned in Despatches.

Very many congratulations to Second Lieut. A. H. T. Lewis on his Military Cross.

Mr. and Mrs. Voller have our sincere sympathy in the loss of their son, Second Lieutenant H. W. Voller, of the Gloucestershire Regiment.

MARRIAGES.

On January 10th, at St. James' Church, Gloucester, by the Rev. J. Martin, Company-Quartermaster-Sergeant J. Meadows, Gloucestershire Regiment, to Ada E. Smith, both of Gloucester.

On January 8th, at St. Mary de Lode Church, Gloucester, by the Rev. W. C. Macklin, 2nd Lieut. Frank Ayliffe, Gloucestershire Regiment, son of Mr. and Mrs. W. G. Ayliffe, Northgate Street, to Phyliss, youngest daughter of Mr. and Mrs. W. C. Mann, The Cross, Gloucester.

On February 6th, at Christ Church, Gloucester, by the Rev. H. M. Braithwaite, Coy.-Sergt.-Major Faville, D.C.M., Gloucestershire Regiment, to Louisa Elliott Moody of Gloucester.

DEATH.

On January 15th, at Olive Dene, 60, Stroud Road, Gloucester, George William Baily, aged 72 years, Captain and Quartermaster of the late 2nd V.B.G.R.

"Deceased had a fine record of 43 years service with the volunteer force and will be remembered by many as a keen and zealous Officer, but a strict disciplinarian withal. He joined the Volunteers on April 3rd, 1862, was gazetted Quartermaster on June 5th, 1886, and Hon. Captain on June 17th, 1892. In July 1882 he was presented by the Officers of the 2nd Gloucestershire Regiment R. V., with a silver cup, "a mark of appreciation of the zeal and energy with which he carried out the duties of his appointment as acting Quartermaster." In November, 1907, he was presented with a purse of money and a clock by the officers of the 2nd V.B.G.R. "upon his retirement after 43 years service in the Volunteer Force. and in grateful appreciation of his work as Quartermaster of the Battalion for 21 years" He also held the Volunteer Decoration for long service. Deceased retired with permission to retain his rank and to wear the uniform."

Gloucester Journal.

A fine record of life-long service in the Volunteers, and one of which any man might well be proud. C.S.M. Baily, his son, has our sincere sympathy in his great loss.

Very many congratulations to Lieut-Colonel J. H. Collett, C.M.G., who has been appointed to the command of a Battalion of the Northamptonshire Regiment.

It was with sincere regret that we heard of the death of the Archdeacon of Gloucester, the Venerable E. C. Scobell. He always took something more than a kindly interest in the Battalion, and came as often as he could to the Week-End Camps in the Summer. On Mobilisation he came to see us off from Gloucester and to wish us well. Nothing used to give him more pleasure than to see a soldier in church at Upton St. Leonards—and those were days when few paid the respect that was due to wearers of the King's Uniform,—and the Territorial Units in Gloucester came from time to time to Parade Services. Soldiers generally, and this Battalion in particular, have lost a very good and faithful friend.

APPOINTMENT.

2892 Pte. (L/c.) Voller, H. W., Appointed Temporary 2nd Lieut. the Gloucestershire Regiment, 18/6/16. (Since killed in action.)

SOLDIERS' SONGS ILLUSTRATED.

"May all your Troubles be Little Ones."

5th Gloucester Gazette.

A Chronicle, serious and humorous, of the Battalion while serving with the
BRITISH EXPEDITIONARY FORCE.

HONORIS CAUSA.

Military Cross.

Lieut. (A/Capt.) E. Conder.
2nd Lieut. F. S. Hill.
2nd Lieut. H. McL. Millar, 7th Bn. H. L. I. (T. F.) attached
    5th Bn. Gloucester Regt.

Distinguished Conduct Medal.

240057   Pte. H. Farmer.

Military Medal.

1139	Sergt. C. F. Harris (since killed in action).
242550	L.-Cpl. C. Hayden.
242289	Pte. F. J. Sessions.
240525	Sergt. H. C. Barnes.
240670	Corpl. W. J. Chandler.
240289	Sergt. A. J. Jackson.
242501	Sergt. G. W. Hobbs.
240153	L/Cpl. E. J. Ryder (since killed in action).
242487	L/Cpl. A. E. Thorne.
240200	Corpl. H. Caudle.
240127	Pte. (L/c.) W. Exell.
202962	Pte. (L/c.) F. Pringle.

PICARDY PARODIES.

III.

T-nn-s-n.

Come into the trenches, Rum,
    For the black bat, night, has flown,
Come into the trenches, Rum,
    I am here in the mud alone ;
And the flying pig has been straffing some
    And the nose of the shrapnel blown.

It is coming, my Rum, my sweet ;
    Were it ever so airy a tread,
My heart would hear it and beat,
    Were cap comforters over my head ;
My face would turn as white as a sheet
    Were it drunk by the Sergeant instead ;
I'd go sick with trench foot, for my feet
    Would blossom in purple and red.

All night like a ceaseless drum
    The heavies have shelled this spot ;
All night has my aching tum
    Been longing for something hot.
(Then a silence fell with the issued rum
    And a hush with the swallowed tot.)

                  W. O. D.

THE BLOODSTAINED BILLHOOK.

Our grand new Serial—Begin now.

New readers can start anywhere and end anywhere. The most powerful and dramatic story ever
written.

READ ABOUT FLOSSIE FLATFOOT.

(*Foreword*.)

(We are able to print this month a further instalment of the thrilling love story from the able and
versatile pen of that famous authoress, Judy M.
Heirs, a name renowned through 6 hemispheres for
her powerful and vivid handling of the problems
and pit-falls of everyday life. We think our readers
will agree that this latest story excels in its simple
splendour and grace of style all former efforts of this
distinguished writer.

For the benefit of those luckless readers who have
missed earlier instalments we print a concise synopsis
of previous chapters, which we trust will enable them
to pick up the thread of the narrative and so help
them to a fuller appreciation of the charm and beauty
of Flossie Flatfoot and the other characters in the
story. With a view to still further enlightening
the least enlightened of our readers we have gone to
some considerable trouble to portray the characters
in the story, and we feel sure that as a result the
exact relationship existing between all parties
concerned will be more fully understood and grasped
by this little deviation from standing practice.

                (Ed. 5th Glos. Gazette.)

Characters in the Story.

SEPTIMUS P. JONES.—A Millionaire of 24 years,
    disguised as a temporary gentleman. Although
    drawing subaltern's pay in addition to his income
    from other sources, is inclined to delay the
    payment of his mess bills. He is passionately
    enamoured of—

FLOSSIE FLATFOOT, a dark haired, olive skinned
    actress of 19 (Summer time) who is the fourth and
    youngest daughter of

GEORGE YOUNG, an impecunious but hard working
    platelayer on the State Railway, France
    Financial distress in his early life led him to throw
    up an important post as D and S. O. E. in a large
    city warehouse, and seek employment far from
    his former surroundings. He has vowed vengeance
    against

ARTHUR CRUMP, a fair-haired pleasant looking,
    middle aged man with a glass eye and a hair lip
    who was a prominent factor in bringing about the
    downfall and disgrace of George Young. He also
    is in love with

FLOSSIE FLATFOOT, a dark-haired, etc., etc.,...
    youngest daughter of

GEORGE YOUNG, an impecunious....................
    vengeance against

ARTHUR CRUMP, a fair haired...........in love
    with

FLOSSIE FLATFOOT, a dark haired, etc., etc., the prospective fiancee of

SEPTIMUS P. JONES, a millionaire............enamoured of

FLOSSIE FLATFOOT, etc., etc., etc., etc.

Synopsis of previous Chapters.

Brought up in an appalling atmosphere of squalor and poverty, Flossie Flatfoot early in life yearns for fame and notoriety on the stage.

To this end she disappears one day from her home and enlists as a chorus girl in the ranks of the Palempiodrome. Returning home late one night on top of an omnibus in the pouring rain to her humble lodging house, she shares a stick of liquorice with Arthur Crump. Warmed by the genial glow imparted to her overdressed but ill-nourished body by the energetic consumption of the sticky sweetmeat, she and Arthur Crump become fast friends and in the excitement she asks him to pay for her ticket. The bell of the ticket-punching machine clangs and, too late, she realises that she is indebted to Arthur Crump more deeply than she can ever hope to repay. Years pass, and while Flossie progresses apace, gaining favour with all her audiences, her Father, George Young, holding the exalted position of D. and S.O.E. (Director and Stamper of Envelopes) in a large city warehouse has been found guilty of embezzling four penny and 23 half-penny stamps.

He decides to disappear and endeavour to win back his name and honour. He is granted employment as a platelayer on the State Railway in France, and at the time of the opening of our story, is engaged on the line between Amiens and Havre. He is living comfortably on his salary of 25 centimes a week and food found (on the side of the track) and gradually qualifying for re-instatement in his old berth.

He is opposed to the marriage of his daughter Flossie Flatfoot (*nee* Young) with Septimus P. Jones, a wealthy millionaire with whom she has become acquainted in the course of her meteoric rise to commissioned rank on the stage. Septimus P. Jones has taken a commission in the A.P.C. for three wars or the duration of the year, and has won the D.S.O., M.C. and been mentioned in despatches 12 times.

Whilst on his 8th Leave he comes across Arthur Crump and in the course of conversation he learns that he also is in love with Flossie Flatfoot. He therefore takes a vow, not to rest until either he or Arthur Crump is dead or married to Flossie.

He takes a pronounced dislike to Arthur Crump's glass eye and the cut of his hair lip, and tells him so. Strangely enough, Arthur resents this and vows a duplicate vow, the third copy being deposited with his bankers, for their information and usual inaction.

Tiring of the comparative inactivity of the A.P.C. Septimus P. Jones decides to transfer to the A.O.D. For this purpose he is granted his 13th Leave and whilst hurtling along in the leave train he finds a Mark III. sandwich amongst his provisions and flings it through the window.

A shriek is heard as he does so and looking out of the window he observes a platelayer lying in the track by the side of the line, with his head smashed by impact with the sandwich. In due course he arrives at Southampton.

Two days later Flossie Flatfoot receives a wire to say her Father has been killed in France whilst in the execution of his duty. This is the first she has heard of the whereabouts of her father for six years.

Simultaneously there is a ring at the bell and her 3rd footman announces Septimus P. Jones.

The latter after a slight bout of small talk proposes to her for the umpteenth time. She tells him of the death of her father and he finding the stumbling block to their engagement thus opportunely removed, presses his suit with renewed vigour and ardour.

Flossie overcome by his great show of affection is on the point of accepting his proposal when the third footman reappears accompanied by Arthur Crump.

CHAPTER CXVIII.

Flossie's face fell several inches and Septimus sucked the air viciously through his false teeth, whilst both regarded the intruder.

" Ha ! ha ! " hissed Arthur, his face working like a jelly, " so I have the pleasure of finding you both in. " 'Tis good, I have here a rough proof which I am sure will interest you, Miss Flatfoot."

Flossie seized the sheet of parchment with dithering hand and devoured the contents with her eyes.

" So you, you, Septimus P. Jones are my Father's murderer. My hat, no, this cannot be. Speak ! Speak ! say yes or no, or I shall faint."

Septimus turned and with bulging eyes clutched the parchment and read. Then turning to Flossie, he said " Apparently I am, but stay, how came this into the possession of our nasty looking friend ? "

" It was sent me this morning in a green envelope," replied Arthur Crump twirling his moustache, and shaking a piece of scrambled egg from his beard.

" Hound, blackguard, scurvy knave and liar," shouted Septimus feeling in his hip pocket for his trusty Wobbly and Slott.

" No, you don't," drawled Arthur producing a Lewis gun from his right trouser leg ; which he rested on the back of a chair and began to traverse the pair with.

" Let us reason together then dearest, and I will try to explain all."

" No, no, Mr. Jones, I cannot marry my father's murderer."

CHAPTER CXXX.

" But wait a second, I too have a scrap of paper here which, methinks, will put the wind up our friend with the knitted lip. Read that, old thing, and see what you make of it," said Septimus extracting a much-soiled piece of paper from his haversack.

As he read, Arthur's face turned an ashen grey. Then suddenly turning on Flossie, he said haltingly, " Miss Flatfoot I must confess that this account of how I brought ruin on your Father is true. I—I embezzled the stamps and fearing the consequences arranged that your Father should suffer. Of course, that was before I knew you, otherwise I should probably have ruined someone else.

" Will you marry me and for ever cast this bloated capitalist from your mind ? Flossie, my own dearest little —————."

" Enough, enough, I say. Listen ! I can never marry you," murmured Flossie, " you, you who am, I mean, are, my father's betrayer. Go both of you, go at once and never show your—er um—faces again. I hate you both, now run along."

CHAPTER CXLVXI.

(We regret that owing to pressure of space we are only able to print a brief synopsis of the closing chapter of this powerful drama. Ed. 5th GLO'STER GAZETTE.)

Synopsis of closing chapter.

As the door closes behind the two rivals—who slink out with downcast eyes, clenching and un-clenching their teeth and hands convulsively,—from behind a Louis XV. screen, steps Ivan Armletski, a Russian general, who has been cashiered from the Russian Army for a deed of great coolness in which the use of a snowball figured prominently.

They get a stranglehold on each other's necks and are left murmuring sweet nothings, the most audible of which are " Flossie " and " Ivan."

H. S. K.

RECALLED.

Lo ! The dread bride again
    Invites me to her arms,
Who knows no joy nor pain
    Of earthly maiden's charms.

Strongly she draws my soul,
    Yet strongly she repels.
My spirit is not whole
    To bind or lose her spells.

Her face is veiled, and her hands
    Empty, but oh ! Her eyes
Shine. And in many lands
    She calls and the men arise.

Men that I loved arose ;
    She would not be denied.
I seek not her, but those
    Bright figures at her side.

C. S. N.

" AT LAST."

See ! What is this figure from the line, tearing headstrong over the open—mad, rushing in broad daylight? No helmet, no equipment. On, on it comes, heedless of the myriad shells that are tearing up the ragged earth. Will nothing stop him ? He is fast drawing closer, now he drops in a shell-hole, now up again and on. That wire ! Will he ever cross it ? Yes, he's through. He has stumbled. Quick ! The stretcher bearers !

They are there now and have lifted him struggling on to the stretcher. How he writhes and struggles, but four strong hands are holding him fast and he is borne to the road and the ambulance. " He is not hit, I cannot diagnose it," the M. O. says. " Send for the A. D. M. S." Still nothing can he find. The man is dumb.

A kindly figure stayed by that bedside till the dawn began to break, when suddenly as the man's eyes opened, his hand shot out and clutched an empty cigarette tin near by.
" At last, at last I've found it," he stammered, " my foot powder ! "

SORROW.

The wind's voice seems to sob and wail
    A chant of doom :
Across the sunshine lies a veil,
    A veil of gloom.

Only our Father's love may cast
    The veil away,
And change the dark hours of the past
    To new-born day.

Where souls will rise in upward flight
    Above the loss,
To meet their loved ones in the light
    Beyond the Cross.

M. L. G.

REVOLTING STORIES OF THE WAR.

1.—" *Laddie in Khaki.*"

The Hon. Mrs. Takett-Smirkoff toyed expansively with a fine specimen of lump sugar and cast her eye around the room. She was alone in her platinum drawing room, sitting on a platimun chair, before a gold and platinum table.

Her husband, Sir Richard Takett-Smirkoff, was away at his Munition Palace vigorously turning out big guns to a grateful country which showed its appreciation by turning out its pockets. Two of her sons were sitting before platinum cash boxes helping their father to win the war and the third son was that day to go into khaki.

He had not been called up and he had not been conscripted. He had been before no Tribunals and he had sent in no appeals. No, of his own accord he would don khaki. He had spoken. He insisted.

The Hon. Mrs. Takett-Smirkoff looked around her and sighed. For a long time she had opposed this desire of her youngest son—had urged him against it, but she had been replused, and as her husband had supported the boy, what could she do ? At the same time, she could not see why her Cuneo should be in khaki when there were still so many young boys in civilian dress. Let him at least wait for a short time. There would be plenty of opportunity later, for her husband took advantage of every occasion for opposing any peace movement to end this wonderful war. But she had been overruled— Cuneo must go into khaki now.

And as she revolved these things in her mind the door opened and Cuneo Takett-Smirkoff, aged 6, entered, dressed as a first lieutenant in his sweet little khaki uniform.

2.—" *The Stout Sergeant.*"

" And, gentlemen, what is more there shall be— there can be—no talk of Peace until Germany is crushed and ground out of existence, until she is dismembered, until there is not a soul but that is serving in bondage throughout the land."

The speaker sat down amidst vociferous applause, which drowned a minority of hisses. He was a short stout man who had evidently never suffered from a shortage of food and the jewels he wore showed that he had never suffered from much else either. He was well over middle age and had naturally, from the outbreak of war, been an earnest advocate of conscription.

He had come here this evening at the instigation of the " War for Ever " League. A fat salary had reluctantly dragged him from a hearty dinner and accompanied by a Sergeant and five men he had been sent to break up a meeting which advocated Peace in 1917. He didn't experience much difficulty in his task for the Sergeant and his men had simply jumped on the platform and snaffled the speaker. For the rest the " War for Ever " League had taken all the necessary steps to see that the hall should be well sprinkled with their supporters.

At the conclusion of the meeting the prosperous gentleman invited the Sergeant to his house for supper, an invitation which was readily accepted.

Six footmen, all exempted by the local Tribunal, of which he was chairman, ushered him into the house and through the luxuriant hall to the well-stocked dining room where his wife sat reposing.

The Sergeant (by name Mugwump) having been introduced, the conversation fell to normal matters. " And what do you think of France ? " asked Mrs. Prosperous.

" Oh, I've never been out of England," replied Sergt. Mugwump. " And may you never go," said Mrs. P. tapping him lightly on the shoulder with her fan.

" Which is a sentiment that I echoes myself, ma'am," replied the Sergeant, as he drained his glass of stout to the dregs.

3.—*War scales.*

The poor munition maker (that is to say he was poor before the War and earned £8 a week now) entered his home with a light step and a joyful heart. In his hand he carried a small parcel, for the following day was his wife's birthday, and it was the first occasion since his marriage that he had been able to afford a little present, for in truth it was but a small present for your big people—even if it did cost a couple of guineas.

His wife ran to meet him as he opened the door and showed a nice comfortable cosy room that indeed merited the name of " home." A snug place it was and very different to what he had previously been accustomed to.

And if he, a poor man, had made his little bit in the war who can blame him for making a comfortable home with it ? Surely not you nor I, and yet apparently someone did, for a few minutes later the door was pushed open and with a great swishing of skirts an angry woman burst into the room.

This was an eminent propagandist of the " Economy League." Having lived on several thousands a year she now considered herself a heroine of heroines because she had cut down her expenditure to a paltry two thousand. Obviously, thought she, I am the woman to parade before the poor who have made themselves comfortable at the expense of their country.

" This is perfectly scandalous," she broke out without introduction or ceremony. " Mr. Smith, have you no decent feelings ! "—she stared the unfortunate munition-maker in the face, whilst he in return cast his eyes down, and nervously fingered the edge of the tablecloth.

" Do you not realise that we are in the midst of a great war ? I've been following you about the last few days. This evening I saw you go into a cheap jeweller's shop. Do you realise the need for economy ? Here am I—trying to do my best to help win the war—I've cut down my expenditure, by four-fifths and you—you calmly go on spending more and more. She glared around with clenched fists—" And that piano," she almost screamed, throwing out her arm, " You have actually dared to buy a paino in war-time ! "

Mr. Smith still remained motionless. How could he know that the rich lady possessed three or four pianos ? True, they were all bought before the war, but he had scarcely ever heard the sound of one then.

" I'm sorry," he said humbly, " Here take this," and he pushed the parcel with the two guinea necklace towards the rich lady.

" No," she said, " You had better send it to the Red Cross and let them sell it—or shall I ? "

" Will you ? " he asked pleadingly.

She nodded and picked up the parcel. Then she swept out again, but as she brushed by the door a nail caught her furs which her husband had given her—oh, before the war, of course—but furs which had cost fifty guineas, and when she saw the damage done she came back and abused again the poor munition worker because he had put up a nail by his door, instead of having an expensive hat stand as she had in her house.

A A. A

THE BATTLE HONOURS OF THE GLOUCESTERSHIRE REGIMENT.

III.

After the Battle of Salamanca in July, 1812, nearly a year elapsed before the Regiment again took part in a first-class engagement.

On June 21st, 1813, Wellington fought and won a great victory at VITTORIA, in the North of Spain.

W

"THE SPRING OFFENSIVE."

For the first time in the history of the Campaign he had superior numbers, having under his command some 80,000 troops, 60,000 of which were British and 20,000 Portuguese. In the former the 28th Foot was included.

The Battle was decisive and resulted in the capture of 143 guns and 1,000 prisoners and a large quantity of treasure. One remarkable feature of this encounter was that the 28th Foot acting on the right flank of the British side found themselves opposed to the French 28th of the Line, the ancient " Regiment du Roi." The eagle of this Regiment was captured and brought to England.

Shortly after the Battle of Vittoria, a great battle was fought at the PYRENEES, the frontier between France and Spain, between July the 28th and August 1st, 1813.

The 28th and the 61st Foot, the latter being under Colonel Coglan, were both engaged.

Marshal Soult was in command of the French Forces, who after very severe fighting, were driven North of the Pyrenees.

Henceforth the fighting in the campaign was in France, the first battle being that of NIVELLE on November 13th, 1813.

In this the 28th and 61st Foot were both engaged.

Lord Wellington's advance had been delayed owing to the attack on, and subsequent capture of, the fortresses of San Sebastian and Pampeluna.

This delay enabled Marshal Soult to create a strongly entrenched position and a hard fought battle took place on the banks of the river Nivelle, with the result that the French were driven out with the loss of some 1,200 men.

The 61st played an important part in storming three redoubts on the high ground beyond the river.

The Battle of NIVE was fought between the 9th and 13th of December.

The 28th and 61st were both present. This was a hard fought action, but victory eventually lay with the British.

The battle of ORTHES followed on the 27th February, 1814, and resulted in a further French retirement to the North. The 28th and 61st Foot took part in the engagement.

The last action of the Peninsular War which opened in August, 1808, was that of TOULOUSE, fought in the South of France, on April the 10th, 1814. The 28th and 61st Foot again were engaged, the latter suffering very severely, losing no less than 20 Officers, including their Commanding Officer, Colonel Coglan.

As mentioned in the first article, the gallantry of the 61st earned for them the name of " The Flower of Toulouse."

This victory closed the long and arduous campaign and the Battle Honour PENINSULA was awarded to those Regiments who had participated therein.

Few had better claim to it than the Gloucestershire Regiment. It took part in 12 pitched battles and its losses in killed and wounded was over 1,700 men.

The situation in Europe now underwent a complete change, as on April 11th, 1814, Napoleon abdicated, and a little later retired to the Island of Elba.

The nations whose peace had so long been disturbed had every reason for believing that wars were at an end, and a Congress was convened at Vienna, in September, 1814, for the purpose of defining the positions of the Powers.

This congress was by no means unanimous and Napoleon, realising there was an opportunity of regaining his old power, left Elba in February, 1815, and arriving in Paris on the 20th March at once raised a large Army.

The Allies again took the field, and on June 16th, Napoleon simultaneously attacked the Prussians at Ligny and the British under Wellington at Quatre Bras.

In this engagement the 28th Foot, under Colonel Belson, greatly distinguished itself, in forming square and resisting the repeated charges of the French Cavalry who threw themselves against its ranks.

On the 18th June, 1815, the 28th fought at WATERLOO, in General Kempt's Brigade, which formed part of General Sir Thomas Picton's Division.

They fought with great bravery and determination. General Picton addressing the Regiment said, " 28th, if I live to see the Prince Regent, I shall lay before him your bravery this day."

General Picton did not live to carry out this intention as he was killed later in the day whilst leading his Division.

The Duke of Wellington in his despatches wrote, " I must particularly mention the 28th, 42nd, 79th and 92nd Regiments."

It will be observed that out of these four Regiments, one, the 28th, was English, the other three being Scottish.

In the afternoon of the great day of Waterloo the Prussian Army, under Prince Blucher, arrived, the final advance of the combined armies followed, and before sunset the French Army was in full retreat.

With the final overthrow of Napoleon Europe settled down to a much wished for peace.

A period of over 30 years elapsed before Gloucestershire soldiers again took the field.

In the second Sikh War, under Lord, Gough the 61st Foot (the 2nd Battalion of the Regiment) were engaged in the PUNJAUB, 1848-49, in putting down the Sikh power. In addition to general operations which gave them the foregoing battle honour, the Regiment took part in two actions of CHILLIAN-WALLAH and GOOJERAT in the latter year.

The 61st were commanded at that time by Colonel McLeod and it was early in January 1849 that Lord Gough decided to attack an entrenched Sikh position at Chillianwallah, which proved one of the hardest fights ever waged in India.

The ground over which the attack was made was much broken and covered with jungle.

In the engagement which ended in a retirement by the Sikhs, the British lost 2338 Officers and men, of which number 114 were of the 61st.

In the action the Regiment was under Sir Colin Campbell and in the course of the day captured 13 enemy guns.

The Battle of GOOJERAT was fought on the 21st of February 1849, and upon this decisive engagement the security of British rule in the Punjaub was assured.

The Sikhs were strongly entrenched and after an artillery attack lasting 2 hours, the British line moved forward about noon and drove the enemy from their positions.

The action resulted in complete victory and, costly though it was, the great efforts made to conquer the Punjaub had not been in vain, as there are to-day no braver soldiers in the Indian Army than the descendants of those men who fought against us so stubbornly in the Sikh wars of 1846-1849.

It was not long before the County Regiment was again engaged in fighting its Country's battles, as in 1853 the Crimean War broke out in which the Forces of Great Britain, France and Turkey were opposed to Russia.

The first action was that of Sinope in 1853 followed by the occupation of the Danubeian Principalities by Russia the following year.

In 1854 British and French Forces decided to invade the Crimea and destroy the Russian Arsenal of Sevastopol.

In September of that year Lord Raglan (a Gloucestershire man) was appointed Commander-in-Chief of the British Force, having under him 27,000 men and 54 guns.

The 28th Regt. (now the 1st Battalion) were under Colonel Adams and formed part of this force being in General Eyre's (6th) Brigade.

At the Battle of the ALMA the Russians held a strong natural position following the crest of a range of hills overlooking the river.

The Engagement lasted between 3 and 4 hours and was of a very heavy character resulting in a Russian withdrawal.

Following this the Russians fell back on Sevastopol, which town was at once invested by the allied forces.

On the 5th November, the Russians taking advantage of a dense fog issued from the town and surprised our troops in the trenches. A hand to hand battle ensued known to history as INKERMAN in which, after heavy losses on both sides, the Russians were forced to retire.

Throughout the Winter 1854-1855 the siege of SEVASTOPOL continued and the privations of our troops, mainly owing to very inefficient rationing and inferior medical arrangements, were most severe.

Early in 1855 operations were again actively renewed and on the 18th June an attempt was made to carry the Fortress by storm.

The attack was unsuccessful and the British and French troops were repulsed with heavy losses.

Shortly after this Lord Raglan died and his place was taken by Sir James Simpson.

On the 8th September another determined attack was made on Redan, an outwork of the fortress, but the Allies were again driven back.

The next day however the Russians abandoned the Redan and the Allied troops entered unopposed : following this the Russians retired from the fortress and the Allied forces took possession.

Soon after the foregoing events the 61st were making a further contribution to the Regiment's fame in taking part in the next rising in India known as the Mutiny.

The Mutiny actually broke out at Merut about 20 miles North East of DELHI on the 10th May, 1857.

The disaffection which existed at the time among the native soldiers was brought to a head by the introduction of a new rifle, the loading of which necessitated the touching of grease on the cartridge.

This offended the religious feelings of the native soldiers and it formed the immediate cause of the rebellion.

At the outbreak the 61st (2nd Battalion) was in India and acted with great promptitude at Ferozepore in seizing the magazines containing ammunition and effectually prevented them from falling into the hands of the mutinous native regiments.

In this matter Major Redmond, later General Redmond, C.B., and Lieut. Deacon took a leading and effectual part.

Delhi itself was taken by the Mutineers on the 11th May and in June a force of 10,000 British and loyal native troops beseiged it, there being in the City about 40,000 of the enemy's troops.

The British force included the 61st Regiment (2nd Battalion) under Colonel Jones.

Between the 7th June and early in September a number of engagements took place and in the latter month it was decided to take the place by storm.

This attack was made on the 14th September and it stands out in history as one of the finest and most heroic actions ever fought.

Whilst leading his men on and in the hour of victory, the gallant General Nicholson was killed.

3626 Officers and men were killed or wounded and of these the 61st lost 151. Surgeon Reade of the 61st won the Victoria Cross. The result of the assualt was that on the 20th of September, Delhi was in the hands of the British and a great step forward had been taken in subduing the insurrection, which was finally quelled after the fall of Lucknow in March 1858.

Many years now elapsed before the County Regiments were again engaged in active operations. The Frontier wars of India and the Campaign in Egypt in the seventies, eighties and nineties of the last century did not offer them opportunities and it was not until SOUTH AFRICA 1899-1902 that the Regiment again added to its long list of Battle Honours.

At the outbreak of hostilities against the South African Republic, the 1st Glo'sters were in India and they were at once despatched to Natal and took part in the initial operations of the War.

The 2nd Battalion went out from England and formed part of the 12th Brigade under Major-General Knox, which composed part of the 6th Division under Lieut.-General Kelly-Kenny.

In this war for the first time in history the volunteer battalions, now the Territorial Battalions, had an opportunity of assisting the regular units.

Substantial drafts were sent to the line battalions from what are now the 4th and 5th Battalions of the Regiment. The 6th Battalion was only formed during the progress of the war and did not contribute drafts as in the case of the two senior volunteer units.

As explained before, the 1st Battalion was sent to the Natal side in October 1899 under Sir George White at LADYSMITH and took part in the successful actions of Elandslaagte and Reitfontein, in which the Battalion suffered heavily, losing among others Col. Wilford, their Commanding Officer.

Owing to pressure from the North the forces under General Yule retired on Ladysmith where Sir George White had under him some 12,000 men.

On the 29th of October, Sir George White decided to attack the enemy at Lombard's Kop and part of the scheme consisted in sending an intercepting force to Nicholson's Nek, along the ridge which lies about 6 miles North of Ladysmith.

This force consisted of 1000 men drawn from the Gloucesters and Irish Fusiliers under Colonel Carleton of the Fusiliers.

It met with a singular and unexpected misfortune owing to a stampede occurring among the mules, during the night march, whereby all the reserve ammunition was lost.

The Lombard's Kop effort was not a success and the force engaged retired to Ladysmith.

Colonel Carleton's force met with very strong opposition, and owing to their isolated position and lack of ammunition were forced to surrender after 9½ hours heavy fighting on the 30th October.

From this date the seige of Ladysmith began and it was not until the 3rd of March, 1900, that it was relieved by General Buller. The Headquarters and main body of the 1st Battalion were in Ladysmith throughout the seige and bore their share in the fighting and privations of the defence.

On the Western side of the operations the 2nd Battalion were engaged in the RELIEF OF KIMBERLEY which was invested by the Cavalry on the 15th of February 1900, who were supported on the South by part of the 6th Division, in which the 2nd Battalion was included.

During the relief operations General Cronje, the Boer Commander, had moved Eastward to take up a covering position South of Bloemfontein, and on the night of the 17th February he had encamped at PAARDEBERG and it was here that he was overtaken by the British Forces. After a very stubborn resistance he was forced by Lord Roberts to surrender on the morning of the 27th February, 1900, with about 5000 men.

The 1st and 2nd Battalions of the Regiment remained in South Africa until the termination of the War in June 1902.

The Regiment has borne, and is bearing, its share in the present Great War and without doubt its long record of Honours will be added to when the time comes for the allocation of its reward of faithful and distinguished service.

E. S. SINNOTT,
Lt.-Colonel R. E. (T. F.)

THINGS WE WANT TO KNOW.

Where do you make slight pause in D. T. M. O.? Is it at "T" or at "D"?

As the result of wearing "windy tunics," is it true that some officers have been mistaken for private soldiers?

Has "B" Company discarded its razors?

If 15 visits in one fortnight to A—— produce one GAZETTE a month late, would permanent residence there make it punctual?

Who is the Staff Officer who goes skating on horseback?

What Sergeant heard a whiz-bang near Bn. H. Q. and said "that must be a minnie"? Is he in "B" Company?

What happened to the Post-Corporal on the night of February 17-18th? And did "A" Company lose a tin of milk?

Why has this war produced so many chits and so much chatter?

In this age of Tanks, Trench Mortars, Bombs, Grenades, Aerial Torpedoes, Howitzers and Blue Pigeons, why does the R. A. M. C. still persist in talking of "Gunshot wounds"?

Who is the Dog Fancier in the Battalion?

Who reported sick to the M.O. with "neurotic wind-swallowing"? Is it a new Trench-disease?

Who are the members of the new Parasite Club?

Is it true that newspapers at home are running short of paper owing to the tremendous amount of chits which arrive at Battalion H.Q.? Has Lord Northcliffe heard of this? Is it not possible to share these chits and thereby save tonnage?

Who ascribed the words—when none was for the Party, and all were for the State—to a Heathen poet?

Who has managed to conceal a couple of Field-Kitchens in their 35 lb. kit?

Have you used powder this morning?

Who is Christopher of whisky fame?

What did the Paddle-Box of the "Mona Queen" do?

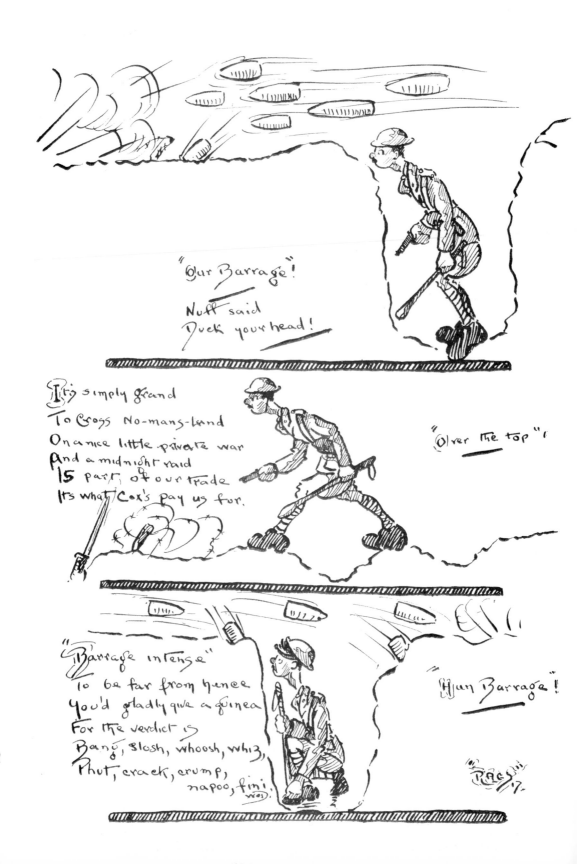

What happened to the Brigade potatoes? And how did they find their way into the pot of the Soup Kitchen? Who was the Sherlock Holmes who traced the peelings? Is it true that the Padre pinched these potatoes? What else did the Padre pinch? Does he compare notes with D. A. D. O. S.?

How many hares and pheasants found their way into the bag on the occasion of the Artillery's " mixed shoot "?

What were the feelings of the two Officers of another Battalion, who, having wandered into No Man's Land by mistake, suddenly heard an excited whisper " Take a steady aim, Bill "?

Is it true that THE time at a certain Field Ambulance still is that of the Sergeant-Major's and NOT that of the C. O.'s clock?

What is the signal for the close?

Who is the Officer who had his head shampooed every day he was on leave?

Is it not a discredit to his many fair teachers that a distinguished member of No. 2 Mess should be ignorant of the meaning of " defense de doubler?"

Who has been guilty of transferring live stock from one Battalion to another? Were the usual Transfer Returns rendered?

Is it true that " Whacker " does not intend touring the States with " Little Tich " cracking jokes after the war? Has he made up his mind as to whether he will take up the duties of Porter-ticket-puncher-chucker-out-and-head-gardener at " Barber's Bridge " Railway Station?

Who described a Boche Cavalry Patrol " as a few of them there German 'ooligans "?

Who is the Officer who came on parade with a bayonet scabbard? Where was the bayonet? Is he in " D " Company?

Did the " high intelligence officer " appropriate many archives? How many kellars in C——— did he allot to horses?

What is the meaning of " Regarded Territory "?

Who is the S. Antony of V———?

Who was up early enough to pinch the G. O. C.'s stick? Was it a gallant Major (R.F.A.)?

Who was the R. E. Officer (Major) who took a bath in the Somme while inspecting a Bridge? Was he looking at the German camouflage overhead?

Who was the R. E. Officer (Major) whose kit fell into the River? Is it true that the waggon and all fell through the Bridge that this self-same Major had constructed?

Why did they send 7 tents with one tent pole to the Mobile Column? Was there a shortage of firewood at H.Q.?

What did a certain Guide say after he had most carefully boiled a tin bearing a label marked " Pork and Beans," and found on close examination that the tin was full of earth, having previously been used as an improvised candlestick? Does he hail from the Cotswolds?

Who is the Private in No. 5 Platoon who remarked " Thems the sort of overcoats, those macks," and did he ask at the Soup Kitchen if they had any " Bully Beef " for sale?

Who said " the party were travelling at two hours per mile "? Was he in " B " Company?

Who is the Corporal in " B " Company who told his men to fall in on the clean mud? And did not the same Corporal call his men to attention, " chests in and stomachs out "? Had he had his rum issue?

Whether the Lewis Gun is cooled by the " rotating of the magazine "?

Did an Officer in " B " Company detail to his Platoon how to powder feet, and whether the course he went on had anything to do with the subject?

Who is the Officer in " B " Company who on arriving at P———, enquired where the mess was, and did he find it luxurious?

" Do some rifles have safety catches and some haven't, are the anxious enquiries of a Lance Corporal in " B " Company. Is he in No. 5 Platoon?

Who is the Staff Captain (Blue Force) who has water laid on to his billet? Did he bring his arm chair with him?

How many Germans did " C " Company really kill?

Who is the man in the Transport who refused a Staff Appointment in order that he might return to the Battalion?

Who is the " Staff Officer in embryo "? Did he get a nice billet at C———?

On O. C. informing a sentry that Baghdad had fallen, did the sentry say that he heard nothing fall near him? Does the sentry hail from " A " Company?

Who is O. C. Football kit at the Base?

Why did the sentry at the War Office present arms to an M. O. (Captain) and to a Chaplain (Fourth Class)? Was it not the climax to their triumphant entry to London?

Is it true that the Drum-Major cleaned his teeth with anti-frost-bite-foot-powder?

How about eleven moves in seventeen days?

TO YOUR ESPECIAL LADY.

(With any piece of shrapnel you may find about, saying how nearly it brought you a Blighty).

I kiss you, Shrapnel, e'er you go,
To take of timid looks your toll,
Beside her trinkets all arow,
When lady mine in camisole
    And dainty wear
Shall loose the fragrance of her hair.

And maybe, Shrapnel, you shall see,
As white a junket in the West,
A shoulder rounded cunningly,
And by her heart may find a nest
    (Where I would be)
Within her dainty lingerie

"SITUATION REPORT."

Enemy ration party seen on the skyline at 5-15 p.m.

And, Shrapnel, if with tender sigh,
  She lay you there, then tell her this :
You cannot render thanks, but I
  Have lips that weary for a kiss.
    Say what you will,
Then nestle to her and be still.

But Shrapnel, e'er your rest you take,
  Say love needs lips as flowers need rain :
Say I would kiss her eyes awake,
  Then kiss them into sleep again.
    Oh ! sorry tale,
When kisses have to go by mail.

And maybe, Shrapnel, some glad hour
  You'll hear her speak, and after drouthe
Of silence, love will be a flower
  And blossom on her splendid mouth ;
    Then you shall teach
My heart true excellence of speech.

               W. O. D.

DINING OUT.

"It's really most annoying," said Clarissa with tears in her eyes, " to think that one cannot get even the necessaries of life now-a-days."

" Why what's the trouble now ? " I asked with as much interest as I could show in my voice. " Everything," was the terse and comprehensive reply. " The baker says we can't have any more rolls for breakfast, potatoes are as scarce as new spring hats, the sugar is still scarcer, and fish is so dear that it sticks in my throat even more than its bones do."

Here she burst into tears and proceeded to sob freely on to my new tunic.

" Well, my dear." I said with a brave show of enthusiasm," let us dine out to-night and try to forget about house-keeping worries." At this she brightened up very considerably, and skipped away to put on her evening clothes. " Where shall we go dearest " ? I asked as we strode along to find a taxi. " Oh ! anywhere, so long as it's nice and has an orchestra."

In due course we found ourselves at a spotless little table for two, and having waited the customary half hour or so to enable the waiter to get accustomed to our presence, we beckoned tentatively to him and began to order. Clarissa chose hors d'œuvres, soup, whitebait, ptarmigan, Scotch woodcock, to be followed by a peche Melba and desert.

Now I never argue with Clarissa for she says I don't appreciate the skill required to order a really nice dinner. So just to please her I said " Very well, I will have the same."

The waiter hereupon turned a delicate duck's egg green and tugged at his collar apparently with a view to improved breathing. At last having recovered a part of his former superciliousness, he replied " Zat ees koite impossible. Monsieur forget zat he may not eat as before. Sree course only are allowed."

This came as rather a shock to us, but without turning a hair Clarissa got in some useful repartee and ordered " Hors d'œuvres, soup (neither with or of meat) mixed grill and peche Melba." Again I concurred and yet again the waiter come perilously near apoplexy.

" I am wairy zorree Sair, but you gannot 'ave zat Sair."

" What the blazes do you mean ? " I shouted, " Are you going to tell me what I can eat and what I can't ? What do you mean ? "

" Eet ees only allowed for ze offisairs to pay 5s. 6d. for zair dinnair, Sair, and you will have ordered too much."

At this point a superior type of waiter without a white shirtfront slid up alongside the table, doubtless attracted by the noise, and explained in a few short sentences just exactly what I could do.

The upshot of it all was that Clarissa was deputed to act as my host and order for me anything I liked. This seemed to appeal to the imagination of our waiter who shuffled off and revived himself from a half bottle of Champagne behind a neighbouring screen.

" I don't hear any music," said Clarissa after a minute examination of everybody within range.

" Oh ! I replied, " They are over there, and they just finished a piece as we came in."

" But they haven't played again since, have they ? she replied. " Oh no " I answered, " you see we've only been here 45 minutes and you can't expect them to do too much."

At this point our waiter returned (looking quite himself again) with plates all up both arms and on his shoulders and proceeded to drop them one by one on to the table.

" Bring me a bottle of No. 24580 " I said, indicating the selected beverage in the wine list.

" I am vairy sorree Sair, but eet ese after 9 o'clock and we cannot supply any alcoholic dreenks after that time. Wartair, geenger ale, leomonarde or cidair, Sair, but zat ees all."

I glanced hopelessly at Clarissa who by now was on the verge of tears again, but was only saved from giving vent to her feelings by the signs of imminent activity manifested by the orchestra.

" Very well " I said, " two ginger ales."

Towards the close of the meal I summoned the O.C. cigars and liqueurs who cannoned violently into the table, at the same time running one of the wheels over Clarissa's foot.

" Give me a box of 25 De Reskes and a couple of Creme de Cacaos."

" I vos zorry, Zir, but ze regulations zay nuzzing after 9 o'clock wheech gontains speerits."

" Oh, very well then, give me the cigarettes and buzz off," I replied, somewhat petulantly.

" I vos zorry Zir but I can only let you 'ave a single cigarette, Zir."

" Why ? Haven't you a box of 25 ? "

" Oh yes, many boxes " he replied affably " but eet ese after 8 o'clock, Zir."

By now I was too exasperated to argue the point so I meekly took the proffered cigarette and commenced to smoke.

As a parting shot the O. C. Cigar barrow remarked " You can 'av as many as you like one at a time, Zir, but not more than one at a time, Zir."

So we sat, Clarissa eagerly waiting for a renewal of activity by the Orchestra, and I smoking cigarette after cigarette for each of which the waiter had to trundle his confection through the maze of tables.

" Well, dear, shall we make a move ? " I suggested as the waiter handed me my bill.

" Monsieur undairstands zat zee laidy must pay zee bill at zee desk as she iss zee host, as if not I get into zee 'ell of a row from zee managaire."

So I carefully counted out the exact money to cover the bill and handed it to Clarissa, who looked at me reproachfully, at the same time realising that only by such means could we clear our consciences.

Once again in the street Clarissa recovered from the embarrassment caused by the glance of the desk-cashier, so we boarded a taxi.

" That " said I, as we let ourselves into our flat " is the last time we dine out until apres la guerre."

               H. S. K.

INCIDENTAL MUSIC FOR THE SOMME FRONT.

Bde. Route March	*There's a long long trail.*
Trench Foot	*Ails o' mine.*
Wiring	*Just we two and the moon.*
The Midnight Cocoa ...	*Another little drink.*
Trench Raids	*Nights of Gladness.*
Leave	*The Golden Legend.*
The 5.9	*Farewell, Isabel.*
Our Dug-out	*I miss the Sunshine and Roses.*
An unpaid Lance-Corporal ...	*Less than the dust.*
A Defaulter's Patrol Report...	*They wouldn't believe me.*
A day's Bombardment ...	*A Perfect Day.*
A Fatigue Party ...	*I didn't want to do it.*
A Patrol	*We don't want to lose you.*
A cushy one	*Please don't take me home.*
War Correspondent ...	*It's only a beautiful picture.*
Our Division on the Somme...	*Here we are again.*
A new issue of clothes ...	*A hunting we will go.*
Kit Inspection...	*Good-bye, my Bluebell.*
A Ration Party	*Oft in danger, oft in woe.*
In France	*Land of Hope and Glory.*
The Leave Boat	*What are the wild waves saying ?*
Chits	*Paper Bag Cookery.*
The Patrol	*With cat-like tread upon our prey we steal.*
The Dud	*The unfiinshed symphony.*
Foot Inspection	*Come with thy naked feet.*
Flying Ducks	*Lo, hear the gentle Lark O Bird of Love, Divine.*
Billets on the Somme... ...	*In cellar cool*
The 18 pounders ...	*Sweet and low.*
The Signal Section ...	*I hear you calling me.*
The Intelligence Officer ...	*They wouldn't believe me.*
On Sentry-go	*Thy sentinel am I !*
Blighty	*When Irish eyes are smiling.*
The Sniper	*I know of two bright eyes watching for me.*

THE NORTHERN RIVERS.

I love these northern rivers that rush and fall and foam
From springs among the mountains, and through the deep
     vales roam.
Fed by thousand streamlets down-dropping from the hills
When Spring from melting snowdrifts their narrow funnels
     fills.

O'er boulders or through limestone they push or carve their
     way
Past little pebbly islands, which urge in vain delay ;
Now leaping full five fathom, now sinking out of sight
In subterranean channels encased in walls of white.

Brown are their pools, yet crystal is not more clear, and fair,
The trees on perilous ledges which are reflected there,
Those trembling silver birches and pines of perfect cone,
Rock-rooted, steeply climbing, each bank a high piled throne.

High spacious lawns receive them emerging from the ghylls
Old towns and cattle-markets and little busy mills,
Castles and ruined abbeys, majestic as they stand,
Where monks might rule the rivers and barons take the land.

Oh, Lune and Dent and Ribble ! Oh, Tees and Wharfe and
     Swale !
What wealth of art and nature adorn each lovely dale,
Through which ye pour your waters and chant your endless
     song !
Like Kings who love their Kingdoms, beautiful, swift and
     strong.
                                        C. S. N.

STARTLING TRUTH DISCOVERY.

From Philip Fibs—Revelations of a Journalist.

Valuable advice free to all readers.

If you know of someone who is troubled as to his future come to ME. The post of special correspondent to one of our greatest journals, the Glo'ster Gazette, is not lightly to be attained. But every man may try. It is up to you to become famous to-day. Amongst my pupils I am at liberty to mention Mr. Bilgesome Bung, Mr. Thomas-Beach Pills, and most notorious of all, Lord Carmelite. Such names speak for themselves. May I add your name to the list ? Read the following hints free of charge and without incurring responsibility and decide for yourself. There can be only one decision.

Journalism is the stepping stone which leads across the flood of current affairs to Sensationalism. Sensationalism is Fame.

Write to-day for full particulars of my Scholarship Course. Below is a portion of an effort of one of my pupils after only six weeks tuition.

Try and copy it or better still send me something of your own. I will send you in return a candid criticism of your work. Meanwhile read the following invaluable hints based on experience.

1. Never stir from safety. An O. P. in Fleet Street is best.

2. Write most of what you know least. This is an unfailing maxim. It appeals to the general public who will believe you implicitly.

3. Remember there are only four kinds of soldiers in the British Army—Scotchmen, Londoners, Lads and Fellows.

4. Cultivate the use of adjectives, " Brawny " is particularly popular. On an average at least every third word should be an adjective.

5. WRITE FOR FULL PARTICULARS OF MY SCHEME TO-DAY.

Extract from an article by one of my pupils after only six weeks tuition.

With the Critics Balmy in the Field.

To-day I have spent among the gaping shell holes on the Western Front. I call them holes but many of them are really torn, swollen craters—and each crater be large enough to conceal a hundred copies of the current number of the Gazette and no one—oh, Horatio !—would be the wiser. And now when this ceaseless artillery barrage goes on from day to day and from night to night, turning the former into the ovens of Hell and the latter into the boilers of Hades, the sentries have indeed an unenviable task. I passed one of these brawny lads, a London boy, on my rounds this morning. He challenged me on my approach : " Who goes there ? " His words rang out loud and clear whilst the Bosch cowered in his trench only a hundred yards away. On my disclosing my identity he welcomed me with a cheery good morning and tripped down from his post for a chat. After I had returned the greeting I offered him an empty cartridge case which I had just picked up in that otherwise speckless trench. I thought he would like it as a souvenir but he merely shook his head and dropped it again. As it fell I heard above me the ominous whirr of a monstrous shell speeding towards me. They had evidently spotted me and instinctively I ducked, but the sentry—that splendid Scotchman—took no notice but held his ceaseless vigil across No Man's Land, never turning his head, and he only smiled at me as he suddenly found himself standing at the bottom of a newly made shell crater. Then without a moments warning he leaped forward and picked up a piece of white hot metal that had caught his attention. " Bon souvenir " he muttered as he placed it under my nose. I withdrew quickly from the hissing heat. Wonderful Scotchmen ! Wonderful Londoners ! Their simpleness astounds me. It is " souvenir " they think of. Ah ! yes. Bon souvenir—Bon souvenir......(Advt.)

                                        FIBULOUS.

Unpaid !

FOR OUR SAILORS.

Lord, they watch day by and night,
　In the North wind's icy breath,
Through the tempest, through the fight,
　Strong and faithful until death.

Fearless, seek the hidden foe
　In the bosom of the deep,
Silent, to their task they go,
　Sleepless, strive that we may sleep.

While they sweep the angry main,
　While the storm-blasts shout and rave,
When the skill of man is vain,
　God of mercy, thou canst save !

In the awful battle hour,
　When beneath Thy heaven unrolled
Fire and strife fling forth their power,
　By Thy Spirit, Lord, uphold !

While the conflict rages high
　These, our sailors, guide and guard,
Lead them on to Victory,
　For their cause is Thine, O Lord !

Let Thine angels, watching, bless
　Wounded men in suffering lain ;
Bring relief to their distress,
　Strength and healing in their pain.

And the fallen, true and brave,
　Who Thy gift of Life have won,
Who their all, uncounting, gave—
　Crown them with Thy great " Well done ! "

Grant that all on land and sea
　May Thy work of love proclaim,
Thanks and glory give to Thee,
　Praise and bless Thy Holy Name.
						M. L. G.

OUR BENEFACTORS.

Brigade H.Q.	Sack of Potatoes
Mr. W. R. Voller	Papers
Miss Parr	,,
Bishop Frodsham	,,
Colonel Marling	,,
Colonel Griffith	,,
The Hon. Mabel Gye	,,
Lieut. Colonel Winterbotham	,,
Miss Karn	,,
Camps Library	Papers and Magazines
" The Echo "	" The Echo "
Pte. Wood	Typing
Pte. Orchard	,,
Mr. Jack Margetson	Cigarettes
Miss Backhouse	Papers
Ladies of Gloucester	Shoulder Badges
Miss McKechnie	Socks
Mrs. Temple Cooke	Papers

THE CURIOS.

It was indeed a great misfortune that owing to the " WAR," only a few from this Brigade had the chance of seeing the " CURIOS " on the opening night of their new Programme. By the time that these lines are in print, (No, we are not saying that by that time it will be August and apres la guerre), we hope that very many more will have availed themselves of two hours excellent amusement. The curtain with its variegated assortment of " local " advertisements is an earnest of the good things to follow. The " Finnegan Fusiliers " parade in immaculate style, and Pte. RAYNOR gives the detail just as it should be given. The claims of " Blighty " are warmly advocated in preference to those of " Tennessee," " Pinafore " is perfectly parodied, while " The Bells of St. Malo " with its haunting

refrain made us long for a glimpse of " The little fishing boat that comes sailing to Brittainy and me." Pte. Herbert sang it in excellent form.

An old friend, Gunner THOMPSON, is as fractious and foolish, in the true and best sense of the word—as ever. You've just got to laugh at and with him. The early-Victorian Parish Clerk is vividly revived by Pte. COOTER ; and the old characters of Dickens are made to speak once more, thanks to a very high class and extremely clever characterisation on the part of Gunner Sleight.

Lastly, " Harry Tate " rolls up in a Rolls-Royce. " Nuff Said."

A crowded and highly appreciative audience, the first of many, was your reward,Lieutenant TEECE,for all your hard work. You are a public benefactor. Thanks awfully.

(We much regret that the Programme was received too late for insertion in this Number.

(*To be taken anywhere*)

DIVISIONAL INTELLIGENCE SUMMARY.

To cover period from Thursday week to Time, Gentlemen please.

I.—OPERATIONS.

Ratting intermittent all the evening. After some reconnaisance work on the part of the A.D.C's, one half couple of the Divisional Bitch Packs effectively silenced two large rats about two degrees N. of the " P " in OLYMPE.

Meanwhile one half-couple of the Padre's dog-pack killed one rat and neutralised two more.

Dug-outs are suspected adjacent to the " P " in " R. E. DUMP."

Good identifications were obtained in each case. Judging by the grey marks on the collar they belonged to the 1914 class. The ice on their whiskers goes to confirm the view that they had very recently come from the Russian Front. They were well fed yet shewed little fight. Our casualties were very slight. One A. D. C. hit on the toe by another A. D. C's. stick and one half-couple of the Bitch Pack a slight bite on the near hind. Groans were heard frequently.

Both packs withdrew on the signal that dinner was " up."

5 p.m. Our 18 PADRE'S fired three salvoes and dispersed a party of men crossing the skyline.

M. G. and L. G. fire was kept up on CAPS in the enemy's wire throughout the night.

Trench mortars fired on a suspended emplacement at X41., b85.

Patrols (Fool reports sent to all those not concerned.)

　Enemy work. It is reported that a little concertina
　　has been thrown into gap...but does not
　　close or open.

II.—MISCELLANEOUS.

Attitude of the Enemy.—Appeared curious. In dug-outs adjacent to OLYMPE Captain Pride-Jones awoke to find a large super-rat nibbling his nose. The rat has not been seen since and its death has been presumed.

　" The rat it was that died."

Lights.—The following Rocket Signals are used by the enemy opposite our rear.

S. O. S.—(Soda or Seltzer) a rocket bursting into Black and White.

Strengthen same.—A square face rocket with Red label.

Signalling.

At 8 p.m. signalling with a white light was noticed about—portion of message read by signallers was———CHINCHIN—CHEEROCHEERO—BANDASBEFORE—Z. No pause between Greetings except in the case of BAND, which was sent as a complete unit.

At one time the following was read "L.G." (apparently "Lloyd George") "is a washout." It is considered probable that the message came from the Irish party.

Identification is very much desired, to prove the arrival or not of the Irish contingent.

> (The above may sound abstruse but reference to the Division Summary from 8th (7-30 a.m.) to 7.30 a.m. 9th March will throw some light on it.—Ed.)

One Very light seen. It appears to have been fired from a Very pistol.

III.—WORK DONE.

Nil.

IV.—ENEMY MOVEMENT.

See infra under "Centres of Activity."

Hostile Artillery.

15 Oyster Shells from direction of GODBERT caused our infantry considerable inconvenience.

A large body of men were seen marching along the road. They afterwards formed single file, and appeared to be walking one behind another.

Centres of Activity. Ref. Map London Tube Map.

Place.	Time.	Remarks.
(1) Empire.	7.30 p.m.—11 p.m.	An ugly rush.
(2) Main road in O. 1. D. 56. 70	Intermittent.	Heavy motor transport one bearing a board in front labelled "TULSE HILL."
(3) Cellar in A-I--S.	10 a.m.-12 noon.	Suspected Field-Cashier.

Information from other sources :—

Telegram received by President Wilson from Mrs. Pankhurst "Disown Adela—drown her."

Austrian official communique announced a very successful raid on the Isonzo front, two mess tins, and one entrenching tool handle Mark 1 X being captured. The booty has been forwarded to Army H.Q.

PART VI.

Examination of a prisoner of the 17h Company, 274 R.I.R. (not R. Irish Rifles.)

At 7-30 a.m., a man of the above Company walked into our lines ; on being warned he was trespassing he stated he would gladly do the month without the option. He is a native of GINGERBEIRHEIM and was G trombonist in the opera there.

In the trenches he was employed as the motive power of a strombos horn. His Company Commander is Lieut. von SAUERKRAUT and Company H.Q. is in the drunken road at O. PIP. BEER. Food is not good and they live mainly on hope. He once fell in the SOMME and received the Iron Cross.

Notes on his further examination will be forwarded in due course.

Examination continued.

Moral.—The tanks made a deep impression on all men they ran over. On being questioned one prisoner stated that he was a married man, with 4 children. He further volunteered the statement that he kept a tame canary, and had now to feed it with Maconachies owing to the lack of potatoes. On being further questioned as to what a maconachie was he said that in his opinion it was a tin full of anything, which when heated was a something that made you feel like nothing.

No further information could be extracted from him so it was concluded that he had recently partaken of one of these rations.

RHYMES.

D-CK-B-SCH

Four and twenty black birds built in a bush
Where they thought that neither side was going to push,
When they hear a five-nine they would only shout
"What a swine the Bosh is ! Tommy turn him out ! "

PL--G STR--T

Plug away, plug away Fritz is nigh beat.
He dont seem to fancy the boys of Pluck Street.
LILLE will not know herself when you march in
And then for a month on the spree at BERLIN.

N--V--GL-S-E

Not many of the Churches behind the line are old.
But there'll be need of new ones before the Kaiser's old.
And God grant the New Church may at last instill
Peace upon earth among men of better will.

C. S. N.

THE WAR AFTER THE WAR.

It is a matter of common knowledge that Germany is as determined as we are—possibly more so—to carry on a Trade War after the Great War. Nations nowadays are tempted by the bait of Trade rather than by the lure of Territory to wage war, and the factories of Germany have been busy turning out millions and millions of goods, which they will endeavour to dump on the markets of the World. It is incumbent therefore for business men to brace themselves for renewed efforts, and for the unbusiness-like to become business-like. In view of the seriousness of the situation we have formulated a scheme to enable those officers who meditate turning their hand to the making of money in the world of Business, to attain that grasp of affairs and business acumen which alone can ensure success. In times past the efforts of retired officers of His or Her Majesty's forces to achieve success in this department have signally failed. Such grip and grasp of Business Technique as in requisite we undertake to instil into the minds of even the most refractory of pupils that ever wearied the most patient of Army Crammers.

Briefly the course will consist of the following studies in departmental Training. Ten days will be spent in each of the different departments, and so varied is the selection we append, that we guarantee with perfect confidence the highest results.

1. *Ten days on the Tube Railway.*—Special attention will be paid to the punching of tickets and to the speed of issuing change a half-penny short.

   General idea : speed and efficiency.

2. *Ten days at Ciro's.*

   (*a*)   Two days attached to doorman to learn tips.
   (*b*)   Two days to the senior waiter.
   (*c*)   Two days to the maître d'hotel.
   (*d*)   Two days to the dancing master to learn the trench foot tango.
   (*e*)   Two days to a table.

3. *Ten days at Messrs. Cox and Co.*
Up-to-date methods of book-keeping.

4. *Ten days Internment at the Hotel Great Central.*
General idea :   Comfort of the guests.
Special Idea :   How to keep your guests at home.

5. *Ten days at any Brigade H.Q.*
The art of letter writing.

6. *Ten days at Docks Rest Camp.*
To learn organisation.

7. *Ten days at Base.*
Special attention will be paid to esprit de corps, the underlying principle being illustrated by the following specimen order.

    " 6666666   Pte————
      1/1 Lamplighters Bn.
           to
  proceed to the 31/1 Jerusalem Lancers."

Names of officers who intend to benefit by attending these courses should be submitted, with reasons for same, to this office at once.

Meanwhile join our Correspondence Courses.

Staff Officer writes : " Since starting your Correspondence Courses I have the reputation of writing the curtist chits and the nastiest notes of any one in this or any other Division "

Efficiency will mean so much to you—it will be the means of placing that elegantly laced top-boot of yours on the bottom rung of the ladder of Fame.

Only a limited number of Officers can attend the courses after the war, but all can join the Correspondence Class Now. No fees till you are placed. Send your names NOW.

FROM THE CLASSICS.

LIFE IN A DUG-OUT.

Higgledy, piggledy, packed we lie
Rats in a hamper, swine in a stye,
Wasps in a bottle, frogs in a sieve,
Worms in a carcase, lice in a sleeve.
Pick up the " Chelmsford book " ! moisten your
    thumbs !
Look out for the Padre—here he comes !

(*Extract from Robert Browning's poem " Holy Cross Day "*
adapted, with apologies).

MUD, MUD, MUD.

Mud, mud, mud,
On the long straight roads. Oh, gee !
And I would that my tongue could utter
The thoughts that arise in me.

Oh, well for the General's job
That he watches us on our way !
Oh, well for the A. S. C.
As they loll in their cars all day !

And the beastly lorries go on
To their railhead miles from the trench :
But, oh, for the touch of a glass of " beer "
And the sound of a voice—NOT French !

Mud, mud, mud,
Day after day, oh gee !
But I hope that the sight of H(e)buterne)
Will never come back to me.

          (*With apologies to Tennyson*). .

THE MERMAID.

(*New Style*).

Who would be
A Wretched Tommy,
Trying to run
In deep con-Sommé
Up to the knee,
In a " has been " trench.
Inhaling the stench
Of a Hun.

AT THE CANTEEN.

And let me the canakin clink, clink,
And let me the canakin clink.
A soldier's a man,
A man's life's but a span;
Why then let a soldier drink.

        (*Othello—Shakespeare.*)

ANENT THE PUSH.

The plain song is most just ; for humours do abound,
Knocks come and go, God's vassals drop and die
    And sword and shield,
    In Bloody field
Doth win immortal fame.

        (*King Henry V.*)

OFFICER PARTING WITH VALISE AND SURPLUS KIT.

When shall we three meet again
In thunder, lightning or in rain ?
When the hurly burly's done,
When the battle's lost and won.
That will be ere the set of sun.
. . . .
Fair is foul and foul is fair
Hover through the fog and filthy air.

        (*Macbeth*).
                H. S. K.

BRICKS FROM THE EDITOR'S PACK.

Gommecourt the Great has gone, the mystery of the house with the semi-ecclesiastical windows at Puisieux has at last been solved. Often times we have looked at it from old Pelisier and wondered and wagered on the chances of it being a Brewery or a Church ! How they used to strafe us, too, from the Bois de Biez ! No more soft hypotheses anent La Ferme Sans Nomme have now to be weaved by Intelligence Officers struggling with their Reports due in the early hours of the morning. How our old friend and comrade Pte. Demmery would have liked to have unravelled the secrets of Puisieux and all its haunts.

At the Battalion Conference. " Pys has been "— there was a slight pause, and the expectant Company Commanders held their breath. It was clear that arrangements were to be made for the transportation of the troops to England. But the final word was not " declared " but " evacuated."

Very many congratulations to another former Censor of the GAZETTE in the person of Captain Lea, M.C., on his promotion to the——Corps. We are glad to see that recognition of the value of the Territorial Officer is no longer a dream but is fast becoming a waking reality.

Have you ever laughed

When the Huns have
        strafed

From dusk to the dewy
                dawn

And you get a chit,

With this "trenchant" wit

"The enemy has withdrawn".

WOJ

Lord Derby, himself a keen Territorial, has given his promise, and he has a way of overcoming the most difficult obstacles.

There is, however, a good deal of lee-way to be made up. It is curious, for instance, that while it would seem impossible for a Major in the Artillery (T.F.) to be promoted to the rank of Lieut-Colonel, in spite of conspicuous ability, promotion to the rank of major within the fold of the Royal Artillery is merely a matter of sequence and comes " in due course." Lord Derby has much to do still.

It has often caused us some surprise to note that the Official Journal of the Royal Regiment does not recognise the Officers of the Territorial Artillery as members of the Royal Regiment. In the R.A. Journal, lists of Honours and Awards and Casualties are duly published, but there is never a place for any Territorial in the above lists.

The roar of our Guns has been heard the world over, at the Dardenelles, in Mesopotamia, Salonica, France, Belgium, Africa—is not their motto truly " Ubique "? The Territorial Artillery naturally volunteered for Foreign Service anywhere. They are everywhere. Yet not to them is granted the badge " Ubique," which is doled out to the latest holder of a Temporary Commission.

Thus *Truth, March 14th, 1917* :—

" There seems to be here and there a silly jealousy of the Territorial Artillery Officers on the part of some of the Regulars who look on them as amateurs. In one case I have heard of, the commander of a T.F. Brigade of Artillery at the front, who was a regular, refused to recommend his three Captains commanding batteries for promotion to Major's rank, on the ground that he had had to wait fourteen years for his crown and they ought to do the same. The C. O. who said this deserves to be scrapped for talking such pernicious nonsense. Half a year's experience of Artillery fighting on the Somme is worth the whole of the fourteen years peace experience which qualified this superior person for the rank of Major."

There are still some old Friends about of Captain E. L. Wright of——Bn. Some of us were lucky to see his 72 against Cambridge at Lords and. they were delighted to hear of his appointment to a Brigade Majorship in the ——Division.

Captain H. P. Snowden, M.C., has been appointed an instructor at a Cadet School in England.

Our best thanks to the " Cheltenham Chronicle and Graphic " for the photographs of Officers and men published in our last number.

In an article entitled " The Artists Rifles " in the " Field " for January 20th, the following remarkable information is vouchsafed.
" Within twelve hours after receiving notice to mobilise—i.e. at 4 p.m. on August 5th, 1914—the Corps 630 strong, was mobilised and in barracks, ready to move off six days sooner than any other Territorial Regiment."

Ah, those London Territorials again ! Isn't it wonderful how it is done. Yet the simple country fellow from Gloucestershire who mobilised with the Battalion, were ready to move off at 4 p.m. on the self-same day August 5th, 1914, and entrained for their war station that very evening, and were at that war station after a sea passage by noon on Thursday, August 6th ! And what is true of this Battalion is, we are certain, equally true of every other Territorial Battalion.

Optimism.

" Several writers have obtained large incomes during the last thirty months by writing optimistic piffle and selling it to an eager public. Such nonsense as

" KITCHENER'S GREAT SURPRISE."

will be remembered by thousands."
Still one could not but feel sorry for the plight of a certain expert writer on The War who found himself in the Bankrupcty Courts. So unduly optimistic as to the speedy termination of the war had he been, that the many papers for which he penned his weekly column finally refused to accept any more of his work. It is undoubtedly true that the false optimism, consistently spread by certain of the politicians, which percolated through the greater part of the Press, has been of ill-service to our Country. No cry, was ever more mischievous than that of " Business as Usual." We are all optimists out here in the sense that we are winning, but England was never allowed to grasp even dimly the magnitude of the task before her. The need of a gigantic effort was never brought home to her, and Lord Kitchener was the solitary herald of a three years War. She was told indeed by one grandiloquent writer of a—(shall we say " the " ?) Sunday Paper—to deal sledge hammer blows on the Somme to relieve the sufferings of Roumania. And those were the days in November when men could hardly move in the trench ! ! ! ! The Military expert for the moment shares the honours with manufacturers of barbed wire, Jams and Bully—and is in great demand *now*. Some of us will be looking for him *and* Mr. Christopher too apres la Guerre.

" Wasted Food in the Army.
No doubt the reduction in the army bread ration is all right, and will not inflict any hardships on the men, but if it was possible to do it why, on earth wasn't it done before ? We have all heard rumours of bread wastage, and it ought not to have taken two years and a half to discover what was the right ration."

Daily Sketch, March 1st.

Only on one occasion in the course of Two years do we remember the Bread ration being in excess of the " right ration " : and only some half-dozen times we are pretty confident, has the issue been up to the " Right-Ration."

Soldiering.

" The Stonehouse platoon had a royal outing last week. A plane had been observed circling around overhead, and shortly news came in that it had alighted at the back of Mr. Jenner's farm, Moreton Valence Lane, and the call came for a guard for it. This consisted of Second Lieut. J. H. Tratt, Sergts. Cole and Gray, Corpl. Larque and Ptes. Mullins, Blick, Hall and Fletcher. These went off at 9-30 p.m. in a taxi, and Fletcher volunteered to bring hot oxo at 2 a.m. Farmer Jenner proved a trump, and gave over his dining room as a guard room, and in addition brought in gallons of cider, and nap was the order till dawn. When the oxo arrived Grey, Larque and Mullins were on duty, and when they were relieved hurried off to partake of the hot drinks, but, alas, found that under the Lieutenant the rest had cleared up the oxo and the cider, and so the poor dog had none. After Mullins had been on duty a quarter of an hour he curled himself up on the lower plane and slept like an infant till relieved, and to his joy when he awoke his guard time was up."

Stroud Journal.

"Good 'eavens! Who indented for you?"

Overheard at a Dinner Party some many miles behind the Line.

"Well, did you get to the Trenches this afternoon? I saw you coming back in the Rolls-Royce!"

"Yes, and the poor fellows are up to their knees in mud!"

"Yes, that's jolly hard, only they have got their waterproof sheets!"

Yet we are *winning!*

It is incumbent on all the Allies, especially on the British in view of our insularity, to look at the War upon all its fronts. It is as difficult for us to grasp the fact that General Smuts has cleared the Germans out of "German" East Africa—a tract of country as large as Germany itself—as to realise that our successful advance from Kut is calculated to menace very seriously the German interests in the East. "Antwerp — Constantinople — Baghdad" inscribed on the Balkan Express has long been the dream of Germany. The Russian and British success in Persia—where a Government in favour of the Entente Powers has been firmly established—and the relief of Kut, the capture of Baghdad and the end of the gross mismanagement in Mesopotamia, are all very favourable signs of the coming dawn.

Naturally, we are inclined to focus our attention on the Western Front, but the importance of movements in the East which will have a far reaching influence on the War, is frequently misunderstood and always underestimated.

"At———one of the enemy was seen jumping up and down seemingly endeavouring to keep himself warm. Stokes Mortars were fired at him."

Division Intelligence Summary from 8th—9th March.

It would appear that Stokes Mortars Bombs have the same Terpsichorean effect as the scent in "High Jinks."

Corps Intelligence Summary.

Covering the period from 7-30 p.m. 13th February to 7-30 p.m. 14th February.

"Two men, each occupying two dixies were seen to come out of trench———and vanish at———"

"His attitude to the war is curious. The ruins of cathedrals and the mediæval glories of Ypres do not greatly move him. The horrors of war—the agonies and deaths and wounds—have, he thinks, been over written. Even the noise of war does not impress him much. "The heaviest bombardment I heard in France," he tells us, "sounded merely like Brock's benefit on a much louder scale, and disappointed me extremely."

Extract from a Review in the *Daily News.* of Mr. H. G. WELLS' latest Book "War and the Future."

We cannot allow two such grossly misleading statements to pass unchallenged or unrefuted. The horrors of war have ever been hid from England. It is impossible to grasp the nature of modern war from behind the Lines. And is is not the amiable journalist comfortably piloted by the Press officer from G.H.Q. who either sees or hears everything. When he compares the heaviest bombardment to a Brock's Benefit, he is talking unmitigated nonsense. To understand the potentialities of the burst of a 5.9 How. (Hun) Shell, you must be "there," and not study a barrage through a telescope some five miles behind the Line.

The reviewer in the *Morning Post* rightly comments on the book when he writes : "The well-meaning attempt to make him (Mr. H. G. Wells) see the war from within has been a fantastical

failure. Throughout his tour of the Front he remains obstinately at home inside himself ; he is outside the war all the time."

"Apropos of the condition into which soldiers' clothes were apt to get, Lieutenant-Colonel Copeman said that the soldiers often turned their shirts in order to get relief. Asked if it gave relief, a soldier replied, Well, I think that the marching and counter-marching up and down breaks the little beggars' 'earts." (Laughter.)

From a Lecture at the Institute of Public Health.

We have often wondered why people at home are often so lugubrious. Perhaps the following information which appeared at the bottom of a page of the "Cheltenham Chronicle and Graphic" for March 10th may afford a clue.

"Lady——wife of Sir John——Bart, and sister of the late———, died at———, on Saturday morning.

Within a fortnight of entering his 102nd year, Francis T. Creech died suddenly at Poplar, where he had lived for a great many years.

Through the breaking of an electric fan in a Rochdale mill, a workman, William Buckley, was killed by an iron rod being forced five inches deep into his throat.

A former conscientious objector told the Hornsey Tribunal that after 20 months' Red Cross work in France he had decided to join a fighting unit.

While at mining rescue practice at Pontyrhyl, South Wales, Edward Thorne, a rescue instructor, and John Evans, master haulier, were suffocated."

Our best thanks are due to Lieutenant-Colonel Sinnot, C.M.G., for his series of articles on the Battle Honours of the Gloucestershire Regiment. He has come to the end of his task for the time being as there are no more official battle honours to describe. But the spirit of the "Old Braggs" is still alive. One Battalion—is it not chronicled by Mr. Buchan in his history of the war?—made history at Loos ; while on one occasion there were several battalions simultaneously on the Somme, occupied in making geography and winning back the soil of France for the French. "SOMME" certainly will have to be added to the already lengthy list. Meanwhile, all ranks have enjoyed Colonel Sinnot's summary.

From the Gloucester Journal," October 2nd, 1759.

City and County
  of Gloucester

To wit. At a Meeting of the Common-Council held on Thursday, the 27th Day of September, 1759. It is unanimously agreed and ordered, That a Bounty of TWO GUINEAS be given by this Corporation to every able-bodied Landman who shall, within One month, voluntarily enter into His Majesty's Service, in the Regiment of the Royal volunteers commanded by the Hon. Colonel Crawford. To every such Man, being approved of by a Magistrate of this City, and delivered to Captain Nugent, or any other Officer of the said Regiment, the said Bounty shall be immediately paid by the Chamberlain of the said City.

Payne, Town Clerk.

And whereas divers good marksmen in the Forest of Dean, and other Parts of the County of Glocester, might be of singular Use at this critical Juncture, and compose a Body of Light Infantry the most capable of annoying our Enemies in their present desperate Designs against the Protestant Religion, and British Liberties ; Therefore the Dean of Glocester, willing to shew a Disposition towards promoting the Publick Service, and for the better Encouragement of such skilful Persons to engage immediately in that Defence of their King and Country for which they are peculiarly qualified, doth hereby offer an Additional Reward of One Guinea to every Volunteer that shall be enlisted by the said Corporation of Glocester in the manner, and according to the Conditions above described ; Provided that such Volunteer will give those Proofs of his Dexterity in shooting at a Mark, within Three Days after his Enlisting, as shall be satisfactory to the afore mentioned Captain Nugent, or to any other Officer of the Regiment of Royal Volunteers : And the said Dean doth further promise to each good Shotsman enlisted and approved of as above, a warm Flannel Waistcoat to defend him from the severity of the approaching Season.

Josiah Tucker, Dean of Glocester.

We are indebted to Mr. Austin, of the Gloucester Library, for the above.

From the " *Daily Mail*, March 28th :

" GERMAN OFFICIAL.

Roisel, on the Cologne brook (*evidently a German Army name for it*), has been occupied by the enemy."

The Fleet Street O.P. again !

Items of Interest from Mr. Beach Thomas's account of the advance.

" High intelligence officers jumped on their bicycles and pedalled furiously miles beyond Bapaume."

" One group sniped a pigeon and cooked it under the eye of an airman at the corner of a wood."

Daily Mail, March 19th.

We have certainly been making history. In years to come the story of the scene enacted in the court-yard of a spacious farm at B——— will be told again and again in the little French village on the far side of the Somme. All ranks were represented— " Whacker " too was there—and Captain Hawkins called the soldiery and signallers to the " Present," what time two dainty maidens emerged from the little crowd of old men and women, and asked the Colonel to accept their gifts of welcome, a Tricolour and three tastefully made floral decorations. They had waited many long and weary months—and there had been very many *jours maigres* in that anxious period, so that there were many pale faces in the wan and weary collection of refugees. However, they were now wreathed in smiles. The Colonel replied in a suitable little speech and called for three cheers for La Belle France ; and the Entente Cordiale was cemented by this gracious interchange of courtesies.

" We'em a winning ! " The British Advance was well on its way and the Flying Column was an army in being. A perspiring Orderly arrives post-haste. The envelope is torn hastily open. The hour of its receipt duly noted on the space allotted and the Adjutant signs the envelope and the Mess anxiously awaits the news.

It is simply this, that Chaplains may no longer have horses.

In our opinion there has been nothing finer done since the signing of Magna Charta than the emancipation of the Chaplains horses.

We congratulate the authorities—it synchronises with the Revolution in Russia, the German Retirement, the British Advance, and is doubtless prophetic, we are sure, of even greater events.

" Two companies of our men were seen entering B———amidst scences of great jubilation."

Corps Intelligence Summary.

This brilliant piece of reconnaissance on the part of our airmen has evidently put others of his Corps on their mettle. We have noticed many aeroplanes swooping down on villages, also looking for the " J " in " Jubilation."

" THE GAZETTE."

The Business Manager would like to thank very much those who very kindly responded to his suggestions of further subscriptions.

The following letter from a Gunner Officer is typical of many—" Enclosed 20 Francs for sub for —— and Myself : if at any time you require any subs to make up deficiences, let me know and I shall be pleased to subscribe. " That's the spirit."

Another Gunner Officer has kindly guaranteed £50 in case there should be any difficulty in the republication of the entire Gazette in book form after the War.

Mr. Amery has very kindly sent a subscription to the Gazette fund in memory of his son, Pte. E. J. Amery, who fell on July 23rd.

We are sorry that some of the last Gazettes, which were sent off, never reached their destination. More than one complaint to this effect has been received.

There was a very great demand for the number, and it was very quickly sold out.

DIVISIONAL LIBRARY.

A number of authors not unconnected with the Artillery have promised to present copies of their Books, as a nucleus of the New Divisional Library. We append a list.

Ice and how to cut it.	Capt. W. O. R.
Nineteen and a half Brace.	2nd Lt. M.W.S.L.
Care of the feet or Thrush and how to cure it and Hows and how to do it.	Major C. P. N.
Drawing Room Etiquette	2nd Lt. D. D. B.
Skeleton Artillery Drill—or when not to drop the pole and Bows and how to use them.	Capt. E. B. L. L.
Mules and their Manners.	Lt.-Col. G. B. B.
Tanks and their Armament.	Major A. L. C.
Official Guide to A——.	C. T. B. M.
The two Bobs	Lts. A. C. & A. W. N.
Promotion made Easy.	Lt. Eric B.
The Dialectical Art.	Lt. H. B.
The complete Section Commander (By one who knows).	Lt. K. A. T.
The Anti-Feminist Movement. ...	2nd Lt. E. S.
Traffic and its Control.	2nd Lt. H. H. L.
A Day with the Grouse.	Lt. H. F. N. H.
My Oath and other Stories. ...	Major C. W. T.
The Adventures of Emma Tock. ...	2nd Lt. Scott, M.
Just one more and how to look the other way.	Major C. F.

We append a brief summary of those Books which we have so far had the pleasure of reading.

Tact.—A brochure dealing with the foibles of Brigade Wagon Line Officers, by Capt. H—— W——.

" Really ? By Jove."—A realistic novel, by Capt. W—— A——.

The Staff Officer.—An eulogy, by Major A. L. C——.

The Regimental Officer.—The sequel to the above, by the same author. Also an eulogy.

Words.—Not a dictionary, but deals, far from impartially with a few Obiter Dicta, culled in France, by Padre C. A. B.

Technical Regime.—A Manual dealing particularly with a regime of this sort by Major C. P. N——.

The Shoebury Course.—Its advantages are here clearly laid out by " SNIP."

The Driver.—Perhaps the best of the books sent us this month for review. It is human, does not place him on too high a pedestal, but is an appreciation, certainly deserved, by any R. A. Officer.

We hope that the Infantry will follow suit and forward some of their publications in due course.

THE LIBRARIAN.

————

PROMOTIONS AND APPOINTMENTS.

Lieut. E. Conder, to be Acting Captain while commanding a Company, 11/9/16.

Sec. Lieut. (Temp. Lieut.) G. Hawkins, to be Acting-Captain whilst commanding a Company, 13/9/16.

392   C. M. C.   Finch, F.

Confirmed substantive rank of C.-S.-M. with pay and, allowances of Warrant Officer Class II. ;

To be Sergeant :—

2532	Cpl.	Fry, F. W.
2374	,,	Barnes, H. C.
20704	,,	Hobbs, G. W.
1476	L/Sgt.	Coopey, A.
8370	Pte.	Griffiths, C. F.
20326	Cpl.	Marment, J.

To be L/Sergeant with pay :—

2428	Cpl.	Butcher, P. H
2088	,,	Hardiman, G.
2705	,,	Rea, W. E.

To be Corporal :—

1760	L/Cpl.	Caudle, H.
1835	,,	Mustoe, M.
2997	,,	Warwick, F.
1171	Pte.(L/C).	Gould, C. A.
3310	,,	Sully, G. E.
2842	L/Cpl.	Hyett, H. W.
1686	,,	Parr, F. J.
2630	,,	Chandler, W.
7163	Pte.	Buckland, J. C.
7473	,,	Pullin, E.
8418	,,	Lewis, G.
2465	L/Cpl.	Martin, B.

To be Lance-Corporal with pay :—

20250	Pte.(L/C.)	Craner, W.
2431	,,	Lait, F. G.
20208	,,	Fisher, W. H.
2751	,,	Curtis, T. B.
2433	,,	White, J. H. C.
1748	,,	Iles, J.
2927	Pte.	Derrick, H. S.
1599	Pte.(L/C).	Exell, W.
1646	,,	Parker, G. G.
20505	Pte.	Shellard, F. P.
4196	,,	Kiddle, A. F.
8417	,,	Brisland, T.
20498	,,	Phillips, F.
7378	,,	Pearce, A.
20765	,,	Thrush, C. S.
7639	,,	Edge, E. A.
7046	,,	Pringle, E. F.

To be Lance-Corporal without pay :—

4893	Pte.	Christmas, E. G.
20731	,,	Tonge, W. J.
5217	,,	McNesby, E. G.
20737	,,	Townsend, T.
2381	,,	Stephens, W. A.
2643	,,	Blackford, H.
4874	,,	Hicks, H. H.
5229	,,	Faithful, A. C.
2637	,,	Woolley, J.
6965	,,	Keeping, A. S.
20465	,,	Eves, E.
1656	,,	Ryder, E. J.
1756	,,	Roberts, R.
2447	,,	Michael, E. A.
1820	,,	Roche, W.
20761	,,	Lee, W.
1858	,,	Brisland, R.
2314	,,	Palmer, W. L.
3412	,,	Fletcher, L.
2640	,,	Wilkinson, T. G.
20281	,,	Cook, W. G.
2294	,,	King, S. R.
7121	,,	Russell, R. H.
7351	,,	Dyer, H. G.
4470	,,	Hodges, G.
4947	,,	Appleton, L. H.

"Bong Jour, Alf! Have you changed your socks to-day? If not, why not?"

5th Gloucester Gazette.

A Chronicle, serious and humorous, of the Battalion while serving with the
BRITISH EXPEDITIONARY FORCE.

HONORIS CAUSA.

MILITARY CROSS

Major D. J. Ward.
Second-Lieutenant N. P. Grubb.

THE DISTINGUISHED CONDUCT MEDAL

240854   Sergeant P. B. Cummings.

MEDAILLE MILITAIRE

240854   Sergeant P. B. Cummings.

MILITARY MEDAL

240050   Sergeant A. Coopey.
241005   Corporal R. Butt.
240887   Corporal P. G. Tolley.

TERRITORIAL DECORATION

Lieut.-Colonel J. H. Collett, C.M.G.

MENTIONED IN DESPATCHES

Lieutenant J. P. Winterbotham.
Lieutenant G. E. Ratcliff.
240545   Co. Sergeant-Major W. W. Bailey.
240289   Sergeant A. Jackson.

The following Officers were among those mentioned in
Despatches, dated April 9th :—

Staff :

Major-General R. Fanshawe, C.B., D.S.O.
Lieut.-Colonel A. I. R. Glasfurd, D.S.O.
Lieut.-Colonel G. H. Barnett, D.S.O.
Major. L. C. Bucknall.

Royal Artillery :

Lieut.-Colonel A. R. B. Cossart, D.S.O.
Lieut.-Colonel Lord Wynford.
Captain H. P. Lane.
Sec. Lieut. D. D. Bassett, A.D.C.
Lieut. J N. Hannam.

Royal Engineers :

Major J. Arrowsmith-Brown.
Major E. Briggs.
Captain J. R. N. Crawford.
Captain V. F. Eberle.
Captain F. E. Marston.

Infantry :

Major J. N. Aldworth, M.C.
Captain A. H. Gibson.
Captain R. G. Ellis (killed in action).
Captain O. M. James. M.C.

R. A. M. C. :

Lieut.-Colonel C. H. Howkins.
Captain J. J. H. Beckton.

Chaplain :

Rev. H. A. Meek.

We were glad to see also that—

Lieut.-Colonel G. N. T. Smythe-Osbourne, D.S.O.
Major E. V. Sydenham, T. D.
Captain Gabb, M.C.
Lieutenant J. B. Watling.

were mentioned in the same Despatches.

BIRTHDAY HONOURS

Staff :

MOST HONOURABLE ORDER OF THE BATH

K. C. B.

Major-General R. Fanshawe, C.B., D.S.O.

C. B.

Brigadier-General W. Strong.

ORDER OF ST. MICHAEL AND ST. GEORGE

Lieut.-Colonel A. I. R. Glasfurd, D.S.O.

THE MILITARY CROSS

Captain J. S. B. Hill.
Captain the Hon. R. D. Kitson.
Lieutenant A. J Muirhead.

BREVET MAJOR

Captain T. J. Leahy, M.C.

COMPANIONS OF THE D.S.O.

R. E.

Major E. Briggs.

R. F. A.

Lieut.-Colonel P. G. Lord Wynford.

R. A. M. C.

Lieut.-Colonel C. H. Howkins.

MILITARY CROSS

R. F. A.

Sec. Lieut. D. P. Morgan.

M. G. C.

Lieutenant R. H. Geldard.

R. A. M. C.

Captain R. A. Broderick.

We were also glad to see the following announcements—

BREVET LIEUTENANT-COLONEL

Major (Temporary Lt.-Colonel) G. N. T. Smythe
Osbourne, D.S.O.

BREVET MAJOR

Captain (Temporary Lt.-Colonel) J. Micklem, D.S.O.,
M.C.

Very many congratulations to M. Henaut, M.M., on
being awarded the Croix de Guerre.

The Rev. W. J. Selby was mentioned among those
who were thanked for their services in England.

Many congratulations to Captains Challoner, Moore,
and James on their Military Cross.

Very many congratulations to our old Brigade-Major,
Captain T. J. Leahy, M.C., on being mentioned in despatches
for the FIFTH time.

Congratulations on receiving excellent reports from
their various Schools to :—

Gymnastic Course : Corporal Tolley, L/Corpl. Hodges,
L/Corpl. Chandler, L/Corpl. L. Lane.

Army School : C.-S-M. Bailey.

Gas Course : L/Corpl. Aston, Corpl. Corlett.

Signalling Course . L/Corpl. Fry, L/Corpl. Trinder.

(Corpl. Corlett has since been severely wounded).

SKIT ON THE "ADMIRAL'S SONG"

from "H.M.S. Pinafore."

When war broke out, I thought I could assist,
So into the Infantry I did enlist.
I finished up my training somewhere down in Kent,
And very, very quickly out to France was sent.
And the bully and the biscuits did so well for me
That now I am the ruler of the King's Armee.

As a private in the ranks I made such a name,
That a Lance-Jack I so soon became,
I marched to the trenches with a step so light
And I carried up the rations in the dead of night.
I went over the top so frequently
That now I am the ruler of the King's Armee.

As a Lance-Jack smart was I upon parade
That a Corporal (Full) I soon was made,
With my wiring parties always I was on " qui vive "
That I soon had Sergeant's stripes upon my sleeve :
And the Sergeant's stripes did so well for me
That now I am the ruler of the King's Armee.

As a Sergeant I became so noted
To a Sergeant-Major I was soon promoted,
And then to make a bid for popularity
I gave away green envelopes so lavishly,
But I issued out the rum so judiciously
That now I am the ruler of the King's Armee.

As a Sergeant-Major who was known to have ambition,
The authorities were pleased to grant me a commission,
And as leader in a bombing raid, I drove the Hun so far
That it wasn't long before I got my second star.
And from that I rose to Captain so easily
That now I am ruler of the King's Armee.

By dodging all the work, and never getting rumbled,
Into further promotion I quickly tumbled,
And the posts of Major, Colonel, General,
I took in quicker time than it takes to tell.
And I " wangled " leave perpetually
So now I am the ruler of the King's Armee.

Now, soldiers all, whoever you may be,
If you want to climb to the top of the tree,
Be advised by a soldier of the old, old school
And you'll be a Field Marshal, if you follow this rule
Just " swing the lead " right lustily,
And you all will be rulers of the King's Armee.

F. O. LYSTER,
Corporal.

April, 1917.

ENGLAND AWAKES.

An Exaggeration in One (very short) Act.

Characters

EMMY RENDLE—the Cook.

MILLIE—the General.

MRS. TUNNOLPH CASSENS—the Ration Man.

A SHY YOUNG GIRL.

SCENE : ENGLAND — TIME : THE FUTURE.

Scene : A Kitchen of a middle class house in the West End of London. Furnished in the genteel middle class way. Time (as shown by a solid kitchen clock handing on the wall in rear) 11 a.m.

On the rise of the curtain there are two occupants of the kitchen ; MILLIE, the general, seated asleep before the fire on the left in a wooden arm-chair, and RENDLE, the Cook, seated at a wooden table in rear before the window. Through the window are seen iron bars proclaiming the fact that the room is in the basement.

RENDLE is busy calculating on a slate, and as she stops frequently to scratch her head the calculations are evidently causing her trouble. She is a stout and plain woman of about 30. MILLIE is a thin and ugly girl of about 19.

RENDLE.—(calculating.)—One thirty-eighths, two thirty-eighths, three thirty-eighths, four thirty-eighths, five thirty-eighths, six-thirty eighths, seven thirty-eighths — (She pauses and looks around, and becomes aware of the sleeping MILLIE). Drat the girl ! Millie ! Millie ! Wake up you lazy thing.

MILLY (yawns, stretches herself, and finally wakes up)—Well, what is it ?

RENDLE.—Why don't you 'elp me a bit instead of sleeping all day in front of the fire. What are seven thirty-eighths of an ounce ?

MILLIE.—Seven thirty-eighths of an ounce ? 'Ow should I know ? What you want to know for ?

RENDLE.—Silly ! I'm making out our pepper allowance, of course.

MILLIE.—I thought we was allowed a thirty-sixth of an ounce.

RENDLE.—So we was, but if you took an intelligent interest in the appenings' of the day you'd know it was reduced to a thirty-eighth of an ounce now.

MILLIE.—Oh !

RENDLE.—Yes, and 'eres eleven o'clock gone and the ration cart due, and I aint got 'alf my calcilations done yet. Really I don't know what things are coming to nowadays. It's enough to drive one silly 'aving to reckon out three days in advance 'ow much this and 'ow much that you're entitled to.

MILLIE.—Well, I always sez and I always 'ave said that I think Missus should make out them reckernings 'erself. Why, she been to school, ain't she ? And what did she learn all about 'em fractions for if she ain't goin' to use 'em now ?

RENDLE.—Well, I call it the fault of the Government. Why do they want to give us them rations ? Short of food in the country are they ? Well, let the poor 'ave what there is. It won't do them rich no 'arm to go without for a change.

MILLIE.—Lor, do talk sense, Emma Rendle. D'you think the Government—the People wot gets four 'undred a year—are going to give the food to the people and starve themselves ? Not likely !

RENDLE.—I didn't say anything about wot they was going to do. I was talking about wot they ought to do. But this chatting won't get my work done. I must get on working out these rashuns. Now, bacon. There's Master, Missus, Miss Dorothy, yerself, myself, and the two kids. That's two, four, six, eight, ten, and two singles—that makes twelve rashers of bacon. (She enters it on the slate.)

MILLIE.—What yer puttin' me down for ? You knows I never touch bacon.

RENDLE (scornfully).—Silly ! What difference does that make ?

MILLIE.—Well, what about the two kids ?

RENDLE.—They're under twelve. They're only allowed 'alf portion each.

MILLIE.—Oh! (There is a pause. Rendle goes on reckoning on her fingers) I thought you said you'd put down seven thirty-eighths of pepper.

RENDLE.—Well ?

MILLIE.—(Triumphantly)—You're wrong. It ought to be six thirty-eighths and that—that's three nine—teenths—

RENDLE.—'Ow do you make that ?

MILLIE.—There's Master and Missus—that's two, Miss Dorothy makes three ; you and I make five ; and the two kids—a 'alf each—makes six.

RENDLE.—Silly ! You don't understand nothing about it. Everybody, man, woman or child, hir-respective of age is allowed a full portion of pepper, of sugar, of milk, and of salt. Of everything else they're allowed a 'alf portion.

MILLIE.—(thoroughly squashed, only remarks) Oh !

RENDLE.—And now don't you get worrying me again. (She calculates for some time). Millie, just see 'ow much jam we've got left in the cupboard, will you ?

MILLIE.—(goes to the cupboard and opens it)— Two tins.

RENDLE.—We must get some more of that in from the Canteen.

MILLIE.—Jam's awful dear now, ain't it ?

RENDLE.—Four shillings a pound.

MILLIE.—No, really ? The Jam Manufactchers ain't 'alf got the wind up, then.

RENDLE (thoroughly inconsistent with her former remarks).—Yes, when things 'ave come to this stage I calls it a darn good job that the country 'as put us on rashuns. Where should we be otherwise, I should like to know ?

MILLIE.—Yes, so should I.

RENDLE.—It would ave been the food hoarders that's have got the lot—and then they'd have been made Lords and Ladies for their services to their country. (Decisively) No, it wouldn't have done. Wot was the good of keeping them restaurants open for the sake of the rich ? Aint Master just as well now when he takes his Ration biscuit into the city, as when he used to sit for two and a 'alf hours every day over chops and steaks and I don't know what not.

MILLIE.—'E got a lust for blood alright through eating them biscuits, but 'e 'aint so 'appy.

RENDLE (winks).—'E may not be as 'appy, but Missus is. That's because 'e can't waste a lot of time with the pretty waitresses.

MILLIE—(jealously conscious of her own lack of beauty)—Well, it's a jolly good thing that the hussies 'ave gone into the munitions at last. It will keep 'em a bit more shut up than they used to be.

RENDLE.—And to think that since last Wednesday they've closed every food shop of every description I can 'ardly credit it now.

MILLIE.—What time is the canteen open ?

RENDLE.—12-2 and 2-4.

MILLIE.—I hear we're to have an F. R. C. up here next week as well.

RENDLE.—F. R. C. What's that ?

MILLIE.—Food Reform Canteen. They're only going to sell nuts and things. It's been opened for the Vegetablians, and conscientious objectors.

RENDLE.—Well, well, I don't know what we shall be coming to next. I do believe they'll be issuing us out our rum before the war's over.
(A pause).

MILLIE.—Mr. Cecil hasn't been sending home so many parcels from the front as usual lately. Why it's over a fortnight since we had the last.

RENDLE.—Ah yes, but it contained a fine big cake. Why that lasted them nearly a week didn't it ?

MILLIE.—Yes, but we could do with some more soup. You can't get it for love or money now, and we're running short of sardines.

RENDLE.—I expect there'll be another one arriving soon. It's wonderful 'ow much food do come from the boys in France nowadays. Why, a friend of mine was telling me only the other day that—

MILLIE (interrupting to save herself hearing a story told already half a dozen times—Sarcastically) Yes, I think it's about time that the Army in France realised there's a War on.
(A pause).

RENDLE.—'Ere's Mrs. Martin's maid coming down the area. I wonder what she wants. Open the door, Millie. (Millie does so and admits. A SHY YOUNG GIRL of about 17).

SHY YOUNG GIRL.—Good morning, m'm. Our cook Clara told me to bring you round this parcel with a note.

RENDLE (glaring).—Don't call me m'm. Call me miss.

S. Y. G.—Yes, miss.

RENDLE.—Well, 'and me over the note.

S. Y. G.—Yes, miss. (Does so).

RENDLE (opens the note and reads).—" Madm—a Mrs. Martin having informed me, her cook, that she and 'er 'usbin, the General, will be dining with your lady to night, she' as gave me instructions to forward you the night's rations which I herewith enclose. I beg to remain, Yours truly, Clara Alling, Cook to Mrs. Martin." Oh dear, oh dear, more company. Millie, open the parcels and see what the rations are like.

MILLIE.—(opens it and produces meat, half a loaf of bread, a soup cube, and four sardines).

RENDLE.—H'm. Not so bad. (To the SHY YOUNG PERSON). Alright, missie, that will do. You can run along away home now.

S. Y. G.—Yes, Miss. (The Shy Young Girl exits).

RENDLE.—(is reading the letter, suddenly calls out) Hi! Missie! Come back a moment! Millie, call her back.

MILLIE.—(goes out and returns again in a moment with the Shy Young Girl).

RENDLE.—You'd better take a note with you, Missie, I'll just write one out for you. (She gets ink, pen, and paper from a drawer in the dresser, then she writes, reading aloud as she does so). " From Emma Rendle, Cook, to Clara Alling, Cook. Parcel and contents received and noted." There ! (as she puts it in an envelope). Will you give that to Miss Alling with my compliments ?

S. Y. G.—Yes, Miss.
(THE SHY YOUNG GIRL goes out again. As she does so she collides with an old man of about eighty who is carrying a wooden box with various things which he puts later on the table).

RENDLE.—Ah! the Rations at last. Millie, call down Madam.
(Millie goes out).

RENDLE.—Are they good to-day, Cassens ?

CASSENS (shakes his head slowly and wearily).—No. They be rotten.

RENDLE.—Dear, dear. What a nuisance, and company coming, too.

CASSENS.—You won't be feeding much company on them rations. (He shakes his head again sadly). (At this point, Mrs. TUNNOLPH, a middle-aged household lady, enters.)

MRS. TUNNOLPH.—Good morning, Mr. Cassens (hopefully) Good rations to-day ?

MR. CASSENS.—'Fraid not, m'm. Only bully beef and biscuits.

MILLIE—(protesting).—That's a shame, m'm. Why Mrs. Martin's just sent round some beautiful meat and bread and—

MRS. TUNNOLPH.—That will do, Millie. I didn't ask for your opinion. You'd better hurry round to the canteen and get those things I told you to this morning or you'll get there after it's closed.

MILLIE (meekly).—Yes, m'm. (She goes out).

MRS. TUNNOLPH.—Don't you think you could let us have a little of something else, Mr. Cassens ? You see, we've got some friends coming to dinner this evening. (Pleading) Just as an exception, Mr. Cassens.

MR. CASSENS.—Sorry, m'm. Rations is rations (He takes the things out of the box as he names them and places them on the table.) There's six tins of bully beef, four and a half pounds of biscuits with an extra quarter pound thrown in, twelve rashers of bacon, tea, sugar, pepper and salt.

MRS. TUNNOLPH.—But the tea, sugar, pepper and salt are all mixed.

MR. CASSENS.—I'm very sorry, m'm, but I couldn't 'elp it. 'Ad a little accident on the way up. My barrow upset and threw everything in the road,

but I wiped 'em all clean again. I'd a been 'ere quarter of an our earlier if it 'adn't been for that little mishap.

MRS. TUNNOLPH.—Oh dear, oh dear, oh dear ! What will the General say ? What are we to do, Rendle ?

RENDLE.—Lor, m'm I don't know.

MRS. TUNNOLPH.—I only hope Millie's successful in getting a good supply from the canteen.

RENDLE.—Yes, m'm.
(Pause).

MR. CASSENS.—Would you please to sign for these things, m'm, and let me 'ave any fresh ration indents as you 'ave so that I may be getting on my way again.

MRS. TUNNOLPH.—Have you got the indents ready, Rendle ?

RENDLE.—Yes, m'm. It's only waiting for your signature and the dining room stamp.

(MRS. TUNNOLPH goes to the table and signs it, after which the cook stamps it, and hands it to CASSENS).

MRS. TUNNOLPH.—One minute. We're going to dine with General Martin the day after to-morrow, Could we arrange to have the rations delivered straight there ?

CASSENS.—Yes, m'm if you give me the map reference.

MRS. TUNFOLPH.—Rendle, the map !

RENDLE.—Here, m'm. (She takes it from the drawer, and MRS. TUNNOLPH opens it out).

MRS. TUNNOLPH (Slowly).—Let me see, it's X one four " b "—no, " c " two nine. Is that correct, Cook ?

RENDLE.—I think that X one four " c " two nine is a reference in No Mans Road, m'm.

MRS. TUNNOLPH.—Well, it's just by the cross roads, isn't it ?

RENDLE.—Mrs. Martin lives about three houses down in Brigade Square, m'm.

MRS. TUNNOLPH.—That's quite right. Then it should be X one four " d " two nine.

RENDLE.—That's right, m'm.

MRS. TUNNOLPH.—Have you got that, Cassens ?

MR. CASSENS (from behind a note-book)—Yes, m'm. Then, with your permission, I'll be getting on now, m'm—Good morning, m'm.

MRS. TUNNOLPH.—Good morning, Cassens (He goes out).

(MRS. TUNNOLPH who has held up under the strain of the bad rations magnificently up till now, at length gives way to wild weeping.)

H. Q. 6th Army.   A. H. Q. 21-12 16.
Army Daily Orders—21-12-16.

DELIVERY TO CORPSE EXPLOITATION ESTABLISHMENTS.

It has become necessary once more to lay stress on the fact that when corpses are sent to the Corpse Utilisation Establishments, returns as to the units, date of death, illness, and information as to epidemics (if any) are to be furnished at the same time,

V. S. d. O. K.   J. A. BRAUN.

MRS. TUNNOLPH.—Well, Rendle, what ARE we going to do for this evening ?

RENDLE.—I'm sure I don't know, m'm.

MRS. TUNNOLPH.—We've got absolutely nothing else, have we ?

RENDLE.—No, m'm, nothing.

MRS. TUNNOLPH.—I can't understand why the food's so bad. I'm sure they must have better rations than this in Downing Street. Well, Rendle, all you can do is to mix the bully beef with Mrs. Martin's rations, and give us a little soup first and custard and sardines on toast after.

RENDLE.—Yes, m'm.

MRS. TUNNOLPH.—And while I think of it, Rendle, will you tell Millie not to sound the dinner gong this evening. The General's just come back from the front and he might think it was a gas alarm.

RENDLE.—Yes, m'm. (She is bending down over the ration box) Oh, m'm, here's a letter come up for you with the rations. (She passes it to Mrs. T.)

MRS. TUNNOLPH.—Ah, it's from Mr. Cecil. (She tears it open). Oh, no ! It can't be ! Rendle ! Mr. Cecil will be arriving home on leave ! any moment.

RENDLE (unperturbed).—Really, m'm. ?

MRS. TUNNOLPH (agitated)—Don't stand there gaping, Don't you realize the seriousness of it ? We haven't indented for any rations for him. Oh dear, oh dear, oh dear ! What shall I do ? Quick, Rendle. Run after Millie and tell her to get all she can at the canteen.

RENDLE.—Yes, m'm. (She prepares to go out, when Millie re-enters again).

MRS. TUNNOLPH.—Well, Millie ?

MILLIE.—I'm sorry, m'm, but the canteen's sold out. They've nothing but cigarettes and tobacco.

MRS. TUNNOLPH.—(with a despairing gasp) Oh : (She sinks into the chair by the fire and slowly sobs. The curtain, still more slowly, descends).

FIBULOUS.

TO SCIATICA.

Sciatica, be by me Friend yclept !
Thou former foe who through dark canvas walls
Into my tent at night with cunning crept
And screwed into my nerves a thousand awls.
They gave me sick leave then—eight weeks in town
To drive you from the nest built in my bones.
A fool—I drove. Since then you've done me down,
For months I've mourned for you with futile moans,
For since I came to France one starlit night
Thinking you in reserve—just tucked in tight
To wait my call. Alas ! Although you hark
To others wanting passage to embark,
Sciatica ! I've sighed to you in vain
To take me back to Blighty once again.

THINGS WE WANT TO KNOW.

Who is the officer with a " broody " tunic ? Is he in " C " Company ?

Are the married officers belonging to H.Q. Mess under orders to write to their wives every day ?

Are not the " Curios " the best show in France ?

Is it true that a certain Company Commander has lost the supremacy in jumping ?

Why did they issue cardigans when the hot weather came ?

Did the issue of rabbits coincide curiously with the mysterious disappearance of cats from L—— ?

Who is the famous " Bairnsfather " in C Company who, on being interrogated by the C. O. as to what he was doing, said he had " lost t'otheruns " ?

If the Padre was very pleased when the C. O. fell into a shell hole during the record breaking walk from—————Camp to ——Wood at 2-3 ak emma on ——— ?

If he was disappointed that there was no slowing down after this catastrophe ?

If he has decided to get up earlier and walk at his own pace in future ?

Who is the War-worn N.C.O. ? Has he done just 3 months ? Is he in No. 2 platoon ?

Who are the A. S. C. Subs who have rowed ? Is it true one officer RODE in a boat at Oxford ?

Who is the author of the " Pont S. Gregoire " ?

Is it true that a potenate in England is one with more than six potatoes in his larder ?

Did you see " Ike " of the G. ?

Who is the sentry who thought an orange light was the signal for gas ? Is he in " C " Company ?

Does the Editor know the best place to buy handkerchiefs ? By the by, did they fit ?

Is it true that the Intelligence Officer (Lieut. C-k) is to be presented with the freedom of L,—— in recognition of his architectural achievement ? When a shell (5.9) burst in close proximity to his slender cellar, did he ask the Pioneers and the Padre if it was " ours or theirs " ?

What did the Brigade staff say when they had to come up to R—— Wood ?

Who is the Field Officer (R.E.) who is expecting a visit from the skies ?

If one pound of rabbit is equal to one pound of meat, what percentage of Hun-extract is contained in a 5.9. ?

Who is the Major (R.F.A.) who lost himself in R——Wood ? Did the Sergeant who accompanied him console him by saying " Sir, we are not lost, but don't know where we are " ?

Who was the Officer who asked if the Very Lights were to light up the cellars. Is he in " D " Company ? Did the same officer try to find the North Star with a flash-lamp ?

Who ordered a " B ". Coy. working party to dig trenches for the Germans in the Hindenburg line ?

Who are " Our Kid " and " Nunky " ? When did " Our Kid " snaffle a week ?

Who got 10 days leave to buy his kilts in London ?

Who is the Chairman Junior ? Does he know the difference between a chat and a horse ?

Were there any trip wires across the ground where A and B played C and D at Rugger ? Or did the C and D full-back fancy a " booby " trap inside the ball ?

Who was " the chap that wanted calling at 2-30 " ?

Why do several officers drop their T's after they have secured positions of prominence ?

How long has No. 2 Mess been a Canteen ?   Who came and asked for a whisky and soda and produced half a crown in payment thereof ?

Why do certain individuals get " wind up " when it is announced that the Divisional Band will play ? Is it a sure sign of coming events ?

Who is the Corporal in A Coy who answers to the name of Corporal Kiss ?

And was it the same Corporal who said that he would bring down the next Bosch plane that came over our lines with a Mills 23 grenade ? And also is he the pugilistic champion who threatened to throw another N. C. O. down the stairs, in a billet at T——— ?

Is he a member of the " Dieu et mon Droit " League, and a strict sticker to the rules of the League ?

Was he the same one who under the role of a hair-cutter, cut a private's ear ?

Has he enough out of haircutting to retire " apres la guerre " ?

What did Jimmy do with the coal, and where was it found ?

Who is the Officer who called a certain Colonel an " Old Blighter " ?

When are the Officers going through the Hoop ?

Who were the two Officers who dismounted when the C. O. cracked his whip ?

Is it true that an Officer in D Company has been engaged to ride in the " Grand National " ?

What did the Padre say when he was warned for Riding Drill ? Did he say " Does the C. O. think this is a Cavalry Regiment " ?

Who got off the stretcher when he heard his Leave warrant had come through ? Is he in the Transport ?

Is it not well to remember, now that the *Nation* is muzzled, that it was the *Nation* who cried out in July 1914.—" Will no one muzzle Lord Roberts ?

Who is the A Company Lewis Gunner who is always bragging about his gun being the best and the cleanest ? When a Hun plane came over, was his the only gun which did not fire ? Is he in No. 3 Platoon ?

Is it true that there was some difficulty in ascertaining a suitable name for the Divisional Artillery Cow ? Had they to change its name after three weeks ?

Who is the M. O. who was ordered to establish an Advanced Aid Post and was informed that his

equipment would follow ? When the equipment arrived, did it contain merely

1. Bottle whitewash.
2. Thomas splints (incomplete) ?

Has the author of this Order proceeded to another Division ?

Who is the M. O. who took as his kit to an Advanced Dressing Station, Mirror gilt-edged, one, and Bed-wire, one ? Has he, too, proceeded to another Division ?

Is it true that the Officer Commanding a North Country Yeomanry Regiment has been decorated by the French for giving 2 tins of jam (borrowed from a cyclist) to the refugees in a village not taken by them from the Germans ?

What happened to the Divisional H. Q. bitch pack for three nights ?

What was to be the reward for one of them, if returned ?

Is it true that one of the pack tried to commit suicide on return by falling over a cliff ?

Who is the Town Major who thinks he can get his boots and puttees free ?

Who is the C. S. M. who wishes the white mule to be camouflaged ?

Did B Company servants enjoy their stroll on Whit-Monday afternoon ?

Who is the A Company Officer who dreams of gas ?

Who is the well-known Officer (Field Rank) who has at last decided that his hair should be cut in accordance with Dress Regulations ? Or is it only the hot weather ?

Who is " Buster " ?

Has not the traffic on the Belfast-Dublin route been a little overdone of late ?

What is the Order of the Soiled Diamonds ? Can a gallant Captain (R. F. A.) inform us ? Have his been replaced by D. A. D. O. S. ?

Who is the only Officer in the Division who refuses to leave the line when relieved ? Is he in the T. M. B. ? And who is Reggie ?

Who is the Officer who refused to believe that the young and dashing R. A. M. C. Officer, complete with crop, was a Lieut.-Colonel ? Is he in D Company ?

Was not Captain McC-nn-ll's attitude in the now famous photograph in the " Tatler " very striking ? Has that proposal from Eve been accepted ?

Has a gallant Officer (R. F. A.) had a second attack of Thrush ?

Now that an experienced Officer has been sent to superintend the building of sand castles, will the B. T. O. shortly proceed thither also to superintend the donkey rides ?

Who rejoices in the euphonious telephonic address of " Cadaver " ?

"Yesterday the Cavalry did some dashing work."—*Daily Paper.*

Who is the N. C. O. who asked—" Is there any more of Number Tea for 12 " ?

Who is the Sergeant who took four francs for one green envelope ? Is he on Headquarters ?

Who is the bandsman who picked up a rifle grenade and said it was a screw-driver ? Was he formerly a bomber ?

Who is the Sergeant who ordered a fatigue party armed with shovels to pile arms ? Is he in D Company ?

Who is the Padre whose favourite book is " Nicholas Nickleby " by Guy Boothby ?

Do the police like hard labour ?

Was it the Divisional Band which played to the Transport ?

Why was there no Cocoa in the Mess ?

Who is the Furniture Remover ?

Who is the Officer (M. G.) who put his foot in the Canal ?

Who is the Officer who fired five rounds from a revolver without the pigeon budging ?

Is it true that a certain unit has adopted a new ceremonial yclept " Ye bucklynge on of ye spurres ? " Is the kneeling position (in the mud) a very popular one ? Why should it be a public performance ?

Who is the Signaller who finds it rather difficult to " do his bally bottom button up " ?

Is it true that the German prisoners in England refused to work side by side with the Conscientious Objectors ? Did not the prisoners (German) say, " We have fought for our country, but you—— have not even done that " ?

Why was the Daily Divisional Intelligence Summary headed " From 6 a.m. May 30th to 6 a.m. June 1st." ? Is it consonant with the principles of the Daylight Saving Bill to try and do the month of May out of a day ?

Why does the " Daily News and Leader " speak of a " hydraphone " as helping the submarines to fire their torpedoes ?

Why is there a picture in this Year's Academy entitled " London Territorials in Pozieres " ?

A PRISONER.

SPRING.

We shiver by the heath's bright blaze
　And safe at home we bide ;
Upon the falling flakes we gaze
　And pity folks outside.

Our way through fog or sleet we grope,
　And hail each sunbeam's play ;
Alas ! with swiftly fading hope
　It might have come to stay.

We long the rustling grass to tread
　Where peeping daisies blush
And wild flowers gaily nod, instead
　Of wading in the slush.

But though the ground's a sea of mud
　We don't bemoan our lot,
And though the leaves refuse to bud
　And grow, we wonder not.

For Spring—with no excuse of war—
　In this our native clime,
Like our GAZETTE's worth waiting for,
　But rarely up to time !

　　　　　　　　　　　　M. L. G.

TO-DAY'S WAR DINNER.

" BULLY BEEF.

BISCUITS."

Recipe for Bully Beef. Beef, salt 203s., onion, tin.

Bully the beef slowly until tender, remove all the bones and cut meat into square hunks. Put in 1 lb. salt and cool in moderate oven for 1½ hours. Then squeeze into tin.

From the *Gloucester Gazette* Meatless Mouthfulls Handbook (30 cms. post free).

— Bn. GLOUCESTERSHIRE REGIMENT

Roll of Officers.

Actually Serving with the Battalion.

Lieut. Colonel A. B. Skinner.
Major D. J. Ward, M.C.
Captain L. R. C. Sumner, M.C.
　　,,　　G. E. Hollington.
　　,,　　R. F. McDowall.
　　,,　　F. F. Francillon.
　　,,　　E. Conder, M.C.
Lieutenant G. A. Lister.
　　,,　　E. J. Cornish.
　　,,　　J. P. Winterbotham.
　　,,　　G. Hawkins.
　　,,　　G. E. Ratcliff.
2nd Lieutenant　N. P. Grubb, M.C.
　　,,　　E. F. T. Fowler.
　　,,　　B. V. Bruton.
　　,,　　C. Logan.
　　,,　　J. F. La Trobe.
　　,,　　K. A. Robertson.
　　,,　　V. B. Bingham-Hall.
　　,,　　H. W. Cruickshank.
　　,,　　R. F. Rubinstein.
　　,,　　W. Walker.
　　,,　　A. J. Deaton.
　　,,　　N. Steel.
　　,,　　C. D. White.
　　,,　　F. S. Wagland.
　　,,　　A. K. Stanley.
　　,,　　W. Lake.
　　,,　　W. E. W. Bamberger.
　　,,　　W. R. Browne.
　　,,　　N. D. Gullick.
Hon. Lieut. and Qr.-Mr. C. F. Foote.
Captain M. St. C. Hamilton (R.A.M.C. (S.R.) Att.)

THE WINGS OF LIFE.

Poems by Cyril William Winterbotham (Printed for private circulation.)—J. J. Banks and Son, Cheltenham.

(Reviewed by Bishop Frodsham.)

Even an experienced reviewer may be forgiven when he acknowledges that, having read this little book with sympathy, he has hesitated long in writing a review upon it. In the first place it was printed for private circulation after the writer had laid down his life with a will for England's sake. Then the verses range over the whole gamut of a life short in years, but crowded with experiences such as were seldom given to young men before this war. The first poem was composed when the writer was a tiny boy ; the last only a few weeks before that Sunday night in August, 1916, when he gave up his life so eagerly. It would be preposterous for an outsider to write much upon the military details of the sacrifice. The Gloucesters, however, will remember long how Lieutenants Winterbotham and Moore, two friends, begged that they might lead their men in an attack on a German trench, and how both were killed.

Two characteristics stand out clearly in this book of poems—a deep devotion to nature and an equally deep religious spirit. A vivid realisation of the manifold beauties of earth and sky and sea is one of the striking features of the most gifted young men to-day. So far as their poetry is concerned this may be due in some sort of secondary fashion to the influence of Swinburne, who rejoiced in living to an extent that is a perennial surprise to all who knew him and his physical limitations. In form, though not so surely in spirit, Swinburne wrote with all the meaning of the things that are seen. The Hebrew poets were equally in love with nature, but they saw at all times the handiwork of the Most High. The heavens declared the glory of God and the firmament shewed his handiwork. Though without speech or language their voices could be heard around them. The rustling leaves of the forest clapped their hands together in worship of Him that walketh upon the wings of the wind. Rupert Brooke, particularly in his earlier poems, reflected the Greek spirit. Cyril Winterbotham from his boyhood appears to have listened for the divine undertone in all earthly music. This religious spirit was realised by his fellow soldiers, who are quicker in such matters than the world realises, even though such men are generally slow to speak. After his death two wrote upon the matter, one saying that his dead comrade had always reminded him of Donald Hankey's " Beloved Captain," the other that his officer was a " real Christian."

There was humour of a good, kindly, warm-hearted, English variety in Cyril Winterbotham, and without such human understanding no man or woman can hope to stir the responsive heart-strings of a race that takes great pains to disguise a deep tenderness, far removed from Teutonic sentimentality. The German can move himself like any Panurge or Pantagruel to copious tears, and yet remain as much a libertine and a drunkard as either of his Rabelaisian prototypes. The Englishman would be ashamed of a catch in his voice, but he would never have ravaged women and children, even in an enemy's country. It is his humour that makes him throw a cigarette to Fritz, though had the cases been reversed, he knows Fritz would have tried to kick him in the stomach. The readiness to pity men when they are down, to see the sad and the funny side of human nature, to do a kind deed with a rough word, has been the mark of the English as far back as the days of Chaucer, and earlier too. Such was Winterbotham's humour. It included inanimate objects like that disappointing " damned awful trench " called " Marguerite," and impersonal cats and starlings. What generous English boy, despite his scorn of " tommy-rot," will fail to understand the shame the poet felt when he had wrought his will upon a starling who had dared to share with greedy man the fruits of the earth ?

> " Poor bird ! I see thee lie,
> Wild pleading in thine eye,
> Thy bill fear-parted,
> Thy plumage piteous spread,
> Raised only thy poor head
> Toward me, harsh-hearted !
>
> Upon thy dread-heaved breast
> On tender grass blades pressed,
> Soft radiance brightly
> Gleams with a tender sheen
> From mingled red and green—
> Yet struck I lightly !
> . . . .
>
> O'er whispering reeds to-night
> Midst loud-winged squadron's flight
> Vacant thy station !
> Moved by thy piteous gaze
> Pity in me doth raise
> Fear to mar, joy to praise
> God's least creation.

The verses are simple enough, but they ring true.

In the valley of the shadow where death walks constantly abroad, it is not surprising that a man like Winterbotham should perceive his form constantly, and while answering to the spirit stronger than death, yet ache with the pity of it all. Here are two examples. The first poem is quoted in full and is entitled " A Casualty."

> " Come, for the cause is good, stout heart, strong hand
> England needs now. Death—for your native land ?
> The cause is good ! "
>
> Poor hackneyed words ! But yet his manhood woke
> And held it true—it matters not who spoke,
> The cause was good.
>
> Poor hackneyed words ! We heard them once again
> From dying lips, teeth clenched against the pain,
> For thus he spoke, and so his loss was gain,
> " The cause is good ! "

The second poem is entitled " The Cross of Wood " —a mark raised over the friends who had fallen during the push forward in July, 1916—and it concludes :—

> " Not now for you the glorious return
> To steep Stroud valleys, to the Severn leas
> By Tewkesbury and Gloucester, or the trees
> Of Cheltenham under high Cotswold stern.
>
> For you no medals such as others wear—
> A cross of bronze for these approved brave—
> To you is given, above a shallow grave,
> The Wooden Cross that marks you resting there.
>
> Rest you content, more honourable far
> Than all the orders is the Cross of Wood,
> The symbol of self-sacrifice that stood
> Bearing the God whose brethren you are."

It was but a very little farther on to the spot where the young poet's body sleeps, but his soul is waiting content—can his friends doubt it ?—in the sure and certain hope in which he lived on earth.

" Boots may be drawn
from the Q.M. on exchange."

ANY NIGHT IN TRENCHES.

With apologies to the author of " Temple Bells."

When the Whistling Pigs are flying
And the Emma G's are crying
    I lie hidden in some deeply sunken lair,
Or I go around the posts
Where the German dead in hosts
    Poison all the dank and humming air.

Ration parties loudly swearing
At the bundles they are bearing
    Form in multitudes about my dug-out door,
And no sooner do they leave us
Than strafes both long and grievous
    Come from the battalion by the score.

An inquisitive R. E.
Comes up our line to see,
    And tells us all the rumours of the War.
Oh ! he makes me nearly swoon
For he says that very soon
    We'll boost, and our objective's O.G. 1.

G. H.

WHITSUN WHITSUN WHITSUN

**Popular Patrols for all Persons. Have you seen the
HINDENBURG LINE ! If not, why not !**

Messrs. FANSHAWE, WATT and Co. beg to
announce that their arrangements for their 3rd
Annual Whitsuntide Patrol are now completed. The
party which will be conducted by experienced guides
will assemble at the CHATEAU in X 10.8d at 12.15
ack emma, and, proceeding by the BOYAU BON
CHANCE, will arrive at the famous LINE at 1.30 ack
emma. On the way the now popular pastimes of
Leaping the Lid, Boring through the Barrage, and
Wangling the Wire may be freely indulged in by all
without extra charge. Arrived at the LINE, the party
will proceed along or through the wire at the discretion of the guide ; here by special arrangement, a
display of MINEN, FLAMEN and other WERFERS
will be given, and the party will be given a unique
opportunity of observing at close quarters howitzers,
whiz-bang, emma-gee and arquebus fire.

Within the LINE, the party will be warmly
received by a band of bomb-boosters, touring under
the auspices of HINDENBURG, FALKENHAYN
and Co. Here the party will separate, part conducting
the B. B's., to the starting point, where they will
hand them over to a representative of Messrs.
ATHLUMNEY and Co. ; the remainder will, without extra charge, be accommodated in the commo-
dious ferro-concrete residences for which the LINE is
famous.   These are replete with every modern
convenience, including gas, and will be vacated by
the present tenants on short notice.

Biscuit-boxes, of the latest fly-proof pattern, will
be carried on a limber driven by the D.A.D.M.S.,
this service is for first-class passengers only ; second-
class passengers will make their own arrangements
in this respect.

Names of those unable to find sufficient excuse for
not joining the party, accompanied by name and
address of next of kin, must reach the D.A.A.G. by
11.0 pip emma on Whitsun Eve.

N.B.—The pastime of swinging the lead is not
included in the programme.

ENGLAND FOR THE ENGLISH ?

Daily Mail, May 2nd.

" Photograph of W. T. HAIKE, who claimed
exemption at FELTHAM as a Mormon Minister. *The
Court was equally divided.*"

Conscientious Objectors at Dartmoor.

AN ENJOYABLE TIME

The 700 conscientious objectors on Dartmoor seem
to be having an enjoyable time (says the " Western
Morning News.") They are mostly sturdy young
men from 19 to 28 or 29 years of age. They apparently
have conscientious objection to the work allotted
them, but they have a large number of privileges
which would be appreciated by the men who are risking
their lives in the trenches. For example, many have
left Princetown this Easter for a six days' holiday,
which they call the " recess," and it may be noted
by a wondering public that the railway fares are
paid by the authorities. It has come as a shock to
people of the district, some of whose menfolk in
khaki have to remain on duty for long periods without visiting home, that these " C.O.'s " get long
leave. The rule that smoking should not take place
during working hours has practically gone by the
board, and the objectors who feel inclined to smoke
do so when and where they please, even in the
cookhouse and bakehouse, and even whilst food is
being prepared " fags " are lit up and the culprits
take no notice of words of expostulation. One warder
did express himself to the effect that he thought
smoking was not allowed during work time, and was
met with the rejoinder, " I know it isn't, but who is
going to stop us ? " The conscientious objectors have
petitioned against the working day of nine and a half
hours, but after the day's work has been done they
are free to walk out, make their private purchases,
etc. A large number have bicycles and have
enjoyable spins on the moors, and many have brought
their womenfolk to the locality."

What an extraordinary people we are.

From the *Saturday Review*, May 5th, 1917 :—

To the Editor of the *Saturday Review.*

28th April, 1917.

SIR,—Sir Alfred Turner has very properly called
attention to the fact that there are in this country
sufficient fanatics to contribute comforts and luxuries
to the value of £31,000 to our overfed and over-
pampered German prisoners, men who a few months
ago were, as likely as not, butchering our wounded
and committing every kind of brutality on the
civilian population of the countries through which
they were passing. Surely the names of the subscribers to this fund should be more widely known.

The list that has been published by the British
Empire Union Monthly Record contains the names
of the following :—

		£	s.	d.
Sir Ernest Schiff ...	...	50	0	0
Baron Schroder ...	...	650	0	0
Sir Edgar Speyer ...	...	5	0	0
Sir Ernest Cassel ...	...	200	0	0
Mr. Barrow Cadbury	...	750	0	0
Cadbury Bros. ...	...	1500	0	0
Mr. Joseph Rowntree	...	270	0	0

Among the politicians we have :—

	£	s.	d.
Lord Courtney	30	0	0
The Rt. Hon. W. H. Dickinson, M.P.	4	4	0
Mr. Aneurin William, M.P.	10	0	0
The Rt. Hon. J. H. Williams, M.P.	10	0	0
The Rt. Hon. Sir J. Simon, K.C., M.P.	20	0	0
Viscount Haldane of Cloan,O.M.	75	0	0

I presume this is a registered charity. If so, who is responsible for allowing such a body to exist ?

Your obedient servant,

WILSON NOBLE."

Of course one does not know everything, but would not the money have gone very well into the war loans ? One cannot help thinking that anyhow it would have looked nicer there, wouldn't it ? The Australians found three of their wounded with their throats cut ! !

REST DURING THE ADVANCE.

We are having a rest, I was told to-day,
We sleep and we eat and we draw our pay,
Of course we deserve it after two years' work,
Work like blazes, we do—we never shirk.

So what do we first, but " breakfast in bed " !
" Come out of it quick," the C. S. M. said,
And if you remained with some folk to brew,
You'd very soon find they'd make breakfast of you.

No work to-day to spoil our good rest—
Parade at 8.30 to give us a test,
On fighting-order duties and things we've forgot ;
I don't see the use of learning such rot.

The O. C. decides that the boys need fresh air,
So we practice a raid—a murky affair—
We start in good order, march all the way,
We've done a good march without knowing to-day.

What ! An afternoon off ?—too good to be true !
I'll mend up my kit and write to Aunt Sue,
No, I've got to play football and rations to get,
I'd sooner be " working " than " resting " you bet.

THE OFFENSIVE SPIRIT.

Arthur Smith joined the Army with laudable speed on the outbreak of War. He thought that he would be furnished with a sword or bayonet and sent immediately to Belgium to get at the Germans. Instead, he was furnished with a Platoon, and told to train himself and it. The comparatively short time of training seemed interminable, and sometimes a doubt arose that the War would be over before he could get out. He almost wept with mortification, for he was determined to win a V.C.

Nevertheless the Division did at last go out, and in fulness of time took over trenches.

Our hero was full of zeal, and spent his time in evolving schemes for the further discomfiture of the Boche. No Man's Land saw him frequently, and he was always " among those present " on the bombing ground. A couple of months passed, and his sector of trench received ever increasing artillery attention.

The Division was eventually relieved, and had a short rest out. The offensive spirit revived, and 2nd-Lieut. Smith thought longingly on an M.C.

After the Division had been fattened, it went into an attack, the remnants being taken out, re-fitted, and reorganized, and drafted up to strength. Among these was Acting-Captain Arthur Smith, whose thoughts ran on the construction of deep dug-outs, and how to save unnecessary casualties. They had a good rest out, and he was again ready to do his bit.

The next attack saw his Division prominently engaged, and supplying War Correspondents with valuable copy about London Territorials and Scotsmen.

Our hero survived this attack also, and has applied for transfer to the A.S.C.

G. H.

THE FATE OF THE NAVY.

" I wish some Member of Parliament would ask Mr. Macpherson for a return showing how many Territorial Officers in France have been given Divisional and Brigade Commands. We should then know whether they are getting fair play or the reverse. It would be impossible to refuse such a return on the ground that its publication would assist the enemy, for the figures would be too small to give him any idea of the number of troops by whom he is opposed.

I feel, with many others, that after three years of war equality of experience must have been established between all officers, whether they belong to the Regular Army, New Army or Territorial Forces, and, this being so, it strikes one as unjust that Regular Officers should monopolise all the higher commands and staff billets, while their Territorial brethren are confined to their trenches.

A suggestion has been put forward that Sir Douglas Haig should have on his staff, as an additional Military Secretary, a senior T. F. Officer, who has the confidence of our citizen army, and who would be able to advise the Commander-in-Chief in regard to the promotion and appointment of officers of the forces. Lord Scarborough performs this duty at the War Office, but now G. H. Q. in France is a more powerful body than the Army Council, and it is desirable in the general interests that the Commander-in-Chief should have other advice at his disposal than that of the Regular Army Officers of his staff, who are all men of picked ability, but naturally disposed to favour the claims of their own caste rather than those of outsiders."

Truth, May 2nd, 1917.

The Office Boy—having had the presumption to read our proofs—has forwarded a cutting from *Strooth*, a paper of which we have never heard.

" We consider it high time to direct the attention of the gold braided Lords of the Admiralty to the shameful way in which Officers of the Royal Naval Reserve are being treated, and to tell them plainly that WE will not stand it any longer.

On OUR suggestion (vide STROOTH, 20th May, 1917), the following questions were put to the First Lord of the Admiralty by the Honourable Member for SLUSH (Mr. GAS BAG)—

" If any Officers of the R. N. R. had been given command of (A) Battle Squadrons, (B) Cruiser Squadrons, (C) Torpedo Boat Flotillas ? "

Sir E——C— replied, " The answer is in the negative." Some further remarks of the First Lord to the effect that ' Officers were selected for high commands on account of their experience of all forms of warfare and of different branches of the service ' met with the contempt it deserved.

Irish Members signified their disapproval with loud cat-calls, and Mr. G——l " cocked a snook " at the Speaker.

This outburst clearly shows the feeling of the Country regarding this matter. It is surely clear to the meanest comprehension that *three years' war experience places all Officers on an equality*, whether they belong to the Royal Navy, R.N.R., or R.N.V.R.

WE have no great fault to find with Sir David Beatty (at present) or his Staff, but the Great British Public must see to it that some well-known Officer of the R.N.V.R. (Mr. G—rg- Gr—ssm—th's name has been suggested) should join the Staff as Assistant Military Secretary to see that Officers of these services are fairly treated."

(STROOTH, 25th May, 1917).
(That's all very well : but no one has complained of the Treatment meted out to the Territorial units— the R.N.V.R.—serving in the Royal Navy.—ED.)

MOBYLYTEE.

Nowe everyman hath of a strycte and of a byndynge necessitee a compulcioun to looke ryghte well unto itte that he hath as fulle and eke as copius a measure of ye goode thynges of Lyfe as he maye come by, whether privylee or openlie it skilleth not a whit. Itte is most certaynlie uppe to hym above ye consideracioun of alle otherne and sundrie thynges to paye ye highest regarde unto ye mobylytee of hymself in ye Warre. Ye Chaplayne, itte followeth, seeth that suche porciounne of ye Bookes of Hymnes as may be convenientlie carried be pleyced—whether privilee or openlie, it skilleth not—albeit they muste be so pleyced—in ye nookes and crannies of ye Lewyse Gunne Lymbers. Somme Chaplaynes of greater daring hath so cozened ye reinsman of Ye Gee S. Carres, that a spotte hath been from tyme to tyme connyved atte beneathe ye very syttynge of ye reinsman, wherein such Chaplaynes be worthie, in myne opinioun, of ye greateste praise and renoune. Howbeith, there lieth upon Chaplaynes who whould endeavour themselves to follow in ye footsteppes of such darynge ones, to stablishe a confederacioune with ye batteman, ye faithful Friar of orders manye, who haplie canne, of his insyghte and discretioun, cause ye porterage of such Hunne fowlynge-pieces as his Master, the Chaplayne, may secretlie come by.

Perchance ye Quartermaster hath packages both great and smalle lurkynge throughoute ye carres of baggage, the which an they brought to revelacioune by suddeyne inspectioun, would dysclose ye consummaciounne of clevernesse. Ye sygnallers too, itte hath been noted, have ye mobyle Musikhall Boxes whereby they have gotten to themselves, and eke to ye troopes, no smalle distractioun and jollificatioun.

But to nonne hath it been granted to behold ye mysteries of ye chest that beareth ye inscriptiun "Ye comforttes of ye Chirurgeon." No marshall hath yet penetrated its mysteriousnesse, to ye greate skylle and witte of ye directorre of ye comforttes, who hath a lyghter load to carry hisself.

Ye devyce, in addicioun, of ye possessioun of a paire of valeeces, certynlie be one of ye greateste subtilltie. So what time ye minions of ye Quartermaster do raise ye valleeces of ye Officers uppe to and eke uponne ye shoulder, certes ye valleece seemeth a lyghte thynge of no undue weyghte, to ye greate and pleasynge gullynge of ye Quartermaster. Sith indeed it be easier to secrete one's goods, chatteyls and souvenires in ye two valleeces, such behaviour is, in very sooth, meritynge ye highest praise and congratulacioun. Wanglynge of such consummate artystrie doth speedilee earne ye hyghest meed of praise.

Lyghtness it apperteyneth to all ye Troopes to acquire againste ye wearinesse of ye marchynges. Howbeit, when ye Brygade doth proceed on its marchynge, it falleth, perchance, grievous upon ye common footmen that they be constreyned to marche at ye steppe which ye Sygnallers shall selecte, sith ye Signallers have ye excellente good fortune to porther their packes on ye velocipedes.

And in connectioun with ye velocipedes there hath, we make confessioun, been of late a case of greede bothe evydente and revoltynge. To the Chaplayne, sith he hath been under compulcioun to discard from strengthe his croppe for ye Pylgryme's staffe, there hath, of ye kyndnesse of ye authoritee, been devysed a velocipede of a certyne great lyghtnesse and subtile artystrie, wherewithalle he maye ye more speedilee, and to hys greater comfortte accomplyshe ye marchynges. Butte, as it doth for ye nonce on occasiouns fall out that such medalles as ye Allye, in whose fayre terrain we be hotlie engaged in ye moyle of ye battles, reache not unto ye common Battalounes, so itte hath been discovered that an Officer of ye Rose Ribbonne hath been disportynge both hisself and his wyly coadjutorre upon ye velocipede of ye Chaplayne.

Howbeit, sith it be incombente on alle to render themselves of ye greateste mobylytee, all men includynge ye Chaplayne, who hath fallen a vyctyme to this exceedynge subtilltye, give a faire meed of praise to ye Rose Ribbonne who hathe therebye achieved ye greater mobylytee.

And ye porterage of hisself and of his chatteyls calleth for subtletie at alle times, and therein lyeth ever ye greate concerne of ye footman.

VON T ORPZ.

How doth the little busy Hun
Improve each gallant dead ?
He turns him into butter
And eats him with his bread !

I'll tell you the glad story
Of Heinrich Fritz von Torpz,
Who served his country living,
And later as a corpse.

Our hero was a Prussian Guard
In Regiment Number One.
He smelt of beer, he had a leer.
The Beau Ideal Hun.
One day he tried to stop a shell,
Now he has gone to—Who can tell ?
Perhaps he's swaggering in ———— ?
We'll hope he finds it's fun !

"The old Sweat"

The MAJOR & TINY

Now very early in the War
He won deserved renown.
He murdered three old women
And burnt their houses down.
Fritz in the hour of danger,
Was never at a loss,
He bayonetted a baby,
   And won the Iron Cross.

He cut down trees, he poisoned wells,
He rifled many a grave.
He killed five wounded prisoners,
   Oh, Fritz was very brave !

One day our hero stopped a shell.
Alas for poor dear Fritz.
He mutter'd " Gott strafe England "
   And blew away in bits.

They put the pieces in a sack
And labelled it " Von Torpz,
Neck 25, girth 53,
   A very useful corpse."

CHITS.

We have much pleasure in publishing the following chit from Sir B. F. Chortle, Bart, and regret that it was received too late for insertion in our previous issue :—

                     April 1st.

" Dear Sir,

Hearing this morning that there is an European War in progress (my wife tells me she can get no potatoes for dinner to-night) I feel it incumbent on me to write immediately to you, the leading Organ of our Army in France. I may mention that during my service in the Boer War (and even now I write with righteous indignation) I volunteered as a General, but the Government refusing my offer, I finally ended up on the Cookers, and I remember with vividness that in spite of the serious decrease in the birth-rate there was an alarming increase in chits, as is exemplified in the following ditty which we used to sing at that time :—

    Jack and Bill went down the Ville
      For fuel, but soon were strafed—A—
    Las ! SOMEONE came and saw their game
      And chits came tumbling after.

I can also even remember the barrage that issued from our mouths one evening when we received a succession of red chits (were they all read ?) and it is in the hope of curtailing this unnatural pest against which as yet no M. O. has found a suitable serum that I am writing to you now. As a preliminary I should like to make the following few suggestions.

(1) No chits to be more than 50 words in length or to make use more than three times of the mystic Arabian hocus-pocus AAA.

(2) That the Officer or O. R. responsible for cancelling a chit be made to impart the information personally to all concerned (I am of the opinion that this alone would encourage a 75 per cent. saving).

(3) That all chits when sent out be labelled either " Read " or " Destroy." The manner of destruction I propose is that frequent paper chases be held in all battalions. Fatigue parties could be detailed on the previous evening to mince the chits.

(4) That in order to economize the personnel employed, dogs should be trained to track down O. C. all Companies, and to return chits either to O. R. or to the incinerator on conclusion of their task. If the O. C. Company proved refractory the dog could easily be trained to remove a piece of puttee.

(5) All chits will be laid out daily in fine weather in the area allotted to Battalions for training. If this space is insufficient, application should be made to the B.C.O. (Brigade Chit Officer) for further allotments. The parade will be taken by the Orderly Officer, who will inspect with drawn sword.

The above few suggestions would, I think, considerably improve the situation, but as the matter is undoubtedly one on which final Victory depends, I have to-day written to the Government offering my services as the President of a " Commission to enquire into the wastage occasioned by Chits and means to be employed to induce economy in this direction " (or " O. C. Chits " as you terse chaps will probably call it). I intend taking over the Ritz Hotel and hope with the aid of not more than a thousand young men to advance my labours to such an extent as to be able to make a report on the subject on the conclusion of the War. This can, however, only be done provided I have the necessary sympathetic co-operation from all battalions, and it is through the publicity of your columns that I appeal to all C. O.'s to forward me all drinks—red and white or black and white, so that they may be collected and collated at our Headquarters. Do not hesitate to send them. The longer our work lasts, the more pleased we shall be !

I must apologise for presuming on your space to this extent, but feel sure that you realise the National Urgency of the question. Letters addressed to the Ritz Hotel, London, W. 105, will find me.

                Yours, etc.,

                Sir B. F. Chortle, Bart.

(*Erratum.*—For " drinks " in last paragraph but one read " chits.")

                    A. A. A.

THE CURIOS.

We have much pleasure in publishing the programme of " The Curios," though we hasten to warn our readers that an entirely new programme has since been arranged. But their success has been so signal since re-organisation, that the Programme of what must be one of the very best, if not the best, shows in France, is worthy of being placed on record.

PROGRAMME

Part I.

1. Opening Chorus.
2. Song and Chorus   ...   " The Finnegan Fusiliers"
                Pte. S. RAYNER.
3. Duet ...   ." Man and Wife "
      Sergt. V. CRUICKSHANK and Corpl. LYSTER.
4. A Revised Version of " Back to the Land "
                Pte. R GREEN.
5. Humorous Song   " My Bally Bottom Button"
             Gunner G. THOMPSON.
6. A Parody of " The Admiral's Song "
              from " *H.M.S. Pinafore* "
            Corpl. F. O. LYSTER.
7. A Quartette ... ..." Mayfair "
    Corpl. F. O. LYSTER Sapper F. PALMER,
      Ptes. R. GREEN and R. CLARK.
8. Picture Number   ...   ... " Bells of St. Malo "
             Pte. B. HERBERT.
9. Song and Chorus   ...   . " Blighty "
          Sapper F. PALMER.

Part II.

1. A Simultaneous Dance.
   Gunner L. SAUNDERS and Pte. B. HERBERT.

2. Character Song ... ... " Parson and Me "
   Pte. E. COOTER.

3. Music Hall Singers Burlesqued.
   Pte. R. GREEN.

4. " Ri-ti-ti-ti " ... ...A Coster Number
   Pte. B. HERBERT, with Sergt. CRUICKSHANK
   and Gunner THOMPSON.

5. Character Trio ... ..." Three Beggars "
   Gunner THOMPSON, Ptes. COOTER and RAYNER.

6. Dickens Impersonations.
   Gunner SLEIGHT.

7. Impressions and Impersonations at the Piano.
   Pte. A. CHIDZEY.

8. " Motoring " ... ... Mr. Harry Tate's Great Sketch
   (By kind permission of the Author).
   Gunner G. THOMPSON, Pte. R. CLARK and OTHERS.

At the Piano : Ptes. W. BROOKS and A. CHIDZEY.

God Save the King.

OUR BENEFACTORS.

Army Council	Back Badge.
Mr. W. R. Voller.	Papers.
Queen Alexandra's Field Force Fund	
	Socks, Shirts and Matches.
Harrowgate Women's Sewing League	Socks.
Sutton Coldfield Women's War Aid League.	Shirts.
Kensington Association for Supplying	
Comforts.	Socks.
Kettering Association of Voluntary War	
Workers	,,
Newbury and District War Hospital Depot.	Shirts.
Somerset Voluntary Help Association	,,
Mrs. Kerr	Papers.
The Hon. Mabel Gye	,,
Bishop Frodsham.	,,
Miss Karn.	,,
Miss Backhouse.	,,
Lieut.-Colonel Marling.	,,
Colonel Griffith	,,
Lady Slater.	Socks and Shirts.
Pte. Wood	Typing.
Pte. Gould.	,,
Pte. Lucas.	,,
Camps Library.	Books and Papers.
Ladies of Gloucester, per Mrs. J. H. Collett.	
	Shoulder-badges.
Sergt. Higgs.	Typing.
Liverpool Civic Service League.	Socks.
Mrs. Rising.	Papers.
Mrs. Temple Cooke.	,,
Mrs. Stanley Tubbs	Cigarettes.
Mr. Jack Margetson.	,,
Mr. G. H. Gothard.	,,

FOOTBALL.

ASSOCIATION

Glo'sters v. D.A.C.

This match was played on 5th May in rather hot weather and on a very hard ground, which made anything like good control of the ball difficult.

The Glo'sters were the better side, and eventually won 3-1, but it is only fair to say that our opponents were handicapped by having to play in their ordinary clothes and Field boots. The game was very fast all through, and plenty of knocks were given. The Glo'sters were the first to score, Pte. Mason at centre forward beating the goal keeper. The D.A.C. now got together, and forced a corner from which a goal was obtained.

During the second half the Glo'sters had most of the game, and scored twice by Privates Mason and Speke, the latter by a beautiful shot near the post.

The Glo'sters backs were very sound, but ballooned the ball too much. They only mis-kicked once, which nearly resulted fatally. The forwards lost several opportunities through lying off side.

The refereeing of Corpl. Parr was admirable, and was a pleasant change from the constant whistling one hears nowadays.

Glo'sters

Goal : Cpl. C. Druce, D Coy.

Backs : L/Cpl. S. Thrush, C Coy ; Pte. Basset, Transport.

Half Backs : L/Cpl. Packer, A Coy. ; Pte. J. Whittingham, B Coy. ; Sergt. H. C. Barnes, C Coy.

Forwards : Sergt. W. Egerton, D Coy. ; Pte. Boyt, D Coy. ; Pte. E. Mason, B Coy. ; Pte. Speke, A Coy. ; L/Sergt. J. Sterry, A. Coy.

D. A. C.

Goal : Dvr. Jones, H.

Backs : Dvr. Colley, G. ; Dvr. Underhill, S.

Half Backs : Dvr. Sydes, W. ; Dvr. Stoker, F. ; Dvr. Smith, S. W.

Forwards : Bdr. Hulme ; Bdr. Stretton, H. G. ; Bdr. Pritchard ; Gnr. Baines ; Dvr. Carrington.

BATTALION CONCERT, April 10th, 1917.

Owing to the unstinted labours of Lieut. Lister and C.Q.M.S. Wilce, a concert arranged for the Battalion passed off with great success.

Lieutenants Browne and Bruton contributed in fine style.

Dmr.-Sergt. Proctor as usual, was in fine form. A sketch, also a monologue anent an interesting wedding caused roars of laughter.

The sentimental and comic elements were well sustained by various N.C.O.'s and men as the programme will show.

Pte. Phillips surpassed himself, and the Humorous Sketch entitled " From Popple Town to Pimple Town is 14 miles," provoked roars of laughter.

PROGRAMME

Part I.

Overture	Lieut. Walker.
Song	Pte. Barnes.
Song	Lieut. Browne.
Humorous Sketch ...	Sergts. Proctor, Hopson, L/Corpl. McNesby, Ptes. Phillips, Pritchard and Crompton.
Comic Song ...	Pte. Crompton.
Song	Sergt. Barnes.
Monologue	Sergt. Proctor.
Comic Turn ...	Pte. Pritchard.
Song	Pte. Aylemore.
Yarns	Lieut. Mardon.

Part II.

Recitation " The County Regiments " ...	Pte. Phillips.
Scotch Song...	L/Corpl. McNesby.
Song	Dmr. Farmer.
Comic Song ...	Sergt. Hopson.
Song	Pte. Phillips.
Song	Pte. Ralph.
Comic Song ...	Sergt. Richards.
Song	Pte. Aylemore.

God Save the King.

High Intelligence Officers jumped on their bicycles and pedalled furiously miles
beyond Bapaume.—*Daily Mail.*

CORRESPONDENCE.

Somewhere in France.

My Dear Mother,

We have left the place we were in before we started to come here, and have arrived at the place to where we were coming before we left : from this you will doubtless be able to gather exactly where we are at present.

We had a short and enjoyable trip here. Started out with a gentle 4 mile breather to the station in full marching order at 6 a.m. after a light breakfast. We felt pretty thin, however, when we reached the station. Here a gentle surprise awaited us in the shape of eight nice box cars with " Hommes 40, chevaux 8 " written on them, and generously provided by our generous O.C. We clambered into them, and after a little delay one of our sappers got off and shoved off the train. It rolled along quite successfully once started.

The billets we left were some billets, but these are Somme billets. They were inhabited before we came by small creatures which are partial to hens, but the species have been augmented since our arrival. Our billets are in a village. The inhabitants of the village consist of cows, horses, cats, dogs and goats, besides these there are human beings. The latter are called French people by our Company authority. These French people are very kind to us and give us eggs, butter, firewood and the French language—at double their face value. We appreciate their kindness very much, and in return clean their streets. These French women assisted by their horses, dogs, cats and goats, live in farms. These farms are different to our English farms and consist mainly of a manure-pile surrounded by stables. The animals are very kind to us and we love them. The cows wander in to see us at all hours, they also wake us up for early parade. If this is not sufficient the hens sing " reveille," assisted by the dogs, cats and goats.

The French people use an enlightened method of driving their teams. Instead of using reins they guide their horses by a series of grunts and groans. If this is not sufficient they get off and shove their carts in the direction they want them to go. This is a very efficient method, and shows their masterful disposition. I must now close as someone has set fire to the billets.

Your loving Son,

Bill.

BRICKS FROM THE EDITOR'S PACK.

From the *Daily Chronicle's* Special Correspondent, April 18th.

" Instead of going into details of the fighting, I venture to strike a sober note.

A ferocious discipline still drives the German Armies to a most desperate resistance. Their bestial excesses have not, as a high idealism might suggest, destroyed their military spirit."

Heaven help us when he's drunk !

The Fore and Afts.

The War Office has just remedied a flagrant injustice which *The Globe* recently denounced and the official right has been conceded to the Territorial Battalions of the Gloucestershire Regiment to wear the " back number," as in the other Battalions of the Regiment. The back number is the Regimental badge—the Sphinx on the back as well as the front of the head-dress, and commemorates the gallantry of the 28th Foot at the Battle of Alexandria in 1801, when the rear rank faced about and withstood an attack of the enemy in front and rear. The distinction is immensely prized because it is possessed by no other Regiment in His Majesty's service.

The article on " The Fore and Aft " in *The Globe* on April, 1916, pointed out the invidious regulation which withheld this privilege from the Territorial Force, repeated protests which had been unavailing throughout the existence of the old Volunteer Force being still disregarded, although the newer Service Battalions enjoyed the right to the back number denied to the Territorials who were their seniors in the trenches. In consequence of our article renewed representations were made by influential friends of the Gloucestershire Territorials, including the Lord Mayor, who is officially honorary colonel of the injured " City of Bristol Battalion," and either the logic of the words or the conspicuous bravery of the men in battle—for the Gloucestershire Territorial Force have been in the fighting line on the Western Front from the beginning—has at last opened the eyes of the military authorities, and the wrong has been righted."

The Globe, April 17th, 1917.

The Australians were doing a raid. On entering the German front line trench they espied a solitary Hun. Cried the Hun " Kamerad ! Kamerad ! I no soldat mann ! No soldat mann ! I Minnenwerfer mann !" To whom an Australian replied "Oh, are you ! Well, you're the——we're looking for," and did him in.

We make no apology for quoting these lines from *Punch*. The truth which they enshrine is too often forgotten, the wrongs they reveal insufficiently realised by the people of Great Britain. The status of the Infantry man is a sad blot on our Nation's History.

FORE AND AFT.

The A.S.C.'s a nobleman, 'e rides a motor car,
'E is not forced to 'ump a pack, as we footsloggers are.
'E drives 'is lorry through the towns and 'alts for fag and beer,
We infantry, we does without, there ain't no shops up 'ere,
And then for splashin' us with mud 'e draws six bob a day,
For the further away from the line you go the 'igher your
   rate of pay.

My shirt is rather chatty and my socks 'ud make you larf,
It's just a week o' Sundays since they sent us for a barf,
But them that 'as the cushy jobs they live in styles and state,
With a basin in their bedrooms and their dinners on a plate.
For 'tis a law o' nachur with the blooming infantry—
The nearer up to the line you go the dirtier will you be.

Blokes up at the Base, they gets their leave when they've
   been out three munse,
I 'aven't seen my wife and kids for more'en a year, not once.
The missus writes, " About that pass, you'd better ask again,
I think you must 'ave been forgot," Old girl, the reason's
   plain,
We are the blooming infantry, and you must just believe
That nearer up the line you go the less is your chance of
   leave."

Major V. N. Johnson, our former Adjutant, who was at the time G.S.O. II. of the 46th Division, has, we regret to see, been wounded.

Major G. F. Collett is now with our Second-line Battalion, as are Sergeants Pepperell and Knight. Sergeant Harding is with the 1/4th.

There seems to be a certain amount of misunderstanding. Some people at home have got the idea that officers and men alike are having a very pleasant holiday—Rations free, too—in France, etc. Sir William Robertson is reported to have said that when he wanted a holiday he went to France, owing to the cheeriness of the British Colony there, which forms a contrast to the long faces sometimes seen at home. The truth is, of course, that were it not for the spirit of bonhommie and cheerfulness, we should all find it very hard to keep going.

" So and So " says A, a Platoon Commander, "is a priceless fellow and always keeps the men in good spirits." It is not quite the joy-ride that some people at home suspect it of being. " You need not worry about your——. He is having the time of his Life." But those who sang " Morituri te salutant " sang with a smile too.

> " They go where England speeds them,
> They laugh and jest at fate.
> They go where England needs them
> And dream not they are great.
> And oft 'mid smoke and smother
> By blinding war-storm fanned,
> Sons of our mighty mother,
> They fall that she may stand."

The self-sacrificing engineers, who went back to work after their noble strike, proceeded at once to demand that the patriots who refused to follow their infamous lead should be dismissed ! What a country ! A man out here gets the wind up, is fed up, and deserts. He is shot after a fair trial, poor fellow, the victim of circumstances. The temptation which assailed him was a strong one. But never a tear would we shed for the shooting of these wretched dagos at home who imperil their country and have to be cajoled back to work. Short shrift and a long rope is the sentence of the B. E. F. But woe to the Officials, should they have been the cause through their pettishness ; for theirs is surely the greater condemnation.

Inscribed on the wall of the Town Major's Office at F———

" Be neither slave nor tyrant to any man."

M. Aurelius Antoninus.

R. T. O's. please note latter half of the above.

More than one correspondent has pointed out that the remarks about the speed which marked the mobilisation of this Battalion—it having been alleged by the writer of an article in " The Field " that the Artists Rifles mobilized six days sooner than any other Territorial Unit—were equally character-istic of the efforts—equally successful—of the other Battalions in the Brigade to be ready and up to time. We apologise for a seeming lack of good taste. It was quite unpremeditated.

We feel sure that we owe " Rags " a special para-graph to congratulate him on his Military Cross and Mention in Despatches. He is, as is well known, Capt. James of —— no, we must not tell. This drawing of "Alas, my poor brother " was executed (rather an appropriate word, that) on May 1st, on the inspir-ation of the Colonel, and at the instigation of that mysterious person " we," whoever he or she may be. " We mention the date, because we received the " Bystander " about two days later with a picture illustrating the same idea. But we believe this is the better picture. Sure thing.

We hope that there will be no need for friction between the Army that returns to its old home in far off England, and the people who inhabit England to-day. We hope and trust that it will not be necessary for the Army to take its stand by the side of the King and Queen in defence of our Constitu-tional Monarchy. We have sung " God Save the King " often enough out here, and we mean it. But

Mr. H. G. Wells has been thinking aloud once again, and has written to the papers raising the question whether we have any further use for the King ! We rejoiced to see the Indian Princes tell him off in excellent style, as has General Smuts. I have seen some speculation recently in the newspapers about the position of the Kingship. This can only be speculations by people who, we are sure, have not thought of the wider issues that are at stake. You cannot make a Republic of the British Common-wealth of Nations.

"If you had to elect a President, he would have to be a President not only here in these Islands, but all over the British Empire, and here you would be facing an absolutely insoluble problem. The theory of the Constitution is that the King is not your King, but the King of us all, and if his place should be taken by anybody else, then that somebody will have to be elected under a process which will pass the wit of men to devise. Let us be thankful for mercies. We have a Kingship here which is not really very different from a hereditary republic," said the gallant South African General in his great speech.

The idea seems to be prevalent in a few people's minds—in the minds of that little fraternity, for instance, which carries little caps in their pockets which they can speedily put on whenever and where-ever " God Save the King " is played—that our Monarchial system is of the same species as that of the Hohenzollerns of Germany and the Romanoffs of Russia. It is nothing of the kind ; it is a Consti-tutional Monarchy or, as has been happily said already—" A Republic with an Hereditary Presi-dent." The Russian business was settled, as far as England is cocncerned, at Runnymede, and in 1832 at the passing of the Reform Rill. We do not identify our Kingship with the obsolete despotic tyranny of the Central Empires. With us the Crown is a moderating and harmonising influence—a golden link and not an iron bond stained with blood.

It is true that disloyalty is only rife in a fraction of the people at home. But we warn them that the Army will have none of it.

" With the support of the whole House, Herr Muller discussed the Iron Crosses scandal. According to Herr Muller, the Iron Cross is now a joke in the Army, which says that the rain of Orders in the rear is as heavy as the rain of bullets at the front. The Infantry at the front are given fewer decorations than those who have never been under fire, men who have never seen prisoners except in the Camps, railway officials, commissariat officers, Clerks in Government Offices in Germany, Army cooks, and officers' servants."

" Through German eyes,"

The Times, May 14th, 1917.

Human nature is the same all the world over.

" That these correspondents have been spared I regard as a miracle, because every day—certainly every day that I had the pleasure of being with them—they are as close to the fighting line as it is possible to get without certain annihilation."

LORD NORTHCLIFFE.

The Times, May 14th, 1917.

Was there not a certain General who recom-mended his chauffeur for the V.C. on the ground that he—the chauffeur—had been everywhere he—the General—had been ?

EVOLUTION.

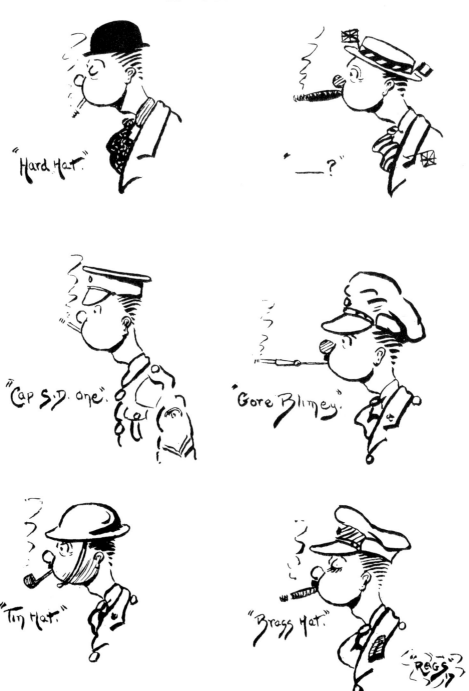

Much sympathy, especially on the part of those who served in the " Third Line " under him, has been expressed for Colonel Jeune on the loss of his younger son, who died from the result of his wounds.

At last.

Extract from letter of a Private—

" I wrote last week to say I had been sent down to the Base on a Field postcard."

(At last, we are glad to see, they have found a good substitute for the French Railways. Ed.)

F. A. T. 1914.
Para. 221.

" (1) It may be possible to locate groups of officers forming staffs either mounted or dismounted. Such objectives should be ranged on rapidly and a quick rate of fire opened for effect till they either disperse or disappear."

Have our Divisional Staff noticed that the Bosche trains his gunners on the same methods ?

It was a difficult situation. It was necessary at all costs—if the " show " was to be a success—to inform the Brigade at once that the barrage must be put off for an hour. It was equally essential that the " Bosche " listener should not pick up the word " Barrage " or anything else to do with the message. So the Colonel and the Brigadier just talked down the telephone in Hindustani, thereby saving the situation. Next morning there were surely insistent calls on the Bosche telephone to expedite returns of the number of men speaking Hindustani.

Company Sergeant Major Tibbles, M.C., is now Regimental Sergeant-Major to the Edinburgh War Hospital.

It is with feelings of real regret that the Editor lays down his Trench stick with which he used to coax unwilling contributors. He would like to take this opportunity of thanking all ranks from the Divisional Commander downwards for the way in which they have supported the Gazette. He is confident that they will extend the same support to his successor on the packing case, Lieutenant G. Hawkins, whose subtle humour and brilliant wit have on more than one occasion been the feature of the Number.

Meanwhile he would point out that although he is unable to state the precise day or hour on which his office closes in France, he can state confidently that it re-opens the first week in September in FENTIMAN ROAD, 400 yards S. E. of the U in VAUXHALL STATION. The SOUTH LAMBETH ROAD communicates with it. There is a re-entrant from KENNINGTON PARK ROAD into FENTIMAN ROAD. The Vicarage window will be readily picked up, as it forms a pronounced salient in the line of houses.

He hopes that all members of the B. E. F.—past or present—will come and have good cheer. All welcome.

The value of the Little Library, supplied through the kindly offices of the Brigadier by the Camps Library, has been great, and the books have been much sought after.

The following " captured " Correspondence may be of some interest.

    " Lieutenant A. S.———
            ——Field Ambulance.
Please see the attached.
        A. H. R.——Lt.-Col. S. S. O.
6/4/17.

To S. S. O.

Col.——will be glad if you will let me know if you can supply him with seeds for planting potatoes and lettuce.

                W. A. S.———, Lieut.
                Q—rt—rm—ster,
                    —S. M. F. Amb.

A. D. of S.   —Army.

No doubt you will arrange to provide the above. I presume a complete gardening outfit will also be required. Perhaps you could arrange with A. D. of S. to supply ? I presume patients suffering from shell shock will be taught the art of gardening, for I believe it has a soothing effect on jaded nerves.

                A. H. R.——Lt.-Col.
1/4/17.

O. C.—Divisional Train.

I regret to say we keep no " line " in seeds and gardening tools.

It is believed that the E. F. C. may be able to oblige your customer.

                F. E. F.——Major.
                    D. A. D. S.

What a war, isn't it !

Divisional Intelligence Summary.

(from 6 a.m. May 29th, to 6 a.m. May 30th.)

AVIATION.

In all 16 enemy machine guns are reported. They flew chiefly N. and S. over our lines."

Anti-aircraft, please note. With a view to obtaining the co-operation of the Artillery, it has been happily suggested that black rockets should be fired.

———

IN MEMORIAM.

It was with sincere regret that the Battalion heard of the death of Major L. G. Parkinson, who was our Second-in-Command for three months during the Winter. We were all very fond of him.

We should like also to express our sympathy with another Battalion of the Gloucestershire Regiment on the terrible tragedy that befell their Headquarters.

" Lieut.-Colonel T. W. Nott, D.S.O. and his younger brother, Captain L. C. Nott, M.C., serving together in a Territorial Battalion of the Gloucester Regiment, one as C. O. and the other as Adjutant, were both killed on the same day (April 18th.)

They were the sons of the late Mr. L. T. Nott, of Stoke House, Bristol, and received their Commissions in the Territorial Force soon after war broke out.

Both brothers repeatedly distinguished themselves in action, and both proved to be fine leaders of men.

The former was promoted Major in July, 1916, and recently got another temporary step in rank to command his Battalion. His brother was appointed adjutant of the battalion in February last year."

Truth, May 2nd, 1917.

The third brother was killed in Tommy Trench, Hebuterne, over a year ago.

We heard with deep regret that our Quartermaster had lost his son, who was acting Company Sergeant Major in the King's Liverpools, during an attack on April 23rd.

He had three times been recommended for a commission.

We turn aside from our traditional custom—a custom necessitated by the inability to publish our Casualty Lists—to say a few words—inadequate as they must inevitably be—in fond memory of Captain W. O. Down, M. C.——Regiment, one of our most brilliant contributors.

He enlisted in the III. Hussars at the outbreak of war, and was granted a commission in the ——Regiment, and earned his Military Cross at Pozieres.

Young as he was, he had already shown promise of a great future before him as a dramatic author, some of his plays being in great demand. But we turn aside to pay this scant tribute to him, not for what he did, but just for what he was.

A character such as his, in which were blended literary charm and soldier-like qualities—he was the most unselfish of men—was indeed one to admire.

Of him, as of Cyril Winterbotham and of others of the band of Literary men who have fallen, we write " Thou hast put a new song into my mouth."

Loving hands laid him to rest by the side of his faithful orderly, and loving hearts will ever hold his memory dear.

————

Much sympathy is felt for the relatives of Major Ward, Lieutenant Hawkins and Captain Hamilton on their recent bereavements.

From the *Times* :

" Second Lieutenant H. E. Hawkins, London Regiment, killed on May 11th, was the second son of the Rev. E. H. Hawkins and Mrs. Hawkins, of Holy Trinity Vicarage, Stroud, Gloucestershire. At the outbreak of war he was a rubber planter in the Malay Straits, and immediately came to England and enlisted in the London Regiment, and received his commission in October, 1916. His brother officers write that " they mourn the loss of a gallant officer and a friend. He was worshipped by his platoon and company. His influence was a power for good."

MAJOR GEORGE DUVAL WARD, R.F.A., who was killed on May 18th, aged 43, served throughout the South African War as an expert on machine guns, receiving at the end the Honorary Rank of captain and both the Queen's and King's medals with seven clasps. He afterwards settled in Johannesburg. Arriving in England on a holiday, just as war was declared in 1914, he immediately offered his services to his country, and after a period of useful service at home was sent to the front in June, 1916, with the R.F.A. He was mentioned in dispatches by Sir Douglas Haig in his last list. The Brigadier General commanding his division writes :—" It was a great blow to me to hear of his death, and the loss of so able an officer will be sorely felt by us. I wish you to know that he died doing (as I have always found him) his duty in a thorough manner." A Brother officer writes :—" He was the bravest of the brave, and in all my experience I have never met a man so altogether trustworthy. He was loved by us all as a friend as well as a brother soldier. I want to tell you that he loved his work, and that if it had to be he would prefer to die at the head of his battery to any other way."

————

PROMOTIONS AND APPOINTMENTS
Part II. Orders.

Granted substantive rank of Warrant Officer Class II. :—

240257	C.Q.M.S. (a/R.S.S.M.)	Lock, W. N.	12/9/16

Promoted C.S.M. with pay and allowances of Warrant Officer Class II. :—

240038	a/C.S.M. Smith, V. G.	21/11/16

Promoted C.Q.M.S. :—

240002	Sergt. Meadows, J.	21/11/16

Confirmed in substantive rank of C.Q.M.S. :—

240013	a/C.Q.M.S. Huxford, J., D.C.M.	1/10/16

Appointed a/C.S.M. with pay and allowances :—

240101	Sergt.	Coward, W. J.

Promoted Sergeant :—

240644	Corporal	Over. J.	24/12/16
241303	,,	Hook, W.	25/12/16
241000	,,	Butt, R., M.M.	26/12/16
240200	,,	Caudle, H.	6/ 2/17
240670	,,	Chandler, W., M.M.	19/ 2/17
203037	,,	Buckland, J. C.	4/ 3/17
240245	,,	Mustoe, H. G.	22/ 3/17
240358	L/Sergt.	Hardiman, G.	13/ 4/17

Appointed L/Sergt. with pay :—

240737	Corpl.	Wise, G.	17/ 1/17
240324	,,	Sterry, J.	29/ 3/17
240867	,,	Kitching, F. F.	13/ 4/17

Promoted Corporal :—

240693	L/Corpl.	Burlton, W. G.	22/ 3/17
240639	,,	Hopkins, P. J.	29/ 3/17
241156	,,	Fletcher, I.	13/ 4/17
240741	,,	Jennings, A. L.	24/12/16
240384	,,	Roddis, F. W.	25/12/16
240127	,,	Exell, W., M.M.	29/12/16
240550	,,	Lait, F. C.	17/ 1/17
240239	Pte. (L/Cpl.)	Roche, W.	13/ 4/17
240488	,,	Cresswell, A.	13/ 4/17
242307	,,	Packer, F.	5/ 4/17
240052	,,	Davis, P.	19/ 1/17
240303	,,	Lane, F.	6/ 2/17
240555	,,	Corlett, G.	10/ 2/17
240202	,,	Oliver P.	19/ 2/17
203706	,,	Hodges, J. T.	25/ 2/17
241085	L/Corpl.	Teale. C. H.	4/ 3/17
240240	Pte. (L/C.)	Fletcher, H. A	10/ 3/17

Appointed L/Corporal with pay :—

241156	Pte. (L/Cpl)	Fletcher, L.	24/12/16
241942	,,	Pearson, W. J.	25/12/16
240736	,,	White, A. J.	26/12/16
240677	,,	Wilkinson, J. G.	17/ 1/17
241914	,,	NeNesby, E. G.	4/ 3/17
203171	,,	Dyer, H. G.	5/ 4/17
240530	,,	Stephens, W. A	17/ 4/17
240481	,,	King, S. R.	21/ 4/17
241103	Pte.	Holtham, A. G.	23/ 4/17
240509	Pte. (L/Cpl.)	Hooper, H.	24/ 4/17
240469	,,	Higgs, A.	24/ 4/17
241040	,,	Miles, F. C.	24/ 4/17
242444	,,	Eves, A. E.	24/ 4/17

Appointed L/Corporals without pay :—   5/ 5/17

241040	Pte.	Miles, F. C.
240251	,,	Jeffris, T.
24087	,,	Martin, E. F.

————

R.I.P.

" In sacred sleep they rest : say not of brave men they die."

CALLIMACHUS.

" Concerning them which are asleep, that ye sorrow not even as others which have no hope."

ST. PAUL.

" Rest quietly, best beloved.
Thou who fellest asleep in thy youth and thy beauty and thy strength,
Rest quietly in thy long slumber.
Though each passing summer scatter its blossom o'er thy head,
Yet art thou ever a changeless memory.
The truest and best of companions."

Capt. R. DENNYS.

" Nothing is here for tears, nothing to wail
Or knock the breast, no weakness, no contempt,
Dispraise or blame ; nothing but well and fair,
And what may quiet us in a death so noble.'

" If to die well is the chief part of virtue, Fortune granted this to us above all others : for striving to endue Hellas with Freedom, we lie here possessed of praise that groweth not old."

Greek Anthology

Study of a Q.M. writing
a treatise on how to
save fat.

No. 20.   AUGUST, 1917.

5th Gloucester Gazette.

A Chronicle, serious and humorous, of the Battalion while serving with the
BRITISH EXPEDITIONARY FORCE.

POEMS FROM A GERMAN PRISON.

To the Editor of "The Times"

Sir,—It will interest many of your readers to know that I have received from Lieutenant F. W. Harvey the manuscript of a new volume entitled "Gloucestershire Friends: Poems from a German Prison Camp." It goes almost without saying that the verses are worthy of the author of "A Gloucestershire Lad," and that they are pathetically illuminative of what the best of our men are thinking and doing to while away the impracticable hours of their captivity.

It is only fair for me to add that the manuscript has been sent without the slightest obliteration or curtailment by the German Censor. I should like to express the gratitude of all Lieutenant Harvey's friends to the authorities of the Kriegsgefangenenlager at Krefeld for this act of literary courtesy.

I am, Sir, yours,

GEORGE H. FRODSHAM, Bishop

(Canon Residentiary of Gloucester Cathedral.)

The Cloister House, Gloucester.

LIEUT. HARVEY'S POEMS.

The many personal friends in Gloucestershire of Second Lieutenant F. W. Harvey, as well as the still wider circle who have had the good fortune to make his acquaintance through the medium of his pleasing poesy, will learn with very real pleasure that arrangements are being made for the publication of another volume of his verses. Although readers of the "Fifth Gloucester Gazette" have for some time been deprived of contributions bearing the familiar initials "F. W. H." that was through no fault of the versatile and gifted young writer, whose poetic fire has not, we are all glad to know, been quenched during the period in which he has been a prisoner of war at Krefeld. The manuscript of about 70 poems which Lieutenant Harvey has written in "durance vile" has recently been received in Gloucester, and we understand that Bishop Frodsham, who is arranging for their publication, will write an introduction to the collection. Many of these verses—which will be published under the title of "Gloucestershire Friends: Poems From a German Prison Camp"—are in Lieutenant Harvey's best and most sympathetic vein, and apart from and in addition to their high literary standard and the lofty sentiments they express, the circumstances under which they were written must of necessity impart to them an added interest. This second venture is a much more ambitious one than that in which Lieutenant Harvey made his debut in "book form" under the homely title of "A Gloucestershire Lad," and it should increase considerably the number of his admirers.

RUINS.

In tangled piles beneath the summer sky
  And laughing sun, the heaps of fallen stone
Each one a house of happier days, now lie
  Abandoned, piteous, desolate, alone.

What simple joy and quiet peace they saw,
  What blissful hours though filled by labour hard,
What memories of faces loved of yore,
  What treasures of the past they hide and guard.

Stones, silent witnesses of grim despair,
  Of shattered hearths, and blindly hurrying feet,
Gone forth the exiles' unknown fate to share
  Where friends no welcome give, nor kinsmen greet.

Symbols of all that men have held most dear.
  E'en though you mark the depths of human woe,
And o'er you falls, uncounted, many a tear,
  You yet may scorn the hate that laid you low.

For on your ruins other homes shall rise
  And joy return, child laughter peal again,
And peace be yours when war's harsh clamour dies,
  Bought by the free-given life-blood of the slain.

M. L. G.

ARMY GROUP OF ARCHDUKE ARCHIBALD.

DAILY NEWS SHEET—June 21st, 1917.

I. OPERATIONS.

(a) MAJOR. Our heavy artillery again shelled enemy listening post 100 yards true N. of the MESS in MESSINES. Our brave gunners achieved many direct hits, one rifle (BRITISH) and one postcard (FRENCH) being projected into our front trenches.

The CORPS COMMANDER has granted permission for the rifle to be retained as a regimental battle trophy by our glorious artillerymen.

Enemy canteens and Y. M. C. A. fortifications were accurately dealt with by our marine guns. A direct hit was obtained on a hostile dripping dump in X 50. e.—muffled explosions were heard.

(b) MINOR. In accordance with rules laid down in Part I of "INFANTRY LEARNING" and para. I (a) Kaisers Regs. our advanced line has been willingly withdrawn from certain unimportant provinces in the vicinity of the Western Front. The enemy, whose losses were especially sanguinary, succeeded, after many fruitless attempts, in occupying some negligible elements of our FATHERLAND.

Fighting continues—some of our Divisions are missing.

2. HOSTILE ARTILLERY.

Enemy's gun fire has been normally terrific during the past 24 hours.

The following map squares have disappeared :—
A. 1, D. 3, B. 4 (Ref. Sheet FRANCE 1/1,000,000).

After preparatory drum fire, the enemy also appear to have mislaid the following small townships :—CAMBRAI, ANTWERP (partially), BRUGES, ZEEBRUGGE (very entirely).

Identification is urgently required of the following: OSTEND, METZ.

3. AVIATION.

Great aerial activity is reported from all fronts.

One of our Zeppelin formations successfully bombed a number of light enemy craft in the Serpentine Lake, LONDON—several small boys were observed retiring rapidly in the direction of the WAR OFFICE.

Yesterday, one of our battle squadrons engaged a hostile carrier pigeon above O. 1. Central—after a sharp contest the enemy bird was seen to nose dive steeply and finally to crash behind our lines.

On the 18th instant a British observation balloon opposite our centre broke loose and bolted towards our lines. The observer who attempted to descend in a parachute was brought down out of control by one of our chaser squadrons under Cavalry Second Lieutenant Baron Bitz von Fissing. The balloon landed voluntarily in our aerodrome at LILLE. One bottle of whisky (Kristoffers), a newspaper and one Tommy Cooker were salved from the basket. On the deflating valve being opened, the balloon exploded emitting vast clouds of asphyxiating gas.

4. DISPOSITIONS.

One of our aerodromes at LILLE has been moved to BADEN BADEN.

5. PATROLS.

On the QUONVILLE sector the enemy is again committing the unspeakable practice of rendering our wire ineffective by applying AMERICAN chewing gum to the barbs. Stern representations have been made through the usual neutral channels.

6. EASTERN FRONTS.

The customary 5 rounds application are reported on the STROMBOS front. A pistol shot was also heard to ring out in the direction of OCHKHI.

The VODKA is frozen—it is very cold.

7. CASUALTIES.

Our own very slight. Ober-General of Reserve, Count von REDTTAP-PRAZZHATT, G.O.C. Lines of Communication is reported " MISSING."

Issued by the Signals at 15 a.m.

Copies 1 and 2 His All Highest.
3 Divine Ally.
4 and 5 War Diary.
5, 6 and 7 C. in C's., East, North and Southern Fronts.
8 1st Div. Prussian Guards (T.F.)
9 15th Div. Pommerarians.
10 169 ERSARTZ (2nd line) Div.
11 19th Div. (LANDWORM).
12 3rd BAVARIBURGHERS.
13 999 GRAVEDIGGERS CORPS.
14 C. in C's. Corpse Factories.

F. D. R.

ABOUT MYSELF.

By an Injured Innocent.

In order to tell you this story I must first explain that I was reduced from Sergeant-Major to 2nd Lieut. in 1915. I was attached to the 8th Boostshire Regt. which formed part of the 999th Brigade. On my arrival the Adjutant scrutinised me closely and took full particulars regarding my life. One of his questions was " Are you a Specialist "? I replied that I had never been in the Medical Profession, but further sallies elicited the fact that he wished to know whether I cultivated war babies, such as Bombs or Lewis guns, etc. I informed him that I had once devoted a considerable portion of my person to Barbed Wire. The Adjutant replied " Oh ! right ; We're not using Wiring Officers at present but I'll put you down as a reserve." Then I bowed, took off my cap, saluted and withdrew.

* * *

The scene now shifts forward three months and changes to Brigade Headquarters. I got the facts from Blass who was Brigade Bombing Officer at the time.

" H'm," said the General turning to the mess. " The wiring in the Brigade is very bad at present. Grinford, you'd better find out whether there are any officers who can instruct in wiring."

Grinford, who was acting for 2 days as Brigade Major, nodded and the conversation flagged. The following correspondence presumably then took place, though I cannnot vouch for it.

1. From Brigade Major, 999th Brigade to O.C. All Battalions.

Please submit to this office your sale catalogue and report anything suitable in the Wiring Line.

2. From O. C. 5th Boostshires to Brigade Major, 999th Brigade.

" Nil Return."

3. From O. C. 6th Boostshires to Brigade Major, 999th Brigade.

" Nil Desperandum."

4. From O. C. 7th Boostshires to G. O. C. 999th Brigade.

" No drink, no drunk."

5. From O. C. 8th Boostshires to G. O. C. 999th Brigade.

" Catalogue enclosed herewith. We have a good line at present in your requirements, but our stock is low. Please fill up enclosed Form at once.

6. From G. O. C. 999th Brigade to O. C. 8th Boostshires.

" Send carriage paid on 10 days approval, sale or return, Wiring Officer as specified. "

I arrived with my valise at lunch time on the following day. All went well until I was told the purpose for which I had been called up.

" Me—er I mean I—instruct in wiring ? Why I haven't done any for—12 months."

" I can't help it " replied Grinford ; the General wants a prospectus drawn up showing instructions for rapid wiring and you'll have to do it."

" Very well," I replied bitterly. " I will " and we parted.

* * *

From dusk of one day to dawn of the same day I worked out my prospectus. I was determined to base it on experience and I did so. I append it herewith.

RAPID WIRING.

Materials required :—

Concertinas
Barbs } wire mark VIIA.

The issue of barbs should be on the scale of 30 per head or 15 per hand.

If mark A is unobtainable, Mark BEE (stinging variety) has been approved.

Skew Pickets :—

Fatigue picquets (S. B's suggested).

1 Clown.

2 Harlequins.

9 O. R. with gloves, skin human. These are the property of the soldier and should not be removed.

(I put in 1 clown as I couldn't help thinking of the occasion when that ass Blud Slag stood up in the middle of a Heap of Concertina wire and asked " Who was the first person in the world to go on pass ? " After five minutes intense silence he gave us the answer. " Eve. She got two leaves for herself and her husband."

Wiring Orders. Sequence.

1. Length. 2. Syndication. 3. Number of yards. 4. Kind of wire.

Wiring orders should be brief and to the barb.

• On the Command " Thirty yards—rapid—wire," All ranks will assume a hasty attitude amid scenes of indescribable confusion.

2. Those below the rank of Harlequin will present pickets.

3. Picquets will stand by, ready to act at a moment's notice.

4. Clown will attempt to play concertina wire.

(He should have at least 2 years' experience at the Theatre de Guerre, France).

5. All ranks will barb themselves.

On the conclusion of the allotted task parties will return to billets and will stand to.

* * *

Now everyone will agree that this was a perfectly sound document, but can anyone tell me why I was sent back to England with a single ticket 2 days later ? Indeed I am as injured as Private Bugg, the Naturalist, who went out into " No Man's Land " to examine a pigeon with blue wings.

OUR AIRMEN.

Swift through the gleaming sky they glide,
  Their soaring flight unswerving,
Or wheel and turn in circles wide
  With sweeping movement curving.

Proudly they sail, to meet the foe
  Worthy our nation's story,
Unfaltering on their course they go
  To danger, death and glory.

Unflinching, face each peril dire
  The deadly shell-blasts flashing,
The blinding smoke, the close-brought fire,
  From angry gun mouths crashing.

They sway, and swoop, and plunge and rise,
  One breathless instant hover
With but the great vault of the skies,
  Above them for their cover.

Unconquered, even though they fall,
  For through the bullets singing,
They hear the note of victory's call
  Far down the ages ringing.

O brave and true, on land or sea,
  Or through air's blue heights flying,
The spirit that made Britain free,
  And keeps her fame undying.

M. L. G.

———

THINGS WE WANT TO KNOW.

Who administered snuff to a captive mouse ? Did the animal sneeze and then " snuff it " ?

When someone asked, if anyone had a looking-glass to lend, who replied " I got a steel 'un " ?

Have any further consignments of Australian Conies, packed in bundles of 10, been seen near the rail-head addressed to the Glo'sters ?

Who is " Wacker's " understudy in the Guides Section ?

Who is the Sergt. in No. 5 who said " There are two empty tins of water here " ?

Who was the Corporal who said " The Germans are now feeding their dead bodies on pigs " ?

Is he in No. 5 — ?

Who was the Sergt. in No. 5 that told the men to " load up five in the chamber " ?

And how many did he want in the magazine ?

Who was the Private in B Coy. that saw the Lord Mayor of London on the sunken road ?

Is he in No. 7 ?

Who was the L/Corporal in No. 5 that said " Bombs have been dropping Aeroplanes on the Railway "?

Who was the Corporal that said " All the jam in this tin is gone " ?

Is he in No. 5 and did he, on handing over his post, enter " Two boxes of No. 23 in bags " on the List of Stores ?

Who was the Private in No. 7 on awakening said " Hello, Jim, I thought Mrs. Collins was on this post."

Who were the Privates in B Coy. that had an argument as to whether the Aeroplanes was firing lumitated or phospurss bullets ?

Which Coy. S.M. arouses his merry men with the remark, " Come on. Yer trance is finished " ?

Who was the L/Corporal in No. 6 that pressed his trousers with his boot ?

And was it only an excuse for lessening population ?

Who was the L/Corporal in No. 5 who said " don't think we shall have any rain to-day ? It has started already."

Who is the man in B Coy. who sings a good song on the piano ?

Who was the Lewis Gunner in No. 5 that said " Don't the flash make a row when that machine guns opens." And did the same man feel the breath of a bullet as it passed him ?

Who was the Corporal in No. 5 that made tea with lime juice ?

And how much sugar did it require for sweetening purposes ?

Who was the Corporal in No. 7 that said " If anyone wants to make a drop of tea, I have plenty of cocoa here ?

Who was the Sergeant in B Coy. that said " Right wheel on your rifles " ?

Did he expect them cleaned for next inspection ?

Who was the Sergeant in B Coy. that said " I will make you laugh the other side of my face " ?

Is he in No. 6 ?

Who is the Sergeant in B Coy. who, knowing a little French, can hardly speak a word of English ?

And is he known as " Totsuit " ?

Who is the Battery position Commander who had a Dutch garden at his Battery position ? Why did the flowers die so quickly ?

Did an Officer's servant volunteer to milk the cow at B——— and was he found later on slumbering peacefully by the animal with an empty milk can by his side. Was he cowed by the magnitude of the task or had the beverage consumed by him on the previous day something to do with the matter ? What were the cows view's upon it ?

Did an excited householder digging his potato patch find a dud shell and exclaim " A bomb-de-terre."

Who was the Domestic on Battalion Mess that fell asleep while Madame was filling the milk jug for breakfast ?

Who was the man in No. 7 Platoon Lewis Gun team that said he had not had a hair-cut since last July's offensive ? Is the Battalion Barber on Strike or does he want paying now ?

BOOK TITLES.

In view of the compulsory library which many officers are now carrying, we are authorised to state that the following books are not necessary :—

(To all Hypocrites and the Credulous this story is dedicated.)

THE SCARLET DROP.

An Adventure of Spitlock Phones by Sir Kadaver Bonan Oyle.

Exactly how Phones and myself came to be in Germany in the year of War 1917 it is not my purpose here to tell ; suffice it to say that we had been installed in COLOGNE for several months prior to the period of this adventure and were engaged on a most delicate and special mission.

It was early one morning that Phones burst suddenly into my room in the Dom Hotel. In his hand he held a pink paper. I had never before in my life seen Phones excited. Now he could scarcely contain himself.

I looked at the telegram he offered me. In bold letters was written : " Potztausend. Graf von Schmerzenkerzendochtgarn und Klufthugel." "What does this mean ? " I asked Phones.

" It's from the Count of Painswick and Cleeve Hill, summoning us at once," he replied. " The Count is the chief shareholder in the Kadaver Factories Ltd.

* * *

On our arrival Phones was closeted privately with the Count for over an hour. Then he came to me.

" Are you ready to leave for France to-night ? " he asked.

" Phones," I said, " I am ready to leave for Hell to-night, if it's with you."

Without another word Phones told me to hurry up, so rushing upstairs I just put together enough shirts and socks to complete to summer scale and in five minutes' time I was ready to start. Not so quickly as Phones, however. He already stood, pipe in mouth and hat in hand, ready for the journey.

"My dear Wonson," he smiled, "I really think you ought not to leave your shaving brush behind."

I stared at him in amazement. The man was a veritable marvel.

Noting my astonishment Phones was amused. "But its perfectly obvious," he said; "from the size of your valise that you have omitted that necessary article of kit."

We left a few minutes later and caught the night-boat from ZEEBRUGGE to OSTEND. From there we rapidly proceeded in the reinforcement train to DOUAI and it was only here that Phones confided to me the motive for our sudden departure.

"It is one of the most interesting cases I have ever met," he began. "Landsturmer Franz, with whose mysterious murder we are concerned, was the Count's Under-Sausage Keeper. He was apparently in perfect health, having been refused exemption on National Grounds and passed fit by the Doctors some months back as A 1.

"He came to France for business reasons and whilst somewhere in the neighbourhood of CAMBRAI he met his death in most mysterious circumstances. He was walking along the B. road one day when suddenly and without warning he was most foully murdered.

"The two friends who were with him describe the scene as terrifying. They were all walking abreast, Franz on the left hand side, when there was a sudden crash. The other two at once fell on their stomachs and when they recovered consciousness half an hour later they could find nothing of their friend. They searched for some moments and at length found what was apparently the sole remnants of the Land-sturmer's mortal remains. It was a scarlet drop of blood which they recognised by the identity disc."

I gasped for horror and after a slight pause Phones concluded.

"And it is this atrocious crime that we have come here to solve."

We left next morning on the 5.15 for C——— which we reached late in the afternoon. The "Grand Hotel" at which I had stayed on a previous visit to the town being no longer in existence we decided to put up for the night at the Rest Camp.

"To-morrow," said Phones, as I was about to retire for the night, "We must go over at dawn."

Happening to run out of tobacco a couple of hours later I ran in to Phones' room. He had his back turned to me as I opened the door, so I stood quietly for a while. He was at the window apparently trying the sash and after a short time I was surprised to see him take a pistol from his pocket. A moment later there was a loud report. I rushed forward. As I did so, a bright red and green light burst in the sky. Before I could reach Phones he had turned round on me smiling.

"A little experiment which has failed, my dear Wonson," he said. "And now let us get to bed."

I knew Phones well enough to understand that he wished to be alone, so getting my tobacco I left his room, though I must confess that it was not without great curiosity as to his motives.

The next morning attired in field-grey we started at dawn as arranged. Phones, with his customary foresight, had warned me to don this uniform so as to make ourselves as invisible as possible.

We soon reached the scene of the crime. In the centre of the road was a hole about 4 feet across and on either side were tall trees. Beyond these the open country stretched away for miles in the distance. The only place for concealment, I thought to myself, would be behind those trees. However it was not I that was to solve the problem and Phones had already started on the job in his inimitable way. He was pacing out various distances from the hole with his eyes half shut and deep in thought. Once he came into a tree with some force and by the sudden look of astonishment that crossed his face I thought for the moment that he had spotted something. He next got down on his hands and nose and examined the whole ground with his pocket microscope. Now and again he would also pick up lumps of earth and bring them under the glass.

We must have been there some two hours before he got up with a sudden grunt and started off rapidly for home. Apparently he had entirely forgotten me, but I knew well enough how unwise it would be to interrupt him, so I followed closely behind him the whole way back whilst he strolled on, his hands in his mouth and his pipe in his pocket.

In the afternoon he drew out his violin and began to play soulful little tunes on it, but he was soon asked to desist by the manager of the rest camp and during the remainder of the day he said no word to me until we parted for the night. Then he remarked.

"I shall be going out again early to-morrow. You need not come with me."

Disappointed as I was I knew it would be useless to argue.

The following day I eagerly awaited Phones' return, but he did not come in until about eleven in the evening, and I saw at once that he had had a day of it. He looked thoroughly worn out and was obviously still baffled.

However, he only murmured "A tough case," and then went to bed.

During the next few days Phones made no reference to the case in hand and I almost thought that he had forgotten it until one morning he came into my room, his eyes shining like Very Lights, and I knew at once that he had spotted a clue.

"Are you ready?" he asked.

For answer I quickly assumed my puttees and jammed my bowler on my head. Then we set off together down the now familiar road.

We had not been at our destination more than five minutes when I heard Phones mutter, " Yes, it is a shell-hole," and the gleam once more lit up his face.

He then walked rapidly across to the nearest tree and waved a white handkerchief. I stared at him in astonishment and for a minute we waited perfectly still. Then there was a sudden whiz and a crash. Phones and I dropped flat from instinct, and a few seconds later, when we got up again, Phones was beaming all over like a small boy.

As for me I felt most annoyed. In bringing my hand into too sudden contact with a sharp stone on the road I had cut it and it was now bleeding profusely. Phones however seemed not to notice it.

" I must apologise, my dear Wonson," he began, " for submitting you to a most dangerous experiment. It was however most essential for the proof of my theories. I must confess that for the first few days the case completely baffled me.

" Last night I happily lighted on a clue, though I must confess it was by a most extraordinary coincidence. I was undressing for bed when suddenly one of my candles began to emit weird little groans and started spluttering. Realising it was in pain I at once put it out, but it was not until some minutes later that I connected it in any way with the case in hand. Then in a moment the whole thing seemed clear. I re-lit the candle, and was just able to recognise in the groans " Franz—Gott straf—" when it went out again of its own accord.

" Landsturmer Franz, my dear Wonson, was the victim of a most peculiarly atrocious crime. Having been partially destroyed by gunshot wound, two of Count Schmerzenkerzendochtgarn's agents kidnapped him and before he had time to protest he had been transformed into a candle. Thus since Franz was his Under-Sausageer the Count's cruelties reflected on his own head. And now I think we may go and have lunch......"

Thus ended one of the most interesting episodes in Phones' career and I am happy to think I have been the means of conveying it to a credulous public.

FIBULOUS.

PRAYER.

The lifting up of heart and soul and mind
In thankfulness and hope, in need, or pain, or grief.
In fret or fear, to where, with sure relief,
The fainting spirit calm and peace may find,
The call of men fast held by doubts that blind
The sigh of longing wrung from hearts that break,
The trustful plea that kneeling children make,
The cry of love in hallowed souls enshrined.
A living force that mounts to heights unseen,
And fearlessly the gate of heaven unbars,
That brings a new-found strength, a new-born power,
A confidence secure, a joy serene,
To guide the weakest through life's battle-hour
And thence unto the world beyond the stars.

M. L. G.

SOME OF OUR UNBENEFACTORS.

1. KITCHENMAID, scullerymaid kept, WANTED for near Bath, and London ; nine servants : good wages ; no charge for this situation.— Apply Mrs. R., care of Mrs. Massey's Agency, 10, Baker Street, W. 1.

KITCHENMAID (Single handed), one in family, seven servants : wages £18-£20 ; must have some experience.—Mrs. Balfour, Sherrards, Welwyn, Hertfordshire.

FOURTH HOUSEMAID of four WANTED, August 4th ; excellent place ; country, 28 miles London ; 11 servants, three in family ; do nursery or schoolroom.—Apply C. 114, care of Mrs. Massey's Agency, Friargate, Derby, or in London, 10, Baker Street, W. 1.

SCULLERYMAID REQUIRED for beautiful place in country, a short distance from town ; age 18 to 20 ; wages up to £20, all found ; 15 servants kept.—Apply H. 104, care of Mrs. Massey's Agency, Friargate, Derby, or in London, Baker Street, W. 1.

Ete., etc.

From the *Morning Post*, 11.7.17.

2. Mr. FORD.

FOOTPATHS.

" It was decided to have cleaned the footpaths in the parish which usually need attention at this time of the year.

Mr. Ford said he knew a man (a discharged soldier) who was willing to do the work for half-a-crown less than it cost last year ; and it was decided that this man should have the job."

From the *Dursley Gazette*.

3. Every West End Firm which advertises—

" New Seasons Furs "

at prices which range from 27 guineas and upwards.

4. **Mr. R. BLATCHFORD.**

" I think the country is rather worried about air raids , but it is not half as worried as I should like it to be, and if anything I can write will add to the general anger and anxiety I shall be very pleased."

5. The ½d. Press which hasn't space enough for publishing Casualty Lists, but manages to print several columns of rubbish daily.

6. The I. C. S. for the cheapest form of commercial patriotism. Small advts. are published in a certain paper as " owing to the paper shortage they have adopted this means of keeping readers acquainted with their products." The I.C.S. have in one issue of the paper, one of these small advts. and a full page advt.

A WAY THEY HAVE IN GERMANY.

KISSCARD

(NOT TRANSFERABLE).

Of the

person entitled to receive

Name : ....

Address : ....

....

Valid for 280 Kisses.

during period from

to

Issued on   1916.

CENTRAL OFFICE
FOR THE DISTRIBUTION OF KISSES.

The Kissing Directorate,
WILLI MUNCHRATH.

Each one of these squares represents the title to the taking of 10 kisses. During the first week of the period of validity only.

I	I
I	I
I	I
I	
2	2
2	2
2	2
2	
3	3
3	3
3	3
3	
4	4
4	4
4	4
4	

(**1**) squares.

during the second week.

only (**2**) squares.

during the third week.

only (**3**) squares.

during the fourth week.

only (**4**) squares.

may be punched.

FIRST WEEK.	SECOND WEEK.	THIRD WEEK.	FOURTH WEEK.
To be completed by the lady after the first kiss.	To be completed by the lady after the first kiss.	To be completed by the lady after the first kiss.	To be completed by the lady after the first kiss.
Name	Name	Name	Name ....
Address	Address	Address	Address ....
After the first kiss tear off. 1 squares.	After the first kiss tear off. 2 squares.	After the first kiss tear off. 3 squares.	After the first kiss tear off. 4 squares.

NOTICE.

1. Ten kisses are to be taken each day.
2. Cardholders very much in need of love can obtain supplementary cards.
3. The lady, who has received the first kiss, is good for the whole week.
   Holders render themselves liable to a penalty, if, during the current week they take a kiss from another lady, They forfeit their card in this case.
4. The lady concerned will tear off the control squares allotted to her and return same to the undersigned official of the Central Office from whom she will receive back the kisses given.
5. One kiss may not last longer than ten seconds. If the period is exceeded, the kiss will count as two.
6. Persons under 16 years of age will not receive cards.
7. On meatless and fatless days no kisses may be given.
8. All those who take less kisses than they are entitled to are not serving the Fatherland.

Brandenburg-Dortmund,   Stein St 21.

MY KINGDOM.

("If even I were as in my boyhood.")

I was a King once long ago
  A happy King was I ;
My sceptre was the wind a-blow.
  My crown the summer sky,
For when I donned my crown, each bird
  Sang songs of love to me.
And homage, when my sceptre stirred
  Was paid by every tree.

And when perforce my crown I doffed,
  My eager hands would play
As though the jewelled stars aloft
  Were poppies in the hay.
Each star I did design to dress
  And gem the glowing hair
Of some princess whose loveliness
  Would grace a realm so fair.

Green hills lay girdle-wise around,
  Midmost a silver stream,
With mysteries of ancient sound
  My minister did seem,
Who oft would croon, as passed the moon
  In drowsy hush and deep,
Of far-off fountains where the moon
  Saw naked gods asleep.

I left my kingdom years ago
  And now what would I give
If my poor exiled heart could know
  The life it once did live ?
If I could spend what years remain
  With wind and summer sky
Then would I be a King again,
  A King, until I die.

NORMAN GULLICK.

BRICKS FROM THE EDITOR'S PACK.

We are sorry to hear that Capt. H. W. R. CHANDLER has been severely wounded in the left arm.

Congratulations to Lieut. Harry Deane, of the Canadian Infantry, whose mother resides at Woodmancote, on having been awarded the Military Cross. He was formerly in this Battalion. He came over with the Canadian Contingent and after serving as a Sergeant was given his Commission.

From the *Times Literary Supplement*, July 12.

" However appreciative Tommy Atkins may be of the Army Chaplain who ' supplies the gentleness of a woman without her seductiveness ' we doubt if he will ever come to regard him as a complete substitute."

Archibald, certainly not.

From the *Daily Express :*

" Public indignation is vigorously expresesd in a North London Suburb at the number of unexploded shells which fell in the district. The subject was raised in dramatic fashion by Sir Henry Dalziel in the House of Commons. He suggested that orders should be given to the Police to report the number of Anti-Aircraft hells found."

Personally we have always looked on the A.A. as being more in the nature of a heaven.

To plagiarise an old saying :—

There are two classes of men out here, the quick and the dead. The former have to be d——— quick.

A Somerset Tribunal story :—

The name of the Clerk to the County Tribunal is Simey. The case of a young farmer appealing for exemption was adjourned " sine die," and the youth reported to his friends and neighbours that he was not to join up till Simey dies !

A genuine howler :—

A girl pupil in a Hampshire Secondary School was asked to give the context of and her idea of the meaning of this quotation :—" For borrowing dulls the edge of husbandry." The girl's explanation was: " This is advice to young women not to borrow money from men or the latter will keep away from them and so they will lose their chance of getting married."

The departure of the Rev. G. F. HELM to the Curacy of St. Anne's, Lambeth, will be regretted throughout the whole Division, in which no chaplain has been so long or so won the confidence of those to whom he has ministered. Attached to this regiment before the war he has been continuously with it since mobilisation, and how much he has done ! One always looked on him as a chaplain, but as more of a friend than a Superior Person. He was so many-sided, and above all no respector of persons. Of never failing cheerfulness himself, he managed always to infect others with the same spirit ; even on a route march the sight of the Padre with a full pack stepping along with the " chaps " (of the company nearest to the band) and administering " comfort " to those who fell by the wayside was a positive joy. In losing the Padre we are losing one of our best friends.

We wish him every good wish at his work at St. Anne's, and feel sure that the qualities which endeared him to everyone here will be no less helpful to everyone there.

"We owe those victories to the firm resolution of Sir Douglas Haig, to the skilful leading of the Army Commanders and their staffs, to the competence of subordinate leaders, to the perfect co-operation of all arms, and, most, perhaps, of all, to the immortal valour of our noble infantry, which continues to bear the greatest burden in the fight, and has once more won imperishable renown. Without it all the labours of other arms would be in vain. It is the infantry with rifle, bomb, and bayonet that both takes and holds, endures the greatest and the longest strain, and suffers by far the heaviest losses. Few lookers-on witness its deeds of valour, but, if we were just, we should distinguish its incomparable gallantry by granting it in future the precedence over all other arms, which it has fairly won by its devotion and its sacrifices."

From *The Times*.

At last. Then why pay the Infantry less than any one else ?

During the King's recent visit to France he knighted two brothers in the Square at Albert. This is we believe unique. The brothers thus honoured were Lieut.-General Sir E. A. Fanshawe and Major-General Sir Robert Fanshawe.

least resistance

INDENBURG'S LINE of

Congratulations to Sergt. Davis, late of B. Coy., now in the 2/5th Gloucesters, on winning the D.C.M.

We are very pleased to see that Major G. F. Collett has been appointed to command the 2/5th Glos. Regiment and has been made Lieut.-Colonel.

———

SOME OLD HAUNTS.

Fonquevillers, Hebuterne, Gommecourt, Serrel. What memories these names call up ! In the minds of many of us they are as familiar as the names of the home. True, the ranks of those who lived in the two villages at first-named, and looked so longingly at the two latter, are sadly thinned, but there must be many who would like to visit their old haunts and to look back on their old trenches from the German side.

The writer proposes to give a short account of a trip he enjoyed round that neighbourhood. He was more familiar with the right sector than the left, and consequently spent more time there.

We approached the neighbourhood via Courcelles and Sailly. These villages were much as we had left them. Leaving the car at Bayencourt, we walked on to La Haie, where it seemed strange to find so much of the Chateau still left.

Arriving at " Fonky," we struck up Thorpe Street, and made for the old Batt. H. Q. there, still in an excellent state of preservation. The Trenches, too, were still quite recognisable. Gommecourt wood was a striking witness to the force of our bombardments, and was in great contrast to the condition of the wood surrounding Fonquevillers and Hebuterne. We met an old man there who had been at his home in Puisieux during the German occupation. He spoke in emphatic terms of the efficiency of our Artillery in that village, and said the Huns " avaient beaucoup de peur te beaucoup de colère contre les Anglais." He described how a German officer came up to him one day and asked him why the French were fighting by the side of the English now. Had they forgotten the Hundred Year's War and Jeanne d'Arc ? Why, it was the English who had defeated Napoleon.—" Attendez," replied the old man, " ils ont vaincu Napoléon par leur tenacité, et c'est leur tenacité qui vous vaincra aussi." I asked him what the German replied to that. " Il est parti vite," was the answer.

We continued our way into Hebuterne down the Bucquoy road, and first made for our old haunts in the keep. Alas ! Keep Cottage is badly knocked about, and the Mess-room filled completely with sandbags to protect the cellar. The cemetery was our next objective, now grown very much larger. Those who have friends buried there will be glad to hear it is in very good condition and is evidently well-cared for. The main street of Hebuterne has been severely handled. Most of the houses are more or less demolished, though it is still possible to say " Here was the R.E. dump, and here Batt. H. Q." The church is nearly levelled to the ground, and most of the trees round it, but the Crucifix still gazes down the street untouched. Leaving the village we took the Serre Road. It had always been our ambition some day to walk boldly and unafraid down the Serre Road into Serre. But unfortunately this cannot be done literally now, as the road becomes a " wash-

out " soon after the first barricade. Instead we climbed on to the top by our old friend Bugeaud trench—known to the Tommies by a less euphonious name—and so up to the front line. Looking to the left we saw what was left of the Sixteen Poplars—6 or 7 broken stumps—and to our front the Christmas Tree—and then as we turned half-right, whatever was that ? We rubbed our eyes. No, it really was a train running peacefully along under Serre towards Colincamps, as though there had never been a war on ! Nothing so forcefully brought home to us the change in affairs.

The front line trench was not so bad, and we could walk along it, bending down at the old spots, and trying to recall the old sensations. It was a joy to walk openly out to the Christmas Tree, the scene of many a scrap, and to see how near it was to the Hun line—and then on to the line itself. Their trenches did not look nearly as good as our own. The parados was not revetted, and one communication-trench, dry though the weather was, was even then half-full of water.

It was interesting to see how far more heavily their front line had been bombarded than our own. And so we went on past The Point, and the remains of John Copse, and up to the site of Serre. Of the village nothing remains. We looked back at Hebuterne and our trenches, and realised how much better placed had been the Huns than ourselves. I do not think, however, that they could see all that we used to imagine they could.

We picked up the car at Serre, and so back through Puisieux—a complete wreck—and Bucquoy, our minds full of memories of our first winter in the trenches. However much we had loathed those trenches at the time, they seemed almost old friends now linked as they are with wistful thoughts of the pals who shared their discomforts with us, and have now passed to the Great Beyond.

———

OUR BENEFACTORS.

Lieut.-Colonel Marling.	Papers.
Colonel Griffiths.	,,
Lieutenant J. Margetson.	Cigarettes.
Sergeant Liddiatt.	Cricket Material.
L/Corporal J. A. Early.	Typing.
Private Wood.	Assistant Editor.
The Hon. Mabel Gye.	Papers.
Miss Karn.	,,
Mr. W. R. Voller.	,,

———

MILITARY WEDDING AT GLOUCESTER.

A very pretty wedding took place at All Saints Church, yesterday, where Pte. Kinder Jones, of the Gloucester Regiment (straight from the front) and Miss Marjory Murkentroy, of Leather Bottle Lane, 17th daughter of Major Murkentroy, of the Salvation Army, were united in Holy Matrimony. The bride who was first to arrive at the church in a tank was accompanied by her father, and looked charming attired in a dress of real sandbag, supported in the centre with a rifle sling and daintily trimmed with 4 by 2. Her head dress was composed of a massive shrapnel helmet (a gift of the bridegroom), nicely dented by a nurf point der, and tastefully trimmed with nosecaps. Round her neck she wore a string of real pork and beans from the centre of which hung a tin of machonachie. On her hands she wore a splendid pair of trench gloves, and her feet were enclosed in a handsome pair of gumboots (both being gifts of the bridegroom). The bridesmaids who were dressed in nargarine muslin, supplied by the Maypole Dairy Company, each carried a bouquet of dandylions. These included Linda Legge, Betsy Twigg, Pretty Polly and Lil Powell.

The Bridegroom, who arrived a little later in a limber, kindly lent by the Transport Officer of the Gloucester Regiment, looked handsome, being bronzed by the sun of France. He wore the uniform of the Gloucester Regiment (which is similar to that worn by conscientious objectors), and his breast was covered with medals, which he had hired for the occasion from Pike and Onleys (Pawnbrokers). An archway of corrugated iron which had been erected outside the church, was gaily decorated with onions and lettuce, and a corduroy path was also laid down from the gutter to the church steps, to prevent the bride from slipping. A large quantity of barbed wire and some trip wires were put out by a specially trained wiring party, (who accompanied Pte. Jones from the front) for the purpose of keeping back the huge crowd which had gathered during the early part of the day. A working party of 20 men (who had also accompanied Pte. Jones from the front) formed the guard of honour. The interior of the church was illuminated by flare lights fired off by the members of the boy scouts, of which previous to the war Pte. Jones had been Intelligence Officer.

The Rev. Nozzle officiated and the service opened out with Fray Bentos's Wedding March on the organ. The choir which consisted of members of the Bantams, then sang two anthems entitled " Never trip up father when he's drunk " and " Never throw the lighted lamp at Mother." The serious part of the service then commenced and it was noticed that during the proceedings Pte. Jones was continually scratching himself, but as we know him to be a real soldier, it was evident he was itching to get back to his comrades at the front. The party were about to return to Leather Bottle Lane, when it was found that the mules had eaten through their iron rations and had also chewed up their harness.

Pte. Jones, grasping the situation, immediately despatched a runner with an indent for a new set and it was some time before this arrived. In the meantime Mrs. Jones began to complain of trench feet. As whale oil could not be obtained, dripping was obtained from the nearest pork butchers and successfully applied by Pte. Jones, who had gained much experience as a stretcher bearer. After waiting several hours the harness arrived and the party then proceeded to the Major's house, where the wedding breakfast was held. On alighting from the limber the happy couple were greeted with a shower of chestnuts and figs, thrown by friends, who had gathered at the door. The breakfast was laid out by the B. E. F. Canteen, and consisted of Machonachie rissoles, bully, 1/3rd of a loaf, a small rum issue. The presents which were numerous and costly were exhibited at Pike and Onley's, and consisted of the following :—

Bride to Bridegroom :—

Tin of Harrison's Pomade.

Bar of Soap.

Clean pair of pants.

Bridegroom to Bride :—

Identity disc, Pay book and Box Respirator.

She was also presented with a nest of performing chats, the gift of some of Pte. Jones' comrades. After the breakfast the party had their photographs taken in the backyard. These were immediately handed to the Police for future reference, and the evening was spent in the taproom of the Monks' Retreat.

This morning the happy couple proceeded to Clapham, where they will spend their honeymoon. The bride's travelling dress was a waterproof sheet and a cap comforter. Iron rations were supplied en route. Pte. Jones has been granted 10 days leave and we wish him the very best of luck.

PROMOTIONS AND APPOINTMENTS.

Part II.

Extracts from *London Gazette*, 22/6/17 :—

Capt. (temp.) A. J. Mitcheson, to be Capt. with precedence as from Oct. 1st, 1914.

Capt. L. R. C. Sumner, to have precedence as from June 1st, 1916.

Lieut. (temp. Capt.) F. E. Francillon, to be Capt. with precedence as from June 1st, 1916.

Lieut. G. A. Lister, to be Capt. with precedence as from June 1st, 1916.

Lieut. (temp) F. K. Foster, to be Lieut. with precedence as from August 19th, 1914, and to remain seconded.

Sec.-Lieut. (temp. Capt.) G. E. P. Hollington, to be Lieut. (temp. Capt.) with precedence as from June 1st, 1916.

Lieut. (temp. Capt.) G. E. P. Hollington, to relinguish the temp. rank of Capt.

Sec.-Lieut. (temp. Lieut.) J. P. Winterbotham, to be Lieut. with precedence as from June 1st, 1916, and to remain Adjutant.

Sec.-Lieut. (temp. Lieut.) G. Hawkins, to be Lieut. with precedence as from June 1st, 1916.

Sec.-Lieut. (temp. Lieut.) G. E. Ratcliff, to be Lieut. with precedence as from August 27th, 1916.

Sec.-Lieut. (temp. Lieut.) E. J. Cornish, to be Lieut. with precedence as from 21st November, 1916.

To be unpaid L/Corporals :—

240450	Pte.	Higgs, W.	18/7/17
241653	,,	Horwood, R. S.	,,
240756	,,	Cook, C.	,,
240184	,,	Wager H.	,,
242504	,,	Simmons, T.	,,
240629	,,	Short, C. E.	,,
240791	,,	Ilry, H. G.	,,
240940	,,	Frinder, L. J.	,,

SPORTS.

1/2 S. M, FIELD AMBULANCE.

15/7/17.

The following N. C. O.'s and Men of the Battalion entered for the Mile Race open to the Division :—

240753	L/Corpl.	Goatman, E.
242309	,,	Watts, W. R.
240395	Pte.	Smith, J. E.
240292	,,	Pugh, F. E.
240576	,,	Hayward, W.
240072	,,	Barnes, G. A. W.
241299	,,	Herbert.

Pte. Smith was in 2nd, being closely pipped by a keen amateur in the Ambulance.

Representing the Battalion the first three in were :— 1st, Pte. Smith ; 2nd, Pte. Herbert ; 3rd, L/Corpl. Goatman.

Pte. Smith had been inoculated the day before !

INQUISITIVE }
RECRUIT }   WHAT THE DEUCE YOU GOT QUARTERS
                                 RUM.?

QM. SGT.   NO, LIME YOU — — !!!

CRICKET.

Glo'sters v. Company Train.

This match was played on the former's ground and a very enjoyable game ensued. The greatest difficulty was in finding a suitable pitch, which although not good, with the help of some matting was quite playable.

The Glo'sters batted first, Capt. Sumner and Pte. Smith alone reaching double figures. Pte. Anderson bowled with great effect.

The A. S. C. started badly, losing a wicket in the first over. They never recovered and were all out for 37, leaving the Glo'sters winners by 21 runs.

Glosters

Corpl. King (D) b. Anderson	...	...	...	2
Pte. Vicary (B) c. Darker b. Simmons	...	...	1
Pte. Hamblin (A) b. Anderson	...	...	...	2
Pte. Burden (C) b. Anderson	...	...	...	5
Pte. Smith (A) c. and b. Anderson...	...	...	14
Pte. Mansell (A) run out	...	...	...	1
Sergt. Butt (B) b. Darker	...	...	...	4
Capt. Sumner b. Anderson	...	...	...	11
Corpl. Burlton (D) b. Anderson	...	...	2
Sergt. Egerton (D) b. Anderson	...	...	0
Corpl Prince (C) c. Darker b. Anderson	...	2
Rev. G. F. Helm not out	...	...	...	3
EXTRAS	...	...	...	10
				—
				58

Company Train

Goddard c. Prince b. Mansel	...	...	...	1
Woods hit wicket b. Sumner	...	...	...	4
Capt. Turner b. Sumner	...	...	...	2
Elderfield b. Sumner	...	...	...	0
Curtis b. Sumner	...	...	...	...	0
Newman c. Vicary b. Sumner	...	...	...	2
Simmons b. Smith	...	...	...	3
Rose lbw. b. King	...	...	...	7
Sergt. Darker b. Smith	...	...	...	0
Sergt.-Maj Williams b. King	...	...	3
S. Sergt.-Maj. Blandridge b. Smith	...	...	1
A Warn not out	...	...	...	2
EXTRAS...	...	...	...	13
				—
				37

R.I.P.

" In sacred sleep they rest : say not of brave men they
  die."
                                        CALLIMACHUS.

" Concerning them which are asleep, that ye sorrow not even
  as others which have no hope."
                                        ST. PAUL.

" Rest quietly, best beloved.
  Thou who fellest asleep in thy youth and thy beauty and
      thy strength,
  Rest quietly in thy long slumber.
  Though each passing summer scatter its blossom o'er thy
      head,
  Yet art thou ever a changeless memory,
  The truest and best of companions."
                                        Capt. R. DENNYS.

  " Nothing is here for tears, nothing to wail
    Or knock the breast, no weakness, no contempt,
    Dispraise or blame ; nothing but well and fair,
    And what may quiet us in a death so noble."

" If to die well is the chief part of virtue, Fortune
  granted this to us above all others : for striving to endue
  Hellas with Freedom, we lie here possessed of praise that
  groweth not old."
                                        Greek Anthology.

" The Trap? "

5th Gloucester Gazette.

A Chronicle. serious and humorous, of the Battalion while serving with the
BRITISH EXPEDITIONARY FORCE.

HONORIS CAUSA.

Military Cross.

Sec. Lieut. K. A. Robertson.
Capt. G. E. Ratcliff.
Sec.-Lieut. A. J. Deaton.

Distinguished Conduct Medal.

240038 C.S.M. Smith, V. G.
240276 L/Corpl. Millichap, P. J.

Military Medal.

203244 Sergt. Pullin, E.
203706 Sergt. Hodges, J. T.
21973   Corpl. Street, C. H.
240750 Corpl. C. Cook.
203696 L/Corpl. Clee, W.

Cards of congratulations for gallantry have been received from the G.O.C. Division by the following :—

Capt. R. F. C. McDowell.
Sec.-Lieut. V. B. Bingham-Hall.
240587 L/Corpl. E. S. Blackwell.
240401 Pte. Cake, W.
240062 Drm. M. G. Jordan.
240890 L/Corpl. T. H. Whitehead.

THE DEVIL DRINKS.

This year my vintage is of the best ;
My cellars are filled from end to end,
And my goblet is splashing o'er,
And dripping on to the floor.
My winepress ? The cannon, my friend.
And my wine ?—But, perhaps, you have guessed.

Modern Civilisation !
I drink to you deep in the bubbling wine,
For yours is many a subtle scheme
Of which this poor brain of mine
Never dreamed, nor will ever dream.
I, too, have been subtle and strong,
But one has come
Who is subtler and stronger still.
I am struck dumb
With very admiration
For you, Modern Civilisation.

Modern Civilisation !
All hail, oh, friend of mine !
My superior, too, I have long suspected,
For have you not filled my head
With a thousand things from the store
Of knowledge that you have collected ?
And what is more—
Filled my belly with scarlet wine ?

                                        P. M.

BALLADE OF INCIPIENT LUNACY.

SCENE.—A Battalion " Orderly " Room in France
    during a period of " Rest."

Runners arrive breathlessly from all directions bearing illegible chits, and tear off in the same directions with illegible answers or no answers at all. Motor bicycles snort up to the door and arrogant despatch-riders enter with enormous envelopes containing leagues of correspondence, orders, minutes, circulars, maps, signals, lists, schedules, summaries and all sorts. The tables are stacked with papers ; the floor is littered with papers ; papers fly through the air. Two type-writers click with maddening insistence in one corner. A signaller buzzes tenaciously at the telephone, talking in a strange language apparently to himself, as he never seems to be connected with anyone else. A stream of miscellaneous persons—quarter-masters, chaplains, generals, batmen, D.A.D.O.S.'s, sergeant-majors, staff-officers, buglers, Maires, officers just arriving, officers just going away, gas experts, bombing experts, interpreters, doctors—drifts in, waste time, and drifts out again.

Clerks scribble ceaselessly, rolls and nominal rolls, nominal lists and lists. By the time they have finished one list it is long out-of-date. Then they start the next. Everything happens at the same time ; nobody has time to finish a sentence. Only a military mind, with a very limited descriptive vocabulary and a chronic habit of self-deception, would call the place orderly.

The Adjutant speaks, hoarsley ; while he speaks he writes about something quite different. In the middle of each sentence his pipe goes out ; at the end of each sentence he lights a match. He may or may not light his pipe ; anyhow he quotes :—

" Where is that list of Wesleyans I made ?
    And what are all those people on the stair ?
Is that my pencil ? Well, they can't be paid.
    Tell the Marines we have no forms to spare.
    I cannot get these Ration States to square.
    The Brigadier's coming round, they say.
    The Colonel wants a man to cut his hair.
    I think I MUST be going mad to-day.

" These silly questions. I shall tell Brigade
    This office is now closing for repair.
They want to know what Mr. Johnstone weighed,
    And if the Armourer is dark, or fair ?
I do not know : I cannot say I care,
    Tell the Interpreter to go away.
Where is my signal pad ? I left it there.
    I think I MUST be going mad to-day.

" Perhaps I should appear upon parade.
    Where is my pencil ? Ring up Captain Eyre ;
Say I regret our tools have been mislaid.
    These Companies would make SIR DOUGLAS swear.
A is the worst. Oh, damn, is this the Maire ?
    I'm sorry, Monsieur—je suis desole—
But no one's pinched your miserable chair.
    I think I MUST be going mad to-day.

                    ENVOI.
" Prince, I perceive what CAIN's temptations were,
    And how attractive it must be to slay.
O Lord, the General ! This is hard to bear.
    I think I MUST be going mad to-day."

THE BALLADE OF THE HUN-CAT.

The Hun-Cat called a Council grand
Upon a summer's day—
A new law through the Fatherland
Had caused profound dismay.

And well it might, for thus it ran :
" On cats of every kind
Tax must be paid by those who can,
The others need not mind.

They'll be exempt—no penalty
In cash at any rate
Is claimed—in kind 'twill be
The cat we'll confiscate ;

And in the country's slaughter-house
Though it may scratch and mew,
'Twill be, like rabbit, hare or grouse,
Converted into stew.

This Tax will bring our victory near
Despite the foeman's plots—
And therefore 'tis a duty clear
For all good patriots."

And so it was the Hun-Cat wept
Within the Council Hall ;
Upon the mantelpiece he leapt,
And thus addressed them all :

—" O Cats ! this is a felon trick,
And goes beyond a joke ! "—
His coat was black and bright and thick,
And bristled as he spoke.

—" The mournful news was first revealed
By England's Daily Press,
Till then it was from us concealed
In all its frightfulness.

The truth our people feared to say
They're forced now to admit.
That's why I've called you here to-day—
We'll not put up with it !

'Tis well, of course, for those whom Fate
Has placed among the rich . . ."
But here the Hun-Cat had to wait
The groans reached such a pitch.

—" Their owners will defray the tax
Without a murmur, lest
Their pets be carried off in sacks—
But what about the rest ?

No need, I'm sure, to dot the i's ;
None can this law defend ;
To think how justice it defies
One's fur stands up on end !

The Government must deem us flats,
I think my record's good,
I've pounced on helpless mice and rats
And gobbled all I could ;

To join a scrap I've never missed,
I've bitten, clawed, and scratched,
I've crouched, and sprung, and clawed and hissed,
With hero Huns well matched.

So until now, you see, I've been
A truly loyal cat ;
But if to eat us up they mean
What is the good of that ?

The British are not half as bad
As some would fain believe,
Such an idea is but a fad
The fiction papers weave.

Their foes are treated royally
I've always understood,
Their land is fair, their people free,
'Tis said they've lots of food ;

So I propose to emigrate
At once to British shores.
Will those who can forget their hate
Kindly hold up their paws ?

'Tis best, of this there is no doubt,
To seek an alien hob
Than stay at home to carry out
The Food Controller's job.

Ah ! every paw is waved I see,
The plan is settled now.
Good luck to all who follow me !
Three cheers for England ! Miaow ! "—

M. L. G.

ADVERTISEMENTS AND ANNOUNCEMENTS WE SHALL EXPECT TO SEE AFTER THE WAR.

TRADE.

I, BUSTER CHARLES JARGON, Tailor, Hosier, and Hatter, 4, Talkscheap Street, invite once again the esteemed patronage of my pre-war customers.

Having served umpteen years in the M. F. P. on a foreign strand, I feel sure you will respect my patriotism by dealing at my establishment.

I have at my disposal a huge indent, just received from DAMAGES & Co., which embraces all the latest fashions.

LOUNGE SUITS made to measure from 11/6.

Come and see the latest Mouse-brown ready-made suits for Night Club " Splash-off's." GUARANTEED not to show beer stains.

A fine range of ties will meet your gaze in the window half-left from the kerbstone, at quite reasonable prices.

SPECIAL behind this window :—
TIES.
Crepe de wag, green background, showing bursts of H. E. Shrapnel in ruddy red, beautifully worked in silk, 1/2.
Extra 3d. for creeping barrage round edge.
SOCKS.
Anti G. S. (converted). Fine colours from blazing orange to a sober pink, going for a mere " song."
Special jet black hose embroidered round ankle with toad-grey entanglements, 1/6. per pair.
Ditto with red, white and blue screw pickets, 3d. extra.

HATS AND CAPS.
I have a large dump of red caps, in fact all hues, 1/- each.
Comfortable riding bowlers (6in. brim), Half-a-dollar.
A chain vizor has been devised, which, when attached to the front of the bowler with a bull-dog clips, affords complete protection against gnats, flies, mosquitoes or horse stingers entering the eye whilst cycling.
Come early and snaffle the bargains.
In view of a great crush it would be advisable for customers to wear Nightfield Body Shields, if available.
We are opening to-morrow.

PERSONAL.

SECRET AGENCY.—WOLFF'S INTELLIGENCE AND EAVES-DROPPING BUREAU.

Expert Detective work expedited at short notice. Money no object.

If you suspect your Husband's real intentions, or vice versa, your Wife's ditto, I will shadow the intruder for a small sum, and render to you a complete narrative of his movements, with map references and true compass bearing in a week.
NIGHT WORK. a speciality.
If ground flares have to be expended 3/6 extra. References galore.
Holder of Military Medal for shadowing Hun working parties during the Great War.
Address all sentimental queries to my understudy :
JIM WEEZEL, attached WI & E B.
CLAPHAM.
Telegrams—" FISHY."

WANTED.

Monkey, small and active, by old Soldier (gassed at MONS) to perch on Barrel-organ.

Would exchange a collection of nose-caps. Write BOX 1434.

LOST.

15 m. m. Calabash Pipe, approximately near " King's Head," NORTON. Owner dropped it whilst executing a spiral vol-plane down to the " RED LION," Wainlodes Hill, Reward. Apply Aerodrome, Twigworth.

VACANCIES.

Male Cook, competent and clean, wanted. Must know how to serve up a sheep's head in six different ways as prescribed in SS. 164 pamphlet issued by the Economy Board. Salary, £36 per annum. Write Hon. MRS. LE SARS, THRUPP.

Lady Marine Engineers urgently needed at Clyde Shipbuilding Yards. Applicants must throughly understand the anatomy of ocean-going liners. Salary, £500 per annum. Write Box 24/1.

CHRISTENING.

There was a distinguished company present at the Christening of ALBERT, MAMETZ and VIOLET HERMIES, the only twins of Mr. and Mrs. CRUMP, at ST. ANNE'S CHURCH, on Wednesday last. Readers will be interested to know MR. CRUMP was one of Bruce Bairnsfather's original studies, under the nom de plume of ALF.

TO HOUSEHOLDERS.

Clinkers to be had for the fetching. Apply Clinker Commandant, Whiteway Colony, near the " Pip " in PAINSWICK. Map CRANHAM 1/10,000.

GOLF.

JOSEPH BRAY offers to teach scientific Golf on modern lines.

Learn to do every movement by numbers in accordance with Field Golf Regulations.

If you wish to become an expert at Golf come to my School of Instruction, and reach the culminating point of fame, i.e. top hole.

Destructive shoots taught.

Remember VARDON.

For prospectus apply—
  The Brayway School of Golfery,
    Le Jokey Links.
        W. J. W.

IN THE PARROT HOUSE.

BY POLLY M.P.

THE SQUEAKER took the chair at 2 p.m.

UMBRELLAS FOR THE TROOPS.

In reply to a question by Mr. Candle Tooth (R Pas de Calais), MR. LONAR BORE stated that the C. in C. did not think it advisable at present to issue umbrellas to the troops on the scale of one per battalion.

MR. CANDLE TOOTH : May I ask why it it considered necessary for our troops to be continually suffering from wet and damp ?

MR. LONAR BORE : I must have notice of that question.

MR. CANDLE TOOTH : Can the Hon. Member not give me a straight answer to a sraight question ?

THE SQUEAKER : The Hon. gentleman has already asked his question and received his reply. I must request him to sit down.

(MR. CANDLE TOOTH then sat down.)

In reply to MR. BLUD (Ind., No-Man's Land), who asked whether the C. in C. sanctioned the acceptance of gifts from the Germans, as he had recently heard from his son in the trenches that the enemy were now sending our troops a number of blue pigeons, MR. LONAR BORE declared this to be an exploded fallacy.

THE EUPHRATES.

MR. PRONGLE (Crouch End) asked whether any action had been taken in connection with the Euphratesian Scandal.

MR. SQUATH (emphatically) : Yes. All concerned have been relieved of their posts and given positions nearer home and with higher pay. (Loud cheers.)

CAPT. FYTER (U., Somme), who had just returned from the Front, then raised the question of pay and leave. The Hon. and gallant Member was speaking at 5 o'clock when the debate stood adjourned, and the House rose on being informed by the SQUEAKER that tea was getting cold.

On the resumption, the SQUEAKER stated that he regretted that Captain Fyter would be unable to continue his speech as the War Office had cancelled his leave. The matter was then dropped, and the House entered into a debate on the question of raising the salary of Members to £500 a quarter. The motion was passed without a division, there being no dissentients.

VICTORY IN THE EASTERN THEATRE.

MR. FROGG then rose to address the House. He stated that he was pleased to say that during the tea interval he had received a telegram stating that the Arabs had inflicted a severe defeat on the Persians. Eight hundred prisoners and one rifle had been reported as captured. Further details were lacking. (Loud cheers.)

A Member : Can the hon. gentleman say which are our Allies—the Arabs or the Persians ? (Derisive laughter)

MR. SQUEAKER : I must remind the hon. gentleman that this House is not a place of amusement. (Loud laughter and cheers.)

MR. PIMPLETON SMELLING (The Parliamentary Pugilist) enquired whether, in view of the fact that no enemy aeroplanes were brought down in the above reported victory, and also since there was an imminent danger of a raid by 10,000 enemy aeroplanes, he would consider the question of having properly traversed and wired trenches dug in the main streets of London.

MR. CHINSTON WURZELL (U., Haut Ayr) replied that he was in communication as to the advisability of employing soldiers on leave who had been specially trained in intensive digging.

MR. SMELLING further asked whether a special medal with the inscription " Some dig, some dec." could be struck for these men.

MR. CHINSTON WURZEL replied that the question would be considered.

MR. THING (U., Cheddar West : Is it a fact that the North Clyde Shipbuilders have refused to work on a ship to convey Mr. Lamsay Smackdonald on a visit to Timbuctoo ?

Sir F. Burnbury (Bath) replied that he was pleased to state that on a further grant of £5 a day the delegates would consider the matter.

The House stood adjourned at 11 p.m.

POINTS OF VIEW.

THE SOLDIER.

Dear Ma,—This War can't last much longer. I have just been reading Lloyd George's speech. We 'ave got the bosch wacked. He runs whenever he sees us, and we shall all be home by Xmas again. From your loving son.

THE MUNITION MAKER.

" One thing is certain. The war *can't* end for another three years at any rate. Why, we've hardly started yet. It's absolutely ridiculous to talk about peace before we've driven the Germans to the Rhine. Yes, my dear sir, three years—three years at any rate."

THE ENGLISHMAN.

" Peace ? Oh, I don't know. It's all very well to talk about it, but then, you see, it would be only the prelude to another war. You see, Germany's out to grab territory—she wants her Colonies back—the idea's ridiculous. Besides, it's no good talking about peace until we get Alsace Lorraine. No, there's only one thing to do—steel our hearts for another year of war."

THE CABINET MINISTER.

" We will fight this War to the bitter end. German militarism must be crushed. The man who talks about Peace at this stage is a traitor to his country. There can be no Peace until the German is driven out of Belgium—until the Kaiser has learned to say the word gestulation without stammering over the Gest.

THE PACIFIST.

" Now, let us go to the root of the thing. Is it peace at any price that we're demanding ? No. We are asking for something reasonable—above all that mere mention of the word Peace—as though it were something filthy and abhorent, should not be treated as a crime in this country."

THE BOSCH.

" Vot ? Vy, of course. I vant peace, my friend. Vy not ? Ve must grow weaker every day. With every push ve lose two thousand prisoners, and you lose one thousand killed. Dat is good for us, but it would be better it ve had peace. Belgium ? Ach ! Zum Teufel mit Belgium."

THE FINANCIER.

" Well, of this, this war's costing a devil of a lot I mean to say—eight millions a day—well, it obviously can't last much longer. At the same time I think it would be a damn good thing if it were all over now. Of course I know the difficulties, but at the same time . . .

THE FANATIC.

" Peace ? Ah ! Murder that man who talks of peace. Who wants peace ? None but those fools the Pacifists. No. War for ever until there is not a Hun left in the world War for ever ! War for ever ! "

DIVISIONAL TRAINING.

SECRET.

Tactical Exercise without Troops.

1. General Idea.

    (A) The Division is in Rest Billets in the Amieville Area, in reserve to a Corps of four Divisions which is holding the line with two Divisions. The latter have recently been withdrawn exhausted from the Training Area.

    The other Reserve Division is receiving contradictory Routine Orders from six other Corps, and is expecting a move.

    For purposes of this Exercise it should therefore be considered neutral.

    (B) The dividing line between Divisions is the line of latitude running through Corps Headquarters.

    (c) Our Division is expecting to attack on a front of about one knot N.N.W. of dividing line. (Read H.M.S. 122, " Co-operation between Services."

2. Special Idea.

    Note.—For Staff, exercise to be carefully worked out with map and compass and a possible previous knowledge of either or both.

    (A) The Artillery, Pioneers, Band and Mess Stewards of the Division are already in position in the Forward Area.

    (B) There is an " X " day and a " Y " day.

3. Extra Special Idea.

    Note.—To be worked out by Battalion Staff.

    The Division is ordered to move up to a position of offensive readiness. Move to be completed by 2 a.m., X-1 day.

    For purposes of this Exercise, " Q " will be presumed to have allotted one half of a lorry per Brigade to supplement existing transport. (Units will have to arrange about their own petrol.)

4. Situations.

    Situations will be issued on the ground by " G " as they arise. (Units must make their own loading and transport arrangements.)

Lessons on Situations 1—6.

1. The Orders to Move.

    These were issued by Division a full hour before the move. Were they fully explained to all ranks ? One cook in " B " Brigade did not know the map reference of " C " Brigade Starting Point.

2. The March.

    Take full advantage of shade and down gradients. Save your men's feet—they will want them in the fight.

3. The Arrival.

    Scouts must be sent on to locate good training grounds and attack courses.

4. Reconnaissance of the Battlefield.

    Most important. Telescopes cannot be too long. Locate O.P.'s first ; officers' messes can wait.

5. The Advance.

    Left Flank in weed—difficult—more training in woodcraft—must bound from tree to tree.

    Right Flank in air—ground Scouts useless.

    One platoon commander halted to consult his A.B.'s, cards, pamphlets and " things one forgets." This held up the advance over four hours.

    Depth—imperative—but it is futile to attack on a front of 300 yards with a Battalion in single file, Headquarters in rear.

Closer liason between all arms—one Battalion Headquarters was accompanied by a pack animal—did the liason officer with this Battalion get all he required.

6. THE AFTERMATH OF BATTLE.

Troops did not show sufficient elan when consolidating—the spade is a noble weapon.

(Sgd.) A. P. ERRISHER, B.F.G.S., —th Corps.

N.B.—Sufficient copies are provided for distribution down to squad commanders.

F. D. R.

A PERFECT NIGHTMARE.

When you come to the end of a perfect day
  That you've spent in a forward post ;
When you've picked the remaining chats away,
  And see who has won the most :
Then you sit at ease and think it fine,
  Such a peaceful evening scene,
When Crump ! Goes the burst of a 5.9
  In your best fly-proof latrine !

When you come to the end of a long, long trench,
  And you walk into No-Man's Land :
If your nose is assailed by a bad, bad stench,
  Why, then you will understand
It's a dead, dead Bosch, and you better strive
  To break fresh ground instead,
For the Bosch has an evil smell alive,
  But a damn sight worse when dead.

TEN COMMANDMENTS.

1. The C.O. is thine only boss, thou shalt have none other C.O. but him.

2. Thou shalt make unto thyself many graven images ; of Officers who fly in the heavens above, of Staff Officers who own the earth beneath, and of Submarine Officers who are in the waters under the earth. Thou shalt stand up and salute them, for the Colonel, thy boss, will visit with Field Punishment unto the first and second degree on them that salute not, and shower stripes on them that salute and obey his commands.

3. Thou shalt not take the Adjutant's name in vain, for the C.O. will not hold him guiltless who takes his name in vain.

4. Remember that thou shalt not rest on the Sabbath Day. Six days shalt thou labour and do more than thou ought to do, but the seventh day is the day of the C.R.E., and in it thou shalt do all manner of work, thou, thy officers, thine N.C.O.'s, thy servants, thy sanitary men, the signallers and the Kitchener's Army that is within thy trench for instruction.

5. Honour the Army Staff that thy days may be long in the land of Corps Reserve where some day they may send thee.

6. Thou shalt kill only flies, rats, Bosch, and other vermin that dwell in dug-outs.

7. Thou shalt not adulterate thy section's Rum ration.

8. Thou shalt steal, but thou shalt not be found out.

9. Thou shalt not bear false witness in the Orderly Room.

10. Thou shalt not covet the A.S.C.'s job, thou shalt not covet the A.S.C.'s pay, nor his billets, nor his motors, nor his horses, nor his mules, nor any other cushy thing that is his.

(The above were written by Lieut.-Colonel (then Capt.) G. F. Collett, at Bus, in October, 1915. As several papers have published them as original, and as many would like to see them entire, they are published here for the first time.—EDITOR.)

TO THE EAST WIND.

Time was, on hot and summer days,
  When if a gentle wind did stream
From Eastwards, one was wont to praise
  Such solace from the scorching beam,
And thanked whatever gods might be
For such benign felicity.

One used to call with cheerful voice,
  While mopping moisture from the brow.
For cooling drinks—ice-balls for choice,
  (Such things are legendary now !)
And bared to view one's manly chest,
Breathing the wind with double zest.

Alas, the times are out of joint !
  Now, when the blooming East wind blows,
Fritz never fails to make a point
  Of trying to up-yurn our toes :—
No breeze is hated so by us,
As that y-clept "Wind Dangerous."

With frantic haste we re-adjust
  Upon our over-weighted chests
That damned "Box" (because we must
  Pay heed to G.R.O. behests),
While hasty lips do not disdain
Words that the pious call profane.

L'ENVOI.

And yet, O Wind (pardon my peroration),
  Oft-times we profit by thy swift volte-face
When, contrary to Bosch anticipation,
  Thou blowest back his beastly clouds of gas :
And if thereby one Fritz should bite the dirt,
I'll cheerfully go weeks "In the Alert."

N. D. GULLICK.

PAY DAY.

For thirteen out of the fifteen days before Pay Day you hear the familiar question : "when the ——'s pay day ? " At last it is whispered—"The ghost she walks to-morrow ! " All's a hustle on the great day ; the estaminet across the way is getting in a supply of beer (the Lord have mercy upon us for calling such stuff by such a noble name), and Madam is looking over her "bestest" frock ; and the gamblers are looking out their cards which have got somewhat dusty in their packs, and the Crown and Anchor people at the Transport are getting their wrists in shape. But what amuses you most is some cook over in one corner polishing his buttons— I suppose he thinks the brilliancy might dazzle the Skipper's eye, and an extra five franc note might slip through his fingers.

At last the welcome parade, and out come the Sergeants pocketing their 30 francs (you wouldn't think to look at them that their capacity was thrice ours, but I suppose it must be, for they get nearly thrice as much—but may be it's for the work they do.)

At last your turn comes ; you soothe your itchy left palm with the two five franc notes, salute the Skipper with the right, pass out and bump up against four creditors. Biff goes half, and a few beers and the last franc on the lucky old mud hook hoping to get a triple—"two lucky old crowns and a spade " dash your hopes to the ground ; off you stroll, your hands in your pockets, and count the days until next pay day.

"There's a pay day coming for every wound and pain,
    Every sacrifice of gain,
    Every waking, aching night,
    Every hour of strenuous fight,
For victory won, when every hope seemed vain."

F. J. W.

SHAKESPEARE : 1917.

Scene : A TRENCH. SOLDIERS. NIGHT.

1ST SOLDIER (*into the darkness*) : How now ? Who are you ?

2ND DO. : Friend.

1ST DO. : Pass, Friend, all's well. Say now, are those the rations ?

2ND DO. : No, no. The fodder will arrive apace. E'en now they load it on the asses' backs.

1ST DO. : That's bon ; for I am passing fit for shackles (1)
To fill my belly to a decent stretch.
And yet a mighty jest is now abroad
How shell-balls, flipping (2) round the village walls,
Nigh hit the cookers, and thereat the cooks
Have scooted half way back to England's shores.

1ST DO. : Ha ! Ha ! But halt ! What's that ? How now ? Who's there ?

LORD FITZ-JOY. : I am the Earl of Monmouth, General. Is there an officer within that trench ?

1ST SOL. : Sir, I salute you, and will fetch him straight.

OFFICER : Who calls ? What want you ? Will you see the trench ?

LORD F. : Ay, for that very purpose am I come.

OFFICER : Then step this way, but mind the steep approach.

LORD F. : Who's this, that works not on the trench defence ?
What man has dared to disobey my word ?

OFFICER : Sir, 'tis an Orderly but now arrived.
Herewith despatched from Company Headquarters.

LORD F. : 'Tis well. But mark you now my willy (3) words,
Each man shall work and dig and carry rations
Both day and night and eve and dusk and dawn.
'Tis only meet the trench should be improved.
" No dig, no dec.," (4) our Lord Napoleon said,
A motto worthy of the House of Monmouth,
For like a man that hath not washed his hands
So is a man that digs not. Idleness
I must have rooted out from my command.
Slackness—the greatest enemy man has
Is but another word for sloth, the which
I never countenance within the ranks.
But what's this here ? This trench is damnable.
It badly needs both width and depth and breadth.
The wire in front is thin, the fire-steps low,
The parados reeks still of dead men's bones.
The soil is muddy—why no trench-boards down ?
The grass is long and shows itself unchewed.
There's nought here schneidig.(5) You and your platoon

OFFICER : Methinks, my Lord, there comes a Blue Pidge (6) nigh,
'Twere best if we in yonder shelter ducked.

LORD F. : Dec me no decs—ahem !—er—as you were !
Duck me no ducks and pigeon me no pigeons.
I will not have it said——(A crash).

OFFICER : Art hurt, my Lord ?
'Twas nothing but a stinking neuf point deux.

LORD F. : Did it belong to us, now tell me quick,
Or came it from those baby-blasting bastards ?

OFFICER : 'Twas theirs, my Lord.

LORD F. : Then show me to your dug-out ! (7)
(Another crash).

OFFICER : Look out, great Sir, they come now, thick and fast,
And cert 'twas best to shelter in this cut-off ; (8)
The dug-out is still many paces off.
(Many crashes follow.)

LORD F. (*in the din*) : The Bosch attacks—now quick—a Very Light !

OFFICER : 'Tis here !

LORD F. : Why don't you send it up, you wonk;(9)
Send up that bloody S.O.S. (10) at once.

OFFICER : I wait, my Lord, until the Bosch attacks.

LORD F. : Thou ass and perisher, pass on the light !

OFFICER : 'Tis here. Your least desire is my behest.

LORD F. : Keep low. I'm just about to fire the charge. (A bang.)
Oh, God ! What have I done ? I've shot myself.

OFFICER : Sire ! Soldiers ! Soldiers ! Come around your Lord !
A sad mishap has recently o'erta'en him.

SOLDIERS : We're here, sir, sergeants all and stretcher bearers.

STRETCHER BEARER (*kicks Lord F.*) : Dead as a bit of bully beef entinned.

LORD F. : Villain, I am not dead, but now expire !
(Dies.)

OFFICER : All is now quiet without. The moon is down.
The straf is o'er. Alone the war goes on.
Bring now a blanket. I will to the 'phone. (Exeunt.)

GLOSSARY.

1 Shackles : A dish made of bones and water, in vogue among soldiers at this time.

2 Flipping : Probably refers to the Shrapnel flying in all directions.

3 Willy : The Christian name of the then Crown Prince of Germany. Denotes here " foolish."

4 " No dig, no dec." : Dec. short for decoration. No trace of this phrase can be found amongst the standard works on Napoleon.

5 Schneidig : It is not quite clear why Shakespeare should have used this German word here. It means " smart" or " keen."

6 Blue Pidge : A peculiar kind of shell with feathers like a pigeon.

7 Dug-out : Phatswyne-Northclieff's Dictionary for 1917 gives the following definition of dug-out—" a shelter for Cuthberts : any cover that gives protection from shell-fire."

8 Cut-off : Here refers to the undercutting of trench sides, which was usually forbidden.

9 Wonk : A fool.

10 S.O.S. : Probably Star of Sunset—a poetical term for Very Light. Fuller Gutz, M.A., the famous Baconian, says it should be taken in conjunction with the initial letter " B " of the previous word "bloody," and that it undoubtedly stood for " Bacon Shakespeare's opera scribit.' I am not inclined to agree with this view.

FIBULOUS.

" Out on Rest."

A. E. FRASER.

" Our ' Tommies' are always cheerful."—
From the " DAILY LIAR."

THINGS WE DON'T WANT TO KNOW

The circulation of the " D—l- M—l."

The impressions of Mr. Ph–ll–p G–bbs.

What the " L–nd–n M—l " wants to know.

Whethe. Loid N–rthcl–ff– is coming back from America.

The war activities of Lady D—n– M–nn–rs.

Mr. P–mb–rt–n B–ll–ng's disclosures.

The religious opinions of conscientious objectors.

The latest government appointment of Mr. W–nst–n Ch–rch–ll.

What Mr. H–r–t— B–tt–ml–y has seen.

THINGS WE WANT TO KNOW.

Who is the Referee who sleeps his fixtures away ?

Who is the reinforcement so anxious to get at 'em, and did it take three years to create the desire ? Is he in D Company ?

Did the T. O. eventually get his breakfast that dark morning at D—— Camp after the shell hole experience, and would it be advisable to borrow a torch from the T. S. in case of future predicaments ?

Who was the Sergeant who said, " Come on, chaps, pair up in three's for Bread " ? Is he in D Company ?

Did the Divisional Bandmaster notice the N.C.O.'s and men who had just returned from leave when the band played " The end of a Perfect Day " ?

Why all the C.S.M.'s are keen on that old song " Fall in and follow me," and what was the opinion of the encore re map reference ?

What was on the notice board ?

A title for a song about a " Tank " ? A Gloucester Scot suggests " Uncanny Lorry " ! !

Has the M. O. indented for a rubber stamp to mark M. and D. on the sick reports ?

Are season tickets going to be issued for sick parades ?

If the following incident had happened to any of our Regiment recently ? :—A certain patient had just been made comfortable for the night, and before going off duty the Nurse asked him if she could do any more for him. " Well, yes," said the patient, " I should like to be kissed good-night." " Just wait till I call the Orderly," she said, " He does all the rough work ! ! "

Has the Q. M. bought another pair of clippers as a precaution against 'air raids ?

If the Medical Sergeant attends to nearly 100 patients daily, how many will he have to attend to before he is an Officer ?

Did the M. G. C.'s make a mistake in challenging the Battalion at Rugby ? Who won the match ?

Did one of the Specialists say they ought to have challenged a Hut instead of a Battalion ?

What species of aeroplane does the Bosch usually select for making good his escape after he decamps from his " Blighty " Cage ?

Who is the Officer who poked his head in a certain tent and ordered the men to " Roll up the flies and put them outside in a neat row " ?

Was the Signal Section perplexed one morning on Physical " Jerks " Parade when ordered by the N.C.O. Instructor to " Carry the left foot off ten paces to the right " ?

Who told " Whacker " the Germans were short of rifle oil ?

Who was the N.C.O. in A Company who, on sighting a Staff Officer on the skyline during Field " ops.," commanded his men to " Bunch out a bit as he's looking at us " ?

Who is the Debonair N.C.O. in the Signals who recently qualified for an active part in Harry Tate's " Fishing " ?

Is it true that Hindenburg has indented for a special pattern of running shorts (field grey) for his troops in order that they may carry out the last phase of the war successfully ?

On a certain Field Day who was the Officer who sent out a heavily-armed private to surround and capture " un homme " stealthily crawling through the grass in the vicinity of the enemy lines ? And did the crawler reply meekly on being challenged that he represented an " intense barrage " ?

Who was the Officer who dismissed the rifle grenadiers five minutes late as " poor chaps, they were wet through." Is he in No. 5 platoon ?

Who was the Officer who when in Field Operations gave the order to the Pack Ponies to Right Dress. Was he in the T. M. B. ?

Which Company is known as " the Soldiers " ?

Which is the Rag-time Platoon, judged by its frequent appearance in " Things we want to Know." Is it No. 5 ?

Who invented the Yukon Pack, and WHERE IS HE ?

How many casualties occurred in the last Hair Raid ?

Who is the " new Officer in B Company " ? Was he posted to the Company at 1 a.m. on " Z " day ? And did the reply to the first question prove somewhat of a bombshell to the Scotch interrogator ?

Did a certain " red cap " in Cheltenham need a severe optical examination, or why is he not satisfied with one furtive glance at a leave man's ticket ?

What Officer on Bn. Headquarters saw milk being drunk at the Canteen ?

Who lost 10 francs at Company drill ?

Can blue-eyed Nell see the bright blue sky ?

On what occasion were we given rabbits for dinner ? What would have happened if the issue had been hares ?

CHATS FROM THE EDITOR'S
FLEA BAG.

General —— wishes to thank the purloiner of his stick from M——. When the stick was found and returned to its proper owner near H—— a ferrule had been added to it.

———

" Mr. Chancellor complained that the crow attacked the pacifists without any attempt at control being made by the police."—*Daily Express*, 31/7/17.
Personally we are glad the pacifists got the bird.

———

We commend the following action of the Worcestershire Committee :—

" The Worcestershire Prisoners of War Committee, who have to raise £12,000 a year to support the county's war prisoners in Germany and Turkey, yesterday decided to return to Mr. Barrow Cadbury his cheque for £5, with the intimation that ' they saw from the leaflet of the British Empire Union that he subscribed £750 and the firm of Cadbury Brothers £1,500 to the fund for alien enemies interned and uninterned in this country.' "—*Daily Mail*.

———

Mr. Phillips Gibbs, in one of his " illuminating " narratives, tells us that " Nieuport in days of peace was a place of SUMMER WAVES AND WIND." We can still recognise it by this description.

———

" And while our gifted rulers talk,
    Deploring wrack and wreck :
And in their Secret Sessions cuss
The Bosche, and fret, and fume, and fuss,
    WE get it in the neck !
Yet Britain umpty millions pays
For AIR SUPREMACY ! (*a phrase*)."

                                        E. L. R.

The italics are our own.

———

Who is this wretch who scoffs at men who risk their valuable lives to save his worthless head ?

———

"NOBODY'S DAUGHTER," specially written for the *Daily Sketch*, by JUNE BOLAND. This brilliant new serial is so unusual in theme . . .

" It tells of a typical modern girl and her soldier lover . . ."

Yes, by Jove, most unusual ; we should certainly never have thought of it.

———

" R. K., no fixed abode, was heard by P.C. Barnes using obscene language on August 13th, in Bell Lane. Defendant was very excited, and the constable had received two complaints that morning of defendant's conduct. A specimen of the language was handed to the magistrate.—Defendant said he had been called names."—*Gloucester Journal*.

We are anxious to know whether the language was produced in tabloid form, or the words in bundles of ten.

" The Quartermaster of the 3rd Batt. G.V.R. presents his compliments to readers of *The Citizen*, and will be glad of presents of green vegetables (peas, beans, cabbages, etc.), and of salads (lettuce,

tomatoes, etc.), to supplement the men's Army rations while in Camp from August 4th to August 11th."—*The Citizen*.

Other Quarter-Masters please note !

———

" Grateful acknowledgments, too, to the staff of the *Glo'ster Gazette* for the last issue of their fine trench magazine that started first of 'em all and has carried on bravely though so many others have gone west under the stress of war, and, alas ! war losses. The Glo'sters' humour is also of the kind you can enjoy on a hot day in a hammock in the garden, with a box of chocs. within easy reach and tea in the near offing."—*Bystander*, August 8th.

We also offer grateful acknowledgments to " Blanche," of the *Bystander*, and trust that the chocs. and hammocks will some day be our lot.

———

" ROMANCE."

" Here is a curious little true story. At a certain rest hut a rather elevated Tommy was giving a good deal of trouble. He was taken to bed, but refused to be pacified until his rifle was brought to him. At last it was decided to bring it, whereupon he kissed it, muttered ' my best friend,' and composed himself to sleep. So does the old idea of romance—the kissing of the sword before battle—perpetuate itself in these iron times ! "—*Daily Sketch*, August 14th, 1917.

It is not stated, however, whether the soldier had a nasty taste of rifle oil in his mouth as a result of his desperate affection for his firearm.

———

SLASHERS.

TWENTY-EIGHT (OR NORTH GLOUCESTER) REGIMENT OF FOOT.

" This name was given to the 28th Regiment during the American War, and took its origin from the following circumstances :—One Walker, a magistrate, in Canada, having refused to give comfortable billets to the women belonging to the 28th, and some of them having perished in consequence of the inclemency of the season, so great was the resentment of the corps, that some of the officers dressed themselves like savages, entered his house whilst he was sitting with his family, danced round the table, and suddenly pulling him back upon his chair cut off both his ears. They instantly disappeared ; nor was the deed discovered until their departure. From this circumstance, and in consequence of various intrepid actions which the 28th performed during the course of the war, the men obtained the name of the Slashers."
—*James' Military Dictionary. The Soldiers' Companion, vol.* I.

———

A FRAGMENT FROM THE CLASSICS.

While engaged in mopping-up operations in Fini Street, in the now famous village of Napiux, one of our bombers found the following written in an unknown tongue. A hasty chit was sent round enquiring for a nominal roll of all men with Greek (Classical) knowledge who had served in Salonika. The following translation was at length obtained :—

OLYMPIAN ORDERS OF THE DAY.

By Father of the Gods, Jupiter.

1. Orderly Officer of the Day.—Mercury.
   O.C. Fire Picquet.—Vulcan.

2. Parades. There will be a Route March at first dawn for all ranks in full kit, nectar bottles will be filled and a day's ambrosia will be carried. Six centaurs will march in rear to collect stragglers.

3. There will be a demonstration in the use of the Flammenwerfer at the mine crater in Vesuvius by Vulcan at noon, and at sunset a demonstration of the use of Liquid Fire at the P in Phlegethon.

   The Commanding Officer will lecture on the use of the Thunderbolt in the Attack at dusk. All Company Discobuli will attend and bring their own Disci.

4. Gods commanding Coys. will render a return to Orderly Room forthwith of all Titans in their Coys. desirous of employment as munition workers.

5. Leave to Atlantis via Scylla and Charybdis is at present cancelled.

6. The following Olympian Routine Order will be read out on three successive parades.

   Sirens are placed out of bounds to all troops except Ulysses.

Part II. Orders.

1. Promotions, Appointments and Postings.—

   The following are sanctioned for employment as stated opposite their names :—

   Ganymede to be Mess Sergt.

   Pheidippides to be Bn. runner.

   Daedalus and Icarus are seconded for duty with the Flying Corps.

   Hercules to be director of Physical Training.

   Cupid to be Sniping Officer.

   Cerberus is taken on the strength as Regimental Pet.

2. Punishments.—Bacchus awarded three days water fatigue for " Soberness on duty."

   L/Corpl. Venus deprived of lance stripe for " Improperly dressed on Parade and creating a disturbance in billets."

   Pte. Prometheus awarded perpetual F. P. No. 1 for " neglect of duty when in charge of Government property, i.e., loss of kit."

3. Leave is granted to Paris for the purpose of marriage.

4. Pay, Allotments, etc.—Aeneas makes an allotment of three obols per day. The child allowance to King Priam is reduced by 50 per cent. on all children in excess of 100.
   No further travelling allowance will be made to Ulysses.

5. Admissions to Hospital.

   Cyclops, now in C. 3, is discharged.
   Achilles, Trench foot.

6. Honours and Awards.—
   Jason, M.C. for conspicuous bravery. He lead a raid into the enemy's lines, destroyed liquid fire projectors, and secured valuable booty including a feather jerkin.

   Ulysses, M.C. When in command of a " Tank " near Troy, which had ceased to function, refused to leave his post, and by night was able to effect a lodgement within the enemy lines, thereby saving the situation.

   (Sd.) CALLIOPE,
   Muse.

HOME.

Haven of calm, abiding happiness,
Of sweet content and sheltered peace untold,
Safe from the world that restless passions hold,
Safe from the rush, the glitter and the stress.
Oft in the throng where passing pleasures press
In weary haste, and quest of fame or gold
Urges to toil your memories will fold
Like music round the heart to soothe and bless.
Home ! Magic name where dwells a deep delight
That thrills with yearning swift the wanderer's dream,
Where waits a welcome warm and warm embrace
The guardian of life's healing sunshine bright
Which sheds o'er darkest days a cheering beam,
Fount of true joy, love's hallowed resting place.
M. L. G.

" GLOUCESTERSHIRE FRIENDS."

By F. W. HARVEY.   (Sidgwick & Jackson.)

The appearance of this, the second volume of verse by 2nd Lieut. F. W. Harvey, is a matter of much pleasure to everyone who read and admired " A Gloucestershire Lad," and who were looking forward to its publication with great hope. They will not be disappointed, for this book is even better than the first. The poems are of the same stamp as before, all short and all sincere. The conventions of war poetry are, as before, flouted. The poems are the true expressions of real emotion that all soldiers who are carrying on in France feel and would express had not utterance been denied them.

Again and again one meets a line or two showing how distasteful the war is, but how worthy the cause. There is but little description of actual fighting, and it is invariably accompanied by a longer description of some Gloucestershire scene. Possibly the two best poems are the two Ballads upon War, which say all that can be said on either side ; though the tribute to R. E. Knight and the last poem of all are wonderfully fine.

The manner of the verse is as excellent as the matter. There is the same flowing grace and clearness and the same flawless form and polish. In sincerity of feeling and in purity of melody Mr. Harvey is worthy to stand with the Caroline Lyrists.

SPORTS.

Many games have been played since the last issue of the "Gloucester Gazette." Owing to pressure of space we have been most reluctantly compelled to cut out many accounts.

The chief matches were in Rugby and Association, an exciting game in which A Coy. of our battalion Regt. beat B. Coy. Glos. Regt. by 1 goal to nil ; and a Rugby match between the Bn. and the M. G. C. Coy. Ten minutes after half-time the Glo'sters were leading by 37 points to nil. Then rain came on and the match was abandoned.

A good game on August 3rd, between D. Coy. and the T. M. B. was a draw, one goal all.

On July 25th an inter platoon tug-of-war competition was held. Some fine pulls were seen. In the final No. 1 Platoon beat No. 6 Platoon.

RUGBY FOOTBALL.
GLO'STER v. R. S. L. I.

This match took place on the Shropshires' ground on July 27th, and a most keen game it was in spite of the heat.

The Glo'sters lost the toss and faced the sun. Settling down quickly they held their opponents well, and led by 8 points at the interval. Huxford and Barnes crossed the line, Cook converting the latter's try.

Hankey for the Shropshires made a great effort, a splendid tackle by Egerton saving the Glo'ster line.

In the second half, playing together better, they scored through Hargreaves. The kick failed, but stimulated by their success they rushed the Glo'ster defence, and Hargreaves scored again, the kick again failing.

A ding-dong game ensued, Woods and Howell for the Shrops, and Boughton and Butcher for the Glo'sters, doing great work. Following some pretty footwork by Hamblin, Glo'ster went down the field, Goatman unfortunately slipping when certain to score.

Good work by the forwards tested the defence, and Hamblin found touch with a fine kick.

From the resultant scrum Egerton made a fine opening for his backs, the ball passed from hand to hand, until with a fine burst Barnes got over with a try.

No further scoring took place, and Glo'ster came away winners by 1 goal 3 tries (11 points) to 2 tries (6 points.)

The Glo'ster team was as follows :—

Full Back :
C. Cook.

Threequarters :
Barnes, Hamblin (L.) Hamblin (W.), Goatman

Half Backs :
Egerton and Lt. Steel.

Forwards :
Boughton, Butcher, Capt. Sumner, Meadows, Hurford, Hobbs, Blount and Parham.

CRICKET.
B. COY. v. T. M. B.

The above match took place on the T. M. B.'s ground on Sunday afternoon, July 29th, and proved very enjoyable in spite of the bad weather conditions. It was a two-innings match, and the T. M. B.'s (who are old friends and opponents of B. Coy.) provided tea during the interval between the two innings.

The result was a win for the T. M. B.'s by ten wickets.

The T. M. B. winning the toss put B Coy. in to bat, and disposed of them for the total of 19, Lieut. Marden taking 6 wickets for 8 runs, and Pte. Hook 4 for 8. The T. M. B.'s replied with 39, Corpl. Gould taking 4 wickets for 12 runs, Pte. Parham 2 for 11 and Pte. Browinng 1 for 6.

B. Coy. on batting again required 20 runs to save the innings defeat, which they managed to do, and left the T. M. B.'s 3 runs to get, and they did this without loss.

Lieut. Marden and Pte. Hook again proved successful, each taking four wickets in the second innings.

B COMPANY.

	1st Innings.		2nd Innings.	
L-Corpl. Jobson, c and b Lieut. Marden	...	0	c Sgt. Martin, b Lt. Marden	2
Pte. Monk, b Lt. Marden ...	...	1	b Pte. Hook...	2
Pte. Tugwell, c and b Lt. Marden		9	b Pte. Hook	5
Pte. Parham, b Lt. Marden	...	0	b Pte. Hook	6
Sergt. Butt, b Pte. Hook ...	...	0	b Pte. Hook	0
Corpl. Gould, b Pte. Hook	...	2	run out ...	0
Pte. Hornby, c and b Lt. Marden		1	st, b Lt. Marden	0
Pte. Browning, b Lt. Marden	...	2	not out	0
Pte. Sturt, not out	...	0	run out ...	2
Pte. Clifford, b Pte. Hook ...	...	1	st, b Lt. Marden	0
L-Corpl. Wager, b Pte. Hook	...	0	c & b Lt. Marden	1
Extras ...	...	3	Extras ...	4
Total ...	...	19	Total	22

T. M. B.

	1st Innings.		2nd Innings.	
Lt. Marden, b Corpl. Gould	...	0		
Pte. James, b Pte. Browning	...	3		
Pte. Lawrence, st Sergt. Butt, b Pte. Parham	...	7		
Sergt. Rogers, b Corpl. Gould	...	4		
Pte. Townsend, run out ...	...	1		
Sergt. Martin, c Clifford, b Corpl. Gould	...	1		
Corpl. Thatcher, run out ...	...	0		
Corpl. Ferriman, b Corpl. Gould	...	1		
Pte. Howe, not out ...	...	6		
Pte. Biggs, run out ...	...	4	not out	2
Pte. Hook, b Pte. Parham	...	2	not out	3
Extras ...	...	10	Extras ...	3
Total ...	...	39	Total	8

BOWLING.

Corpl Gould, 4 wickets for 12 runs.
Pte. Browning, 1 wicket for 6 runs.
Pte. Parham, 2 wickets for 11 runs.

OUR BENEFACTORS.

Miss Tomlinson	...	...	...	...	Books.
Camps Library	...	...	...	...	,,
Moreton-in-the-Marsh Committee			...	Vests.
Harley Butt, Esq.	...	...	...	Tobacco.
J. Margetson, Esq.	...	...	...	Cigarettes.
Lieut.-Colonel Marling	...	...	...	Papers.
Colonel Griffith	...	...	...	...	,,
Pte. Wood	...	...	...	...	Typing.

PROMOTIONS AND APPOINTMENTS.

Coy.	Regtl. No.		Rank and Name.	

Promoted Sergeant :—

D	240737	L/Sgt.	Wise, R.	29/7/17
B	240867	,,	Kitching, F. F.	16/8/17
C	240161	a/L/Sgt.	Parr, F. G.	17/8/17
A	240239	Corpl.	Roche, W.	18/8/17
C	240931	,,	Palmer, F.	25/8/17

Appointed a/Sergeant with pay —

B	240549	L/Sgt.	Butcher, P. H.	16/8/17
A	242557	a/Corpl.	Lee, W.	16/8/17
A	240109	Corpl.	Bundy, W.	16/8/17
B	203706	,,	Hodges, J. T.	16/8/17
C	240202	,,	Oliver, F.	16/8/17
C	203244	,,	Pullin, E.	16/8/17
D	240693	,,	Burlton, W. G.	16/8/17

Appointed L/Sergt. with pay :—

D	240717	Corpl.	Paget, T. W.	29/7/17
B	260087	,,	Gooday, G. C.	16/8/17

Absorbed into establishment of L/Sergts. :—

C	240540	L/Sgt.	Fowler, R.	31/8/17

Promoted Corporal :—

B	203171	L/Corpl.	Dyer, H. G.	29/7/17
B	242489	,,	Wilkins, G.	16/8/17
D	241925	Pte. (L/C.)	Hobby, A. E.	17/8/17
A	240258	L/Cpl.	Brisland, R.	18/8/17
C	240859	,,	Derrick, H. S.	18/8/17
D	240670	,,	Blockford, H.	25/8/17

Appointed a/Corpl. with pay :—

A	240559	L/Cpl.	Michael, E. A.	16/8/17
A	21973	Pte. (L/C.)	Street, C.	16/8/17
A	242307	Pte.	Packer, F.	16/8/17
B	240481	L/Cpl.	King, S. E.	16/8/17
B	240192	,,	Iles, J.	16/8/17
B	240750	Pte. (L/C.)	Cook, C.	16/8/17
B	242504	,,	Simmons, T.	16/8/17
B	240236	L/Cpl.	Smart, G. C.	16/8/17
C	241103	,,	Holtham A. G.	16/8/17
D	240033	,,	Langley, R.	16/8/17
D	240824	Pte. (L/C.)	Pobjoy, G.	16/8/17

Confirmed in rank of L/Corporal :—

B	241725	Pte(a/Cpl.)	Appleton, S. H.	12/8/17

Appointed L/Corporal with pay :—

A	240372	Pte.	Doyle, P. B.	29/7/17
A	241623	Pte. (L/C.)	Lewis, J. A.	16/8/17
B	240703	Pte.	Parham, W. G.	16/8/17
C	203696	,,	Clee, W.	18/8/17
D	241301	,,	Gill, G.	18/8/17
D	240708	,,	Johnson, C. F.	25/8/17

Appointed a/L/Corporal with pay :—

A	240223	Pte.	Hamblin, A. E.	16/8/17
A	242188	Pte. (L/C.)	Wright, C. F.	16/8/17
A	240991	Pte.	Swanborough, A. F.	16/8/17
A	242503	,,	Pritchard, P.	16/8/17
A	240276	,,	Millichap, P. J.	16/8/17
A	214722	,,	Leach, W.	16/8/17
B	203691	,,	Booten, F. T.	16/8/17
B	240298	,,	Tilley, E.	16/8/17
B	242436	,,	Ball, H.	16/8/17

Coy.	Regtl. No.		Rank and Name.	
B	203202	Pte.	Dyer, A. V.	16/8/17
B	203017	,,	Winter, F. M.	16/8/17
B	241024	,,	Tackley, W. G.	16/8/17
B	242254	,,	Smith, S.	16/8/17
C	260139	,,	Earl, R. J.	16/8/17
C	241970	,,	Sellick, H.	16/8/17
C	241962	,,	Gillies, H. G.	16/8/17
C	203658	,,	Rumsey, F.	16/8/17
C	240172	,,	Hokpins, W.	16/8/17
C	240876	,,	Price, A. E.	16/8/17
C	241714	,,	Fraser, A E.	16/8/17
C	203680	,,	Lane, G. H.	16/8/17
C	241954	,,	Travett, C. H.	16/8/17
C	242533	,,	Wagner, A.	16/8/17

To be L/Corporals, without pay :—

B	241473	Pte.	Wakefield, A.	16/8/17
B	240360	,,	Comfort, W. J.	16/8/17
B	240228	,,	Durrant, A. E.	16/8/17
B	240413	,,	Hemmings, C.	16/8/17
B	241425	,,	Clifford, R. S. T.	16/8/17
B	242488	,,	Tugwell, F. A.	16/8/17
B	203726	,,	Pryce, W. J.	16/8/17
B	240102	,,	Apperley, C.	16/8/17

To be L/Corporals without pay :—

D	241460	Pte.	Mallard, L. F.	16/8/17
D	242214	,,	Maggs, C.	16/8/17
D	241685	,,	Norton, G.	16/8/17
D	240417	,,	Taylor, A.	16/8/17
D	240705	,,	Hiam, E. J.	16/8/17
D	240043	,,	Bruce, O.	16/8/17

The following N.C.O.'s and men are to be congratulated on having done exceptionally well at Courses of Instruction :—

240466	Sgt.	Reeves, F. W.	(Qualified as Asst. Instructor of Signalling).
240743	Pte.	Whittingham, J. E.	do.
241103	L/C.	Holtham, A. G.	
260244	Pte.	Davis, J. L.	
240902	Cpl.	Warwick, F.	(Since killed in action).
203012	L/C.	Russell, R. H.	

R.I.P.

" Rest for evermore rest,
Upon a mossy shore
Till time shall cease."

CHRISTINA ROSETTI.

" So he passed over, And all the trumpets
sounded for him on the other side."

" PILGRIM'S PROGRESS."

" Nor blame I Death, because he bare
The use of virtue out of earth :
I know transplanted human worth
Will bloom to profit, otherwhere."

" IN MEMORIAM," TENNYSON.

5th Gloucester Gazette.

A Chronicle, serious and humorous, of the Battalion while serving with the
BRITISH EXPEDITIONARY FORCE.

FLANDERS THOUGHTS FROM BLIGHTY.

Oh to be in Flanders
   Now that winter's there
And whoever lives in Flanders
   Sees, each morning, full of care
That still more trench and dug-outs, too,
Have with the rainfall fallen through.
But the German they are dry, I vow,
   In Flanders, now.

And after Frost, when the Thaw follows,
And in waist-deep mud each soldier wallows !
While each relief is a perfect terror
With the long long march on trackless ground
For the fear that the guides have made an error
Till at last the trench they've found,
And just when you think a strafe is ended
The Bosch encores a practise splendid.
The next night sees the ration
Lost and trench foot and fever in fashion.
Chances of rest and leave all seem napoo
To the fed-up-fellow who sticks it through.
   In Flanders now.

                                        G. H.

THE TRUTH ABOUT THE GERMAN NAVAL
MUTINY.

It was reported recently in the Reichstag that there had been a mutiny among certain units of the German Navy. The announcement was followed by the resignation, both in Flanders and Germany, ef VON POEL CAPPELLE, who apparently committed a grave indiscretion when he commenced to tell the truth.

However, the counter batteries at work in Germany immediately silenced him, and it has only been at the greatest expense, and by means of the most active Patrol work that we have been able to collect the full details of the Mutiny, which we produce in their entirety below.

The trouble started in May of this year, when the Kaiser reviewed his Navy in the vicinity of KIEL CANAL (Sheet 155a, X. 24, d. 19). One of the short-hand typists who took down an account of the proceedings was subsequently conscripted into the army, and has since been fortunate enough to fall into our hands. Round his neck, in an empty beer bottle, he carried, as a mascot, a complete copy of the above mentioned proceedings. This is what the Kaiser said :—

" My brave Blauemütze, I have the greatest pleasure in addressing you here to-day. All the British efforts have not yet succeeded in driving us from the Kiel Canal, which remains firmly in our hands, after the most terrific struggles. (Loud cheers.) It is with the most godworthy pride that I have inspected every unit of my fleet, and I am more than rejoiced to find them in such excellent condition. From the top of the mastheads to the bottom of the keels, I have no fault to find. Every plate is polished, every boiler unblemished. In recognition of my pleasure I propose to make a grant of a Mark a day Sausage Allowance to every officer of the fleet, well realising that no sacrifice is too great for the men who are saving the country to-day. I feel sure that my brave Blauemütze will appreciate this recognition of their officers, but with the true " Demokratische Instinkt " I also propose to award the Iron Cross to every N. C. O. and man of the fleet. The actual presentation of the cross will be deferred until after the war, but every man may, from this moment, consider himself entitled to wear the ribbon, and I understand that an indent for a million yards of it has already been forwarded by the F.Q.M.S. (Fleet Quarter Master Sergeant) to the C.D.R. (Chief Distributor of Ribbons.")

Here the Kaiser paused, and beamed around him wagging his moustache with pleasure. But a moment later the same moustache grew rigid, and the Kaiser with a sudden tug of rage, inadvertently pulled it off. At the same time the recoil, after the first shock of separation, caused the Kaiser to fall head first on to the deck. Unfortunately, in falling, the pike of his Pickelhaube got wedged between two planks, and the unfortunate man had to remain in an undignified, inverted position, with his feet vainly struggling in the air, until he was released by the cutting away of one of the planks.

On resuming the standing position, the origin of his sudden displeasure was made known, and after the additional indignity he had suffered his wrath knew no bounds.

It appears that whilst looking around him he had suddenly spotted a gigantic spider's web, stretched right across the harbour mouth. It was obviously of several months' growth, but some unfortunate blue-cap, who had been detailed on dock clearing fatigue, had entirely overlooked it.

The fatigue man was hauled out, but the only excuse the poor wretch could give us was that he thought it would stop the British Fleet breaking through. However, such a feeble pretext was of no avail, and he was forthwith sentenced to three years' imprisonment, or in the alternative, to be transferred to a Counter-Attack Division on the Flanders Front. The man at once chose the three years' imprisonment. In addition a party of one N.C.O. and six men were sent to capture the spider responsible for the mesh. At first this proved too much for the squad, but on receiving a couple of machine guns and a 15 cm. howitzer they were able to capture it complete, with all its equipment. The Kaiser therewith ordered the unfortunate animal to be placed in the next mustard gas shell fired, and it is said that the poor beast is still smarting under the sentence.

Nevertheless, the Kaiser, not satisfied with these examples immediately ordered the queue of men who were waiting to receive their ribbons outside the F.Q.M.S.'s Stores to disperse, and cancelled all awards of the Iron Cross for six months.

He then jumped ashore without waiting for the Imperial gangway to be swung aboard, and strode off in his motor-car, where he was last seen pacing up and down the interior.

These summary proceedings were by no means pleasing to the rank and file of the fleet, and that same evening one man, who commenced to sing " Die Wacht am Kiel " was promptly transferred to the U-boat Corps.

During the next few weeks it was evident that the Kaiser had not forgotten the incident. The officer commanding the unit to which the offender belonged shortly received orders to sail up the Thames in a Submarine, and torpedo all river parties between Boulter's Lock and Maidenhead. He was not to return until his mission had been accomplished. In the official casualty lists he has since been reported as missing.

On another occasion the Captains of certain cruisers were ordered to sail down the LEKKER-BOTTERBEEK, and to rendezvous at the point where this river meets the STEENBEEK. Here they were to combat the English Tanks which at that time had just been formed into a Corps, and were expected to arrive in Column of Fours.

All these things did not serve to improve the temper of the men, and when finally the Sausage Allowance granted to the Officers was cancelled, it was felt that the Prussian spirit could bend no further.

Accordingly, meetings were convened daily in the local estaminets, from twelve to two, and six to eight, and after the maximum quantity of beer had been drunk at each session, the following demands were formulated and presented to His Imperial Majesty—

(1) The Invasion of England be cancelled.

(2) The transfer of Ships Drivers to the Infantry to cease.

(3) All men of the Navy to be recalled from the Counter Attack Divisions.

(4) The Kiel Canal to remain closed for the Duration of the War.

After a consultation with Bethmann Hollweg and Heaven, the Kaiser refused these demands, and ordered everyone concerned to be put under arrest and shot. However, Hindenburg refusing to spare men from the Western Front to carry out these orders, the sailors simply pulled their guns to pieces and danced hornpipes on the Quays.

It was at this point that Hollweg resigned, and Michaelis was appointed Prime Minister. The situation was at this time very serious, and it was only with the aid of the most rigid censorship that the whole affair was kept quiet.

During the next few days things only grew worse. The Kaiser himself visited the Canal Bank again, but for his trouble only received a tweak of the nose from one specially daring unter-offizier. In addition the men even started parading the streets singing, " We won't sail submarines again till sausages are cheap."

Obviously it was high time to put an end to it all, for, apart from the effect on the Morale of the men, the Kaiser was beginning to feel the effect of having no fish for dinner. (It will be remembered also that at this period, the beginning of October, the U-boat sinkings were the lowest on record since intensive warfare began.)

Consequently, after a consultation with the leaders, the Kaiser at length had to give way on every point, and to accede to the demands made by the men.

Immediately this was done order was restored, and the Blauemütze goose-stepped down to the quayside and boarded their boats once more, singing patriotic tunes.

This, and this only, is the true story of the Naval Mutiny in Germany in 1917, and those who think otherwise had better tell a better story themselves.

FIBULOUS.

OUR LITERARY COLUMN.

" GLOUCESTERSHIRE FRIENDS."

By F. W. HARVEY.   (Sidgwick & Jackson.)

Referring to the paragraph in our November number under the above heading the following extract from the " Morning Post " of 3/10/17 will be read with interest.

The poems signed F. W. H. in the " Glo'ster Gazette," the first paper ever published from the trenches, and still the liveliest of all the little soldiers' journals, revealed the existence of a soldier-poet of power and a subtle distinction. His new volume of the poems from a German prison camp—he is now at Gütersloh—will be welcomed by the many admirers of his simple and sincere work. He has used the weary days of captivity to good purpose, for his new poems show an advance in technique, and also a fuller and deeper sense of the function of poetry as a " criticism of life." He now sees all things—even the homely beauties of his own dear Gloucestershire, a certain tree-encircled house at Minsterworth, and all the hills and meadows that are friendly and familiar—against the darkly-bright background of his tremendous experiences in the fighting zone, and every piece in his new volume shows that the English heart is unconquerable in adversity, that there is for us an essentially English truth in the lines of an elder soldier poet of ours :

> Stone walls do not a prison make,
> Nor iron bars a cage.

Many of the Poems in " Gloucestershire Friends " are inspired by sad, glad memories of sights and sounds and odours of the English countryside. The poet sees familiar flowers in a German garden :

> Snap-dragon, sunflower, sweet-pea,
> Flowers which fill the heart of me
> With so sweet and bitter fancy.

or hears familiar birds :

> Thrushes, finches, birds that beat
> Magical and thrilling sweet
> Little far-off fairy gongs ;

and his heart is filled with sorrow and joy, the joy at last prevailing. He longs for freedom to roam at his leisure by one of those little Gloucestershire by-ways, the like of which are not to be found in any of the penurious and wholly commercialised German lands :

> I will not take the great road that goes so proud and high,
> Like the march of Roman legions that made it long ago ;
> But I will choose another way, a little road I know.
> There no poor tramp goes limping, nor rich poor men drive
> by,

Nor ever crowding cattle, or sheep in dusty throng
Before their beating drovers drift cruelly along :
But only birds and free things, and ever in my ear
Sound of the leaves and little tongues of water talking near.

More intimate a record of his own land and its peoples is a series of five dialect pieces, of which the lament of Seth over the death of the oldest inhabitant shall be quoted.

We heard as we were passing by the forge :
"'Er's dead," said he.
"'Tis Providence's doing," so said George.
"He's allus doing summat," so I said,
"You see this pig ; we kept un aal the year
Fatting un up and priding in un, see,
And spent a yup o' money—food so dear !
I wish 'twer 'e ;
I'd liefer our fat pig had died than she."

In two well-wrought Ballades (he handles the old French verse-forms with delightful dexterity) he contrasts the squalor and the splendour of warfare, but the most touching of the poems that present the passions of war-time in retrospect are those that commemorate dead comrades :

You never crept into the night
That lurks for all mankind !
Joyous you lived and loved, and leapt
Into that gaping dark, where slept
Our Fathers all, to find
Old honour—jest of fools, yet still the soul of all
delight.

War is still for him, as in one of the first of his "Glo'ster Gazette" lyrics, "Honour's high festival, to which all Earth's chivalry is now bidden." Quotation is the sincerest form of criticism, and one is much tempted to go on quoting from this beautiful and various little book. But let a final quotation be given—the "Ballad of Army Pay," in which he deals with a mean and ridiculous mania for unworthy economies on the part of our civilian war-lords with a satirical vigour not unworthy of Mr. Kipling :

In general, if you want a man to do a dangerous job ;
Say, swim the Channel, climb St. Paul's, or break into and rob
The Bank of England, why, you find his wages must be
higher
Than if you merely wanted him to light the kitchen fire.
But in the British Army, it's just the other way,
And the maximum of danger means the minimum of pay.

You put some men inside a trench, and call them infantries,
And make them face ten kinds of hell, and face it cheerfully ;
And live in holes like rats, with other rats, and lice, and
toads,
And in their leisure time, assist the R.E.'s with their loads.
Then, when they've done it all, you give 'em each a bob a
day !
For the maximum of danger means the minimum of pay.

We won't run down the A.S.C., nor yet the R.T.O.
They ration and direct us on the way we've got to go.
They're very useful people, and it's pretty plain to see
We couldn't do without 'em, nor yet the A.P.C.
But comparing risks and wages—I think they all will say
That the maximum of danger means the minimum of pay.

There are men who make munitions—and seventy bob a
week ;
They never see a lousy trench nor hear a big shell shriek ;
And others *sing* about the war at high-class music-halls
Getting heaps and heaps of money and encores from the
stalls.
They "keep the home fires burning" and bright by night
and day,
While the maximum of danger means the minimum of pay.

I wonder if it's harder to make big shells at a bench,
Than to face the screaming beggars when they're crumping
up a trench ;
I wonder if it's harder to sing in mellow tones
Of danger, than to face it—say, in a wood like Trone's ;
Is discipline skilled labour, or something children play ?
Should the maximum of danger mean the minimum of pay ?

Here is a little book of the munitions of memory and hope, which will be a proof to after ages that even a German prison camp could not tarnish the bright valiancy of English soldiers.

WHO ?

Who is the C. Q. M. S. who played with a bottle of Champagne until the cork came out ? Did he then remark : "I couldn't help it, Sir, I'll put it back again !" Was he successful ?

Who is the servant in H. Q. Mess who tried to pick up the mile-stone to build a trench fire ?

Who is the A/C. S. M. who told his men that puttees would be worn 4 inches over the trousers ?

Why did a certain Press Correspondent in Flanders only get as far as Div. H. Q. ?

Who sent two orderlies into the ruined village to find a German Helmet for his fiancêe ? What did he say when they returned with a French fire helmet

Who is the signaller who asserts that when a cat is forcibly submerged in water a host of bubbles come to the surface followed by a groan ?

Who gave a lecture on "Native Patrols," and said : "They creep up to within two or three yards of you without making a sound. It's a treat to hear them ?"

Who is the man who asked if the Very Lights were to see if the Line was straight ? Is he in 13 Platoon ?

What kind of dog have they got in 14 Platoon ?

Who is the man that said, "I want to write a letter ; that's all I have to read" ? Is he in 14 Platoon ?

Who said "that Caterpillar is a Machine Gun " ? Is he in 14 also ?

Who is the cook that puts up D. Coy's. Rations ? Did he put in a tin of pepper instead of jam ?

Who are the men that "do overtime in the Front Line " ? Are there many in D. Coy. ?

Who was the Private in No. 5 that said he was "that tired coming off the working party that he held on to the rail with one hand and dropped off to sleep with the other ?

Who was the Corporal in B. Coy. who said that "listening posts were used for the purpose of seeing what one could hear ? " Is he in No. 5.

Who was the notorious "gentleman" who was being shown round the Front, and when proceeding down a sunken road three miles from the line went flat when someone appeared on the top, thinking it was a German sniper ? Does not the story deserve more publicity than it has received ?

THINGS WE WANT TO KNOW.

When Mr. Maconachie will wind up his business and go to sleep ?

What percentage of cement is used in the manufacture of *some* kinds of biscuits ?

And whether tile merchants are on the look out for "buckshee" samples with a view to setting up opposition ?

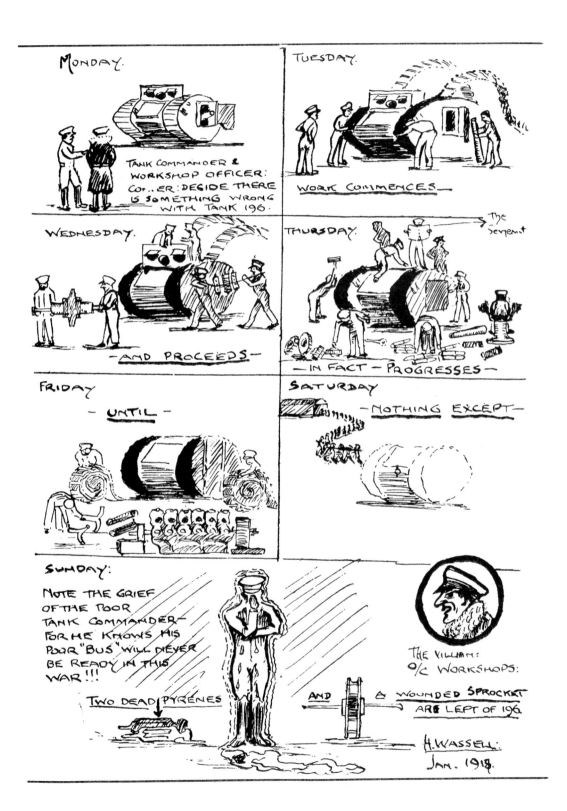

DE PROFUNDIS.

" Here, you ! Pick up that can of water and take is to 13 Platoon. You'll find it on the extreme right. Look sharp about it, too ! "

Jimmy made a grab at the converted petrol tin, and hurriedly started off. So hurriedly, in fact, that he had proceeded half a mile in pitch darkness toward the line before he wondered what 13 Platoon was the extreme right of. Was it Belgium ? Perhaps Jimmy's geography was not a strong point, but he appreciated the difficulties in that event. Again, " the line " consisted of a system of shell-holes, and as every other square foot of ground for miles was part of a shell-hole—the identification of any particular one would have puzzled an Australian aborigine. Progress was difficult also, and Jimmy, as he struggled laboriously up the side of a " neuf point der " (?) repository, wished that 13 Platoon had the stomach (as well as the " hump ") of a camel, and only needed water once a month.

Sepulchral voices at his very feet brought Jimmy to a sudden halt. Peering down, he had a bird's-eye view of shrapnel-hats of unmistakable shape.

" Hello ! You 13 ?" Jimmy queried, and the tin hats suddenly fore-shortened, giving place to white dabs of upturned faces.

" Thirteen ? No, we're 7."

" Nay, master : we are seven," added a wag in the shell-hole.

" Are you ? " answered Jimmy, recognising the quotation. " Well, I'm as dubious as the poet was. I can only see four of you anyhow. Better put more water with it next time, old sport, or you'll be seeing a blooming battalion in every section. Where's 13 ? Do you know ? "

" Up there. Along the line somewhere," was the answer.

" Bit vague, ain't it ? Jerry's along the line somewhere, and I don't want to walk into him."

" Can't help it. I'm not a Cook's guide to Belgi-um. Keep on walking, and you'll come to it all right I expect. S'long."

Jimmy started off again, peering thro' the darkness as well as he was able, looking for 13. Then he fell over a piece of barbed wire.

" Damn ! " he ejaculated as he measured full length.

" Halt ! Who's that," came the subdued challenge from the bowels of the earth.

" Who the devil do you think it is," answered Jimmy peevishly, as he scrambled to his feet. " Are you 13 ? "

" Thirteen ? No ! Three shell-holes up, and don't make such a bally row. Don't want Fritz's fire over here. Hop it ! "

Jimmy went on again firmly covinced that the superstitions concerning the number 13 had adequate reasons for their existence.

He paused in front of a block-house, determined to question the sentry on duty when he could descry in the darkness. Then the moon came out from behind a cloud and showed " the sentry " for what he was.

" Ah ! " said Jimmy, turning away with a shudder. " No good asking you, mein herr Fritz. You've finished your soldiering on this earth anyhow. Where the great howitzer can 13 be ? "

He struggled over a heap of rubble, the sharp handle of the petrol can cutting his fingers as he stumbled along.

" I shall be over with Jerry in a minute strikes me. Wonder what the German for " surrender " is. Shall have to——. Damn it ! What's—— who are you ?·"

The business end of a bayonet gleamed not twelve inches from his feet. Tin hats also evolved from the depths of a yawning hole.

" Who are you ? " repeated Jimmy.

" Thirteen Platoon. What are you doing there ? "

" Thank the Lord for that ! Here's your bally water. Thank your lucky stars it aint milk, or you'd have had a pound of butter to drink. I've walked nearly all over Belgium looking for you. Here, take it," and Jimmy let the can slide down the side of the shell-hole and grinned cordially to himself as a smothered growl indicated that the heavy can had come to rest on somebody's pet corn. Then he turned and made his way back.

H. J. B.

CHATS FROM THE EDITOR'S FLEA BAG.

Xmas. 19— ?

A merry Xmas, and a Happy New Year on a Field Post Card to all our Readers.

We herewith defeat all efforts ever yet made by our contemporaries by producing our Xmas Number ten months before the happy event. Note the above 19— ? The intelligent printer feeling sceptical when we wrote him that we wanted our Xmas, 1918, number produced has taken the matter into his own hands. This drastic early production is really the outcome of a row in our Editorial Offices with the Office Boy, who was unable to produce our August number until October. We trust, however, that the hardest blocks of frigidity which may have been formed towards us in any of our subscribers' noble hearts will be liquefied when we say that the delay was entirely due to the war.

THEY DID NOT BUDGE.

While all our own line battalions, freely mentioned in last night's communique, fought with traditional valour, the stand made by the **Gloucesters** was Homeric. Under the great superiority in weight of a German counter-attack the troops flanking the famous west-country regiment were forced back, the line forming a sharp bend. But the Gloucesters did not budge ; they stood as they had done in the days of Abercrombie, when they gained the unique distinction of wearing their headgear plaque both in front and behind. Before their unyielding resistance the Hun effort came to a standstill, and the pressed-back line was able to some measure to recover itself.—*Daily Mail*, 24/10/17.

Comment is needless !

Before we go further we should like to wish our permanent Editor, Capt. G. Hawkins, who of a sudden exchanged the gold nib for the gold stripe, a most speedy recovery, and may we soon see him again in Blighty. Had he but known how by his departure he set the Editorial Staff wringing its hands and gas gongs with alarm, we feel sure he would not thus have left us. Our best wishes also to others who have temporarily left our ranks for similar causes. May we see them all again soon somewhere in ——.

More thanks ! This time to our noble House of Commons for the vo'e of thanks which they have passed to the soldiers. May we, however, point out that Votes of Thanks won't end the war, and we should appreciate them as much unexpressed even if only on grounds of economy—but after all members must presumably do something to earn their £400 a year. £400 is twenty times the pay of a private soldier per annum. That vote of thanks was certainly worth twenty times as much to the country as 640 men who are in trenches holding the line for twenty-four hours, wasn't it ?

Oh, those air raids on England! May we be allowed to give our point of view? By bombing one German MUNITION FACTORY you may be SAVING hundreds of lives. By bombing German TOWNS you may be CAUSING the loss of hundreds of lives. In the former cases you may be conceivably shortening the war. If you bomb COLOGNE or BERLIN until you're blue in the face it won't affect the duration of the war by one day. We have seen how little effect is caused by the bombing of London. Except for the wailing of a few senile idiots everyone realises that a few bombs on London are contemptible compared with a barrage in Flanders. The German people may produce some senile idiots, too, if we start bombing them, but as a mass they are not going to " Kamerad" after their men have been through the Hell that the Germans surely have had this year at Vimy, Messines and Flanders. And, please, remember, good people of England, that what we want is to END this war, and by going for a petty system of revenge (which is all that reprisals on German civil towns amount to), you are merely intensifying warfare, and not bringing Victory a single day nearer. The war to-day is being fought in France, not in England! Concentrate on France, and to Hell with Senile Idiots!

We notice with pleasure that the Lord Mayor had a dinner last year so that he might just show his contempt for all the Economy Campaigners. At the same time we should have been still more delighted had he honoured us with his presence in Flanders. We could have offered him a splendid brand of Bully Beef (1906, Extra Sec) and biscuits which are the pride of the army. We had several tins of the former and several pounds of the latter to spare, so it is all the more pity that he did not turn up. However, as he has started off in the best manner possible for prolonging the war, perhaps next year we may have the pleasure of his company, for we always like to honour those for whom we are fighting.

THE RELIEF.

"We're up the line to-night. Parade at ten."
The Sergeant curses, and at night our men,
With struggling, tumble into twisted kits
The while we curse abominable Fritz.
We start, and o'er our ankles plonks the filth
As down the shell-holed road we step with stealth.
Sudden, a shrieking shell with brazen blare
Tears forward through the mild-protesting air
And lands—some fifty yards in rear—a dud.
Now, bodies bent, we slower through the mud
Pursue our way, whilst o'er us longing falls
To reach the Trench. Once we're within its walls
A kind of safety-shroud's around us spread.
Alas! We reach the trench and find instead,
That on a timid footstep being placed
Upon its floor, it is withdrawn in haste,
For otherwise, the floor sinks softly down
Circling the leg with mud-slime soft and brown.
Yet down this filthy lane we have to plod
Dragging each leg as though an iron rod
Until a halt—and then we meekly grunt,
Awaiting for a move-on up in front.
Pin-quiet we stand, peeling off mud in strips
Till frantic torrents from blaspheming lips
Are poured forth from the rear. " God! let's get past! "
The reason for delay comes down at last.
"There's someone up in front got stuck," they shout,
So there we wait the while they dig him out.
And then again a move—again a pause.
This time, another's in those clammy jaws.
And so could multiply itself this stunt
For many hours; but someone up in front
Takes both the matter and the mud in hand
And with an effort, slippy, sloshious, grand,
Climbs out the trench, then leads the way anew
Along the top edge of that muddy stew

Till striking 'gainst the front trench (not so quick
As in this narrative our way we pick),
We sink in this time deeper than before,
For now our thighs are in this mud-soaked floor.
We reach our post at last. Exhausted now
From all our efforts in this nightmare slough
But thankful to be there, where'er we are
We ease our worn-out souls and curse the war.
And gazing round, think with an awesome dread,
" Fools do step in where angels fear to tread ! "

OF PETS—AND A CAT.

If we were asked what were our feelings about the war, most of us would probably say we were bored to tears. We are like the " old man of Dundee, who was horribly bored by a bee," and who remarked that it was a " regular beast of a bee." We have our moments of thrill and excitement, of course, when we hear the enemy planes overhead at night, or when we are told there is a rum issue. But the ordinary routine, whether in the front line, or in support, or even in rest-billets, becomes very monotonous in time. And so the British soldier, whether officer or man, being cut off from the variety given to life by the opposite sex, finds his consolation in pets of all kinds. You cannot go into any Company lines or cantonments without stumbling over a kitten or seeing a dog of some kind, be it " puppy, mongrel, whelp or hound, or cur of low degree." You may see the aristocratic grey-hound, or its plebian counterpart the whippet, the rat-catching terrier, and every species of animal whose only claim to recognition is that it is a dog. Some are useful for the larder, others provide sport, but all serve to afford Tommy (and his officers) an outlet for his softer feelings. Birds, of which one sees so many kept as pets at home, are not common in that capacity here. Probably the impossibility of adding a cage to his equipment prevents the soldier from indulging his whims in this direction. The writer has seen a magpie in captivity in one camp, which swore volubly at every one who passed. And a friend of his told him that on taking over the duties of a Staff Officer who was going on leave, he found that one of these duties, and that not the least important, was to look after a young owl.

One of the most curious whims in the pet-line was a litter of fox-cubs. These had been found by an officer by the side of a dead vixen, and he had carried them off. There were five of them, but one soon succumbed. They were given a good run of rabbit-wire, and frequently let out for exercise in the open, when they sometimes nearly proved one too many for their keeper. They were fed on meat and fresh milk. The officers' mess had to be content with the Swiss variety, but fresh milk was always forthcoming for the cubs, fresh from " the " cow every morning. They were pretty little chaps, but one could not help asking oneself what would be the upshot. They solved the question by digging themselves out—all but one, who still remains with his master, and so escaped a worse fate.

Kittens, of course, make charming pets, but when they grow into cats they are not satisfactory. The cat has a great sense of her own importance, and sets a vast store by her own comfort. Whereas a dog will follow his master anywhere, and efface himself when not wanted, turning up smiling later on, a cat will ruthlessly desert a home where she can't have the best place and the best food. And yet at moments of stress she is quite willing to attach herself to a human protector.

Some time ago when Divisional H. Q. was being shelled by one of the Hun's long-range guns, a cat, which had been living under a Nissen hut with her two newly-born kittens, decided that the hut did not provide sufficient security for her family. So she formed herself into a reconnoitring patrol, and went out to find a " better 'ole." Passing the A. and Q. Clerks' office, she espied a tempting array of wooden boxes. She stepped in and examined them, and finding an empty one, she at once streaked off and fetched first one kitten and then the other, and settled down happily in her new abode and there remained. Of course, the kittens are called A. and Q., and when one witnessed the domestic squabbles that sometimes took place, one was tempted to say " How human ! " They became great pets, and when one of the staff returned from leave and found that one had been presented to another office he wrote and demanded its restitution. He was puzzled to receive in reply the following letter : " Ref. your letter of x/7/17, you are referred to G. R. O., 7349." Turning this up he found it headed, " Officers' Kits, instructions for recovery of." And Homeric laughter shook the halls of Olympus.

One wonders what will be the fate of the many pets when the time comes for their masters to return to Blighty. Will they be smuggled home in the pack, or will they remain in the land of their birth to recount to their off-spring tales of the strange—but kind—mud-clad, muddy-coloured masters who so unaccountably left them and never came back ?

A CHRISTMAS WISH.

I cannot give you happiness
For wishes long have ceased to bring
The fortune which to page and king
They brought in those good centuries,
When with a quaint and starry wand
Witches turned poor men's thoughts to gold
And Cinderella's carriage rolled
Through moonlight into Fairyland.

I may but wish you happiness,
Not Pleasure's dusty fruit to find,
But wines of Mirth and Friendship kind
And love, to make with you a home.
But may our Lord, whose Son has come,
Now heed the wish and make it true
Even as elves were wont to do,
When wishing could bring happiness.

F. W. HARVEY.

Reprinted from " Gloucestershire Friends," which is reviewed in this *Gazette*.

MESS-TABLE GOSSIP.

BY THE JUNIOR SUB.

IN CORNWALL COVES.

The Hon. Margerine Melce has chosen Cave Canem, the pretty little village amidst the cave and coves of Cornwall, as the scene for her marriage with Captain Richard Butters, who is now in khaki. The marriage is, I hear, to be quite quiet, and that is why they are running away from Town for it.

KADAVER.

An amusing story reaches me from the Canary Islands. A certain cannibal King was sitting down to his lunch when a dish of kidney beans and pork was brought to him. Not realising that the kidneys belonged to a bullock he ordered the dish to be removed, saying, " Bah ! You know I never eat anything from those Kadaver Factories ! "

THE ORIGIN OF THE TANKS.

I was told yesterday that it was Mr. Churchill who was the original inventor of the Tanks. One day, during a holiday in France, he had occasion to examine his shirt, so my informer tells me. He was not a little surprised to find a louse sojourning on one of the seams. He removed it with all haste and whilst conveying it to the incinerator he dropped the chatling on the floor. It fell on its back.

THE SEQUEL.

On looking down he was astonished to find that the animal didn't seem to mind the change a bit, and was going along quite merrily in that position. He then turned it on its side with the same result. In fact, he found that nothing he could do seemed to dishearten it. It was this incident that gave him his first idea of what is now one of our greatest war inventions.

IN TOWN.

I saw Major Warlong, of the General Staff, the other evening on his arrival in town from France. He is staying at present in Calais Castle, and looks in perfect health, though I cannot imagine he is very pleased to leave such a beautiful place for a dull house in London—and English War Bread !

CURIOS.

The other night at the Curios I saw quite a big bevy of pretty girls. They had a new programme, and it was still as sparkling as ever. I can prophesy a long run for the new show.

A WAR WORKER.

Pte. Atkins is devoting nearly all his time to his labours on behalf of a lasting Peace just now. Save for a short walk in the Boyaus de France he often spends entire days in the Front Line.

NEW STYLE.

I heard this a few days ago : " The Man who Stayed at Home. Senior Wangler, 1914-1918." And true, isn't it ?

AND THIS.

Epitaph to a Profiteer : " He made his bit."

WHO ?

Have you read the opening chapters of " Who ? " our new serial ? If not, hasten to, for there is a pleasure in store for you. If you have I am sure you will agree with me that it is grand. In fact it must be grand for we are paying the authors £2,000 an instalment for it. So hurry up and read it !

M. C.

Lady Viole Manners is arranging a delightful novelty at her Bazaar next week in aid of the Tommies who lose their Tickets to France. She is holding a hat-trimming competition for men, which alone is sure to be an amusing sight, but in addition she is offering for the best trimmed hat a Millinery Cross (M. C. See ?).

"Cheero! Cook. 'Ere's another bit of meat for the stew."

CONCERTS.

We have been fortunate lately in having been in the vicinity of a number of Concert Parties, and we have lost no opportunity in visiting them.

We must give thanks to the " See Too's " for providing us with one of the best evening's amusement we can remember, " depuis la paix." " Ginger " and " Sebastian " are two comedians who may well rank with George Robey and Alfred Lister, and the remainder of the Company provided a programme which never gave us a dull moment.

" The Tonics," whom we also had the pleasure of visiting, gave us, too, a thoroughly enjoyable evening, and we all appreciated the singing talent which this troupe has succeeded in bringing together.

Last but not least " The Curios " remain still as enjoyable as ever, and we are never too tired to go and see them " just once more."

———

A successful concert was held by the Battalion on the 17th October, and once more we heard the talent which we have come to expect on these occasions.

It is hard to signalise any individual on these occasions when all are worthy of mention, but in the comic line we think our old favourite " From Pimpleton to Poppleton " still retains first place. Appended is the full programme. Our best thanks are due to Rev. C. A. Clark for organising and arranging the concert.

PROGRAMME.
Part I.

Song	...	...	...	Pte. Young, F.V.
Comic Song	...	...	...	L/C. Shellard.
Song	...	...	...	Rev. C. A. Clark.
Song	...	...	...	Pte. O'Brien.
Song	...	...	...	Pte. Walker, E.V.
Conjuring	...	...	...	Pte. Pittaway.
Song	...	...	...	L/C. Pritchard.

Part II.

Song	...	...	...	Pte. Farmer.
Song	...	...	...	Pte. Young.
Song	...	...	...	Pte. Walker.
Song	...	...	...	Sergt. Proctor.
Comic Song	...	...	...	L/C. Shellard.
Song	...	...	...	Pte. O'Brien.
Humorous Sketch	...	...	Sgt. Proctor,
				L/C. Pritchard and Co.

" God Save the King."

———

SPORTS.

HORSE SHOW.

A Brigade Horse Show was held at ——, on 23rd September, 1917. It was a great success, and thoroughly enjoyed by a large crowd, of whom no small proportion were French civilians who made the Show the occasion of a Féte.

In the results our Battalion came out first with the Bucks a good second.

The following events were won by our Battalion :

Best Pair of Mules.
    1st Prize.   2nd Prize.

Divisional Jumping Competition.
    1st, Capt. G. Lister.

Brigade Jumping Competition.
    1st Prize, Capt. G. Lister.
    3rd Prize, 2nd.-Lieut. C. E. W. Rawlings.
Water Cart Turn Out.
    2nd Prize.
Best Pair of Light Draft Horses.
    2nd Prize.
Wrestling on Horseback.
    1st Prize.
Tug of War.
    1st Prize.

———

MUSKETRY COMPETITION.

In a Field Firing Competition, held at ——, in which every Company of every Battalion in the Division took part, D. Company, of our Battalion, took first place. We convey to them our heartiest congratulations on this success.

———

QUESTIONS FOR YOUNG SOLDIERS.

In future it is proposed to hold a short examination before allowing men to expose themselves to shell fire. For the benefit of those who have yet to prepare themselves for this ordeal we append the waste paper set at the first examination. As a general guide the model answer to the first problem is also given.

Problem 1. You have been detailed to proceed on leave at 7 a.m. on April 1st, having been 17 months and 20 days in this country. At 11.59 p.m. on March 31st leave is cancelled for all men who have been under 18 months in France. Detail your instructions to the orderly who brings you the message.

Answer. I should tell him to unpack again as I have decided that owing to air raids on London and the absence of trenches in that city I have decided not to take a holiday this year.

Problem 2. You are in a trench and hear approaching you—
    (1) A Whiz-Bang.
    (2) A Blue pigeon.
    (3) A 5.9.
    (4) a. A machine gun bullet.
        b. A rifle bullet.
    (5) A dud.

What action would you take in each of the above cases.

Problem 3. You have been court-martialled for using a steel helmet for cooking purposes, and the decision of the Court has been promulgated sentencing you to imprisonment for three years or the duration of the war. Taking into account the probability of the entrance of Timbuctoo and Tennessee into the war which sentence would you choose ?

Problem 4. You are to attack at dawn on the morning of December 25th. At 7 p.m. on the evening of December 24th you are offered 2 hot meals consisting either of (a) duck and green peas, or (b) bully beef. The doctor has warned you that duck and green peas are bad for you, and you know yourself that an attack of indigestion is bound to ensue. Which dish would you choose ? Give reasons for your answer.

PROBLEM 5. The Divisional Band plays on a Saturday afternoon. The following is the programme of music played :—

1. " If you're waking, call me early."
2. " Oh, for a ride in a Puff-Puff ! "
3. " Soldier's Chorus " (Faust).
4. " Somewhere a 5.9's calling."
5. " 'Midst Shot and Shell."
6. " A Perfect Day."
7. " Where are the lads of the Village to-night ? "
8. " Take me back to Blighty."
9. " Nights of Gladness."
10. " I live in Trafalgar Square."

What comments have you to make ?

(Had we not a certain amount of regard for our readers' feelings we could go on quoting indefinitely, but we cannot allow it to be said of us that we are lacking entirely in " noblesse oblige."—ED.)

R. I. P.

" Who, doomed to go in company with Pain,
And Fear, and Bloodshed, miserable train,
Turned his necessity to glorious gain."

WORDSWORTH.

A WAR WORKER.

Kennedy Davin was on leave from France. There were many things to be done and little time, but he had promised to go and deliver some messages to an unknown friend of a brother officer. One afternoon he called. The call was rather a surprise to the good lady, who was of that age which friends call mature and enemies ripe, and who waited till the afternoon should be a bit darker and till she should have time to be more becomingly clothed. Accordingly Davin was shown into a room, and left to cool his heels for half an hour. His glance wandered idly round till his attention was arrested by a large bookcase. He glanced at the books, and found that all were concerning war. He pulled out several books and endeavoured to form an estimate of the lady's character by the nature of her reading. The books were arranged haphazard, and must have been got because she knew the author or had had them recommended, or had ordered a job lot. Anyhow they showed either an astonishing catholicity of taste or an undiscerning omnivourousness.

They were :—

The Grear War	By Bernhardi.
Men, Women and Guns	Sapper.
Poems	By Rupert Brook.
Richard Chatterton, V.C.	By Ruby Ayres. Which opened of itself at the last chapter.
First Hundred Thousand.	Ian Hay (well thumbed).
The Great Push	McGill (several pages uncut).
The Tunis History of the War	With a pin between the leaves at the chapter on the Belgian atrocities.
A Gloucestershire Lad At the War	Harvey.
No Man's Land	Lord Northcliff.
Kitchener Chaps ... ·	Sapper.
	Neil Lyons.

Several Government blue books and white papers, rather dusty.

Davin was looking at the books, and was wondering why Miss Blandish should have at least three hundred books, but had read less than a dozen, when she came in. Davin jumped to his feet, and immediately stammered some apologies for calling, and delivered his messages. Miss Blandish was very charming, and very charmingly and tastefully led the conversation to the war.

" Do tell me about the war," she said. " I have read all those books " (with a wave of her hand to the bookcase) " and my soldier friends tell me I know more about the war than any woman they know ; but I should love to hear what you think."

And then began not so much a conversation as a parade of knowledge. It was like a catechism, save that Miss Blandish, not content with asking the questions, would not stay for an answer, but replied to them herself.

" Have you heard a shell ? " she asked.

" Have you seen the Kaiser yet ? "

" Aren't you glad when Sir Douglas Haig gives the word to advance ? "

" Aren't you thrilled with the music of the guns ?"

" When will it all be over ? "

" Do you have much fun in the trenches ? "

" I suppose you can get leave to visit the large towns on Saturdays ? "

Davin also learned that the government of this country should be handed over to the soldiers ; that Mr. Asquith was a traitor ; that our dug-outs were very comfy ; that the Germans had no shells ; that the air service was doing badly in letting us be raided ; that her cousin in the motor transport was in the thick of it, and won the Military Cross on a raid ; that he himself was itching to get back, and that Sinn Feiners, Conscientious Objectors, Bolos, and Socialists should be burnt ; that she was quite wearing herself out helping the soldiers on flag days.

Davin sat patiently and quietly while the monologue was delivered. Taking advantage of a temporary lull he rose and took his leave, regretting a wasted afternoon, but glad to meet the *couleur du rose* attitude of mind common in phlyarocratic England.

ACCORDING TO SHAKESPEARE.

JOINING UP.
    Honours thought reigns solely in the Breast.—
Henry V.

RECRUIT DRILL.
    I was never so bethumped with words since first I called my brother's father dad.—*King John.*

KIT INSPECTION.
    What a disgrace it is to me to take note how many pair of silk stockings thou hast.—*Henry IV.*

FIELD DAY.
    More rushes, more rushes.—*Henry IV.*

SICK PARADE.
    I know a trick worth two of that.—*Henry IV.*

No. 9.
    I have a cure will mend all ills.—*Lear.*

THE CONSCIENTIOUS OBJECTOR.
    But for those vile guns he would himself have been a soldier.- -*Henry IV.*

GENERAL INSPECTION.
    And ere they be dismissed let them march by.—
Henry IV.

GG

IN FRANCE.

England we love, and for that England's sake with burden of our armour here we sweat.—*King John.*

FURLOUGH.

I pray thee give me leave.—*Macbeth.*

RETURNING TO FRANCE.

There are other men fitter to go out than I.—*Henry IV.*

—PR—S.

I'd sooner live with cheese and garlic in a wind-mill.—*Henry VI.*

GAS.

If you have tears prepare to shed them now.—*Julius Cæsar.*

A DUD.

Full of sound and fury, signifying nothing.—*Macbeth.*

SENTRY.

Take your places and be vigilant.—*Henry VI.*

AFTER GUEST NIGHT.

He arose with lank and haggard cheek.—*Lucrece.*

A BLIGHTY.

And to England then, where ne'er from France arrived more happy men.—*Henry V.*

FOOTBALL.

A soccer match was played between the Glo'sters and the Second Army Troop Coy. of the Canadians, which ended in a win for the former by one goal to nil. Our opponents were a fine team, and held an unbeaten record. The goal was scored in the second half by Pte. Speke from a centre by C.S.M. Middle-cote, who played in fine style. The game was very fast with plenty of head work. Noticeable players were Sergt. Jones (Captain), L/Corpl. Nichools and Sergt. Sterry.

Sergt. Parr performed the duties of referee.

A Platoon Football Competition has been arranged and below are the results to date. In each case the winning Platoon is given first.

3 v. 15	...	2 goals to nil.
13 v. 7	...	4 goals to nil.
1 v. 4	...	6 goals to nil.
5 v. 2	...	3 goals to 1 after, extra time.

A Rugby football match was played between our Battalion and R. Siege Park on November 19th, and resulted in a win for us by 2 tries (6 points) to 1 try (3 points).

We were represented by :—

Back :
Sergt. Egerton.

Three-quarters :
2nd.-Lieut. Carrol, L/Corpl. Hamblin, Pte. Hamblin, Pte. Eden.

Half Backs :
Pte. Monk, Pte. Cook.

Forwards :
Capt. Sumner, Lieut. Coote, C.Q.M.S. Meadows, C.Q.M.S. Huxford, Sergt. Butcher, Sergt. Boughton, L/Corpl. Ansell, Pte. Blunt.

(The above accounts were in the Press before our departure for Italy.)

HONORIS CAUSA.

Military Cross.

2nd-Lieut. E. A. R. Josephs.
Capt Rev. G. F. Helm.

Distinguished Conduct Medal.

240715 C.S.M. Middlecote, W.

Military Medal.

240662 L/Corpl. Jordan, M.

Mentioned in Despatches.

Lieut.-Colonel A. B. Skinner.
Lieut. (a/Capt.) G. Hawkins.
Corporal R. A. Burton.

The following N.C.O.'s and men have received excellent reports from their Schools :—

242504	Cpl. Simmonds, T.	...	...	L. G.
240525	Sgt. Barnes, H. C.	...	...	General.
242552	Sgt. Lee, W.	...	...	P. T.
240181	Cpl. Burton, R. A.		...	Signalling.
240600	Pte. Blackwell, H	...	...	,,
260081	Pte. Bardell, W. F.	...	...	,,
241300	Cpl. Niblett, W. E.		...	Musketry.
241000	Sgt. Butt, R.	...	. .	General.
242306	Sgt. Marment, J.	...	...	Musketry.
242661	Sgt. Hobbs, G. W.	...	...	,,
240680	Sgt. Blackford, H.	...	...	,,
	Sgt. Carter, C. H.	...	...	Signalling.

We offer our congratulations to Capt. C. R. Coote, M.P., who has been returned unopposed as the Member for Wisbech.

NURSERY RHYMES OF THE MOMENT.

1.—IN THE TRENCHES.

Sing a song of sixpence, married Tommy's pay,
Four-and-twenty long debates brought eighteenpence a day,
When the Tommies heard of it they all began to sing,
That's the right and proper stuff to set before the King.

The Commons in their Council House are very bright and sunny,
Munitioneers and Profiteers are making pots of money,
Poor Tommy in the trenches dodging Fritzs' hate,
Wonders when the X. Y. Z. he'll get his increased rate.

2.—ON LEAVE.

Subaltern, subaltern, why do you sing ?
I've received an M.O. at the hands of the King.
Subaltern, subaltern, why do you glare ?
An A.P.M. strafed me for having long hair.

3.—ON REST.

Poor Private Bert, he lost his shirt,
'Twas found in an incinerator ;
An Officer came and took his name,
He got Field punishment later.

THE SEAGULL.

Feathered wanderer of the sea,
Ever roaming, wild and free,
Who 'neath smiling skies and bright
Speed your smooth, unhurried flight.

Under heavens dull and grey
Battle in the storm and spray ;
With your shaded wings spread wide
Down the breezes drift and glide.

Or, with weary wings at rest,
Float upon your water nest,
Pillowed in the soft sea foam,
Sea and wind and sky your home.

Restless spirit, on life's sea—
Like the sea-bird wild and free
Guided by the Father's hand—
Seeking far your promised land.

Through the tempest and the night
Until faith is lost in sight,
Sheltered on your way unknown,
Lonely oft, yet not alone.

Though life's tide may rise and fall,
Hearing still the distant call.
Wandered, whene'er you roam,
Love, and joy, and peace, your home.

THE REFLECTIONS OF A RAT.

The human being we call men don't seem to have much sense,
They spend most of their energy and wits and time and pence
In digging trenches in the earth and making dug-outs, too,
Then wonder their new dwelling place gets like a sea of glue.

By those whose Kultur's unrefined 'tis said to be like hell.
The point of view is everything—it suits *me* very well.
Life was uncertain in the past with dogs and boys and traps,
But little skill is needed here to pick up lots of scraps.

Though meddlesome, when unemployed, and not at all polite,
The men are fairly harmless now—they've got some Huns to fight ;
And often have I ventured out when all was quiet and still
To find a first-class supper laid, and feasted at my will.

I think it due to age or damp—perhaps I may be wrong—
But anyhow their cheese is good—the brand is extra strong.
I'm very fond of sausages, they make you sleek and fat,
Besides 'tis getting back one's own against the hated cat.

If I were man I would not choose to live in this queer way,
But for a rat 'tis just A.1., and so I'm glad to stay.
Some talk in hopeful strain of war and say 'twill end an n ;
The point of view is everything—I hope it's going on

PROMOTIONS AND APPOINTMENTS.

Coy.	Regtl. No.	Rank and Name.	

To be Sergeant :—

D	240824	L/Sgt.	Pobjoy, G. A.
D	241177	Cpl.	Phillips, C.
B	8687	,,	Turfrey, J.
C	241103	,,	Holtham, A. C.

To be a/Sergeant :—

| C | 240276 | Cpl. | Millichamp, P. J., D.C M.,M.M. |

To be L/Sergeant —

| D | 241460 | Cpl. | Mallard, L. F. |
| C | 203680 | ,, | Lane, G. H. |

To be Corporal :—

D	240062	L/Corpl.	Jordan, M. G.
D	10958	,,	Woods, T.
D	9812	,,	Bennett, A. G.
A	20465	,,	Eves, A. E.
C	203638	a/L/Cpl.	Lee A. G.
C	21296	,,	Cairns, J.
C	242529	,,	Townsend, T.
B	242254	L.Cpl.	Smith, S.

To be Lance/Corporal, with pay :—

D	240043	L Cpl.	Bruce, C.
D	37536	,,	Baker, H.
D	3311	,,	Hutchings, F.
D	20277	,,	Kahn, P. R.
A	240197	Pte. (L/Cpl.)	Roberts, R.
A	240587	,,	Blackwell. E. S.
A	214468	,,	Griffiths, S.
C	260236	,,	Ainge, G.
C	240174	,,	Aylmore, M.
A	240600	Pte.	Blackwell, H.
B	206540	Pte.(L/Cpl.)	Cook, F.
B	203726	,,	Pryce, W. J.
A	38820	Pte.	Bedford, T. A.

To be Lance/Corporal, without pay :—

. C	241847	Pte.	Ladyman. A.
C	203685	,,	Jones, A.
D	34234	,,	Foster, E.
D	203703	,,	Gladwin, T.
D	241886	,,	Plascott, J.
D	38808	,,	Ogden, L. K.
D	203648	,,	Preece, M.
D	260146	,,	Bowerman, A. B.
D	242500	,,	Johnson, F.
D	241443	,,	Taylor, H.
D	38812	,,	Walker, E. V.
D	39153	,,	Webster, G.
D	1837	,,	Matthews, W. G.
A	39191	,,	Martin, E. N. J.
A	201821	,,	Cook, W. J
A	241392	,,	Taylor, E. J.
A	20034	,,	Comer, F.
A	39239	,,	Dix, W.

5th Gloucester Gazette.

A Chronicle, serious and humorous, of the Battalion while serving with the
BRITISH EXPEDITIONARY FORCE.

HONORIS CAUSA.

Military Cross :—
    Capt. Rev. G. F. Helm.

Distinguished Conduct Medal :—
    C.S.M. Coward, R.

Croix de Guerre :—
    Capt. F. K. Foster.
    240258 Sgt. Brisland, R.

GERMANY'S DANCE WITH DEATH.

(From a Picture by Raemakers).

Death (*loquitur*) :

"Three years and more we have danced together ;
    We cover the miles by tens and scores ;
What do we care, you and I, for the weather—
    My arm about you, my lips to yours ?

What though we dance through the rain and the wind,
    Under a sparkling or sunless sky ?
Acre and acre we leave behind,
    I am a tireless partner, I.

But you, beloved, your cheek grows pale ;
    Your gay voice slips into sobbing tones ;
You pant for breath, and your footsteps fail,
    Your lips are colder than sea-washed stones.

Once, vine-crowned, and with song, we passed
    The towns strewed starkly at our command ;
But now you sigh, and sick looks you cast
    At the bones which whiten the ravaged land.

Then with mad laughter your form was shaken ;
    Now o'er my shoulder you furtively strain
Your eyes to the towns we have pillaged and taken,
    And your wild mouth is twisted and torn with pain.

No use, beloved, to falter and sicken ;
    Needs must dance onwards wherever I choose,
Till your cheeks burn red, and your footsteps quicken,
    Albeit they follow in worn-out shoes.

No use to call on your Gods for pity ;
    We are linked by an indissoluble tie.
Dance, till you dance through the Gates of my City ;
    We are blood relations, are you and I."

                        P. M.

WHAT WE THINK OF OURSELVES.

The papers have long contained accounts from war correspondents and other journalists—notorious and otherwise, who from time to time have visited the back areas of our fighting forces.

It was left to an enterprising provincial paper to give an account of what battalions think of themselves.

To do so, this paper sent out a journalist who, quoting from his account, " visited fifteen units under severe limitations of time and distance, and the minds of officers explored as well as may be. It is from these separate investigations that these articles have been constructed." Moreover, this reporter was more candid than some of his notorious contemporaries, for he tells us that his information was "not got on the Ypres sector. No correspondent could yet enter that with a reasonable chance of coming out whole."

It is obvious, therefore, that what is found in the articles will reveal what some of us think of ourselves.

Without further introductions quotations will be taken from the Midland Daily Post.

Territorial Engineers.

An engineer is the skilled artisan of the Army and can do anything from bridging a river to stopping a leak in a water pipe. Men are highly trained and officers also. It is the engineers who say how a prospective trench line shall be dug and revetted, and themselves dig and revet . . . that is where the brains of an engineer comes in.

The theory—and practice—is that a private in the Engineers is competent to tell the Officer commanding a company which has captured a line of shell holes how it may best and most quickly be converted into a good trench.

The Gloucesters.

The Gloucesters think of themselves as West countrymen. . . they are an exceptionally good lot, the pick of the physique and the intelligence of the city . . . having the natural modesty of West countrymen.

Worcester Regiment.

Of the Midland men in the fields of France, there are none finer than those of the ancient cathedral cities and counties. . . Were they dispirited ? Not at all. Failure to achieve the full success which they would have attained to . . . made them more eager to be at the enemy again . . . physically they were a fine lot of men . . . the enemy must have thought them supermen.

The Warwicks.

The standard was high in those days, and many a volunteer was stronger in patriotic instinct than in body. A good deal of weeding out and re-shaping had to be done . . . henceforth these Birmingham Warwickshires had a reputation to maintain . . . men will come back to the trenches after a raid in the dead of night with dripping bayonets and dilated eyes.

(Note.—*Is the following in routine orders : Bayonets will be cleaned and eyeballs returned to the normal before the morning's inspection ?*—Ed.)

ITALY-CS.

(Our departure from France having synchronised with our arrival in Italy makes us realise that there is a war on. The Editors of the GAZETTE wishing to mitigate its hardships as much as possible have compiled a small guide book to the latter country and its language for information and necessary action of all ranks. Besides giving the incorrect pronunciation of all Italian villages, this little Guide contains all the useless out-of-date phrases and idiotic expressions which are invariably met with in handbooks of this nature. In fact it is quite valueless in every respect, and the extent to which it is appreciated may be gauged by the fact that it is already in its 99th Edition, the previous 98 editions having been exhausted in complimentary copies and copies for the Press. The Guide has been arranged in tabloid form, and one cube, which should be taken in a mess-tin of rum, is given below for the benefit of readers who's A.F.B. 64's are incorrectly balanced and who are therefore unable to obtain these little manuals for themselves).

CUSTOMS OF THE COUNTRY.

1. *Money* is freely circulated among the Field Cashiers, whose office hours are somewhat limited. It is advisable to apply for money at least four weeks in advance of requirement.

2. *Currency.* The popular coin is the LIRE (pron : Lyro). It is worth about 6d. and does not go very far, in fact seldom beyond the Field Cashier's office.

3. The National *Drink* is CHIANTI (pron : Key-auntie). If the wish is to pass as an Italian ask for VINO (pron : Vyno). Water is sometimes used for washing purposes. Visky is a strong drink, and should only be taken on the advice of the Medical Officer.

4. The National *Food* is POLENTA—an a-maizing mixture. Spaghetti and macaroni are no longer eaten, as they have been requisitioned for the manufacture of ropes for mountain warfare. Ice Cream is not recommended as it melts in the mouth.

5. *Posts* are rather scattered and are seldom successful in reaching their destination. It is reported that on one occasion a motor lorry despatched on a three days' journey to fetch mails returned with letters that had been despatched from railhead on their way to England a week previously.

6. *Climate.* Cold and very cold. If the thermometer is below freezing point it may be implicitly trusted. The sun is hot.

7. *Railways* run in network across the country. There are four Classes : 1st Class, 2nd Class, 3rd Class, and cattle trucks. The latter are the most comfortable. If a train leaves a station it may usually be relied upon to arrive at another one.

8. *Accommodation.* Chiefly barns. Hotels are not frequently met with, but are very comfortable.

9. *Dress.* Optional. Evening dress is seldom worn. Khaki is recommended. Puttees should not be crossed. Steel helmets are useful in summer for keeping off the sun. It is advisable not to throw away shirts or socks.

CHIEF CITIES AND SIGHTS.

BACCACICCACISSIMA (Pron : Back-a-cheek-a-chiss-i-mar). A village of two inhabitants chiefly celebrated for its name, which rivals any Welsh village. Contains one grocer's shop (always sold out). Chianti may sometimes be obtained, beer never.

TURKEY MOUNTAIN.—A prominence of note. A magnificent church has been erected at the summit which is alone worth a visit. Not recommended for mules.

VENICE.—A town of some importance, but difficult of approach.

GUIDE TO THE LANQUAGE.

Below are a few useful phrases which the authors trust will suffice for the most unintelligent reader.

Where is my Aunt ...	Dove e la mia Zia (Dough-vay eh la mee-ah zee-ah)
Oh, Oh, Antonio ...	O-O-Antonio.
Ice Cream Cart ...	Il carro della crema ghiacciata.
(Owing to lack of space we are unable to print the pronuncaition of this phrase).	
Vin Blong	Chianti (Key-Auntie).
Napoo	Non piu (Non-pew).
Officers' Mess ...	Ufficiale Mangiore.
Good-night	Buona Notte. (pronunciation optional).
I want my ticket ...	Voglio il mio biglietto (pron : An-may-I-get-it).
No. 9	(Italian unnecessary ; the M.O. speaks English).
Bring me some oysters, turtle soup, lobster, duck and green peas, fruit salad, Stilton cheese, coffee, liqueurs, and champagne ...	Donotoh tempto Satanoh.
Take away the Stilton	Alley tootsweeto il stiltonoh.
Charlie Chaplain ...	Karlo Kaplino.
What time does the Leave train go ...	Quando partito il treno di permissione. (pron : Kwondo par-tee-toh eel train-oh dee per-mission ay).
There is no Leave train	Non e un treno di permissione.
Damn...	Sapristi.

The above few phrases will give the reader a general gasp of the Italian language. For anyone who really wishes to see the country we recommend a walking tour with frequent foot inspections. The scenery is unrivalled.

HOW LORD TOPWIND WON HIS STAR.

A Romance in Six Revolutions.

Specially written and typed for the " Gloucester Gazette " by BOADICEA BROADSTREET.

REVOLUTION I.

The Lord Horace Topwind revolved in his revolving chair, his lighted Woodbine delicately poised between his upper and lower lips. He was engaged in deepest calculations and from time to time made mental notes on his shirt cuffs.

" Two and two is twenty-six—pence, and one is two and three," he muttered as he came to the end of an abstruse calculation, and with a look of self-satisfaction he commenced to revolve once more.

Lord Horace Topwind was a charming youth of 23 summers and 28 winters. The slight discrepancy was due to the vagaries of the English climate. His correct title was really Second Lieutenant the Lord Horace Topwind, for he was one of Britain's khakied sons, and it was only his natural modesty that with-held from the people the fact that he had been one of the first to join up—in 1917. In fact he was the first of the long list of Topwinds to join the Army. He was at present employed at an A.B.C. Tea-shop which had been taken over by the War Office for work in connection with the raising of soldiers' pay, and it appeared that Fortune was indeed smiling on this happy and clever youth. But, alas ! this was not so, and even at this moment Fate was at his doorstep.

He was still revolving when there came a flip at the door and a moment later a Boy Scout appeared.

" Lady to see you, sir," said the latter, saluting with the thumb and forefinger of his right hand.

Lord Horace stopped revolving.

" Tt ! How annoying," he said in a voice accustomed to command. " You know I cannot see ladies during office hours. Show her up."

A moment later and he gasped in surprise as a face he knew, a face he adored, appeared through the swing door.

" Gwendolen," he gasped, " What are you doing here ? "

Dame Gwendolen Ransome, for the visitor was none other than she, his fair fiancée, did not reply for a moment. She was a beautiful girl—3 years 6 months and a few hours younger than her affianced, and had well deserved the title of Dame which a grateful country had bestowed upon her in the Grand Order of the British Empire, for on flag days she was indefatigable, whilst her collection of war medals was considered one of the finest in the country, including as it did the V.C., M.C., A.S.C. and R.S.P.C.A. ribbons.

Aye, she was silent for a few moments after her dramatic entry. Then she spoke.

" I am here," she said simply.

" Yes, but why ? " His breath came in short pants. She paused just for the fraction of a second whilst the gold-mounted clock on Lord Horace's mantel-piece chimed twelve.

" My luncheon hour," she cried, then suddenly, " But before I go I will tell you why I came."

He waited in breathless expectancy.

" I can never marry a man who has not been to the Front." Then she gurgled softly and leaning forward she put every stone of her weight into her next words.

" Go," she neighed hoarsely. " Go ! I command you. Away to France to earn the star you wear upon your sleeve."

REVOLUTION II.

There was an intense air of excitement through-out the War Office as it gradually became known that someone had volunteered for Active Service.

As yet, in the general buzz of the confused murmurs, it was impossible to distinguish the name of the hero, but as it leaked out that it was none other than Second Lieutenant the Lord Horace Topwind—for it was indeed none other than he—the astonish-ment of the Boy Scouts and Girl Guides knew no bounds.

But it was growing near closing time, and as Lord Horace appeared at the door of his room a tremendous burst of applause rent the vast building.

Smilingly he returned the salute, and as he strolled down the corridors—those familiar corridors—for the last time, there was one prolonged cheer.

At the door the policeman saluted him.

" Taxi, sir ? "

" Yes." There was not a quiver of emotion in his reply—a reply which meant so much to Lord Horace, for he knew that this summons to the Petrol Kings would mean the commencement of a stern fight.

" Victoria Station," he said in a firm voice to the driver, as the taxi rolled up.

The driver began to protest.

" Victoria Station," repeated Lord Horace firmly, and he could not have been more magnificent had he been commanding his battalion on parade.

The taxi-driver nodded.

Lord Horace had won his first battle. It was a favourable omen.

REVOLUTION III.

The scene at the station was brief.

Not even for Love would the train wait.

Gwendolen was there and looked ravishing in a soft green velour with a dainty lace collar and black satin belt.

" Good-bye," she whispered, as Lord Horace jumped out of the taxi, and she pressed a sealed package into his hands.

" Sweetheart," he murmured into a wave of hair coiled round her ear.

" You won't forget me ? " she urged, as the guard sounded his bugle and waved his green flag as a signal for the departure of the train.

" Forget you   .   .   .   ? "

But the train was already rolling away from the platform, and the remainder of the sentence went scattering along in the wind like leaves on an Autumn day.

It was only after some hours that he remembered her present. He unclenched his fist—the packet was still there—and as he discovered her gift, staggered at her generosity, he performed a complete revolution.

Gwendolen had sacrificed her margarine card.

REVOLUTION IV.

'Midst shot and shell, Second Lieutenant Topwind, for as such we must now know him, found his way to Divisional Headquarters.

" The Glawsters ? Oh, they be oop in front," replied the sentry on duty, in reply to our hero's query as to the location of that unit.

Topwind walked through into the office.

" Ah," he thought, " I may as well wait until they come out of the line, then," and turning to a Captain, he explained his position.

" And I suppose you can just manage to put me up for two or three days ? "

But, alas, for the horrors of war, Topwind was informed that he must proceed to his unit at once.

In vain he gnashed his teeth. He must go.

Topwind was angry—and justly so. To be ordered out at eleven at night was preposterous, but— Our hero recovered his self-possession as an inspira-tion struck him.

" Very well then," he barked fiercely to himself. " I will go. They will see that I do not fear to face five hundred thousand Germans single handed," and grasping his six-inch revolver—a present from his mother—he strode out into the night.

There was a battle raging that night. We cannot conceal the fact. All day long shells had fallen here, bullets had fallen there, and aeroplanes had fought gigantic battles in the air. And now as Topwind strode down the shell pitted road the reverberating roar of the guns was still revolving. Suddenly he drew his revolver. What was that coming down the road ? Carefully covering it with the barrel of his weapon he stepped to one side, but a moment later he breathed a sigh of relief. It was only a motor lorry, and as the mud from the wheels splashed his new trench boots he grew angry for the second time that night.

"Ha!" he grunted to himself, "I wish the German Army would break through this evening. My God, if I met a German to-night."

We must forgive him these blasphemous thoughts. Who can say whether they are justified or not? Let us be patient with Lord Horace.

On he strode, the forefinger of his right hand ever pressed against the trigger of his revolver. On, on he went until—until—

Suddenly he heard a sound that he had never before in his life heard. A dull sound first, which gradually increased to an ominous one, a rumble, a roar, and . . .

"My God," murmured Topwind, "The Germans . . . they have broken through."

He pressed the trigger of his revolver.

Resolution V.

Before he knew what was happenning he found himself surrounded by Germans. Several of them were booing and hissing at him, but he stood proudly in their midst with his revolver pointing towards them.

"You will yourself up give?" A short fat German came waddling towards him.

But Lord Horace was an Englishman.

"Take that," he said, as he discharged the revolver full in the German's face, which the bullet missed by inches only. "I will never surrender," he hissed.

But the shot had an effect which he had not anticipated. In a trice six hundred German hands had gone up. Three hundred prisoners had fallen to him.

At least Topwind thought it was three hundred. He had, however, not quite finished numbering them when—

The stretcher bearers arrived and found a man lying insensible on the duck boards counting in a monotonous voice:

"Two hundred and eighty, two hundred and eighty-one, two hundred and eighty-two . . ."

Revolution VI.

"Drink this."

A feminine voice as soft as the cooing of a tame rabbit was by his side, and opening his eyes Lord Horace, for we may once more call him by his title, found himself looking into the eyes of . . . oh, could it be . . . of his only Gwendolen.

"Where am I?" he muttered thinly.

"Hush," she replied. "You have been seriously wounded. By a miracle your life has been spared . . ."

"How? When? Who? Why? What?"

Lord Horace was justly bewildered.

"Hush," repeated Gwendolen. "The doctor has ordered you complete rest. You were hit by a revolver bullet on the way to your Battalion from Divisional Headquarters. By a miracle . . ."

"My Gwendolen—my Gwendolen . . ."

"Horace, I have never forgiven myself for sending you away . . . Can you forgive me?"

"My darling—what have I to forgive. But say, will you now be mine?"

"Horace . . . Horace . . . This is sudden—terribly sudden."

"But will you?"

Gwendolen hung her head.

Second Lieutenant the Lord Horace Topwind, B.E.F., had won his Star.

FIBULOUS.

WAR MUSIC.

At a classical concert a short time ago I fell into a sleep, induced doubtless by reading the analytical programme. It was an unwise thing to do, because the dinner at the Convalescent hotel where I had been sent had ended for four successive days with prunes and custard, and into the sleep crept a nightmare—that the Author of the descriptive notes of the music had turned war correspondent and was giving an account of

"Trench Raids."

This (he wrote), the second and possibly more popular of Atkins' method of obtaining the offensive, is in a Major D—. Its opening movement is prefaced by orchestral introduction in which the two main themes which suffice for its construction are clearly stated, Surprise and Pain. The first and plaintive marking shell, a pathetic little 18-pounder, is followed by a rhythmic pulsation in the base, which after a few bars works up to a fortissimo, the theme being taken up by the divisional hows, the corps heavies, and other "wind instruments." Full use having been obtained by most successful orchestration, synchronisation, and co-ordination, the bangalore then enunciates the second phase, accompanied by a protective barrage on the second line. The full orchestra again enters with a burst and softens down later after a few full-toned passages.

The grenade in a rising and falling movement then heralds the third phase. Interest in this movement is confined almost entirely at first to bomb and bayonet in a few brilliant and rapid passages. Trench mortars and Stokes take up the theme with gradually increasing colour till the whole glitters with a bright staccato springy figure, the effect being heightened with a wonderful entry of flares. Very lights, golden rain and rockets. One can imagine a night revel with cries and laughter and the flash of the torch. This theme is taken up by one instrument after another as the climax of this movement is reached, our men getting much effect from "percussion instruments," and the Germans appearing "on strings."

Soon a tremolo from the full orchestra announces the fourth stage, The Return. Rapid action from the 18-pounders and increased activity with the heavies leads to a more passionate and fuller rhythm, while the infantry, having accomplished a beautiful tour-de-force and having swept the whole gamut of the trench, fade into the background.

The last movement is of the responsive order and indicative of retaliation. As befits its title, it is stern and severe in character, though somewhat uncertain in operation, emphasis and stress, for example, often falling on the wrong place. The bright colouring of the flares in previous movements dies down, while sullen and loud arpeggi and scales proceed in the scale of B and F to take up the challenge of the earlier motifs. The air is stated in loud shuddering chords and double notes. Several of the phrases are recapitulated and again the whole orchestra attacks the melody with Minnies, Blue pigeons and machine guns deepening the tonal effect. This lasts for some time till in a series of chord passages of extraordinary intensive power—(such as the regiment on the right flank who are receiving an undue share of the retaliation get heartily tired of)—the whole movement dies away and tonal harmony is eventually restored. . . .

I woke during the applause to some particularly classical figure, glad to be rid of the nightmare, and glad to feel that unsatisfactory as present war correspondents are one might go further and fare worse.

G. HAWKINS.

THINGS WE WANT TO KNOW.

Who was the A Coy. Sergeant who found the stones in his pack ? Who was the donor ? And is it true that he was seen on sentry the same evening ?

Whether a certain Editor and Self-Advertiser now knows what under fire means ? Whether he enjoyed the experience ? And whether he now knows the meaning of " Somewhere in Hell ? "

Who was the man on the transport who combed the horse with the bully beef tin ? What did the T.O. say ?

Did the Christmas Carol really get the R.Q.M.S. to Blighty ? Who really sang that Carol ? Was it in Scotch ?

Who is known as the Limber King ?

Who is the fair Haired Corporal who talks in his sleep—and is it true he was overheard to remark " Sign Quarter Master Sergeant, please."

Why was B Coy. afraid to Play A Coy at football ?

Why " Biscuits " is always so keen to return to his stable alone ?

Was Ninella sorry to see the Glo'sters depart ?

Who refereed a football match wearing spurs and armed with a revolver ? Did he have a horse ready ?

What Sergeant described his hair as " Holborn ? "

A SHORT DICTIONARY OF MILITARY DISEASES.

Cursus linguae, or verbal dysentery.—This insidious disease claims its victims from all ranks, but is particularly rampant among officers holding high commands and junior subalterns from cadet schools. The symptoms are inability to control the tongue, leading to hoarseness of the throat, and carmination of the visage. These are largely aggravated by the consumption of alcoholic beverages. The patient is seized with violent chattering and rapid palpitation of the lips, and gives utterance to a large and ceaseless flow of unintelligible utterances. This disease is extraordinarily infectious, and whole Messes have been known to fall victims to it for long periods.

TREATMENT.—The patient should be strictly isolated and his tongue kept in position by a gag made preferably from the editorial pages of *John Bull*. Short sharp exclamations from his companions, such as " Golden ones," " Ear 'oles," etc., are recorded to have had a beneficial effect by recalling the patient to his senses.

Inflatio capitis, or swelling of the head.—A disease originating probably in Government offices, but one to which many are liable immediately on return from Corps or Army Schools, Gas-Courses, etc. Many cases occur among members of the R.F.C. The patient suffers from persistent delusions as to whom he is and what he has done, and tells the most wild and impossible stories of his achievements with every appearance of veracity. In patients advanced in years the disease shows a distressing tendency to extend to the abdomen, hence the kindred ailment of extensio tummi, or middle-aged spread.

TREATMENT.—The patient should on no account be humoured. Firmness is essential. If the ordinary treatment of expressing disbelief or even contempt is of no avail, the application of some hard object to the patient's posterior is almost invariably efficacious

Fungus visiagnis, or bristles.—An epidemic rampant chiefly in the lower ranks. On waking the patient finds his face covered with a thick growth unpleasant alike to the sense of touch and sight. There is no occasion, however, for alarm ; an immediate scraping, though painful, will remove the growth. In advanced stages, during the morning parade, the patient experiences a sinking feeling on the approach of an officer or senior N.C.O., and shows a distinct tendency to hide himself. Indeed, an old sufferer will invariably fall in the rear rank, where he is less likely to be observed. This disease is often allowed to rage unchecked in civilian life, and is particularly prevalent among elders of the Scottish Church, anarchists and ladies of strong mind and masculine proclivities.

TREATMENT OF ADVANCED STAGES.—The part affected should be well washed and cleansed, and scraped every morning for five minutes. The use of pincers, tooth nails and Army razors, or anything of a blunt nature, is not advocated.

Desideratio cushi laboris.—This is not so much a disease as an obsession. The patient exhibits strong disinclination to work of any kind, while at the same time expressing great affection for it in every other form than that on which he is employed. He also has a mania for collecting small pieces of coloured ribbon and cloth, with which he adorns his person, and surrounds himself with numbers of servants, motor cars, etc., which he uses to give the impression that he is hard worked. He is not infrequently found also to be suffering from *inflatio capilis* and *cursus linguae*.

TREATMENT.—The patient should be told the war is going to end, or alternatively that he is going to be inspected by the G.O.C. in C.

C. R. C.

A PERFECT SOLDIER.

Is your uniform clean ? Have you polished your boots?
  Have you brushed from your putties all dirt ?
And last evening did you remember to sew
  All those buttons on trouser and shirt ?

Is the strap of your hat on the point of your chin ?
  Have you given the buckle a thought ?
If you're curtly requested to take off your cap
  Are you sure that your hair is cut short ?

Is your mess tin outside of and under your pack
  With the round surface outwards inclined ?
In your hurry you didn't p'raps chance to forget
  That your putties you've outwards to wind ?

Is your bolt cover on and the safety catch back ?
  Is the bore of your rifle well oiled ?
Where the magazine rubs on your Company tab
  Are you sure that the latter's not soiled ?

Is your jerkin rolled neatly and tied on the pack ?
  Are you sure that your kit's all correct ?
And after a march are your feet always clean
  When the Officer comes to inspect ?

Is your box respirator worn at the alert ?
  And your tube helmet close by your side ?
And during a march do you always keep step
  And take a full thirty inch stride ?

Do you hope day by day for the end of the War ?
  Do you curse ? Do you swear ? Do you grouse ?
And then start again with a b——y and damn
  As you pick off the ninety-ninth louse ?

Are the hundred and one other jobs done ?
  Do you compree the Old Soldier's way ?
If " Yes " is your answer to all the above
  You deserve one and sixpence a day.

" AREFAR."

THE QUEST OF THE GERMAN HELMET.

With apologies to Malory's " Morte d' Arthur."

When that there was certayn debate and bickering betwixt George and Wilhelm there were in the goodly fellowship of the Platoon two Knights, Sir Thomas night, also a sarg and Sir Bill th Olde. Now sithen these Knights had fought valorously for many moons they thought soon to return home a space to a far land called Blighty and have there much joyance and feasting. But inasmuch as the times were hard and they had little tofore been sore shent by a company of recreant Knights at a tourney called " Banker," it beseemed them good to endeavour if peradventure they might come by the wherewithal.

Now there were many Knights who belonged not to the famous fellowship of the platoon but thought it more profitable to belong to fellowships where, if the honour were less, certes, the pay were more. And these Knights all with one accord lusted after souvenirs wherewith to show their sweet Damozels or haply to justify them to their children if that their children should rise up and ask them

" What did you do in the great War, Daddy ? "

but of all the souvenirs ne was there not one more desired by everychone than a German helmet. So Sir Thomas Le Sarg spoke and said,

" Wit you not well that we might barter some souvenir ? Why not let us adventure our persons honourably and see if we may not come by a German helmet ? Shall us ? "

" Lets," said Sir Bill th Olde.

Then these twain tarried a space till undurne night come and when dark night was come they bad let fetch their armour and girded them. And they sought sweet counsel with a pleasant and trusty friend called Rum. After that they were comforted, they fared quietly forth to a place so foul, noisom and Forsaken of God that all men verily called it No Man's Land. And when they came there, there was much curious noise and bruiting so that Sir Bill felt a wind and was afeard.

" Also me sore repenteth I came ever here," he said, " Never name shall I ne do this stunt again, let them keep their blinking helmets."

" Be of good cheer," said Sir Thomas, " and fare quietly, for even now I see a perisher with a helmet that beseems me passing well."

So took he his good weapon, Lee-Enfield, and delyvered so sure a stroke that the false traitor Knight, Fritz of Prussia, was dead in a moment.

Then came they with all speed and wrested away the helmet. And they hied them quick at a great wallop all besweat after the fight back to the goodly fellowship of the platoon and had great joy for the helmet was most curiously and cunningly wrought so that all were enamoured and orgulous thereof and it fetched full many francs.

This right valorous emprise so pleased the fellowship of the platoon that they went straightway for a short sojourn in Blighty wherin was all mirth and merriment.

G. HAWKINS.

CHATS FROM THE EDITOR'S FLEA BAG.

We have now settled down in Italy and, we may safely say, if use may be made of the vernacular, " It's a bit of orlright." Glad as we all were to get away from the dreary plains of Flanders, we little suspected that such a good time was in store for us as we have experienced since our arrival in this country. Whilst admitting that our main pleasure has been to have a rest from the War, we think the bon time we are having is in no little measure due the reception we have everywhere received at the hands of the Italian people.

* * * * *

Heartiest congratulations to two of our former Editors who have recently gained War Honours. The Rev. G. F. Helm has been awarded the Military Cross, and Capt. G. Hawkins has been mentioned in despatches. The latter has now transferred to the I.W.T. Good luck to him ! With four gold stripes up, he well deserves it.

* * * * *

Recently Parliament has cast a more benevolent eye upon soldiers than was formerly its wont. The rise of pay has been greeted with acclamation by all ranks. The mails we now receive are both regular and rapid. The announcement made for the first time that Brigade Commanders are in future to be chosen more freely from the New Armies is also very welcome. This lack of a well earned right was a " grouse " which we made notice of twelve months ago in this column. Unlike some of our contemporaries in like circumstances, however, we will not claim credit for its achievement ; we rest content that it is so. There is one point still, however, on which we should like to ventilate a young " grouse." We read recently in a Weekly that they were pleased to state that they were mainly responsible for the fact that soldiers were now granted leave regularly every twelve months and officers every six months.

Whilst realising that a great deal has been done in this direction we think we might respectfully call attention to the fact that several of us came down here with eighteen months and more continuous service in France without leave, and that this is at present only being very, very slowly worked off— and we are a great way from that twelve months leave.

* * * * *

There is also one point in connection with the increased rates for pay of soldiers which does not strike us as quite right. The announcement stated that in future the grant of proficiency pay would be given after six months instead of two years. What has really happened is nothing of the kind when once the Act is denuded of its flowery language. This is the real state of affairs. On joining the infantry a man receives 1/- a day Regimental Pay, plus 6d. a day to make up the War minimum of 1/6 a day. After six months he receives 1/- a day Regimental Pay, plus 3d. a day proficiency pay, but only another 3d. (instead of 6d. as before) to make up the War minimum—total, as before, 1/6 a day ! And then, after two years, he may be put in for Class I. proficiency pay and receive another 3d. whilst he has by this time earned 2d. War pay, making a total of 1/11 per day. We do not like to make a complaint about the new rates, but we think the Proficiency Pay point might have been expressed clearly to begin with, instead of disappointing hundreds of thousands of men to the tune of 3d. a day, or 16 per cent. of their total income !

Also, by the way, cannot something yet be done to wash out the out-of-date Unpaid Lance-Corporal system. In Peace days when a man was given a stripe on probation and probably had several months in which to learn his job this may have been all right, but nowadays when a man is given a stripe it means very much more than looking on and learning. It is quite probable that he may do the work for three or four months without a penny. Even if he gets killed whilst doing the job, he has died a Private in the eyes of the Army, and his wife gets pensioned accordingly:

A REGIMENTAL PARABLE.

Atte one time it came to pafs that there was a Great War. And the chief men of Albion with alle their following went forth to give battle to William the Teuton in the Lande of Gaul.

And there were divers slaughters.

Now atte that time there dwelt in Albion a certain young chieftain, lusty and fair toe look upon ; and he said within himself, " Verily, I also will be a soldier, butte I will have nought of this fiteing lest, peradventure, I be slain ! "

And he trained the levies, and sent them forth toe fite. For his liver was as milk within and he had noe bowells.

Now one daye, about the setting of the sun, the Devil appeared untoe the young man and took him intoe a solitary place aparte. And in a vision he showed untoe him alle the wangles of the world and the cushy jobbes thereof. And the fine women, and the wine, and the houses of the great men.

And the Devil spake untoe him saying, " Alle these things canst thou have untoe thyself if thou wilt but give me dominion over thy soul." And the young man answered him saying, " Done, O ! Devil."

Then gave the Devil untoe the young man a bande of cloth. And the length thereof was one halfe a cubit, and the breadth thereof was the breadth of an average sworde. And the colour thereof was redde.

And the Devil spake, saying, " Go forth, and wear these tokens ; and great favour shalt thou find in the eyes of faire women, and for thine amusement thou shalt have sovereignty over many brave men."

Soe he went forth and ere many months had pafsed he rose to a place of great power in the Armies.

Now after the War had ceafed the young man betook him toe his house. And a man childe was born untoe him, he having married a wife.

And the childe grew uppe and he was the delight of his father's eye ; and great was the young man's pride in his offspring.

Now after the fourth winter the childe came untoe him and said, " Tell me, I pray thee, O ! my Father ! What didst thou in the Great War ? "

And the young man answered, saying, " Of a truth, O ! my firstborn, I was a D.A.Q.P.M."

And the childe was exceeding wroth and did spurn hys father and spake untoe him, " Verily it is as the soldiers tell of thee, saying, ' Behold ! he was embufque.' Father, O ! my father ! thou art a perisher."

And father knew it ; and such was the sorenefs of his hearte that he never smiled again.

F. D. R.

A LETTER FROM ITALY.

December, 1917.

DEAR WIFE.—Just a few lines, dear, hoping this finds you as it leaves me at present with a bad leg. We have just had a long journey, and I am not allowed to say we have left France, but I may say that we have now arrived in Italy. The scenery here is beautiful, and all the mountains is covered in snow, dear, they is a long way away, dear, but look quite near until you start to march to them, and then they are a long way away, and when you get there you haven't got to them.

Well, dear, yesterday, we climbed one of them ; it is much further to go up than to come down, the one who got to the top first won a turkey. I didn't win the turkey, dear wife, but I wouldn't go up again for a hundred b—— turkeys. My mate would have won it, but he stopped to pick chestnuts to stuff it half way up. Well, dear, the last man did not get back until the next morning. Out here it is very cold, dear wife, but they have no fireplaces, only stone ones, and them is not for sitting by, only for cooking, they gets too sticks and a corn cob and then lights them and keeps on blowing down a bit of gas pipe and when they gets him alight he goes out and they use the red hot ashes for cooking and if they has much cooking they blows again, dear wife.

Well, dear, we aint allowed to drink water out of the stream as the women washes there clothes in them, they don't use no soap but hits them on a board, these streams run by the sides of all the roads and if you have too much vino you falls in them, our sargent fell in one to-day, dear wife, as the road was not so wide as he thort it were. Well, dear wife, we had a good time at Xmas, they wun us a pig and wen it was dead we had pork and beans for dinner, there was also chicken with nuts and oranges and we had some vino.

Well, dear, we had some boxing in the evening. I did not box because of the pig and then we had a concert and I sung, but I would not sing again for a hundred b—— pigs. There was a large sick parade the next morning.

Well, dear, the people here all drinks vino which is the Italian for wine but much cheaper. I tells var ole dear it is good stuff for you can get blind for a liro, but I never does. A Liro is Italian for a franc which is French for money, but not worth quite so much, it is worth about sixpence. Well, dear wife, I could write a lot more, but will do so next week. Well, dear, good afternoon, and may God bless you and keep you safe from your ever loving husband till we meet again.

P.S.—Please do not send me anything just yet, but I should like some fags as soon as you can get them. We cannot get fags for love or money, dear wife, out here so please send them to me as soon as possible.

(We regret that the above letter, sent us on a registered field post card, was delayed for six months in transit and finally found in No Man's Land.—ED).

FIRING.

A Battalion Musketry Competition was held at —— Range, and there was a large number of entries. In the Platoon Team Contest No. 4 and No. 11 Platoons tied—each with 193 points. On a re-fire taking place No. 4 Platoon won by 135 points to 133. Their team was Lt. Shears, Sergt. Hobbs, Ptes. Bennett, Hand, Gale and Cockram.

The Individual Competition (200 yards snap-shooting, 200 yards application, and 400 yards application), was won by Corp. Smith, of B Company.

SPORTS.

A very pleasant sports meeting was held at the beginning of April, which provided some good running. The 120 yards hurdles provided the most exciting contest of the afternoon, 2nd-Lt. Sanders beating Sergt. Hardiman by inches only. At the conclusion the Colonel presented the prizes and also awarded the medals to No. 6 Platoon football team, who won the final of the Platoon Football Competition. Results :—

100 yards.—1st, Pte. Barnes.
Mile.—1st, Pte. Smith, J. G.
High Jump.—1st, Sgt. Hardiman.
Broad Jump.—1st, Sergt. Hardiman.
¼-Mile.—1st, Pte. Barnes.
½-Mile.—1st, Pte. Smith.
Boat Race.—D Company Team.
120 yards Hurdles.—1st, 2nd-Lt. Sanders.
Tug-of-War.—D Company Team.
No. 11 Relay Race.—D Company Team.
No. 12 Band Race.—Pte. Godwin.

BATTALION BOXING TOURNAMENT.

This was held on April 14th. Good form was shown by all competitors and an interesting evening was spent. The winners were as follows :—

Welter Weight.—Sergt. Sterry, A Company.
Light Weight.—Sergt. Butt, D Company.
Feather Weight.—Corpl Woods, D Company.

The final of the middle weights, between L/Corpl. Comer, A Coy., and Sergt. Blackford, D Coy., could not be fought owing to persistent rain. No one could be found of large enough calibre to tackle Sergt. Boughton, D Coy., in the catch weight, and he accordingly sparred a couple of amusing and clever rounds with a member of the audience, in which both hands and feet were freely used. The contest between Pte. Love and Corpl. Woods provided the most interesting and pretty boxing of the evening.

FOOTBALL.

INTER-PLATOON CUP MATCHES.

Some exciting games were witnessed in the Semi-Final and Final of this competition. No. 6 Platoon eventually proved the winners, beating No. 14 Platoon in the Final.

BRIGADE CUP MATCHES.

All except A Company had the misfortune to be knocked out in the first round of this competition.

In the match our B Company v. C Company Oxfords the latter won by 3 goals to 2 after extra time. Our D Company was beaten by C Company Berks, who turned out a strong team, by 3 goals to 2 after D Company had scored the first two goals of the match. Our A Company beat our C Company, after a stiff game, by 2 goals to 1.

Under the heading of Sports we should like to offer our congratulations to our Battalion Band, who have made great strides in the last months. Under the leadership of Capt. Rev. C. A. Clarke, assisted by Sergt. Millichap, D.C.M., M.M., we are now provided with " right merry musick," and their daily performances are much appreciated.

OUR BENEFACTORS.

Camps Library—Books.
Col. Griffith—Papers.
Lt.-Col. Marling—Papers
Pte. Wood—Typing.
Queen Alexandra's Field Force Fund—
                                    Christmas Gifts.

R. I. P.

Say not good-night—but in some brighter clime
Bid me good morning.—*Barbould.*

We shall rise to peace anew
An earth where every dream is true and
Nothing is unknown but pain.—*Harvey.*

And over all this wind and wet
His soul sits safe with God.—*Harvey.*

Why make us moan
For loss that does enrich us yet.—*Lowell.*

Upon thy hearse I shed no useless tear,
For us we weep rather thou in calm divine.

5th Gloucester Gazette.

A Chronicle. serious and humorous, of the Battalion while serving with the
BRITISH EXPEDITIONARY FORCE.

HONORIS CAUSA.

*Mentioned in General Sir H. Plumer's Despatch
dated 18/4/18—*

    CAPT. B. V. BRUTON.
    LT.-COL. W. ADAM.
    CAPT. F. E. FRANCILLON.
    CAPT. G. A. LISTER.
    A 240109 SGT. BUNDY, W.
    D 240697 SGT EGERTON, W.
    D 240358 SGT. HARDIMAN, G.
    D 240705 CPL. HIAM, E. J.
    C 241103 SGT. HOLTHAM, A.
    B 240282 PTE. OSMAN, F.
    D 203664 PTE. THOMAS, W.

*Awarded Meritorious Service Medal. Extract London
Gazette, dated 3/6/18—*

    A 240037 SGT. JONES, H. V.
    A 240089 CPL. PERRY, G.

Awarded Distinguished Service Order, 3/6/18—

    LT.-COL. W. ADAM.

Awarded Distinguished Service Order, 28/6/18—

    CAPT. C. R. COOTE, M.P.

Awarded M.C., 28/6/18—

    THE REV. C. A. CLARK, C.F.
    2/LT. G. F. CHURCHILL.

Awarded D.C.M., 28/6/18—

    B 240181 SGT. BURTON, R.A.

Awarded M.M., 28/6/18—

    A 240877 SGT. PARKER, H.
    C 241942 SGT. PEARSON, W. J.
    C 242523 L/CPL. TONGE, W. J.
    C 240896 L/CPL. WHITEHEAD, T. H.
    C 13373 PTE. PEGLER, B.

THE FLAG.

Banner, drooping in graceful folds,
  Floating or furled by the wind's caress,
What is your magic that thrills and holds
  And fills our hearts with the tears that bless ?
Banner, for you men have fought—and fight—
  For you will die while the ages roll ;
Emblem of freedom, honour, right,
  Banner ! you stand for a nation's soul.—M.L.G.

FAILURE.

To watch hope slowly fade, to realise
That others reach the mark from out the press
By chance or favour, see with bitterness
That toil which fruitless seems, men but despise
Or pass unheeding by, and nought arise
To bring the golden fruit of hoped success
Within the tired grasp. Only the stress
Of cheerless work, a goal without a prize.
Yet he who stedfast stands may surely know
His work and patience have not been in vain,
That effort unrepaid has greater power .
For good than victory won without a blow,
That there the labourer toils to sow the grain
And in the Harvest Day will reap the flower.—M.L.G.

FLOWERS OF LIFE.

The flowers of life are the smiles that charm and chase away
The greyness and the gloom of a dreary, sunless day.

The flowers of life are the hands outstretched for a brother's
  need,
The words that in sympathy for another's weakness plead.

The flowers of life are the tears for others' sorrow shed,
That help to lift the load and bear it in their stead.

The flowers of life are the songs that every glad heart sings,
Their gift of joy is borne to the world on shining wings.

The holiest flower is Love, to all men freely given,
The light of life to set our feet on the surest road to Heaven.
                            M. L. G.

PEACE.

The prayer of every heart by pity torn
For all the bitter anguish and the pain,
The young lives in their last long sleep now lain,
War's cruel toil in silence nobly borne,
Yet few there be of those in grief who mourn
But would fight on if danger still remain,
Lest War's dread curse darken the world again.
Lest we forego the purpose we have sworn.
And they know peace—though thunders loud and long
The cannon's roar on battlefields storm-tossed
Where ruined homes bestrew the broken sod—
Who faithful stand to fight against the wrong,
Giving their all unheeding of the cost,
The higher peace, the changeless peace of God.—M. L. G.

TRAVELLERS' TALES.

POSSIBLY our readers may think that the following
specimens of typical conversations at the Front
are rather ideal than actual, more potential than
dynamic, as who should say overdrawn, or—in a
word—untrue. Certainly it is admitted that at first
sight it should seem that they have been lifted from
that alas too little known brochure " Etiquette for
Infantry " by a Regular Adjutant (Ball and Golden,
1/6), yet, nevertheless, there has been no such
immoral scrounging. In asking our readers to believe
them we are putting no greater strain on their
credulity than the pen-pictures of the special war-
correspondent already impose.

CONVERSATION 1.—By an Officer who has just
received a pink chit containing the curt sentence,
" All leave cancelled, for your information."

" What ! My leave cancelled ! This is indeed
singular. I have already had it stopped twice,
delayed three times, promised four months and I was
beginning to think I should have to undertake the
long and arduous journey to Blighty. It is with
unalloyed pleasure that I receive the good tidings
that owing to the war, I will be taking no holidays
this year. Not only do I miss the hardships, discomfort and uncertainty of the journey but I feel,
also, that I save tonnage for the nation."

CONVERSATION 2.—An Officer writes to an
Adjutant :—

" I note with regretful surprise, that by some
unfortunate oversight the return asked for in my
E.D. 33x.x. d/15/1415/12, has not been submitted
by you. I can quite realise how busy you must be,
but so much do I value this return of Hindus taken

on the strength last week that I must really ask you to let me have it at your convenience. As this mishap on your part must be due to overstrain and consequent lack of health, I am sending you a leave warrant for one month in England. I trust that the brief respite will do you much benefit and that you will return to the business of chit-supplying with added vigour and renewed ardour."

CONVERSATION 3.—A private to his Platoon Sergeant :—

" Really, Sergeant, my being put on fatigue again is an unexpected joy. As I have been out digging for six nights running now, I certainly counted on this evening off as several of my comrades-in-arms who have been out only four times are not going to-night. Pray do not deem me insubordinate if I say that I am glad that some understanding has arisen which enables me to do this further service towards the vigorous and successful prosecution of the war."

CONVERSATION 4.—An Artillery Officer speaks to a nervous Subaltern of the Bn. which his battery covers :—

" It is with unalloyed pleasure that I have to inform you that our guns will shortly open on the point on which you ask for retaliation. Do not hesitate to call us up another six times to-morrow night if you feel we may be of the slightest assistance. If it is true as you say, that the grantenwerfer which you wish silenced cannot reach you and does you no damage, that is no real reason why you should hesitate to ask for artillery support. It is a real pleasure for us to wake up at any hour of the night, and on even this unnecessary retaliation, to fire off some shells—which are, by the way, quite expensive."

CONVERSATION 5.—Company-Sergt.-Major to last joined recruit.

" I trust you will not take it amiss if I ask you slightly to accelerate your movements, inasmuch as the Bn. parades in ten minutes, and we are already somewhat late. I fear you must give over for the nonce the task of adjusting your pack, and with the final precaution of removing the half-smoked cigarette from your ear, I must request you to take your place in the ranks and look like the ne plus ultra of soldierly beauty."

G. H.

A MATTER OF BUSINESS.

" I say, Clarence, this is absolutely ghastly ! Here we are, slap-bang in the middle of Italy, and not a blooming sou, franc, lire or whatever it is, to spend. Rotten, I call it ! "

And Jimmy hurled a tobacco quid viciously about ten feet away with a dexterity that told of long practice.

" Its humiliating too," agreed Clarence thoughtfully. " A pennyless army lowers the national prestige, and—and all that kind of thing. I'm as hungry as a hunter and have got an inside that's in the throes of rebellion against bully and biscuits. If there were a pawn-shop here I'd pop my watch for a loaf."

" Some of 'em manage without the three balls, anyhow. Look at that chap—loaves in every bally pocket, and yesterday he hadn't a cent. Regularly cornered the wheat all on his own ! "

" H'm," ejaculated Clarence, musingly, " How the deuce do they do it ? "

Jimmy looked at his pal meaningly and then winked.

" Quite so," said Clarence. " After all we're a nation of shopkeepers, as one of our old-time enemies said once. But what the deuce have we got to sell here, and who's going to do the talking when we HAVE got anything ? They forgot to teach me Italian when I went to school."

" Me, too," answered Jimmy. " And the people can't understand French either. I don't mind joining the British Army when the Old Country gets herself in a hole, but to become a bally linguist as well is asking too much. Pity, too, for I've got an old razor which, if we polished him up a bit and showed it in the dark, might raise a—what-d'ye-call-it ? "

" A lire ? " queried Clarence. " Let's have a look at the thing anyhow. You polish it up a bit and I'll practice Italian. I saw " vendita " on a shop-window just now. " To vend " is to sell in English, and I expect the 'ita' at the end is a participle or some other grammatical case ending. I'll have a shot at it, anyhow."

" That's up to you. I don't know anything about grammars or particles or whatever it is. Let's go in and see."

So they went in the billet. Jimmy ferreted out the razor, and Clarence, seated on his pack, cudgelled his brains and covered dozens of envelopes with elementary Latin roots, to which he added what he believed were Italian case endings. A quarter-of-an-hour went by.

" There, how's that ? " remarked Jimmy, holding the razor in one hand and the leather brace of his pack in the other. " This thing makes a ripping strop. The razor looks a treat now ; it'll do anything but shave, but that's for the blighter who buys it to find out. This is made to sell ! How are you getting on with the lingo ? "

" Ni havas razoro vendi, senor—what the devil's 'buy' in Italian ? " remarked Clarence abstractedly.

" Blowed if I know—stick an 'o' on the end of the French 'ashtray' and chance it. They know we ain't going to give it 'em, anyhow. Let's try it. Come on ! "

Clarence agreed in despondent mood, None knew better than he that a fluent tongue is needed to sell a faulty article, and none knew better than he that his Italian was anything but fluent. He was not hopeful of success. And nothing but stern necessity could have made him undertake such a forlorn hope.

The village street by now was pitchy dark, but there were plenty of civilians about. They seemed to throng in little groups around various objects of interest it was too dark to see the nature of. The two pals made their way along and presently, much to their surprise, found they were surrounded by an excited, whispering crowd.

" Cigarettes, cigarette vendi, senor ? "

" What's that mean ? " saked Jimmy.

" They want us to sell cigarettes," answered Clarence.

" They can jolly well go on wanting anyhow. If I've got to go hungry I'm hanged if I'm going without a smoke. Shove the razor into 'em. Make 'em buy it. What's the good of being a British soldier if you can't make a foreigner do what you want him to."

Jimmy's creed has its devotees in more exalted circles.

" No ; no cigarettes, senor. Mi havas razoro vendi."

The darkness hid the expression on the Italians' faces. Then a burly form pushed through the crowd. " You have a razor to sell ? " came the query in quite good English. " Say, let's see it ! "

Covering his astonishment as well as he could, Clarence handed over the razor. The would-be-purchaser made his way to a lighted window and examined the article critically. Clarence and Jimmy followed dutifully and anxiously awaited developments.

" Where did you learn English ? " asked Clarence of the burly soldier.

" Chicago, sure. Say, call this a razor ? Barber's my trade. I know a good one when I see it."

" Then you'll recognise that one," said Clarence, inspired by a brilliant brain-wave. " A good, first-class English razor."

" —With the German mark on the blade, eh ? " remarked the stranger, laughing at the obvious discomfiture of the two. " Well, how much ; make a price."

" A liar," said Jimmy, in his haste, imitating the old psalmist.

" Una lire, senor," put in Clarence quickly, fearing his pal would be taken literally.

" Um. Not worth ten cents. Army issue."

" Certainly not " (duet.)

" Thought it was," meanly remarked the too-knowing stranger. " All right, here's your lire. S'long, boys ! "

Clarence pocketed the coin, and the two promptly lost themselves in the crowd.

" He, he," laughed Jimmy, " he thinks he's got a bargain ! Why the bally thing wouldn't cut a wet newspaper. Here, let's go in here and have a vino. That's Italian for vinegar, I think."

They entered the shop and called for a vino 'toot sweet (?) and Clarence tendered the coin.

Signora took the coin, looked at it, smiled, then handed it back with a voluble explanation.

" What's up, Italian lire, ain't it," said Jimmy ; " here, chum (turning to a khaki-clad near him) this is a ' liar,' ain't it ? "

Chum regarded the coin in Jimmy's paw critically.

" No," he said brusquely, " a tuppenny piece," —and it was.

H. J. B.

CHATS FROM THE EDITOR'S FLEA BAG.

It has never been possible, because of military reasons, to publish a list of casualties. We cannot, however, allow this occasion to pass without paying our respect to our late companions, loyal and true to death, and also to offer our deepest sympathy to their relatives.

We mourn and regret their loss, but are thankful to have had the privilege of living amongst such fine men.

To their parents we uncover our heads, that their sons at the last could say, " Thank God I have done my duty."

* * * * *

An alteration has recently occurred in our Editorial Staff. One Editor, most reluctantly, has been compelled to spend a holiday—we trust a short one—in Austria. Upon his return you may expect a bumper GAZETTE. In the meantime we carry on.

* * * * *

In conjunction with our gallant allies, the Italians and French, we have gained a brilliant victory over the Austrian forces.

The Italians fought magnificently and have good reason to be proud of their achievements.

THE CONFERENCE.

Scene : Derelict strong point 1 *finger* 2 *o'clock the Z in the-Hedge of Hebuterne.*

It was almost in progress. Straining at its starting point it only needed the presence of the convening officer to enable it to dash straight away through the usual channels in the proper orthodox manner.

The Staffs (*sic.*) of twelve Battalions had been invited and all had accepted. They had come mounted, and the conspicuous convexities of their pockets suggested sandwiches and the expectation of prolonged proceedings. Some of the more ardent blades were already removing elastic from A.B.'s, and a few of the younger soldiers had even betrayed the possession of maps. The older soldiers were tentatively fingering their flasks and looking that look of concentrated and obviously hereditary boredom which only old soldiers can sustain for any appreciable time.

The three Brigadiers were there, too, each with his following of crimson upholstery. Yes ! it was certainly a great day. The staff and the regimental officer had gathered together for a common purpose.

The situation was almost unique. True, neither appeared to derive any great satisfaction from being in each other's company, but that may have been due to the phlegmatic reticence of a notoriously insular race.

Au contraire, it may not. The Brigadiers were just beginning to look as impatient as was consistent with good order and military discipline, when a wind-spread crimson pennant in the middle distance heralded the approach of the convening officer, who was, incidentally, the G.O.C. Division and possessed of a phenomenal reputation for the gastric assimilation of fire. The enthusiasts hastily produced pencils and carbons, the Staff assumed defensive positions around their commanders, and the old soldiers screwed on stoppers and looked round to see if the others were still smoking.

" Good morning, Gentlemen ! " said the G.O.C., and the sentiment was echoed by one salute per officer and the stirring clash of hopelessly entangled spurs.

There followed a pause. The G.O.C. leaned on his stick, carried off a foot to the on guard position, stooped slightly forward in an attitude of alert appreciation of the matter in hand, faced his front and beamed pleasantly on all present. Then with one hand resting lightly on a diminutive firearm attached to his belt, and chin earnestly thrust out, he commenced ; and for two long hours he spoke wisely and feelingly of blood, and fire, and iron.

" Now was their opportunity, now was the appointed time. They had been fighting a different war in a different country. Now they had returned to their old haunts in France and very soon they would be going into the trenches. He had seen the sector they would take over and topographically it was identical with the area in which the Division was now resting. Never in his experience had he met a happier coincidence. The enemy was hard pressed, his reserves were exhausted, his economic situation was desperate. The Division was about to take part in operations—operations the results of which would be of far-reaching consequence. Here at their very doors was the parade ground for their fighting, a facsimile of the actual battlefield. They would practice the attack."

The younger soldiers again made intense play with their stationery, the Staff looked as though they knew but could not tell, and the older soldiers sighed and thought their horses were getting cold.

Suddenly a signaller appeared and handed a message to G.S.O.3. The latter passed it on to G.S.O.2, who forwarded it to G.S.O.1., who presented it with a verbal minute to the G.O.C. Returning the envelope via the same channels, the G.O.C glanced at the contents, gasped, looked again, turned white, and stood mute in an atmosphere of final and staggering catastrophe. Evidently something serious had happened—something unusually terrific.

The Staff looked very concerned about it. The younger soldiers were bloated with suppressed excitement. The older soldiers merely scented trouble of some sort and hoped that zero wouldn't be before breakfast.

With an effort the G.O.C. found voice and breath and gave proof of both. " Gentlemen ! " he exclaimed, " I must read you this urgent wire just received from Corps. " Peace declared—hostilities will cease forthwith—Central Empires accepted all Allied terms."

News of this sort is calculated to create a sensation. It did. A five-nine couldn't have done it better. The conference broke up in a confused welter of dust and noise—everyone shouted and laughed and told each other that the war was over. Hands were shaken, backs were slapped and one Brigadier was distinctly seen to part with his cap.

After considerable time and difficulty, the G.O.C. restored order. Somehow he seemed to have aged rapidly during those last few minutes.

" Well," he said, " I suppose it cannot be helped. The enemy has declared Peace on us. There will be no more fighting."

He paused heavily, and the look of him was the look of a man who looks back along the path of life and would fain retrace his steps. He sighed ; and excited and elated as they were, the others felt a deep sympathy for their leader in this strange sadness which had come upon him in the very hour of victory.

And then, as yet they looked upon that well-known face, they saw a wondrous transformation. There again shone the old fire, the lips parted in the old smile—the merry smile of battle, smoke and flame—the old sparkle of pleased and pleasant understanding was dancing in those eyes—again that whole frame radiated with a spirit of tireless energy !

" Gentlemen," he cried—and it was the old voice —" Gentlemen, now is the time to show our mettle ! Man-mastership ! Discipline ! Morale !—now is the time to prove their worth ! Despite the lack of an enemy we will carry on. To-morrow we will practice our attack over this natural course. It will be a dawn attack and units will be in position one hour before Zero. You never know, Gentlemen ; in another war this exercise may prove very useful ! "

F. D. R.

——BGDE. INTELLIGENCE SUMMARY.

COVERING ANY OLD PERIOD.

1. OPERATIONS.

(a) ARTILLERY.

7.42 A.M.—One 18 Pdr. (said they) fired on B. 419, 743, on hostile movement. No movement was seen by observers, and no shells arrived there.

9.00 A.M.—6 Shrapnel shells burst 300 yds. NORTH of the M of MOUNTAIN.

11.15 A.M.—Our Heavies engaged our Reserve Bn. H.Qrs. with marked success, smashing all windows and causing the position to be evacuated as untenable.

2.30 P.M.—5 A.A. Shells (6 mile group, 1 wide) immediately SOUTH of the S of SUN. Result— Total Eclipse.

(b) PATROLS.

Patrols went out from everywhere in all directions obtaining no information. They were, however, able to discover from other patrols where they had been themselves.
Identifications, Prisoners—nothing to speak of.

(c) AVIATION.

4 enemy aeroplanes flew over our lines at 9 a.m. A ground observer in an O.P. made a noise like a British Fighting Machine, with the result that two crashed in no man's land and the remaining two were seen to descend out of control behind the enemy's lines.
Our observer is not missing.

2. INTELLIGENCE.

(1) HOSTILE ARTILLERY.

Heavy shelling by 5.9 H.E. at X. 418.397. Fire apparently drawn by dummy water point, conveniently filled by thunder-storm.

(2) ENEMY MOVEMENTS.

11.7 A.M.—An Austrian was seen to enter house at 2, 704, 913 closely followed by 18 pdr. shell.

Neither were seen to come out again.

3.16 P.M.—Enemy aviator seen to fall out of an aeroplane about 4,000 ft. from the ground. This point has been registered, and guns will fire on any similar movement. Tracing has been taken.

3. GENERAL.

It seems probable that enemy trenches are sometimes held. This is considered all the more probable as no one has ever been seen there.

The situation remains cold, rat-infested and obscure. Visibility, not so as you'd notice.

S. O. N. SLEUTH,

Lieut. I. O.

for Brig.-Genrl.

Comg. ——*Bgde.*

" BONO."

Italian is an easy tongue,
It's no use saying " Oh ! no."
You've only got to learn one word
Just B. O. N. O.—Bono.

It's Bono if the bread is good,
And Bono suits the weather,
It's Bono when you say good-bye,
Or when you talk together.

" No Bono " is the opposite
(Like ration tea and cocoa)
And much is " Molto Bono," while
No good is " Bono Poco."

It's Bono when Reveille sounds
(And Bone-o time at dinner !)
So when in doubt just " Bono " shout
For Bono spots a winner.

C. B. F.

C.-Q.-M.-S. : Two hundred men got a 6 inch gun up that hill.

PTE. FRESH : How ? By pulling ?

C.-Q.-M.-S. : No ! They each took it in turn to carry it up on their shoulders.

THINGS WE WANT TO KNOW.

Who is the N.C.O. who said, " Extend a bit more, one of you is all in a bunch ? "

Who tried to blow out the electric light ? Is he in No. 4 Platoon ?

Who, when sent to Battalion Headquarters for the correct time, wrote it on a piece of paper because he had no watch ?

What is the use of Potassium Permanganate ? And who swallowed a tablet as if it were a pill ? Did it ease his throat ?

Who asked " and WHO is Sweet Fanny Adams ? " Anyhow, who is she ?

Who remonstrated with his confreres for being too familiar before 9 p.m. ? Is he in the Berks ?

Is there anyone in Blank Brigade who knows the difference between X.Y.Z. schemes in any sector ?

Is Morar held ?

Who pulled up Maize roots to obtain Macaroni ?

Why was the picquet lines at night so popular with B.H.Q.?

What Sergeant gave the order " Into ones get " ? Do the Signals know ?

What sentry said " Advance one and give the counter attack " ?

What Corporal stuck the S.O.S. in the ground to fire it ?

Who stated that " Bayonets could be fixed on Lewis Guns " ? Was he in B Coy. ?

Why a cook in B Coy. so urgently required his waterproof sheet from a dug-out, and whether his story was believed.

Who read out " Any man saluting with the left hand after this date will be abolished " ? Is he a Sergeant on B.H.Q. ?

Who was it that made " tea " on B.H.Q. and forgot to put the tea-leaves in, and what did the Padre say ?

Who ventured out to " No Man's Land " to collect Souvenirs ? What did he find ?

Who remarked, " Do they explode," when H.V. Shells were whizzing about ? Was he above the rank of Sergeant ?

Whether it is claimed for the new German gas that it is of most deadly effect, and even is capable of destroying all the next of kin.

DOPO LA GUERRA.

In view of the fact that some day or other this war must end, even if this does not occur until the commencement of the next one, we offer the following " leader," etc., gratuitously and absolutely free of all cost, to any contemporary, to print, publish, or otherwise reproduce after all Peace Treaties have been ratified.

POLITICS AND PEACE.

Once again we feel forced, in the national interest, to protest against the action—or rather inaction—of the present Government. For years we have warned the people, and we have urged to our uttermost this same Government, that sooner or later peace must be declared. And what heed have they paid ? Absolutely none, and yet to-day Peace is upon us. The enormity of their offence cannot be too strongly reiterated. Whilst they have been occupied with their political bickerings, we have, in spite of all obstacles, been slowly winning the war and drifting towards Peace. Germany knew it—Germany recognised it. For twenty years they have been preparing for this Peace, and have been turning every factory to the manufacture of the Munitions of Peace, and now—as usual—they have caught us absolutely unprepared. How long this Peace may last, we are not in a position to say, but it is not likely to be a short one. We have the authority of LORD NORTH-CLIFFE for saying this. But what are we to do to save the country—where are we to commence ? The question is urgent—the nation is serious. POLITICS MUST GO OVERBOARD, and we would suggest as immediate measures :—

1. The compulsory enlistment from the army into civil life of all men between the ages of 60 and 90. The Civilian Service Act, which practically only deals with persons over the age of 90, carries us a very little way.

CIVILIANS!

The DAILY HAIL is YOUR friend.

The DAILY HAIL has secured for you :

1. The right to enter Public-houses.
2. Permission to live.
3. All security from taxation of 5 per cent. of your income.
4. Ships and yet more Slips.

And we are now agitating for the immediate comb out from the army of all men between the ages of 60 and 90.

BUY THE DAILY HAIL,

THE CIVVIES' FRIEND.

---

2. The immediate formation of a new Government, with LORD NORTHCLIFFE as Premier and MR. BERNARD SHAW at the head of the Peace Office.

The country needs no reminder as to the services rendered by these men. We once held different opinions from MR. BERNARD SHAW. We will frankly own it. But times have changed. We are now at a national emergency when all differences must be placed in the melting pot, and there is not a man more efficient than MR. BERNARD SHAW to run such a gigantic Peace Campaign as we have before us. As for LORD NORTHCLIFFE, Nature has never conceived a more brilliant and able statesman, so, FOR THE LORD'S (NORTHCLIFFE) SAKE LET US WAKE UP. 40,000,000 men are resting idle in the army to-day, whilst the prospects of war grow hourly more remote ; and one other thing, do not let us forget the enemy in our midst. There are thousands of spies in the country to-day, who, as a result of pernicious teaching, are shouting for war at any price. We give a final and last warning to the Government that the country has reached its last stage of tolerance, and unless urgent steps are taken to carry out every single one of our suggestions they must GET OUT OR GET UNDER.

"THE CIVVIES' FRIEND."

Answers to Questions concerning the Civilians Service Act.

D.S.—Mothers are exempt from all civil service, provided they have received a certificate from their local tribunal.

A.B.—Under Schedule 105, Clause 18, Paragraph 93 of the Act, "Soldiers or other Men of War under the age of 90 may at present remain in the Army." We are agitating for the reform of this clause. No mention is made of Naval Ratings.

Old Soldier.—If you have been granted conditional exemption from Civilian Service, you must join one or other of the Civilian Volunteer Depots.

FIBULOUS.

CORRESPONDENCE IN BRIEF.

SIR,—The country is being flooded by enemy Peace Agents with millions of copies of that pernicious paper, THE HUMBUG NACHRICHTEN. When will we learn that the only method to counter these attacks is by reprisals? For instance: Why not send a million copies of the DAILY HAIL to Germany every day?

Percy Woolybourne,

Rose Cottage, Sandfields.

———

SIR,—With all your influence, cannot you get this rationing system abolished? Thousands of tons of food are being wasted daily owing to insufficiency of Ration Cards. I myself, although living twenty miles from the docks, smelt a boatload of stale cheese yesterday.

" Disgusted,"

Very Upper Finsbury Park.

———

SIR,—I think it only right to inform you, as the Civvies' Friend, that the following invention of mine has been turned down by the Peace Inventions Committee, without comment. " Patent No. 003005/004001. A projector of 100 inches diameter to protect silk, cotton, horse-hair, etc., for export from Dover to Calais." I shall be pleased to supply full particulars to any patriot.

Yrs. Fly, Thomas Screw,

Loose-on-Avon.

———

THE GREAT AWAKENING.

NOTE.—" An Objective Line " is an imaginary line running at the usual pace across the surface of a battlefield. Prior to an attack it appears in the flesh on military maps and indicates to the attacking forces what they have to attack.

I.

The Company Commander shared a pill-box with his Second-in-Command. His affection for both was genuine and he called them Vibration Villa and Tom respectively.

The Battalion was in close support and taking an uncommonly keen interest in the war. The artilleries of both sides were keeping most of both sides of the battlefield up in the air most of the time. And the quantity of mess-stores bore to the quantities of maps " Lessons of Recent Offensives," and addenda to amendments of Operation Orders about the same proportion as the pork does to the Beans in the Pork and beans.

All of which meant, of course, that a battle was in the offing, and not far off at that.

II.

Carefully holding a candle at the high porte, the Company Commander was examining a map with the tender solicitude of a mother watching her sleeping child. It was an ordinary trench-map, but the Company Commander had adorned it with a re-freshing network of lines of varying length, shape and hue. To an ordinary civilian, or even one not engaged upon work of desperate national importance, these lines would probably have indicated nothing more than a pleasant but childish passion for things pretty. But the Company Commander, in the honest, simple way of regimental officers, recognised and tactfully respected them as symbols of the branch that is " G "—objective, boundary and barrage lines.

To him they were what the writing on the wall was to the other man in the other story, the what-is-to-be and the how-you'll-do-it, the product of masses of highly-trained grey matter—super-grey-matter—grey-matter behatted, betabbed and bechateaued.

Now in keeping with all those fine, old tawny and crusted traditions of the British Army, the Staff had affably consented to share their labours with the Company Commander. His job had been to keep his map absolutely up-to-and-including-date, i.e., to arrange and re-arrange his cherished lines to keep pace with an ever changing situation and the staff plans, which changed about as often. It had been sticky going. For weeks he had worked—worked like a tired woman who tries to keep a hat fashionable for a whole season —and it had cost him an infinity of perspiration and pencils and oaths.

But now, praise be! All was in order, the fait was accompli, and the lines could stand more or less at ease.

The Company Commander mused. He was not a habitual muser, but just then he was pleasingly aware that something had been both accomplished and done and on such occasions a muse is inevitable. Little by little he remembered the high ideals for which he was fighting—the little countries, civilisation and the Great Peace. They were mostly in the form of explosive quotations from the historic war-prose of Bellario Hottumly (soldier and sailor, too), but they made him feel a prouder and a better man.

Again he lifted the candle and looked at the map, this time with the air of a conqueror running through the booty states. Yes! There was no doubt about it. At last he had achieved something great, something of war on the Hindenburg scale, something that would make largely for the decline and fall of the Central Empires, something that would enable Our Special Correspondent, head-quartered in a shell-hole, to peer over the last ridge and gaze upon the promised land.

Now to the average rough soldier of Foot such high-class sentiments are fatal—they are as leave warrants, substantive promotion, 200lb. valises, lifts in Staff cars, hot food in battle, gaps in barrages and rides in trains—they intoxicate! They crump! They utterly floor!

And the Company Commander was average; moreover, he could liaze with Lethe even in Vibration Villa. Of course he put down the candle.

III.

The Company Commander awoke. Somewhere someone was saying something. It was the 2nd-in-Command. " Marked Urgent—from Batt. H.Q.—runner just brought it! " Sitting up, he yawned a blurred oath, opening the envelope and read:—

" All Divisional Objective Lines have been altered in accordance with attached amendment to O.O. 999 of to-day's date. To-morrow the Battalion will attack, capture and consolidate the Blue, Black, Red, Yellow, Green, Chestnut and Roan Lines. Zero will be notified later. Detailed orders to follow."

It was ten pip emma. Turning to his 2nd-in-Command, " She's a great war, ain't she, Tom? " said the Company Commander.

F. D. R.

———

DEATH.

Death be not proud, though some have callèd thee
Mighty and dreadful, for thou art not so:
For those whom thou think'st thou dost overthrow
Die not, poor Death; nor yet canst thou kill me.
From Rest and Sleep, which but thy picture be,
Much pleasure, then from thee much more must flow;
And soonest our best men with thee do go—
Rest of their bones and souls' delivery!
Thou'rt slave to fate, chance, kings and desparate men,
And dost with poison, war and sickness dwell:
And poppy or charms can make us sleep as well
And better than thy stroke. Why swell'st thou then?
    One short sleep past, we wake eternally,
    And death shall be no more! Death, thou shalt die.

(JOHN DONNE, 1573—1631.)

INSPECTOR-GENERAL OF MUSKETRY :   Tell me, my man, why do you fire at 6 o'clock ?

RECRUIT FROM THE COUNTRY :   Well, zur, I s'pose it would be a bit too dark to fire at 7 o'clock.

5th Gloucester Gazette.

A Chronicle, serious and humorous, of the Battalion while serving with the
BRITISH EXPEDITIONARY FORCE.

HONORIS CAUSA.

Awarded V.C., Dec., 1918—
> 17324 PTE. MILES, F. G.

Awarded Bar to D.S.O., 27/11/18—
> LT.-COL. DUDLEY LEWIS, D.S.O., M.C.

Awarded D.S.O., 27/11/18—
> CAPT. R. DE W. ROGERS.

Awarded Bar to M.C.—
> CAPT. F. S. HILL, M.C. (27/11/18).
> CAPT. V. B. BINGHAM HALL (24/12/18).

Awarded M.C., 27/11/18—
> LT. P. A. MORFEY.
> 2ND.-LT. A. J. COX.

Awarded M.C., 18/12/18—
> CAPT. V. B. BINGHAM HALL.
> 2ND.-LT. V. SCROGGIE.
> 2ND.-LT. G. H. WEST.
> 2ND.-LT. C. L. OVENDEN.

Awarded M.C., 1/1/19—
> LT. S. BRYANT.

Awarded D.C.M., 28/11/18—
> 28074 PTE. COBB, G.

Awarded D.C.M., 18/12/18—
> 240079 CPL. PEACEY, W.
> 240665 C.S.M. BROMAGE, W.
> 242501 SERGT. HOBBS, G. W., M.M.
> 11749 L/CPL. HORNIGOLD, A. J.

Awarded D.C.M., 1/1/19—
> 240078 L/CPL. PIKE, H. G. A.

Awarded M.S.M., 1/1/19—
> 280358 SERGT. HARDIMAN, G. H.

Awarded M.M., 7/11/18—
> 242307 SERGT. PACKER, F.
> 39945 L/SERGT. HEWSON, C.
> 203664 PTE. THOMAS, W.
> 39757 SERGT. EDWARDS, E. T.
> 266698 PTE. COLE, R.
> 242547 PTE. DAUNCEY, W.
> 240297 SERGT. FLETCHER, L., D.C.M.
> 240530 SERGT. STEPHENS, W. A.
> 240859 SERGT. DERRICK, H.
> 242267 L/CPL. CLEAVER, F.
> 240192 PTE. ILES, J.
> 240647 L/CPL. IRELAND.

Awarded M.M., 28/11/18—
> 240017 C.S.M. FINCH, F.
> 38781 PTE. COLES, W.
> 17804 SERGT. OMWEN, H. J.
> 240287 L/CPL. TRIGG, L. D.
> 240292 L/CPL. PUGH, F. E.
> 260297 PTE. WILLIAMS, T.
> 38823 L/CPL. PAYNE, C. G.

> 241962 CPL. GILLIES, H. J.
> 240298 PTE. TILLEY, E. F.
> 9740 CPL. KING, F., M.M. (*Bar*).
> 242530 PTE. WEBBER, F.
> 240236 SERGT. SMART, G.C.
> 203696 CPL. CLEE, C., M.M. (*Bar*).
> 240291 CPL. SWANBOROUGH, A. F.
> 39899 PTE. SNOWLING, G. W.
> 241300 SERGT. NIBLETT, W.
> 262264 PTE. CHIDGEY, E.
> 240163 CPL. VOSPER, W.
> 240310 CPL. FLETCHER, W. C.
> 31352 PTE. BULLOCK, A.
> 15568 CPL. FOWLER, E. H.
> 242470 PTE. MATTHEWS, J.
> 240339 CPL. CURREY, F.
> 260089 CPL. COULSON, W.
> 39229 PTE. PROUDFOOT, P.
> 242356 PTE. WOODMAN, J.
> 263025 PTE. SCANLON, J. T.
> 39200 PTE. JARVIS, S.
> 260244 PTE. DAVIES, J. S.
> 200094 CPL. EDGWORTH, W. T.
> 12516 L/CPL. LEWIS, G.

Awarded Italian Bronze Medal for Valour, Sept., 1918
> PTE. CAKE.

His Majesty the King has awarded the Victoria Cross to the undermentioned :—

No. 17324 PTE. F. G. MILES, Glos. Regt.

For conspicuous gallantry and initiative in attack. On the 23rd October, 1918, during the advance against the Bois L'Evque, his company was held up by a line of enemy machine-guns in the sunken road near the Moulin L'Jacques. Private Miles, alone, made his way forward for about 150 yards, under exceptionally heavy fire located one machine-gun and shot the man firing the gun. He then rushed the gun and kicked it over, thereby putting it out of action. He then observed another gun firing from 100 yards further forward. He again advanced alone, shot the machine gunner, rushed the gun and captured the team of eight. Finally, he stood up and beckoned to his company, who, following his signals, were enabled to work round the rear of the line and to capture 16 machine-guns, 1 officer and 50 other ranks.

The courage, initiative and utter disregard of personal safety shown by this very gallant private soldier was entirely instrumental in enabling his company to advance at a time when any delay would have seriously jeopardised the whole operation in which it was engaged.

WALKING WOUNDED.

Still I see them coming, coming
In their broken ragged line,
Walking wounded in the sunlight,
Clothed in majesty divine.
For the fairest of the lilies
That God's summer ever sees
Ne'er was robed in royal beauty
Such as decks the least of these ;
Tattered, torn and bloody khaki,
Gleams of white flesh in the sun,
Robes symbolic of their glory
And the great deeds they have done :
Purple robes and snowy linen
Have for earthly kings sufficed,
But these bloody, sweaty tatters
Were the robes of Jesus Christ.
"WOODBINE WILLIE."

THE DEAD.

When the long-waited day of peace shall dawn
    And hope arise to lift a world's despair,
Among the throng whose thankful hearts upborne
    The God of Battles praise—will they be there ?

To share the joy of comrades who have stood
    Staunch and unflinching through the storm and wreck
In one great, loyal, fearless brotherhood,
    And see their labour crowned—will they come back ?

Unto the loved ones left who bade them go
    So bravely, and in sorrowing memory yearn
For the hushed voice, while yet with pride they glow,
    In this most solemn hour—will they return ?

Ah, surely, one with us, the souls at rest
    In reverent thankfulness to Him abide
Who gave the world deliverance, and blest
    The sacred cause for which they fought and died.
                                            M.L.G.

- - - - - - -

FRIENDSHIP.

True friendship is a lovely thing and rare,
    Made up of understanding, mutual trust,
And sympathy, patient and sure, the rust
Of years can never touch nor time impair.
A part of our own soul, the part most fair,
For who is true unto his friendship must
Live to his highest, faithful, kind and just,
Nor fail each burden with his friend to share.
Ready to give, uncounting, of his best,
Treasure or toil, the help of hand or brain,
And if the need arise his name defend.
Whose love will meet e'en shame or sorrow's test,
Rising triumphant, nobler for the pain,
And shine more pure and bright beyond life's end.
                                            M.L.G.

- - - - - - -

No 1 (and only).

GENERALLY ROTTEN ORDERS

BY

 GENERAL *DAME* **ALICE, K.B.E.,**

Commanding-in-Chief, British Force

in Wonderland.

General Headquarters,
July 2nd, 1918.

ADJUTANT GENERAL'S BRANCH.

0—Use of Motor Cars.

The mileage done by motor cars is now so very small
There must be many officers who don't go out at all ;
At least a dozen Lancias are eating off their heads,
And at least a dozen drivers spend the morning in their beds.

The shocking waste of public funds in letting motors rot
Will lead to questions in the House as probably as not ;
The G.O.C.-in-C. regards the matter with dismay
And wishes every officer to go out every day.

00—Leave.

In view of epidemic influenza
No passes will be granted to Vicenza.

Owing to an outbreak of small-pox
Leave is prohibited to Bampton (Ox.)

In consequence of typhus and enteric
Troops will not proceed on leave to Berwick,

In fact, there is so much disease about,
Troops going on leave will have to go without.

QUARTERMASTER GENERAL'S BRANCH

000—Bakers' Clothing.

Approval is given for bakers' men
Who bake their bake and bake again,
To draw a snow-white jacket apiece
And snow-white trousers complete with crease.

This only refers to men who bake
A nice white loaf or a nice white cake,
And men whose bake is brown must still
Continue to bake in their khaki drill.

0000—Compensation for the Loss of Officers' Kit on Active Service.

—Except in exceptional cases compensation is not payable in respect of summer and winter clothing lost at one and the same time, and officers should therefore take such steps as are necessary for safeguarding under private arrangements their warm clothing in summer and their cool clothing in winter, and in the event of an officer losing winter clothing in summer or summer clothing in winter he is not entitled to claim compensation in respect of his lost winter or summer clothing until the ensuing summer or winter as the case may be, but in this connection it should be noted that winter and summer do not necessarily correspond with the dates officially fixed for the commencement of the seasons, but are governed for the purposes of this G.R.O. by the prevailing temperature at the time, *e.g.*, there may be summer temperatures in winter and winter temperatures in summer, and in all cases the actual mean temperature of the day on which the clothing was lost will be stated in the application for indemnification, although in cases where speical hardship is involved applications *may* be submitted for the loss of both winter and summer clothing—where, for instance, after a cold spring, an officer is changing from winter to summer clothing and an enemy shell explodes in the dug-out in which the change is taking place, destroying both sets of clothing ; but all concerned are notified that in no case will cases be submitted except as the case may be.

With acknowledgments to Poet Laureate,
British Forces in Wonderland.

- - - - - - -

MEMORIES.

For seven weary hours I've gazed
    Into the gloomy far beyond,
Heard rattle of bullets that grazed
    The unkept grass like a magic wand.
To stare into uneven light
On a chilly disturbed Italian night ;
Soon it will end—this weary time—
To retire and rest near by the line—
                                    The Outpost.

We go on tiptoe, crawl and worm
    Our way toward the man of might ;
No one will even shake or squirm
    The duty only kept for night.
And wander through the unclaimed strip
Of land to which we hold the whip,
To creep along the unknown way
And rest contented one more day—
                                    The Patrol.

One good long sleep before we start
    The round of duties that are here ;
Quite soon and joyfully we'll depart
    From out this strenuous life so queer.
We climb and scramble on our way
To start our task at dusk of day,
And work until the break of dawn ;
Return to dug-out, spent and worn—
                                    The Support.

Once more we don our pack with glee,
    For very short will be the time ;
The flat low plains again we see,
    So soon we'll quaff the sparkling wine.
Before the heat our parade is done,
Instead of work we'll have some fun ;
Forget the worries of the line,
To spend our cash in fine red wine—
                                    The Rest.
                                            M.B.A.

- - - - - - -

AN ACCIDENTAL DISCOVERY.

(With apologies to Alfred Dunhill).

Early in 1915 the R.Q.M.S. had brought to his notice a shipment of Gloucester Cheese, then for the first time imported.

Impressed by the beauty and richness of the colour, he experimented with this new substance, only to find that owing to its spongy qualities the results were disappointing.

The unused blocks of food were consequently put aside and forgotten. As it chanced, the room in which they lay adjoined the Sanitary Section. Happening to examine these blocks many months later the R.Q.M.S. was struck by the fact that the odour stood out in relief. Since then he has been experimenting with various means of seasoning the cheese, and found that by the application of heat and sand to the freshly carved rind, most remarkable results were achieved. The bulky spongy substance could be shrunk to a mere shell, the rind assuming a novel and fascinating appearance, whilst the smell or odour completely baffles description.

Price £1 1s. 0d. per block.　　Every block unique.

"ALGERIAN."

"THE PACK."

The Blackest Criminal of the Age stood by the side of the road and saw the troops march past in fighting order. He noted the free swing of their shoulders and the light lift of their feet, and he scowled, grinning like a bilious dog. Anon came clattering along the road a string of lorries, each with a nonchalant cigarette equipped Jehu, and stopped opposite him, their engines churning and groaning with an infinite variety of sounds and smells. Scenting a familiar spirit, the Blackest Criminal of the Age approached the foremost Jehu. "Oh, man," said he, "whither goest thou with this wagon of stinks?" "Sir," replied the Jehu, "I carry the equipment of yonder marching men linewards. But the way is long for me and my wagon. Mark the dust upon my clothing and how she groaneth and complaineth—for in sooth we are loaded with stuff even unto the eaves of the covering." Then was the heart of the criminal touched, callous though it was, and he laid his head upon the radiator and wept bitterly, for it was hot.

And he went thence and tarried a long time, communing with himself. . . .

He invented the pack. . . .

C.R.C.

"PAPER SHORTAGE."

In view of the G.R.O. and the necessity of economising paper—not that there is much to economise on, in the front line (I.E.F.), the following description of Leave shows how our lads can rise to the occasion.

Expectations. Hopes. Excitement. Dusty. Cramped. Suspense. Upheavals. Joy. Embraces. Stories. Merriment. Farewells. Fatigues. Weariness. Alpine. Greetings. When are you going on leave, Bill? Fini.

M.B.A.

ARMY TALK.

It is a common fact to human experience that words acquire new and added meanings under abnormal circumstances.

There are people who consider war as normal now and likely to continue; at the same time there are others who think the war will end some day, these are optimists, and still others who are afraid it will end—these are profiteers, and munitioneers, who continually strike for higher pay.

To cut a long story short, civilians at home have realised a growing difference in the English as spoken in the Army from that at home.

A guide to Army talk would, therefore, be of great use to all, and particularly to those who wish to hide their lack of Army experience apres la guerre.

In this number we publish a few hints on grammar and familiar words.

Adjectives. The importance of these cannot be too strongly impressed on all aspirants to Army conversation.

The number employed are few, and can be counted on the fingers of one hand. The spelling of them is variable, the most common way being by derivatives of blank, e.g., blank, blankety, blanking.

This spelling is by no means phonetic. Adjectives must be employed whenever possible or not, and their meaning varies according to emphasis and number. No sentence appears to be understood unless one or more Army adjectives are used, as the following incident will show :—

"Pte. Smith, be quick and fetch the rations." "What's that, Sergt?" "You blankety blank, be blank quick and fetch the blankety blanking rations." Pte. Smith jumps to it.

This incident further illustrates that proficiency is only acquired after long practice, as the sergeant's remarkable ability in their use serves to show.

Swinging the lead is not a nautical term and has no connection with any other water besides that of the English Channel. It is a phrase referring to a nervous and moral aberration. This disease is frequently met with by medical boards at the base. The majority of sufferers, however, are dealt with by tribunals at home. It is not unknown to regimental M.O.'s in the forward areas.

[Since writing this the armistice has been signed, and cases are known of those nervously afflicted applying to join a battalion.]

Sweating. In civilian life applied to horses only, perspire being reserved for human beings; to apply the word perspire to leave simply would not do.

A man's home address has been asked for, and he is warned for leave. From that time on each shell seems to have his name written on it, each bullet seems to be made for him. Someone's hair might be too long, or another might wear a soft cap in the trenches, etc., etc., and leave will be stopped.

The billet may be such that the necessary certificate from the M.O. of that which is next to Godliness might be refused.

Another advance may be contemplated and all leave cancelled, etc., etc., etc. No, dear reader, perspire would not do, one simply sweats.

To win. Verb, trans, most irregular. Clothes, food, rifles, tin hat, rum, excluding the jars, etc., all that a man has belongs to the Army, and however and in whatever manner he may come by the article or articles he uses or possesses they still remain employed by the military. Winning means obtaining goods, for personal use otherwise than by indent, it is much simpler, causes fewer explanations about lost kit, and is decidedly quicker, but irregular.

The verb to steal has thus become redundant and obsolete.

HOW IT HAPPENED.

We called her Bona, and claimed the knowledge of another language in our little blue-books. She was short and fat and passing ugly. After a while she became a great favourite in our circle.

This is about what happened during the while.

She was understood to possess a twin sister whom she never saw. We called her Sera.

We saw a good deal of *Bona*. She was a 12-inch Italian Trench Mortar, and accommodated missiles of enormous bulk. She came to live behind a crag in our sector, and when we passed that way we felt grateful that she was on our side.

Nobody imagined she would deign to fire without due cause—a big attack or Christmas Day or something. Really important guns always lie doggo like that. Besides, the orgin of a 4 foot bomb intrigues the enemy furiously.

We were sitting in the Mess criticising the climate of the Plateau. This is frequently done in lots of the Messes.

There was a devastating activity on the part of the crockery, an appalling roar, a blast of hot air, and some keen remarks about the Dual Monarchy.

Several excited troops appeared at the door. "*Bona*," said one, "See'd 'er coming all the way."

We straightway took the matter up several hundred feet of difficult country, and laid it before the Battery Commander. He was a *Capitano*, entirely charming and spoke interesting French. After very precise salutes, we indicated *Bona* and polite protestation. "Our troops were accustomed to shell fire although it wasn't their fault." He bowed in comprehending acknowledgment.

"A mortar bomb was of course nothing—we almost liked them. But of three hundred pounds, and from the rear? yes, it was apt to disturb. However, no harm had been done, and without doubt *Signore il Capitano*—everybody saluted—would graciously arrange for the practice to cease. Our own T.M.'s were a trifle lighthearted."

He was awfully sorry and looked it. Hands, eyebrows, shoulders and pleasing voice produced such a convincing impression of utter mental desolation that we saluted again, out of pure sympathy.

He spoke earnestly. "He regretted so very much, but so little to him, it was understood. The mortar was new and of the latest mode." He regarded *Bona* with wistful admiration. "But only one time before had it fired. That had been for the registration, and then, O! it had been most superb. To the second line of Austrian trenches it had fired!!! Just one thing alone had been not just correct, and to-day he had resolved to shoot a spot yet finer than the first." To which end he explained, "More of charge had been placed in the mortar, and the muzzle had been adjusted—so." And he patted *Bona's* barrel with the air of one who believes that, sooner or later, good will out. "Yes," he sighed, "Much had been hoped of than shot, but alas, it had fallen behind our own line. *Crux dolorosa.*"

It was all very sad. Nothing more could be done. We withdrew quietly, and left him with his grief.

That first shot had been a dud.

A week later and we were again in the Mess. He was dining with us and answering to the name of Ludo.

The youngest subaltern had just confessed to the criminal acquisition of a portion of loosely packed charge of cordite. His intentions had been honourable. He had been on a two-day rock-blasting course, and he had wanted to show his platoon all about it. Incidentally there had been an inconvenient boulder in his own personal dug-out. He promised not to do it again.

Ludo took it magnificently. He rose in his seat, and, holding aloft a chipped enamel mug of execrable vino, he swore by all his vivid-hosed, poison-mixing, pope-defying ancestors, that such a nation couldn't possibly lose the war.

He was probably right.

F. D. R.

"I 'ear as 'ow Jerry is to 'and over all 'is gnns '*in situ.*'"

"Lumme! Where's that, in France, or Belgium?"

A "RUM" STRATEGY.

Pte. Raikes and Pte McGillivray were under suspicion. The previous night the ration party had brought up two jars of rum and one had been lost owing to the bearer (Pte. Raikes) tripping over something as he reached the front line trench.

As the Platoon-Commander remarked to his sergeant, " It may have been a pure accident, but it is a curious thing that they could only find one jar, although the Corporal came along at once to my dug-out and borrowed a flash-lamp and searched all round. There was certainly a smell of rum about the place, but if the jar had been broken there should have been pieces lying about, and I don't remember seeing any. I am prepared to bet *umpteen lire* that Raikes and McGillivray know something of the whereabout of that jar."

Suspicion usually, and not often unjustly, fell upon these two, inasmuch as their conduct sheets contained as many entries as any ten put together in the Platoon.

The remarks of the Platoon Commander were overheard round a neighbouring traverse by Pte. McGillivray and were promptly communicated to Pte. Raikes.

The latter's first comment was, " Me motives is always misconstructed like." He then confided his plan to Pte. McGillivray. Briefly, it was as follows : In the course of night patrols in a broad " No Man's Land," he had come across a shell-hole showing obvious signs of recent occupation. He had divined that it was an Austrian observation post occupied by day. If he could capture a prisoner single-handed it might ease the situation with the Company Commander, and mitigate that objectionable institution known as " F.P."

" It's strategy wot does it, me cross-eyed kid," remarked Pte. Raikes affectionately. " You an' I are again' ter met that there observer teller off our own blooming bat, an' we aint goin' ter take no unnecessary risks."

So it happened that when, just before dawn, Karl Schumacher esconsed himself in his post to carry out his daily task of observation, he found a brown jar, with the mystic letters S.R.D. printed on it, lying at the bottom of his shell-hole.

His first thought was that it was a simple booby-trap, and he left it severely alone, after a careful investigation as to the presence of any attached wires. Later, curiosity overcame discretion, and he gently lifted the jar and shook it. The swish of liquid inside sounded reassuring, so he poured out a few drops of the brown fluid on to his hand, smelt it and licked it.

Then he put the jar away from him and once more peered through his telescope.

As the day progressed and he bcame cramped and cold in his position, his thoughts continually reverted to the jar. By 4 p.m. he had experimented with two more licks. " Facilis descennus tieoni ! " The licks gave place to gulps ; the gulps to a long draught which emptied the jar. Thus it came about that when he should have been returning to his own lines under cover of dark, bearing his daily report of enemy movements, he was lying in his post unmistakably drunk in the military sense of that much-debated and hotly contested word.

The work of Ptes. Riakes and McGillivray, who had obtained permission to " try and secure a hidentification, sir," was easy.

It is perhaps best described in Pte. Raikes' own words as he stood before his Company Commander : " It was as easy as picking out winkles with a pin, sir. We just crawled up to 'im and lifted 'im out of 'is cubby-'ole neat and quiet like. I know as 'ow I was wrong in not asking of yer it us could use the rum wot I 'appened to find lying about, but the hidea took me all of a sudden like, as I was goin' along of the trench afore starting on patrol. I 'opes as 'ow you thinks as I done right, sir. It were a bit of that 'ere strategy wot the Colonel was a-talkin' about last week."

At this point Pte. Raikes relapsed from the stiff attitude of attention and fumbled in his pockets, finally producing the day's observation report which he had found tightly grasped in his prisoner's hand.

This document was handed to the Brigade Intelligence Officer, who came in to question the prisoner. The last three entries were deciphered as follows : " 3-50 p.m., enemy movement near church towers "; " 4-30 p.m., ditto near both church towers "; " 5-5 p.m., ditto near both revolving towers."

* * * * * * *

But Pte. Raikes was not altogether satisfied. As he climbed into the bunk above Pte. McGillivray that night he whispered in a melancholy voice, " I believes as 'ow we could have taken out another 'arf-pint afore we give 'im the jar."

Sergt. V. F. E.

CHATS FROM AN EDITOR'S FLEA BAG.

Events have moved fast since our last issue, a fresh page has been turned over in the world's history, a bloodstained page turned down, never, we hope, to be revised, unless, perchance, to cure any war fever politicians of that fell complaint.

* * * *

All of us received letters stating what a jolly time we must have had on Armistice Day. The feeling was far too deep for that, and the sense of our own preservation, and the loss of many of our comrades, produced nothing but a deep feeling of thankfulness that the end that all had fought for had been attained at last.

* * * *

The demobilisation arrangements are now rapidly reaching completion, and soon we shall all be separating and going to our old homes.

* * * *

The Battalion left Italy for France in September, and has since been incorporated in the 25th Division. Its record in the recent fighting has been brilliant, as will be seen by the following account, and also by the Honours list on the first page.

* * * *

In the middle of September the Battalion moved at very short notice from Italy to France. After 10 days or so of refitting and reorganisation to meet the conditions of service on another front, the Division to which the Battalion was posted commenced moving forward.

* * * *

On October 5th we went into action at Beaurevoir, and together with another unit captured the village. On October 9th we attacked again at Maretz, with like success. The following day the Battalion took part in the advance towards Le Cateau. After a few days' rest we again attacked near Bamel, and subsequently held the line there for a few days

* * * *

On October 23rd the Battalion took part in the full dress attack ot the 3rd and 4th Armies, attacking the Bois L'Eveque.

Again, on November 4th. we shared in the success of the Brigade at the attack on Landrecies.

* * * *

The last time the Battalion was in action was on November 7th, forming the advanced guard during the advance from Marbaix towards Avesnes.

* * * *

A subscriber desires to complete his collection of *Glos'ter Gazettes*, and lacks Nos. 1—5 and 8—13 inclusive. If anyone can spare all or any of these numbers, will he kindly communicate with the Editor?

THINGS WE WANT TO KNOW.

Who always takes a bottle of ammunition into the line ? Is he in the Berks ?

What servant on picket said to his officer, "Sir, I think we are blankety blanks for staying here?" And how much that windy barrage of the Austrians cost ?

Who was the member of a new draft who said that the L.G. did not agree with his health ?

What cook said "Dinner is late, sir, because my foot is bad ?"

What T.O. in the I.E.F., when criticising skinny horses, said that they were too long to take the hairpin turnings ?

Who offered his application for special leave to the editor as a jolly good yarn, and whether G.H.Q. agreed with him ?

Is it true that a silver cup has been put up for a "catch-as-catch-can competition among the 48th Division, and whether G fancies its chances?

What were the casualties in a famous pillow fight at Granezza ?

Who went to the canteen to buy some field postcards ?

Who was the N.C.O., when asked the time, pulled out his pay-book ? Was he in D. Company ?

Who souvenir-ed some Bosche cigarettes, and were they the brand he usually smokes at home ?

Who was the officer who asked how the ventriloquist made the dummy speak ?

Who wrote, "Any keeping step with me in civil life will suffer a serious injury?"

Why the M.O. always drinks to the health of Charles ?

What subaltern told the C.O., "I think you are very wise, sir ?"

Who was the man who did not possess a watch or some other souvenir after the last attack ?

"TALES FROM THEATRELAND."

By A. C. TORR.

For his production of "The Merchant of Venice," the late Sir Herbert Tree engaged the services of several Jews--not particularly well-bred—paying each the sum of one guinea per week.

At the first rehearsal, the stage manager informed these gentlemen that they must not object to the actor playing "Antonio," pretending to spit at them. Forth stepped one, "If Sir Herbert will make it *two* guineas, Mr.— can *really* spit at us ! "

* * *

A young actor had played his first engagement with the late Sir Henry Irving. He then left the company, and played small parts with Sir John Hare for a year. At the end of the year his conceit knew no bounds. Sir Henry met him in London, and enquired after his welfare.

"Ah yes ! I remember you," said the young gentleman,— "Oh, I'm playing at the —— Theatre, don't you know !" "Indeed," replied Irving,—"By the way, is there a man by the name of Hare playing with you ? "

* *

It was in the Third Act— the convict had leapt from the wall of his prison—but no rifle shot rang out to impede his flight—the property man being fast asleep.

For the moment dismay seized the actor, and then an inspiration came to his forced brain. His hands clutched his throat, and a terrible cry rang out into the auditorium, "Shot ! Shot !— by an air gun."

* *

A propos of a quaint idea entertained by ostriches, is told the following story of the late Sir Henry Irving's stage manager.

It was at a dress rehearsal, and the members of the orchestra were practising underneath the stage, thereby drowning the voices of the actors. Their strict attention to the conductor's baton was suddenly interrupted by a voice from the trap-door, "Hi ! You down below there !— I s'pose you think because we can't see you, that you're ostriches ! " Delightful muddle, isn't it ?

*

The scene was the rampart scene in "Hamlet." "Horatio" and "Hamlet" awaited the coming of the "Ghost" (played by a certain Mr.—).

"Horatio," unfortunately, had dined "not wisely, but too well," (*not* a common fault of actors, as some misguided people are apt to think. But then, how many *do* know the true actor ?).

Enter the "Ghost." "Horatio" clutched "Hamlet" by the arm, "Look, my lord, it comes—hic —it's old M—!"

* *

And then A. C. Torr enters the Army Of a certain young actor, an accomplished elocutionist, is told the story that when training in an N.C.O.'s class for his lance stripe, the Sergt.-Major corrected his first attempt at giving a command with the following words : "You doesn't know 'ow to use your voice ! What you wants to learn first and foremost is 'ow to in'ale, and then to give your word of command, *clear and dis'tinc* ! " Joy of the actor.

LT. SHELLFIRE, T.F.

(*With apologies to Lt. Shellback, R.N.R., of* PUNCH).

NOW he wasn't a husky born and bred,
'Twas a different life to the one he'd led—
Seven years in a nursery, ten at school,
The rest on a soft-seated office stool ;
Nurtured in comfort, sleeping on feathers,
Changing his clothes with the changing weathers ;
Never went hungry nor yet lacked a bed —
That's the pre-war sort of life that he'd led.
But on August the fourth, one nine one four,
When the roughs and toughs were wanted for war,
And Belgium was falling and things at their worst—
About-town Shellfire was there with the first.

They gave him khaki and boots and a gun,
And told him that war was the best of fun—
September would see him booting the Boche !
November would end it !—and such-like tosh.
Pushed in a train and sent to the coast
He soon found he knew a lot less than most.
But strength of spirit faltered no trifle,
Linked to flesh that could not slope a rifle.
It was drills, and parades. and hellish marches,
Sore feet, galled back, and throat that parches,
With nothing to drink—and it's dusty and hot—
But Private Shellfire he went thro' the lot.

He learnt the ways of the army at war,
To shoot, and march, and a good deal more ;
Muscled like whipcord, and browned by the tan,
He soon looked the right sort of soldier man ;
For he had had the way and the will to win,
And worked like the devil and trained like sin.
The Retreat, Marne and Aisne—he missed them all,
Of red chevrons and stars he got dem-all !
But he got out in time for Neuve Chapelle,
And marched from railroad straight into hell ;
And snaffling a post (without permission)
Got him a rep. and the King's Commission.

Six days kit leave, and he never touched ground ;
Town !—living *la vie* and knocking around—
Rejoined at Hill Sixty—hollow with mines—
Found his platoon in a whirl of *five nines* ;
Carried on fighting till most had gone west,
Then led the survivors out for a rest.
Soon after at Wipers the Boche, en masse,
Found him still kicking in spite of the gas.
And from north of Wipers to south of Somme,
From the Dunkirk dunes down to old Peronne,
In the stickiest shows, were they lost or won,
He's suffered and fought in every one.

Yes, he's learnt the ways of the men on land,
Who live, fight and die on that foreign strand ;
Body dog-weary and senses areel,
With bullet and bomb and the keen, cold steel,
He's doing his whack like the seasoned tar
In that opposite branch—the R. N. R.
And there isn't a sector of line in France
Where Hell plays the music of Death's own dance,
In the roofless hall where the floor is mud—
And the walls are fire and the drink is blood—
And all is red with the cups aspill—
But Lieutenant Shellfire has drunk his fill.

F.D.R.

THE R.T.O.

A Play recently produced at Connemara Court, ITALY.

Dramatis Personæ.

Miss Ruby Queen	... ...	
Capt. Tootsweet, o.b.e.	... ...	New R.T.O.
Gnr. In de Pink, r.f.a.	... ...	R.T.O.'s Orderly
Pte. Rip Van Winkle	... ...	An Aged Soldier

Time—The present—about dusk.

Scene—Railway Station, Slapperhinge, Somewhere in Flanders.

The curtain rises displaying Pink, sitting on chair, going over his shirt and soliloquising.

Pink : Old soldiers never die-ee, they simply fay-eed ayee-wayee. Got 'im ! [*He kills imaginary louse with hammer and shakes Keating's over its corpse.*]

Hi, you there ! Put it down, I said, put that engine down. We've lost things like that before. No, you can't have that lunch basket. What's that ! Eaten your iron rations ? You'd better 'op it before the quarter bloke 'ears you. [*Continues soliloquy.*]

Yess ! Horderly to the new R.T.O., that's what I ham, last one went on leave, and was sent up the line. Still, I'll tell the new bloke as how he met an 'orrible end. [*Kills another chat and says to it, "You'll have to conclude a separate peace."*] It's a cushy job being an R.T.O., though one does have the responsibility of standing the racket if trains don't go right, not as 'ow I ever seed a R.T.O. what was brought to justice, not properly anyways. Only the other day I was. . . . .

[*Enter Ruby Queen.*]

Ruby : Excuse me, are you the R.T.O.?

Pink : Ham hi the R.T.O. ? Well, miss, hi ham and I ham not. I'm 's local beanends.

Ruby : His local what ?

Pink : His local beanends, miss : I hacts for him like.

Ruby : His *locum tenens* I suppose you mean ?

Pink : Ah, well, miss, have it your own way. Well he is hout, miss, at present.

Ruby : How long will he be?

Pink : Well, he might be so long, then again he might be so long. [*Indicates length with his arms.*]

Ruby : How absurd you are.

Pink (surveying her) : Do you know, miss, I wish I were R.T.O.?

Ruby : Why is that ?

Pink : Well, miss, you could travel all over my railways for naught.

R.T.O. (Capt. Tootsweet) : Orderly ! Orderly !

Pink : There 'e is, miss. That's 'im.

Ruby : Him ! Who !

Pink : Why, the new R.T.O.

R.T.O. : Orderly (crescendo). Orderly, ORDERLY.

Pink : 'Aint 'e got a lovely voice, miss? Coming, sir, coming.

[*Exit Pink and re-enters with R.T.O. and his valise.*]

R.T.O. : Orderly, put my valise down there. [*Pointing.*]

[*Exit Ruby Queen.*] [*R.T.O. removes his cap. mops his brow, divests himself of impedimenta, piling it up on Pink.*]

R.T.O. : Tell me, orderly, what sort of a place is this. [*Whistle—bang—crash.*]

Pink : Quiet, oh quiet, sir, very quiet. [*Frightful noise and repeated sounds of shells arriving, during which R.T.O. and Pink duck frequently.*]

R.T.O. : D——n it, Orderly. [*Mops his brow.*] I thought you said this was a quiet place. Put my valise over there. [*Indicates fresh position.*]

Pink : 'E don't seem to no what 'e do want.

R.T.O. : Now just point out the country to me, orderly, places of interest, and so forth.

Pink : Well, sir, see that mound over there?

R.T.O. : Yes.

Pink : With the wooden cross on it?

R.T.O. : Yes. [*Impatiently.*]

Pink (very slowly) : That's where we buried our last R.T.O.

R.T.O. : Good Lord ! How did it happen ?

Pink : A shell, sir. Only a whiz-bang.

R.T.O. : Where did it happen ?

Pink : Just where you are standing, sir.

R.T.O. : Orderly, just put this valise somewhere else. [*R.T.O. moves to another place.*]

Pink : To continue, sir, look over there as far as you can.

R.T.O. : Yes, I'm looking.

Pink : Well, look a little farther.

R.T.O. : What do you mean, man ; do you realise to whom you are talking ?

Pink : Well, sir, you see that bully beef tin ?

R.T.O. : Yes.

Pink : Well, that's the Town Hall where the mayor lived

R.T.O : Has he gone, too ?

Pink : Gone, sir, why he's there now.

R.T.O. : No, you don't understand. I mean is he living now.

Pink : I don't know, sir, he asn't come back to hearth since the Beetle 'it 'im.

[*Enter Ruby Queen.*]

Ruby : Good evening, can I speak to the R.T.O. ?

R.T.O. and Pink : Good evening.

Pink : Just my luck. [*Exit, humming " apres la guerre finie."*]

R.T.O. : Pray, be seated. Can I possibly be of service to you? [*Offers chair.*]

Ruby : Thank you. [*Sits down.*] I want to sell buns on your station.

R.T.O. : What a topping idea ; of course you shall.

"For information & necessary action".

Ruby : And tea, to the dear boys.

R.T.O. : Certainly, certainly. [*Sits down at the table and adopts the professional attitude.*]

Ruby : You know I do so admire you men, who rush up our troops to the front.

R.T.O. : We rush them up all right. We rush them up [*Enter Pink.*] What do you want ?

Pink : Please, sir, there's a man that wants to know what time the 2-15 train goes.

R.T.O. (to Ruby) : Excuse me. [*Goes to telephone and buzzes and speaks.*] Hello, hello. Give me G.H.Q. [*Thinks.*] Hello, Duggie, is that you ? Quite fit. Oh, so glad. Any luck last time ? Yes, rather, in fact there's a charming one here now. English and all that. Oh, bun selling, etc., etc. Cheerio. Oh, Duggie, are you there ? [*Buzzes. . .*] Qive me G.H.Q., again signals. Oh, Duggie, sorry to trouble you. What time does the 2-15 train go ? Quarter past two ; don't be funny. Very good.

(*To Pink*) It goes at 4-20 to-day.

Pink (to Officer) : The R.T.O. ses as that it goes at 4-20 to-day, but he isn't certain.

R.T.O. : There you are. That's the sort of thing they expect me to know, what time the train goes. What's my orderly for ! However, these things can't interest you.

Ruby : But they do. You interest me enormously. [*R.T.O. rises and comes and takes seat close to Ruby.*] Oh, I meant your work interests me. [*R.T.O. looks downcast.*]

R.T.O. : Would you like to know about my work ? [*Ruby nods.*] Ah, yes, my work. [*Pause, in which he thinks hard.*] [*Aside.*] What the dickens do I do ? [*Aloud.*] Um-ah-oh-yes, of course. Well, as I was saying ———.

Ruby (encouragingly) : Yes !

R.T.O. : Well, I get up sometimes. [*Ruby looks surprised.*] I mean sometimes about 10-30 a.m., and Pink brings me my breakfast. Invaluable feller, Pink is.

Ruby : Funny name, isn't it ?

R.T.O. : Yes, his full name is In the Pink, as he always writes and says I hope it finds you as it leaves me in the pink.

Ruby : I see.

R.T.O. : Well, then, when I've dressed, about 12 noon I go and attend to all the fellows who want to know about the leave train, and of course the strain is awful. At 12-30 I am quite exhausted, so I give the order to carry on, and I go to Skindle's to be refreshed.

Ruby : You poor dear. [*R.T.O. moves his chair a little closer.*]

R.T.O. : Well, then, I have to entertain hundreds of generals. [*Ruby shows interest.*] For instance, yesterday I had a corps commander to lunch, and you wouldn't believe the stupid things he talked about. For instance, he said that. . . [*Hesitation.*]

Ruby (very encouragingly) : Yes ?

R.T.O (embarrassed) : Well, I don't think I can remember it all

Ruby : Oh, do. [*Simultaneously lowers parasol, and R.T.O. and Ruby approximate, laughs, giggles, and other sounds are heard.*]

[*Enter Pink.*]

Pink (laughs) : Excuse me, sir. [*Sudden commotion.*]

R.T.O. : Well, what is it ?

Pink : There's a man here who ses as how he's been waiting years for this train.

R.T.O. (to Ruby) : Impossible, my dear, I assure you.

(*To Pink*) : Bring him in.

[*Exit Pink and re-enters with aged soldier.*]

Pink : Come along, old bluebeard.

R.T.O. : What's your name ?

Aged Soldier : Winkle. Pte. Rip Van, sir.

R.T.O. : Date of disembarkation ?

A.S. : August 5, 1914, sir.

R.T.O. : Any papers ?

A.S. : Yes, sir. [*Hands over huge bundle of A.F.'s of various colours, shapes and sizes, neatly bound with red tape.*]

[*R.T.O. goes to table to correct papers*]

Pink (to A S.) : Do you think if I was to hit you on the back a robin would come hout ?

R.T.O. : These papers are in order. You will leave by the 2-15 train, report here at 3-45.

[*A.S. remains*] Is it quite clear ; well, what are you waiting for ?

A.S. : I'm very sorry [*breaking down*], but I have been on the R.E. dump and got no rations, so I ate my iron rations.

Pink : Blimy, you're for it.

R.T.O. (thunderstruck) [*Goes over to table and produces red volume—Manual of Military Law*] : Ah, I feared it. Here are the very words. [*Reads.*] As iron rations are liable to deteriorate rapidly when unprotected damp, it is important that only such as are required for immediate use should be uncovered. Maximum penalty—death.

[*Hands revolver to Pink, bought in Padua, 80 lire, specially made to carry without inconvenience on a Sam Brown.*] Take him away, orderly, you know your duty.

[*Exit Pink and A.S. Six shots are heard in rapid succession. Pink reports each shot. No. 1 fired, sir. No. 2 fired, etc.*]

Pink (re-entering) : Good Lord, sir, I've missed 'im, but I've got a rabibt. [*Produces tin of Australian multiplier.*]

R.T.O. : Very good. Inform the D G.R.E.'s unit. [*Pink still waits.*] Why are you waiting ?

Pink : A movement horder, sir. [*He gets a good one from the R.T.O., runs out, rubbing the afflicted part.*]

R.T.O. (to Ruby) : Well, as I was saying. [*They mutually approach each other.*]

[*Pink re-enters hesitatingly, and seeing how the land lies rushes out again.*]

R.T.O. (jumping up) : I hear a train coming.

Pink : Train reported at Pop In, it left Hop Out three hours ago.

R.T.O. : It's coming.

Ruby (Rushing for basket) : It's coming.

Pink : It's going, sir.

R.T.O. : It's going.

Ruby : It's going.

[*Pink blows his whistle three times, runs round station, altering boards " arrive " and " depart."*]

R.T.O. : This has been a terrible blow for me. My only train, the 2-15, has gone and never been stopped. [*Sobs.*]

Ruby : Don't take it so to heart, I so wanted to please the boys, but they preferred St. Julien. Never mind, you can always have your Ruby Queen. [*He places her to his lips and draws long breaths.*] But see a messenger approacheth. [*Pink draws near.*]

Pink : Rations have just come down, and a special one to you, sir.

R.T.O. : What is it, speak, for heaven's sake, speak.

Pink : The ration O.B.E. for taking affectionate care of the King's gifts to the troops.

[*The R.T.O. embraces Ruby again, and adjourns to Skindle's to celebrate the event.*]

S.

SPORTS.

Since the Armistice was signed, our energies have been divided between rolling up barbed wire and other salvage work, education and sport.

Under the latter head, we are having inter-platoon, inter-company and inter-battalion football competitions, rugby matches, cross-country running, and boxing competitions.

FOOTBALL (Association).

XIII. CORPS INTER-COMPANY COMPETITION.

1. The Corps are running an inter-company football competition, in which we first have to play off our own companies against each other. Results of matches in the preliminary round :—

26/11/18   D Company beat C Company, 3-1.
27/11/18   A Company beat H.Q., 2-1.
28/11/18   B Company beat D Company, 4-1.
1/12/18   B Company beat A Company, 2-0.

B Company (the winning Company of the Battalion) played C Company (winning Company) 1/8th Warwicks on the Warwicks football ground, on December 6th, at Carnieres, the Warwicks winning by 1-0.

INTER-PLATOON COMPETITION.

2. We are also having an inter-platoon competition within the Battalion, which is evoking much keenness, as it gives most people who can kick a ball a chance of playing.

The prize is a set of silver medals for the members of the winning team.

No. 1 beat No. 3.   Played 21/11/18.   Remainder byes.

First Round.

23/11/18   No. 1 beat B.H.Q. "Rest."
23/11/18   No. 6 beat Signallers.
23/11/18   No. 15 beat Band.
23/11/18   Transport Drivers beat No. 7.
24/11/18   No. 5 beat No. 14.
24/11/18   No. 2 beat Transport "Rest."
25/11/18   No. 13 beat No. 10.
21/11/18   No. 9 beat No. 11.

Second Round.

14/14/18   No. 5 beat No. 1.
14/12/18   No. 6 beat No. 13.
15/12/18   No. 15 beat No. 2.
18/12/18   Transport Drivers beat No. 9.

Semi-Final.

24/12/18   Transport Drivers beat No. 15.
24/12/18   No. 6 were unable to raise a team, and gave the game to No. 5.

Final.

The final was played on Christmas morning, and resulted in a win for the Transport Drivers by 3-0.

3. The Brigadier has very kindly offered a cup and set of silver medals to be competed for in an inter-company competition within the Brigade, the Transport and Q.M. Stores counting as one Company, and the rest of the Battalion Headquarters as another. This competition has not started at the time of writing as it is waiting for the Corps Competition to get on a bit.

4. There is also a promise of an inter-battalion competition in the Division, but this is still in a nebulous form. At any rate, our players will be busy for some time to come.

5. On December 7th a football match was played between the Officers and Sergeants of the Battalion, and resulted in a win for the Sergeants by 3-1.

December 29th we played the first Battalion match of the season against the 1/8th Warwicks. The result was a draw, no goals being scored.

RUGBY FOOTBALL.

Our Rugby XV. has been revived again after many months, and a certain amount of new blood has been discovered. We took on the Divisional Artillery on Thursday, the 28th November, and managed to beat them by 2 converted goals, 1 dropped goal, 4 tries to 1 try.

The game was almost entirely a forwards' one, the ball being far too greasy for the backs to handle well, and our forwards, as of old, proved themselves a magnificent pack.

CROSS-COUNTRY RUNNING.

We have made a start with an inter-company run, held in two parts, on the 20th and 22nd November.

The distance was about 3,000 yards, over rather a sticky course. Every available man in each company ran, the company having the largest number of finishers in a fixed time (18 minutes) in proportion to their ration strength to be the winner. C and D companies ran on the 20th November, and A and B, two days later ; C and D were unfortunate in having to contend with a thick mist, in which it was impossible to see more than a hundred yards, which made it difficult to follow the course. The result was as follows :—

	Finished in 18 mins.	Ration strength (less Sick, etc.)	Percentage.
1st B Company	61	107	57.00
2nd D Company	46	98	45.91
3rd A Company	48	107	44.85
4th C Company	29	107	26.16

"THINGS TEMPORAL."

Pass through them, they are not your lasting life,
Means to the end, or warning shadows they ;
Lose not for them, the things of timeless day,
Go quietly on through darkness, care, and strife—
Your strength the word of light and love and peace,
Pour out your thought like oil upon the sea,
Be firm in moving forward, fearless, free,
    The world is his, who knows the world must cease.

Only a fool could fail to love the earth,
This teeming earth, the lives of men, the fields,
The sun, the rain, the sweetness nature yields,
The noble joys of art—and homely mirth ;
    But wisdom ever sees the highest star,
    Ultimate Beauty beckoning afar.

                              ARDAN CLARKE.

(With acknowledgments to " The Commonwealth.")